Modern Indian I

'This is a book which defies generic classification . . . one cannot but marvel at the fine balance editor Amit Chaudhuri has struck between critique and admiration, between documentation and a sense of social history and change . . . If Chaudhuri had not written a single line outside this book, he could have, rightfully, claimed a place in the history of Indian literature for producing this anthology'
Chitralekha Basu, *Statesman*

'Chaudhuri's translation of *Pather Panchali* suggests that it is . . . a literary masterpiece'
Charles Allen, *Spectator*

'Most of the pieces included are excellent and the translations are invariably done with sensitivity . . . the editor's head notes to some of the pieces surprise us with unexpected illuminations . . . this priceless volume is guaranteed to give many hours of pleasure'
Meenakshi Mukherjee, *Deccan Chronicle*

'The immediate benefit of this liberating perspective is that it opens up the very culture of Indian modernity to a vertiginous variety of voices and views . . . the clarity of editorial purpose and the elegance of most translations are exemplary, and invite us to welcome the anthology as a major literary event'
Leela Gandhi, *Hindu*

'The items are well chosen, and what there is, is very good indeed . . . There will be few readers who will not make pleasant discoveries here . . . Chaudhuri has succeeded remarkably in focussing attention on the inevitably unfinished nature of such an exercise . . . The really valuable thing, then, that Chaudhuri accomplishes – with the selections, the headnotes, and his thoughtful Introduction – is to enable us to frame the question of what an Indian literature – not an object but a horizon – might look like'
Alok Rai, *Outlook*

Amit Chaudhuri was born in Calcutta in 1962 and brought up in Bombay. He is a graduate of University College, London, and completed his doctorate at Balliol College, Oxford. He was later Creative Arts Fellow at Wolfson College, Oxford, and Leverhulme Special Research Fellow at the Faculty of English, Cambridge. He has written five books, *A Strange and Sublime Address*, *Afternoon Raag*, *Freedom Song*, *A New World*, and, most recently, *Real Time*. He has won first prize in the Betty Trask Awards, the Commonwealth Writers Prize for Best First Book (Eurasia), the Society of Authors' Encore Prize for Best Second Novel, the Southern Arts Literature Prize, and the *LA Times* Book Prize for Fiction, 2000. He is the editor of Picador's Modern Indian Library, a new series that aims to bring hitherto inaccessible works of Indian literature into the mainstream. His work appears in various publications all over the world, including the *London Review of Books*, the *Times Literary Supplement*, *Granta*, the *New Republic* and the *New Yorker*. He lives with his wife and daughter in Calcutta.

THE PICADOR BOOK OF

Modern Indian Literature

Edited by Amit Chaudhuri

PICADOR

First published 2001 by Picador

This edition published 2002 by Picador
an imprint of Pan Macmillan Ltd
Pan Macmillan, 20 New Wharf Road, London N1 9RR
Basingstoke and Oxford
Associated companies throughout the world
www.panmacmillan.com

ISBN 0 330 34364 5

1 3 5 7 9 8 6 4 2

A CIP catalogue record for this book is available from
the British Library.

Typeset by SetSystems Ltd, Saffron Walden, Essex
Printed and bound in Great Britain by
Mackays of Chatham plc, Chatham, Kent

For Saikat, Shantanu, Soumya, Palash,

and other future writers and readers

I later asked about Asian writers in general and got a similar rebuff. He described reading most Pakistani and Indian writers as 'wading through gibberish', and added, 'Their work is usually no more than rhetoric.'

Thou art translated.

Quince the carpenter, in *A Midsummer Night's Dream*,
on discovering Bottom has acquired an ass's head.

India is not *an* important country, but perhaps *the* most important country for the future of the world ... All convergent influences of the world run through this society: Hindu, Moslem, Christian, secular: Stalinist, liberal, Maoist, democratic socialist, Gandhian. There is not a thought that is being thought in the West or East which is not active in some Indian mind.

E. P. Thompson

Contents

xiv / *Acknowledgements*

INTRODUCTION

xvii / **Modernity and the Vernacular**

xxiii / **The Construction of the Indian Novel in English**

xxxii / **A Note on the Selection**

THE BENGAL RENAISSANCE AND AFTER

3 / **Michael Madhusudan Dutt (1824–73)**

5 / from *'The Anglo-Saxon and the Hindu'*

7 / *Two Letters*

12 / **Bankimchandra Chatterjee (1838–94)**

13 / *'A Popular Literature for Bengal'*

19 / *'The Confession of a Young Bengal'*

24 / from *Rajani*

26 / **Rabindranath Tagore (1861–1941)**

29 / *'The Postmaster'*

34 / *Five Letters*

39 / *An Essay on Nursery Rhymes*

42 / from the Introduction to *Thakurmar Jhuli*

45 / **Sukumar Ray (1887–1923)**

46 / *'A Topsy-Turvy Tale'*

66 / **Bibhuti Bhushan Banerjee (1894–1950)**

68 / from *Pather Panchali*

88 / **Parashuram (Rajshekhar Basu) (1880–1960)**

89 / *'Blue Star'*

97 / *'The Jackal-Faced Tongs'*

106 / **Buddhadev Bose (1908–74)**

107 / from *Tithidore*

114 / from *An Acre of Green Grass: A Review of Modern Bengali Literature*

122 / **Mahashweta Devi (b. 1926)**

123 / *'Arjun'*

HINDI

133 / **Premchand (Dhanpat Rai) (1880–1936)**

134 / *'The Chess Players'*

145 / **Nirmal Verma (b. 1929)**

146 / *'Terminal'*

156 / **Krishna Sobti (b. 1925)**

157 / from *Ai Ladki*

URDU

187 / **Sadat Hasan Manto (1912–55)**

188 / *'Peerun'*

193 / *'The Black Shalwar'*

205 / **Qurratulain Hyder (b. 1927)**

206 / *'Memories of an Indian Childhood'*

220 / **Naiyer Masud (b. 1936)**

221 / *'Sheesha Ghat'*

THE SOUTH

239 / **U. R. Anantha Murthy (b. 1932)**

240 / *'A Horse for the Sun'*

266 / **Vaikom Muhammad Basheer (c. 1908–94)**

267 / *'Walls'*

290 / **O. V. Vijayan (b. 1930)**

291 / *'The Rocks'*

297 / **Ambai (C. S. Lakshmi) (b. 1945)**

298 / *'Gifts'*

PAGES FROM AUTOBIOGRAPHIES

309 / **Fakir Mohan Senapati (1843–1918)**

310 / from *Story of My Life*

330 / **Nirad C. Chaudhuri (1897–1998)**

331 / from *The Autobiography of an Unknown Indian*

347 / **Aubrey Menen (1912–89)**

347 / from *Dead Man in the Silver Market*

355 / **Pankaj Mishra (b. 1969)**

356 / *'Edmund Wilson in Benares'*

ENGLISH

375 / **R. K. Narayan (b. 1907)**

376 / from *The English Teacher*

397 / **Raja Rao (b. 1908)**

398 / from *The Serpent and the Rope*

414 / **Ruskin Bond (b. 1934)**

415 / *'The Night Train at Deoli'*

419 / **A. K. Ramanujan (1929–93)**

420 / *'Is There an Indian Way of Thinking? An Informal Essay'*

438 / **Dom Moraes (b. 1938)**

439 / from *Answered by Flutes*

455 / **Arvind Krishna Mehrotra (b. 1947)**

456 / from *'The Emperor Has No Clothes'*

478 / **Adil Jussawalla (b. 1940)**

478 / *'Make Mine Movies'*

Contents

484 / **Salman Rushdie (b. 1947)**

486 / from *Midnight's Children*

508 / **Vikram Seth (b. 1952)**

509 / from *The Golden Gate*

538 / **Amitav Ghosh (b. 1956)**

538 / *'Tibetan Dinner'*

542 / *'Four Corners'*

547 / **Upamanyu Chatterjee (b. 1959)**

548 / from *English, August: An Indian Story*

563 / **Vikram Chandra (b. 1961)**

564 / *'Siege in Kailashpada'*, from a novel in progress

582 / **Sunetra Gupta (b. 1965)**

583 / from *Memories of Rain*

595 / **Aamer Hussein (b. 1955)**

596 / *'The Colour of a Loved Person's Eyes'*

605 / **Ashok Banker (b. 1964)**

606 / from *Vertigo*

617 / **Rohit Manchanda (b. 1963)**

618 / from *In the Light of the Black Sun*

632 / *Notes on Translators*

635 / *Permissions Acknowledgements*

Acknowledgements

I'd like to thank people who've helped me at different times with their suggestions, and for pointing me in the direction of works and translations that have been of use to me: Arvind Krishna Mehrotra, Rupert Snell, Aamer Hussein, Pankaj Mishra, Saikat Majumdar, Ayappa Paniker, Srikumar Kampurath, Anjum Katyal, Samik Bandhopadhyay, Geetha Dharmarajan, among many others. Peter Straus is to be thanked warmly for his support, and congratulated for the stoic calm he displayed during the many years in which this anthology took shape. My deepest gratitude is reserved for my wife, Rinka, not only for her involvement in this project, but for considerably enriching my knowledge of nineteenth-century Indian writing, her field of expertise; and for my parents, especially my mother, who, since I was a child, has conveyed to me, through her vast reading in Bengali and her enthusiasm, something of the magic of our writers.

INTRODUCTION

Modernity and the Vernacular

What would happen if almost all of Britain's modern and ancient cultures were, for some reason, largely unavailable to the rest of the world, and the only means non-English people had of gauging, judging and even celebrating the uniqueness of English literature – its achievements and barren phases, the tensions that have shaped and enriched it – were the works of Julian Barnes, Martin Amis, Fay Weldon, Angela Carter and a few names chosen at random from the Granta 'Best of Young British Novelists' roll-call? What if they were ignorant of the existence of Clare, Blake, Dickens and Lawrence, and believed the central texts of English literature, of English consciousness, to be, say, *Flaubert's Parrot* or *Last Orders*? We would have a situation that approximates the one we have now in relation to what is loosely called 'Indian writing' (to which are appended, occasionally, in a seemingly arbitrary desire to be accurate, the words 'in English'). Can it be true that Indian writing, that endlessly rich, complex and problematic entity, is to be represented by a handful of writers who write in English, who live in England or America and whom one might have met at a party, most of whom have published no more than two novels, some of them only one? More importantly, is it possible to assess properly and appreciate the merits of this handful of writers without any recourse to the diverse intellectual traditions to which they do or do not belong?

We are, apparently, in the midst of some sort of resurgence in Indian writing (in English). Few writers themselves will feel confident, in their hearts, that they are living and working in a creative boom, though they may be forgiven if they take advantage of the probably short-lived monetary benefits of its supposed existence; but journalists and publishers are busy assuring us that there is good cause for excitement. In the meantime, the glare of publicity is not the best way of ensuring the possibility of good writing, let alone its resurgence; writers need years and need patience to develop and to create their imaginative worlds, and readers need much the same as they wait and watch these worlds take shape. How much of the resurgence has to be with what publishers in England consider the marketability of Indian fiction, and how much of it is genuine achievement, will take at least twenty or thirty years, or more, to decide.

The continuing marketability of India should come as no surprise; nor should it surprise us that intelligent people appear to lend, fitfully, their support to this phenomenon. The first global superstar or celebrity in literature was not an Englishman or an American, but an Indian, Rabindranath Tagore. A series of problematic and strange English translations in the *Gitanjali* came to represent, in the West, this poet's work; and it is instructive to recall that these 'translations' (whose fidelity to their Bengali originals was often tenuous) were celebrated as the high lyric utterance of an Eastern sensibility by respectable people like Yeats and Pound. Much more shockingly, these people lost interest in Tagore's work in about a year, soon after Tagore got the Nobel Prize; and Tagore's reputation seems to have been permanently damaged in the English-speaking West thereafter. Notwithstanding some excellent translations by Ketaki Kushari Dyson and others, notwithstanding the fact that, with so many Bangladeshis settled in Britain, Bengali should be fairly easy to learn, Tagore's oeuvre in Bengali remains unknown in the West, as does his place in the Bengali literary canon and India's intellectual and literary history.

The reason for this lack of curiosity is simple: to be interested in a canon, you have to be interested in how a nation or community sees itself. You have to be interested, in other words, not only in what you think is a nation's history, but also in how a nation sees its own historical process – an area of knowledge that the West, in connection with India, has enquired into very little. (On the other hand, how the West sees itself continues to be the basic point of enquiry in exhaustive studies of its intellectual and cultural output in academic departments all over the world.) Regarding Tagore's works themselves, there has been a fundamental but illuminating misunderstanding which is related to this ignorance or failure of perception. Tagore's writings, which, once rendered into English, were supposed to be representative of an authentic Easternness, in reality both belonged to and contributed to a bourgeois-secular sensibility and class that were then coming into being in India, a new space in which old feudal and familial loyalties, Western liberal humanism, education and folklore, Hinduism and Protestant-style reform, Bengali, English, Sanskrit and other languages all could coexist in a way impossible before, and in ways that often blurred the distinctions between what was 'native' and what 'foreign'.

Of course, Western people, with very few exceptions, continue to think that all the major intellectual and cultural movements of the century have happened in the West; and that is because history happens in the West. India, by contrast, is 'different' and mythic and non-Western; 'history', in the Western sense of the term, does not pertain to it; the West still has problems with accepting that indigenous class-structures, rather than caste-structures, might be an important factor in its development. How, then, can the West have any sense of, let alone interest in, canons and literatures in modern India, when these are part of movements and redefinitions in class and history, neither of which India possesses, apparently, in the 'Western' sense? Post-colonial literary theorists, with their playing down of class in India, and emphasis on the ontological 'difference' of India's cultural patterns, are, in their way, guilty of consigning India to a historical vacuum.

The only way India enters history is, evidently, via colonialism; and as colonialism is seen basically as an encounter between Western colonizer and native colonized, it is perhaps fair to say that colonial India is interesting because, at least in one crucial sense, it is a part of Western history. In what way colonialism and its manifestations – education, the railways, the emergence of a new class-structure and new urban centres – represented a troubled, but rich, phase in the Indian's sense of self, and his or her relation to tradition, history, community and change, remains largely unexplored and unknown in the West. And yet, rather than a simple conflict between native and foreign cultures, this phase of self-enquiry and self-redefinition is, substantially, what colonialism meant in India, so that, importantly, even categories such as 'native' and 'foreign' were confounded or realigned.

The Bengal Renaissance, that great flowering of writers, poets and thinkers from the mid-nineteenth century to the early decades of the twentieth, represents, largely, a record of the intellectual and, above all, the creative response of Indians coming to terms with, and shaping, changes in their history and identity. It involved, on the one hand, unprecedented leaps of technique and of the imagination in literature, and, on the other, issues of social and religious reform, of nationalism, education and the mother tongue; all this was happening as a new bourgeoisie came into existence, and a new class-structure replaced or inflected, in cities and towns, old hierarchies of caste, while new patterns of ambition, of social and geographical movement, replaced old ones.

If a Western reader should turn to this extraordinary literature in Bengali and expect to find some sort of simple response to colonialism, he or she will be disappointed; the response is complex, subtle, varied and profound; the colonial world is represented, in these fictions, as history, contemporaneity, memory and change, by, for instance, the post office and the railways, by the names of roads, by professions, and old and new ways of life, rather than the figure of the British oppressor. This peripherality of the Western figure might be unsettling to the Western reader; unsettling that a historical process, engendered partly by Western intervention, should continue, even in its profoundly original and creatively unprecedented engagement with Westernization, making little or no direct acknowledgement of the Western colonizer. If an oppressor or target is identified and subjected to critique, or satirized, it is either the old feudal landlord caste or the emerging upper middle classes. One thinks, for instance, of examples as diverse as Tarashanker Banerjee's short stories, where a critique of the old feudalism turns into a meditation on decay (one short story, 'Jalsaghar', became Satyajit Ray's film *The Music Room*); of the paintings of the Kalighat *patuas*, with their vibrant and satirical depictions of babu life; of some of Sukumar Ray's nonsense verse for children, with their covert laughter at the enlightened and pious members of the Brahmo Samaj. Interestingly, on the matter of the Indian upper classes, post-colonial theory and, to some extent, Indian writing in English – by contrast to vernacular literature – have remained largely mute, raising, instead, the bogey of the colonizer again and again as a windmill to tilt at, while saying little about the predominance of a native upper class for the past fifty years, and hardly subjecting to imaginative scrutiny the poignance and comedy of the new class tensions, the pathos of the social yearning of the educated lower middle classes, the threatening but exuberant appearance of the new rich.

Most unsettling of all for the Western reader, and the reason why he probably refrains from enquiring too deeply into India's indigenous modern traditions, is perhaps not the oft-cited problem of untranslatability, but the problematic questions raised by concordance and kinship; the unsettling fact that native colonial and post-colonial literatures in India are not 'different', but that they, in many ways, share many of Western culture's own concerns and problems, and that the differences from Western culture are subtle and challenging rather than obvious; that there is a shared history and even narrative idiom in common, the idiom of modernity.

Of course, one of the most common reasons offered to explain away the inaccessibility of Indian literatures is that India possesses an alarmingly and endlessly multifarious, confusing number of tongues; it was into this Babel that the English language arrived and established a semblance of coherence and unity. English comes to be identified, thus, with modernity, and the proliferating, uncontainable vernaculars with the 'natural' state of things in India. In actual fact, the rise of the vernacular was directly and profoundly connected to the rise of the Indian middle classes. The 'traditional' state of affairs in India, itself a result of centuries of cross-fertilization, was a multilingualism akin, in at least one way, to the state of things now in its urban centres: official or devotional literary languages such as Sanskrit, Persian, or Braj Bhasha, rather than mother tongues, were usually employed for the purposes of writing and composition, just as, these days, some people speak in one language and 'choose' to write in English. The first vernacular grammar, in Bengali, was written by Nathaniel Halhed in the late eighteenth century for the instruction of British administrators; the missionary William Carey, in collaboration with the Brahmin Mrityunjoy Vidyalankar, produced textbooks in Bengali for the same purpose a few years later. But the rise of the Bengali language, the subsequent Bengal and Indian Renaissance, and the creation, in Bengali, of the first modern Indian literature were related directly to the fact that Bengali became a respectable, and then the principal, medium of expression among the educated Bengali middle classes, who had, before, in the early days of English education, preferred to write in English. The story of other vernaculars and their increasingly significant literatures is more or less similar; as the indigenous, educated middle classes in different regions became more entrenched, so did their modern literatures flourish. The vernaculars – which were, in truth, paradigms of a new consciousness – emerged from a feudal-religious world into a secular one; this emergence was connected to the cross-fertilization that took place during colonization, largely due to the receptivity and the intelligence of the local population and the local intelligentsia, and of which the colonizers, whose concerns (after the initial efflorescence of Orientalist scholarship) seem constricted and provincial in comparison, were almost completely unaware. Thus, while the Babel of tongues often lends itself, misleadingly, to the representation of India as a many-headed, many-voiced, inchoate Hindu behemoth, it would serve more accurately as an emblem for the increased embourgeoisement of India in the twentieth century. And, in order to study the most profound impact of Western, and English, culture on a non-Western one, in order to study the most complex response to that cross-fertilization in India (which, in itself, represents one of the most important, and neglected, intellectual developments in the modern world), one must turn not to the English language and the way it is used in India, but to Bengali, Hindi, Urdu, Marathi, Tamil and the other vernacular tongues.

One of the reasons for the good health of the vernaculars in pre-Independence India had been the spread of good education and, paradoxically, the teaching of good English in even some of the remotest areas. Those dreaded figures, the missionaries, were often responsible for this –

people like E. J. Thompson, who went and taught in small towns and villages (in his case, in Bankura in Bengal) and were conversant with the local language. Thus, Indians from a variety of backgrounds learnt English as a second language and acquired a deep feeling for it; English represented to them social mobility and choice. Many of the greatest and most interesting writers and poets in the vernacular languages were, or are, students or teachers of English literature: Jibanananda Das, Buddhadev Bose, Harvanshrai Bachchan, U. R. Anantha Murthy, Mahashweta Devi. After Partition, the best English education has been restricted to a tiny minority in the major cities and towns. This has meant the constriction of choice and access for the less privileged, and, with this constriction, the depletion of the power of the vernacular in whose name the teaching of English has often been abolished.

The position of English, in India, is both inescapable and ambiguous, an ambiguity that is perhaps insufficiently mapped in its fiction and criticism. It is a unique ambiguity; for it is misleading to compare the way English is used in India, by a small but substantial group, not all of its members by any means well-to-do or privileged, with the space that the language occupies in, for instance, Africa or America. Moreover, to say that English is now an Indian language – while that may be true – requires all kinds of qualifications and a careful re-examination of that claim; for English is not an Indian language in the way it is an American language; nor is it an Indian language in the way that Bengali or Urdu, for instance, is one. The position and meaning of English in India is still on the verge of becoming clear; it is still part of a process that is far from being complete. But to understand, fully, the story of the English language and its most profound impact and extraordinary outcome in India in the past 150 years, one has to turn, paradoxically, from English and the issue of colonialism to the vernacular languages and indigenous history.

'*Modernity and the Vernacular*' *was originally published in the* Times Literary Supplement *in 1997.*

The Construction of the Indian Novel in English

In the past eighteen years, after the publication of *Midnight's Children* and the rise of the Indian novel in English, Indian fiction in English has not only come to seem central to the idea of Indian literature in the minds of both the popular media and the academic intelligentsia, but has also edged out from everyday consciousness those indigenous languages and their modern traditions that seemed so important a few decades ago, and were so crucial to the evolution of modern Indian identity or identities. Neglected, too, now, is the narrative of how the poets and writers in English who preceded Rushdie (*Midnight's Children* having been erected as a sort of gigantic edifice that all but obstructs the view of what lies behind it) practised their craft when conditions at home and abroad were, in several senses, inimical to the enterprise they were involved in. The two words, 'Indian' and 'English', which sat next to each other so uneasily, their juxtaposition looked upon with as much suspicion from every side as if they were the progeny of warring families (which, in a sense, they were), are now wedded in a marriage that not only seems inevitable but health-giving; what might have been a tragedy has been turned, apparently, into a happy ending with numberless possibilities. In fact, the word 'Indian' is almost only ever used, as a taxonomic term in contemporary literature, in connection with the word 'English'; no one speaks of the Indian novel in Bengali, or Urdu, or Kannada. There is an implication here that only in the English language do Indian writers have the vantage-point, or at least feel the obligation, to articulate that post-colonial totality called 'India' (on the other hand, it sometimes seems that the post-colonial totality called 'India' only exists in the works of Indian English novelists, or in the commentaries they engender). The construction of the post-colonial Indian English novel, after Rushdie, has, in critical and popular discourse, become inextricably entangled with the idea and construction of 'Indianness' and post-coloniality; it is an idea that has taken on new and, in some way, more prescriptive meanings since the days of the poet A. K. Ramanujan, the novelist R. K. Narayan, and the memoirist Nirad C. Chaudhuri (to name, at random, three important Indian practitioners of the English language).

The publication in 1981 of *Midnight's Children*, a Nehruvian epic, coincided, oddly, with the beginning of the end of Nehruvian India. Since then, Indian writers in English have become increasingly visible, especially the English-language media in India, and have become less like God's spies and more like members of the English royal family, involved in trivial curiosity and national prestige, and receiving inordinate amounts of attention. In the way Rushdie's work, or an idea of that work, is interpreted and represented perhaps lies a key to the way Indian writing is supposed to be read and produced – Rushdie both being the godhead from which Indian writing in English has reportedly sprung, revivified, and a convenient shorthand for that writing. It is probably possible to look individually at some of the assumptions which inform the expectations of publishers, writers and critics, even when they haven't been consciously articulated by them.

The first is the tautological idea that since India is a huge baggy monster, the novels that accommodate it have to be baggy monsters as well. Indeed, different Indian writers in English have taken different routes to the goal of hugeness. Rushie and others have created 'magical', bustling, post-colonial narratives, while Vikram Seth and Rohinton Mistry have annexed the nineteenth-century European novel. It is their privilege to do so. But while the large novel might have come to seem typical of the Indian literary enterprise, it is actually not. It contrasts with forms that writers of fiction have chosen in, say, Bengali, where the short story and novella have predominated at least as much as the novel, often in the hands of the major novelists of the first half of the century, such as Bibhuti Bhushan and Tarashankar Banerjee. The writer and critic Buddhadev Bose reminds us that Tagore brought the modern short story into Bengal in the late nineteenth century, some time before it was introduced to England. In a South Indian language such as Kannada, the novella became a seminal form in the hands of a major contemporary, U. R. Anantha Murthy; in their choice of form, these writers hoped to suggest India by ellipsis rather than by all-inclusiveness. Paradoxically, the large, postmodernist Indian English novel, while apparently eschewing realism, pursues a mimesis of form, where the largeness of the book allegorizes the largeness of the country it represents. It is worth remembering that those who write in the languages of India, whether that happens to be English or one of the modern 'vernaculars', do not necessarily write about 'India' or a national narrative (that narrative, anyway, wasn't present in any clear way before Independence), but about cultures and localities that are both situated in, and disperse the idea of, the nation. They write, to take examples from only twentieth-century vernacular traditions, about villages (such as the Bengali village, Nishchindipur, of Bibhuti Bhushan Banerjee's great modernist novel *Pather Panchali*,

published in 1929; later to become Satyajit Ray's first film), or particular
cities and places, like, say, the Lucknow or London or Sylhet in Qurratulain
Hyder's Urdu stories, or even the Czechoslovakia of Nirmal Verma's Hindi
short fiction, or the Africa that Bibhuti Bhushan wrote about in *Chaander
Pahaad (The Moon Mountain)*, an Africa he had never been to. None of
these fictional landscapes is, thus, necessarily India; yet none of them is
situated outside the consciousness of what it means to be Indian; they
extend our idea of what 'Indianness' is, while opening that idea to question.

Post-Rushdie, the Indian novel in English has been constructed, in both
popular and critical terms, as something distinct from – indeed, as an
alternative to – the conventional English novel. Rushdie's writing is not
my subject here; the nature of its achievement and legitimacy is a separate
issue altogether; it is the construction, after *Midnight's Children*, of a
particular idea of both the post-colonial novel and Indian writing in
English, where the heterogeneity of the genre is glossed over and where
these terms are used as a substitute for a more demanding form of
engagement, that is intriguing. Rushdie's style, robustly extroverted, rejecting nuance, delicacy and inwardness for multiplicity and polyphony, and,
moreover, the propensity of his imagination towards magic, fairy tales and
fantasy, and the apparent non-linearity of his narratives – all these are
seen to be emblematic of a non-Western mode of discourse, of apprehen-
sion, that is at once contemporaneously post-colonial and anciently,
inescapably Indian. Again, although the emphasis on the plural and the
multivocal, in this reading, is postmodern, the interpretative aesthetic is
surprisingly old-fashioned and mimetic: Indian life is plural, garrulous,
rambling, lacking a fixed centre, and the Indian novel must be the same.
Delicacy, nuance and irony apparently belong properly to the domain of
the English novel and to the rational traditions of the European Enlightenment; and inasmuch as these traditions have been involved with the
history of colonialism, nuance and irony must be looked on with suspicion.
A cursory glance at the ancient and modern literary traditions of India –
one thinks even of translations such as Ramanujan's English renderings of
ancient Tamil poetry or Arvind Mehrotra's versions of Prakrit love poetry
– will confirm that delicacy and nuance are not the prerogative of the
rational, bourgeois West alone, but are central to, and manifested with
great skill and beauty in, all significant examples of Indian writing. To
celebrate Indian writing simply as overblown, fantastic, lush and non-
linear is to risk making it a figure for the subconscious, and to imply that
what is ordinarily called thinking is alien to the Indian tradition – surely
an old colonialist prejudice.

A related way of assigning a fundamental Indianness to the post-colonial Indian novel in English is to place its 'magical' subject matter and its expansive, non-realist narrative mode in the lineage of epics such as the *Ramayana* and the *Mahabharata*, and texts like the *Thousand and One Nights*. While there are many differences between the traditional Indian epic and the post-colonial Indian English novel, one seems to be of particular importance; the mythic imagination from which those epics sprang was disturbingly amoral and estranging (I recall some of the British critics of Peter Brook's *Mahabharata* noting in wounded tones the Machiavellian, unfathomable nature of the Hindu god Krishna), and it is through this amorality that the epics reveal to us the mystery of human nature and the universe. The post-colonial novel, on the other hand, is frequently rooted in the liberal middle-class conscience and founded in the liberal humanist verities: multiculturalism is good; colonialism and fundamentalism are bad, etc. Further, it often rehearses a national narrative that every middle-class Indian child has learnt in school and which every member of the Indian ruling class is defined by: the narrative about colonialism and independence, and the idea of India as a recognizable totality. William Carlos Williams said of *The Waste Land* that it had returned poetry to the classroom; and there are those who, when reading some post-colonial narratives, will feel that they have gone back to their Indian Certificate of Secondary Education history textbook.

There is yet another way in which the post-colonial Indian novel is interpreted mimetically: in the proposition that, because the post-colonial, often diasporic, Indian is a hybrid entity, the language of the post-colonial too must be hybrid, with a scattering of untranslated Indian words and phrases and odd sentence constructions. What is perceived to be, or even constructed as, standard English is seen to be linked to an alien sensibility and to the verbal traditions of colonialism, and perhaps less adequate to the hybrid, multilingual nature of post-colonial, Indian consciousness. Hybridity, however, can frequently enter texts in subtly disruptive, rather than obvious, ways; it need not be worn like national constume. In his famous story, 'Pierre Menard, Author of the *Quixote*', Jorge Luis Borges, himself a multilingual, Anglophile Argentinian writer who was preoccupied with the idea of what constituted difference, and with a multiplicity of voices, invents Pierre Menard, a modern French writer who 'did not want to compose another *Quixote* – which is easy – but the *Quixote* itself'. Borges, who was shaped both by English and Spanish literatures, meditates, mischievously, on the nature of translation and artistic creation, and the subtle ways in which a hybrid, multilingual sensibility relates itself to language. Menard is French; but he does not attempt to appropriate Cervantes's language, nor Gallicize it; instead, he creates the *Quixote* by producing it verbatim. Let me quote two passages by other writers. The first is from a biography:

> It was a curious town with one long main street running through it, called Cavalierstrasse. The street was very long and had pavements on both sides. But so little traffic passed over it that it had to be weeded from time to time to get rid of the grass which came up through the chinks of the stones. The houses generally had only one storey, and some of them were mere cottages. Almost every house had a mirror fastened outside the main window, like the driving mirrors of today, so that the inmates could get notice of an approaching visitor.

The second is from an autobiographical novel:

> Rabbits came out to play on the snow, or to feed. A mother rabbit, hunched, with three or four of her young. They were a different dirty colour on the snow. And this picture of rabbits, or more particularly their new colour, calls up or creates the other details of the winter's day: the late-afternoon snow-light; the strange, empty houses around the lawn becoming white and distinct and important.

The first passage offers a description of a nineteenth-century German town, and is from Nirad C. Chaudhuri's life of Max Müller, *Scholar Extraordinary*; the second is a description of Wiltshire from V. S. Naipaul's novel *The Enigma of Arrival*. Both the passages could have been written by an English writer, in which case they would have been elegant and unremarkable; their peculiar meaning, however, operates in the fact that they are the products of hybrid sensibilities and histories, sensibilities belonging in one case to an Indian writer, and in the other to a writer of Indian origin; and these sensibilities and histories are not present in the writing in any obvious way, but are immanent in it. These writers, like Menard, create a new language by seemingly reproducing the old, a language of altered meanings in which hybridity and post-coloniality reside like the colour of snow and the rabbits in Naipaul's passage, on the border of absence and recognition.*

*

---

* R. K. Narayan wittily introduces the theme of 'copying' and its relationship, in the context of post-coloniality, to creativity, in the extract from *The English Teacher* included in this volume.

One of the subtlest ways, indeed, in which the multilingual imagination enters an Indian text has to do with the use of English words – not transmuted or 'appropriated and subverted for the post-colonial's own ends', as the current dogma has it, but, estrangingly, in their ordinary and standard forms; yet this is a practice whose import has been insufficiently acknowledged or studied. The peculiar excitement of the poetry that Ramanujan, Arvind Mehrotra or Dom Moraes (to take only three examples) wrote in the 1960s and 70s derived not so much from their, to use Rushdie's word, 'chutnification' of the language, but, in part, from the way they used ordinary English words like 'door', 'window', 'bus', 'doctor', 'dentist', 'station', to suggest a way of life. This was, and continues to be, more challenging than it may first appear; as a young reader, I remember being slightly repelled by the India of post offices and railway compartments I found in these poems; for I didn't think the India I lived in a fit subject for poetry. The poets I have mentioned appeared to make no overt attempts to 'appropriate' or 'subvert' the language, because the English language was already theirs, linked not so much to the colonizer as to their sense of self and history; these poets' use of language had less to do with the colonizer than with the modern Indian's exploration, and rewriting, of himself.

English words had entered Indian languages, their original shapes and meaning intact; and when Satyajit Ray, in his film *Kanchenjunga*, had his characters switch constantly between Bengali and English, he was neither, as his first American viewers concluded, depicting a set of deracinated Indians, nor celebrating as a curiosity Indian 'hybridity', but speaking directly to a middle-class Bengali audience in a language they already understood, a language of different linguistic, cultural and emotional registers. Buddhadev Bose notes the excitement he felt in the 1940s on encountering the English word 'bulb' in a poem by the great Bengali poet Jibanananda Das; not because it illustrated some notion of hybridity still decades from coming into fashion, but because Das's use of the word revealed some ordinary, inevitable, but resonant constituent in the intellectual and emotional texture of modern Bengali life that was then in the process of being articulated. Bose's recording of his excitement is not unlike Larkin's contentious and characteristically self-confident comment on Auden in an essay that appeared in 1960: 'He was, of course, the first "modern" poet, in that he could employ modern properties unselfconsciously ("A solitary truck, the last / Of shunting in the Autumn") ...' The 'modern' was not only an era, but a language, and poets everywhere had set about defining it, and discovering the ways in which they were defined by it.

Fredric Jameson has called the 'national allegory' the most characteristic form of the post-colonial novel, and has deemed pastiche the most characteristic literary form of postmodernism. This leads us to the way in which the construction of the post-colonial Indian novel in English – with its features of hybridity, national narrative, parody and pastiche – is connected to the movements and changes in the history of the West itself, especially in the late twentieth century, and to the possible notion that, in the Indian English novel, the West had found a large trope for its own historical preoccupations at least as much as it has discovered in itself a genuine curiosity for, and engagement with, Indian history and writing. From the 1970s onwards, and, in Britain, from the early 1980s, which was also, as it happens, the time of the publication of *Midnight's Children* and the rise of the new Indian English novel, the West has seen a decisive and sometimes invigorating assault on what Derrida has called 'the metaphysics of presence in the history of Western thought', in the form of Continental philosophy and American and European cultural movements; specifically, post-structuralism, postmodernism, and post-coloniality, the latter a discourse created mainly by migrant intellectuals. The impulse behind these schools and movements, if they can be called such, has been a sometimes necessary overturning of old certainties and hierarchies; the blurring of the line dividing 'high' from 'popular' culture; the rejection of authenticity in favour of 'difference' and hybridity; the preference, after Bakhtin, of the parodic over the original; in cultural studies, after Foucault and Said, the shift towards historical discourse and away from the literary; and the deconstruction of the idea of the author. Some of the reasons for this are clear and are related to Western history. Colonialism, for instance, has been based on a misrepresentation of the culturally different, as Said has shown, and the politics of exclusion and misrepresentation are involved in the creation of canons, which are formed by leaving out the 'different'. Any kind of 'authenticity', whether canonical, cultural, or textual, is thus in question. And this has to do not so much with the history of countries like India, where, during the nineteenth and twentieth centuries, a sense of the authentic was indispensable to the sense of self and the past, and where it has also been imbricated with a sense of hybridity and evolving plurality that has characterized its cultures for centuries, but with Western history, where 'authenticity', or 'purity', and 'hybridity' have not only existed, since the nineteenth century (if not since the Enlightenment), in mutually exclusive intellectual and cultural compartments, but where, more recently, after Auschwitz, 'authenticity' is associated with extreme right-wing politics and the destructive nature of masculine fantasy. At this point in Western history, hybridity is morally preferable to the authentic, quotation or discourse to 'presence', and post-colonial culture, in particular, the post-colonial novel, becomes a trope for an ideal hybridity by which the West celebrates not so much Indianness, whatever that infinitely complex thing is, but its own historical quest, its reinterpretation of itself.

When Derrida and the post-structuralists, taking as their forebears those philosopher-subversives, Nietzsche, Marx and Freud, began their attack on the relationship of the word to the world, of the text to presence, they were perceived as raising a critique of Western logocentric thought and creating a space for marginalized, even non-Western, cultures and voices. Ironically, in one respect this critique belongs to mainstream Western tradition, and goes back to its source: Plato. In a chapter in the *Republic*, Socrates reveals two orders of reality to his disciples; one, the reality of the phenomenal world, in which exist concrete objects like, say, a table, and the other the world of ideal form, in which the idea of the table exists immutably and timelessly. The idea of the table, Socrates suggests, is truer than the actual table. But, Socrates goes on to say sardonically, there is another, third table distinct from either of these; and when his fuddled disciple enquires what this is, Socrates furnishes a rather beautiful Protean description of the poet, and says that the third table exists in the work of the poet, and that the poet, incredibly, claims it is as real as the other two. Plato, here, is Derridean; any claim that the creative text or language makes magically to represent the world or capture reality is looked on with suspicion. Derrida's and Plato's quarrel concerns the ideal form, which Plato considers the only truth, while Derrida would see it as a logocentric construct or a 'transcendental signified'; however, they are both in agreement about the duplicity of the poet's claim that he can somehow represent, and in doing so convey, reality, or presence. This is worth remembering whenever we think that realist art is a profound constituent of the Western tradition, and that fantasy is somehow non-Western. Realism – the relationship that modes of representation have to the seasons, human life and the universe – has been a fundamental and unquestioned component of Indian art, from classical dance to the epics of Valmiki and Vyasa, the court poetry of Kalidasa, and the modern lyrics of Tagore; on the other hand, in Western culture, realist art, with its special claim to renovate our perception of the world, has always resided somewhat uneasily at the centre, repeatedly called on, like an immigrant, to justify the legitimacy of its existence.

The post-structuralist philosophers and postmodernist writers taught us to be playful and at the same time to disbelieve in the real with the ferocity and scepticism with which the atheists and materialists of old disbelieved in God. In the global, postmodern world, we live in the materialism of the sign. The old command economies pretended to cater to the wants of the needy; in the free-market economy the needy remain, an intractable and unaddressed signified, while money generates itself around the signifier, the idea of wealth and desire; wealth does not feed the poor, but itself. In a world of representations, what happens to the practices of reading and publishing? One hears, in relation to the novel, especially the Indian novel in English, that commerce and art have come together, that literary works of quality are becoming commercial successes. Can this be true? It doesn't really matter. In a culture of signification, the issue of what a 'real' masterpiece is, or whether such a thing can even exist, is an irrelevance; what matters is the marketing and consumption, after each successful publicity campaign and the awarding of each prize, of the signifier, the idea of the masterpiece, the idea of the Indian novel in English. What Indian fiction is, what the traditions and histories and languages are from which this real and heterogeneous entity emerged, is a signified that, paradoxically, almost has no presence.

'The Construction of the Indian Novel in English' was originally published in the Times Literary Supplement *in 1999.*

A Note on the Selection

There are eighteen writers in English in this volume, and twenty in the other Indian languages; this slight tipping of the scale towards 'regional' or 'vernacular' writing is not strategic or premeditated, but a numerical fact that has emerged after the completion of the selection. The single language with the most writers in this book is, however, still English. This is not because its literature, in India, exceeds the other Indian literatures in importance, but because this anthology happens to be in English – which means material in English is most readily and easily available – and because suitable translations are still hard to come by, though far less so than before. I should point out here that the number of pages allocated in this book to a writer, or a language, is not indicative or his or her, or its, standing in my eyes: a writer or a language with ten pages is not necessarily less significant than a writer or a language with twenty. The criteria for the inclusion of a piece have been its ability to give us a persuasive sense of the writer's work, and to reveal something new to us about the literature to which it belongs.

This is not a representative anthology; there is nothing, for instance, from Assamese, Gujarati, Marathi, and Punjabi, to take four languages at random. This is so partly because I couldn't find enough translations of quality in these languages from which to make a selection, and partly because there wasn't enough space to accommodate all the important writers in any one language in this anthology, let alone include something from every language. A representative anthology of Indian literature would have to be an ongoing project, and would probably run into several volumes; an attempt to present everything at once would risk either engulfing and overwhelming the reader, or missing him or her altogether, like one of those meteorites that hurtle past earth without making any noticeable difference to its atmosphere. I hope this selection, with its inevitable omissions, still gives, to the reader, in its trajectory and narrative, a sense of something of the quite amazing shape of modern Indian literature and narrative, and its provocative and engaging heterogeneity. Some famous names are, regrettably, missing, but those can easily be found in other anthologies, and in bookshops. Some writers I admire very much are absent, again for reasons of space. The literary form I most love, poetry, is absent too, for the same reason; the extract from Vikram Seth's *The Golden Gate* is in verse, but it is included here as an example of hybridized narrative fiction, rather than of poetry.

Finally, this anthology is not a riposte to any other anthology; it has taken shape, slowly, for the last five or six years, and the substantial inclusions from the Indian languages were planned from the beginning. Given my own multilingual cultural background, and the extent to which my sensibility has been formed by both the English and the Bengali languages, any other plan of selection would have been not only unthinkable, but would have required a complete change in my personality and outlook. One of the most positive by-products of the recent attention focused on Indian writing has been the small but increasing number of publishers, such as, for instance, Katha, Seagull, and Manas, committed to publishing translations, and translations of a better quality than has ever existed in India before. In part, this book is a homage to that work, and a record of my own discovery of these writers; the sophistication and the variety of techniques with which they deal with the subject-matter called 'India' has often been an education for me. The fact that some of the most rewarding work in English has been done outside of the domain of fiction, in the essay and the memoir, has also been reconfirmed to me during my work on this project. Another thing that has emerged for me during the making of this anthology, not as an idea but as a material determinant that must influence and shape the way each one of these works is written and read, is that modern Indian writing is no single, definable tradition, but multiple, occasionally competing, traditions embedded within traditions. We can see this in, for instance, Buddhadev Bose's essay on literary and colloquial language, or in his relationship to Tagore, or in the different directions that the figures of Rushdie and A. K. Ramanujan point to in post-Independence Indian culture, of multilingualism and the subconscious on the one hand, and postmodernism on the other. It is more important to acknowledge these contesting traditions within traditions than the imagined battle between the margin, or the once-colonized, and the colonial centre; they are a fundamental source of creativity as well as of, of course, fatuous quarrels. Both the shape of Rushdie's work, and his throwaway comment that little of value has been written in the Indian languages in the last fifty years, must be put within the context of such contestation to begin to be understood. Rushdie's remark is an interesting one, and also somewhat mystifying; less interesting, and equally mystifying, has been the sanctimoniously outraged and self-congratulatory response to the remark in liberal, middle-class India. Anyway, I can't remember another time in the recent past when the Indian urban middle classes extolled the virtues of regional writing at such length.

Among the writers here are those who are established nationally and internationally, those who are well known in their own languages but relatively unknown outside them, and new, sometimes underrated, writers who deserve to be better known both in India and elsewhere, and who have not been included in recent anthologies. There are, of course, others I might have included; but while I have already stated the reasons for my omissions, I can also declare that every piece in this book has been selected because it is, in my opinion, a literary work of a high order; nothing has been included to make a gesture towards representing a certain language or a phase in history. If there is anything this anthology says, it is that it is possible, in this time of post-colonial theory on the one hand, and trivial curiosity on the other, to place authors and their texts at the centre, rather than on the margins, of a discussion and reassessment of how we think about India.

THE BENGAL
RENAISSANCE
AND AFTER

Michael Madhusudan Dutt (1824–73)

One of the most profound and creative cross-fertilizations between two different cultures in the modern age took place in Bengal in the late eighteenth, the nineteenth, and early twentieth centuries. The first province to feel the full weight of the British presence in the eighteenth century was Bengal; and Calcutta, once three neighbouring villages by the river Hooghly in the south-western part of that province, emerged as probably India's first colonial city, its capital and the second city of Empire.

Collaboration, in the early days, between Bengalis and the British took, primarily, two forms. The first was trade and commerce, with entrepreneurs like Tagore's grandfather, Dwarkanath Tagore, benefiting immensely from acting as middlemen for the East India Company. The other was the phenomenon of scholarly and intellectual collaboration in the first half of the nineteenth century, before the so-called Mutiny in 1857 polarized colonized and colonizer permanently, as historians such as C. A. Bayly and others have shown; collaboration which produced, among other things, the first Bengali grammar, the reconstruction of Indian history by Orientalist scholars, and institutions like the Hindu College, where Western-style education was imparted. These complex phenomena – trade, the reconstruction of Indian history, the teaching of English, the creation of the Bengali grammar, the Indian students at these colleges – brought into existence a new, indigenous bourgeoisie and intelligentsia. This bourgeoisie set about redefining tradition in radical ways even as its members frequently led private or domestic lives more in keeping with conservative Hindu or Victorian mores; from the beginning, then, there was a self-division in this social class, a concern with genuine change but also with role-playing and concealment, all of which became part of a continual crisis of identity but a fundamental source of creativity as well. Intellectual and social change was precipitated in roughly two ways; first, for instance, by breaking caste or dietary taboos (by eating beef), and, more seriously, by instituting social reform (say, in support of widow remarriage). On the other hand, there was an attempt, on the part of this bourgeoisie, at recovering the very tradition that, at other times, it seemed intent on redefining or even disowning. In other words, this bourgeoisie created, for the first time in India, a secular space in which tradition was no longer an autochthonic, hierarchical set of codes that must be adhered to, but an inseparable part of the Indian self and memory that was being reconstructed in the nineteenth century, the renewing power of that tradition sanctioned by no higher an authority than the individual himself.

The figure of Michael Madhusudan Dutt (1824–74) belongs to this context. In his personal and creative life, we see again the twin impulses towards, on the one hand, the disowning or, at best, redefinition of tradition, and its recovery as a creative constituent of the secular self on the other; contradictory but persistent and linked impulses that would contribute to the shape of the Bengal Renaissance, and of modern India itself. Dutt studied at the Hindu College, and wrote poetry in English (he sent a poem to *Blackwood's Magazine* dedicated to William Wordsworth, but there was no response from the journal; see also the extract below) in his quest to become a canonical 'English' poet. When still at the college, he converted to Christianity; whether as a perverse reaction against the Hinduism he'd come to dislike, or in defiance of his father, or in his desire to become more completely 'English', it is not known (at any rate, he does not seem to have led a particularly 'Christian' life). If he then disowned his past, his past, or, more specifically his father, disowned him as well. He was striking in personality and appearance, and reminded those who knew him of Othello; his life compensated in eventfulness what it lacked in stability. He abandoned his Eurasian wife, an indigo planter's daughter, and his children in Madras, in 1855, the year in which his father also died. Returning to Calcutta, he started from scratch; took another Englishwoman, Henrietta, as his life's companion; took up a series of jobs; wrote Bengali plays and translated two of them into English. Now, after the long process of disowning, came the process of recovery. In the letters below (both the extract from the essay and the letters are originally written in English), one sees how the Hindu gods and goddesses return to Dutt, but not as they would to a believer; instead, they inhabit the secular stage of Dutt's consciousness, as they would, increasingly, that of modern, secular India, in a way such that their significance is never quite fathomable, but never quite lost. At the age of 37, then, he remade himself as the first modern Bengali, and Indian, poet of true importance. Dutt chose as subject-matter for his epic *Meghnada Badha Kabya* (1861) an episode from the Hindu epic, the *Ramayana*, which he had heard from his mother as a child, but made the son of Ravana, the hero Rama's traditional adversary, the tragic protagonist of his poem. Dutt was an admirer of Milton, and while approximating Miltonic blank verse in Bengali with startling effects, he used the Miltonic inversion of *Paradise Lost*, where Satan is a contested but unforgettable protagonist, to make the transition from the certainties of a religious epic, and religion itself, to the ambivalences of a secular work and the construction of a new secular self as reader and writer, caught between the simultaneous processes of disowning and recovery. 'I hate Rama and all his rabble,' said Dutt; perhaps neither this statement nor the epic poem would have been quite possible in today's BJP-ruled India, which has witnessed the demise, in one sense, of the struggle for a kind of redefinition which began in the early nineteenth century. The diverse provenances of Dutt's epic – the oral transmission, in Bengali, of the *Ramayan*; classical Bengali metre; Milton; Miltonic and Greek epic simile; the progressive culture of the Bengali bourgeoisie – remind us that the cosmopolitanism and multilingual, eclectic modernism that would come to Europe in the twentieth century had come to Bengal and India in the nineteenth, at a time when Victorian England was still relatively provincial and inward-looking. In 1862, indeed, he left for England, registered at the Gray's Inn, was joined there later by his wife and children, and spent a miserable period studying law. Running out of money, he moved to Versailles in France, but returned to England eventually to take his exams at the Bar. He returned to Calcutta in 1867, and began practising law at the High Court. Dutt led an extravagant life, and spent more than he earned as a barrister; he often borrowed money from his indulgent friends, some of whom were towering presences in their own right. His health deteriorated in 1872, and he died tragically at the age of fifty in a hospital, three days after Henrietta died at home. He is buried in the Park Circus cemetery in Calcutta.

* * *

from *'The Anglo-Saxon and the Hindu'* (1854)

I stand before you – not as a Columbus, proudly claiming the meed of a discoverer of unknown worlds; I stand before you – not as a Newton, whose god-like vision penetrated the blue depths of ether and saw a new and a bright orb, cradled in infinity; I deal in no mysteries; I am no sophist, ravishing the ear with melodious yet unmeaning sounds; captivating the eye with sparkling yet meretricious ornamentalism – beautiful, yet artificial flowers, glittering yet false diamonds. No! – the fact I enunciate, is a simple one; – even he who runneth may read it. But its simplicity ought not to destroy its grave importance You all know it – you all see it. Why has Providence given this queenly, this majestic land for a prey and a spoil to the Anglo-Saxon? Why? I say – It is the Mission of the Anglo-Saxon to renovate, to regenerate, to Christianize the Hindu – to churn this vast ocean, that it may restore the things of beauty now buried in its liquid wilderness; and nobly is he seconded – will he be seconded, by the Science and the Literature of his sea-girt father-land – the Literature of his country – baptized in the pure fountain of Eternal Love![1] And here let me pause for a moment.

When a man suddenly stands before her, to the golden shrine of whose beauty, his impassioned soul kneels in the sinless idolatry of love; the lustre of whose eyes is dearer far to him than the light of sun, or moon, or star; the sound of whose voice is sweeter far to him than strains from angel-harps; a lock of whose raven hair – in the enthusiastic words of the Prince of the Persian Lyre – is far more priceless to him than Samarkand and Bokhara – he is as one dumb. What tongue can utter the thoughts of delirious joy, which oppress his bosom? I acknowledge to you, and I need not blush to do so –. that I love the language of the Anglo-Saxon. Yes – *love* the language – the glorious language of the Anglo-Saxon! My imagination visions forth before me the language of the Anglo-Saxon in all its radiant beauty; and I feel silenced and abashed.

I have heard the pastoral pipe of the Mantuan Swain;[2] I have heard that Mantuan strike, with a bolder hand, the lyre of heroic poesy and sing of arms and the man whom the hatred of white-armed Juno imperilled both by land and by sea! I have listened to the melodies of gay Flaccus, that lover of the sparkling bowl, and the joyous banquet; I have heard of bloody Pharsalia,[3] and learned to love Epicurus, the honour of the Greek race;[4] I have sighed over the sad strains of him, who in his cheerless exile, sang of the hapless and the absent lover;[5] the harp of the blind old man of Scio's rocky isle,[6] singing of the wrath of Achilles, the direful spring of woes unnumbered to Greece, has often hushed my soul to awe; I have seen gorgeous Tragedy, in sceptered pall come sweeping by presenting Thebes' or Pelop's line;[7] I am no stranger to the eloquence of fiery Demosthenes, of calm and philosophic Cicero; I am no stranger to marvel-relating Livy; to sententious Thucydides; to the delightful out-pourings of the father of historic novelists – the man of Halicarnassus;[8] I have heard the melodious voice of him[9] who from the green tree of Poesy sang of Rama like a Kokila; I have wept over the fatal war of the implacable Courava and the heroic Pandava;[10] I have grieved over the sufferings of her who wore and lost the fatal ring; I have wandered with Hafiz on the banks of Rocknabad and the rose-bowers of Mosellay: I have moralized with Saddi, and seen Roustum shedding tears of agony over his brave but hapless son; I have laughed with Molière; the melody from the dismal prison-cell of Torquato Tasso, has soothed my ears. I have visited the lightless regions of Hades with Dante; I know Laura's sad lover[11] who gave himself to fame with melodious tears; but give me the literature, the language of the Anglo-Saxon! Banish Peto, banish Bardolph, banish Poins, but for sweet Jack Falstaff, kind Jack Falstaff, banish him not thy Harry's company; banish plump Jack and banish all the world![12] I say, give me the language – the beautiful language of the Anglo-Saxon!

I have heard would-be Quinctilians talk disparagingly of this magnificent language as irregular, as anomalous. I disdain such petty cavilers! It laughs at the limit which the tyrant Grammar would set to it – it nobly spurns the thought of being circumscribed. It flows on like a glorious, a broad river, and in its royal mood, it does not despise the tribute waters which a thousand streams bring to it. Why should it? There is no one to say to it – thus far shalt thou go, and no farther! Give me, I say, the beautiful language of the Anglo-Saxon.

1. Cowper   2. Virgil   3. Lucan   4. Lucretius   5. Ovid   6. Homer   7. The Greek Tragedians (Milton)   8. Herodotus   9. Valmiki   10. The *Mahabharata*   11. Petrarch   12. *Henry IV Part I*

* * *

Two Letters

My dear Raj Narain,

I ought to apologize to you for not having replied to your kind and welcome letter so long; but I must warn you not to expect anything like regularity in me as a correspondent. I am by nature a lazy fellow, besides, I have a great deal to do. I have my office-work to attend to; I generally devote four or five hours to Law; I read Sanskrit, Latin and Greek and scribble. All this is enough to keep a man engaged from morn to dewy eve and so on. However, here you are – as I just half an hour to devote to the pleasant task of writing to an old friend whom I have at last learnt how to value.

Some days ago I wrote to my publisher to send you a copy of the new drama; I am very anxious to hear what you think of it. I am of opinion that our dramas should be in Blank-verse and not in prose, but the innovation must be brought about by degrees. If I should live to write other dramas, you may rest assured, I shall not allow myself to be bound down by the dicta of Mr Viswanath of the Sahitya-Darpan. I shall look to the great dramatists of Europe for models. That would be founding a real National Theatre. But let me know what you think of Padmavati.* I am sure I need not tell you that in the First Act you have the Greek story of the golden apple Indianized.

Tilottama† is printed, though the Printer has not yet sent it out. You shall have a copy as soon as possible. As I believe you are one of the writers of the Tattwabodhini Patrika, will you review the Poem in the columns of that Journal? That would be giving it a jolly lift indeed. If you should review the work, pray, don't spare me because I am your friend. Pitch it into me as much as you think I deserve, I am about the most docile dog that ever wagged a literary tail!

I feel highly flattered by the approbation of your wife. She is the first lady reader of Tilottama and her good opinion makes me not a little proud of my performance. I did not read that part of your letter to Rangalal, who is often with me, for we were boys together at Kidderpore and he used to call my mother (God rest her soul!) mother. He is a touchy fellow, but, I have no doubt, is ready to allow that, as a versifier, I ought to hang my hat a peg or two higher than his. My opinion of him is – that he has poetical feelings – some fancy, perhaps, imagination, but that his style is affected and consequently execrable. He may improve. Tilottama seems to have created some impression on him, as you will find in his very next poem.

I am glad, my dear fellow, that your domestic discomforts are gradually disappearing. I pray God to bless you and make you happy. You fully deserve to be so, for you are an honest-hearted and guileless fellow, full of enthusiasm and in some points what the world in its wisdom would call – a fool. You may rest assured that I am longing to see you.

I am going on with Meghanad by fits and starts. Perhaps the poem will be finished by the end of the year. I am glad you like the opening lines. I must tell you, my dear fellow, that though, as a jolly Christian youth, I don't care a pin's head for Hinduism, I love the grand mythology of our ancestors. It is full of poetry. A fellow with an inventive head can manufac-

---

*   Editor's note: Bengali play by Dutt, 1860.

†   Editor's note: 'Tilottama Sambhava Kabya', Dutt's first long poem in Bengali, 1860.

ture the most beautiful things out of it. When you get your copy of Tilottama you must send me a regular Aristotelian letter about the fable, the characters, the sentiments and the language. You must also review it in such a way (publicly) as to initiate our countrymen into the mysteries of a just and enlightened criticism. What a vast field does our country now present for literary enterprise! I wish to God, I had time. Poetry, the Drama, Criticism, Romance – a man would leave a name behind him, 'above all Greek, above all Roman fame.' I wish you would take up the subject of criticism. Aristotle, Longinus, Quintilian, the Sahitya-Darpan, Burke, Kames, Alison, Addison, Dryden and a host of others, not forgetting old Blair's lectures or the German Schlegel. If you don't read Sanskrit with ease, get a Pandit to work under your direction.

Where is the fat old Deputy Magistrate of B— now? I have not written to him for a long time and that is why he is vexed with me. Pray send him my love. That, I hope, will soothe his irritated feelings as a tub is said to do with reference to a whale or Leviathan.

When do you mean to come to Calcutta? By the Bye, can you induce the Educational Superintendent of your side of the world to take Tilottama by the hand for the higher classes of your school? With you for a teacher, the book is sure to make a tremendous impression.

You must know, my good friend, that I am in mourning for a relative of my wife's – that died in England five months ago. I am sorry I have no news to give you. I lead the life of a recluse, conversing with the mighty dead through the medium of their works and caring as little for the living world as possible. I hate most of the newspapers of the day – Native and English. They do contain such rubbish! And now adieu, my dear fellow. Write to me always but don't expect me to keep pace with you. Gour has given me up as a hopeless job. Pray, don't follow that fellow's example. With sentiments of the sincerest affection.

15th May, 1860   Ever yours most sincerely.

P.S. – Your good wife, by the bye, is not the first lady-reader of Tilottama. The author's wife claims to have read it before her.

*

My dear Raj Narain,

I don't know how it is, but I fancy that you have been writing to me a long letter but that I have lost it through the carelessness of the Post Office folks. If I am correct, then you must take the trouble of writing to me again for I am anxious to know what you think of the Tragedy; but if not, you must allow me to ask you the meaning of this long silence. Has the book disappointed you? Here people speak well of it; tho' I must say that men of your stamp are anything but common here.

The 'odes' are out, and I have requested Baboo Baikunta nath Dutta (a co-religionist of yours) who is the proprietor of the copyright, to send you a copy. You must also tell me what you think of them. We are now printing the last Book (IX.) of Meghanad. So you may expect him by the beginning of the next month (English).

How you are, old boy, a Tragedy, a volume of Odes and one half of a real Epic poem! All in the course of one year; and that year only half old! If I deserve credit for nothing else, you must allow that I am, at least, an *industrious dog*. I am thinking of blazing out in prose to reduce to cinders the impudent pretensions of the 'mob of gentlemen' who pass for great authors. Great authors!! great *fiddle-sticks*!! But of that by and by. You may take my word for it, friend Raj, that I shall come out like a tremendous comet and no mistake. Pray, what are you doing? Where is that grand Theological Book of yours that is to convert all manner of sinners to *Brahmoism*.*

We have just got over the noise of the Mohurrum. I tell you that: – if a great Poet were to rise among the Mussulmans of India, he could write a magnificent Epic on the death of Hossen and his brother. He could enlist the feelings of the whole race on his behalf. We have no such subject. Would you believe it? People here grumble and say that the heart of the Poet in Meghanad is with the Rakhasas. And that is the real truth. I despise Ram and his rabble; but the idea of Ravan, elevates and kindles my imagination; he was a grand fellow.

I showed your letter in which you say that you prefer the I and IV Books to the rest, to a friend. He said your silence about *Pramila's* entry into *Lanka* in the III Book surprised him. The silly fellow went on to say that the episode roused him like the clang of a martial trumpet! But *De gustibus non est disputandum*.

I must now conclude. Pray, hereafter address your letter to the 'Care of James Frederick Esqr. Kidderpore' or at the Police Office. I have given up 'No 6 Lower Chitpore Road.' Hoping you are quite well, old boy, with affectionate regards.

Yours affectionately.

---

* Editor's note: The Brahmo Samaj, a Hindu reformist sect, was founded by Rammohan Roy in 1828 in Bengal. Its Protestantism was an important basis for the middle-class liberal humanism of modern Bengal.

P.S. Harish is dead. They are kicking up a row on the subject and propose to establish a 'Scholarship'. Fie! why not a Statue? However, I shall subscribe. I loved and valued the man. *Vale,* as the Latins used to say or *au revoir* as the French say.

Bankimchandra Chatterjee (1838–94)

Bankimchandra Chatterjee (1838–94), son of a Deputy Collector, belonged to the first, small batch of graduates from Calcutta University in 1858. He was, later, a magistrate in the government's employ when he started writing his essays (two of which are included below), in both English and Bengali (both essays below were written in English), about, among other things, colonial Bengali society, ancient Hinduism, and babu culture. (The 'Young Bengal' in the essay 'Confessions of a Young Bengal' below was a group of radical young men, students of Henry Vivian Louis Derozio at the Hindu College, who were also, thus, called the Derozians. The group was formed in the late 1820s, some time before Bankimchandra Chatterjee's birth, and earned notoriety by breaking dietary taboos – by eating beef, for instance – and denigrating idolatry and superstition, and championing free will. They were not infrequently a subject of satire.) In 1864, Chatterjee wrote *Rajmohan's Wife*, his first novel and one of the very earliest Indian novels in English. Crucially, by the time the seminal figures of Dutt and Chatterjee were emerging, the Mutiny had already occurred in 1857; this, and some other political changes, including the passing of colonial power from the Company to the Crown, brought into existence a polarization between colonizer and colonized such as had not existed before. Thus, the efflorescence of modern Bengali literature and the emergence of modern India went largely unremarked and unnoticed in Britain and in colonial society. This did little to dampen the vigour of that great efflorescence, which came to be known as the Bengal, or Indian, Renaissance, which would proceed, in its open-ended, cosmopolitan fashion, with unprecedented creativity, before the very eyes of the English in the second city of the Empire. Chatterjee wrote his first novel in Bengali, *Durgeshnandini*, in 1865, inaugurating the first major fiction oeuvre in a modern Indian vernacular. His fiction is a mixture of realism and fantasy, of the historical yarn from which he moves to, gradually, the uncharted territory of middle-class Bengal. His novels, complex both in terms of their diction and their plot, are difficult to extract from. This did not prevent the avid readers of the periodical *Bangadarshan* (which he'd started himself in 1872), among whom was the young Tagore, from reading his novels eagerly, instalment by instalment, as they appeared in serialized form (the fictional Apu was an impatient reader, in an obscure village, of a different periodical, *Banga-basi*: see the section from *Pather Panchali* below). There is some justifiable controversy over Chatterjee's anti-Islamic views; these, like the subject-matter of his historical novels, Chatterjee partly owes to the work of the Orientalist scholars, and their reconstruction of Hindu, pre-Moghul antiquity as the 'true' India. Interestingly, Chatterjee's fiction, with its occasional anti-Muslim rhetoric, was, for the delights it offered, still, in Urdu translation, an important body of work for Urdu readers, as was the writing of the Bengal Renaissance; a comic account of how the ethos of the latter influenced the educated Muslim elite in Lucknow is to be found in Qurratulain Hyder's melancholy story in the Urdu section. Chatterjee, however, was himself a product of Bengali cosmopolitanism, and the short extract from his novel *Rajani* extracted below (fairly faithfully translated, notably, by Nirad C. Chaudhuri, a later, hybrid product of that Renais-sance, with a characteristically Chaudhurean comment from him at the end) is a tribute to such a cosmopolitan figure, the sort of figure that Kipling would later savagely caricature in *Kim*.

* * *

'A Popular Literature for Bengal' (1870)

By a popular literature for Bengal I mean a Bengali literature. Bengali literature must for a long time to come be nothing more than merely the popular literature of Bengal. As long as the higher education continues to have English for its medium, as long as English literature and English science continue to maintain their present immeasurable superiority, these will form *the* sources of intellectual cultivation to the more educated classes. To Bengali literature must continue to be assigned the subordinate function of being the literature for the *people* of Bengal, and it is as yet hardly capable of occupying even that subordinate, but extremely import-ant, position.

I believe that there is an impression in some quarters that Bengali literature has as yet few readers, and that the few men in the country who do read, read only English books. It must be admitted that there is a certain amount of truth in this supposition, but it is by no means wholly true. It may be that there are few systematic readers of Bengali, because there are so few Bengali books capable of being read through. But it is not altogether correct to entertain the idea that the absolute number of purely Bengali readers are in reality so few. The artisan and the shopkeeper who keep their own accounts, the village zemindar and the mofussil lawyer, the humbler official employé whose English carries him no further than the duties of his office, and the small proprietor who has as little to do with English as with office, all these classes read Bengali and Bengali only; all in fact between the ignorant peasant and the really well-educated classes. And if to these be added the vast numbers who are likely to benefit by a system of vernacular education, extended and developed so as to suit the requirements of the country, we may be in a position to appreciate fully the importance of a literature for the *people* of Bengal; for these classes constitute *the people*.

And we Bengalis are strangely apt to forget that it is only through the Bengali that the people can be moved. We preach in English and harangue in English and write in English, perfectly forgetful that the great masses, whom it is absolutely necessary to move in order to carry out any great project of social reform, remain stone-deaf to all our eloquence. To me it seems that a single great idea, communicated to the people of Bengal in their own language, circulated among them in the language that alone touches their hearts, vivifying and permeating the conceptions of all ranks, will work out grander results than all that our English speeches and preachings will ever be able to achieve. And therefore it is that I venture to draw the attention of this Association* to a subject of such social importance as a literature for the people of Bengal.

A popular literature for Bengal is just blundering into existence. It is a movement which requires to be carefully studied and wisely stimulated, for it may exert a healthy or a pernicious influence on the national character, according to the direction it takes. The popular literature of a nation and the national character act and react on each other. At least in Bengal there has been a singular harmony of character between the two since the days of Vidyapati and Jaydeva. Jaydeva was the popular poet of his age and the age which followed him. It may seem absurd to say so now, but it must be remembered that all who read at that period, read in Sanskrit; and, besides, Jaydeva's poems used to be sung, as they are even at the present day.

And it would be difficult to conveive a poem more typical than the

Gitagovinda of the Bengali character as it had become after the iron heel of the Musalman tyrant had set its mark on the shoulders of the nation. From the beginning to the end it does not contain a single expression of manly feeling – of *womanly* feeling* there is a great deal – or a single elevated sentiment. The poet has not a single new truth to teach. Generally speaking, it is the poets (religious or profane) who teach us the great moral truths which render man's life a blessing to his kind; but Jaydeva is a poet of another stamp. I do not deny him high poetical merits in a certain sense, exquisite imagery, tender feeling and unrivalled power of expression, but that does not make him less the poet of an effeminate and sensual race. Soft and mellifluous, feeling tender and as often grossly sensual, his exquisitely sounding but not unfrequently meaningless verse echoed the common sentiments of an inactive and effeminate race. And since then all Bengalis who have ventured on original composition have followed in his footsteps. The same words may be used to describe the writings of Madhava, the second best of the Bengali Sanskrit poets. The writings of the poets who wrote under the patronage of the Nuddea Raja were the same in character, and worse perhaps, for they had all the faults of Jaydeva in an exaggerated form and but few of his redeeming beauties. Till lately, the Bidya Sundar, the best known production of that age, continued to be the most popular book in all Bengali literature. After the Nuddea poets, we come to the day of the *kabis, jatras* and love-songs, the only species of literary composition to which the nation confined itself for generations. And fit intellectual food they were for a race who had become incapable of comprehending any other class of conceptions!

Along with this species of poetical literature, Bengal was developing within itself two other systems which were the peculiar property of the Bengali intellect – Law and the Nyaya Philosophy. The Bengali had lost all dignity of character and all manliness; but he had not lost his acuteness of intellect. So from the days of Kulluka Bhatta to those of Jagannath volume after volume and commentary after commentary were written to interpret and expand and alter and mystify a system of law, which already in the hands of its original framers had gone beyond the proper limits of legislative interference, and set unbearable restraints on individual freedom of action. And this unlimited expansion and development of an already ponderous system of law, or rather of law and religion welded into one

---

* Editor's note: Chatterjee repeats a typical British racial construction of the period, where the 'effeminate' Bengali is contrasted with, say, the 'manly' Pathan, a construction that would be used by Kipling in his fiction four decades later.

solid mass, tended only to multiply *ad infinitum* the iron bonds under which the Bengali already groaned – until all his pleasures and his aspirations became restricted to his hookah and his love-songs. In weightier matters the spiritual guide and the interpreter of law regulated, even still regulates, his destiny.

And the splendid Nyaya Philosophy which flourished side by side with it, and to have matured and developed which constitutes the sole claim of Bengal to intellectual pre-eminence in any department over the other provinces of India, had little influence on the people, for it did not reach them. It was to them an unintelligible jargon with which they had no concern, which nobody cared to interpret to them, and the inherent rationalism of which therefore remained a secret with its exclusive professors. What a blow to the immense mass of Bengali superstition would that philosophy have been, if it had been allowed to see the day! But the only effect which it had on the destinies of the people was the importation of its subtleties into the endless mazes of Hindu law, and its endowment with a borrowed strength which it never could have commanded of itself.

And thus the national character and the productions of the national intellect acted and reacted on each other. Indolent habits and a feeble moral organization gave birth to an effeminate poetical literature; and then for ages the country fed and nourished itself on that effeminate literature. The acute but uncreative intellect of the Bengali delighted to lose itself in the subtle distinctions of the law, and he indulged in the favourite pastime till he had succeeded in making his own bonds tighter and more intimate.

And so the Bengali stood, crushed and spiritless, insensible to his own wrongs, till a new light dawned on him, to rouse him, if that were possible, from his state of lethargy. And with this new dawn of life came into the country one of the mightiest instruments of civilization, the printing-press. Gradually the change set in, and a demand began to be made for a literature of another character than that of the *Gitagovinda* school. It is not my wish to pursue the history of the national mind any further, for the facts are known to all. It is my object to point out to those who wish to bestow attention on the subject, *first*, that there is already a certain demand for a popular literature for Bengal, and that the demand is likely to be greater very speedily; *secondly*, that both the quantity and *quality* of the supply is of vital importance to the community; *lastly*, that, whatever the quantity is, the quality is very inferior at present.

If you will look over the quarterly returns published by Government, you will find that the Bengali mind is anything but unproductive. But its productions are remarkable for quantity alone; the quality is on an average contemptible – often they are positively injurious. Excepting a few books of recognized excellence, they are, when they are nothing more mischievous, either clumsy imitations of good Bengali models, or abject copies of the silly stories of the later Sanskrit writers, or a string of harmless commonplaces. I beg leave to point out two causes as conducive to this state of things.

The first is the disinclination of the more educated classes to write for their country in their own language. Authorship is with us still the vocation of the needy and fawning pundit, or the ambitious schoolboy, or the idle scribbler who must needs be an author simply because he cannot be anything else. Those who can teach their country, consider it beneath their social position to do so. It is degrading for the dashing young Bengali who writes and talks English like an Englishman, to be caught writing a Bengali book. And if anything induces him to stoop to this vulgar course, the book comes out stealthily, without the great man's name on the title-page, and hence many of our best books are anonymous. There are a few honourable exceptions, and these men have done an immense good to Bengali literature. It is a fact that the best Bengali books are the productions of Bengalis who are highly cultivated English scholars. The matter for regret is how few these books are, and how few the scholars who have written them.

The second cause is the absence of sound and intelligent criticism.* Intelligent criticism may be said to be a thing unknown to the Native Press. There is some inherent defect in the Bengali character which renders the task of distinguishing the beautiful and the true from the gaudy and the false, a task of even greater difficulty than the higher effort of creation. This deficiency in the culture of the cultivated Bengali reacts on the literature. The blundering critic often passes a verdict, which, if he happens to be an authority accustomed to command respect on literary matters, misleads by its error and strikes at the root of all excellence. Those who have seen, as I have, an audience of Bengali gentlemen sitting patiently to listen for hours to the flash and froth and rant which is poured forth in native theatres, and calling the whole thing a good drama, will doubtless understand why the Bengali drama is so inferior in its character. And the same sort of criticism keeps down other branches of literature to the same low level.

---

* Editor's note: A persistent problem, alas, even one hundred and thirty years after Chatterjee made this statement.

Another great impediment to the formation of a respectable and read-able popular literature for Bengal is the extremely low idea some people entertain of the capacities of the Bengali-reading public. It is assumed that books intended for them must contain childish stories and information suited to children only and treated in a childish style,* or they will not suit the understanding of the adult reading population of Bengal. No kind of literary excellence, no sentiments of a manly and elevating character, must be permitted to creep into such books; no glimpse of that wondrous world of scientific knowledge which European research has revealed; nothing but its dry details and naked skeleton can be allowed to the Bengali reader. He will not understand them, he will not read books which contain such things. This idea is a great mistake. The fact is that the Bengali will read only such books as contain anything worth reading; and books manufac-tured on a principle which ignores him as an intellectual being he will not read, and he does not read. Our most popular authors have succeeded by following precisely an opposite course. It is by following the principle of so-called *simple* publications, that so respectable a body as the Vernacular Literature Society have failed to make any contributions to the popular Bengali literature worth the name. It is, however, due to that body to say that the Bengali periodical published under their auspices offers a remark-able exception to this criticism, and that it is the most useful publication of the kind in all Bengali periodical literature.

I have to suggest only another topic in connection with the subject for discussion – the creation of some suitable agencies for the circulation of readable books in the mofussil. Books will doubtless reach the most remote village in the interior when it will pay tradesmen to carry them there, but that day is distant yet. The mofussil mainly depends at present on supplies brought by itinerant hawkers. Their visits are always few and far between; their stock scanty and ill-selected. I mention the subject because I have often heard complaints from residents in the mofussil. The Vernacular Literature Society has special agencies of its own at many places; and these agencies are, I believe, available on certain conditions to the general public for the sale of books not published by the Society, but I am not aware that the public make use of them to any considerable extent. Cannot the system be utilized to a greater extent?

To me it seems that all that can be done at present is the establishment of village Public Libraries. I know that a few such institutions have been already called into existence by public-spirited residents in the mofussil. It

---

*   Editor's note: Another typical colonial construction.

is desirable that they should become more general. A beginning may be made in every village where there is a Vernacular or Anglo-Vernacular School. One of the teachers of the school under the supervision of the School-Committee may keep charge of the books, and in the school-house room may be found for the bookshelves. Thus village libraries may be formed at once without more cost than the price of the books and the shelves. Educational officers who travel so much, and officers in the executive and administrative departments who command so much influence, may do much in this direction if they think fit. I do not think the suggestion is one difficult to carry out – it has been already carried out in several places.

* * *

'The Confession of a Young Bengal' (1872)

That, in the outward circumstances of social and personal life, English-educated Bengalis are rapidly getting Anglicized, few English-educated Bengalis will deny. The stamp of the Anglo-Saxon foreigner is upon our houses, our furniture, our carriages, our food, our drink, our dress, our very familiar letters and conversation. He who runs may read it on every inch of our outward life. We build, and fit up, our houses, according to English ideas of architectural beauty, ventilation and general comfort. Our ancestors, in building houses of any pretension to grandeur, invariably postponed all considerations of the ease and comfort of the human inmates to a pious regard to the befitting accommodation of the various celestials during their thirteen appointed visits in the course of the twelve months. The *Poojah Dâlân*, the apartment dedicated to the idols, was invariably that portion of the house upon which the lion's share of the whole estimated cost was spent, which was most adorned with the architectural decorations of the time, which, in its dimensions, surpassed every other apartment – which, in short, determined by its style and magnificence, the owner's position in society. In the houses built by English-educated Bengalis, the *Poojah Dâlân* is conspicuous only by its absence, so much so that it would not, perhaps, be altogether superfluous to refer to a piece of philological evidence to prove that it was not always so: – in many rural villages in Bengal, *Dâlân* is, to this day, synonymous with a brick-built house. Chairs, tables, punkahs, – seldom meant to be pulled,

American clocks, glassware of variegated hues, pictures for which the *Illustrated London News* is liberally laid under contribution, kerosene lamps, bookshelves filled with Reynolds' Mysteries, Tom Paine's *Age of Reason* and the *Complete Poetical Works of Lord Byron*, English Musical-boxes, compose the fashionable furniture of the sitting-rooms of Young Bengal. Not to speak of Calcutta and its suburbs; it was only the other day that the Lieutenant-Governor congratulated the enlightened gentry of Rajshaye upon what struck His Honour as the most prominent concrete manifestation of English civilization in that district, – dog-carts, to wit. The solemn assurance of His Honour that he was not joking was perfectly needless. Whatever might be the degree of confidence which said enlightened gentry reposed in His Honour's declarations touching his complete code of self-government for Bengal, there is not the shadow of a shade of doubt that their own opinion was only too faithfully echoed by His Honour's observations touching the dog-carts. We have ceased to be strict vegetarians and teetotallers. We have no objection, – on principle, – to dine on roast beef or veal cutlets, nor any, either on principle or in practice, to *drink*, in the idiomatic English sense and after the English fashion. Our conversation is nine parts broken English, and one part pure Bengali. We have exchanged the cumbrous forms of Bengali epistolary correspondence for those of Cook's Universal Letter-writer, and the tight-fitting jackets and loose-flowing *chapkans* of our grandfathers for shirts *á l'anglaise* and *chapkans* that are every day steadily approaching towards the shape and size of English coats, to say nothing of our English shoes, the eyesore of official Anglo-Indians.

English education, administered with the most rigid economy and the example of Englishmen, wrapped up with the threefold covering of national, political and religious exclusiveness have, in a single generation, sufficed to work these changes in the external features of Bengali Society. Paradoxical as it may seem, the second is by much the most powerful agency of the two, though, without *some* share of the first, it cannot have free scope for its operation. A six months' visit to England, accomplished with the lightest possible equipment of English, does far more to Anglicize one's taste, manners and fashion than a lifelong devotion to English literature at home. Cases of conflict between the action of English education and that of English example are not rare, in which the result has proved to demonstration the superior energy of the latter.

The very idea that external life is a worthy subject of the attention of a rational being, except in its connections with religion, is, amongst ourselves, unmistakably of English origin. In spite of their emphatic inculcation of the duty of self-preservation, the prevailing tendency of our Shastras was towards a severe asceticism, founded upon a profound feeling of the transitoriness and unreality of this world.

Our ancestors thought and felt, with the immortal poet of universal human nature, with the one man in the world's literature whose works hold up a mirror to every possible phasis of man's inner life, –

> Pour soul, the centre of my sinful earth,
> Fool'd by those rebel powers that thee array,
> Why dost thou pine within and suffer dearth,
> Painting thy outward walls so costly gay?
> Why so large cost, having so short a lease,
> Dost thou upon thy fading mansion spend?
> Shall worms, inheritors of this excess,
> Eat up thy charge? is this thy body's end?
> Then, soul, live thou upon thy servant's loss,
> And let that pine to aggravate thy store;
> Buy terms divine in selling hours of dross;
> Within be fed, without be rich no more:
> > So shalt thou feed on Death, that feeds on men,
> > And Death once dead, there's no more dying then.*

No doubt, they did not, – without ceasing to be human beings, they could not, – quite act up to these sentiments; but they could never justify to their conscience any care bestowed upon food and raiment for their own sake. English civilization has pulled down the three hundred and thirty million deities of Hinduism, and set up, in the total space once occupied by them, its own tutelary deities, Comfort and his brother, Respectability.

We lack the candour and the courage to confess this change of faith, but whichever way we look at the matter – whether by direct self-examination or by indirect study of our inner in our outer life, we are forced to admit that it is to this complexion we have come at last.

We are labouring in downright earnest to break down the joint-family system. We are endeavouring to raise the national standard of living and to foster independence of character. Fine phrases. Have you reflected for a moment on their real signification? You are tearing asunder the only bond of social union in a society which has yet to learn the very first lessons in

---

* Editor's note: William Shakespeare, Sonnet 146.

the art of co-operation. Or do you, after all, in spite of your petitionings and memorializings and the incessant outpourings of your newspaper press, really suppose that the 'Village Municipality' will, as a school of co-operation, supersede the antiquated joint Hindu family? What, again, have you to say to the inhumanity of defeating the rational expectations of your relations – expectations founded on the uniform experience and traditions of ages? To take the lowest ground, are you blind to the economical convenience – if you have an arithmetical turn of mind and some knowledge of money-matters, you can easily estimate it in solid rupees, annas and pice, – are you blind to the economical convenience of dwelling and messing together to the bulk of your countrymen who are little removed from a condition of abject pauperism? You are bringing into fashion a habit of heartless isolation which, very unlike your highly volatile 'High Education', is steadily filtering into the inferior strata of the community. Fostering independence, forsooth! Do not lay that flattering unction to your soul. Your interest and your duty are so happily in unison in this same matter of fostering independence of character in your poor relations that you ought really to pause and consider what you are about. One thing is quite clear: this zeal for the formation of a national habit of self-reliance never shows itself, except in the sunshine of comparative prosperity.

We have cast away caste. We have outlived the absurdity of a social classification based upon the accident of birth. But we are not such ultra-radicals as to adopt for our watchword the impracticable formula of 'Equality and Fraternity'. Thank God, we are not so far Frenchified as that. We have received a High English education. Our culture is thoroughly English and we mean to reconstruct society according to English notions. Do you wish to know our definition of a respectable man? Here is one which will give you as correct an idea as any other.

> Q. What do you mean by 'respectable'?
> A. *He always kept a gig.*
>
> (Thurtell's Trial)

It is the balance at the banker's which fixes a man's place in society; the cumulative humanities of a hundred generations are nothing to the purpose.

Such of us as are gifted with exceptionally disciplined minds and have appreciatingly imbibed the best and the most recent English teaching concerning individuality and non-conformity, eat, dress and conduct ourselves in society exactly like Englishmen, the usual allowance for the imperfection of a first attempt being, of course, made. The Bengali accent refuses to be quite forgotten, the English idiom every now and then proves quite treacherous, above all, the transmigration from 'black' to 'white' defies the existing resources of chemistry and cosmetics, but as regards the main points of first, a scrupulously exact English costume, with its collateral incidents of occasional invitations to dinner from Englishmen and occasional salaams from Railway porters and cabmen, and secondly, a habitual manifestation, by word, look and gesture, of a thorough contempt for 'niggers', their attempt is usually crowned with success. Who shall censure them? If the national constume of Bengalis has become a badge of subjection, surely the sooner it – the costume – is cast aside the better.

Our Deism, our Theism, our Brahmoism,* progressive or ultra-progressive, our Comp (sic) teism – apparently an indigenous religious development, the morality of which was recently discussed, under that strange designation, with equal ability and learning in more than one issue of a Calcutta newspaper, – what are all these isms at bottom but merely so many different embodiments of a strong desire to exempt ourselves from the obligations of Hinduism? No enlightened human being can endure semi-barbarous restrictions concerning food – and drink; no enlightened human being can afford to forgo the commonest comforts of life for finding means for the extravagantly expensive superstitions of benighted parents; no enlightened human being can find it in his heart to respect a man whose only claim to respect is founded on an old-fashioned ascetic purity of life, and an intimate acquaintance with a literature, full of false history, false geography and false physics; no enlightened human being can bring himself to believe in the moral excellency of perpetual widowhood; and soon to the end of the chapter of grievances. The necessary minor premises being assumed, sound logic compels us to cry with one voice, Hinduism must be destroyed.

Agreed. But the spiritual nature of man abhors a vacuum. Between our various isms, the Hindu code of personal and social ethics has been wellnigh wholly repealed, and its precepts are universally seen and felt to be more honoured in the breach than in the observance. Where is our new code of morality? Where is the new public opinion to enforce its rules? Where is the man amongst us who in personal purity, in meekness, in self-forgetfulness, in genuine non-political patriotic feeling, in tenderness for the least sentient thing, in lifelong and systematic devotion to knowledge

* Editor's note: See footnote in Dutt, p. 10 and Tagore, p. 26.

and virtue for their own sake, can stand a moment's comparison with the better order of minds nurtured in the cradle of Hinduism? Let the tree be judged by its fruit.

* * *

from *Rajani* (1877)

translated from the Bengali by Nirad C. Chaudhuri

He did not disclose his business, nor could I ask him outright. So we discussed social reform and politics. I found him an accomplished conversationalist. His mind was cultivated, his education complete, and his thought far-reaching. There being a pause in the conversation, he began to turn over *The Shakespeare Gallery* on my table. In the meanwhile, I had a good look at him. He was a most handsome man; fair, rather short but neither stout nor lean; his eyes large, hair fine, curly and carefully arranged; he was not over-dressed but was perfectly neat; a man with an exquisite conversational style and a beautiful voice. I could plainly see that he was a sophisticated person.

Amarnath did not come to business even after the plates of *The Shakespeare Gallery* had been gone over, and began to discuss the pictures. His thesis was that it was an audacious conceit that tried to depict in a picture what was expressed in language and through action; such attempts could never be successful, nor were these pictures successful. He opened the picture of Desdemona and observed: 'You get her patience, sweetness and modesty, but where is her courage with the patience, and her pride of constancy with the modesty?' He pointed to the illustration of Juliet and said: 'You have here the figure of a beauty in the first flush of youth, but you miss youth's irrepressible restlessness.'

Amarnath continued in this vein. From Shakespeare's heroines he came to Sakuntala, Sita, Kadamvari, Vasavadatta, Rukmini, and Satyabhama, and he analysed their characters. The discussion of ancient literature led in its turn to ancient historiography, out of which there emerged some incomparable exposition of the classical historians, Tacitus, Plutarch, Thucydides, and others. From the philosophy of history of these writers Amarnath came down to Comte and his *lois des trois états*, which he endorsed. Comte brought in his interpreter Mill and then Huxley; Huxley brought in Owen

and Darwin; and Darwin Buchner and Schopenhauer. Amarnath poured
the most entrancing scholarship into my ears, and I became too engrossed
to remember our business.

*

[Nirad C. Chaudhuri comments in *The Autobiography of An Unknown
Indian,* 1951]

This passage is significant not because it came to be written by a man
who probably had the most powerful intellect and the best intellectual
equipment of any Indian in the nineteenth century, and who was the
creator of Hindu nationalism and the writer of the *Vande Mataram* song,
but because it embodied an ideal which even an ordinary educated
Bengali felt compelled to pursue. The social compulsion was such
that the volume of pretence sometimes exceeded the volume of real
education, but on the whole it served a good purpose. It kept in check
that display of ignorance, airy or arrogant according to the character
and manners of the exhibitor, which today makes informed persons
thoroughly ashamed of themselves in company.

Rabindranath Tagore (1861–1941)

Born in Calcutta, Rabindranath Tagore (1861–1941) was, as a boy, an admirer of Chatterjee, and was, in turn, admired by him on the publication of his first book of poems, *Sandhya Sangeet* (*Evening Songs*) in 1880. It was a precocious debut; but Tagore belonged to one of the most extraordinary families in the cultural history of modern India. His grandfather was 'Prince' Dwarkanath Tagore (1794–1846), an entrepreneur who became one of the richest Indians of his time, during the early phase of colonial trade, and then went on to amass great debts which he left, along with his estates, his son Debendranath (1817–1905) to inherit. Debendranath, Tagore's father, moved in another, unworldly direction, and became a sort of Platonic philosopher-king, both managing the estates and exploring, increasingly, the spiritual life. He was also one of the pillars of Raja Rammmohun Roy's Brahmo Samaj, the Hindu reformist movement which was to be so crucial to the formation of both modern Bengali middle-class *bhadralok* (literally, 'civilized person' or 'civil person') society, and of secular India. The Samaj espoused a form of Protestant Hinduism; it rejected the idolatry and innumerable divinities of Hinduism, replacing them with the transcendental, nameless god of the *Upanishads*. This god fitted in quite well with, and presided over, the new puritan work ethic of the Bengali, which directed him towards education, science, and rationality. It was the Brahmo temperament that Tagore inherited, that he articulated, and whose limits were also severely tested by him.

As if it wasn't enough to have a grandfather and father of such stature, Tagore came from a family that produced pioneering composers, painters, and poets, and also the first Indian member of the Indian Civil Service. He was something of a black sheep himself; the youngest of fourteen children, he grew up with something of the solitariness of an only child; there are pages devoted, in his memoirs, *Jiban Smriti* (*My Reminscences*) to the activity of day-dreaming in childhood, and he would have possibly been the first to acknowledge the uncomfortably close association day-dreaming has with creativity. In 1878, he was sent to England by his father; he attended some lectures at University College, London, but returned without completing his studies or taking a degree. In this regard, too, he was an anomaly in that family of intellectual achievers, and in the new *bhadralok* society as a whole, with its high regard for education and professional qualifications. As a poet, he was intermittently held in the highest esteem, and also repeatedly reviled by older poets like D. L. Roy, and not a few critics. His core achievements as a writer begin to become apparent only now; that, as one preoccupied from the start with the fragmentary moment of heightened sensory and intellectual perception, he was probably one of the first Modernists of the Victorian age.

'The Postmaster', included below, written in 1891, is one of his earliest stories, and enters uncharted terrain in a number of ways. Firstly, it introduces the insignificant citizens of the colonial world – the postmaster, the servant-girl – into the centre-stage of fiction. On the other hand, it relegates the more 'significant' actor of colonization, the Englishman briefly mentioned in the first paragraph, to the backstage. The story, for its time, is astonishingly modern, in spite of the exacerbated Victorian emotionalism towards the end; there are no twists in the tale, no complexities in the plot. It is more absorbed in image and memory, with smell and sound, with the idea of exile and belonging, than with progression and denouement. It also introduces themes to be found in many of the pieces in this volume: the ambivalent social (and, implicitly, creative) relationship the Indian middle class has with its rural or feudal antecedents, turning to them for spiritual sustenance, while rejecting, materially and intellectually, the way of life they represent.

The letters below are among those he wrote between 1886 and 1895, during, in his own words, 'the most productive period of my literary life, when, owing to great good fortune, I was young and less known'. These were written when Tagore was looking after the family estates, moving down the river on a houseboat, the auditory and sensory world he was confronted with finding its way into his poetry, and the ordinary people he was coming into contact with on his estates entering his fiction. The letters, juxtaposed with the story, provide a fascinating record of how a literary oeuvre, and a modern tradition, emerges. One of the letters describes a postmaster on whom he might have based the character in his story; another letter describes the postmaster reading the same story in a magazine. These are casual but extraordinary records of the creation of a space in which a modern culture comes into being and lives; 'reality' becoming transmuted into imagination, and then the all-important element of *recognition*, as a reader, in the early days of an evolving sensibility, discovers his altered incarnation within the fictional world.

Tagore's life was a relatively tranquil one for the first fifty years of his life; although it was a tranquillity that had been repeatedly pierced by tragedy. When Tagore was 23, his sister-in-law, Kadambari Devi, whom he was probably in love with, committed suicide, and her absence haunted him all his life; later he was to lose some of his children – two daughters, Rani and Bela, and a son, Shamik – and then his wife Mrinalini. In 1912, the painter William Rothenstein 'discovered' Tagore through the poems the latter had translated into English, a series of loosely structured prose poems whose fidelity to the originals is tenuous, and which do not in any way reflect their tone, form, or language. These translations were circulated in literary London, and found champions in Yeats and Pound; soon after, in 1913, Tagore was awarded the Nobel Prize for the *Gitanjali*, a collection of these translations, and Pound and Yeats and the London literary establishment promptly lost interest in him. Tagore was thrust into an international celebrity (based on a misprision of the nature of his work) such as few poets had known before; as were his poems and, in a sense, modern Indian literature. Unfortunately, both Tagore and modern Bengali literature were reinvented to represent an unbroken lineage of religion and wisdom, rather than situated in the modernity and middle-class culture to which both belonged; Tagore dressed in long robes and long beard (in Buddhadev Bose's words, a 'whiff of incense' emanating from his proximity), while his 'translated' poems were dressed up in a quasi-biblical, mystical, often mystifying, diction.

While Tagore played his part on the international stage as a 'world poet' (*bishwakabi*), he also continued to be engaged, in Bengali, in what was his most profound undertaking: the delving into the subconscious of the middle-class, secular Bengali psyche. The little essay on Bengali nursery rhymes included below records his exploration of the stirrings of the subconscious, of the power and mystique of words, rather than religion, in a secular world. It, and the tender but combative introduction Tagore wrote to the book of fairy tales that is now every Bengali child's staple, is indicative, too, of how important the construction of childhood, and the landscape of childhood, was to the formation of the modern Bengali identity, and of nationhood.

* * *

Rabindranath Tagore

'The Postmaster' (1891)

translated from the Bengali by Amit Chaudhuri

As soon as he took up employment, the postmaster found himself sta-
tioned at Ulapur. It was a village of no consequence. There was an indigo
planter's home nearby, and the sahib had made every effort to get a post
office established in the environs.

Our postmaster was a young man from Calcutta. Arriving in this village
left him feeling not very unlike a freshwater fish that has been lifted onto
a riverbank. His office was a dark thatched shed; not far away there was a
weed-infested pond with a jungle on its borders. The agents and workers
at the plantation had little time on their hands and were anyway unfit to
mix with genteel people.

Moreover, the young man from Calcutta was particularly lacking in
social skills. Unfamiliar places found him become aloof or awkward. Which
was why he didn't mix too easily with the local people. On the other hand,
he didn't have enough work to occupy him. From time to time he
attempted to write a poem or two. The sentiments he expressed in them
were largely that life passed in great happiness in the day-long proximity
of the tremor of trees and leaves and of the cloudy sky – but the lord of
his innermost self knew that if some giant out of an Arabian novel were to
come there and uproot, in one night, the trees with their green branches
and leave a macadam road in their place, if several tall buildings were to
obliterate the clouds in the sky that were now clearly visible, this half-
dead progeny of *bhadralok* society would receive a new lease of life.

The postmaster's salary was negligible. He had to cook himself, and a
parentless girl from the village would do his household work, in exchange
for a little food. The girl was Ratan. She would have been twelve or thirteen
years old. There seemed to be no great possibility of her getting married.

When, in the evening, smoke, curving and coiling, rose from cowsheds
in the villages, crickets began to be heard in the bushes, and intoxicated
Baul mendicants in the distance struck their drums and cymbals and
launched into song in high-pitched voices – when, sitting in the dark
porch, there would be a small palpitation even in a poet's heart, then,
lighting a slender wick in the corner of his room, the postmaster would

Ratan would be sitting by the door awaiting the call, but come into the room when she first heard it; she'd say, 'What is it, you, why are you calling me?'

The Postmaster: 'What are you doing?'

Ratan: 'I have to go right now to light the stove – in the kitchen – '

The Postmaster: 'Oh you can do your kitchen-work later – would you first bring me my hookah?'

A little later, Ratan would enter, blowing into the hookah, her cheeks inflated. Taking the hookah into his hands, the postmaster asked suddenly: 'Ratan, do you remember your mother?' That was a lengthy matter; what she remembered, and what she didn't. Her father loved her more than her mother; she remembered him a little. He would return home in the evening after a day's hard work; one or two of those evenings, for no good reason, had remained imprinted like pictures in her mind. As she spoke of these things, Ratan would gradually lower herself onto the floor beside the postmaster. She would recall she had a younger brother – on a monsoon day years ago they had stood by a pool and, pretending a broken branch was a fishing-rod, played at a make-believe game of catching fish – this memory came back to her more frequently than more important events. They would talk in this way late into the night sometimes, and the postmaster would feel too lazy then to cook any more. The morning's leftovers would still be there, and Ratan would quickly light the stove and make a few chapattis – in this way they'd both make do for the night's meal.

On certain days in the evening, the postmaster, sitting upon the office bench in one corner of that large shed, would introduce the subject of his own family – his younger brother, mother, elder sister, those people for whom his heart ached as he sat by himself in a foreign place. Things that he always remembered but couldn't speak of in any circumstance to the agents at the plantation were what he would talk about with this illiterate, insignificant girl, without thinking it in any way inappropriate. As a result, the girl, in the course of the conversation, began to refer to the people in his family as 'mother', 'elder sister', 'elder brother', as he did. She even drew, from imagination, their forms and features upon the small canvas of her heart.

One day, during the monsoons, a tender, slightly warm breeze was blowing on a cloudless afternoon; a sort of fragrance had risen from the wet grass and trees in the sunlight; it seemed as if the warm breath of the exhausted earth were falling against one's skin; and somewhere a persistent bird repeated its complaint in one long-drawn note before the court of nature's creation the afternoon long. The postmaster had no work on his hands – the movement of the rainwashed leaves on the trees, become smooth and satiny that day, and the vanquished rains' ruins – the piles of many-levelled clouds made white by the sun – were truly something to look at; the postmaster was contemplating this sight and thinking, If at this time there were someone near who was truly my own – at one with my heart, a human figure that was a tender object of love. Gradually it appeared to him that that bird too was saying this very thing repeatedly, and that what the branches were murmuring in the midst of that human-less seclusion of forest shade was of more or less the same nature. No one would believe it nor come to know of it, but, in the midst of profound silence on a long off-day, thoughts like these arose in the mind of a negligibly-salaried sub-postmaster in a small village.

The postmaster sighed deeply and called: 'Ratan.' Ratan was then, legs outstretched, beneath a guava tree, eating a guava; hearing her master call she ran to him without delay – out of breath, she said, 'Dadababu, did you want me?' The postmaster said, 'I'm going to teach you to read a little every day.' So saying, he spent the entire afternoon teaching her to speak the alphabet. And in this way, in only a few days, they had gone past the stage of the compound letters.

There was no end to the rain in the month of Sravan. Canals, lakes, and drains filled with water. For twenty-four hours the sound of frogs and of rainfall. The paths of the village, in one sense, out of use – people had to go in canoes to the market square.

One day it was very cloudy at dawn. The postmaster's student had been sitting expectantly for a long time at the door, but, not hearing the call, which on other days was punctual as could be, slowly entered the room with her small bundle of books. She saw the postmaster was lying on the string-bed – supposing him to be resting she began again to leave the room while taking care not to make a sound. Suddenly she heard – 'Ratan!' Quickly returning she said, 'Dadababu, were you asleep?'* The postmaster said in a woeful voice, 'I don't feel very well – would you touch my forehead and see?'

Here, in this quite companionless foreign place, in the heavy downpour, the afflicted body longed for a little looking after. What came to mind was the touch of a mother or an elder sister by one's side; and this migrant's desire didn't remain unfulfilled. The little girl Ratan didn't stay a little girl. At that instant she was transformed into a mother. She got the local *vaidya*[†]

---

* Dadababu: master: but with familial resonance, as 'Dada' can also refer to an older brother or a grandfather.
† *vaidya*: traditional doctor.

to pay a visit, gave the postmaster the medicinal pills at the right times, remained awake all night by the bedside, cooked the sick man's food by herself and would ask repeatedly, 'Tell me, dadababu, are you beginning to feel a little better?'

Many days later the postmaster, much thinner, abandoned the sickbed; he'd decided, No more, I have to get a transfer out of here somehow. Citing a local illness, he immediately sent a formal request to the authorities in Calcutta for a transfer. Her service at the sickbed having come to an end, Ratan returned to her old place outside the door to the room. But she wasn't called in as before. She'd occasionally peep in to see that the postmaster, in an extremely absent-minded way, was sitting on the bench or had lain down on the string-bed. While Ratan sat waiting in hope of being summoned, he was impatiently awaiting the reply to his request. The girl sat down by the door and reread her old textbook numberless times. What if she was suddenly called again and, on that day, found herself completely confused about the compound letters: this was the cause of some trepidation. In the end, after about a week had passed, there was a call for her one evening. Her heart brimming with excitement, Ratan entered the house and said, 'Dadababu, were you calling me?'

The postmaster said, 'Ratan, I'm leaving tomorrow.'

Ratan: 'Where are you going, dadababu?'

The postmaster: 'Home.'

Ratan: 'When will you come back again?'

The postmaster: 'I won't come back.'

Ratan didn't ask him any other questions. The postmaster informed her of his own accord that he had applied for a transfer, and that the application had been denied; and so he was putting in his resignation and returning home. No one spoke for a long while. The light of the earthen lamp began to flicker weakly and in one part of the room rainwater fell drop by drop, through an aperture in the ageing roof, upon an earthenware vessel below.

After some time, Ratan rose slowly and began to knead some dough in the kitchen. Her task wasn't finished as quickly as it was on other days. Probably thoughts travelled in and out of her head. When the postmaster's dinner was over, the girl asked him, 'Dadababu, will you take me home with you?' The postmaster laughed and said, 'How can I do that?' He didn't think it necessary to explain to her the reasons that made it impossible for him to give any other answer.

All night long, in her sleep and dreams, the sound of the postmaster's laughter rang in her ears – 'How can I do that?'

Early in the morning the postmaster woke up to see that the water for his bath was ready; in keeping with the customs of Calcutta, he used to bathe in water that had been collected in a pail. For some reason, the girl hadn't been able to bring herself to ask him at what time he'd set out; she'd gone late at night to the river to collect the water in case he needed it at dawn. When the bath ended, Ratan was summoned. Ratan entered the house soundlessly and, awaiting a directive, gazed silently upon her master's face. Her master said, 'Ratan, I'll tell the man who's going to come in my place, he'll take care of you just as I did; you don't have to worry because I'm leaving.' That these sentiments came from a most tender and compassionate heart there was no doubt, but it's difficult to fathom a feminine heart. Ratan had for many days silently tolerated many sharp remarks from her master, but couldn't endure these gentle words. Overcome, she cried, 'No no, you don't have to say anything to anybody, I don't want to stay here.'

The postmaster had never seen Ratan behave in this way; he was astonished.

The new postmaster arrived. After explaining to him his responsibilities, the old postmaster was ready to make his journey. Before leaving, he called Ratan and said, 'Ratan, I've never been able to give you anything. Today, before going, I'm leaving something for you, you'll find it'll last you a few days.'

He took out his salary from his pocket, all of it except what would be necessary for the expenses of the journey. Then Ratan fell to the dust and embracing his feet said, 'Dadababu, I fall at your two feet, I fall at your two feet, you don't have to give me anything; I fall at your two feet, no one needs to worry about me' – and then, in a burst of speed, fled from that place.

The ex-postmaster sighed, hung the carpet-bag from one arm, balanced the umbrella on one shoulder, having lifted the white-and-blue-painted trunk onto a coolie's head, and slowly walked towards the boat.

After he'd got onto the boat, and it had sailed forth, the river, full with rain, brimming at the bank like teardrops in an eye, he experienced in his heart an intense ache – as if the suffering face of an ordinary rural girl-child had brought to light a great, world-encompassing, inarticulate pain. At one point he felt a great desire, 'Let me go back, let me take that world-abandoned orphan child with me' – but by then the wind had reached the sail, the monsoon current was flowing swiftly, and, the village behind them, the cremation pyres on the banks could be seen – and, carried by the river, the traveller, afloat, found a sorrowful insight taking birth in his mind, There are so many such separations, such deaths, in life, what will come of turning back? Who belongs to whom in this world?

But no such insight came to Ratan's mind. She, weeping unstoppably, was only wandering again and again about the building of the post office. Perhaps there was a tenuous hope in her heart, to do with dadababu coming back – trapped, she found herself unable to go far from where she was roaming. Alas, the mistaken human heart! Its delusions never end, the laws of reason enter the mind after much delay, disbelieving incontestable evidence it embraces false hope with both arms and all its might to its breast; in the end one day, severing the umbilical cord and sucking the heart empty of blood, it flees, there is then a return to one's right senses, and the mind grows restless again to embrace its next delusion.

* * *

Five Letters

translated from the Bengali by Krishna Dutta and Andrew Robinson

Calcutta, 27 July 1887 (12 Shravan 1294)

I have reached my twenty-seventh year. This fact keeps intruding on my thoughts – nothing else seems to have happened in the last few months. But is having reached twenty-seven a trifling thing? – to have passed the meridian of one's twenties on one's progress towards thirty? Thirty. Maturity: the age at which people naturally expect fruits rather than green shoots. Alas, where is the promise of fruit? When I shake my head it still feels full of frivolity, without even a kernel of philosophy.

People are beginning to complain:

Where is that which we hoped of you? For quite a while we have been expectantly watching the tender green of the unripe state and it has pleased us, but we cannot put up with immaturity forever, you know. It is high time that we learn what we may extract from you. We require an estimate of the amount of oil that an unblinkered unprejudiced critic can squeeze out of you.

My old excuse will not wash any longer. As long as I was youthful people trustfully gave me credit until I should come of age. Now that I am nearly thirty I ought not to keep them waiting. But what am I to do? Words of wisdom will not come! I am incapable of satisfying the general public. Beyond a snatch of song, some tittle-tattle and some harmless fun, I have been unable to advance. Those who had high hopes for me will undoubtedly turn on me; but did anyone ever beg them to nurse such expectations?

These are the thoughts that have preoccupied me ever since waking on that fine spring morning in Baishakh amidst new leaf and flower, light and breeze, to find that I had stepped into my twenty-seventh year.

*

Shahzadpur, 7? February 1891 (26? Magh 1297)

Just in front of my window, on the opposite side of the stream, a band of gypsies has settled and constructed shelters out of bamboo frameworks hung with split-bamboo mats and pieces of cloth. There are only three of these little structures, so low one cannot stand inside them upright. The whole of gypsy life is lived in the open, except at night when they creep under these shelters and sleep huddled together. That is the gypsy way: no fixed abode, no zemindar requiring rent, they just wander about as they please with their children, their pigs, and a dog or two, watched constantly and vigilantly by the eyes of the police.

I have been keeping my own eye on the doings of the family nearest my window. By no means bad-looking they remind me of people from north-western India. Though dark, they are handsome, strong and shapely. Their women have tall, slim, taut figures; with their independent air, confident carriage and quick, straightforward movements, they strike me as swarthy Englishwomen.

One of the men has just put a cooking-pot on the fire and is now splitting bamboos and weaving winnowing trays, baskets and other items. The woman first balances a small mirror in her lap, then carefully moistens a towel and wipes her face several times, adjusts and tidies each fold in her upper garment, and finally goes, spick and span, to find her man, squat beside him and help him now and then in his work.

They are truly sons and daughters of the soil, in constant touch with it. Born in some unknown place, brought up on the road, they will die in an equally unknown place. Night and day is spent under the open sky, in the open air, on bare ground. It is a unique existence – and yet work, love, children and domestic duties are all included.

They do not sit idle even for a trice but always are doing something. When her own task is finished, a woman suddenly plumps down behind another, unties the knot of her hair and begins delousing and arranging it for her. Whether they fall to discussing the affairs of the three little mat-covered households I cannot say for certain at this distance, but I shrewdly suspect it.

This morning the carefree camp experienced a great disturbance. It happened about half past eight or nine, while the gypsies were spreading out their tattered bedding quilts and sundry other rags to sun and air them. The pigs and piglets were lying in a hollow like blobs of mud, relishing the morning sunshine after the cold of the night, until routed out by the two canine members of the ménage and sent squealing in search of their breakfasts. I was writing my diary, absently looking out from time to time, when a real hubbub suddenly began.

I got up and went to the window, and saw a crowd gathered around the gypsy residence. At its centre was a personage flourishing a stick and using the choicest language. The leader of the gypsies cowered in front of him, apparently trying to offer explanations. I gathered that suspicious happenings in the area had attracted the attentions of a police constable.

The woman had so far remained seated, busily scraping lengths of split bamboo as serenely as if she had been alone and there was no row in progress. All of a sudden she sprang to her feet, strode up to the constable, gesticulated violently in his face with her arms, and loudly gave him a piece of her mind. In the twinkling of an eye three-quarters of the officer's haughtiness subsided; although he attempted to say a word or two in mild protest he got little chance. He backed off in a manner much different from that of his arrival. When he had retired to a safe distance, he shouted back: 'All I say is, you'd better get out of here!'

I expected my neighbours to pack their mats, roll up their bundles, rustle up their pigs and their offspring, and make their exit forthwith. But there is no sign of it yet. They are still nonchalantly splitting bamboos, cooking food, and picking lice.

*

Shahzadpur, 9? February 1891 (28? Magh 1297)

Some evenings the postmaster comes upstairs to have a chat with me. His office is on the ground floor of our building – very convenient, for we get our letters as soon as they arrive. I enjoy our talks. He tells of the most improbable things in the gravest possible fashion.

Yesterday he informed me of the reverence towards the Ganges shown by the people of the locality. If someone dies, he said, and the relatives do not have the means to take his ashes to the Ganges, they powder a piece of bone from the funeral pyre and keep it until they come across a person who at some time or other has drunk the water of the sacred river. To him they administer some of this powder, hidden in a courteous offering of *paan*, and are so content to think that their deceased relative has finally made his pilgrimage to the blessed waters – or at least a portion of him has.

I smiled as I remarked: 'This must be a yarn.'

He pondered for quite a while and then admitted: 'Yes, it probably is.'

*

Shahzadpur, 29 June 1892 (16 Asharh 1299)

Earlier I wrote that tonight I had an engagement with Kalidas the poet. At seven o'clock, my appointed hour, I lit a lamp, drew up my chair to the table, and sat ready, book in hand – when instead of Kalidas the postmaster walked in. A live postmaster cannot but claim precedence over a dead poet. I could not very well say to him: kindly make way for Kalidas, who is due any minute now – and if I had, he would not have understood me. So I pulled out a stool and quietly said goodbye to old Kalidas.

There is a kind of bond between this postmaster and me. When the post office was on the ground floor of the estate building, I used to meet him every day and in this very room upstairs I wrote my story 'The Postmaster'. When it came out in *Hitabadi* our postmaster touched on it after a series of bashful smiles. I must say I like the man. He is a fund of anecdote into which I dip and silently enjoy. He also has a nice sense of humour.

It was quite late when he left and I got started on the *Raghuvamsa*. I read about the *swayamvara* of Indumati. Seated on rows of thrones in the marriage hall, splendidly attired, striking-looking princes are kept waiting. Suddenly blasts of conch-shell and bugle sound, and Indumati, in bridal finery supported by Shunanda, enters and stands between the rows of suitors. What a superb picture!

Then she is introduced by Shunanda to the princes one by one, and to each of them Indumati bows low, touching his feet in a loveless *pranam*, and passes on. How beautifully she does it! Though she rejects each one she is so respectful that her gesture seems like reverence. They are all princes and all her seniors, for Indumati is a mere girl: and yet she passes over them. Had she not wiped away that stain with the humility of her *pranam*, the scene would have lost its grace.

*

Shahzadpur, 5 September 1894 (20 Bhadra 1301)

All of a sudden I realized how hungry for space I had become and so now I am taking my fill of it. Here I am sole monarch of these rooms and have thrown open all the doors and windows. I feel the mood and the will to write here as nowhere else. The living essence of the outside world floats in freely in verdurous waves of light and air and sound and scent that mingle with my bewitched mind and mould it into story after story after story.

The intoxication is especially strong in the afternoons. Heat, hush, solitude, birdsong – especially the cawing of crows – and languid, limitless leisure together remove me from reality.

I believe, though I have no proof, that the *Arabian Nights* came into being upon such sun-baked afternoons, in Damascus, Samarkand and Bokhara. I can see the bunches of grapes and the wild gardens of roses, hear the melody of bulbuls, taste the wines of Shiraz. In the desert there is only a file of camels, an itinerant horseman or a crystal spring beneath a date palm to be seen. But in the city, below bright canopies overhanging narrow alleys in the bazaar, there sit turbaned loosely attired merchants selling melons and pomegranates, while not far away in a great palace perfumed with incense, on bolsters and kincob-covered divans within balconies, reclines Zobedia or Amina or Sufia, dressed in a gaily decorated jacket, flowing pyjamas and gold-embroidered slippers, her hubble-bubble pipe coiled at her feet, and her person guarded by gorgeously liveried Abyssinians. Such a prodigiously grand and mysterious setting in such a faraway country was bound to lead to a thousand tales – credible and incredible – of the deepest hopes and fears of mankind.

Noontime in Shahzadpur is high noon for story writing. It was at this time, at this very table, I recall, that my story 'The Postmaster' took over my thoughts. The light, the breeze and the movement of leaves on all sides combined and entered my writing.

* * *

An Essay on Nursery Rhymes (1907)

translated from the Bengali by William Radice

For some time I have been engaged in collecting all the Bengali rhymes that women currently use to divert their children. These rhymes may indeed have special value in the determination of the history of our language and society, but it is the simple, natural, poetic quality in them that has made them especially attractive to me.

I am fearful of making my simple likes or dislikes my critical starting-off point, because those who are expert critics condemn such writing as egoism.

I would humbly submit to those who make this judgement that there is no conceit in such egoism, rather the reverse. Those who are proper critics carry a pair of scales; they ascribe to literary works a fixed weight by weighing them against certain fixed maxims; whatever composition is before them, they can give it an appropriate number and stamp.

But those who through ignorance and inexperience are unable to determine weight in this way have to base their criticism on pleasure or displeasure; so for them it is arrogant to introduce gospel truth into the discussion of literature. They find it better to say which piece of writing they like or dislike than to say which is good or bad.

If anyone asks me who wants to hear such things, my reply is that everyone comes to hear them in literature itself. The word 'criticism' is reserved for literary criticism, but most literature is nothing but a criticism of nature and human life. When a poet expresses his own joy or grief or surprise concering nature, mankind or events, and tries to convey his feelings through passion and literary skill alone to another mind, no one condemns him. And all the reader does is to see, equally egotistically, 'whether the poet's words agree with my way of thinking or not'. So if the critic of poetry is also prepared to abandon logical argument and value-judgement and present to his readers the feeling of a reader, then it is not right to find fault with him.

In particular, what I have sat down to communicate today will have to contain some autobiography. It is impossible for me to distinguish the aesthetic delight that I find in nursery rhymes from my own childhood memories. The present writer does not have the analytic power required to decide how much the sweetness of these rhymes is based on my own infant memories and how much on eternal literary excellence. It is best to admit this at the outset.

'The rain falls pitter-patter, the river has overflowed.'* This nursery rhyme was like a magic spell to me in childhood, and I still cannot forget its enchantment. I am unable to appreciate clearly the sweetness and appropriateness of nursery rhymes unless I remember that spellbound state of mind. I cannot understand why so many poems great and small, so much philosophical and moral discussion, such intense human endeavour, such sweated exertion should vanish every day into futile oblivion, while all these incongruous, nonsensical arbitrary verses remain perpetually current in popular memory.

There is a timelessness in all these nursery rhymes. They never carry any indication of who wrote them, and no one ever thinks to ask on which day or in which year they were written. Because of this inherent timelessness, even if they were written in our own day they are ancient, and even if they were written thousands of years ago they are new.

If you look closely, you see that there is nothing as ancient as infancy. Adults have been changed in many different ways by place, time, education and custom, but infants are the same today as they were a hundred thousand years ago. Unchanging ancientness is born into human homes again and again in the form of a baby, yet the freshness, beauty, innocence and sweetness it had at the beginning of history is the same today. The reason for this eternal newness is that infants are the creations of Nature. But adults are to a very great extent man's own making. In the same way, nursery rhymes are infant-literature; they are born spontaneously and naturally in the human mind.

There is a special significance in saying that they are born spontaneously. In their natural state, our minds are filled with images and echoes of the universe wandering about in a broken, disconnected way. They can take on a variety of shapes, and can suddenly shift from one subject to another. Just as the wind contains dust from the road, flower-pollen, countless odours, various sounds, stray leaves, drops of water, vapours from the earth – all the strange, uprooted, aerial bits and pieces of this swirling, churned-up world wandering around without meaning – so too our minds. There too in the ceaseless stream of consciousness many colours, scents and sounds, puffs of fancy, snatches of thought, broken

---

* Editor's note: In Bengali, 'Brishti pare tapur tupur, nadey elo baan.'

pieces of language – all the many hundreds of abandoned, forgotten, detached materials of our experiential world – float about aimlessly and inconsequentially.

When we aim our thoughts consciously in some particular direction, then all this humming activity suddenly stops, the web of particles flies away, the entire shadowy mirage is removed in a trice, our imagination and intelligence concentrate themselves into a unity, and proceed intently. The substance that we call Mind possesses such superior mastery that when it wakes and asserts itself then most of our inner and outer world is overwhelmed by its influence: under its discipline, rule, language, and by the commands of its servants, the whole world is reduced. Think of all the thousands of kinds of small and large noises that are perpetually sounding – bird-calls, rustling leaves, gurgling waters, the mingled noises of human habitations – and think of all the shaking, stirring, coming, going, the restless stream of moral existence playing and swirling on and on: yet what a tiny part of it do we notice. The main reason for this is that, like a fisherman, our mind is able to throw only a single net and take up only that little bit that is caught in one throw: all the rest eludes it. When it sees, then it does not hear well; when it hears, then it does not see well; and when it thinks, then it does not see or hear well. It is able to a great degree to exclude all unnecessary materials from the path of its attention. This power is the chief thing that preserves its supremacy even in the midst of the boundless variety of the world. In the Puranas one can read that in ancient times certain great souls were able to achieve the power to live or die at will. Our mind has power to be blind or deaf at will, and because we have to use that power at every step, most of the world from the time we are born to the time we die carries on outside our consciousness. The mind takes up what it prepares for itself; it perceives whatever is formed by its own needs and nature; with what is happening or developing all around it – even in its own inner regions – it is not much concerned.

If the reflected stream of all the dream-like shadows and sounds that wander about like endlessly-forming clouds in the sky of our mind in its simple state, sometimes combining, sometimes separating, going through various shapes and colours, moving at the chance dictate of invisible winds, could be projected onto some non-conscious screen, then we would see a considerable resemblance between that projection and these rhymes that we are discussing. These rhymes are nothing but the shadows of our ever-changing inner sky; they are like shadows projected onto the clear waters of a lake by clouds playing in the heavens. That is why I said that they are born spontaneously.

Before I quote some nursery rhymes here by way of illustration, I must beg for my readers' indulgence. Firstly, how can the sound of the affectionate, sweet, natural voice that always went with these rhymes issue from the pen of a man like me, sober, old and conscious of my position? My readers must recall to mind from their own homes, from their own childhood memories, that soothing sweetness of voice. What magic spell do I possess to bring before my readers the love, the music, the evening lamp-lit pictures of beauty that are forever intimately associated with it? I trust that the spell will lie in the rhymes themselves.

Secondly, to place all these homely, unkempt, unsophisticated nursery rhymes in the middle of a guarded and conventional literary essay is to do them some unfairness – like putting an ordinary housewife in the witness-box of a court of law for cross-examination. But I have no choice. Courts have to work according to the rules of courts; essays have to be written according to the rules of writing essays. Some cruelty is unavoidable.

* * *

from the Introduction to *Thakurmar Jhuli* (1907)

translated from the Bengali by Amit Chaudhuri

Is there anything quite as *swadeshi* in our country as *Thakurmar Jhuli*?* But, alas, even this delightful bag of tales was coming to us not so long ago manufactured in the factories of Manchester. These days, English 'fairy tales' have begun to become the only recourse for our children. Our own *swadeshi*† Grandmother Company is utterly bankrupt. If you shake its bags, Martin's *Ethics* and Burke's notebooks on the French Revolution may

---

* *Thakurmar Jhuli* means, literally, 'grandmother's bag'. It is a book of fairy tales collected and transcribed into Bengali by Dakshinaranjan Mitra Majumdar, published in 1907, and has been for several generations the staple of every Bengali child and, presumably, parent and grandparent.

† '*Swadeshi*' means 'that which originates in one's country' or 'indigenous', and was also a key term in the Indian nationalist movement; it sought to emphasize the moral duty of every Indian to buy and sell Indian-made goods, and to voluntarily ban goods that came from England. Tagore's relationship to this demand was ambivalent and ironical, as he wasn't sure if the banning of 'foreign' goods was always in the interest of the poorer sections of the population.

fall out now and again; but whatever happened to the Royal Prince, the Royal Minister's son, to Bangoma and Bangomi,* to the seven kings' precious jewel that lies beyond the seven seas and thirteen rivers?

Festivity, *jatra*, song have all gradually dried up like the dead river, and Bengal's villages, where the current of delight used to flow in various tributaries, have become a wasteland of dry sand. Because of this, the hearts of the grown ups are becoming hardened, selfish, and mean. And thus our children too have been excluded from delight through no sin of theirs. Why are today's bedtimes so silent? In study-rooms, the hum you hear by their kerosene-lit table is the traumatic sound of English spelling. Can a child be happy if you remove its mother's breast from its lips and feed it with only tasteless and nourishing food?

All this talk of books! What of the tender words our mothers uttered? And of the heartfelt words of the goddess who presides over our country?

These, our land's fairy tales, for many ages passing restlessly over the Bengali child's consciousness in the midst of so many revolutions, the ends and beginnings of many kingdoms, these have remained indestructible, and they have all been born of the maternal tenderness that exists in this land of Bengal. The affection on which everyone was raised to manhood, from the land's king of kings to its most destitute peasant, which, on a bright evening, has pointed out the moon to each one of us to enchant us, and sung us to sleep – in all Bengal it is that timeless and ancient and profound love that has given birth to these fairy tales.

So, when the children of Bengalis listen to fairy tales, it's not as if they feel happy to listen to the stories, and no more – the melody of Bengal's eternal affection penetrates their youthful consciousness, and suffuses them with the delight that belongs to this land.

When I received Dakshinaranjan babu's *Thakurmar Jhuli*, I was afraid to open it. I suspected that it would be difficult to sound that melody on the harsh metal of modern Bengali. It's very hard to capture that melody in today's bookish language. If it had been me, I would never have had the courage to begin this endeavour. In the recent past, I have asked a few educated women who also happen to be accomplished storytellers to rewrite these fairy tales – but though it be a feminine hand, the spell of English style is so strong that even if the tale is told, the fairy tale is not; an eternal possession becomes merely a contemporary one.

---

* Editor's note: Bangoma and Bangomi, male bird and female bird who talk in human voices in Bengal's folktales.

But blessings on Dakshinaranjan babu! He has planted grandmother's words in printed letters, and yet his pages are almost as green, as fresh; in the way he has been able to rescue, to such a considerable extent, the special language, the special manner, and that age-old simplicity of fairy tales, he has revealed his subtle aesthetic instinct and an effortless expertise in his craft.

At this moment my suggestion is: let a school be opened, without delay, for the modern grandmothers of Bengal, and, making Dakshinaranjan babu's book their principal manual, let them once more regain their pride of place in the child's kingdom of sleep.

Sukumar Ray (1887–1923)

Childhood, with its fluid power-relations, its constant transposition of meanings, its secrets and discoveries, provided a metaphor, for Bengali writers, for the unexpected secular redefinitions and repressions of the Renaissance and the colonial world. It is, thus, perhaps no accident that one of the greatest creative writers of his time, Sukumar Ray, should have chosen what is loosely called 'children's literature' as the genre in which to conduct his experiments in creating a code to describe Bengali society in flux. Ray was the son of the writer, printer, and innovator Upendrakishore Ray, and father of the film-maker Satyajit Ray; though not a trained illustrator like his father, his pictures, like his compound words and his compound creatures, form an outrageous allegory of the hybrid, cosmopolitan origins of the Bengal Renaissance. This hybridity, within the matrix of which Ray's sensibility was formed, is both parodied and celebrated, as in the following couplet about mutant animals engendered by compound words:

> A porchard and a porcupine, defying the grammarians,
> Combined to form a porcochard, unmindful of their variance.

('Hodge-Podge' trans. Sukanta Chaudhuri)

The penchant and predilection Victorian England had for 'fabulous creatures', as a code with which to record its contact with the Orient in the age of colonialism, is appropriated by Ray, in both his illustrations and his writings, to delineate a comic history of the Bengal Renaissance. Moreover, his compound words can be seen to belong to the parodic margins of more significant, and serious, compound words created by poets like Tagore. For instance, the title of Tagore's Nobel-prize-winning collection, *Gitanjali*, is itself a compound of a word with religious resonances, *anjali* (which is a floral offering to a deity), and a secular one, *geet* (which means 'song'), creating a third word with connotations appropriate to a secular, *bhadralok*, cultured ethos: 'offering of songs'. Such a compound word mirrors the Renaissance's adjustments of meaning as Bengali society moves from a pre-colonial reality to a secular one; and Ray's own compound words, like 'haanshjaru' or 'porcochard', and several others, like anarchic scribblings on the margins of the great book of the Renaissance, both reflect and caricature these adjustments of meaning.

The story below (its original title is 'Ha-Ja-Ba-Ra-La', which are consonants of the Bengali alphabet arranged in no particular order – now, after Ray, synonymous with a 'muddle' or a 'jumble') appropriates and parodies Lewis Carroll in order to give the reader a sense of the chaos inherent in a *bhadralok* Bengali society – comprising clerks, solicitors, and barristers – that loves order, education, rote-learning, and rationality. Carroll's narratives, with their keyholes and looking-glasses, their tiny doors and rabbit holes, are about the repressed sexuality of Victorian England. Ray's story (which was published in the year that another 'jumble', *The Waste Land*, first appeared, 1922) is about the modern Bengali identity in flux. It is an identity that, as I have said, began to be formed with the unprecedented transactions between languages and cultures enacted in the lives of figures such as Rammohun Roy, Madhusudan Dutt, Bankim Chatterjee, and Tagore; and the opening paragraphs of the story, like the couplet quoted above, are a cunning commentary on the Renaissance universe in which one identity seems to give birth to, while cancelling, another. Ray died at the age of 34 of the dreaded *kala azaar*.

* * *

'A Topsy-Turvy Tale' (1922)

translated from the Bengali by Sukanta Chaudhuri

It was terribly hot. I lay in the shade of a tree, feeling quite limp. I had put down my handkerchief on the grass: I reached out for it to fan myself, when suddenly it called out, 'Miaow!'

Here was a pretty puzzle. I looked and found that it wasn't a handkerchief any longer. It had become a plump ginger cat with bushy whiskers, staring at me in the boldest way.

'Bother!' I said. 'My handkerchief's turned into a cat.'

'What's bothering you?' answered the Cat. 'Now you have an egg, and then suddenly it turns into a fine quacky duck. It's happening all the time.'

I thought for a while and said, 'But what should I call you now? You aren't really a cat, you're a handkerchief.'

'Please yourself,' he replied. 'You can call me a cat, or a handkerchief, or even a semi-colon.'

'Why a semi-colon?' I asked.

'Can't you tell?' said the Cat, winking and sniggering in a most irritating manner. I felt rather embarrassed, for apparently I should have known all about the semi-colon.

'Ah!' I said quickly. 'Now I see your point.'

'Of course you do,' said the Cat, pleased. 'S for semi-colon, p for handkerchief, c for cat – and that's the way to spell "spectacles"! Simple, isn't it?'

It didn't seem simple at all, but I nodded to stop him from sniggering again. Instead, he stared at the sky for a while and suddenly exclaimed, 'Why don't you go to Tibet if you're feeling the heat?'

'That's easily said,' I retorted, 'but it's quite a job getting there.'

'Why, what's the problem?' asked the Cat.

'Do you know the way?' I asked him in return.

'Of course,' he said with a grin. 'Here's Calcutta, and here's Diamond Harbour a little to the south, and here's Ranaghat a little to the north, and then presto! you're in Tibet! Straight roads, an hour and a quarter's drive – just say the word.'

'Do show me the way,' said I.

He suddenly turned very grave, shook his head and said, 'That's beyond me, I'm afraid. If only I had Cousin Treehopper here, he'd be able to tell you.'

'Who's Cousin Treehopper?' I asked. 'Where does he live?'

'Up in the trees, of course,' the Cat replied.

'Where can I find him?' I asked again.

'Oh, you can't do that!' he cried. 'Quite out of the question.'

'Why?' said I.

'It's like this, you see,' said the Cat. 'Suppose you're looking for him at Uluberia: you'll hear he's in Motihari. So you go to Motihari only to find he's at Ramkrishnapur. Off you go again, but they tell you there he's left for Cossimbazar. You just can't run him to earth.'

'Then how do you manage to meet him at all?' I wondered.

'It's quite a job,' said the Cat. 'First you've got to work out the places where he can't possibly be. Then you work out the places where he just possibly might; and *then* you calculate where he actually is. After that you plot where he's going to be by the time you get to where he is now. Next after that—'

I cut him short and said, 'How do you work out all these calculations?'

'It's hard work,' he replied. 'Like to see?' And he took a stick and cut a long furrow in the turf, saying, 'Suppose this is Cousin Treehopper.' Then he sat silently for a long time.

Then he cut another furrow in the same way and said, 'Suppose this is you,' and crooked his neck and fell silent again.

Then he cut yet another furrow and said, 'Suppose this is a semi-colon.' And he went on like this, pondering and drawing more and more furrows, saying things like 'Suppose this is Tibet.' ... 'Suppose this is Cousin Treehopper's wife cooking dinner.' ... 'Suppose this is a hole in the tree-trunk.' ...

After a while I felt annoyed and said, 'You're talking nonsense, and I'm getting quite bored.'

'All right, I'll make it simpler for you,' said the Cat. 'Shut your eyes and work out the sums I call out.' So I shut my eyes.

I sat like that for quite a long time without being set a single sum. In the end I got a bit suspicious and opened my eyes, only to find the Cat escaping over the garden wall with a smirk on its face.

There was nothing I could do, so I sat down again on a big stone under the tree. At once I heard a hoarse croaking voice call out, 'What's seven times two?'

I wondered what it could be this time. As I looked about me, the voice came again: 'Why aren't you answering? What's seven times two?' I looked up and saw a jungle-crow scribbling something on a slate and bobbing his head towards me.

'Seven times two is fourteen,' I answered.

He shook his head very hard and said, 'Wrong answer! No marks!'

I felt very peeved indeed. 'Of course I'm right!' I protested. 'Seven ones are seven, seven twos are fourteen, seven threes are twenty-one.'

The Crow didn't answer for a while, but just sat there sucking his pencil. Then he began muttering, 'Seven twos are fourteen, put down four and carry the pencil.'

'Well then!' said I. 'What made you say seven twos didn't make fourteen?'

'It wasn't quite fourteen when you spoke,' answered the Crow. 'At that point it was only 13 rupees, 14 annas and 3 pice. If I hadn't very cannily put down 14 just at the right moment, it would have got to be 14 rupees 1 anna and 9 pice by now.'

'I've never heard such rubbish,' I told him. 'If seven twos make fourteen, it's always fourteen, an hour ago or ten days from now.'

The Crow looked shocked and said, 'Don't you count the cost of time in your country?'

'What do you mean, the cost of time?' I asked.

'You'd know if you lived here a few days,' he replied. 'Time's terribly expensive here, we daren't waste one little bit. Here had I scraped and scrounged a bit of time together, and now I've lost half of it talking to you.' And he set to work again on his sums, while I sat by feeling rather guilty.

Just then something slithered out of a cranny in the tree and dropped to the ground. It was a little old man just three feet tall, completely bald but with a long green beard that reached down to his ankles, holding a hookah without a bowl. Somebody had scribbled on his bald head with a piece of chalk.

He took two hurried pulls at his hookah and asked very concernedly, 'Well, are the accounts ready?'

The Crow shuffled this way and that and finally said, 'Almost.'

'This is absurd,' said the Old Man. 'You've had nineteen days and they still aren't ready.'

The Crow sucked glumly at his pencil for a few minutes. Then he asked, 'How many days did you say?'

'Nineteen,' answered the Old Man.

At once the Crow called out, 'Going twenty!'

'Twenty-one!' cried the Old Man.

'Twenty-two!' cried the Crow.

'Twenty-three!' cried the Old Man again.

'Twenty-three and a half!' yelled the Crow, exactly as if they were bidding at an auction.

Now the Crow turned to me and frowned. 'Why aren't you bidding?' he demanded.

'Why should I?' I replied.

The Old Man hadn't noticed me all this time. Now he began spinning round and round at the sound of my voice, and finally came to a stand facing me. He then fixed his hookah to his eye like a telescope and observed me for a long time. Next he took some bits of coloured glass out of his pocket and looked at me through these. Finally he brought out an

old tailor's measure and began to measure me, calling out as he did so 'Height 26 inches, arms 26 inches, cuff 26 inches, chest 26 inches, collar 26 inches.'

'Impossible!' I said. 'How can my chest and collar both be 26 inches? I'm not a hog.'

'See for yourself,' said the Old Man.

I saw that all the figures on the tape had faded away. Only the '26' could still be made out, so everything he measured came to 26 inches.

He then asked me, 'How much do you weigh?'

'Don't know,' I replied.

He prodded me a little with two fingers and called out, '2½ seers.'

'Impossible,' I protested again. 'Patla weighs 21 seers, and I'm a year and a half older.'

'You've got a different scale of weights,' said the Crow hurriedly.

'Take this down,' the Old Man told him. 'Weight 2½ seers, age 37.'

'Of course not!' I cried. 'I'm only eight and a quarter, and I won't have you saying I'm thirty-seven!'

The Old Man considered for a moment and asked, 'Upward or downward?'

'I beg your pardon?' said I.

'Is your age increasing or decreasing?'

'How can one's age decrease?' I asked back.

'Do you mean to say it'll keep going up and up?' he exclaimed with a shudder. 'Good heavens, that way you'll end up sixty or seventy or eighty, and even grow old and die some day.'

'Of course,' I told him, 'One's very old by the time one's eighty.'

'But that's stupid!' he answered. 'Why should you ever get to be eighty? Over here, we turn our age back when we're forty. Then we don't go on to be 41 or 42 but start growing younger at 39, 38 and so on. When we've got down to ten in this way, we turn upward again. I've quite lost count how often I've grown young and old in this way. I'm thirteen now,' he added. It seemed too funny for words.

'I wish you'd talk more quietly,' said the Crow. 'I could finish my accounts that way.'

The Old Man sidled up to me at this, sat down dangling his legs, and began to whisper, 'I'll tell you a lovely story. Just let me think.' He closed his eyes and began to think his story out, scratching his bald head with his hookah all the time. Then he suddenly hissed, 'Splendid! I'm ready now. Just listen: Meanwhile the Head Vizier had swallowed the Princess's spool of thread. Nobody knew about it. And just at this moment along came the man-eating giant, roaring as he rolled off the bed in his sleep. At once there was a hideous din of drums and bugles and cymbals and bassoons and guards and gunners and dragoons and cavalry, clash, clash, bang, bang, boom, boom, rattle, rattle – when suddenly the king cried out: "What's this magic horse doing without a tail?" And the pastors and masters and doctors and proctors began telling each other, "A very good question. What's happened to its tail?" Nobody knew the answer: they all tried to slink away.'

The Crow interrupted at this point to ask me, 'Have you got my handbill?'

'No,' I said, so he drew out a piece of paper from a big wad and gave it to me. It said:

Corvus Sylvanus Protect Us

CROWORTHY COLE-BLACK, Esq.

Chartered Accountant

41 Raven Row, Woodmarket

We undertake all kinds of accounting work, business and unbusinesslike, wholesale and retail; on scientific principles. Rate: 1 rupee 5 annas per inch. Children half-price. For free brochure by return of post, send all relevant information such as size of shoe, colour of skin, propensity to earache, whether alive or dead, etc., etc. . . .

BEWARE! BEWARE!! BEWARE!!!

We represent the reputed house of Sylvan Corvines or Jungle-Crows. It has been brought to our notice that inferior practitioners such as House-Crows, Gor-Crows and Carrion Crows are currently imposing upon the public with base profiteering intent. Do not be deceived by their vulgar publicity.

'What do you think of it?' asked the Crow.
'I don't fully understand it,' I told him.

'Yes, it's rather difficult. Some people can't follow it at all,' he remarked. 'I once had a client with a bald head . . .'

The Old Man flew into a rage. He made for the Crow, yelling, 'I won't have all this talk about bald heads, d'you hear? Just once more and I'll crack your slate across with my hookah.'

The Crow was somewhat taken aback. He thought for a moment and said, 'I didn't say bald – I said *balled* head, meaning round like a ball.'

Even this didn't calm the Old Man, who sat muttering to himself. The Crow finally said to him, 'Want to look at the accounts?'

The Old Man thawed a bit and said, 'Oh, have you finished? Let me see.'

'Here you are,' said the Crow, and dropped the slate straight onto the poor man's bald head. He collapsed at once with a hand held to his head and began to howl like a baby, 'O Mummy, O Auntie, O Cousin Shiboo!' He flung his limbs about as he blubbered.

The Crow gazed at him vacantly and finally said, 'Hurt again, old chap? I never saw such a one.'

'Two, three, four,' the Old Man began counting, stopping his tears straight away.

'Five,' cried the Crow.

I thought they were going to start bidding again, so I quickly stepped in: 'You haven't seen the accounts yet.'

'Quite so, quite so,' said the Old Man. 'Just read what you've got there, will you?'

I picked up the slate and found it was scrawled over closely in this way:

Be it known unto all men by these presents that whereas I Croworthy Cole-Black licensed legal practitioner accountant and notary public having considered surveyed assessed and evalued the assets fixed and unfixed movable and immovable of the principal party (hereinafter referred to as 'the party') in the case at issue hereby declare and requisition for and on behalf of the said party the right of decree right of action right of arbitration right of appeal . . .

The Old Man cut me short and turned to the Crow. 'What's this drivel?' he asked.

'You've got to write all that,' said the Crow. 'How do you expect your figures to last otherwise? You need all that for a nice solid set of accounts.'

'Very well,' said the Old Man, 'but let's see the actual figures.'

'They're there at the end,' said the Crow; and then to me, 'Why don't you read the whole thing out?'

I found that he'd put down in big letters at the end:

$7 \times 2 = 14$

Age: 26 inches

Cash in hand: 2½ seers

Expenditure: 37 years.

It's obvious,' said the Crow, 'that this is neither LCM nor GCM. So it's either Fractions or the Rule of Three. 2½ seers is a fraction, so the rest is the Rule of Three. You'd better tell me which one you'd like to have.'

'I'll have to ask,' said the Old Man. He stooped and laid his mouth to the foot of the tree, and called, 'Brother! Brother!'

After a while someone growled from inside the trunk in a huffy kind of way, 'Wha'd'you want?'

'Croworthy wants to know something,' called the Old Man.

Again came the growl, 'What's he saying?'

'Fractions or the Rule of Three?' shouted the Old Man.

This time we heard quite a roar. 'Who's he calling a fraction? You or me?'

'No, no, he's asking whether the accounts should be in Fractions or the Rule of Three.'

After a while came the answer: 'Tell him to make it the Rule of Three.'

The Old Man gravely stroked his beard and began shaking his head. 'Just like silly old Brother! Rule of Three indeed! What's wrong with Fractions? I really think you'd better make it Fractions, Croworthy.'

The Crow began to calculate: 'Take away two from two and a half seers and what's left is the fraction, half a seer. So your accounts come to half a seer. Half a seer of accounts costs 2 rupees 14 annas if it's neat, and 6 pice if it's mixed with water.'

The Old Man said, 'Three teardrops fell on your figures while I was crying. So here's six pice, and here's your slate.'

The Crow seemed very pleased to get the money. He began dancing and drumming on the slate, singing 'Oh bold and brave . . .'

'Did I hear you say *bald* again?' the Old Man roared. 'Well, you've asked for it. Brother, Brother! Quick now, he's just said *bald* again.' Even as he spoke, a huge bundle of rags tumbled out of a hole in the tree. I could see an old man trapped beneath it, waving his arms and legs in an agitated manner. He looked exactly like the Old Man with the hookah. But *he*, instead of coming to his brother's help, leapt on top of the bundle instead, and sat there crying 'Get up at once, you clod,' while he beat the poor man with his hookah.

The Crow winked at me and said, 'Don't you see? This new chap would like to pass the bundle to his brother, but he won't take it, of course. They keep quarrelling about it all the time.'

By now the old man with the bundle had managed to stand up. He lifted the bundle in a threatening way and said, clenching his teeth, 'You stupid old Other!' While Other, rolling up his sleeves, roared, 'You hateful old Brother!'

'Go on, go on,' yelled the Crow. 'Have a good fight.'

And they went at it hammer and tongs, biff, biff, thud, thud. After a minute Other lay gasping on the ground, while Brother rubbed his bald head and shivered.

Then Brother began to bawl, 'Oh my poor, poor Other, what's happened to you?'

And Other also started howling, 'Oh my precious, precious Brother, what have I done to you?'

So they fell on each other's necks and wept for a while, then went off chatting arm in arm, as friendly as you please. Meanwhile the crow had also shut up shop and left. I was just thinking of going home myself, when I suddenly heard a strange sound in a nearby bush, as if somebody were laughing himself into stitches. I looked and found a most peculiar creature – part man, part monkey, part owl, part goblin – thrashing about with laughter and spluttering, 'It's too much – I'll burst, I know I will.'

He paused a little on seeing me, and gasped, 'Thank goodness you've come, or else I'd really have died of laughing.'

'But what makes you laugh in this monstrous way?' I asked.

'Why, it's like this,' said the creature. 'Imagine the earth were flat, and all the water in the sea were to drain onto the land, and it grew all muddy and slippery, and every one kept slipping and breaking his bones – ho, ho, ho, ho.' Again he began tumbling about with laughter.

'Surely you aren't laughing like this for such an absurd reason?' said I.

He paused again and said, 'Well, not only for that, of course. Suppose there's a man coming along, with an ice cream in one hand and a lump of clay in the other, and he takes a bite out of the clay instead of the ice cream – ho, ho, ho, ho.' He started laughing again.

'Why on earth,' I asked him, 'are you hurting yourself by laughing at such impossible things?'

'Oh, they aren't as impossible as you may think,' he replied. 'For instance, suppose there's a man who keeps lizards, and he feeds them and baths them and puts them out to dry, and along comes a billy goat and gobbles up the lot – ho, ho, ho, ho.'

He really was a most extraordinary creature. 'Who are you?' I asked him. 'What's your name?'

He thought for a while and said, 'My name's Higgle-Piggle-Dee. I'm called Higgle-Piggle-Dee, my brother's called Higgle-Piggle-Dee, my father's called Higgle-Piggle-Dee, my uncle's called Higgle-Piggle-Dee . . .'

I cut him short. 'Why don't you simply say the whole family's called Higgle-Piggle-Dee?'

He pondered the matter again. 'Oh no,' he said at last, 'I'm really called Tokai. My uncle's called Tokai, my nephew's called Tokai, my cousin's called Tokai, my father-in-law's called Tokai . . .'

'Are you sure?' I asked sternly. 'Or are you making all this up?'

He grew quite confused and stammered, 'Well, actually my father-in-law's called Biscuit.'

This really made me very angry. 'I don't believe a word you say,' I declared.

Just then there was a rustle behind the bush, and a big bearded goat came stomping out. 'I believe you were talking about me?' he enquired.

I was going to tell him we weren't, but he'd already launched on a long speech. 'You can argue as much as you like,' he said, 'but I tell you there are some things that goats don't eat. I would therefore like to deliver a short discourse on "The Diet of Goats".' He then stepped forward and began: 'Assembled children and dearly beloved Higgle-Piggle-Dee, you can see from the label round my neck that my name is Grammaticus Horner, BA. Nutritional Consultant. I am very fond of gram, so I am known as Grammaticus, and my horns are plain to behold. I have been honoured with the degree of BA for my widely acclaimed skill in going ba-ba. I have personally investigated the nature of Things That Can Be Eaten and Things That Cannot, hence my merited profession of Nutritional Consultant. I know it is proverbial to say "Fools bleat everything, goats eat everything," but this is a foul libel. You have just heard this miserable – *creature* saying that goats eat lizards. This is utterly mendacious. I've had a lick at all kinds of lizards, and they simply aren't worth eating. It is true, of course, that we consume many items that other species refuse – like paper bags, or coconut fibre, or newspapers, or good magazines. But we wouldn't dream of eating costly bound books. We may sometimes savour a quilt or a blanket, or perhaps a mattress or pillow, but those who accuse us of

devouring beds, tables and chairs are no better than liars. When we feel inspired, the muse may induce us to face all kinds of challenges – like india-rubber, or bottle-tops, or old shoes, or canvas bags. It is reported that my grandfather chewed up half a surveyor's tent out of sheer high spirits. But of course we do not partake of knives, forks, jars or bottles. Some of us are fond of soap, but usually they are the vulgar sort with cheap tastes. And yet my own young brother once swallowed a whole bar of washing-soap . . .'

At this he looked up at the sky and began to bleat in a melancholy way. Obviously his brother hadn't survived the experiment.

The Higgle-Piggle-Dee had fallen asleep, but the Goat's dreadful wailing awoke him: he sat up with a start and began to splutter and choke. I was quite afraid he'd die, but there he was again a little later, sprawling with laughter in the same old way.

'Now what's the joke?' I asked him.

'There was once a man with a most fearful snore,' he said. 'And one stormy day there came an enormous clap of thunder, and everyone began to thrash him because they thought it was his snore ... ho, ho, ho, ho.'

'Rubbish!' I said, and was about to turn away, when I noticed a man with a smooth shaven head, wearing a collarless coat and a pair of baggy

trousers, looking at me with an insufferable grin on his face. The moment he caught my eye he began to buck and simper and rub his hands saying, 'Please, my dear fellow, don't ask me to sing right now. My voice is a little off today.'

'Here's a nuisance!' I exclaimed. 'Whoever's asked you to sing?'

But he simply kept on whining, almost into my ear: 'Now you're getting angry. Don't tell me – I can see you're angry. Come, come, old chap, I'll sing you a few songs if you like. No need to get worked up.'

Before I could get rid of him, the Goat and the Higgle-Piggle-Dee called out together, 'Yes! Let's have a few songs!' In a twinkling, Smoothpate took out two large songbooks from his pockets, held them up to his eyes, hummed a little to himself, and suddenly began to bawl, 'A rose-red song with sky-blue tune, a little scent of laughter.' He sang this single line over and over once, twice, five times, ten times.

'This is getting tiresome,' I told him at last. 'Don't you know any other words?'

'I do indeed,' he replied. 'But they're out of a different song. It goes like this:

> On pavement and alley
> The revellers rally
> And paint the walls pink
> With blacking and ink.

I hardly sing this one nowadays. There's another one that begins "O the hills where they grow new potatoes ..." You have to sing it in a Mealy and Mushy Manner. I can't manage that either these days. What I do sing quite often now is "Peacock Plumes".' And he began at once:

The darkness looms with peacock plumes that whisper in the welkin's
  ear,
And bottle-tops with tuneful pops go sailing up so thin and clear.
The lisping light that rambles right around the bright and tender air
Through black and white in dreamy flight, through thick and thin goes
  floating fair.

'What kind of a song is this?' I asked. 'I can't make head or tail of it.'

'Yes, it's awfully hard,' said the Higgle-Piggle-Dee.

'What's hard about it?' remarked the Goat. 'Except the bit about the bottle-tops, of course.'

Smoothpate began pouting as though we'd hurt his feelings very much, and said, 'Well, if you want a simple song, you've only to say so. There's no need to make rude remarks. I'm perfectly capable of singing simple songs.' And he started off:

> The Bat said to the Porcupine, 'Old Spark,
> We're going to have a proper little lark.
> The owlets and the batlings will assemble,
> The froggies and the tadpoles all a-tremble,
> The shrew will shriek, or even faint with fright:
> The wretched mouse awaits his doom tonight!'
> The Porcupine responded, 'Here's the rub:
> My missus lies asleep beneath this shrub.

> You'd better tell the Owl and all his fellows,
> If she's disturbed by screeches, croaks or bellows,
> I'll draw my quills and spank and spike and spear:
> You'd better make that absolutely clear.'
> The Bat replied, 'I couldn't in all conscience.
> The owls will simply hoot to hear your nonsense.
> The inky eve's a funny time to snore:
> Your better half's a lazybones and bore.
> And you, dear chap, are daily growing dafter:
> A soot-faced sot and batty butt of laughter . . .'

I don't know how much longer he'd have gone on, but a great hubbub arose at this point. I looked about and saw quite a crowd around me. A porcupine stepped forward and began sniffling and crying, while a Crocodile wearing a wig patted him on the back with an enormous book and whispered, 'Now don't cry, don't cry, I'll see that you have your rights.' And a large Toad in livery raised his baton and announced, 'Action for libel!'

At these words a Screech-owl in a long black gown clambered onto a big stone and fell to nodding and drowsing quite openly, while a hefty Shrew fanned him with a very dirty fan.

The Owl blinked round with his bleary eyes, fell nodding again, and mumbled, 'State the charge.'

The Crocodile now rose, puckered up his face to look as sad as possible, and poked at his eyes with his claws until he'd squeezed out a few tears. Then he began to speak in a hoarse, rasping voice: 'My Lord, it behoves us to get to the root of the matter. First, then, a few words about roots. Roots are of two classes, edible and inedible. The yam is an edible root. It comes in several varieties, and is a celebrated nutriment.'

At this point a Fox, also wearing a wig, jumped up and said, 'My Lord, the yam is a toxic and execrable weed. It irritates the throat, and "Go and eat yams" is a vulgar insult. Only pigs and porcupines consume yams.'

The Porcupine was about to sniffle again, but the Crocodile shut him up with a rap from his book and asked, 'Can you produce witnesses or documentary evidence of the charge?'

The Porcupine pointed to Smoothpate and said, 'He's got all the documents.'

The Crocodile snatched Smoothpate's songbooks, opened one at random and began to read:

> One, two,
> What shall we do?

> Lie on our backs,
> Tie up our packs:
> Roses in posies,
> Fishes in dishes,
> Beans and greens,
> Floors and doors,
> Wash them with soap:
> What makes you mope?

'Not that one,' protested the Porcupine.

'Isn't it?' said the Crocodile. 'Well, what about this?' And he turned up another page and read:

> The moon shines bright, the witches light upon the drumstick tree
> Where mimbling schools of grubby ghouls go crackle-crunch with glee.
> The banshee swings and shakes her rings because she's feeling
>   slighted:
> She pouts and squeaks through painted cheeks, 'I want to be invited.'
> The hairy hag, just see her wag in upsy-daisy fashion:
> She'd like a slice of soft and nice young human for her ration.

'Rubbish!' cried the Porcupine. 'You don't know what you're looking for.'

'Perhaps it's this one then?' said the Crocodile.

> Cream and curd
> Your case is heard
> A wily bird
> Just say the word –
> It's quite absurd.

'Not that one either? Well, try this – "I lie in a fright in the attic at night, and find that I'm feeling quite famished." No? What's that? A poem about Mrs Porcupine? Why didn't you say so all this while? Here you are:

> Ram Bhajan's wife
> Is a creature of strife:
> Tossin' and pitchin'
> The pots in the kitchen.
> And thumping and sloshing
> The clothes in the washing.

Don't tell me I'm wrong! Then it's bound to be:

My old man wheezes and coughs and sneezes, he's suffered a couple of
  strokes:
He shudders and jibs at a crack in his ribs, it shouldn't be long till he
  croaks.'

The Porcupine positively began to wail, crying, 'I'm done for! All that
money down the drain! Here's a worthless lawyer for you, can't find a
document when it's handed to him.'

Smoothpate had stood by all this while. He now asked, 'Which song do
you mean? "The Bat said to the Porcupine"?'

'Yes, yes, that's the one,' said the Porcupine excitedly.

The Fox jumped up again and said, 'What *did* the Bat have to say? My
Lord, I wish to call upon the Bat as a witness.'

'First witness – Bat!' croaked the Toad.

But everybody looked around, and the Bat wasn't there at all. So the
Fox went on, 'In that case, My Lord, I supplicate for the death penalty to
be passed on all the accused.'

'Not on your life,' said the Crocodile. 'We're going to appeal.'

The Owl, his eyes still shut, growled, 'Appeal admitted. Summon the
witnesses.'

The Crocodile glanced round warily and said to the Higgle-Piggle-Dee:

'Like to be a witness? You'll get four annas in good money.' The Higgle-Piggle-Dee seemed only too pleased to get the money, so he jumped into the witness-box and started to giggle immediately.

'What are you giggling about?' asked the Fox.

The Higgle-Piggle-Dee answered: 'There was once a man whom they'd coached to be a witness. They'd taught him to say that a certain book had a green cover with a blue leather spine and a blotch of red ink at the top. So when the lawyer asked him "Do you know the accused?" he replied "Yes, your honour: he has a green cover with a blue leather spine and a blotch of red ink at the top." Ho, ho, ho, ho!'

'Do you know the Porcupine?' said the Fox.

'Yes, your honour,' said the Higgle-Piggle-Dee. 'The Porcupine, the Crocodile, the whole pack of 'em. The Porcupine lives down a hole and has long sharp quills. The Crocodile has big bosses on his hide; he eats goats and suchlike.' At which Grammaticus Horner began to weep.

'Now what's the matter?' I asked him.

'A crocodile chewed up half of my youngest uncle but one,' he wailed, 'and so the other half died too.'

'Well, good riddance,' I snapped. 'Now just keep quiet.'

The Fox turned again to the Higgle-Piggle-Dee. 'Do you know anything about the lawsuit?'

'About lawsuits of all kinds,' said the Higgle-Piggle-Dee. 'There are two parties to a lawsuit. One's called the plaintiff, and he has a lawyer with him. The other's called the defendant, and he's got a lawyer too. There are ten witnesses on each side. And there's a judge who sits down and goes to sleep.'

'I haven't gone to sleep at all,' protested the Owl. 'I've got my eyes shut because there's something the matter with them.'

'Yes,' said the Higgle-Piggle-Dee, 'I've seen a lot of judges and they'd all got something the matter with their eyes, poor things.' And he began giggling again.

'What's wrong with you?' said the Fox.

'There once was a man,' said the Higgle-Piggle-Dee, 'who had something the matter with his head, and he used to give names to things. His shoes were called Pusillanimity, his umbrella was called Perseverance, his bucket was called Plenipotentiary – but he'd no sooner named his house Paradox-icality than it fell down in an earthquake. Ho, ho, ho, ho . . .'

'How interesting,' said the Fox. 'And what may you be called yourself?'

'At present,' he replied, 'my name is Higgle-Piggle-Dee.'

'What d'you mean, at present?' asked the Fox. 'One always has the same name, I suppose.'

'Indeed not,' said the Higgle-Piggle-Dee. 'In the morning, my name is Coconut-and-Spuds, and later in the afternoon I'll be Scarecrow Major.'

The Fox turned to the Owl and sid, 'My Lord, here's a fine pack of dolts and lunatics. Their evidence has no value at all.'

The Crocodile flared up and began to lash his tail. 'Who says it has no value?' he shouted. 'I'm buying it at four annas a time.' He made a great show of counting out the money and gave it to the Higgle-Piggle-Dee.

Someone announced from over our heads: 'Witness no. 1, price 4 annas.' I glanced up and saw Croworthy Cole-Black at his accounts again.

The Fox asked once more, 'Do you know anything else about this dispute?'

The Higgle-Piggle-Dee thought for a while and said, 'I know a song about foxes.'

'Let's hear it,' said the Fox.

The Higgle-Piggle-Dee began to croon:

> O come and view these rousing scenes,
> Foxes wolfing aubergines.
> And all they lack by way of spoil
> A pinch of salt, a dash of oil . . .

The Fox hastily stopped him, saying, 'That's about a different lot of foxes. I have no more questions to ask this witness, My Lord.'

There now began a regular stampede for the witness-box, as it seemed witnesses were being paid good money. While everybody was milling and jostling, I suddenly saw Croworthy hop down from his perch and climb straight into the witness-box. Before anyone could ask him any questions, he began: 'Corvus Sylvanus Protect Us. Croworthy Cole-Black, Esq., Chartered Accountant, 41 Raven Row, Woodmarket. We undertake all kinds of accounting work, business and unbusinesslike, wholesale and retail . . .'

'Stop that rot and answer my questions,' said the Fox. 'What's your name?'

'Croworthy Cole-Black,' said the Crow, 'I've just told you.'

'Place of residence?'

'Woodmarket,' said the Crow. 'I've told you that as well.'

'How far away is that?' asked the Fox.

'Hard to say,' said the Crow. '4 annas per hour, 10 pice per mile, discount of 2 pice for cash. 10 annas by addition, 3 annas by subtraction, 7 pice by division, 21 rupees by multiplication.'

'Don't show off,' said the Fox. 'Do you know your way home?'

'Of course I do,' said the Crow. 'It's the road just in front of you.'

'How far does it go?' asked the Fox.

'Why should it go anywhere?' replied the Crow. 'It stays right where it is. Roads don't roam about. They don't go for holidays in the hills.'

'You're a pretty piece of goods,' sneered the Fox. 'Do you know anything of this case in which you're supposed to be a witness?'

'I like that!' parried the Crow. 'Who's been keeping the accounts all the while, I'd like to know? Apply here for any information you need. First, there's a yam at the root of the matter. Yams belong to several species. They hurt the throats of foxes but not of crows. Next we have a witness, price 4 annas net, whose spine used to turn black and blue. Then there was a man who gave everything names. He called the fox Oil and Grab, the crocodile Old Twister, the owl Gloomscreech...'

At this, complete pandemonium broke out in court. The Crocodile went berserk and swallowed the Toad, the Shrew began to gibber with terror, the Fox tried to drive Croworthy out with an umbrella.

In the middle of this, the Owl started intoning: 'Silence in the court! I shall now deliver the judgement.' He turned to a rabbit with a pen stuck in his ear, and said: 'Take down what I say. Libel case no. 24. Plaintiff: Porcupine. Accused: – who *is* the accused?'

Everybody was taken aback and began saying, 'Goodness gracious! There's nobody accused!' So they quickly hustled poor Smoothpate into being the accused. The silly fellow thought the accused would also get some money, so he happily agreed. Instead he was sentenced to three months' imprisonment and seven days' hanging.

I was just thinking of protesting against such an unfair sentence, when suddenly the Goat bleated 'Gr-r-r-rammaticus!', butted me in the back, and then began to bite my ear. Next everything got a bit blurred, and the Goat came to look more and more like my uncle. When I could see plainly again, there he was, hauling me up by the ear and shouting, 'Caught you, boy! Sleeping away when you're supposed to be learning your grammar!'

I was quite taken aback. Could I have been dreaming? But honestly, when I looked round for my handkerchief, I just couldn't find it; and there on the wall sat a cat preening its whiskers, who scurried away as soon as I caught its eye. And just then a goat began bleating beyond the garden fence.

I told my uncle the whole story, but he only said, 'Nonsense, my boy. You're making up stories out of some silly dream you've had.' People turn funny as they grow old: they just don't believe things any more. But you aren't very old as yet, so I thought I'd tell you all about it.

Bibhuti Bhushan Banerjee (1894–1950)

Childhood persists as a trope in many of the pieces in this section. Bibhuti Bhushan Banerjee published his first novel in 1929, although it originally appeared in serialised form in a periodical such as Apu waits for so impatiently in the extract below. Here, again, childhood is the filter through which death, nature, the Bengali village, and, most notably, the romantic possibilities of the secular world penetrate the imagination of an inconsequential and impoverished Brahmin boy. As in Tagore, the activity of day-dreaming (see the note on Tagore above) becomes a trope for the liberation that art seems to offer; part of the poignance of the analogy with Tagore derives from the fact that the boy-Tagore, as portrayed in his memoir *My Reminiscences*, and Apu are on opposite ends of the social scale that came to exist in colonial Bengal. Unique for its tenderness and poetry (Buddhadev Bose once observed that it proves that 'it is still possible for an artist to be at once innocent and intelligent'), *Pather Panchali* rejects both nineteenth-century realism and social realism (the social milieu described in it would have logically lent itself to the latter) for an enquiry into perception and memory. Like his hero Apu, whom he would write about again in *Aparajito*, the sequel to his first novel, Banerjee too came from an impoverished Brahmin family, and grew up in a village in West Bengal; like Apu, he lost his first wife early. Before his own death at the age of 56, he had written several novels and stories, his protagonists often old women, girls, and children, his sensibility, when he wrote of them, preternaturally tender, curiously androgynous, and yet maternally sexless; it was as if he sometimes imported an old woman's vision to look at the world. In one regard he differed from the more rational impulses of the Renaissance; he was genuinely interested in the supernatural, used to wander cremation grounds and converse with Tantrics, and reportedly foresaw his own death.

The following extract occurs in the last third of Banerjee's novel, and forms its twenty-seventh chapter. By this time, Apu is a young boy who seems gradually about to enter his father's priestly profession. His elder sister, Durga, is dead, the small family is in decline, and, though they still don't know it, will leave Nischindipur village before long for Benares.

To translate Banerjee is to rediscover his complex, deceptively seamless, long sentences, with their musical pauses and transitions. These sentences introduce a subtly exploratory speaking voice into Bengali, and also a very modern form of suggestiveness. They are capable of accommodating, in one breath, the diverse, conflicting realities of Apu's universe: the facts of rural poverty, the names of local plants and deities, the Arabian Sea, the story of Joan of Arc, the detail about the anthill and the bamboo forest.

Three passages below are perhaps worth commenting on separately. The first, which occurs midway through the text, describes Apu reading, and being greatly moved by, Bengali romances. Banerjee, here, both celebrates and lovingly mocks the melodramatic literature of his childhood, with its strain of home-grown Orientalism and exoticism that has been such an important constituent of our modern popular culture. In celebrating it, he also distances himself from this literature, implying that this enchanted direction was no longer one his own fiction, with its Modernist impulse, could take. This literary device, by which Banerjee acknowledges a tradition in order to alert us to the fact that he is distancing himself from it, can be compared to the moment in Tagore's short story, 'The Kabuliwallah', first published in 1892, in which the narrator reveals he is a writer of romances involving medieval heroes and heroines (possibly princes and princesses), even as he is in the midst of unravelling a story that is realist and Modernist in its intent.

The second passage, which comes later, has Apu reading the story of Joan of Arc, a peasant girl reflecting on 'the sad state of her country', France. This is the only time in *Pather Panchali* that the writer invokes, through this subtle echo, the matter of colonial subjugation, to which otherwise Apu seems indifferent. There is also the suggestive parallel between the peasant girl, Joan, who had divine guidance, and the village boy, Apu, who, living in the secular world, has nothing more than his daydreams. One of the earliest instances of a modern Indian literary text mourning 'the sad state of the country' is Henry Louis Vivian Derozio's English sonnet, 'To India – My Native Land', published in 1827, one hundred and two years before *Pather Panchali* was published.

Finally, there is the epiphany towards the end, which occurs when Apu and his friend Potu have ventured out on a skiff on the river Ichhamoti, the river which ran as a leitmotif through both Apu's and Banerjee's lives. Apu dreams he is voyaging through oceans to distant places – Aden, England, France – and the vision of moving 'onward! – onward!' which the passage ends with is a striking echo, and inversion, of Whitman's 'Passage to India', especially its closing stanza, 'Sail forth – steer for the deep waters only .../... O farther, farther, farther sail!' Whitman wrote his poem in 1892, some time after the opening of the Suez Canal had made journeys to the East relatively easier, and inaugurated greater trade and expansionism for the West. For Whitman, the journey to India was the great dream of, or metaphor for, the liminal; about forty years later, in *Pather Panchali*, Apu completes this transaction and inverts this profound trope. For him the dream of the liminal, in almost the same words that Whitman used in his poem, is the voyage to the West. It is impossible to know if Banerjee had actually read Whitman.

* * *

from *Pather Panchali* (1929)

translated from the Bengali by Amit Chaudhuri

The days had gone by before they knew it. Winter, too, was about to come to an end.

Ever since Durga's death, Sarbajaya had tirelessly urged her husband to arrange for the family to leave the village for good, and Harihar himself hadn't been remiss in his various efforts to make this happen. But nothing had come of his efforts. And so Sarbajaya, these days, had in a way abandoned hope of leaving. Meanwhile, the widowed wife of Nilmoni Roy, Harihar's distant cousin, had arrived here last winter, and, finding her family house thickly overgrown with a forest of weeds, put up at Bhubon Mukhujje's house. Harihar had displayed considerable enthusiasm about bringing his *boudi* to his own house, but Nilmoni Roy's wife had declined. Accompanying her at present were her daughter Atasi and her youngest son Sunil. The elder son, Suresh, studied at a school in Calcutta; he wouldn't be able to come before the school closed in the summer. Atasi was fourteen years old; Sunil was eight. Sunil wasn't especially good-looking; but Atasi was fairly pleasant to look at, though you couldn't say she was beautiful. All the same, they'd spent much of their life in Lahore – Nilmoni Roy had worked there at the commissariat – there they'd been born, there brought up; thus the Western country's perfect health resided in their very bodies.

When they first arrived here, Sarbajaya tried to socialize with her affluent, well-established sister-in-law.* After she'd heard that Sunil's mother was the owner of ten thousand rupees in cash and shares, her heart filled with reverence for her sister-in-law, and, at her own initiative and with a degree of over-familiarity, she spared no effort at getting to know her; eventually, foolish though she might be, Sarbajaya had realized that Sunil's mother was not ready to give her a great deal of importance. Her husband had always been a high-ranking employee; she and her children were used to a different way of life. From the beginning, she maintained such a clear difference of status between the family of her poor cousin and her own that Sarbajaya herself had no choice but to withdraw. In conversation, behaviour, day-to-day business, and all kinds of trivial ways, she informed Sarbajaya that she was in no sense fit to consort with them as an equal. The fact that they came from a well-to-do family was brought constantly to light in the things they said, their clothes, their manner of existence. The children were perpetually well-dressed, no speck of dust permitted to stain their clothes, their hair perennially combed, a necklace circling Atasi's neck, gold bangles round her wrists, gold earrings on her ears; no one went anywhere in the morning without having breakfast and a round of tea, and they had with them a servant from the Western provinces, and it was he who performed all the domestic chores – in every respect, there was a great difference between the ways of Sarbajaya's impoverished household and theirs.

Sunil's mother didn't let her son get too friendly with any of the village boys, not even with Apu – in case, finding themselves in the company of this backwater's ignorant, rude urchins, her children should be corrupted. She hadn't come to this village to live here; the one objective of the visit was to supervise and take stock of their own estate and property during land measurement. The Bhubon Mukhujjes had some of their property on lease, and for this reason had reserved a couple of rooms in the western wing of their house for their use, and even their cooking and meals were kept separate. There was no perceivable difference in the behaviour of the Bhubon Mukhujjes and Sunil's mother; for Bhubon Mukhujje was wealthy, although he wouldn't count Sarbajaya as a human being at all.

During Dol, Suresh, the eldest son of Nilmoni Roy, came down from Calcutta and stayed at the house for about ten days. Suresh was about Apu's age; he studied in the fifth grade in an English school. He wasn't

---

* Editor's note: In Indian familial relationships, cousins are referred to as 'brothers' or 'sisters', and a male cousin's wife is a 'sister-in-law' by relation.

very fair; he had what might be called a wheatish complexion. Regular exercise had made his body strong, healthy. Though merely one year older than Apu, he resembled, in his outline and structure, a fifteen- or sixteen-year-old boy. Ramnath Ganguly's son – of the Ganguly family of the neighbouring locality – was his classmate. The Dol of Ramnabami was much celebrated at the house of the Gangulys, and he'd come on a visit to his maternal uncle's house to mark the occasion. Suresh spent the greater part of his time there; he too probably considered none of the other boys of the village worth mixing with.

The dark piece of land which, overrun with weeds and the wilderness, used to lie next to the deserted house, and which Apu had seen ever since he'd come to consciousness, was these people's land. For this reason, they held, for him, a mysterious attraction. Suresh, his contemporary, studied in Calcutta – and for a long time he'd been waiting for his arrival during the holidays so that he might get to know him. But Suresh, upon his arrival, didn't mix with him as one might have thought he would; besides, his behaviour and his manner of speaking were such that he seemed ready to exhibit his superiority to the village boys at every step. Though a peer in age, the shy and tongue-tied Apu would feel daunted by such behaviour and wouldn't dare come near him.

Apu hadn't yet been to school; when Suresh asked him about studies, he said, 'I study at home with my father.' On the day of Dol, sitting under the Jalpai trees at the ghat of the pond owned by the Gangulys, Suresh was asking the village boys questions on various topics in the manner of a world-vanquishing authority and pundit. To Apu he said, 'Let's see if you can tell us what the "boundary" of India is. Do you know "geography"?'

Apu couldn't answer. Suresh asked again, 'What sums have you solved? Can you solve a decimal fraction?'

Apu didn't know all these things. But even if he didn't, the books in that tin box of his weren't few. A handbook on everyday rites and observances, an old volume of physical geography, one Subhankari, a page-torn volume of the poem 'Virangana', that old copy of the *Mahabharata* which belonged to his mother – these were the books in the tin box. He had read all these books; and would reread them even though he'd read them repeatedly. His father, asking at every quarter, dreaming of every avenue, tried to procure his son books whenever he could; for his deepest wish was that his son should be well-educated, that he should become a scholar, that he should be brought up well – like a patient in delirium, his thirst in this matter was indomitable, insatiable. But he had no money, utterly lacked the means to keep his son at a distant boarding school, and didn't have much of an education himself. And yet whenever he was at home he'd sit with his son and teach him this and that, talk about different things, and, in order to teach his son arithmetic, would, with the aid of a Subhankari, return to the once-perused, forgotten knowledge acquired in childhood to once more sharpen and revive it and then assign his son arithmetic problems to solve. Whenever he thought something would enrich his son's knowledge, he'd either give it to him to read, or read it out to him himself. For a long time he'd been a subscriber to *Bangabasi*; the old copies of *Bangabasi*, collected over many days, had accumulated in their room; Harihar had, with great care, tied them into bundles and set them aside so that his son might read them one day; now these were coming into use. Not being able to meet the cost of the subscription, they no longer received new issues of the periodical, and the newspaper vendors had stopped delivering it. Harihar knew very well just how crazy his son was for this magazine, *Bangabasi*, how, on Saturday mornings, abandoning his games, he'd sit on Bhubon Mukhujje's puja platform near the postbox, open-mouthed, in expectation of the postman, and his heart would tingle with pain at not being able to get his son this most beloved of things.

And yet Apu had learnt several stories reading the old *Bangabasi*s. He'd tell Potu about them – Leuka and Raphael, the volcanic eruptions on Martinique island, stories of magicians who could make gold, and so much more. But his studies at school came to nothing. He knew arithmetic only up to lessons on divisions, nothing of history, nothing of grammar, hadn't even heard of geometry or mensuration, and his knowledge of English extended to the page with the picture of a horse in the First Book.

His mother had slightly different ideas about her son's future. Sarbajaya had grown up in a backwater. She had no elevated expectation that Apu would study at school and grow up to be an educated man. No one among her acquaintances knew what a school looked like. Her great hope was that after a while her son would start frequenting the houses of the disciples they had, keep them in hand. Sarbajaya had yet another hope. The village priest, Dinu Bhattacharya, had grown old. None of his sons was suitable for the job. Rani's mother, Gokul's wife, and the eldest daughter-in-law of the Ganguly household had all been of the view that henceforth they'd have their rituals performed by Apu, that in Dinu Bhattacharya's absence, they'd have, instead of his ganja-smoking son Bhombal, this unspoilt, simple, beautiful boy preside over the arrangements for the village Manasa puja and Lakshmi puja; this was what the women of the village wished. Apu was loved by all. Sarbajaya had heard this wish expressed many times, on the river ghat, on pathways, on the lips of the women who were her neighbours, and this, at present, was her highest hope. She was the child of a poor family, she'd been married into a poor one; she had no conception of a future brighter than this. If what she wished were to come true, she would have in her grasp what she'd dreamed of in her waking dreams.

The subject had come up one day in Bhubon Mukhujje's house. It was afternoon, and not a few people from the neighbourhood were present there to play cards. Sarbajaya said, in a voice intended to keep everyone happy, 'Here's Boro khuri, here's thakuma, here's mejdi; if they're kind maybe my Apu can take the sacred thread in the coming Fagun and try his hand at the village puja. I won't need to have any more cares about him then! There are eight to ten families of disciples, and if by Ma Sidheshwari's will the puja at the house of the Gangulys becomes a permanent job, then ...'

Sunil's mother suppressed a smile. Her son Suresh would grow up and study law, and then practise with her cousin, who was a well-known lawyer in Patna. This uncle of Suresh's was childless, but a lawyer with a thriving practice. It had become their wish, in time, that he take Suresh under his wing and educate him – but, saying, 'Why should we keep our child in someone else's house,' and words to that effect, she, instead of blabbering the truth like Sarbajaya, had already, in asides during casual and desultory conversation, explained to everyone why her son still wasn't with his uncle.

Emerging from Bhubon Mukhujje's house, Sarbajaya told her son, 'Listen to me' – then said surreptitiously, 'Why don't you go up to your jethima and tell her – jethima, I don't have shoes – buy me a pair, won't you?'

Apu said, 'Why, Ma?'

'Oh, tell them, they're rich people, if you ask, they'll probably give you a good pair of shoes today – like the ones Suresh wears; haven't you seen them? Such red shoes quite suit you ...'

Apu said with a shy look, 'I feel very ashamed – I won't be able to say it – who knows what'll they think – I ...'

Sarbajaya said, 'But what's there to be ashamed about! ... your own people – oh, tell them – what's wrong?'

'Ooo ... oonh – I won't be able to say it, Ma. I can't speak in front of jethima ...'

Sarbajaya said angrily, 'Why should you? You demonstrate all your might in your little corner at home – wandering about everywhere bare-foot, and for two years there haven't been good shoes on your feet; they're rich people, if they wanted they might have bought you a pair – but not a word will come out of your lips – king of the tongue-tied ones...'

*

On the day of the Purnima moon, Apu went to Rani's house to receive the prasad for Satyanarayan puja. Rani, calling him, said with a smile on her face, 'You used to come to our house so often before, why don't you come these days?'

'Why shouldn't I come Ranudi – I do.'

Rani said in a hurt voice, 'Of course you do! You mean you don't come at all! I think of you so much. Do *you* think of me, of us?'

'Don't I! Oh that's too much – why don't you ask my mother and see?'

No other satisfactory excuse was available to him. Leaving him standing there, Rani went in herself and, bringing him fruit, prasad and sandesh, transferred them to his hands. Smiling, she said, 'Take these, plate and all; I'll go tomorrow and bring it back from *khurima*.'

At the smile on her face, a sense of absolute trust in her came to Apu. How beautiful Ranudi had lately become; he was still to see a girl as beautiful. Atasidi always appeared impeccable, but her looks bore no comparison to Ranudi's. Besides, Apu knew that none among the girls of this village had a heart like hers. If he loved anybody after didi,* then it was Ranudi. And Apu knew too, didn't he, that something in Ranudi went out to him as well.

As he was leaving with the plate, he said, a little hesitant, 'Ranudi, Satuda doesn't let me read the books you have in the cupboard in your west-facing room. Will you give me one to read? I'll return it as soon as I've finished it.'

Rani said, 'I don't know which books, though; wait, I'll see—'

It was impossible to persuade Satu at first, but eventually he said, 'All right, I'll let you read the books if you do one thing for me. Everyday someone steals fish from the pond in our field – Jethamoshai has asked me to go there and keep guard in the afternoons – I don't like being there, all alone; if you go there in my place, I'll let you read the books—'

Rani protested, 'Oh that's fine! He's just a boy – he has nothing better to do than sit in the forest and guard the fish, does he? You're an overgrown boy and you can't, so he has to go! Forget it, you don't have to give him your books, I'll ask Father—'

Apu, though, agreed. Rani's father Bhubon Mukhujje lived in another

---

* Editor's note: Durga, Apu's late elder sister, is being referred to here.

part of the country; it would be a long time before he returned, while Apu, on the other hand, desired these books deeply. In his greed to read the books, he'd loitered, with a covetous heart, in Satu's west-facing room on many occasions. He'd even browsed through one or two. But Satu, who didn't read at all himself, didn't let him read either. Snatching the book from his hands just when he'd arrived at the protagonist's most critical moment, Satu would say, 'Put it back, Apu, these are Chhoto kaka's books, they'll tear, give it to me.'

Every day in the afternoon, selecting a book from the cupboard, and taking Satu's permission, he'd leave; and, spreading some tender branches from the Seora tree in the shadow of the bamboo forest, he'd lie on them on his stomach and read undisturbed. There was no shortage of books – *The Icon of Love, Saroj-Sarojini, Kusum-Kumari, The Illustrated Drama of the Young Yogini, The Bandit's Daughter, The Fate of Love or Poison in the Elixir, Gopeshwar's Secret* ... how many more names need he utter! He'd begin with one; he wouldn't be able to let go of it until he'd finished it. His eyes would ache, the vein in his temples throb gently; in the meanwhile, the shadow of the empty bamboo forest by the pond would, at some point, deepen, and descend on the cluster of weeds on the muddy surface, and he wouldn't even be aware in what way the afternoon had gone!

What stories! Saroj, taking Sarojini with him, going to Murshidabad by boat ... on the way, the Nawab's men plundered the boat and took them prisoner. At the Nawab's orders, Saroj was sentenced to death; and Sarojini was imprisoned inside a dark room. Deep in the night, the door to the room opened; the Nawab, stepping into it in a state of inebriation, said, 'O beautiful one, Saroj has been put to death at my directive; why then ...' et cetera. Sarojini, turning proudly, said, 'Demon, you still know nothing about Rajput women; until there is breath in this body ...' et cetera. At this moment, a great kick shattered the prison window. The Nawab started and saw – a sannyasi with knotted hair whose very physical proportions radiated strength, and with him four or five men who seemed powerful as death's emissaries. The sannyasi, his eyes red with anger, looked upon the Nawab and said, 'O lowest of humans, have you turned from being saviour to savourer?' And then, turning to Sarojini, he said, 'Mother, I am your lord's guru, Jogananda Swami; your lord is not dead; my *kamandulu's* water has given him life a second time; come with me now, mother, to my ashram; my disciple Saroj is waiting for you ...' The writer had a beautiful facility of style – in order to give a more elaborate sense of the wonder of Saroj's new life, he would stimulate the reader's curiosity about the next chapter by saying, 'Come, reader, let us see by what means, after being put to death in the place of execution, was it made possible for Saroj to have a second life . . .' et cetera.

At the end of each chapter, Apu's eyes would begin to blur – something would be stuck in his throat. Looking at the sky, he'd seem to think something for a minute or two – his ears would emit, in joy, in wonder, in agitation, a stream of fire; his breath stopping, he'd turn to give his attention to the next chapter. It would become evening, shadows would congeal on every side, all kinds of birdcall would begin to be heard in the bamboo overhead; he'd continue to read, thinking all the while, I must get up, his eyes an inch above the page – as long as the letters remained visible.

But he'd never read such books before! What were Sita's exile and Duval's story after these?

When he'd come home, his mother would scold him – 'How did you turn out to be such a silly fellow? You go and guard other people's fish sitting alone in a forest in your greed to read a book? They've discovered a fine fool in you.'

But his mother had no inkling whatever of the direction from which benefits were coming to the stupid Apu. These days he'd acquired two books: *The Dawn of Life in Maharashtra* and *The Evening of Life in Rajasthan*. Against the visible canvas of anthill and *baichi* forest, in the silent afternoon's enchantment, picture after picture kept changing – Zulekha, ministering to the injured Naren upon the river; Shivaji, finding himself placed on equal footing with the Mansabdars who led five thousand men, swelling with anger and thinking – Shivaji, a leader of five thousand? Go to Poona once, and count how many Mansabdars with five thousand there are in Shivaji's army! . . .

His entire day would pass on the desert peaks of Rajbara, in the Rang mahal and Sheesh mahal of Delhi and Agra, among groups of beautiful women wearing scarves and Peshowaj skirts. What world was this – where there was only moonlight, swordplay, lovely faces brought together in friendship, and, long spear in hand, men galloping across barren valleys and fields of corn on horseback during the Aheria festival? . . .

Pratap Singh had achieved all a hero, a Rajput, a human being could. His story was written on the face of every stone on Haldighat's mountainous roads. The story was inscribed in the imperishable glory of the blood spilt from the hearts of twelve thousand Rajput men on the battlefield of Dewar.

Even after years had passed, the ancient warriors would sit by the fire on a winter's night and narrate the story of the astonishing heroism at Haldighat to their grandsons and granddaughters...

A spear was thrown by an invisible hand. Apu, who'd grown up by the perpetually dark shadows of the trees in this village, among hidden creepers and leaves, and the wet earth's smell, still knew every place in the province of the Bhils in Rajputana, or in Aravalli Mewar; he was intimate with the incomparable wild beauty of Nahara Mogro ... How beautiful was the image of Tejsingha, descending from the mountains, weapon in hand!...

'There, in Chappan Pradesh, for many days at midnight, a song sung by a woman could be heard issuing from the uninhabited cavern and the utmost summit of that Bhil village. Very early in the morning, in that lonely place, passers-by could sometimes see a woman's pale face and her restless eyes; people used to suppose it must be some forest goddess, unhappy and bereft of repose' ... It was as if the indistinct, mournful echo of that song would come to Apu's ears from behind the *kaash* flowers!...

Kamalmir, the battle at Suryagarh, General Shabaaz Khan, Noor Jehan the beautiful, Pushpakumari, the wild province of the Bhils, the child-hero Chandansingh – those remote, remote imagined places. And yet how near, how real it seemed. In the deserts of Rajbara and the blue Aravalli, the chenar trees on the peaks of the high mountains had flowered and shed their blossoms; the footprints of the goddess Mewarlakshmi, red as if with lac and blood, were printed on the bits of stone on the banks of the rivers Bunas and Ravi, on the rocks beneath waterfalls, on fields of bajra and *jowar* and the Moul forests...

Chittor could not be saved. Rana Amar Singh bowed before the sovereignty of the Badshah. And in what way did his father Pratap Singh, who had lost everything, who for twenty-five years had fought with legions of Bhils in forest and on mountain, bear witness, his heart raging with sorrow, to this?...

With hot tears, anthill, the *baichi* forest, the bamboo, would all grow indistinct.

*

That afternoon, his father, displaying a parcel, said, smiling, 'Tell me, son, what d'you think this is?'

Apu swiftly sat up in the bed; in an eager voice, he asked, 'A paper? Isn't it, baba?'

Of the three rupees Harihar had got the other day from Bihari Ghosh's mother-in-law for writing down the Ramkabach, he'd sent two rupees (keeping it a secret from his wife) towards a subscription for the newspaper; if his wife had known, the want of another five things in the household would have meant that there would have been absolutely no way of salvaging those two rupees.

Apu, quickly taking the parcel from his father's hands, opened it. Yes – it *was* a paper. The word 'Bangabasi' was written on it in those same, large letters, and here was that very smell of new paper, that very newsprint – it was for this that, about a year ago, he, like a scavenging crow, would go impatient and eager, every Saturday to sit by the postbox, near Bhubon Mukhujje's porch where festivals were celebrated, in open-mouthed expectation of the peon! A paper! A paper! Who knows what news had appeared in it this time? What unheard-of things were printed on its large pages?

Harihar thought, 'The satisfaction derived from releasing some pawned earring surely couldn't exceed the joyous smile that's come to my son's face by the grace of two rupees.'

Apu read for a while and said, 'Look, baba, they've published a letter from a "Traveller in England"; its first instalment's come out today. We've got our paper just at the right time – haven't we, baba?'

Yet it still made him sad to think that, on the subscription being stopped suddenly last year, he hadn't read the last part of the story about the Japanese demon-spider; he hadn't been able to find out what happened after Raiko visited the emperor's court . . .

One day Rani said, 'What's that you've been writing in your notebook?'

Apu said in a tone of astonishment, 'Which notebook? How did you—'

'Didn't I go to your house the other day in the afternoon? You weren't there: I sat and talked with *khurima* for such a long time! Why, didn't *khurima* tell you? That's when I saw you'd scribbled all kinds of things in your red notebook among the books in your "library" – my name's there, and Devi Singha or somebody—'

Apu went red with embarrassment. 'That's a story.'

'What story's it, Apu? You'll have to read it out to me.'

The next day Rani handed a bound exercise book to Apu and said, 'Write me a story in this, Apu – quite a good one. You will, won't you? Atasi was saying that apparently you write well! Write it, I'll show it to Atasi . . .'

Apu used to write in his notebook at night. He'd say to his mother, 'Do give me another spoonful of oil, Ma. I'll just write a little more and stop.'

His mother would say, 'Don't read any more tonight – there are only another two spoonfuls left; what'll I cook with tomorrow? I'm cooking here, come and read in this light.' And Apu would quarrel with her.

His mother would scold him: 'Oh, all the enthusiasm for reading and writing comes to this boy at night – there's no sign all day even of his forelock! What d'you do in the morning? Go away, I won't give you any more oil.'

In the end, Apu'd come and sit down with his notebook at the edge of the stove, in the light of the burning wood. Sarbajaya would think, 'When Apu's a little older I'll get him a good bride. Let's give him his sacred thread next year; and then if the puja at the Gangulys could become a regular affair . . .'

When he returned the exercise book to Rani four or five days later, she asked, opening the book in excitement, 'Did you write it?'

Apu, a hint of laughter on his face, said, 'Why don't you open it and see?'

Rani looked in and said happily, 'Oh, what a lot you've written! Wait, let me call Atasi and show it to her.'

Atasi looked at it and said, 'Apu's written it or has somebody else – Ha! It's all copied from a book.'

Apu said in protest, 'Oh yes, from a book, of course! I *make up* stories – let's see, why don't you ask Potu, Atasidi? Haven't I sat by the river with him in the afternoon and made up all those stories to tell him?'

Rani said, 'No, I know he's written it. That's the style he writes in. He once read out a wonderful play he'd written in his notebook to me.' Later, she said to Apu, 'Haven't you written your name inside? Write your name on it.'

Apu, as if slightly compromised, said that his story wasn't quite finished yet; he'd sign it the moment he had. Although he'd begun the story in the style of the play, 'The Life of a Young Yogini in Pictures', he hadn't been able to altogether decide how he'd finish it; on the other hand, if the exercise book stayed with him for too many days, Ranudi – Atasidi in particular – might begin to doubt his creative powers; it was this fear that caused him to return the story in its unfinished state.

His father wasn't at home. Waking up in the morning, Apu, with everyone else from the village, went to a funeral ceremony in the neighbouring village they'd all been invited to. Sunil went with them as well. Brahmins from various villages who made it their business to feed at such ceremonies walked as much as ten or twelve miles to their destination. Each person had brought about five or six children with them; seating everyone conveniently seemed to lead to the possibility of a riot. After dispatching five *luchis* on everybody's plate, the organizers, beginning to distribute fried aubergines, discovered the plates were void of *luchis* – everyone was sitting pretty, having deposited them on to the cloth or the *gamchha* they had by their side! ... Little boys, not knowing enough to grasp these manoeuvrings, were breaking the *luchis* on their plates – Bishweshwar Bhattacharya swooped towards his son's plate and, putting the *luchis* on the cloth next to him, said, 'Why don't you leave those alone! They'll give you some more soon, eat them then.'

After this, for a while, there was a great disturbance – 'Bring the basket of *luchis* to this row'; 'By the way, there's absolutely no pumpkin on my–'; 'Hey, see that they're hot'; 'Sir, touch and see what you've given me, will you, it's raw flour' ... et cetera. With regard to the bundle of things to be given to the Brahmins to take home, there was noisy disagreement! Someone began to shout, 'In that case you mustn't invite *bhadralok*. Five or six heaps of *luchis* is the accepted "rate" for take-home bundles – it's been established since the time of Kallol Sen. I don't want your bundle; in a place like this, Kandappo Majumdar would never–'

The organizers set about appeasing Kandarpa Majumdar in earnest.

Apu too brought a bundle home. Sarbajaya, quickly emerging from the house, said with a smile, 'O ma, what a lot you've brought back – let's see, open it! *Luchi, pantua, gaja* – how many, Apu! Let me cover them and put them away; you can eat them in the morning.'

Apu said, 'But you'll have to eat them too, Ma – I asked for a double helping of *pantua* for you.'

Sarbajaya said, 'What, did you tell them, Give me some, my mother'll eat them? O you're really too greedy!'

With a movement of his neck and arms, Apu said, 'As if I'd say something like that! I asked them in such a way that they thought I was going to eat the lot.'

Sarbajaya, full of happiness, picked up the bundle and took it inside.

Apu went to Sunil's house after a while. Stepping on to the porch, he heard Sunil's mother telling her son, 'Why did you drag all those things back home? Who asked you to bring them?' Sunil, too, following everyone else, had brought with him a take-home bundle; he said, 'Why, Ma, everyone took one – Apu brought one back too.'

Sunil's mother said, 'Why shouldn't Apu bring one back – he's the son a Brahmin who survives on the food at such ceremonies! In the future he's going to preside over pujas and take home many more bundles – that's the course they've taken in life. His mother's just as pathetically greedy.

That's why I didn't want to bring you two with me when I first came to this village. Bad company's setting you a bad example! Go, call Apu and leave these with him – go; or at least throw them away, go. You were invited to a feast and you ate at a feast – what was the need for bringing back all those things like low people.'

Frightened, Apu decided against entering Sunil's house. On his way home, he thought, Ma was so happy to get those odds and ends; why was Jethima so angry upon seeing them? Was the food blobs of earth, that it had to be thrown away? His mother greedy? He the son of a Brahmin who survived on feasts? But Jethima might have had many *pantuas* and *gajas*; his mother had little opportunity to eat them. And how often had he eaten these things himself? How could what was reprehensible for Sunil be reprehensible for him?

He didn't get a great deal of studies done; this was the way he spent his time. Eating at ceremonial feasts, tying up bundles of food to bring home, accompanying his father to a disciple's house, fishing. That small boy Potu – the one who'd been beaten up when he'd gone to the fishermen's quarters to play with cowries – was Apu's companion in all these things. These days he was bigger, and had grown taller; and he'd go everywhere his Apuda did. He'd come from another locality to this one only to play with Apu; he didn't mix a great deal with anyone else. He still hadn't forgotten that it was while rescuing *him* from the fishermen's sons that Apu had taken a beating.

Apu had a great passion for fishing. The mouth of the Kanchikata canal, by the river Ichhamati that ran down the Sonadanga field, was often full of fish. He'd go there frequently and sit down under a large *chhatim* tree on the riverbank to catch fish. He was very fond of this place; it was absolutely lonely; on both sides, the river was bordered with all kinds of foliage and branches leaning over the water; on the other side were the deep green thickets of *ulu* grass, the intermittent stirring of the leaves of the creepers on *kadam* and *shimul* trees, bushes over which had spread purple *bankalmi* blossoms; further on, Madhavpur village's bamboo forest; amidst birdcall, forest shadow, the *ulu* thicket's gloom, this mingling and merging with this tender loneliness!

Since that day in early childhood when he'd first come to the *kuthi* field, what an allure did field, forest, river have for him! The moment he'd drop his line and, sitting beneath the shadow of the *chhatim* tree, look on all sides, an amazing contentment would flood him. Whether he caught a fish or not, whenever the afternoon's deep gloom was suffused with the smell of the half-ripe dates on date palms on the edge of the field, and a soft breeze broadcast in all directions the cries of the *bou-katha-kao* and the *papiya* bird, and the great sun, scattering silver and vermilion on branches, would droop behind the corner of that banyan on Sonadanga field, the river's water grow black, flocks of river-shalik return home amidst their own noise, it was then he'd become engrossed, and look on all sides with eyes heavy with joy; he'd think, 'Even if I don't catch a fish, I'll come here and sit every day, right here under this *chhatim* tree.'

Most of the time there was no fish; the float on the line in the still water would, hour after hour, remain as immovable as the windless, tremorless flame on the wick of a lamp. He didn't have the patience to stay in one place for so long; he'd go wandering about restlessly in the vicinity, in search of birds' nests in the bushes; returning, he might notice the float was tembling a little. Drawing the line in, he'd say, 'Rubbish! There's a shoal of *jheya* fish here; it's no good fishing here now . . .' Later, drawing the line, he'd go and drop the bait in the weed-covered surface a little further away. The deep blackness of the water might make one suppose that, what else, large *rui* and *katla* fish would swallow the bait straight-away! It didn't take a long time for this delusion to end; the float on the line would attain a state of transcendental samadhi . . .

On certain days he'd take a book or two to settle down with.

He'd throw in the line and open a book. From Suresh he'd borrowed an English book with pictures meant for younger children, and also its glossary. He couldn't understand English; turning to the glossary he'd read, in Bengali, what the story was about, and then only look at the pictures in the English book. Narratives about distant countries and all kinds of human greatness had always moved his heart since he'd been a child, and this book had several stories on such subjects. How, in some featureless landscape, a traveller had lost his way in a terrific snowstorm and, going round and round in circles, lost his life in the cold; in what way, crossing an uncharted ocean, Christopher Columbus had discovered America – stories of this kind. The English girl and boy who'd climbed up the side of a mountain by the sea to collect eggs from a seagull's nest, and found themselves in danger; the courageous girl, Praskovia Lapulof, who, in order to repeal her father's exile, had embarked alone on a journey to the ice-girded land of Siberia – it was as if he'd recognize them at once if he saw them.

Reading the little story about Sir Philip Sidney, his eyes filled with tears. He went and asked Suresh, 'Sureshda, d'you know this story? Would you please tell me more?'

Suresh said, 'Oh, about the Battle of Zutphen!'

Apu, amazed, said, 'What, Sureshda? Zutphen! Where's that?'
Suresh could tell him no more about it.

*

One day, a few months later.

He'd been trying to catch a fish, and somehow a big *sarputi* had attached itself to the line and he'd reeled it in.

Expectant, now, Apu could no longer abandon that place – he'd break some twigs and branches and, spreading them, sit there.

Time unravelled gradually, and once more that incomparable stillness would come to the field by the river; on the other bank, by the border of Deyar's field, in the green expanse of *ulu* grass, in the thickets of *kaash* flowers, and on the tops of the *kadam* and *shimul* trees, all extending into the distance, was once more that most-familiar, old friend of the blessed time of his childhood happiness – the afternoon's disappearing, final sunlight!

He'd recall the beautiful story he'd read in the 'Letter From A Traveller in England' in the *Bangabasi*...

He'd seen in Sureshdada's English map where the Mediterranean ocean was; and he knew that, beyond it, was France. Many years ago, a foreign army had borne heavily upon the heart of France; the country was in danger; the king powerless; there was lawlessness everywhere; looting and pillaging! At this time when the nation was being gravely wronged, an impoverished peasant girl, in a tiny village situated in the province of Lorraine, went out to graze her father's herd of sheep, and letting her sheep wander here and there, sat down upon the green earth of that remote rural landscape, and, lifting her blue eyes to the sky, pondered, alone, on the sad state of her country. After several days of deep thought, a voice was born in her untainted, tender maiden's mind, which said to her, You are France's saviour; go and gather the royal army; the nation's deliverance is in your hands. St Mary was the one who granted her courage – day after day, her call would come to her from furthest heaven. Then, in what way the reinvigorated French army had repulsed the enemy from the country, how an otherworldly maiden herself took arms and restored the throne to the king, and then how ignorant, blind men, accusing her of witchcraft, had burnt her alive – all this he'd read today.

In what a wonderful way his heart would fill to the brim as he thought over the story on this afternoon, by the serene river's side! It wasn't as if he thought a great deal about the tales of the maiden's battles and her victories. But the picture that came to his mind again and again was of the young girl, deeply pondering, in that uninhabited landscape, and the sheep on all sides wandering of their own volition, the green earth below, above her head, the open blue sky. On the one hand, the terrifying foreign enemy, the cruelty, the arrogance of victory, the streams of blood; on the other, a simple, celestial, otherwordly, blue-eyed peasant girl. This picture absorbed his boy's growing mind.

More pictures came to his mind. The faraway, blue-sea-encircled Martinique island. Sugar-cane fields on every side, the blue sky above – so, so distant – only the blue sky, and the blue sea. Blue and only blue! And much more, which you couldn't convey – or communicate.

Drawing in the fishing-line, he'd prepare to go home. Clusters of *babla* and *saibabla*, their heads bowed before the river, lowered their burden of flowers upon the soothing, dark water. The immense, blood-red sun had drooped behind the corner of the banyan tree in the middle of Sonadanga field – it was as if some heavenly child had, in play, blown a bubble from Alaka's* burning, curdling, golden ocean into the sky, which at this moment was descending on the western horizon, into the interior of the earth's forests!

Someone covered his eyes from behind. As he forced the hands from his eyes, Potu broke into peals of laughter and, confronting him, said, 'I couldn't find you anywhere, Apuda; then I thought, I'm sure he must have gone fishing, and so here I am. Didn't catch a fish? . . . not even one? Come, let's untie a boat instead and go exploring – coming?'

Many boats from distant places came to Saheb ghat at Kadamtala – boat after boat moored to the bank, loaded with the leaves of the fan palm, with grain, with oysters. The fishermen on the oyster-catching boats had cast large nets on the river. Each year, at this time, they'd come from the South to catch oysters; they'd tied several boats to each other in the river's midst. Apu was watching from the bank – a darkish man was diving into the water again and again in search of oysters, and, surfacing by the boat after a few minutes, was retrieving the few oysters he'd collected from the bag in his hand, and then, sifting them from the heap of sand and mud they were in, throwing them into the boat. Apu, full of joy, said to Potu while pointing with his finger, 'D'you see, Potu, how long he can stay

---

* Editor's note: The city in which Kubera, the god of wealth, resides; it is also a name that means 'heaven', or the 'paradisial city', especially in the sense Kalidasa used it in his long Sanskrit poem, 'Meghdut' (*c.* fifth century AD). The name has a paradisial resonance in modern Bengali literature also because of the importance Kalidasa's poem had for Tagore.

underwater? Come, let's count one, two and see. Could you stay under-water for so long?'

The bank, carpeted with *durba* grass, became a slope as it descended to the water's edge; cargo-laden boats were tethered, here and there, to posts – their anchors lowered. They had passed through so many lands, crossing great rivers and canals, drinking in the high and low tides and storms of so many salt-waterways as they travelled – Apu yearned to sit with the boatmen to listen to the tales of those countries. He desired nothing but to travel from river to river, sea to sea. It was reading about the sailors of various nations in Suresh's books that had awakened this powerful wish within him! Potu and he went near the boat to bargain: 'Boatman, what price is a bundle of these leaves? ... Where does this grain-carrying boat of yours come from, boatman? ... From Jhalkathi? In which direction's that, how far is it from here?

Potu said, 'Apuda, come, let's go to Tetultala ghat and get ourselves a skiff, and go out into the river – come.'

The two of them untied a small skiff from Tetultala ghat, and, giving it a shove, climbed on to it. The cool, moist scent of the river-water was rising into the air, *jalpipi* birds were adrift on masses of bindweed, and farmers were weeding fields of *patal* by the sandbanks; some were tying the grass they'd cut into sheaves; a group of river-shalik were clamouring, by Chaltepota, in the bushes on the bank; a many-coloured heap of clouds had gathered against the eastern sky in the dying light.

Potu said, 'Apuda, why don't you sing a song? The one you sang the other day!'

Apu said, 'Not that one. I've learnt the tune of a very good song from baba. I'll sing that one, but after we've gone a little further, though; there are all these people on the bank – not here.'

'You're too shy, Apuda. A few people somewhere in the distance, and you don't want to – rubbish, let's hear it!'

After they'd gone a little further, Apu began to sing. Potu lifted the bamboo paddle and, sitting quietly on the stern, listened, rapt; there was no need to row, because the skiff went by itself with the current, meander-ing towards the bend at La-bhanga. When Apu finished his song, Potu began singing one. Now Apu started to row. The distance the boat had covered wasn't negligible – the bend at La-bhanga was about to come into sight. Suddenly Potu, pointing to the north-east, said, 'Hey Apuda, have you noticed the way the clouds have piled up? The storm's almost here – should I turn the boat round?'

Apu said, 'Oh let the storm come – it's during a storm that rowing and singing's most fun – let's go on.'

As they talked, the dense black clouds, advancing towards Madhavpur's fields, filled the whole sky, and their black shadows spread upon the river's water. Potu, with eager eyes, kept staring at the sky. Far away there arose a windy, sibilant sound, an indistinct noise accompanying the cries of many birds; a cool breeze began to blow, and the smell of wet earth floated towards them. The winged seeds of the sun-plant began to fly towards the field in thousands; and before you knew it, the tops of trees tossed, swayed, and broke with the tremendous *kal-baisakhi* storm.

The river's colour turned deep black, the branches of the *saibabla* and big *chhatim* trees looked about to break, and a band of white cranes escaped, making a long line in their flight beneath the black sky! Apu's chest swelled; in enthusiasm and agitation he abandoned the boat's helm, and began to look around him to review the spectacle of the storm; no sooner had Potu opened the creased end of his dhoti and lifted it to the storm like a sail, than it ballooned with the wind!

Potu said, 'It's really a harsh wind, Apuda, the boat won't go any further. And what if it capsizes? Thank God we didn't bring Sunil with us!'

Apu, though, was unmindful of Potu's words; his ears and mind didn't register what he was saying. Sitting on the stern of the boat, he was staring, unblinking, at the river in turmoil and at the sky. The effervescent water of the black river surrounding him, the cranes in flight, the piles of storm-clouds, the heap of oysters collected by the fishermen from the South, the mass of water-hyacinths set afloat in the current – it was as if none of these existed! In his imagination, he was that traveller in England he'd read about in the *Bangabasi*! His ship had departed from Calcutta; leaving Sagardweep on the mouth of the Bay of Bengal behind him, passing many unknown and tiny islands in the midst of the ocean, beholding the dark coconut groves on the coast of Ceylon and then going beyond the blue mountains and horizons of so many marvellous countries, anointed by the red light of sunset, he was moving onward through the fresh and changing scenery of new lands! – onward! – onward!

Like this Ichhamati's black, deep, angry water was the water of that faraway, unseen ocean; and like the green of these bushes and thickets was the green of that island in the Arabian Sea. There, on an evening like this, he'd sit beneath a tree at the port in Aden and, like that traveller in England, take a glass of water from the hand of an Arab girl. When he looked at the bend at Chaltepota, it was as if he could clearly see the flock of water birds in flight behind the ship that had been described in the paper!...

He'd journey to all those places, see all those things, go to England, to Japan, he'd embark on commercial voyages, he'd be a great merchant, travelling constantly through the seas of the world, facing, occasionally, great danger; if his ship started to sink in a storm in the sea of China as terrific as today's intoxicating *kal-baisakhi* storm, he too, like the sailors he'd read about in *My Wonderful Voyage*, would get into a jolly-boat and, roasting the oysters and shellfish he'd picked up from the sides of submerged rocks, cross an ocean that seemed to have no shore! Over there, above the top of Madhuvpur's bamboo forest, was a congregation of turquoise clouds, leaning slightly forward – just beyond them were those blue seas, unknown seashores, coconut groves, volcanoes, provinces upon which snow fell, Zulekha, Sarayu, Grace Darling, Zutphen, the beautiful English girl and boy who'd gathered a seagull's eggs, the magician Batgar who could produce gold, Lorraine's blue-eyed village girl, Joan, who sat pondering in a lonely landscape – and so much more! The few books in his tin box, the books in Ranudidi's house, the one he'd borrowed from Sureshdada, the old issues of *Bangabasi*, had spoken to him of those countries; it was as if someone was waiting for him expectantly somewhere in those places. From there a call would come to him one day – and he would go!

It didn't even occur to him to think how distant those countries were, nor to wonder who'd take him there, or in what way his journey would be made possible! He, who'd have to go from house to house performing ceremonial duties in a few days in order to support the household, who had to listen to his mother's reprimands because he needed oil for the light by which he read at night, who still, at his age, hadn't seen what a school looked like, and didn't know what good clothes or luxuries were – who would invite this ignorant, insignificant village boy, who had neither wealth nor support, to take part in the celebrations of a greater life?

If these questions had arisen in his mind, the chariot-speed of his boyish imagination – the irresistible glamour of the hope-filled avenue of life he walked down – would probably have conquered all his fears and doubts; but these things didn't even occur to him. He only thought that everything would come to be once he grew up, and that, as he advanced onward, he'd find all opportunities and conveniences in his path ... all he had to do was wait till he was grown up! As soon as he'd grown up, the opportunities would come, as would enthusiastic invitations from various places – he'd discover the world and come to know all humanity on his triumphal journey.

The rest of the way he spent absorbed in the colour of the dreams that showed him his future life. It had stopped raining; the storm, blowing away the pile of black clouds, had cleared the sky. The spell he was under broke as the skiff approached Tetultala ghat; tying the boat, he walked ahead of Potu on the path through the bamboo forest, whistling exultantly as he went homeward. He, too, had learnt to dream like his mother and his sister.

Parashuram (Rajshekhar Basu) (1880–1960)

Parashuram was the pen-name of Rajshekhar Basu, probably the greatest twentieth-century humorist in Bengali. The pen-name is not, apparently, a homage to the Parashuram of mythology, the Brahmin sage who made it his mission to decimate the Kshatriya, or aristocratic, caste with his axe; although Basu directed his satire towards his contemporaries, his humour was regenerative rather than destructive. For his pen-name, Basu simply borrowed the surname of someone at hand, the family goldsmith, Tarachand Parashuram, revealing that, from the beginning, his interest lay in the hidden potential for idiosyncrasy in local and ordinary actors, rather than in the grand mythologies. He came from a distinguished family; he took a Master's Degree in Chemistry from Calcutta University in 1903, joined Bengal Chemical and Pharmaceutical Works Ltd, founded in 1901, as a chemist, and rose, before long, to the high-ranking position of 'manager'. Basu once said that he began his literary practice through writing copy for his company's advertisements; he is not only one of the early pioneers of the medium of advertisement in Bengali, but, moving into the private realm of 'high' art from copywriting, points to a direction that many later writers and artists, from Satyajit Ray to Rushdie, would take. His brother, Girindrashekhar Bose, was the first Freudian psychoanalyst of the non-Western world. Basu's means of engaging with a rather odd contemporary reality of *bhadralok* propriety and comic subterfuge was not to consign his subjects to a psychoanalyst's couch, as his brother might have, but to treat them with an indulgent but penetrating satire, often leading them to confess to oddities they might have been too embarrassed to do so to a doctor. He, like Sukumar Ray, is extremely difficult to translate, although for different reasons; while Ray puns and plays with words, Basu records the diverse ways in which Bengali is spoken, and loquaciously transformed, by the various communities settled in Calcutta, not least the Marwari entrepreneur. In the second story below, we have, as in the extract from *Pather Panchali*, a portrait of a boy reading, although the account here is anarchic and parodic. The first story, in which a well-known figure from Western culture (in this case, popular English culture) comes into contact with a real or imaginary Bengali figure, belongs to a tiny sub-genre in Bengali fiction;

another example is Bibhuti Bhushan Banerjee's 'Einstein o Indubala' (not included here), where the great scientist meets a Bengali singer hugely popular in her time. As it is the task of literature to both celebrate, and ridicule, certain forms of wishful thinking, these fictional but vivid meetings acknowledge and parody the contact between India and the West in the modern age, the sort of contact that the West itself cared to know little about: an air of secrecy and anonymity, thus, is apt to these appointments.

* * *

'Blue Star' (1954)

translated from the Bengali by Ketaki Kushari Dyson

I am talking about a time sixty years behind us, during the reign of Queen Victoria. In those days Calcutta did not have electric lights, motor cars, radios or loud-speakers; aeroplanes did not fly in the sky; Tagore was not yet famous; and Hemchandra was called the best poet. But Rakhal the schoolmaster fancied himself to be a superior poet and held that he could write better stuff than the *Lament of Disappointment*. To his devoted student Naran he would say, 'Want to hear what I've written today? – The wind, enraged, smears his body with dust. Want to hear another one? – Where, on a dry tree, is the effect of a tempest? Can anybody else write like that?'

Rakhal Mustaufi was educated only up to the pre-university stage, but he was a learned man. He had read plenty of Bengali and English books. Apart from writing poetry, music and chess were also his hobbies. In his early youth Rakhal was the Third Master in Behala Jubilee High School. Then by chance he attracted the notice of Rajabahadur Raupyendranar-ayan Raychaudhuri of Rupchandpur and worked as his private secretary for two years. For some reason he had to leave that job. After that ten years passed. Now Rakhal lived in his paternal house in Behala and was once again a teacher at the Jubilee School.

At that time Rakhal was nearly thirty-three years old. He was good-looking, but took no care of his appearance. His hair was tousled; he did not shave; his beard was streaked with grey as well. People in the neigh-bourhood used to refer to him as the crazy schoolmaster. In those days people used to marry young, but Rakhal was still unmarried. He lived alone, his mother having died two years before that.

It was eight o'clock on a Sunday morning. Rakhal was sitting on a *taktaposh* on the veranda outside his front room, smoking a hookah and writing a poem. A half-paved street twisted and turned about a hundred yards from the house. Rakhal saw a hired phaeton come and stop, and two Europeans and one Bengali alight from it. While the carriage waited, they advanced briskly towards Rakhal's house.

One of the Europeans was tall and thin, clean-shaven, the cheeks a little sunken, his receding hairline making his forehead look bigger than it was. The other man was of medium build, neither fat nor thin, had a moustache and limped a little. Their Bengali companion was dark, of firm athletic build, hair cropped short, the tips of his moustaches curled, dressed in a dhoti and a white drill coat. Rakhal put his hookah down and stared at the visitors with amazement.

Coming nearer, the tall sahib took off his hat and said, 'Good morning, sir.' The other sahib did not take his hat off, just said, 'Good morning, babu.' Their Bengali companion remained silent.

Rakhal got up deferentially, salaamed, and said, 'Good morning, good morning, sir. I am very sorry there are no chairs in my house. Please sit on this *taktaposh*, this wooden platform.'

The tall chap said, 'That's all right, we shall sit down. Please sit down too. Am I speaking to Rakhal Mustaufi himself?'

'Yes, sir.'

The two sahibs each gave Rakhal his card and sat down on the *taktaposh*, and Rakhal sat down too. The visiting Bengali gentleman remained standing – he couldn't sit on the same seat as sahibs.

The sahib with the moustache threw away his cigarette and said, 'This Bengali babu is our interpreter Banchharam Khanja. Perhaps we won't need his services, since it seems you know English. We can talk to you directly. Well, Mustaufi babu, you have probably heard the name of this famous friend of mine?'

Rakhal studied the two cards intently and said, 'Very sorry, sir, I don't think I have.'

– How strange. You are an educated man. Haven't you read of him, in the *Strand* magazine?

– I'm a poor man, sir. Where will I get hold of the *Strand* magazine? I just read the *Bangabasi*, the *Janmabhumi*, and occasionally the *Hindu Patriot*.

– Don't you read English fiction?

– I've read a lot – Scott, Dickens, Lytton, George Eliot.

– You don't read crime stories?

— I've read many novels by Reynolds, including *Mysteries of the Court of London*.

— For shame, Mustaufi babu. One shouldn't touch his books. He is a wicked man, a traitor to his country.

— What has he done, sir?

— He's written that the French are the most civilized nation, that no man as great as Napoleon has ever been born, and that the British ministers are so worthless that they get hold of German scoundrels and marry our princesses off to them. But let that pass. So you know nothing about this famous friend of mine?

A little embarrassed, Rakhal said, 'I only know that this is his first visit to this country, but that you are not a newcomer.'

Amazed, the tall sahib said, 'That's fine! What else do you know, Mr Mustaufi?'

— That the two of you didn't sleep well last night.

— Very very good. What else do you know?

— That you ate *lanka* last night.

— Lanka? You mean Ceylon, the island of Ravan?

— No sir, not that Lanka. It's called *mirchai* in Hindi. Can't recall the English name. Red and green pods — ah yes, I remember — chilli, red pepper, capsicum, a very hot spice.

The tall sahib said to his friend, 'Do you see, Watson? This Bengali gentleman is well-versed in the science of deduction. No, Sherlock Holmes won't be able to attract many clients in this country.'

Watson said, 'Mustaufi babu, do you practise yoga?'

Rakhal said, 'The Yoga-shastra? No, I don't know that. My father used to practise *kaviraji*, the Indian system of medicine. I learned a few things from him. Observing all symptoms carefully and inferring the cause therefrom has become a habit with me.'

Watson asked, 'How did you guess that we didn't sleep well last night?'

Sherlock Holmes said, 'Elementary, Watson. It's very easy. Our faces have traces of mosquito bites. We didn't sleep under a mosquito net, and the punkah-puller too absconded in the middle of the night. But how did you make the two other guesses?'

Rakhal said, 'Very easy. As soon as you came you took your hat off and addressed me with a "sir". Experienced sahibs don't treat natives with so much courtesy. That told me you were newly arrived from England. Dr Watson didn't take his hat off, called me "babu", so I knew he was not a newcomer, but a pukka sahib, well-versed in the customs of this country.'

— How did you know we'd been eating chillies?

– You've got tobacco stains on your fingers. It's clear you smoke a lot of cigarettes, cigars, or a pipe. Dr Watson was smoking a cigarette, but you were not. From time to time you were exposing the tip of your tongue, that's to say your tongue was smarting. When someone not used to chillies eats them, this is what happens. He can't smoke a cigarette afterwards. Dr Watson is a pukka person – he hasn't been affected by chillies.

Holmes laughed and said, 'Wonderful! It was on Watson's recommendation that last night I had mulligatawny soup, chicken curry, and Bengal Club chutney at the hotel. All three were extremely hot. Well, can you say anything about this companion of ours, Mr Khanja?'

Looking at Banchharam, Rakhal said, 'He works for the police. It is clear from his haircut, style of moustache, and drill coat. Besides, under his chin one can see the mark made by the ribbons of his topi.'

Banchharam Khanja said in his mother tongue, 'Ha, you are a very smart guy indeed. Tell us something more then.'

– You are from Panchakot. Recently you got beaten. You had lathi-bashings on your hands and shoulders. Wire-lashed Mircapuri lathi. Your skin still shows the marks.

– Is that all you can see – the marks on my body? Do you know the bashing I gave that scoundrel Baldeo the *paan*-wallah?

Holmes said, 'Mustaufi, it's clear from the expression on the face of our friend Khanja that your guess about him is correct too. By the way, what's the tobacco you were smoking? I can tell sixty-three different types of tobacco from their aromas – Virginia, Turkish, Manila, Java, Cuba, Coimbatore and so on. But I don't recognize yours. Smells good.'

– It's called *da-kata* [cleaver-chopped] tobacco – very cheap and pungent.

– Dakota? Smells better than the shag I smoke. Where can one get it? I would like to take some with me.

– I could myself give you two or three seers, prepared in my own home. But you can't smoke it from a pipe. You need a hubble-bubble like this, a hookah or a *gurgura* with a long water-pipe. You'd have to learn the technique. A beautiful scientific invention, sir. The smoke comes refined through water, and the tongue doesn't smart.

– I shall learn it from you. But let's talk business now. You've probably guessed why we are here?

– You too work for the police?

– No, I'm a private detective, but I do help the police if necessary. And my friend here – Mr Watson – is my colleague.

– Kumar Swarnendranarayan of Rupchandpur has sent you, hasn't he?

But I'm telling you in advance that I know nothing. You won't get any info out of me.

Holmes said, 'Mr Khanja, I won't need your help. Please go and sit in the carriage.'

Banchharam rolled his eyes and said to Rakhal, 'Hey, Mister, don't prattle too much. I am warning you, by making a statement to the sahibs you'll land yourself in a trap.'

After Banchharam left, Holmes said, 'Mustaufi, please rest assured that it is not my intention to harm you in any way. In fact, you will benefit from my efforts.'

Rakhal asked, 'Does the Kumar Bahadur wish to obtain information from me by bribing me through you?'

– He wishes to attain his object anyhow, by fair means or foul. But that's not my policy. I would like to look after both his interest and your welfare. I know that you are a simple, honest, educated person who has been much put upon. I wish you well. You don't have to say anything. Whatever I've heard before coming to this country and have found out through my investigations since arriving here – let me just relate it all to you. If I make a mistake, let me know.

– OK then. Go ahead.

Sherlock Holmes started speaking. 'Mr Griffith, the agent of the Kumar of Rupchandpur, saw me in London about a month ago. He said that the late Raja Ropender–'

Rakhal said, 'Raupyendranarayan.'

– Yes, yes, it's hard to pronounce that jaw-breaking name. I shall just call him the Raja. What Griffith told me is this. It's now a year after the Raja's death. That old man had married a young girl while his first wife was still there. To please the new Rani he'd given her large amounts of jewellery, the most expensive item being a brooch with a huge star sapphire.

Rakhal said, 'It's called Neel Tara, Blue Star. It's a priceless jewel. Whoever has it benefits enormously. An ancestor of the Raja bought it from a Portuguese pirate two hundred years ago. It's supposed that the jewel was looted from some temple in Ceylon.'

– That's right. Did you see that jewel?

– No, just heard about it. And then?

– Just a few months after his second marriage the Raja had a fall and broke the bones of his legs and hips. He was bedridden for nearly eight years and then he died. Then suddenly one day the new Rani disappeared. The Raja's successor, the Kumar Bahadur, has done much searching, but has found neither the Blue Star nor any news of the Rani who has fled. An advertisement was put in the papers, urging the Rani to come back, saying she could live with honour in her own quarters within the royal palace, and get a sizeable pension as well. But there were no results, and the police of this country have no clues either. Am I right, Mustaufi?

– Indeed, this is as I've heard it. But the business of the Raja's marriage was more complicated.

– I am aware of that, and have solved all the riddles. Listen then. The Kumar Bahadur is not worried at all about his stepmother, he just wants to retrieve that jewel. Soon after the Blue Star passed into the hands of the new Rani, the Raja was injured, and after suffering for many years, died. Then the new Rani disappeared. All kinds of inauspicious things are happening in the estate – bad harvests, difficulty in collecting the land revenues, defeats in three major lawsuits, the peasants rioting, and the Kumar suffering from dyspepsia. He believes everything is the result of the disappearance of the Blue Star.

– You don't believe that?

– No. No matter how expensive it may be, the Blue Star is just a stone, a lump of alumina. It can have no effects, whether good or bad. In our country too there are superstitious beliefs about precious stones. Griffith, the London agent of the Kumar, told me that the Blue Star could not be the dowry or bridal gift of the junior Rani. It was the property of the royal family, an heirloom, a jewel to wear on the turban. Whoever becomes the Raja is entitled to it. The Kumar Bahadur is to receive the royal title soon, hence the Blue Star should belong to him and no one else. The junior Rani has stolen it and run away with it.

Rakhal said, 'That's false. The old Raja did have the right to give away or sell any part of his property according to his own wishes. What he gave the junior Rani is indeed her dowry.'

– I consulted the Advocate-General here. He too is of the opinion that this is her dowry, though it is hard to say what verdict would be reached in the end in the High Court and the Privy Council. Be that as it may, the Kumar Bahadur has entrusted me with the task of retrieving the Blue Star.

– The Kumar has sent a messenger to me too, and had used threats as well. He believes that I know the junior Rani's whereabouts. Have you been able to find out anything since coming to this country?

– Immediately after my arrival I went to Rupchandpur. Investigations there revealed that our late lamented Raja Bahadur was a scoundrel, as addicted to women as to alcohol, and a terrible oppressor of his people. Ten years back someone called Ramkali Ray used to work in his estate. This man had no offspring and had fostered an orphaned niece named Savitri. The girl was uncommonly beautiful and at that time was aged about sixteen. A marriage had been arranged for her with a good match from Rupchandpur itself. There was some distant connection between the families of the bride and the groom, and because they lived near each other they had even developed an intimacy. The bride used to do her studies under the direction of the groom. When the Raja found out about the marriage proposal, he said to Ramkali, the girl's maternal uncle, that on no account must he arrange a marriage anywhere else, that he, the Raja, would marry the niece himself. The uncle was a brave man and did not listen to the Raja; he made all plans for the wedding to go ahead with the groom with whom marriage talks had been held. The bride's party and the groom's party were all assembled, the girl's maternal uncle was ready to give her away, the priest was about to read the mantras, when the Raja entered with his gang. Nobody dared to offer resistance, because the Raja was so powerful, and besides, he was accompanied by a police inspector who had come to keep the peace. The Raja's followers tied up the hands and feet of the girl's uncle and the groom, and removed them from the scene. The parties of the bride and the groom scattered in terror. Then the Raja sat down on the groom's seat, his own priest read the mantras, and one of the Raja's sycophants pretended to be the bride's paternal uncle and gave the unconscious Savitri away. After the wedding, the Raja took his new wife to the palace, the maternal uncle went into exile, and the groom and his mother went off to Calcutta.

— Are you aware of the identity of that groom?

— I am speaking to him right now. He is called Rakhal Mustaufi, is a schoolmaster, thinks he is a very great poet, though not a single one of his poems has been published as yet.

— Is it a fault to think highly of oneself?

— It is for a stupid person, but not for clever blokes like you or me.

— Continue.

— The new Rani Savitri was sick for a long time. The Raja spared no effort to please her and bring her under his sway. He gave her vast amounts of jewellery including the Blue Star, a separate wing of the royal residence for her accommodation along with a large retinue of menservants and maidservants. For her education he appointed Sister Theodora of the Mission School. But within five months of the marriage the Raja suffered a fall when he was drunk, was injured, and took to his bed. The new Rani spent her time with her teacher.

— Tell me where Savitri is now.

— Don't get agitated, I am giving the whole story in the right sequence.

After the Raja's death the new Rani was put under a strict surveillance. She was very clever, and in consultation with Sister Theodora arranged her escape. One day in the middle of the night she left the royal residence with some money and jewellery and one loyal maidservant. She didn't want to take the Blue Star with her, but took it because of Theodora's earnest requests. Then she came to Calcutta and lodged in the house of a Bengali Christian lady named Miss Cecilia Banerjee. It was Theodora who had arranged it.

— Have you met Savitri?

— Yes, I have. The Rani said, "I have won my release from the palace and am now free, and have also got myself a job in a girls' school. I don't want to retain the Blue Star. You can take it away and give it to the Kumar." I said, "Why should you give it up for nothing? First you have to claim compensation for the harassment yourself and Mustaufi have suffered, and only then should you part with it." The Rani said, "I have no steam left to decide anything. Nor are Uncle and Aunt alive, so I can't consult with them either. You can talk to Mustaufi. Whatever he says is OK by me." Mustaufi, she holds you in much esteem, has a great regard for you.

— Has she turned Christian?

— Sister Theodora tried to convert her, but in no way would the Rani agree with that.

— Don't call her "the Rani", call her Savitri Devi.

— Very well. Savitri Devi. The Goddess Savitri. See, Watson, how when one's in love, one's point of view becomes so elevated, the mind's magnifying power increases. I saw the same process before your own marriage.

Holmes got a casket out of his pocket, opened it, and revealed the Blue Star in a golden frame. It was shaped like an areca nut, but bigger. Its colour was a pale cloudy blue, and within it was a figure like a bright star, radiating six rays in six directions.

— Crores of years ago,' said Holmes, 'hot liquid alumina slowly congealing within the earth's womb, produced this gem. Its market price won't be that much – ten thousand rupees at the most. But since the Kumar believes in its supernatural powers and is desperate to get it back, he must pay a high price. Tell me, Mustaufi: how much should I extract from him?

Rakhal said, 'My head feels confused. You decide whatever has to be decided.'

— Poets have very little worldly sense. There are honourable exceptions, of course, such as Lord Tennyson. Listen, Mustaufi, I shall extract four lakhs from him, two lakhs for Savitri Devi and two for you. If we ask for more, the Kumar may panic. Besides, he must pay for our fares to this country and remunerate us for our pains. Savitri has an account in the Bank of Bengal. As soon as the Kumar deposits four lakhs there, I shall hand over the Blue Star to him. He is seeing me this evening.

– What's Savitri's address?

– Number three, Cornwallis Third Lane. Mustaufi, do go and see her this very afternoon. I hope you are free of prejudices. She is a widow now, but are you prepared to marry the woman to whom you were solemnly engaged before? ... Well then, no more worries. Go, woo and win her. Come and see me tomorrow morning in my hotel. Goodbye.

Watson said, 'Excuse me, Mustaufi babu, please shave off that beard of yours. Goodbye.'

*

Rakhal went to visit Savitri at four in the afternoon, returning at half past eight in the evening. His student Naran was sitting in the veranda. Rakhal said, 'Who's that? Is it Naran? Brighten the hurricane lantern, will you.'

Turning up the flame, Naran said, 'What's this, sir, one can hardly recognize you!'

– I've shaved off my beard. What are you doing here so late in the evening?

– Bah, you've forgotten? You said you were going to read *The Battle of Sedgemoor* with me this evening.

– The devil take *Sedgemoor*. We'll do that another day. Want to hear what I made up today, coming back on the tram? – The rain comes down, cool is the ground; the heat-scorched tree has its water found; the thirsty roots suck up the juice; leaves will appear and flowers bloom. Can those poets you people admire – Hem Banerjee, Nabin Sen *et al.* – write like that?

* * *

'The Jackal-Faced Tongs' (1955)

translated from the Bengali by Ketaki Kushari Dyson

Removing the thermometer from Jhintu's mouth, his mother said, 'Ninety-nine point four. Just milk-and-barley gruel for you tonight. No roaming about. You have to stay in this room. It won't be all that long before we're back. Say, midnight.'

'Not fair,' Jhintu said, pouting. 'You are all going to have fun, having a Madrassi feast, and I have to stay at home, all on my own – hmm–'

– Nonsense. It'll hardly be a feast! No fish, no meat, just tamarind pulao, chilli curry, and sour yogurt. It's just that Yajnuswami Ayar is the big boss in your father's office, and it's his daughter's wedding, and Mrs Ayar has also specially asked me to come, that's why I'm going. I'm leaving you this Meccano; build a Howrah Bridge with it. Here are three books by Sukumar Ray; you can look at the pictures. But don't do too much reading – it'll give you a headache. I'll tell your aunt to give you milk-and-barley at half past eight in the evening. Just have it and then go off to bed. Auntie will sleep near you.

– No, Pishima doesn't have to sleep near me. She snores too much, I won't be able to sleep. I want to sleep by myself.

– All right then. As you wish.

Jhintu was ten years old, bright enough in his schoolwork, but very active and restless. His mother, father, and little sister went out to the wedding dinner, and he stayed at home. This was intolerable. He had a little touch of fever. So what? He could run two miles right now, or play a game of badminton, or leap up the stairs to the terrace on the fourth floor. There was not a soul at home with whom he could have a chat. His Pishima, his father's sister, was such a strange creature. She went to her office in the middle of the day, and spent mornings, late afternoons, and evenings just reading novels. Jhintu's classmate Jitu's Pishima was such a nice elderly lady and could tell so many different kinds of stories. Jitu would say, 'Tell me, Jhintu, why does your Aunt Sarasi get togged up and go to office? She should tell her beads, shape little cones from dhal-flour paste to dry in the sun, make sweet ground-coconut balls, cakes of dried mango-paste, and jujube pickles: that's what makes a Pishima.'

*

Jhintu made several different kinds of bridges with his Meccano pieces, and dismantled them again. At half past eight Aunt Sarasi made him have his milk-and-barley and said, 'Now go to sleep, Jhintu.'

'Do people go to sleep at half past eight?' retorted Jhintu. 'You read so many books, don't you – why not tell me a story from one of those?'

Sarasi replied, 'You won't enjoy those stories.'

– All love stories, are they?

– You're a very cheeky boy, you are. Do youngsters enjoy stories for grown-ups? Just the other day your mother was reading *The Last*

*Poem.** You heard it and said it was horrible. I'm going to turn off the light now. Go to sleep.

After Aunt Sarasi left him, Jhintu went to bed, but sleep eluded him. After tossing and turning in bed for an hour, he jumped out of bed. He had a brainwave, he had to have an adventure. He had read many stories about detectives, robbers, pirates, hidden treasures, and so forth. What fun it would be if he could discover some hidden treasure tonight! He had heard from his mother that one of his great-great-great-uncles, that's to say, an uncle of his great-grandfather, was a tantrist who was a *pishach*-expert. He had died long since, but his trunk was still there in the fourth-floor attic. Why not open that trunk and have a look?

Jhintu had a torch, and also a pistol costing a rupee and a half. Torch in one hand, the pistol slung from his waist, he climbed to the fourth floor. There was just one room by the stairs, where only useless, rubbishy items were stored. Entering that room, Jhintu switched on the light. The trunk of his great-great-great-uncle Karalicharan Mukherjee was in a corner. Made of rattan and covered in buffalo hide, it had a peculiar shape, resembling a huge tortoise. The padlock attached to it was peculiar too. A bunch of old keys hung from the wall. One by one, Jhintu tried each key on that lock, but couldn't open it. Disappointed, he was about to turn back, when he noticed that the trunk's back hinges were corroded with rust. Just a little tugging caused them to slip off. Jhintu then swung open the trunk lid from the opposite side, the back.

There was a musty disagreeable smell. Right on the top there were some dirty saffron cloths, beneath them a bunch of palm-leaf manuscripts and three fat rosaries made of dried fruits. Beneath those there were cloths again, a pair of ritual copper vessels, one for holding water, the other for sprinkling, a vessel that looked like a white earthenware pan lid, a small rusty knife, a narrow tobacco-holder for a hookah, a very dirty rag, and a pair of tongs. Had Jhintu been smart enough, he would have known that the white pan lid was the skull of a corpse, and that the knife, the tobacco-holder, the rag, and the tongs were equipment for smoking ganja.

Jhintu was annoyed. 'Hang it,' he said, 'there's nothing here – no rupees, cowries, diamonds, or rubies. But that pair of tongs isn't bad.' It was about a foot long, with a ring-shaped handle at the top, which had three more rings in a bunch attached to it. The instrument had a funny shape: when one squeezed the sides the face looked like a jackal's, with a pair of eyes on each side, and a pair of ears too. Though an artefact of considerable

---

* Editor's note: *Sesher Kabita* (1929), one of Tagore's later novels.

age, it hadn't rusted and was quite shiny. Jhintu closed the trunk and returned to his room with the tongs.

*

With the light on, Jhintu sat up in bed for a little while, looking at the Sukumar Ray books. The clock in the next room chimed ten. Now he was sleepy. Before lying down, he examined the tongs once more. The handling caused the rings at the head to clang loudly. And immediately something extraordinary happened.

Pushing the door, a strange figure entered the room. He was of short stature, his body the colour of pale blue-black ink, his hair in a tufted topknot, his face like a monkey's, with a certain resemblance to Nandalal's picture of Nandi. He wore a saffron loincloth and a pair of wooden clogs. The figure said, 'What do you want, little boy?'

At first Jhintu shuddered in terror. But he was a brave boy. Adventure incarnate had presented itself before him. He couldn't afford to be afraid now. Jhintu asked, 'Who are you?'

– Dhundudas Chanda. You've heard that your ancestor was a *pishach*-expert? I am that *pishach*.

– It was you he cooked up then?

– Silly, who has the power to cook me! He served his spiritual apprenticeship and became an expert, and thus he established his power over me. It was I who gave him the jackal-faced tongs. We had this arrangement between us that as soon as the tongs would be rung I would appear and do as bidden. But Karali Mukherjee was an honest man, not greedy at all. He never asked me to supply him with riches. He would only command thus: "Bring me tobacco! Bring me ganja! Bring me European liquor – the primeval liquid that bestows warmth! Bring me delectable Shivaite anchoresses!" Ever since he died I have no work to do. Listen, lad, today is the new moon of Baishakh. This very day a hundred years ago, at the hour of midnight, Karalicharan Mukherjee, the uncle of your great-grandfather, attained his expertise. According to the terms of our agreement, today at the same hour I shall be released from my bondage. After that, I shall not respond, no matter how many times you ring the tongs. A couple of hours to go still. I heard your call, and here I am. Tell me what you want.

Jhintu thought a little and replied, 'Can you get me a duckupine?'*

---

* Editor's note: One of Sukumar Ray's imaginary, compound creatures, the *haanshjaru*, a cross between a duck and a porcupine. Ray's translator Sukanta Chaudhuri, translates the word as 'porcochard'. See biographical note on Sukumar Ray.

— And what's that?

Jhintu opened his book and showed him the picture. 'A creature like this, halfway between a duck and a porcupine.'

— I see. But such a creature won't be available ready-made. It would have to be created, and that would take time. I'll send you a duckupine in an hour's time.

Jhintu said, 'It doesn't matter if it takes an hour. I can sleep until then. But don't be too long. Ma, Baba, and the rest will be back.'

The *pishach* vanished.

*

Jhintu was fast asleep, when suddenly a tapping noise woke him up. The light was on, and Jhintu saw a grotesque creature running about in the room. It had the head and neck of a duck, the trunk of a porcupine, and the quills erect all over its body. It was running about on four feet and quacking like a duck. Jhintu sat up and called it gently, as one speaks to a pet, 'Ah ah, chu chu!' The duckupine jumped like a pet dog and tried to climb to his lap with his paws. Jhintu felt the prick of the quills on his knees. Annoyed, he exclaimed, 'Move off! One can't even stroke you a bit, can one?'

The room directly below that room belonged to Aunt Sarasi. After her dinner, Sarasi had devoured an entire novel and fallen asleep. The thumping noises overhead woke her up. Irritated, she said, 'Ah, that scallywag isn't asleep yet. He is scampering about all over the place.' She came upstairs, but no sooner had she entered Jhintu's room than she gave an astonished shriek, 'Mamma mia! From where did this thing come?'

Jhintu said, 'It's my pet. Don't be afraid. He won't say anything to you. Tomorrow I'll get a barber to shave off all his quills, then he won't prick your hands. Please, Pishima, get him some milk and biscuits! The poor thing is so hungry!'

Sarasi got up on Jhintu's bed to protect herself and said, 'Jhintey, say at once from where you got this thing!'

Waving his hand and grimacing, Jhintu said, 'Why should I, eh!'

— Good boy, say from where it has come.

— First swear that you won't tell anybody.

— I swear by Mother Kali of Kalighat that I won't tell anybody.

Thereupon Jhintu explained the whole business, but Sarasi wouldn't believe him. She said, 'You're making it up, Jhintu. Indeed, I did hear that Uncle Karali was a *pishach*-expert, but this is bunkum.'

— Bunkum! Then see for yourself—

No sooner had Jhintu rung the tongs clang-clang than Dhundudas Chanda appeared. Stupefied with terror, Sarasi watched with her eyes wide open. The *pishach* asked, 'What d'you want, lad?'

Jhintu ordered, 'Crunchy-fried dried peas, large ones. Lots, please, for Pishima's having some too.'

The *pishach* vanished. In a little while a paper packet fell plonk on the floor, from nowhere. It was full of large-sized freshly dried peas, still hot. Taking a handful, Jhintu said, 'Why not try some, Pishima.'

Sarasi placed a hand against her cheek and said, 'Amazing! Never saw such a thing in all my life, nor in my father's, nor even heard of it. But you are such a silly boy! You should have asked for some money – a few lakhs, a big house, an expensive motor car, and such things. Instead of that, you go for a duckupine and fried dried peas! Honestly! OK then, let me have that pair of tongs just for once.'

Jhintu had never been much attached to his aunt. He made a wry face and said, 'Yeah, give it to you – indeed! I'm not giving this pair of jackal-faced tongs to anyone. Tell me what you need, and I'll get it for you.'

– You are a kid and won't be able to explain.

– OK, let me call Dhundudas. You can tell me what you want and I'll repeat it to him word for word.

Sarasi had to agree. As soon as Jhintu shook the tongs, the *pishach* appeared once again and asked, 'What's needed?'

Jhintu said, 'Quick, Pishima, hurry up and say it. Ma and Baba may be back any minute.'

What Sarasi applied for through Jhintu's mediation was as follows. First, that freakish animal had to be packed off. Next, a gentleman named Durlabh Talukdar had to be fetched. He worked in the Kanpur Woollen Mills, and his residential address was unknown to her.

The duckupine and the *pishach* both vanished.

Jhintu asked, 'What would be the point of fetching the gentleman from Kanpur, Pishima?'

– I'm going to marry him.

– What d'you mean you'll marry him? You are past it now, aren't you?

– Who says I'm past it? I am just twenty-five.

– But Ma says you are thirty-four or thirty-five.

– That's a lie. Your mother's jealous. That's why she says so. And anyway, I am a single girl. Whatever my age, why shouldn't I get married?

Before the *pishach* comes back, let's recap some past history. Some twelve or thirteen years ago, when Sarasi was a college student, she was friendly with Durlabh Talukdar. Durlabh had told her, 'I am likely to get a good job. As soon as I get it, I'll marry you.' After some time Durlabh got the job and went to Kanpur. From there he occasionally wrote letters. 'This is a very expensive area. I haven't found a residence suitable for you either. My salary is only two hundred rupees. How can two people live on that? I hope soon to be promoted to the grade that carries a salary of three hundred and fifty, and to get good living quarters also. Sarasi, my dear girl, please be patient until then.' Then his letters became infrequent, and at last they stopped altogether. Sarasi realized that Durlabh was a liar, but still couldn't forget him.

The *pishach* returned, between his arms a fat man grabbed at the waist. Dropping the bloke on the floor with a thump, he said, 'Here you are, son. Here's a bridegroom for your Auntie. He's unconscious now, but will soon liven up.'

Drawing his own face close to Durlabh's, Jhintu commented, 'Ugh, he smells rather like my Uncle, my mother's brother, when he comes back from his club. I say, Mr Dhundu, why not wake him?'

The *pishach* said, 'He's totally pissed. He was having a good time with his mates in a slum in Kanpur, from where I picked him up just now. Hey there, man, get up quick, wakey-wakey.'

The push returned Durlabh to a wakeful state. He opened his eyes and said, 'Who on earth are you lot?'

Jhintu said, 'Pishima, tell him what has to be said.'

— I can't. You say it, sweetie.

— Mister, can you hear me? This is my Aunt Sarasi, a single girl. Please marry her.

'Aha, what a charming proposition!' said Durlabh. 'I have to marry her just because you ask me to?'

'What d'you mean you won't?' said the *pishach*. 'We'll get your father to marry if need be.'

Given a horrendous smack on his face by the *pishach*, Durlabh said, 'Please don't hit me. I apologize. Very well then, I'll get married. Call a priest. But I must set the record straight. I already have a Bengali wife and an up-country spouse. If Sarasi wishes to be my helpmate number three, why should I object? But all must sleep on the same bed.'

'Get rid of that wretched drunk,' said Sarasi.

On Jhintu's command, the *pishach* picked Durlabh up and went off. Jhintu said, 'Listen, Pishima, there are loads of nice gents in your office. Why not fetch one of them?'

Sarasi reflected a little and then said, 'Our Head Assistant Jogin Banerjee lost his wife two years ago. Joginbabu is a nice guy, but not cultured. He's also getting on a bit. Smokes far too much, gives off a hookah-like smell when he speaks. What can one do? All this fault-finding won't get me anywhere. All males are more or less dirty. But will Joginbabu agree? Perhaps if he was given a substantial groom's dowry—'

'And what's a groom's dowry?' asked Jhintu. 'Is it money and jewellery? Don't you worry about that, Pishima. I'll fix everything.'

Sounding the tongs and summoning the *pishach*, Jhintu said, 'There's this guy Jogin Banerjee who works in my Auntie's office – what's his address, Pishima? – Number three, Bechu Mistri Lane – get him from there. And listen, give Pishima tons of jewellery and loads of cash.'

All of Sarasi's body became covered with chunky gold jewellery, and five bags of money fell at her feet with clunks. The *pishach* went away.

Picking up one of the bags, Sarasi said, 'Must be at least five or six seers.'

Jhintu said, 'Five hundred rupees make six seers and a quarter, a thousand rupees make twelve seers and a half, and a lakh of rupees make thirty-one maunds and ten seers. It says so in the book *The Chest of Knowledge*.'

The *pishach* arrived, his arms around Jogin Banerjee's waist, and dropped him on the floor.

'Is he drunk as well?' asked Jhintu.

'He's not drunk,' said the *pishach*, 'I just made him unconscious in order to bring him here. He'll revive if given a little push. Hang on, let me slip off first, or else he'll swoon again if he sees me.'

Given a push, Jogin Banerjee sat up. He yawned, clicked his thumb and middle finger, and exclaimed, 'Durga, Durga, what's this, where am I? Goodness, Miss Sarasi Mukherjee's here! O my, what a quantity of jewellery you're wearing! Have I been invited to your wedding?'

Her face bent down, Sarasi said, 'Go on, you say it, nephew.'

'Sir,' said Jhintu, 'please marry my Aunt Sarasi. She is a single lady, just twenty-five years old. You can see how much jewellery she has. She's got five bags of money as well, each weighing five to six seers.'

'Wow, young man,' said Jogin babu, 'are you yourself giving away your bejewelled aunt? Must say I don't mind, I did have my eye on Miss Mukherjee a bit. But she's a modern lady, so I didn't have the courage to proceed. The jewellery is very old-fashioned, but looks heavy. We can sell the stuff and have other things made in new designs. But I just don't understand what's going on. How did I get here?'

Sarasi said, 'You'll hear that later. Now go home. Come back tomorrow morning and present the proposal of marriage formally to my elder brother. Wear this ring so that you don't forget.'

– How can I forget? I'll surely come tomorrow morning and speak to your Dada. What's the time now? What d'you say, a quarter to twelve? Good God, how shall I go home? Trams and buses have all stopped now, haven't they?

'Don't you worry at all, sir,' said Jhintu. 'Just lie down and close your eyes for once.'

Jogin Banerjee lay down and closed his eyes like a well-mannered child. Summoned by the sound of the jackal-faced tongs, the *pishach* came once more. Jhintu gave him an order by means of a gesture, 'Take him back to his own house.'

The clock struck midnight. Sarasi said, 'Dada and Bowdi will be back any minute. Let me go and take these pieces of jewellery off. The money bags must be put away too. Really, you aren't clever at all, are you? Why didn't you ask for paper money, instead of all these coins? Jhintu, dear boy, don't breathe a word of this to anybody.'

– No no, why should I? Damn it, I forgot to ask Dhundudas to give me a mongoose. Rambhajan, our school porter, has a very nice one. It's ever so tame, clings to his shoulders.

– Don't worry, my pet. Your Pishima's husband will buy you as many mongooses as you want. You shouldn't stay awake any longer with that fever. Go to bed now.

– Fever! Where's it gone? It vanished when I saw Dhundudas.'

– My dear boy, we are not dreaming by any chance, are we? What if we wake up in the morning and find that all the jewellery and money have flown away?

– Doesn't matter. Jogin babu will have new sets made for you. He'll give you dosh too.

– What if Jogin babu also flies away?

– Let him. Why don't you try some of these fried dried peas? See how crunchy they are. Chew them thoroughly and then swallow them. Then they won't be able to fly away – no way.

Buddhadev Bose (1908–74)

The admirers of Buddhadev Bose claim he is Tagore's true successor, at least for the range and quality of his writings; short stories, poetry, essays, criticism, novels. Bose had immense gifts, and the incisiveness and occasional acerbity of his criticism was commensurate with the enthusiasm he showed, and encouragement he gave, to the contemporaries he admired – both as critic and editor. He was himself involved with the magazine *Kallol*, with which an energetic post-Tagorean movement was once associated. He represents a break with, and reassessment of, Tagore, with whom his relationship was, if not Oedipal, at least both worshipful and contestative. He once said of the poets of the post-Tagore generation, 'It was impossible [for them] not to imitate Rabindranath, and it was impossible to imitate Rabindranath.' His ambivalence towards, and immense love for, the older writer is reflected in the extract below from his long novel *Tithidore* (1949), by consensus his greatest fiction; the extract records the movements of two of the novel's characters, a man and a woman (who will marry each other later in the novel), on the day of Tagore's death in Calcutta. Bose uses Tagore's own radiant but melancholy sensibility to describe the time of his passing, as if he were intermittently ventriloquizing, through Tagore's voice, the poet's own demise; the section is replete with concealed metaphors for, and tributes to, Tagore's poetry. In the constant reference to light and shade in this section, Bose plays with the meaning of Tagore's name – 'Rabi', or 'the sun' – and the alternating eclipse and rebirth of that meaning. Bose was also a remarkably sophisticated literary critic. The extract from the essay included below, written in English, opens a window, with characteristic humour and an animating intelligence, upon a literary ethos no less real for having vanished; and reminds us that the hegemonies Bengali writers were concerned with subverting in the interests of their own artistic well-being had less to do with Empire, the colonizer, or the English language, but with traditions and hierarchies embedded in the Bengali language itself.

* * *

from *Tithidore* (1949)

translated from the Bengali by Ketaki Kushari Dyson

Svati said at once, 'No, I'm going as well.'

She ran indoors, wrote a brief note for her father and pushed it into the hand of Ram's mother, changed her dress and footwear, grabbed a handbag, and when she was out in the street with Satyen Ray the first thing she noticed was that the day was still as happy, lovely and radiant as before.

The bus filled even before it reached Kalighat. Nevertheless more and more people kept boarding it: male and female college students, school-boys, shopkeepers, the unemployed, young men who spent their days chatting to one another. The congestion was stifling. But Svati's seat, one of those reserved 'for ladies', was safe, and she was sitting by the window, looking intently outside. The streets were crowded – as if the time was late afternoon. Gangs of schoolboys were walking, but without making a racket; elderly people were wandering around as if they had nothing to do; before each shop that had a radio on there was a crowd; and at street corners there were crowds of people hoping to get on a bus or a tramcar. Cinema posters were pasted over with black paper; the doors were closed. Women, their hair down, babies in their arms, were standing in balconies or by windows, watching the street as much as they could. Today all eyes, all minds were focused on the street.

Clouds gathered, and by the time they reached the Chowringhee, rain came down. But when the bus stopped at the Esplanade, it was bright and sunny again. And in that soft-moist light Svati saw an amazing swirling of people, amazing even for the Esplanade: office executives in suits, lawyers in black coats, middle-aged gents with umbrellas in their hands, slim young clerical workers, Englishmen, Chinese, Madrassis, Christian priests, Parsis. People were rushing from every direction to every other direction – Chowringhee, Dhurrumtola, Curzon Park, Corporation Street – but it was as if they were not quite sure where they were going, as if they had somewhat lost their sense of direction. Many seemed to have forgotten what they knew by heart – that as soon as the office was closed, one had to head for home. However straggling they may appear, Calcutta's crowds are never aimless; everyone knows whither he is bound and why; but today all people had lost their goals, the certainty of their destinations, which is why these crowds were amazing, extraordinary.

Someone was standing erect and staring straight ahead; another was wandering up and down aimlessly; another seemed to make up his mind suddenly and take a few steps, then stopped again; yet another was standing, reading a newspaper, while a few others read over his shoulders. A special issue of a newspaper arrived and was an immediate sell-out.

Satyen, sitting behind Svati, stretched out his hand and bought a paper. He just glanced at it once and gave it to Svati. Svati gave it one glance and placed it on her lap. The fifteen-ish girl sitting next to her picked it up without even a 'may I?', and as her eyes moved from the top to the bottom of the page, her tears dripped on the black print, rubbing off some of the ink which was fresh from the press.

At Jorasanko* the bus almost emptied. Everyone ran towards Dwarakanath Tagore Lane, but Satyen, about to cross the street, suddenly paused. He had seen a barrage of people – what had happened to them? Why was no one about? 'Taken away already?' – the words slipped from his lips.

'Yeah, been taken away – if you want to have a look you have to go to College Street–' said someone as he passed by.

Svati had never visited Chitpore before; amazed, she was looking at the traffic of trams and buses pushing through that narrow lane. There were lanes within lanes – twisted and dark; tall buildings jostled against each other, shutting out the sky; the pavements were marvellously crowded and were selling the most amazing wares. She nearly forgot why she was there, when Satyen's words reminded her of it: 'Been taken away. Let's go to College Street. You'll be able to walk fast won't you?'

Fast and silent, the two of them began to walk, avoiding the pushing and shoving crowds on that pavement that was a pavement only in name. After a few minutes they turned left into Muktarambabu Street. To Svati these areas of Calcutta seemed to belong to another country, another world; here the light, the air, even the smells were different. She tried to cast her glances around her, but couldn't see anything very well, so fast was Satyen babu walking.

The long, dark, curving Muktarambabu Street ended in Cornwallis

---

* Editor's note: Area in Chitpur in North Calcutta, where Tagore's ancestral house is located.

Street; and in a little while the junction of College Street and Harrison Road appeared.

On reaching the covered pavement of the College Street Market, Satyen stopped and climbed the steps of a shoe shop. Many more were standing there, most of them college students. 'Coming any minute now' was the message passing from mouth to mouth.

'Was the walk too much for you?' asked Satyen.

'N-no.'

'Are you wishing you hadn't come?'

'No.'

Their exchange of words stopped there, and once again they fell silent. On the opposite side, on the roof of a one-storeyed shop – without any railings, dangerously unsafe – a few were standing with their cameras ready; the adjoining first-floor balcony was packed with women and children; there wasn't a single window in the area from which three or four faces weren't looking out; and no one was walking on the street, everyone stood still. Once again Satyen experienced the pressure of that waiting, that dumb waiting.

'Coming . . . coming . . .' a murmur rose in the crowd.

Svati had imagined a procession – long, slow, solemn, bowed, over-whelmed, stupefied; but it was just a handful of people who came bearing the burden on their shoulders, seemingly in a hurry, going from north to south, with a few straggling followers behind them. The sight flashed like lightning in front of Svati's eyes and disappeared; long white hair and a huge, pale, tranquil, meditative brow gleamed in the sun. That was all Svati could glimpse; she could see nothing else.

Satyen saw that Svati was standing rigid and straight, her hands clenched, lips tightly pressed; saw the trembling in her throat and lips, the deep colour of her cheeks; saw how her bright black liquid eyes became brighter, became twin shining mirrors, how then the mirrors broke, turned liquid again, overflowing, while the head was bowed.

And seeing that, Satyen felt a new tightness in his throat, a blurring in his eyes, and was ashamed of himself in his own eyes. For this death did not solicit weeping; this sorrow, this grand, precious sorrow, this final jewel of eighty years of supreme toil – was it something to be wasted frivolously in tears?

'Come now,' said Satyen.

Svati did not try to hide the fact that she was crying. She wiped her eyes with the end of her sari, coughed once, and said in a slightly husky voice, 'Let's go.'

But the trams and buses were choked. Along various streets, following various routes, everybody was rushing towards Nimtola.* The two of them stood helplessly; they stood so long that their legs ached.

Svati said, 'Hadn't we better walk? Perhaps if we went ahead a little–'

'Going ahead a little won't make any difference. Only if we could get to the Esplanade–'

'Is the Esplanade very far?' asked Svati, unsure of the geography of this region.

'Not that far,' said Satyen with some enthusiasm. 'One could go via Chittaranjan Avenue. Will you walk then?'

'OK then.'

No sooner had they crossed Kolutola and reached Chittaranjan Avenue, than the sky darkened and suddenly the rain came down once more. They took shelter under a portico. The rain was heavy, poured with a clatter, and getting wet in that downpour, a group of Chinese went by, calm and quiet, solemn and slow, each with bowed head and bare feet.

Svati stared at them as long as she could see them. Then she said, 'How beautiful they are!'

Satyen nodded in assent.

'Where are they going?'

'To Nimtola, surely.'

Svati had heard of Nimtola, so understood. 'Aren't you going?'

'I would have – but–'

'Can't I go there?'

'You could, but I wouldn't take you there.'

'Why not?'

'You can't imagine how crowded it's going to be.'

Svati didn't like that reply. She felt Satyen babu was being too cautious, too circumspect, too rule-bound even on a day like this. Meanwhile the rain did not cease.

Another group came along: European priests, bearded and elderly, in long white robes, flowers in their hands, peace upon their faces, prayers in their eyes. They walked through the rain, getting wet.

The rain slackened, then ceased. When the rain was still dribbling, they started walking once again, drops of rainwater falling on their hands, lips, heads. The sun came out; the oblique yellow light of the late afternoon shone on the wet black street, shimmered in the soft-moist wind.

*   Editor's note: Major cremation ground.

Satyen said, 'If you are feeling tired, say so. I think we could get on a bus here.'

Svati said, 'I'm quite enjoying the walk.'

No sooner had she spoken than she felt regret and guilt. On a day like this, at a time such as this, was one allowed to 'enjoy' anything? Or even if one did, should one say it out loud? Timidly, out of the corner of her eyes, Svati gazed at Satyen Ray's face, but the grief-stricken lecturer seemed not to notice the unseemliness at all, but rather, said in a cheered voice, 'Well then, nothing to worry about.'

Quietly they went on walking, but not as before, when, disappointed in Jorasanko, they had walked silently along Muktarambabu Street. Then their pace had been fast, the lane had been narrow, and their minds had been anxious, whereas now they faced the straight expanse of Chittaranjan Avenue: a huge broad generous road, uncrowded, without tramcars, the motor cars gliding along quietly, as if they were floating. On either side of the road there were tall buildings, but the sky here was vaster, higher up, and the road was so spread out that the buildings appeared lightweight, as if the piles on the two sides belonged to two separate neighbourhoods. And above the road's entire stretch trembled, swung and shone a film – that of the rain-washed yellow-green late-afternoon's fine transparent radiance. They walked slowly, for there was no hurry now. The high-water mark of time had happened when they were standing on the veranda of the College Street Market shoe shop: it had now passed. The mind's bow, drawn so taut before, from ear to ear, was now slack. Now there was time to look at the afternoon, to gaze at the light, at the bright, beautiful sky. Svati felt a vague sense of happiness within her; a little later all her feelings of guilt vanished as well. But it was as if she did not herself take in the news of this change of weather within her own mind. She didn't think about it, didn't think much, just sank slowly into a new consciousness of happiness. And Satyen – a man mad about poetry, a Tagore fan since childhood – he too felt an obscure sense of happiness. Just as at that very instant in Tagore-less Bengal, over Calcutta overflowing with grief, the flag of blueness flew on the sky's incorruptible gateway, so too in his mind the green of the living moment, of the here and the now, covered the deep black tomb of historical grief: and it all happened so easily that he himself did not take it in. Both of them quietly accepted this blurred sense of feeling good, he his, she hers, and each the other's as well. Before this they had been quiet because they had nothing to say, and now they were quiet because there was no need to talk.

Reaching the Esplanade, they once more faced the screeching of wheels, the whirl of the crowds, the impact of humanity rushing about. They had to stop several times when crossing the road. On the Chowringhee, Satyen said, 'Would you like some tea?'

'You haven't had a bite all day, have you,' said Svati, remembering.

'If you think it'll delay you—'

'Not that much more.'

'You mean, it's very late already?'

These words made Svati realize that all this time she hadn't once thought of home, of returning home, of her father. What was Father thinking? How long had she been out? What was the time now? She tried to look at the clock on Whiteaway Laidlaw, but from where she stood it was difficult. Never mind. 'Which one would you go to?' she asked.

All the little restaurants in rows were absolutely packed with people. In the middle there was a large English hotel, with frosted glass panes facing the road, ensuring privacy, and rubber matting on the steps. Satyen took Svati into that one. From the turmoil of lights, crowds, noises they were suddenly transported into a smooth, silent, solemn, spacious darkness. Once again Svati sensed a new smell, a smell that was kind of English – dry, light, warming – unfamiliar, yes, but good – it was good!

Walking along the edges of several empty tables, they were making their way towards a corner table, when suddenly someone seated at a table said, 'Hi there!'

Satyen stopped, raised his hands in greeting. Without returning the greeting in any noticeable way, the gentleman said, 'From where? Nimtola?'

'No, didn't get that far – Svati, haven't you recognized him?'

Svati had indeed. Dark, dishevelled, gloomy, Dhruba Datta was sprawled on a chair, a cigarette between his fingers, and in the glass before him a pale brown drink like – Svati suddenly remembered in a flash – like she had seen in front of an elderly Eurasian in Chang-An Restaurant. Having noticed the futility of Satyen babu's greeting, she made no similar attempt. Through a soft expression on her face, she just tried to convey that she had had the good fortune of being introduced to this celebrity once.

But she needn't have bothered. Dhruba Datta didn't notice her presence at all. Looking at Satyen, he said, 'How did it go – the business of weeping and wailing, all that racket?'

Satyen couldn't find an immediate answer, and straight away Dhruba Datta began again, 'I am feeling sorry for Tagore. He tried so hard to die in Europe, said that so many times, and put it in writing, but in the end – "I was born in this very land, may I die in this land too"!' Dhruba Datta smiled a bitter, diminutive smile, and his voice sounded too harsh and shrill in the dimly lit quiet of that big empty restaurant. It seemed that Satyen was about to say something, but realized in an instant that this man didn't want to hear anything, just wanted to spill out all the thoughts that had gathered within him. Puffing away at his cigarette, but leaving his drink untouched, the poet continued to speak, twisting his lips a little: 'I was out, and wandered in the streets for a long time, then I couldn't take it any more and escaped here. Oh, what an opportunity! Those who haven't read any Tagore except *Katha o Kahini*, or if they have, haven't understood any of it, or even if they have understood the stuff, haven't accepted it, and all those wily smart nitwits who repeat "Gurudev" on their oily lips, yet whose entire existence is an act of opposition to Tagore, and all those countless sensation-mongers who all their lives will never know – nor want to know – what Tagore is all about, the why and the how of his being: for all such people up and down the land what a marvellous opportunity it is today! The equivalent of ten IFA matches, one hundred Kanans and Saigals singing together! What a carnival for the newspaper-wallahs, what a peak season for the meeting-wallahs, and what a chance for the top business executives to make a lot of noise, puffing out their own names! What enthusiasm, what frolicking, what fun! Those people to whom it makes no difference whatsoever whether Tagore is alive or not – those are the very people who are the most drunk on this grief's Holi! Ha!'

Pausing, deliberately weighing every word, thus did the successor deliver the funeral oration of his predecessor in a shrill, harsh, severe voice. After the last sound of his voice he stopped at the right spot, bent forward and stretched his hand, partook of his drink a little, then leaned back on his chair to clarify that he had nothing further to say on that subject.

* * *

from *An Acre of Green Grass:*

A Review of Modern Bengali Literature (1948)

from 'Pramatha Chaudhuri' – an essay

I

Pramatha Chaudhuri, in his seventies, said goodbye to Mayfair and all that, and a visitor to Santiniketan, while straying in the Uttarayan grounds, could have caught a glimpse of him in one of the lovely little houses designed and built for Rabindranath. If the visitor was intrepid, or curious, or a lover of literature, he would perhaps have walked in and for a few moments sat face to face with one of the master artificers of Bengali prose. Sharp eyes, a dagger-like nose, a clean-shaven handsome face wreathed with wrinkles, a splendid body of a man shattered by illness, looking for all the world like a great mountain eagle, wounded in combat, wings broken, alone. As the long trembling fingers reached out for the golden cigarette-case lying on a little table amid books and cups and things, the bright eyes, pouncing on the visitor, lingering, questioning, would so unnerve him that he would forget to strike a light for the cigarette and begin to think of taking his leave. If he was lucky, however, Indira Devi Chaudhurani would appear at the right moment and immediately start the right sort of conversation. A niece of Rabindranath's, herself gifted in music and *belles-lettres*, tall, ivory-complexioned, splendid in an old-world way, she was the lesser known half, and is now the only half, of Bengal's most distinguished couple. The eagle, if alone in his last days, was not companionless.

Despite his two-fold connection with Rabindranath, personal and liter-ary, Pramatha Chaudhuri had never lived in Santiniketan before, nor had he been a frequent and interested visitor. This, I think, is significant, for Pramatha Chaudhuri was the most urban writer of his time, and that in the best sense of the word. No ashram, however leafy and serene, could ever have been his Land of Heart's Desire. His choice of pseudonym meant much, for in adopting the name of Birbal, Akbar's Hindu wit, he not only made an already famous name more famous, but affirmed his own affinities. Indeed, he was born to the role of a courtier, and would happily have shone a jewel in the crown of either Vikramaditya or Akbar. Krishnanagar, where his boyhood was spent, stimulated his congenital courtliness. Once the capital of Bengal, the seat of the great art-patron Maharaja Krishnachandra, whom his protégé, Bharatchandra, the poet, has made memorable in our literary history, Krishnanagar still retains (or retained till half a century ago) a tradition of court culture, of fragrant indolence and witty repartees. True, it is a decadent tradition, out of place in the context of modern life, and perhaps it is to be counted among the casualties of the Second World War. But there was still some life in it when Pramatha Chaudhuri was young, and it instilled in him a love for the delicacies of life, including classical music and the *bon mot*. His lifelong admiration for Bharatchandra is an indication of his mental climate – Bharatchandra, the typical court poet, a master of the craft of verse, and not at all the sort of poet whom Rabindranath could care for. The interrelation of Rabindranath and Pramatha Chaudhuri is a fascinating subject: when they first met, the former was still young and the latter very much so, but mature enough to recognize the older man as 'surpassingly great'. His elder brother, who had married another of the Poet's nieces, was one of the earliest lovers of Rabindranath's poetry, and the young Pramatha was often a passive listener, and sometimes an eavesdropper, to the brilliant conversations that flower in the elders' circle. Time only strengthened the impression of that first acquaintance; a more devoted friend Rabindranath had never had. A friend, yes; an admirer, certainly; but not a disciple. In Rabindranath, Pramatha Chaudhuri saw a genius, a greater master, but not The Master. In spite of the closest association which terminated only with Rabindranath's death, in spite of long years of literary comradeship, Pramatha Chaudhuri never came directly under Rabindranath's influence, either in his work or in his life. This is remarkable, but not strange. Herein we discern not only Pramatha Chaudhuri's great integrity, but also his natural lack of sympathy for the *type* of mind Rabindranath embodies. There is nothing in him of that parching nostalgia which is the ultimate source of most lyrical and all mystical poetry; he is perfectly at home in this world; his fulfilment is here and nowhere else, whereas Rabindranath's cry has ever been 'Elsewhere!' In fact, Rabindranath and Pramatha Chaudhuri represent two altogether different worlds: one, the winding stair of imagination panting up to the starry tower; the other, the comfortable well-lit drawing-room of the intellect. Rabindranath is ever drunk with dreams; Pramatha Chaudhuri is incorrigibly sober. Yet Rabindranath, with his all-absorbing mind, found in his younger colleague a model of excellence and even an inspiration. This, certainly, is a singular distinction for Pramatha Chaudhuri, for he alone of Rabindranath's juniors influenced the poet without being influenced by him. One feels that Pramatha Chaudhuri is an alien in Rabindranath's world, whereas Rabindranath has free access to the Pramathean drawing-room: he visits, dines and lingers, but does not *stay*. The perfect guest he, and Pramatha the perfect host. This guest-host relationship culminated in *Sabujpatra* ('Green Leaf'), whose unstinted hospitality Rabindranath honoured in princely fashion. The green leaf faded, the lights in the drawing-room grew dim, the Guest, gratified and grateful, departed. But to the last day, his respect for Pramatha Chaudhuri's intellect remained undiminished.

II

After taking his Master of Arts degree at Calcutta University, Pramatha Chaudhuri spent a few years in England. He returned as a barrister, but never practised. Professionalism he shunned, either in law or literature. Private means, ample at that time, formed the necessary background to his life as a man-of-leisure-and-letters. He built up a gorgeous library; he read, he smoked; he thought, he talked. Steeped in French literature, knee-deep in Sanskrit, as much at home in English as in his own language, far and near he fared with zest and discernment, drinking at many springs, gleaning the harvests of centuries and countries. His house at 20 Mayfair, Ballygunge was an intellectual centre; Rabindranath came there often, and C. F. Andrews, and other celebrities of the day. He studied art and music, history and philosophy, the geography of India and the Tenancy Act of Bengal. Politics he liked, polemics he loved; he was interested in Sports, ghosts and gossip. Those who matter at once felt that a rare spirit had come to our literature. To those who do not, he was unknown.

Fame came on the trail of *Sabujpatra*, which he founded and edited and burnt a lot of money on. This monthly magazine started as a revolt and soon became an institution. Its name and its green cover suggested that spirit of youth which emanated from its pages. Gloriously insouciant, it discouraged both circulation and stability by every possible means: it never printed an advertisement, appeared at wilful intervals, reproduced no drawings or watercolours, and published whatever the editor liked and as he liked it. Canons were flouted, conventions defied; there were no 'features' or eye-catchers; no gadgets or trinkets. The editor and Rabindranath filled more than half the pages and there was once an issue containing, cover to cover, Rabindranath's song drama *Phalguni* ('Spring'), the whole of it, and *nothing* else. This is the only instance I have known, or heard of, of a magazine coming out with only one 'article' in it. Of course *Subujpatra* did not live long, it was not meant to. A second series appeared after an interval of some years: the flood rose for a second time, flagged, ebbed, and stopped.

In Bengal we think *Sabujpatra* unique, and are apt to forget it was like Rabindranath's *Sadhana* in many ways. *Sadhana*, too, with its stubborn chastity, was eminently unsaleable. In those pre-Santiniketan days, when Rabindranath lived in a houseboat on the Padma, alone with his dreams, his prodigious quantities of verse and prose were flung down the corridor of a magazine before they emerged into the great world in final book form. It had to be so; that magazine was his link with the outer world. *Sadhana* was his very own, a vehicle for his own *sadhana*,* his literary exercises and experiments, a medium for his meditations. Thus was it different from its successor: for while *Sadhana* was really a running anthology of new writings by Rabindranath, *Sabujpatra* founded a school of new writing, started a movement and saw it through. Inspiration, the cause of *Sadhana*, was *Sabujpatra*'s effect. Pramatha Chaudhuri, with his taste, discipline and critical acumen, was the model editor: and inevitably, in the heyday of *Sabujpatra*, a group of young disciples rose round him, some of whom, in later years, have more or less distinguished themselves as critical writers. That he was born to leadership Rabindranath himself had felt and acknowledged; it was not personal affection, merely, but literary admiration that made him send his best works of the period to *Sabujpatra*. Two novels, *Chaturanga* and *Ghare-Baire*, appeared in it, the majority of the *Balaka* poems and the prose poems of *Lipika*, besides plays, short stories, songs. It is possible that the paeans to youth in *Balaka* were written specifically for *Sabujpatra*, and certainly it has the distinction of having published more of Rabindranath's work than any other contemporary periodical within the same span of time.†

---

* Editor's note: spiritual discipline.

† Bengal has been fortunate in editors; Bankimchandra, the literary dictator of his time, launched and captained *Bangadarshan*, the first serious literary journal in Bengali: and Rabindranath in his earlier years conducted quite a number of magazines (including a new series of *Bangadarshan*), fitfully, it is true, but seriously and even strenuously while the fit lasted. Rabindranath, it should be noted here, was as good an editor as it is possible for a creative writer of his proportions to be: for, although his own work was work enough, he found time to mould those of the younger Tagores who threatened

For yet another reason is *Sabujpatra* memorable: it is the hero in our War of Words. Bengali prose, rough-hewn by Rammohan Roy, hammered by Iswarchandra Vidyasagar, became readable and writable with Bankim-chandra, who set the standard for next fifty years or so. The rococo extravagances of his style began to drop off in his own lifetime, but the essentials persisted for long after: Bengali prose continued to be written in a manner artificially removed from actual spoken language. It would be precise to say that it retained traces of the spoken language of the past and of some dialects of the present, and was artificial inasmuch as it assumed a form not actually spoken in any part of Bengal, either by the illiterate or the most cultivated. This was felt to be a handicap very early in our literary history; even before Bankimchandra, the Serampore missionaries wrote and printed specimens of Bengali as spoken at that time in south-west Bengal. (This dialect, by the way, because of the overwhelming influence of Calcutta, has formed the base of the standard spoken Bengali of today.) The next step in this direction was taken by the author who called himself Tekchand Thakur. He made a brave attempt to give literary status to contemporary common speech, but failed, because he was merely colloquial, and to be colloquial is to be a little vulgar. It was that brilliant contemporary of Bankimchandra's, the translator of the *Mahabharata*, and the princely lover of literature, Kaliprasanna Sinha, who, in his *Hutom Pyanchar Naksa* ('Sketches by an Owl') first brought literary grace to the spoken tongue. If he had lived reasonably long, the dispute between the two styles might have been settled long ago. But he died unpardonably young, and Bankimchandra was the only author worthy of imitation. His style, known as *sadhubhasha* (the chaste tongue), was adopted by every self-respecting author; for the style of *Hutom*, known as *chalitbhasha* (the current tongue), the world of letters and learning had nothing but contempt.

Rabindranath himself, in his prose fiction and essays, was close on the tracks of Bankimchandra, with Saratchandra in hot pursuit. Prose, in the works of the latter two, became increasingly vivid and buoyant, but the structure of *sadhubhasha* remained. The main point of contention between the two styles is the conjugation of verbs: in *chalit*, they are as actually

---

to become writers. More apposite here is the fact that he seems actually to have collaborated in the editing of *Sabujpatra*; his letters to Pramatha Chaudhuri reveal that he was actively, ardently interested in its career, worried about finding new writers for it, and agonized by its misprints and inordinate delays. This, together with the quantity and variety of his contributions, definitely declares that *Sabujpatra* was Rabindranath's creation no less than Pramatha Chaudhuri's.

spoken today by the cultivated classes; in *sadhu*, as they probably were spoken a few centuries ago and are partly spoken today in provincial dialects. This, of course, implies other differences, so varied and fundamental that to change from *sadhu* to *chalit*, or vice versa, it is not enough to change the verb forms; the whole has to be rewritten. In his earlier fiction, Rabindranath followed Bankimchandra even to the extent of making the characters speak in the 'book' language. In other words, he sacrificed verisimilitude to convention. Later on, however, he realized this sacrifice to be too great and introduced *chalitbhasha* in dialogues while keeping up the older style in narration. This is the manner accepted by Saratchandra and almost all writers of the last generation: 'book' language for narration and the spoken tongue for dialogues. It is notable that there is only one short novel of Saratchandra's written throughout in the spoken tongue.

From the very beginning of his literary life, Rabindranath rebelled at heart against the prim respectability of *sadhubhasha*, though for long he was unable in practice to break away from it. The spoken language strongly attracted him; he was in love with its music, its colour, its warmth; he felt in it an abundance of vitality which he hoped to exploit. And he used it in his 'unofficial' writings, in hundreds of letters, in humorous sketches, and – of course – in his plays and sermons. When he first visited Europe at the age of eighteen, he sent home a series of letters, later collected and published under the title of *Europe-prabasir Patra*, written in lovely and lively prose, the prose of everyday speech. An air of joyous freedom pervades these letters, freedom from the cold formality of *sadhubhasha*; there is in them a ripple as of bright waters, a sunny playfulness as of young leaves. These qualities Rabindranath cherished, but, for some strange reason, he did not officially adopt the spoken tongue till the appearance of *Sabujpatra*.

He was over fifty then, laurelled by the Nobel Prize, internationally famous. But he had still much more to achieve – how much, neither he nor anybody else could at that time possibly imagine. Bengali prose, tired, bored, much more used than tended, was panting for a rejuvenation.

The reader may compare the following verb forms.

	sadhu	*chalit*
I was going	Ami jāiechhilām	Ami jāchchhilām
He was doing	Shé karitéchhilo	Shé karchhilo
She was saying	Shé balitéchhilo	Shé balchhilo
You will go	Tumi jāibé	Tumi jābé

The advantage is entirely on the side of *chalitbhasha*.

Pramatha Chaudhuri, incarnated in *Sabujpatra,* started the process and at once Rabindranath was passionately with him. Of *sadhubhasha* he was getting tired on his own account, he was craving for freedom from its fetters, his long repressed yearning for the spoken tongue had begun to overcome the force of habit. It was exactly at this junction that the Green Leaf unfurled its banner, sending out its call for courage. Rabindranath responded as a harp to the wind; he was released. *Chaturanga* was his last novel in the old style, *Ghare-Baire* his first in the new. But he was still hesitant, for though this new claimed him more and more, he was unable for some years yet to ring out the old. It was only in old age that he could finally make up his mind – for Rabindranath grew older and bolder at the same time – and persuade himself to write every bit of prose in the spoken tongue, whether fiction or criticism, textbook or Convocation address. His total rejection of *sadhubhasha* completed his conquest of prose, and that on an unpredictable level; he discovered incalculable shapes, shades and depths, and so quickened the process of evolution that in the last ten or twelve years of his life his prose, or Bengali prose, took on more new forms than it had done in the preceding fifty. Across emblazoned *Ghare-Baire,* beyond bejewelled *Sesher Kavita,* his prose, as the years passed, grew sweeter and simpler and more harmonious till, in the very last phase, an utter beauty was born. It would be a grievous wrong if, in our admiration for his poetry, we ever allow ourselves to forget what a great prose-writer Rabindranath is, what a master of rhythmic prose.

I am old enough to remember the battle I have alluded to as the War of Words, the battle that raged over the new style of prose. The pundits were shocked, their pupils scandalized. *Chalitbhasha* was an object of derision and slander. Calcutta University, in its examination papers, set passages from Rabindranath asking would-be passers to turn them to 'chaste and elegant Bengali'. Periodicals bristled with controversy. And in this, Pramatha Chaudhuri was the principal figure. He flung himself headlong into the fray; he tilted, he thrust, he parried, he preached, he practised. His serenity was chilling, his flippancy killing. A lightweight Chesterton, a light-hearted Shaw, he had neither the ponderousness of the former nor the latter's frenzy. Throughout the battle, both long and furious, he was cool – and deadly. His poise unnerved, his dignity devastated. While opponents foamed and raged, his voice was suavely conversational. He made fun of pedantry till it was torn to bits; he turned his artillery of wit against the Castle of Conservatism till it trembled, and tottered, and fell. The battle was won; the claims of the spoken tongue were at least tacitly recognized. It was possible to argue endlessly in theory, but to Rabindranath's examples there was no reply. The author-baiting University itself quailed. Pramatha Chaudhuri, through his writings and his personality, worked as an incessant stimulus, and was thus able directly to influence Rabindranath; so much so that, for a brief period, Rabindranath was infected by the Pramathean characteristic of puns and other verbal tricks – his *Sabujpatra* stories have a greater measure of them than his prose before or after. It is worthwhile to remark here that though the battle concluded as it did, Pramatha Chaudhuri's direct imitations soon palled – for wordplay is a delicate and dangerous game – and it was only when Rabindranath, his period of indecision over, formally enthroned the spoken tongue that it really began to do its work in the entire body of current literature. The quantity and quality of our recent spoken-tongue prose indicate that though Pramatha Chaudhuri broke the ice, Rabindranath set the stream flowing. Today more and more writers are taking more and more to the new – but no longer new – style, and there are many living who use it exclusively. To those who maintained that *chalitbhasha*, permissible in fiction and light literature, is unthinkable in 'serious' works, a crushing reply has been given by both Rabindranath and Pramatha Chaudhuri who have written in it on philosophy, philology, physics and the agrarian problem: the former magnificently, the latter exquisitely. For all this, newspapers, textbooks and works labelled 'research' are even now clinging to *sadhubhasha*: conventions die hard. But they do die – life would have stopped if they did not – and a time may come when everybody will look upon *sadhubhasha* as what it is: a museum specimen. After all, the influence of literature on language is far stronger than that of either newspapers or school-masters.

Mahashweta Devi (b. 1926)

Mahashweta Devi (b. 1926) is now probably the most considerable of living Bengali writers. As a student and teacher of English literature, she shares a formal and pedagogic relation with that tradition with many other writers in this anthology. However, unlike most other writers in these pages, she has been a writer-activist, living close to the tribals she writes about. Her fiction – several short stories and novellas (the present story was first published by *Katha*) – are sometimes seen as an extension of her activism; some commentators find her writings lend themselves to the concerns of post-colonial theory. The latter find in her fiction the figure of the subaltern woman, and the unwritten history of an oppressed people. But her articulations also represent a critique of the Bengal Renaissance she was formed by; in her absorption with the non-Sanskritic universe of the tribals, right down to the non-Sanskritic names and words they use and pronounce, she marks a break with the high cultural, sometimes Brahminical impulses that informed the secular sensibility of the Renaissance. The occasionally violent and mythopoeic nature of her imagination can also be read as a kind of assault upon the Renaissance's humane lyricism. Yet, in another sense, she is carrying on the work started by Tagore, for whom the songs of the Baul mendicants who lived on the fringes of society, and the Santhal tribespeople, were a crucial constituent of the aesthetic he was creating. There is some debate about Mahashweta's prose style; some readers think it lacks the music of the great Bengali writers of the first half of the twentieth century; but it possesses the unexpectedness of a terse piece of journalism that is being transformed into poetry.

* * *

'Arjun' (1984)

translated from the Bengali by Miridula Nath Chakraborty

Aghrayan was almost over and the month of Poush was just round the corner. It was not cold enough yet for the sun's warmth to be welcome.

The ripe paddy crop in Bishal Mahato's farm had been harvested the previous day. All day, along with the harvesters and casual grain pickers, Ketu Shabar too had been collecting the leftover grains of paddy in the fields. Now, in the foggy twilight, he needed a little liquor to warm him and to relax his aching body. The desire was sure to remain ungratified, but, he told himself, there was no harm in fantasizing.

His wife, Mohoni, was not with him. She came to the fields only when he was not around – Ketu was frequently in and out of jails. His offence – clearing the jungles for the paddy crop.

It was no use trying to reason with Ketu Shabar about this. Ram Haldar gave him the job and Ketu did it. Haldar collected the profits from the felled trees, and Ketu and others like him went to jail. But what could he do? All that mattered was the four pice at the end of the day – be it for chopping down a tree or chopping up a man. In fact, it might be easier to chop up a man! Why hadn't anyone asked him to do that? wondered Ketu. He might even earn four whole rupees that way! But he quickly corrected himself – I didn't mean it seriously, of course.

*

Ketu does not ever question his predicament. If you were born in the Shabar tribe of Purulia, you *had* to cut down the trees. And you *had* to go to jail. It could be no other way. If one Ketu was in jail, and something needed to be done, Haldar could always find another Ketu. Nothing lost – except that, the woman in the house had to go looking for work.

The last time Ketu had been jailed for cutting down the trees of the Forest Department, Mohoni had gone out looking for work. And who knows what happened ... In spite of the inevitability of the situation, Ketu couldn't face the prospect of returning to an empty hut. No wonder the mind and the body demanded liquor. A little intoxication, a little oblivion ...

Lost in reverie, Ketu was suddenly confronted by Bishal Mahato. 'I have some work for you,' he said.

'Is it about the votes, babu?'

'No, no! I'm not worried about that. The people will have to elect whoever I nominate, won't they?'

'Hanh, babu.'

'Well? What did Ram Haldar tell you?'

'The same thing that you said.'

'And what was your reply?'

'Just what I told you.'

'What kind of an answer is that?'

'I am just a fool, babu,' said Ketu.

'Never mind. There is something I want you to do. Are you interested?'

*

Ram Haldar and Bishal Mahato belonged to different parties. But for Ketu and his companions, they were two of a kind. One had to appear dumb whenever they were around. Both these deities had to be pleased, if one were to make a living in this area. But who among them would dare to say 'No' to these party members? Haldar and Mahato too knew that the Shabars were indispensable – they held the world record for jail terms, after all.

Now, Bishal Mahato had indeed managed to arouse Ketu's curiosity. Elections were round the corner. Bishal babu had been busy – attending meetings, giving speeches. So if the matter didn't concern votes, what could it possibly be? Whatever it was, it must be something shady.

'You have to cut down the arjun tree,' Bishal said.

'Why, babu?' Ketu was startled.

'Just do what I say.'

'Please babu, I've just come out of jail, babu.'

'If I wanted to send you back, would you be able to prevent it?' asked Bishal Mahato.

'No, babu.'

'This is not like one of Ram Haldar's contracts. Only through his illegal operations do you land in jail. Who'd dare to arrest you if I ordered the removal of the tree from the main intersection at the government road?'

Ketu's mind went blank. He had never thought about it, but it was true. You worked for Ram Haldar and you promptly got caught. That meant another trip to the jail. But Bishal babu's word was law. He actually ran the country, you know! So, who would send you to jail if, under his instructions, the shady tree no longer stood at the government road?

An idea flashed through Ketu's mind. 'Babu, are you making a pukka road this time, to ensure the votes?'

'Pukka road? Here? Ketu, you must be mad! It has not happened in thirty years. And it won't happen now. No, I need the tree.'

'A full grown tree?'

'Yes, the whole arjun tree.'

'And how would you transport it?'

'Ram babu's truck, what else.'

It was as if the clear sky, the pure, cold, air and the Santoshi Ma bhajans blaring out on the cassette player were prompting Bishal Mahato to speak the truth.

*

It was that magical hour when earth bids farewell to the day and twilight disappears into the arms of night. The wind carried the smell of ripe paddy from the fields of Bandihi. But Ketu was oblivious to all that. Mahato's request had stunned him. It was as if a huge stone had been placed on his chest. This is what Chandra Santhal must have felt when, during the harvest revolution, they had pinned him down with a half-maund measure. That weight ... Frightening.

Bishal Mahato and Ram Haldar belonged to two different parties. But only in word did they represent opposite camps. One conducted the Panchayat, the other ran the sawmill just outside the borders of the district. If one ordered the arjun to be cut down, the other happily provided the transport to carry it away.

Hai! The tree couldn't be saved. It was the only surviving relic of the Bandihi jungles from the zemindary era. It still evoked memories of the past in the minds of Ketu and his friends.

When the jungles were not jungles in name only, the Shabars had been forest-dwellers. Gone were those days when they scampered off like rabbits into its dark depths the moment they heard or saw a stranger approaching. Was that why they had been identified as Khedia Shabars, in the census records?'*

The elders of the tribe still revered the arjun tree. They believed that it

---

* Khedias and Shabars are two distinct tribes in West Bengal. But in the census records they have been classified as one. 'Khedia' means 'runaway' in one of the dialects of West Bengal.

was a manifestation of the divine. Now Ketu was to be responsible for its death.

'Yes, babu. I'll cut it down,' Ketu Shabar said. He stretched out his hand for ten rupees.

What a strange evening this way. He was even given what he had asked for.

'Go, go drink,' Mahato said. 'You won't be able to manage the job on your own, so get all those just released from jail. I'll see to it that you are all taken care of.'

Ram Haldar's business did not stop with one or two trees. First, he put up posters, 'Save the Forests,' then vandalized the jungles. Hands that wielded the axe were rewarded with torches, wristwatches, gleaming radios, cassette players, cycles, and of course, unlimited quantities of liquor. Each according to his capacity and capability. But the fallout was that whether innocent or guilty, the Shabars were repeatedly persecuted by the Forest Department or the Police.

Mahato's offer was much more promising. Who else would offer them so much?

'Very well, I'm going to the town now. For a meeting . . . I must get some posters. How on earth can one conduct a campaign without walls?'

'Get some for me too, babu.'

'Why, do you have a wall to stick them on?'

'No, no, babu. I'll spread them out on the floor when I sleep. Then I won't feel the cold in my bones.'

'All right, all right. See that you cut down the tree in two or three days. I'll have it removed when I return.'

'The arjun tree, babu?'

'Yes, yes, that one. Of course, it will be like the death of a mahapatra, a noble soul . . .' the monkey-capped, sweater-clad Mahato muttered as he disappeared into the foggy darkness of the night.

*

Ketu was deep in thought. He went to look for his friends – Banamali, Diga and Pitambar – to see if they could offer a solution.

Since he was carrying liquor, they welcomed him warmly. All of them had wielded the axe. All of them were just out of jail. He who wields the axe goes to jail – that was the rule of the land. Just as it was understood that Ram Haldar would get palatial mansions built in Purulia and Bankura. That was fate. So what could they possibly do to change the order of things?

'Let me think,' said Diga. Among them, Diga was treated with a little more respect. He had actually attended four whole days at the non-formal education centre! And learnt the alphabet too.

The four Shabars drowned themselves in thought and liquor. During festivals and weddings, they went around the arjun tree, beating their *dhol-dhamsas*. After a certain wish had been granted, the tribals made the ritual sacrifice of their hair and buried it under the tree for good luck. Hadn't Diga's father said that the tree had medicinal properties?

Drunkenly, Pitambar exclaimed, 'Even the Santhals come here during the Badhna Jagoran for the cow dance.'

What a predicament! Cut the tree, you go to jail; don't cut the tree, you still get jailed. What is the Shabar to do? This prosperous village of Bandihi sits where once the jungle used to be. Now it falls under the jurisdiction of the Forest Department. But of course the Shabars don't have any claim to it.

After much contemplation, Diga said, 'So why should we alone take the blame? Why should only Shabars get trapped in a false case? I'm going to tell the others. After all, they too revere the arjun. What do you say?'

*

Who knows how long the arjun had stood at that intersection. No one had really noticed it all these years. It was as if the tree had been there from time immemorial and would be there for time eternal. But now, all of a sudden it had become enormously important for everyone. As if it was a symbol of their existence!

The Forest Department did not control only the jungles, but the fallow land too. So where could the Shabars go? They had simply begun to wander from place to place. Wherever they saw a green patch of jungle land, they would settle down. Then the jungles would start disappearing. The fallow land would be sold off. Once again the Shabars would be homeless.

When the arjun had been a young tree, the Shabars had offered prayers to it before going on hunting expeditions. Now that it was mature, how grand it was! A shiny bark, the top touching the sky. On full-moon nights, the tree and moonlight seemed like one. During Chaitra and Baishakh, its spread of leaves provided such shade. It meant so much to them. That arjun at the crossing...

Pitambar asked, 'For how long has the arjun been guarding us? That one tree is the entire jungle for us. And our few families, the children of the forest. Now Mahato wants that very tree?'

'What can we do? Everything belongs to Bishal babu and Ram babu.'

'Till we had built our huts, we lived under the arjun. Only later did Mahato give us the land to build our huts . . .' went on Pitambar.

Diga put in his bit, 'Didn't the Santhals come to it for shelter and consolation after Haldar had burnt their shanties?'

One by one, they began to recall stories about the arjun tree. Each one realized that their lives and fate were inextricably linked with that of the arjun. Society and the system had continually persecuted, exploited and almost obliterated this handful of tribals from the face of the earth. Now the same fate awaited the arjun tree, the last mute symbol of their existence.

'Bishal babu is going to town. We must collect the cash from him before he leaves,' said Diga.

'You will cut the tree then?'

'Five people should be enough to do the job. We'll ask for one hundred rupees, what do you say?'

'You may have to go to jail.'

Frequent visits to the jail and constant exploitation by society had taught the Shabars to mask their true feelings and intentions. One face was presented to the Mahatos of the world, while the other one remained hidden. In the days of the British, the Shabars were the only ones who could be relied upon to set police stations and checkposts on fire. Today the babus were dependent on them, for these same Shabars performed the all-important tasks of land encroachment, crop theft, disposal of corpses and clearing government-owned forests.

So who would be so dumb as to go to jail for cutting one single tree?

Diga gave a shrewd, cunning laugh. 'You don't worry about it,' he told the others. After all, he knew the alphabet, had been to the jails of districts as far apart as Jamshedpur, Chaibasa, Medinipur and Bankura.

Bishal babu was assured that by the time he returned from the town, the job would be done. 'Go and conduct your election meetings with an easy mind. Give us the money. When you come back, you'll see that the tree is not there.'

'Make sure that Ram babu doesn't get a hint of what is happening.'

'Why, isn't he giving you the truck?'

'Yes, but he'll still create a big fuss. Also, take care that no one outside the district gets news of it.'

'We'll see, babu.'

On the surface, politicians hoisted different flags, but underneath, they were like sugar in milk. No conflict of interest when it came down to brass tacks.

Bishal babu, you have taught the foolish Shabars many a lesson, haven't you – what they call non-formal education!

The leaders of the two opposite camps abuse each other in public meetings. The cadre members do not understand all this. Abuses, petty quarrels and occasional bloodshed are all part of the political system. There is bound to be some dispute over the arjun too. But then, how many people would really support Ram Haldar? The entire village was under Bishal Mahato's sway.

*

A trip to the town really becomes frenzied, thought Bishal Mahato. On the way there are speeches and gatherings at the public halls and bazaars to be attended to. In the town, so many chores have to be taken care of. Get the moped light repaired, buy a new lantern, a shawl for the wife, some medicines . . .

Satisfied with his trip, Bishal Mahato was returning to Bandihi. The problem of votes had been taken care of. Oh god! When would they build a proper road to the village? Nengshai, Tetka, stream after stream, and then the descent down the bamboo bridge. After that, the tortuous way through slippery paths and uneven roads.

But as he neared the village, his head reeled.

*

Against the backdrop of the deep blue sky, the majestic arjun tree stood with its head held high – like a guardian of the village, keeping vigil from its lofty vigil post. Once upon a time, this land used to be guarded by hundreds of leafy sentinels. One by one, they have all gone, leaving no trace. Only the arjun is left now. Alone, to guard this devastated, neglected, humiliated land of his.

Unbidden, a proverb flashed through Bishal Mahato's mind, 'The leaves of the arjun tree are like the tongue of man.'

All around boomed the sounds of the *dhol-dhamsa-damak* and the strains of the *nagra*. An agitated Bishal Mahato rushed into the village. A huge crowd had gathered around the arjun. Its trunk was covered with *aakondo* garlands.

Haldar was standing at the perimeter of the crowd, holding on to his bicycle.

'What happened?' asked Mahato.

'The gram-devata has made them do it,' answered Haldar.

'What? Which ill-begotten fellow says so?'

'Diga had a dream, it seems. You paid him money in the dream and instructed him to build a concrete base around the trunk. People from all the tribes – Santhal, Khedia, Shohish, Bhumij – have now gathered to make their offerings.'

'To the gram-devata?'

'Yes, and the crowds have not stopped coming. There is practically a mela on. We'd thought these fellows were fools. But they have made fools of us, Mahato!'

Bishal stepped forward to taste the full flavour of his defeat.

What a stupendous crowd! Ketu was dancing away like a maniac, going round and round with his dholok.

Bishal was suddenly afraid. This tree, these people – he knew them all. He knew them very well. And yet, today they seemed like strangers.

Fear. An uncomprehending fear gripped him.

HINDI

Premchand (Dhanpat Rai) (1880–1936)

Premchand, born in a village near Benares, was the pen-name of Dhanpat Rai. He belonged to an educated, if not greatly well-to-do, family of the Hindu kayastha community, and his own education was in Persian and Urdu. To him, as his translator David Rubin claims, 'belongs the distinction of creating the genre of the serious short story, as well as the realistic novel, in both Hindi and Urdu'. Hindi (or Hindustani, as some would call it) and Urdu were, indeed, the twin languages he inherited; though he moved from the latter to the former, he never stopped writing in both – 'Hindi in the morning, Urdu in the afternoon,' he apparently said once. The lay conception of Hindustani and Urdu is that they are virtually identical languages, except that the former has a predominance of Sanskrit words while Persian and Arabic predominate in the latter; similarly, that Hindi is written in the Devanagari script while Urdu is written in Arabic. A further extension of this view would be that Urdu is the language of the Muslim speaker and Hindi that of the Hindu one. But, as Rubin reminds us, 'Premchand described his own background as deriving more from Muslim culture (particularly Persian and Urdu culture) than from the Hindu, and indignantly rejected the popular myth that Urdu was for Muslims while Hindi was for Hindus.' Since Partition, however, Hindi has, increasingly, been ethnically cleansed, especially in its incarnation on the Indian television channels and radio stations that are state-run, of its Persian and Arabic words, till it has come to be an Esperanto or pan-Indian lingua franca no less artificial than babu English; and perhaps some such process of purification has taken place on the other side of the border as well. But the figure and career of Premchand tell us that Hindi was not so much situated at the origin of a culture or tradition, but at the interface and junction of two or more cultures. As Premchand is usually seen as the 'father of modern Hindi literature', it would be instructive to discover in what way he has been appropriated and reinvented by those who see Hindi as the articulation of some sort of authenticity and authority.

Premchand's first book of stories was published in 1909 in Urdu. He turned from Urdu to Hindi circa 1916 because, Rubin tells us, of 'a dearth of Urdu publishers willing to publish his work, his lack of sympathy for

the elaborate Urdu style fashionable at the time and his belief that writing
in Hindi would reach a wider audience'. One wonders about the condem-
nation a writer would have to face today from the tsars and zealots that
write for the Indian papers if he or she confessed to writing in English for
the last-mentioned reason. Premchand made his reputation as the father
of social realism in Hindi, mirroring the era of social trauma and reform in
North India, with its problems of caste, widowhood, and the impoverished
peasantry, by both chronicling that world and transforming it into a
purgatorial landscape. The story below, one of his best known and made
into a film by Satyajit Ray, is, however, different in tone and subject-matter.
Here, Premchand, with great passion but an equal lightness of touch,
acknowledges the very Urdu language and Muslim court culture that were
so important to his formation, and remained a significant, if implicit, part
of his artistic endeavour. (This story, like others, is available in two versions
– Hindi and, later, Urdu – though Rubin translates the earlier, Hindi one.)
But it is an elegy as well, for a way of life and a hegemony, with its excesses
and refinements, that was coming to an end – not only because of the
break in history that the British soldiers marching in represent, but
because of the more subtle transition from the past to modernity that
Premchand's invisible eye – ironic, observant, but itself situated at the
crossroads of history – symbolizes.

* * *

'The Chess Players' (1924)

translated from the Hindi by David Rubin

It was the era of Wajid Ali Shah.[1] Lucknow was plunged deep in luxurious
living. Exalted and humble, rich and poor, all were sunk in luxury. While
one might arrange parties for dancing and singing another would find
enjoyment only in the drowsy ecstasy of opium. In every sphere of life
pleasure and merry-making ruled supreme. Indulgence in luxury pervaded
the government, the literary world, the social order, arts and crafts, industry, cuisine, absolutely everwhere. The bureaucrats were steeped in gross
sensuality, poets in describing lovers and the sufferings of separation,

---

1.   The last king of Oudh (Avadh); the story takes place in 1856.

artisans in creating intricate patterns of gold and silver thread and embroidery, merchants in selling eyeshadow, perfumes, unguents and colouring for the teeth. All eyes were dimmed with the intoxication of luxury. No one had any awareness of what was going on in the world. There were quail fights, betting on matches between fighting partridges, here the cloth for *causar*[2] spread out, there shouts of 'What luck, I've made an ace and twelve!' and elsewhere a fierce chess battle getting under way.

From king to beggar all were swept with the same antic spirit, to the point where when beggars were given money they spent it not on bread but on opium or *madak*.[3] By playing chess, cards or *ganjifa*[4] the wits were sharpened, the process of thought was developed, one became accustomed to solving complex problems – arguments of this sort were presented with great vehemence. (The world is not free even today of people of this persuasion!) So if Mirza Sajjad Ali and Mir Raushan Ali spent most of their time sharpening their wits, what reasonable person could object? Both of them were masters of hereditary estates and had no worry about their income, so they could lounge around at home enjoying their idleness. After all, what else was there to do? Early in the morning, after breakfast, they would sit down, set out the board, arrange the chessmen, and warlike stratagems would begin. From then on they were quite unaware of when it was noon or afternoon or evening. Time and time again word would be sent from the kitchen that dinner was ready and the answer would come back: Get on with it, we're coming, set the table. It would reach the point where the cook, desperate, would serve their meal right in their chamber and the two friends would go on with both activities, eating and playing simultaneously.

In Mirza Sajjad Ali's household there was no elder, so the games took place in his drawing room. But this is not to say that the other people of Mirza's household were happy with these goings-on. And not only the members of his household but the neighbours and even the servants were constantly making malicious comments. 'The game's ill-omened! It's destroying the family. Heaven forbid that anybody should become addicted to it, he'd be utterly useless to God or man, at home or in the world! It's a dreadful sickness, that's what.' Even Mirza's wife, the Begam Sahiba, hated it so much that she sought every possible occasion to scold him. But she hardly ever found the chance, for the game would have

2. A game of dice.
3. An intoxicant prepared from opium.
4. A type of card game.

begun before she woke and in the evening Mirzaji would be likely to
appear in the bedroom only after she had gone to sleep. But the servants
of course felt the full force of her rage. 'He's asked for *paan*, has he? Well,
tell him to come and get it himself! He hasn't got time for his dinner?
Then go and dump it on his head, he can eat it or give it to the dogs!'
But to his face she could not say anything at all. She was not so angry
with him as with Mir Sahib, whom she referred to as 'Mir the Trouble-
maker'. Possibly it was Mirzaji who laid all the blame on Mir in order to
excuse himself.

One day the Begam Sahiba had a headache. She said to the maid, 'Go
and call Mirza Sahib and have him get some medicine from the doctor. Be
quick about it, run!' When the maid went to him Mirzaji said, 'Get along
with you, I'll come in a moment or two.' The Begam Sahiba's temper flared
at this. Who could put up with a husband playing chess while she had a
headache? Her face turned scarlet. She said to the maid, 'Go and tell him
that if he doesn't go at once I'll go out to the doctor myself.'[5] Mirzaji was
immersed in a very interesting game, in two more moves he would
checkmate Mir Sahib. Irritated, he said, 'She's not on her deathbed, is she?
Can't she be just a little patient?'

'Come now,' said Mir, 'go and see what she has to say. Women can be
touchy, you know.'

'To be sure,' said Mirza, 'why shouldn't I go? You'll be checkmated in
two moves.'

'My dear fellow, better not count on it. I've thought of a move that will
checkmate you with all your pieces still on the board. But go on now,
listen to her, why make her feel hurt for no reason at all?'

'I'll go only after I've checkmated you.'

'Then I won't play. Do go and hear her out.'

'I'll have to go to the doctor's, old man. It's not just a mere headache,
it's an excuse to bother me.'

'Whatever it is, you really must indulge her.'

'Very well, but let me make just one more move.'

'Absolutely not, until you've gone to her I won't so much as touch a
piece.'

When Mirza Sahib felt compelled to go to his wife the Begam Sahiba
was frowning, but she said with a moan, 'You love your wretched chess so
much that even if somebody were dying you wouldn't think of leaving it!
Heaven forbid there should ever be another man like you!'

5. For an aristocratic lady in purdah this would be inappropriate.

Mirza said, 'What can I tell you? Mir Sahib simply wouldn't agree. I had a most difficult time of it putting him off so I could come.'

'Does he think everybody is just as worthless as himself? Doesn't he have children too or has he just let them go to the dogs?'

'He's utterly mad about chess,' said Mirza. 'Whenever he comes I'm compelled to play with him.'

'Why don't you tell him off?'

'He's my equal in age and a couple of steps above me in rank, I'm obliged to be courteous with him.'

'In that case, I'll tell him off! If he gets angry, let him. Is he supporting us, after all? As they say, "If the queen sulks, she'll only hurt herself." Hiriya!' she called her maid, 'Go out and take up the chessboard, and say to Mir Sahib, "The master won't play now, pray be good enough to take your leave."'

'For heaven's sake, don't do anything so outrageous!' said Mirza. 'Do you want to disgrace me? Wait, Hiriya, where are you going?'

'Why don't you let her go? Anybody who stops her will be simply killing me! Very well, then, stop her, but see if you can stop me.'

Saying this, the Begam Sahiba headed for the drawing room in high dudgeon. Poor Mirza turned pale. He began to implore his wife: 'For God's sake, in the name of the holy Prophet Husain! If you go to him it will be like seeing me laid out!' But the Begam did not pay the slightest attention to him. But when she reached the door of the drawing room all of a sudden, finding herself about to appear before a man not of her household, her legs felt as though paralysed. She peeked inside, and as it happened, the room was empty. Mir Sahib had done a little shifting of the chess pieces and was now strolling outside in order to demonstrate his innocence. The next thing that happened was that the Begam went inside, knocked over the chessboard, flung some of the pieces under the sofa and others outside, then clapped the double doors shut and locked them. Mir Sahib was just outside the door. When he saw the chessmen being tossed out and the jingling of bangles reached his ears he realized that the Begam Sahiba was in a rage. Silently he took his way home.

Mirza said, 'You have committed an outrage!'

She answered, 'If Mir Sahib comes back here I'll have him kicked out straightaway. If you devoted such fervour to God you'd be a saint. You're to play chess while I slave away looking after this household? Are you going to the doctor's or are you still putting it off?'

When he came out of his house Mirza, instead of going to the doctor's, went to Mir Sahib's and told him the whole story. Mir Sahib said, 'So I guessed when I saw the chess pieces sailing outside. I took off at once. She seems to be quick to fly off the handle. But you've spoiled her too much, and that's not at all the way to do things. What concern is it of hers what you do away from her part of the house? Her work is to look after the home. What business does she have with anything else?'

'Well, tell me, where are we going to meet now?'

'No problem, we have this whole big house, so that's settled, we'll meet here.'

'But how am I going to placate the Begam Sahiba? She was furious when I sat down to play at home, so if I play here it could cost me my life.'

'Let her babble, in a few days she'll be all right. But of course you ought to show a little backbone yourself.'

*

For some unknown reason Mir Sahib's Begam considered it most fitting for her husband to stay far away from home. For this reason she had never before criticized his chess playing, but on the contrary, if he was late in going she reminded him. For these reasons Mir Sahib had been deluded into thinking his wife was extremely serious and humble. But when they began to set up the chessboard in the drawing room and Mir Sahib was at home all day the Begam Sahiba was very distressed. This was a hindrance to her freedom, and all day long she would yearn to be at the door looking out.

Meantime, the servants had begun to gossip. Formerly they had lain around all day in idleness, if someone came to the house, if someone left, it was no business of theirs. Now they were living in fear all twenty-four hours of the day. Orders would come for *paan*, then for sweets. And, like some lover's heart, the hookah had to be kept burning constantly. They would go to the mistress and say, 'The master's chess games are giving us a lot of trouble. We're getting blisters on our feet from running all day. What kind of a game is it that starts at dawn and goes on till evening? Diversion for an hour or two, that's enough for any game. Of course we're not complaining, we're your slaves, whatever you command naturally we'll do it; but this game is positively sinister! Whoever plays it never prospers, and surely some disaster will befall his home. It can reach the point where one neighbourhood after another's been known to go to rack and ruin. Everybody in this part of town is gossiping about it. We have eaten your salt, we're grieved to hear bad things about the master, but what can we do?'

Hearing this, the Begam Sahiba would say, 'I don't like it myself, but he won't listen to anybody, so what can be done?'

In their quarter there were also a few people from an earlier generation who began to imagine all sorts of disasters: 'There's no hope now. If our nobles are like this, then God help the country! This chess playing will be the ruin of the kingdom. The omens are bad.'

The entire realm was in an uproar. Subjects were robbed in broad daylight and nobody was there to hear their appeals. All the wealth of the countryside had been drawn into Lucknow to be squandered on whores, clowns and the satisfaction of every kind of vice. The debt to the East India Company kept on growing day by day, and day by day the general misery was getting harder to bear. Throughout the land, because of the wretched conditions, the yearly taxes were no longer collected. Time and again the British resident warned them, but everyone in Lucknow was so drowned in the intoxication of sensual indulgence that not a soul gave any heed.

Well then, the chess games continued in Mir Sahib's drawing room over the course of several months. Newer strategies were devised, new defences organized, and ever new battle formations planned. From time to time quarrels broke out as they played, and they even reached the point of exchanging vulgar insults; but peace was quickly restored between the two friends. At times the game would come to a halt and Mirzaji would return home in a huff and Mir Sahib would go and sit in his own chamber. But with a good night's sleep all the bad feelings would be calmed; early in the morning the two friends would arrive in the drawing room.

One day when they sat engrossed in thorny chess problems an officer of the royal army arrived on horseback and enquired for Mir Sahib. Mir Sahib panicked, wondering what disaster was about to come down on his head. Why had he been summoned? The case appeared desperate. To the servants he said, 'Tell him I'm not at home.'

'If he's not at home where is he?' the horseman demanded. The servant said he didn't know – what was this all about? 'How can I tell *you* what it's about?' said the officer. 'Maybe soldiers are being levied for the army. It's no joke, being the master of rent-free estates. When he has to go to the front lines he'll find out what it's all about.'

'Very well, go along, he'll be informed.'

'It's not just a matter of informing him. I'll come back tomorrow, I have orders to take him back with me.'

The horseman left. Mir Sahib was shaking with terror. He said to Mirzaji, 'Tell me, sir, what's going to happen now?'

'It's a great misfortune! What if I'm summoned too?'

'The bastard said he was coming back tomorrow.'

'It's a calamity, no doubt of it. If we have to go to the front we'll die before our time.'

'Now listen, there's one way out: we won't meet here at the house any more. Starting tomorrow we'll have our game in some deserted place out on the banks of the Gomti. Who could find us there? When that fine fellow comes for me he'll have to go back without us.'

'By Allah, that's a splendid idea! That's certainly the best way.'

In the meantime, Mir Sahib's Begam was saying to that cavalry officer, 'You've got them out of the way very nicely,' and he answered, 'I'm used to making such jackasses dance to my tune. Chess has robbed them of all their common sense and courage. After this they won't stay at home, whatever happens.'

*

From the next day on the two friends would set out from the house at the crack of dawn, carrying with them a rather small carpet and a box of prepared *paan*, and go to the other side of the Gomti river to an old ruined mosque which had probably been built in the time of Nawab Asafuddaula.[6] Along the way they would pick up tobacco, a pipe and some wine, and spread their carpet in the mosque, fill the hookah and sit down to play. After that they had no care for this world or the next. Apart from 'check' and 'checkmate', not another word came out of their mouths. No yogi could have been more profoundly plunged in trance. At noon when they felt hungry they would go to some baker's shop and eat something, smoke a pipeful, and then return to engage once more in battle. At times they would even forget all about eating.

Meantime, the political situation in the country was becoming desperate. The East India Company's armies were advancing on Lucknow. There was commotion in the city. People were taking their children and fleeing to the countryside. But our two players were not in the least concerned about it. When they left home they took to the narrow alleyways, fearing lest some government official might catch a glimpse of them and have them forced into military service. They wanted to enjoy the thousands in income from their estates without giving anything in return.

One day the two friends were sitting in the ruined mosque playing

---

6. Ruler of Oudh, 1775–97; his reign was noted both for debauchery and for the construction of many buildings, especially mosques.

chess. Mirza's game was rather weak and Mir Sahib was checking him at every move. At the same time the Company's soldiers could be seen approaching. This was an army of Europeans on their way to impose their rule on Lucknow.

Mir Sahib said, 'The British army's coming. God save us!'

Mirza said, 'Let them come, but now get out of check.'

'Maybe we ought to have a look, let's stand here where we can't be seen.'

'You can look later, what's the rush? Check again.'

'They have artillery too. There must be about five thousand men. What odd-looking soldiers! They've got red faces, just like monkeys, it's really frightening.'

'Don't try to get out of it, sir! Use these tricks on somebody else. Checkmate!'

'What a strange fellow you are! Here we have the city struck with calamity and you can only think of ways to checkmate. Do you have any idea how we're going to get home if the city's surrounded?'

'When it's time to go home we'll see about it then. This is checkmate, your king's finished now.'

The army had marched by. It was now ten in the morning. A new game was set up.

Mirza said, 'What are we going to do about food today?'

'Well, today's a fast day – are you feeling hungrier than usual?'

'Not in the least. But I wonder what's happening in the city.'

'Nothing at all's happening in the city. People are eating their dinner and settling down comfortably for an afternoon nap. The King's in his harem, no doubt.'

By the time they sat down to play again it was three. This time Mirzaji's game was weak. Four o'clock had just struck when the army was heard marching back. Nawab Wajid Ali had been taken prisoner and the army was conducting him to some unknown destination. In the city there was no commotion, no massacre, not a drop of blood was spilled. Until now no king of an independent country could ever have been overthrown so peacefully, without the least bloodshed. This was not that non-violence which delights the gods, but rather the sort of cowardice which makes even great cowards shed tears. The king of the vast country of Oudh was leaving it a captive, and Lucknow remained deep in its sensual slumber. This was the final stage of political decadence.

Mirzaji said, 'Those tyrants have imprisoned His Majesty.'

'I suppose so. Look here – check.'

'Just a moment, sir, I don't feel in the mood now. The poor King must be weeping tears of blood at this moment.'

'I'm sure he is – what luxuries will he enjoy as a prisoner? Checkmate!'

'Everybody has to suffer some change in his fortunes,' said Mirza. 'But what a painful situation!'

'True, that's the way things are. Look, checkmate! That does it, you can't get out of it now.'

'God's oath, you're hard-hearted. You can watch a great catastrophe like this and feel no grief. Alas, poor Wajid Ali Shah!'

'First save your own king, then you can mourn for His Majesty. It's checkmate now. Your hand on it!'

The army passed by, taking the King with them. As soon as they were gone Mirza again set up the chess pieces. The sting of defeat is bitter. Mir said, 'Come now, let us compose an elegy for His Majesty.' But Mirza's patriotism had vanished with his defeat. He was eager for vengeance.

*

It was evening. In the ruins the swallows were returning and settling in their nests, the bats began to chitter. But the players were still at it, like two bloodthirsty warriors doing battle together. Mirzaji had lost three games in a row; the outlook for this fourth game was not good either. He played each move carefully, firmly resolved to win, but one move after the other turned out to be so ill-conceived that his game kept deteriorating. For his part, Mir Sahib was singing a ghazal and snapping his fingers from sheer high spirits, as though he had come upon some hidden treasure. Listening to him, Mirzaji was furious, but praised him in order to conceal his exasperation. But as his game worsened his patience began to slip out of control until he reached the point of getting angry at everything Mir said.

'Don't change your move, sir,' he would say. 'How can you go back on a move? Whatever move is to be made, make it just once. Why is your hand on that piece? Leave it alone! Until you figure out your move don't so much as touch your piece! You're taking half an hour for every move, that's against the rules. Anyone who takes more than five minutes for a move may be understood to be checkmated. You changed your move again! Just be quiet and put that piece back there.'

Mir Sahib's queen was in danger. He said, 'But when did I make my move?'

'You've already made it. Put the piece right there, in that same square.'

'Why should I put it in that square? When did I take my hand off the piece?'

'If you wait till doomsday to make your move, you'll still have to make it.'

'You're the one who's cheating! Victory and defeat depend on fate, you can't win by cheating.'

'Then it's settled, you've lost this game.'

'How have I lost it?'

'Then put the piece back in the same square where it was.'

'Why should I put it there? I won't!'

'Why should you put it there? You *have* to put it there.'

The quarrel was getting worse. Each stuck to his position, neither one would give an inch. Their words began to move to irrelevant matters. Mirza said, 'If anybody in your family had ever played chess then you might be familiar with the rules. But they were just grass-cutters. So how can you be expected to play chess? Real aristocracy is quite another thing. Nobody can become a noble just by having had some rent-free estates given to him.'

'What! Your own father must have cut grass! My people have been playing chess for generations.'

'Come off it, you spent your whole life working as a cook in Gaziuddin Haidar's house and now you're going around posing as an aristocrat.'

'Why are you defaming your own ancestors?' said Mir. 'They must all have been cooks. My people have always dined at the King's own table.'

'You grass-cutter you! Stop your bragging.'

'You check your tongue or you'll be sorry! I won't stand for talk like that. I put out the eyes of anybody who frowns at me. Do you have the courage?'

'So you want to find out how brave I am! Come on then, let's have it out, whatever the consequences.'

Said Mir, 'And who do you think is going to let you push them around!'

The two friends drew the swords from their belts. It was a chivalric age when everybody went around carrying swords, daggers, poniards and the like. Both of them were sensualists but not cowards. They were politically debased, so why should they die for king or kingdom? But they did not lack personal courage. They challenged one another formally, the swords flashed, there was a sound of clanging. Both fell wounded, and both writhed and expired on the spot. They had not shed a single tear for their king but gave up their lives to protect a chess queen.

Darkness was coming on. The chess game had been set up. The two kings each on his throne sat there as though lamenting the death of these two heroes.

Silence spread over all. The broken archways of the ruins, the crumbling walls and dusty minarets looked down on the corpses and mourned.

Nirmal Verma (b. 1929)

Nirmal Verma was born in 1929 in Simla. He took an MA in History at St Stephen's College, Delhi, and between 1959 and 1968 lived in Prague, studying Czech literature and also translating it into Hindi. The impact of the culture, landscape, and weather of Europe, and of the *nouveau roman*, on his sensibility led to the birth of some extraordinary Hindi stories, which he wrote in the fifties, stories that inaugurated a new genre in Hindi literature, the *Nai Kahani*, or the 'new story'. There was nothing ostensibly 'Indian' about the subject-matter of many of these stories; neither did they go out of their way to identify, or name, the alien terrain they described; although the world in them was often European, there was no attempt to narrate, in these stories, the life of an Indian in exile, as one might have expected, because no specifically 'Indian' characteristics would be given to the protagonist or other characters, and characters might be even left unnamed. The only real cultural specificity attaching itself to these stories, and which distinguished them from being just Hindi versions of the *nouveau roman*, emanated from the name 'Nirmal Verma', that translated these European fictions from a private symbolic landscape into a cultural exploration of what it means to be Indian and to write in Hindi at a certain point in history, and brought to the foreground the whole process of cultural translation as an act of creative expression. The stories seem to be realist enough in their mode, and, occasionally, their particulars are rendered with great beauty; but the aura of the real is an illusion; the features of their world are no more definite or recognizable than the mysterious daubs of colour that form certain Cubist paintings. Just as those daubs of colour congeal, and are translated, into a scene only once we know the name of the painting – say, 'Night Fishing At Antibes' – so the features of the world of these stories hang suspended in the locus of the name, 'Nirmal Verma', and the language, Hindi, and its traditions. In his more mature years, Verma has moved to apparently less symbolist and more recognizable territory. But he has also proved, ironically, that it is possible to map, on the suburban capital city, private and nebulous quests; he

writes, a publisher's note informs us, 'from a rooftop room that appears
in some of his stories'.

* * *

'Terminal' (1992)

translated from the Hindi by Alok Bhalla

1

She did not say anything, but he always knew when she had drifted away
from him. He shook her by her shoulder. 'Are you angry?' She let herself
be shaken like a wax doll. The same thing used to happen when they
made love, her body would become malleable, and she would let him do
what he liked with her, yield completely to him. Even when she sobbed, it
seemed as if she had emerged, wrapped in sorrow and joy, from a third
body which existed in some boundless present on which the future had
cast no shadow. Perhaps that's where the thistle of ill omen had begun to
grow – can one simply refuse to look into the future? 'We should find out
about the future,' she insisted, 'find out what's going to happen.' He folded
her in his arms. Wondered what she saw in the dark which was invisible
to him. 'You say there is nothing. Are you sure there is nothing, are you
sure that nothing will happen?' She pushed him from her. Turned away
from him in rage; became hard like stone. She felt hot when he touched
her. 'Your hands are always feverish,' he said. Unmoved, she continued to
look away. He realized that he could do nothing at such moments. Over
the last seven months he had known all the different seasons of her soul,
but the coldest, the most chilling was the one in which he found himself
sitting holding her hand while she drifted somewhere far away from him.

When they met the following day it was like a new morning after rain
and storm. Her face began to glow the moment they stepped out of the
hostel. She took off her scarf and her hair scattered over her shoulders.
Away from the city, in the direction of the setting sun, there was a bend in
the river where they sat on their usual bench on the embankment which
was always vacant. There was a skating rink across from it where delirious
music and the excited shouts of children could be heard mingled together.
Most often they sat there before returning home. After a stormy day, it

was a quiet, clean and dry place where the threads of things left half said could be picked up again. But she was silent. She watched some women, who were busy gossiping, as they strolled along pushing the prams in which their children were asleep. A man, smoking a pipe, ambled past them. Blue smoke from his pipe swayed in the light of the setting sun like a snake and then disappeared. She watched till the man was out of sight, and then she turned towards him and smiled. A small tremor ran through her hand as if all that was good had just passed in front of them in the form of gossiping women, sleeping children and a man smoking a pipe.

'Isn't this like a hallucination?'

'What is like a hallucination?'

'This feeling that all that is faithful merely touches us and then passes by?'

'Yes, that's true,' he said, as he laughed. 'I must find out why you always distrust me. Is there a cure for distrust?'

'If my parents were alive, I could have asked them. If they had told me not to meet you, it would have been a comfort to know that they had decided for me. Even if they hadn't, at least I would have known they supported me – now there is nothing.'

'Why does this absence cause you so much anxiety; why does it torment you so much, oppress you so much?'

'It's a question of trust,' she said, as she gazed into the darkness of her heart. 'We'll somehow have to find out if what we are doing is right.'

'Who will tell us that?' he asked irritably. 'Who will you go to see in order to find out?'

She brushed his unshaven cheek with her lips and whispered, 'I know where to go. Will you come with me?'

'Again the same madness.' As he turned his face away, her bruised lips left a thrilling damp stain on his cheek. 'I won't go anywhere,' he moaned sorrowfully. 'I don't want to go anywhere.' He repeated himself like a rotating tyre stuck in mud.

'Why not?'

'I have already told you but you refuse to listen.'

'Tell me again. I can't remember what I haven't heard, can I?'

'I don't believe in such things. If you are so keen, go yourself. I won't go.'

The finality of 'I won't go' made her refrain from urging him any further. She never begged, she only backed off a little. 'Whom do you trust?'

He wanted to say, I trust no one. When I met you, I didn't think that our meeting was such an unfortunate accident that we needed the approval of others. Do you know that whatever I have belongs to you; whatever I am is a result of you. In this dark city, every heartbeat of mine glows in your body – I can see nothing beyond that. After I leave you at the hostel, I find the presence of my self very oppressive. I take my clothes off as quickly as possible so that I can get rid of my self. I try to forget my self till you remind me of my presence the next day . . . Is that such a sin that I must cleanse myself before someone else?

But he didn't say anything to her. To have said anything would have meant acknowledging her suspicions, drawing them into the circle of sin. His words would have so terrified her that she could have done anything. She was like a somnambulist, who instinctively turns away from the edge of the roof, but falls when startled awake by someone's warning. There were no guarantees with her. Therefore, at moments like this he preferred to stay silent. He did, of course, talk to himself in the hope that at some future time she would find out what he was actually feeling now. Immediately, however, it occurred to him that his thoughts were a bad omen – black magic – and he wanted to forget them.

'Alone?' She looked at him with tears in her eyes. 'All right, I'll go alone. There is no need for you to come with me.'

She got up from the bench. Tied a scarf around her hair. Dusted her clothes and looked at the bench to see that she had not left anything behind – apart from himself, still sitting there. His presence did not concern her. She climbed down the embankment to the street. Started walking. She did not look back to see the city lights sparkling on the surface of the river whose banks were lost in the evening shadows.

He sat rooted at the same spot for a few moments, and then ran after her anxiously. He caught her hand which was still burning hot. He was afraid that she would pull it away with a jerk. She didn't do that, but neither did she respond in any way. Her hand lay in his like a soft and limp glove. There were no women, or children, or shops, or bars on the street. They seemed to pass from one end of the town to the other through a tunnel, only to find themselves at her hostel where the lights were still burning on every floor. Had it been daytime, he would have overcome his anger and gone in with her, but at that dead hour of night, all he could do was to leave her there and turn back. She stopped at the porch. 'You can go now,' she said, without looking at him, as if she was addressing the night.

'Shall we meet tomorrow?'

'That depends on you.'

'Why on me?' He was grateful that in the darkness of the porch she couldn't see his face.

He started walking towards his house. He lived in the old city across the bridge. The bridge had been built a long time ago. It was said that the Emperor had mixed the yolk of thousands of eggs in mortar to build it. That is why it was still in as good a shape as on the day, three hundred years ago, when the Empress had driven across it in her horse-carriage for the first time ... One day as they were walking across it and going towards his house, she had told him that on moonlight nights when the city was silent, one could still hear the sound of carriage wheels on the bridge. Before marriage, the Emperor, instead of telling the Empress that he loved her, had said that he was tired of crossing bridges alone and that from that day onwards he only wanted to cross the bridges he came to in his journeys with her. Do you know what the Empress replied? She said, bridges are meant for crossing rivers, not for building homes ... The Emperor didn't understand what she wanted to tell him. Years later, the Empress jumped from that bridge into the river which still flows under it.

2

The next day, when she reached the tram-station, he was already there waiting for her. Even though it was not winter yet, he was shivering. It was difficult to tell if he was shivering because it was cold or because he was nervous. The sun was hidden behind the clouds. The morning rain had washed the tramlines clean and they were gleaming. After last night's conversation both were so self-conscious that the arrival of the tram was a relief. Without saying anything to each other, they quickly boarded it.

There were very few people inside, and even they were sitting crouched in their raincoats. All of them sat with their feet raised a little above the floor so as not to touch the mud left behind by the previous passengers. Instead of looking at each other, the two of them sat and stared out of the window even though there was nothing to see outside. The windows of the tram were covered with such thick layers of dust that the trees on the footpaths, the lamp-posts and the people walking on the streets seemed to slip by like dirty smudges on some old film. A few passengers got off at every stop. Whenever the conductor pulled the bell-rope, the tram hiccuped and dragged itself forward.

When the conductor came, she quickly took some money out of her purse and bought two tickets. After he had gone, she did not shut the bag. Instead, she took out a hairbrush and began to brush her hair. She turned to look at her face in the glass window, out of habit at first, and when she could see it clearly, with some anxiety, for she saw him there staring at her instead of sitting beside her. When she smiled, his reflection smiled back. But the moment she turned away from the window and looked at him, he wasn't smiling. He was sitting quietly. Suddenly nervous, she squeezed his hand so hard that he winced and pulled it away. Her nails scratched his hand so deeply that they left small trails of blood on it. She quickly pulled a handkerchief from her bag and wiped away the blood . . . Both of them started laughing and, pushing the previous night aside, moved close to each other. She put her head on his shoulder and shut her eyes.

He looked out of the window. Her warm breath caressed his cheek. Nothing will happen, he thought, we'll go and return by the evening. There were two tickets for *The Magic Flute* in his pocket, which he had bought many days ago. He wanted to surprise her. It was the opera they had seen together exactly seven months ago, when they had hardly known each other. Now it seemed as if that was years ago. He had reached the auditorium well ahead of time so that he could get a ticket with ease. But when he got there, the advance-booking counter had closed and the queue had begun to disperse. He had stood around despondently. He had waited for that day for a long time and was not yet convinced that he would have to return home disappointed. He had found his tie and black coat, which he wore only when he had to go to a concert, a bit amusing. Irritated, he had been reading the list of future performances on the board outside so that people would not think that he was merely hanging around, when he heard a soft voice behind him ask, 'Do you need a ticket, I have an extra one . . .' When he turned around, he saw her. She seemed tall in her black dress and rather young. After they had got to know each other, he realized that she was shorter and older than he had taken her to be. There were two tickets in her fist which were clutched so tightly that it had been difficult to separate them for some time. It was only later, when they had sat down next to each other, that he realized he had forgotten to pay her for the tickets, but by then it was already too late.

Her hand was warm and soft. She seemed to have a fever. As he gazed at the misty and rain-washed city through the tram window, he wondered if all her actions were not performed in some feverish delirium, so that she heard the sound of each approaching event in the throbbing of her veins, in the pulsating flow of her blood, in the pounding of her heart.

One day, after they had got to know each other, he had asked her, 'That night when we met at the Mozart opera, who had you bought that other ticket for?'

'For you,' she had replied with a laugh.

'No, tell me truthfully, who were you waiting for?'

She was silent for a while. She had neither laughed nor said anything. 'There is nothing to tell ... I won't tell you because you won't believe me.'

Suddenly anxious, he had said, 'Don't make excuses ... You don't want to tell me who you were waiting for ...'

'For you ...' she had said.

'But we didn't even know each other.'

'That's why I didn't want to tell you. Such things happen to me often. I feel as if something is about to happen, like a signal from a distance. I see it only once, but I know it is asking me to be ready. That day I was the first in the queue to buy tickets. When a voice from the ticket-window asked, "How many?" I replied, "Two". After I had bought them, I wondered who the second ticket was for. It was then that I saw you.'

They had reached the terminal. The tram didn't go any further. It returned from there, went back to the city which was lost in the afternoon haze. They got off the tram but for a while he was confused about where they were ... All he could do was to follow the girl, who was walking very fast. After walking some distance, the girl left the main road and turned into a small lane. It was then he remembered that he had been there before.

It was a narrow lane. The houses on both sides seemed to lean into each other. The sky above, masked by smoke and mist, was like a dirty rag spread over the houses. She stopped at every turning and waited for him to catch up with her. Every now and then they came upon the ruins of some old houses. Their broken walls, their swaying rods of iron, seemed like the skeletons of forgotten corpses. She avoided the rubble with such confidence that it seemed as if she was walking, not through some strange part of the town, but towards her own home. But suddenly her steps faltered. She stood uncertainly before a door, and when he caught up with her, she looked at him as if she was terrified of losing the very thing which she longed to possess. But before doubt could take root, she crushed it under her feet and knocked at the door. Instead of waiting for an answer, she took him by his hand and pushed him against the door. It began to open by itself with a strange low whine. It would perhaps have continued to whine for a long time had she not suddenly shut it with a bang.

The first thing he noticed was the dirt in the house. It leapt out at him

from every corner. It had the sharp smell of old, damp and moth-eaten
clothes which have been locked in a trunk for a long time, or of unwashed,
lice-infested hair. Strangely enough, instead of being repulsive, the house
seemed to invite him in, urging him to cut himself off from everything
and walk in, calling to him like a wild forest which offers shelter from the
harsh glare and deception of the world to anyone who seeks it. If she had
not impatiently signalled to him to enter, he would have forgotten why he
was there.

Did he know? He didn't know that desire would make him walk
through twisting and turning lanes and bring him here. The courtyard was
surrounded by dimly-lit jute curtains. In the middle of the courtyard there
was a low table, dark as ebony. There were two candles burning at each
end of the table.

'Come closer,' a voice called from a distance. When he approached the
table, he saw a pale white face framed by long hair on the other side
staring at him. He realized that the girl was not beside him.

'She'll be back soon,' the woman said, as if she had guessed his fear.
'Please sit. Not there, but here beside me ...' Then she pushed the red
velvet-covered stool, which was on the left of the table, towards him.
When he sat down, she said in a strangely high-pitched voice. 'You are
different from what I had imagined.' He continued to sit with his head
bowed.

'Were you afraid of coming here?'

He raised his head. In the pale light of the candle, her face seemed to
be carved of marble.

'I didn't know what to expect.' he replied.

'I am glad that you came,' she said gently. 'Do you know where one's
longest journey begins? With one's first step!' She laughed for the first
time – softly, without kindness or sarcasm. Full of knowledge and trust.
'Look at me,' she said, and when he gathered the courage to look at her,
he felt that he had never seen a face which was wiser or more beautiful.
He leaned forward a little so that he could see the other side of her face
which was hidden in the shadows cast by the candles. Suddenly he saw
the girl emerge from one of the dark walls in the back. Joy surged through
him as she sat down on a cushion across from him. Unable to restrain
himself, he leaned forward to whisper something to her, when he felt
someone gently touch him. The woman had placed her hand on his head.
It was still and cold like death, covering his inner being like a black lid.

'Do you love this man?' The woman's eyes were fixed on the girl. The
girl nodded. The woman then turned to look at him. 'And you?' She waited

for a reply for some time and then sighed deeply. He was still wondering what he should say, when he suddenly realized that the girl's hand, which had crept under the table like a thief, was clutching his fingers, and anxiously urging him to reply. He wondered if there was a word between yes and no which could express his feelings? 'Yes,' he said.

'What is your name?'

'Name?' The moment it escaped his lips, the woman caught it in her hands like a flying kite – imprisoned it in her five fingers which were glittering with rings. It was then that he felt a slight tremor in his soul. The hand, which had felt like death on his head a few moments ago, was now encircled with diamonds and mocking him. The woman wrote out their names on two pieces of paper. She did not ask the girl her name because she already knew it. Then she crumpled the two pieces of paper, shook them in her cupped hand and dropped them on the table … For some time their names lay trapped in those crumpled pieces of paper. Then she picked them up with her bejewelled hand and held them to the flame of the candle till they slowly unfolded. In the light of the sparkling diamonds, their two names glowed on the charred remains of paper. She stared at them for a while, and then suddenly clapped her soot-covered hands and watched grey flakes of ash slowly fall on the table … She shook her head, as if she had seen a vision of something fated, something which had been ordained before the two of them had been born. She shook her head sadly, once, twice, thrice, like a pendulum wildly oscillating on its axis, or like an epileptic patient. She stopped only when the girl placed her head on the woman's hand lying on the table. When the woman opened her eyes, they were as calm and peaceful as they had been in the beginning.

She began to caress the girl's hair with her white marbled hands. 'Silly girl, you should be happy … You have been saved from a grave misfortune. And he too … This man who has come with you.'

She lifted her head from the table and looked at the woman with defeated eyes. 'What misfortune? Won't we live together?'

The woman was silent. For the first time a trace of anguish passed over the remote sadness of her face, as if she wanted to banish the shadows that had emerged from the walls of darkness and were standing around her. 'I can't describe what I have seen, I can only show it to you. Would you like to see it?'

The girl's hand, which was still grasping his under the table, trembled a little and then was steady … Perhaps that was when they should have left the place because, at that moment, what was hidden, and at stake, was not only the future of their love but the seduction of seeking to attain it.

Perhaps that was what the woman also wanted them to do, but she could neither tell them to do so nor prevent them from finding out. She could not help them in the region which she had opened up before them. In fact, she was herself only an observer of the vision she wanted to show them.

3

The woman withdrew the hand on which the girl's head had been resting. The woman's hand, which now lay on the table, seemed like the hood of a snake glittering with diamonds. Slowly she slid her hand across the table till it lay before the girl's eyes, which were still, like the eyes of a fish under the surface of water watching the sun glowing in the sky. 'Is this what you wanted to see?'

He did not remember what happened after that even though he had often tried to do so. He heard the girl's scream, sharper and brighter than the edge of a knife. The candles flickered and were then extinguished, and ghostly shadows jumped off the walls and surrounded the woman. After that, he saw nothing except that scream which continued to flash in the darkness. 'Now that you know, decide.'

He felt like jumping up and strangling the woman. Instead, he dragged the girl by her hand and hugged her. 'Let's get out of here.' This time she did not resist. She allowed herself to be dragged away like a log of wood, but when they emerged from behind the jute curtains, she stopped, hesitated at the threshold of the door. She pulled him towards her and kissed him, kissed him in a frenzy – her tongue sought his as if she was in search of something in a deep and dark well.

4

It must have been a coincidence that they returned to the city in the same tram they had taken to the woman's house. The ticket conductor smiled when he saw them. He recognized them as the couple who had got off at the terminal in the afternoon.

Everything was as it had been before. They occupied the seat they had earlier and which had perhaps remained vacant. The only difference was they were now sitting a bit apart, and the misty afternoon had given way after the rain to a bright evening light in which the roofs and the towers of the city seemed to glow with beauty. No one could have guessed that they had recently emerged from the shadows of a candlelit room and the darkness of an old house.

Before they reached her hostel, the girl looked at him for the first time, touched his hand, gave him his tram ticket, and said, 'Never try to see me again. Forget all that happened today.'

When the tram reached her station, she collected her bag, adjusted her scarf and got off. She walked along the tramlines for some distance, then turned into a brick building which was her hostel and where she had a room on the third floor.

When the tram reached the other terminal, he gave the conductor his ticket which still carried the warmth of her hand. After he got off the tram, he slowly walked towards the bridge which he used to cross every evening on his way back home after dropping her at her hostel. It was an ancient bridge and the red light of the setting sun was sparkling over the river that ran under it ... Absent-mindedly, he put his hand in the pocket and discovered that he still had the two tickets for the opera that evening. He felt that they belonged to another world. He started walking again, but stopped when he reached the end of the bridge. He watched the river, which was now partly lit by the setting sun and partly covered by the evening shadows, flowing peacefully under the bridge. Then, suddenly, in the confusion of light and shadow, he saw a face floating on the surface of the water, staring at him, gazing up at the place where he was standing, and he couldn't decide if it was the face of the Empress who had drowned at that same spot under the bridge three hundred years ago or of the woman he had seen in candlelight three hours past and who had saved them from drowning.

Krishna Sobti (b. 1925)

Krishna Sobti was born on 18 February 1925, in a part of Punjab which is now in Pakistan; she was brought up in New Delhi, where she still lives, although the ancestral *haveli* in Punjab in which she spent part of her chidlhood is an important constituent of her creative makeup. Like Qurratulain Hyder, she has never married, and devoted herself entirely to the written word. Sobti has said that she is 'a writer who happens to be a liberal, middle-class woman. I need to have my freedom so that my creative apparatus functions smoothly.' But she is a believer not so much in functioning smoothly as in unexpected evolutions; from her first novel, *Zindaginama*, with its chronicling of Partition and its recreation of a vanished ethos, to *Mitro Marjani*, where she experimented with the dialect of rural Punjab, to her later works, her fiction has been a polyphony of styles and subject matter, a sort of dialogue between different parts of herself. Dialogue, then, is both change and identity in Sobti; and it is as an interrogation of change and identity, the dissolution of age and the continuance of memory, that we might read the dialogue in the novella *Ai Ladki*, from which an extract is presented below. In the main part a conversation, a series of questions and answers that are both evasions and confessions, between a mother on a sickbed and her daughter, the restrained, elusive beauty of the piece had a considerable impact on the Hindi literary world when it first appeared. The imperiousness and plaintiveness of the cry that forms the title, which means, 'Hey, girl', capture perfectly the intermeshing of the contradictory emotions and realities crystallized in the narrative.

* * *

from *Ai Ladki* (1991)

translated from the Hindi by Shivnath

These extracts from the novella consist of its opening pages, and of the second half of the novella.

— Ai Ladki, why is it dark in here? Saving electricity? Has it come to that?

— All the lights are on, Ammi. Even the table lamp.

— So, you think that I see darkness where there is light, do you? No, no, I haven't taken leave of my senses yet. But yes, it is a different matter if you people can see silver snakes in the dark.

Why are you silent? Afraid of saying something? Even Susan can't see. What are you people afraid of?

— Ammu, relax. Aren't you suffering enough?

— You're right. But don't forget, I haven't let illness depress me. Otherwise, it would've sucked me dry by now.

Tell me, why are you looking away?

— Ammi!

— The door of my cage is already open. One knock and out I'll fly. But listen to me. I am holding on. Disease and sickness are great enemies of man — they can shatter the relationship between the mind and the body. Even one's own body has no odour. Medicines get into the blood and shrink the body to a dry reed. I don't know what's got into my head.

Ladki, this reeks of illness. All that I had, seems to have disappeared . . .

— Should I burn some incense?

— No. Have you taken leave of your senses? This is a patient's room. Not a prayer room. You may put some roses in the flower-vase; they are fragrant.

Where did I see so many red roses? Just can't seem to remember? I hope my brain cells aren't dead!

— Ammu, don't worry about all that. One sees flowers everywhere. It's not important to recall each and every place.

— The medicines are playing havoc inside. I'm confused. But tell me, what has come over you? Your voice doesn't have the same timbre. It is losing its mellowness.

– Ammu, would you like to drink something cold?

– You've change the topic! All right, go ahead. Anything will do – anything from the generosity of your heart!

Ai Ladki, listen to me, our roles have been reversed. You were my daughter, now you are my mother and I ... But forget it ... That patient of mine ...

– Who, Ammi!

– My doctor!

Ammi chuckles.

I can understand my illness, but he can't. The soul has to leave the body somehow or the other.

Dozes off.

Telephone rings.

Ammu, startled –

– Who called?

– Someone from Chacha's* house.

– Ai Ladki, be specific, your Chacha or mine?

– Chotey Chacha called.

– Oh! my Devar!† You should've put him on to me. Now he is more your Chacha than my Devar. You talk about him as if he's unrelated to me. I'm still alive and alert.

– Chacha asked about your health.

– I hope you are not exaggerating my illness to everybody! When I came here as a bride, he was very small. Maybe four or five years of age. Some mischievous girl placed him in my lap.

– Were you embarrassed?

– I was the bride, but he was just a child. My little Devar! I fondled and kissed him. It was a charmed moment. The girls and the elderly women collapsed with laughter. My lap was filled with gifts – coconuts, almonds, dried dates ...

It's enough to ask about an old person's health once a week. I'm going to be here for quite some time.

I've worked hard to toughen this body. It will take time to give in. Are you listening?

– Yes.

– Ladki, there is no place for old people either in someone's heart or in

---

*   Editor's note: paternal uncle.
†   Editor's note: husband's brother.

someone's house. And here am I, occupying an entire room. After I am gone, spread a carpet and play your music here.

– Ammu, why must you say such things?

– No. I'm just beating my wings in vain.

I am glad you have looked after me in my last days. As your mother, I had to suckle you and as my daughter you had to drink my milk.

Ladki, our relationship is not merely one of flesh-and-blood, but of the soul. Both are intertwined. I don't know why you turned out to be so different.

Where are you going? Why have you got up? Sit with me for a while.

Ammu begins to doze.

After a short nap –

– I dozed off. Your Nani's* face kept flickering before my eyes. I don't know how many years have passed since I dreamt of her. The same olive green dress and peeping through her odani, her breasts.

Ammu laughs.

I was wondering why I didn't suck a little more milk.

I was still young when my sister was born. I was entranced by the sight of my mother suckling her.

One day, Mother finally asked – hey you, why are you staring? When you were a baby, you too lay in my lap and sucked at my breast.

I asked – may I have it once more?

Ma didn't get annoyed. She touched my chin and said – Munniya, once a child stops drinking her mother's milk, she never does it again. Now it's your little sister's turn. Don't crave for it. That is the law of nature. You'll understand it all when you grow up.

Ladki, it seems as if it was only the other day! Mother was suckling my little sister!

With a child at one's breast, all the three worlds seem steeped in ambrosia! Yes, a mother has to eat nutritious food. The child sucks it all.

Suddenly glaring at her daughter –

How can you understand this miracle? Books can't tell you about it. One can't paint pictures by staring at walls! If that were possible, you would've created so much. No, Ladki, apples can't grow on semal trees!

Irritated, the daughter rises from the chair.

I am not trying to hurt you. Surely friends can talk freely.

– I don't say such things to anyone nor do I listen to them . . .

---

* Editor's note: grandmother.

— How can you? It is all blank. Vacuum. I don't see anything else. Do you?

The daughter leaves the room in a huff.

Ammi, to herself —

First, one makes things. Accumulates them. This is mine. That too is mine. Then slowly, the grip loosens. Everything begins to slip away,

The body is a cloth. Wear it and enter the world. Take it off and go to the other world. The other world – the world of others. Not one's own.

Who knows how many planets there are in this Universe! One for the living. Another for the dead. And one for people who are ill like me.

Susan, listen. Old age robs one of dignity. It's hard for anyone who enters it. Operations, doctors, medicines, injections, oxygen! The doctor probes the whole body – jabs hundreds of needles. What is left of this body now? Only my voice remains.

What is a patient supposed to do – lie in bed and stare at the ceiling or gaze at the past with closed eyes?

Sometimes it seems as if I have descended into a dungeon. I am haunted by shadows from the distant past.

Why be afraid of the past? Smoke always precedes fire!

Nature made the body to last for a hundred years! I was fine till I slipped and broke my leg!

Susan gives her the dose of medicine and turns down the light.

— Ammiji, sleep for a while.

— Susan, you have served me so well – how will I repay you? Sometimes I feel guilty.

Seeing her daughter looking into the room —

Come. Come in. Sit with me for a while.

Listen, I am walking through bushes and brambles. Have you seen that thorny bush on the hillside? It has sprung up in my head too.

— Ammi. This is the effect of the sleeping pills.

— Ladki, it seems as if it's raining dry leaves inside my head. Not water. But dry leaves.

Listen, Ladki, in the beginning parents hold their children's hands and teach them how to walk. But, when the parents grow old, they become the children of their children.

I understand your burden. Are you exhausted? Why don't you go out for a few days?

— No, not exhausted, Ammu! I feel caught, entangled.

— Ladki, you are worried about my illness. I know you well. Sorrow and happiness – neither suit you. Pray for an early break and release for your mother.

– Ammi, why must you think like that? Have courage and get well. Even the doctors admire your will power!

– You're right. As a child, I could fly. I was physically strong.

We all have a fire within. The body draws its energy from it. But both my doctors are determined to extinguish it.

After sleeping for a while –

You people have seen me only in my old age. Not as that girl who was about to be your mother. It happened so long ago! In another epoch. Yes, a different age.

Neither the sky nor the earth have an end. Only our race comes to an end.

Suddenly, self-conscious –

Ai Ladki, am I talking nonsense? Please stop me if I am.

The daughter makes a move to leave.

Don't go yet. Sit for a while. What is there in that room? Is there something? I must know. I want to know.

– No, there is nothing.

*

– Ladki, your mother looked beautiful as a bride. Seeing me, people felt a certain fondness for me.

How one decays with time! There is a time for going up the ladder. And there is a time for coming down. No one remains beautiful forever.

– Ammu, after marriage, how did you find your new family?

– Don't you flaunt your family. When I arrived, the fortunes of your family were already in decline.

There is no lack of pride and vanity. But there was a lot of humility and meekness also. The grandeur of the large mansion had faded, but it was there all the same. There was affluence and penury.

– Ammu, tell me about my father.

– Yes. Once families begin to decline, they continue to do so till they are completely ruined.

Your father was very calm by nature. Sober. I was a bit stern. But I was keen to learn and I did. I learnt a lot from him.

Ammu, suddenly excited –

You're making me talk and talk, but why?

Are you trying to distract me or amuse yourself?

Old age deprives one of all grace. Makes one graceless. Its darkness engulfs all human beings.

I'm a burden on all of you. Who needs such a long life!

My daughter's son died at the age of twenty-seven. Oh! How handsome, tall and well-formed! It was a terrible blow! There was no appeal, no protest against that – neither here, nor up there. He didn't die, he was murdered.

Ladki, just show me his photograph. I can see him standing before my eyes. You were needed here very much, son! Why were you snatched away? It was the day of your betrothal. Your fiancée, bedecked in her best, kept waiting. The engagement ring never reached her finger!

Ladki, there's someone else who makes us play a part in this lila.

And see what my other grandson, his elder brother, did. He followed the same road as if to challenge fate. He brought home the same girl as the promised daughter-in-law of the family.

They spared no effort to save you, Chitra. Your share of life was over! The game came to an end within a year. She couldn't see the one whom she brought forth!

Susan, put some drops in my eyes! I don't know why they are watering. My eyes have become old!

– Ammiji, will you have Horlicks with some chocolate in it or tea?

– Give me whatever you like. Has Didi left this room?

– She has gone to lie down for a while.

– Cover me with the double bedsheet.

– Double bedsheet? It is very hot, Ammiji!

– Do what I tell you to do. You don't know anything about the tune and the rhyme of this song! You stick to your own timetable. Give the medicine. Apply the bandage. Give the injection. Take the temperature. Ring up the doctor. Make the patient turn to one side.

Why are you smiling? Your records will go into the wastepaper basket! Everybody's record goes there.

– Ammiji, I'll go and get the Horlicks.

– No, no! You should attend to my head first. It feels hollow inside! Put some oil in my hair, Susan!

Susan applies oil to Ammi's hair. Ammi closes her eyes.

After a nap –

– Hasn't she got up! Is Didi still sleeping?

– Yes, Ammiji.

– My nails are bothering me. Cut them.

– Ammiji, I cut your nails only yesterday.

– You may have cut them, but do as I say. Just to please me.

Are your brothers married, Susan?

– Yes, both of them.

– Do you send money to your parents?

– Yes.

– Do you know a boy whom you want to marry? You've to find one yourself.

– No, Ammiji, not yet. I'll do a course in nursing first.

– Good idea, Susan. Stick to it. Don't drop it. You surely have a friend?

Susan smiles.

You don't spend too much on him, I hope?

– No, Ammiji.

– Listen to me. See that neither you nor he bears the entire expenses. You should share the expenses. Otherwise you'll find yourself being taken for a ride. You understand what I mean?

– Yes, Ammiji.

– Susan, after marriage, don't become a plaything in the hands of anyone. Try to be strong ... See who has come. Somebody has rung the door bell.

– No, Ammiji. There's nobody.

– Go and see again. It's time for Shobha Ram to come.

– Ammiji, he has been in the kitchen for quite some time.

– Go and find out if the kheer is ready. You remember we had decided to cook it in the morning.

– Ammiji, pranaam!

– May you live long.

– The kheer is ready. Will you taste it?

– Bring me some. Just two spoonfuls.

– Here it is, I have added some roasted nuts.

– You know that I still have my original teeth and they're strong.

– Ammiji, shall I make puaas in the evening?

– No, no. Even kheer is pretty heavy!

Someday I'll tell you what goes well with what. I have coped with all sorts of demands in this regard.

The daughter, standing close to her –

– Ammu, what's this talk about demands? Should be interesting. Please tell us.

– Shobha Ram, the kheer is very delicious. May you continue making delicious halwa, puri, pakodas, kheer, puaas for our delight. But, remember you have one more task to perform. Don't make any excuses. You have to take Amma up to that place.

The daughter, light-heartedly —

— What was that about demands?

— Nothing special. Squabbles over food and cooking. What else? Whenever there was a long argument on that subject, I had a solution. I would place the tea tray before your father — tea is waiting for you. Here is your cup. Please have it first.

Your father appreciated good tea. It would make him forget everything else.

— Ammu, did you really have many clashes with father?

— Perhaps. I don't remember all that now. Why are you provoking me? Is it necessary to know all that?

— Ammu, what's the harm in knowing?

— Ai Ladki, everyone's life passes through a series of encounters. In a family, the game is never amongst equals; it's between unequal players. The master of the house provides for the family; he grows in strength and authority. The children's mother is a hostage to his authority.

— Ammu!

— Yes, after marriage, a woman takes over the oars of a family. You have seen boats and gondolas floating on the lake. The family, seated in the boat, enjoys the boat ride, while the woman works at the oars. She rows the boat all her life.

Her situation improves only when she starts earning her own livelihood.

Think about it — when a man works, he gets money in return.

A woman toils day and night and earns nothing. She loses herself in love and attachment. Ignorant. Unmindful. If she doesn't look after herself, who is going to bother about her?

— Ammu, you are so enlightened!

— Keep quiet, girl. You are quick to pounce upon my words. Why? I know your trick. The journey is mine but you enjoy the scene!

Looking towards the window —

Change these heavy curtains. Let fresh air come in. Ladki, let me be quiet for some time. My own past is unfolding within me.

Ammu closes her eyes.

After some time, seeing her daughter seated in front —

You're stll sitting there! Tell me, girl, what are you doing in this world? Show me a single thing that you've earned in this life. What are your own achievements? On top of that you want to judge what I have done?

The daughter, getting up —

— I'm going to the other room.

— No, please sit down. Keep me company.

I'll tell you something which will interest you. I have very little time left. Tell me, where do you stand? At what turn? Do you have anyone waiting for you? You are not welcome in the family circles of your brother and sisters.

— Ammu, the same topic again?

— Ai Ladki, don't interrupt me. Let me say things clearly. See, I've a son and daughters, grandsons and granddaughters, a whole family and yet I'm alone.

And you? You're outside that time-worn tale in which there is a husband and yet I'm alone.

You may not have the support of a family structure, but you are independent.

Ladki, it's great to be independent, noble. If you also had to run a family, you would've realized by now that a family's glory rests on relationships.

A woman is either somebody's wife, daughter-in-law, mother, nani, or dadi. And again the same round of food, clothes, jewellery. Ladki, she is the mistress of the house only in name. When she is no longer of any use, she is shown her place.

The daughter, smiling —

— Ammu, you're unbeatable!

— If you think carefully, there's an answer to every question.

— Susan! Get some juice for Ammu and for me too.

— You are a girl in tune with your times. You are wasting your sap on something which is dry.

— Get something really cold. My throat is parched.

It was nice, Susan. My thirst is quenched. You should also have some.

Ladki, you have no idea how much tact a woman with a family has to develop and how much restraint she has to exercise!

You are free. No one restrains or controls you. You do as you please. Remember that one needs to be independent of one's own self too. Do you ever let yourself go? I'm not talking about wilfulness. Have you ever been able to do something that you really wanted to do?

— Ammu, what shall I say?

Long silence in the room.

— I ran this house with clockwork efficiency, but I did nothing worthwhile for my own fulfilment.

Now, I regret it very much.

The daughter, surprised —

— What is it that you wanted to do, Ammu?

— I wanted to climb mountains, stand on their summits, but how could I have done that and yet performed the daily chores of the home? Who would have listened to me? He couldn't even cope with the family problems. What's more, he was a stickler for punctuality, everything had to be on time. I was turned into a clock.

The daughter looks out of the window.

Susan starts folding the clothes.

Ammu snaps at her —

Why are you piling up those clothes, Susan? As though a new baby has arrived in the family.

This old woman is going to leave this world. The pile of old clothes . . .

The daughter gets up and puts on a record of sitar music.

Ammu listens to the music for some time with her eyes closed, and with a sense of wonder. Then in vexation —

Stop it. This noise is not good for me. Try to understand things. My veins have dried up. Music plays havoc with my body.

Why are there black spots before my eyes? Ask someone.

As Susan tries to cover her, Ammu, with a start —

Why are you people troubling me? Pull the curtains apart. Let some fresh air in. Hurry up. I'm feeling suffocated.

Why are you silent? Listen to me carefully. I'm not asking for the moon. I'm only demanding my rights. Give them to me. Let me breathe fresh air.

Susan draws the window curtains apart.

— Ammiji, the glare will come in from outside.

— This is a cave, a cave! Why have you closed me in? Open the doors. Who has bolted them? Call the girl who is playing these tricks on me! Call my daughter! Take me to the balcony. I won't stay in this room even for a moment.

— Susan, give Amma glucose. I shall make a bed for her to lie on in the balcony.

— Ai Ladki, don't put me off. You have to make me sit in a chair. I don't want to lie down. I won't lie down. I'll sit. Ladki, let me decide today.

— Ammu, any movement will open the sores.

— I don't need your sympathy — don't worry either about me or my sores. Do as I say.

Susan places an easy chair in the balcony and spreads a mattress and a bedsheet on it. Places a cushion for support. Then both of them lift Ammi and take her out.

Ammu, after being seated in the chair, excitedly –

What season is it now? The trees are still. Not a leaf moves. What month is it?

The daughter, not paying attention to what she has said, remains quiet, with her hands resting on the railing.

I asked you something. Answer me! It's not nice to ignore me.

– Ammi, it's the third week of May.

– Now there'll be dust storms. Look at the sky – its colour has turned dusty. It looks so alien. Has its strength been drained away by its grown-up children? It looks ancient.

Ladki, the sky appears to have aged.

Ammu raised her head and looks at the electric poles. Then keeping her eyes fixed on the trees below –

Neem trees have a longer span of life than the golden flesh-and-bone tree of man's life.

– Ammu, the neem trees are full of fresh leaves. The one outside your room has grown so tall!

– In this season, neem trees are full of fragrance. When they blossom, they give out a sweet smell. Their fragrance makes the daughters of the earth throb with desire.

– What then, Ammu?

– Then what, silly? They go to the ones they long for. Physical desires have their consequences!

Ladki, I feel like a fish out of water again. The blood in my body has dried. Terrible thirst! Give me some soda with ice cream and fetch one more chair. My son is about to come. He comes here straight from the office.

The daughter remains silent.

What is a woman, who can't supplant a son's mother, worth?

– Ammu, you too have passed through such a phase.

– Yes. I too must have. All women do.

– Is it necessary to do so?

– I think so. Only then can a woman put her stamp on the mind and body of her husband, possess him. She has to do it. Otherwise she can have no peace and comfort.

Ammu smiles.

Everyone's temperament is different. Some are more suspicious and some more trusting!

Men understand all this. The rule of family life is – give and take. The one who gives must also take.

Susan feeds Ammu ice cream with a spoon.

May you live long. I'm gratified.

Ammu, back in the room –

– This ice cream reminds me of pistachio kulfi. We had it at Chandpal Ghat.

– What was special about it, Ammu?

– The time and the place. That place took one's breath away. Sirens were screaming. Lights glimmered on the water. There were boats. The shores were full of festivities. There was a canopy of moonlight overhead. Stars twinkled. The moon was in full splendour. Ladki, the exuberance of life on earth and water was awesome. Who would like to leave this earth after such a vision? But one has to depart when it is time.

When I went to Calcutta, I visited a number of places. Ladki, one evening my elder daughter took me and her little granddaughter there!

Three lines of families got together. You can call them three generations. My daughter, the daughter of my grandson and I.

Ladki, children in families rejuvenate the old, elderly people. Thus, the elders first become aware of their own ages and then forget them. They lose themselves in children.

That evening, your sister acted as though she was the elder one and I, her mother, the younger.

On the other hand, her naughty granddaughter, an only child, gave the impression that her papa's nani was not only odd but also a child. She entreated me again and again – Nani-Amma, have one more ice cream. Let us share it – half-half . . .

There are occasions when off-shoots of families get together.

Wait daughter. I can see a vision . . .

– What's it, Ammu?

Ammu gives a toothless smile –

– A horse! Fleet-footed! Strong! You haven't done any horse riding. You've neither developed your capacity to rein in a horse nor known its vigour and speed.

Ladki, only the one who understands his own times is favoured by the gods.

Only the hand that earns, dispenses according to its wishes.

The daughter looks beyond the walls and closes her eyes.

If you are feeling bored, why don't you go out for a stroll?

– Ammu, I'm going out for a cup of coffee. Do you want me to bring back something? Pineapple pastry?

– Yes, I'll have some. Come back when you like. Don't worry about me. You'll fnd me here. I'll still be here.

Yes. If you go for a haircut, ask the hairdresser to come and trim my hair too. My hair feels heavy on my head. It weighs me down. A trim will give me relief. I find it difficult to manage my hair.

– Susan, keep the towels, shampoo, hair oil, everything ready. She won't have much time. If she comes before I return, get Mammu's hair trimmed. Ammu, is that all right?

– Yes.

Silence! Without my daughter!

Did you notice, Susan? After she left, the room has become cheerless.

– Ammiji, Didi loves you very much.

– She not only loves me but also understands me. There is a difference between the two. It is one thing to love, quite another to understand. She is always sensitive to the needs of others.

Susan, your Didi looks rather vexed. I don't know what is bothering her.

– Nothing, Ammiji, Didi gets tired.

– Will you be able to take care of her, after I'm gone? She needs a lot of rest. When she works, she forgets everything else. She is not afraid of hard work. It'll be good if you stay on. Susan, she has an austere exterior but she gives everyone his or her due.

Do me a favour, Susan. Go outside and see the colour of the sky. Are there any signs of rain?

Once it rains, I'll bathe in the open and be washed clean. My back is in bad shape, no doubt. Medicines, bandages and who knows what else!

– The sores appear to be healing, Ammiji.

– Don't try to fool me. You see the sores when you dress them. I can't see them. Still, I know better than you because I feel the pain.

Smiling –

One can't see one's own back. But I know its condition because I have to suffer.

Leave it. Tell me, if you have ever had a bath in a river. Cold and hot showers are nothing in comparison. I have bathed in a baoli, a river, a lake and in the sea. Profound pleasure! Immense joy! I bathed in the sea at Puri to my heart's content. It was my elder daughter who took me there.

– Ammiji, do you miss Badi Didi?

– Why shouldn't I? She is my first born.

– There were more boys in my in-laws' family. When she arrived, there was great rejoicing.

– And the youngest daughter, Ammiji?

– She is very intelligent. But once she gets annoyed, it is very difficult to bring her round. Parents pass on their qualities and eccentricities to their children. Children exhibit the characteristics that they acquire from the soil in which they grow, and the elements that go into their making.

Listening carefully –

I hear something. See if there's somebody at the door. Must be my son.

– Ammiji, there's nobody at the door.

– Go and see again . . . Maybe it's Prabha . . . My eldest daughter's eldest girl! She takes after her father. She manages her affairs efficiently.

Listen, Susan, you have seen Mira too, her younger sister. She is very elegant and charming. She often comes to meet me.

Now wipe my face with a cold towel. The neck too. Susan, this neck of mine has to carry the weight of my hair now.

The daughter, on returning –

– Ammu, you're looking better. Your hair has been well set.

– You have had an outing, that's why I look cheerful to you!

– No. Shorter hair suits you.

– I don't know why I didn't think of it before. If I had got my hair trimmed earlier, it would've given me some relief. It's so much lighter on the neck now.

Listen, formerly, at the time of marriage, the bride's hair used to be braided in such a way that it seemed as if all the world's constraints had been woven into her hair.

When I arrived at my in-laws' house, your father asked me at the very first opportunity – don't you find it bothersome to plait your hair like that? Your head must feel very heavy.

I said – I like a single braid, but this is according to custom.

Your father said – look there is no convention or custom that can't be changed in this family. You can certainly do whatever is comfortable and convenient and what pleases you.

– Ammu, how did you feel when you heard that?

– I liked it. It felt good. I thought I would be able to pull on well. Your father was soft and disciplined by nature. There were no unnecessary restrictions on me. But there was a certain family tradition and I had no freedom to modify it or tamper with it. The family upheld it strictly.

– Ammu, that was plain stubbornness!

– No, I'll call it discipline. Your Dadaji's sense of discipline and balance was amazing. Both father and son were alike in that. I learnt about equality after coming to this family. I observed that they didn't discriminate between boys and girls.

– And Ammu, in your parents' family? In our Nana's* family?

– Leave that out. There's no point in comparing the two.

– Tell me please, Ammu.

– There was no dearth of love and affection in your Nana's family, too. Plenty to eat and drink, plenty of time to play and dresses to wear. But even then, there was always a sharp line drawn between boys and girls.

During your Nana's terminal illness, we sisters used to take turns to be with him, but whenever he had to call someone, it was always his son. It made me very sad. I felt disheartened and wondered why there was such attachment to a son.

Ladki, at a time like this, one tends to lose track of things. Everything looks frayed.

What was I saying? Let me recollect. Our brother was sent to a college and we sisters were made to take lessons from a Granthi and a Maulvi.

Just imagine, what I would've become, if I had only studied like my brother. How I would have shaped and how my children would've developed! The fact is that girls are prepared for a life of drudgery.

Brother is studying. Go and give him milk.

Brother is sleeping. Go and cover him with the blanket.

Hurry up. Place the plate of food before your brother. He is hungry.

Your brother has eaten. Now you may also eat.

Ammu is quiet for some time.

Susan bends close to her.

– What's the matter, Ammiji?

Ammu, in a subdued voice –

– My eyes are smarting.

Something like smoke is spreading across them. See, what's happening?

The daughter goes to the kitchen and returns quickly.

– It seems someone is spreading a layer of fog over my eyes. I am not able to see anything clearly.

– Ammu, this will give some relief.

– What are you placing on my eyes?

– Mammu, these are pads of cream.

– Come close to me.

* Editor's note: maternal grandfather.

— Did you ever experience the sort of cool comfort you are giving to my eyes? Tell your mother honestly.

— No, Ammi.

There is silence in the room for some time.

Ammu, all of a sudden, unmindful of herself —

— When will it be a full moon night? When did the new moon appear? Tell me. I'm asking you.

The daughter, nonchalantly —

— Ammu, I don't know anything about the phases of the moon.

— That's why you're carrying this load on your shoulders. Throw it away. Hurl it far away. Don't allow your time to turn into dust. Pull yourself up. Things are on the decline.

The daughter gets up and leaves the room. Susan gives Ammi some glucose in water.

When I conceived this daughter of mine, I don't know why I felt so lost, so solitary in my heart and mind. A feeling of loneliness possessed my whole being. I wished to go on walking alone on dusty paths. I felt as if a tall pine tree was growing inside me. And it was indeed a tree that I gave birth to. It is swaying in the wind, just swaying. There is nothing in front of it. Don't consider this girl to be cold at all; there's fire in her veins. She keeps herself under control, I don't know how.

Susan, the bell is ringing. Someone has come. Must be my grandson and granddaughter.

— Ammiji, they have gone to their Nana and Nani's place.

— Yes, to cheer up their Nani. Since I'm about to leave this world, my son's mother-in-law must be feeling disconsolate. They've gone to comfort her. Susan, have you seen my grandson? He takes after his Dadaji. He sits and gets up like him, moves his hands like him, even in his preferences for food . . .

Ammi dozes off.

On opening her eyes, Ammu immediately looks all around the room.

Seeing her daughter standing near the bed.

Well, who are you? You are tense when you come in and you charge out like a bullet. I've seen your face somewhere. The spitting image of your father. Ladki, he wasn't arrogant. But, you are conceited. That's why you never shared anything with anyone.

The daughter tiptoes out of the room.

Susan, there is a piggy bank lying on the top of the cupboard. It is my granddaughter's. Don't move it from there.

I've hung a hunk of silam yarn on the peg. I'm making a doll for my granddaughter. I'll make the doll's hair with it. See that you don't tangle it.

Why are the shutters of the windows banging against each other? Whose anchal is fluttering there again and again? Oh! it is my odani. Catch it. Otherwise it will be blown away by the storm.

Susan goes out and returns with Didi.

Both of them bend over Ammu.

– She has gone to sleep. She is in deep sleep.

– Susan, you rest for a while. I'll sit here.

Ammi, on waking up, in a sharp voice –

– Susan, where are you? Change my bedsheets. They are wet.

Susan cleans up Ammi and changes the bedsheets.

After a long deep sleep, Ammu wakes with a start.

– Do you hear the sound of the train? The station is quite some distance away, but the screeching sound of the engine reaches this far. It pierces deep into me.

The daughter fondles Ammi's hair.

When your father was preparing for his departure, he used to sit up, startled by the four o'clock train.

I used to observe him silently. I never questioned him about anything. What was there to ask?

One night, he sat up on hearing the vibrations, and resting his elbow against the pillow, bent towards me – Can you hear that sound? It terrifies me!

I kept quiet. What could I say?

When the journey's end is near, one doesn't know what pulls at the heart-strings.

Clusters of past pleasures make one look back while the soul pushes towards the infinite. Back again.

The daughter feels her mother's pulse on the pretext of adjusting the covering sheet.

Ammu, gently –

This old woman is faring well. Go and take some rest.

The daughter, in order to avoid embarrassment –

– Ammu, I'm going to prepare coffee for myself. Shall I get a cup for you too?

– No. If you wish, you may bring me some fresh fruit.

– Mango or plum?

– Let it be a mango. Its very name spells deliciousness.

Ladki, your elder sister cuts fruit with the finesse of a machine. She cuts a mango into two halves; taps them with the point of a knife and puts cream over them. It's as much a delight for the eyes as for the heart.

– Ammu, she must've learnt it from you.

– No. This ability to cut with finesse is characteristic of your family only. Not of mine.

The daughter, smiling –

– Ammi, what's all this talk about my family and your family?

– Why? What's surprising about it? After marriage, when a woman strikes roots in her new home, she buries the days at her mother's in the backyard of her mind.

Look at me, I'm recollecting those days today after spending a whole lifetime.

– Ammu, there's no fear of a clash now. Then, how did this thought of comparison arise in your mind?

– Don't be naive. Where was the time to think or speak about it? Now, lying here, I can see clearly the colours of the two, distinct from each other.

– Which side looks better, Ammu?

– Don't you boast, girl! My family wasn't less gifted.

– You come from the same branch. You kept all of us under firm control!

– No, your family doesn't mingle with anyone. It swallows up the qualities of everyone.

– Ammu, don't say that. This family has been dancing to your tune for a long time.

– Everything in your family, the pleasant and the unpleasant, is confused, scattered. I don't know what your family thinks and does. It is too absorbed in itself.

– Ammu, do you find all of us like that?

– What else? Look at what you are. You were always like that. My parents' relatives did not give themselves airs the way you do. In your family, everyone thinks no end of himself or herself.

– Ammu, why are you saying all this?

– Let me talk. I'm not coming back again to tell you all this.

The beating and pounding that a woman endures after she becomes a housewife, are not less than the upheavals of an earthquake. A woman is able to stand them because she has to.

– Ammu, if you were to come to this family again, how would you like it?

Ammu first scowls at her daughter and then begins to laugh –

– Well, I'm the old woman of this family. If someone does ask me before sending me to this world, I'll come back only to this family. Your ancestors have accumulated a rich tradition in this house. This is my own family, why should I knock at somebody else's door?

The daughter restrains herself with some effort and kisses her mother's forehead.

I've lived in this world for years and years. But during these last few days, it has occurred to me repeatedly that if I had known I was going to live for so long, I would have done something worthwhile. Seen this wide world. But I spent my days enmeshed in family responsibilities.

– Ammu, you've done so much; you've created a whole family.

– Ai Ladki, don't exaggerate. I'm your mother, no doubt, but I'm different from you. I'm not you and you're not me.

– Ammi, why don't you listen to me?

Ammu, irritated –

– No. Keep quiet. Your show of concern will not do me any good now. Children swallow up all the time allotted to their mothers.

– Ammu, surely you must get some satisfaction – happiness from someone at least?

– I'm not talking of that. Mother produces. Nurtures with love and care. Then why is she alone sacrificed? The family divides her into fragments and scatters her here and there. Why? So that she may not remain whole, spring back in one piece. A family keeps a mother like a cow or a nurse. She should go on working, catering to the comforts of its members; is that all she is good for? She can conjure any image she wants of herself, but for her children she is no more than a housekeeper.

Susan switches off the table lamp behind Ammi's head and Ammi shuts her eyes.

Midnight. Ammi, on waking –

– Susan, what time is it? Is it dusk or dawn?

– It is two o'clock at night, Ammiji.

– This night doesn't seem to end! Yes. Do something about my throat. I don't know what has happened. I have nothing to do. I lie here and my memory leaps back across time. Talks about the days gone by like a speeding train.

Susan gives Ammu some water to drink.

See if there is some misri lying around.

– I'll get it Ammiji.

– The human body has been formed and structured to last a hundred years. I was doing all right. Had I not fractured my bone, I would have been fit.

– What's this Ammiji? You've undone the bandage again.

– Yes, I've opened it. I've only untied what was tied.

Susan helps Ammi turn on one side, wipes the sores and starts applying the dressing again.

– Susan, listen to me. Let it remain unbandaged.

– Ammiji, the sores will get lacerated. They'll start oozing pus.

– Don't talk rubbish! – I know how much it hurts. I'm not wearing armour; I'm sprawled on a bed of arrows.

Susan, has the pick-up van passed by?

– What pick-up van, Ammiji?

– Susan, you're not doing your duty properly. You have become careless. You've been in this house for months, and you don't even know when the pick-up van comes and goes.

– Ammiji, the station is far from here.

– I'm not speaking about the station. The pick-up van which comes from the depot to pick up the empty milk bottles and then returns to deliver bottles of fresh milk.

Susan picks up the thermos.

– Ammiji, milk or Complan?

– Nothing. I don't need anything. You take me to Didi's room.

– I'll go and ask Didi.

– Ask Didi? Why? That room is also part of my house. Don't let me feel I am handicapped. First take me to the small room so that I can offer my prayers. Then to Didi!

Susan picks up Ammi in her arms.

The daughter raises her head on hearing the sound of footsteps –

– Susan – what're you up to?

Ammu here? At this time?

– Yes, haven't you gone to sleep yet?

Ladki, is there any harm if I lie down in your room and talk to you?

– No, Ammu.

The daughter places a cushion on the divan.

– Susan, carefully, here . . . it's all right. Ammu.

– Yes!

Have you started anything new?

– No, Ammu, an old piece was lying unfinished. I thought I would look at it.

– Now, stop thinking about too many things. Complete whatever you have in hand. Ladki, life is transient. Remember, do not consider this work any less important.

Ladki, this is also creation. Not inferior to the other. Life-forces have a thousand channels. They may spring from anywhere and flow in any direction.

Ammi, after a moment –

It seemed to me as I lay there, and just as day and night get separated from each other, mother and daughter also drift apart. I kept looking around to make sure that I was in the same room. In my own room. In this very world. Then I thought, why shouldn't I go and see my daughter? So I came. Susan was not inclined to . . .

Ammu smiles –

The greatest blessing is to be able to do what one wants. Don't miss your mother too much. Go out for a few days. You're exhausted.

After a long silence –

– Will you retain Susan?

– No, Ammu.

– And the cook?

– He'll also have to go.

– Can't you keep at least one of them?

– It'll be difficult.

– If you've vegetables, milk, curd and cheese in the refrigerator, you can manage on your own somehow. Doing your own cooking and serving is refreshing in a way.

– Yes.

– You must think of the future? It is already too late, Ladki. How will you manage alone?

– Somehow, Ammu.

Ammu, perplexed –

– If you are really determined, there's nothing that you can't do. There's nothing so small or so big that you can't manage.

The daughter keeps looking at her mother.

Don't try to go against your grain.

– Ammu, if you have something important in mind, please tell me.

– No one will get jewellery, gold, cows, horses and fields from me. Only advice.

Ladki, the headship of a family does not pass to a daughter. According to the sacred texts, your brother alone will wear the turban. And the family flag will pass into the hands of the daughter-in-law.

The key of the locker is in my cupboard. You'll find it in a round box on the upper shelf. Ladki, I had gold in kilos, now you'll find it only in grams. Whenever the need arose, it got used up. You know . . .

I have prepared a will in my own hand. Show it to your brother and sisters.

The daughter-in-law has a locker of her own. Whatever belongs to her, is already with her. At the time of my departure, if her mother-in-law's gift does not reach her, I shall ask Bhavani to forgive me.

Families don't really possess all that they appear to have, to outsiders. What belongs to whom, why and how much – the same old story! The subject of gossip among relatives!

Don't argue with anyone. All the others are complete units in themselves, only you are outside every circle. Ladki, you are bound to find yourself alone.

The daughter lights a cigarette.

With a smile –

– Ammu, would you like a smoke?

– Yes, but you'll have to raise my head with the help of the pillow.

– No problem.

Ammu, relishing a smoke –

– If your heart tells you to do something, you must go ahead and do it. It was good that I came over here. If I hadn't, I would've continued to wander in the same murkiness.

The daughter, light-heartedly –

– Ammu, it was really difficult to lift you off the bed. Susan wasn't wrong.

– Ladki, I just wanted to move from one room to another! I can't come back from the other world to see you even if I want to! Can I?

– No, Ammu.

– Several moments are entangled in this smoke. Ladki, may I ask you something?

– Yes, Ammi.

– Whose flat is this?

– Ammu, in my absence, it is yours!

– In that case, I give it to you.

Both laugh together–

Ammu in a strange, changed voice –

— If you ask me, it's not a matter for laughter but for tears.

— Ammu, it's not such a big issue that one should turn laughter into wailing.

— It's not so small either that one shouldn't think about it. I see myself in you. The picture is more or less the same, although your temperament is more like that of your father's family.

— Ammu, is that a virtue or a flaw?

— Ladki, it's neither a virtue nor a flaw.

— You've put a seal of ambiguity on it. That doesn't prove anything.

— Ladki, what will you establish by travelling alone? When you live with someone, something remains, something is washed away. If you live alone, nothing remains, nothing is washed away.

Are you listening?

— Yes, Mammu.

— Ladki, a field of action surrounds a family. There a woman realizes herself and perceives others. When she becomes a mother, she lives through past, present and future. Since you are not attached to a family, you live only for yourself.

— What about the others, Ammu?

— They're busy feathering their own nests.

Ladki, what you have done for this family doesn't bring you any compensation. Only your mother's blessings.

Susan, peeping through the door —

— Shall we take Ammi to the other room?

— Susan, let Ammu remain here for some time. And, yes, get some cold water, ice, a lemon and two glasses. Take some rest. I'll wake you up if I need you.

Susan places a tray on the table.

— Ladki, your room looks full.

— Ammu, because of your presence here.

The daughter squeezes the lemon into the two glasses, adds ice and fills them up with water.

Ammi looks on fixedly.

The daughter places a cushion on the pillow and provides support to her mother.

— Ammu, will you be able to hold the glass?

— Yes, I'll hold it.

— Ammu, Cheers!

Ammu shakes her head.

Taking a sip —

– Ladki, somewhere, sometime, we'll meet again. We'll recognize each other. Even in such a wide world. You can be sure of that. No matter where the mother is and where the daughter is, and no matter who the mother is and who the daughter is – mother and daughter will always remain mother and daughter till the end of time.

The daughter restrains her tears and continues to look at her mother. Then she fixes her gaze on the glass; empties it in one gulp; refills it.

Next morning.
Ammu is lying quietly. In no mood to talk. She removes the bangles from her wrist and pushes them under the pillow. Bundles up the sheet covering her and throws it on the floor. Removes the pillow from under her head and keeps it aside. Tosses the cushion towards the door. In an attempt to pull out the bedsheet under her, she tosses her head right and left.

Susan, on entering the room –
– Ammiji, what are you doing?
– You can see what I'm doing.
– Ammiji, you shouldn't do it.
– One has to do it when it becomes necessary.
– I'll change the bedsheets, Ammiji.
Ammu starts taking her bandages off, quietly. Throws the cotton, gauze and bandages into the pan.
Susan goes and calls Didi.
The daughter, drawing near, in a gentle tone –
– Ammu, well, what are you doing?
– You know what I am doing!
– By pulling the bandages off like this, the sores will start oozing. Are you feeling hot?
– No, I'm feeling cold.
The daughter switches off the cooler.
Ammu, angrily –
– Hot or cold, whatever it is, now remove everything from here and put it outside.
Ammu tries to remove the chain from her neck.
Remove it. I don't need it. Now I don't need anything.
The daughter, lovingly –
– Ammu, not like this.
Ammu keeps staring with eyes opened wide.
Ammu, anything you wish to have . . . ?
Ammu, sharply –

– Quiet!

– Ammu, what is bothering you? Please tell me. Do tell me.

Ammu keeps looking towards the door for a long time.

Then she signals to her daughter to come near her and says, as though whispering in her ears –

– Remove my body in the same way as I have removed the bedsheet covering me. Fling my body away from me. I can't bear it any more.

The daughter continues to bend over her mother, alert, silent.

Do not keep my clothes in the house. Throw all of them out. Somewhere far away. So that you don't see them.

The daughter, in a flash, as though she has instinctively caught something from the inner recesses of her mother's mind, in a controlled voice –

– Things will be done according to your wishes. But I, too, have to say something and you must listen to me. I will not give your clothes to anyone. I'll wear them.

Ammu, did you hear me?

In this matter, even if you order me, I will not listen to you.

The tension on Ammu's face dissolves and she buries her face in the pillow.

The next morning, Ammu appears alert.

– Susan, you are dragging your feet today. Didn't you sleep well last night?

– I slept well, Ammiji.

– Was I feigning sleep then? Susan, you sleep only if your patient sleeps. If the patient remains awake, you also have to keep awake.

Susan smiles.

Listen to me, Susan. Come close.

The papers have been signed.

Now it's time to get ready.

The documents are all ready.

Susan, just go and peep outside.

Can you see any patch of cloud in the sky?

Susan goes out and returns from the balcony.

– Ammiji, the sky is absolutely clear. No cloud. There is bright sunshine.

– Well, prepare my bath. Today, I will not get my body sponged. I'll have my bath in the bathroom under the shower.

– Ammiji, shouldn't we first consult the doctor on the telephone?

– No. His advice is limited to medication. His task is over. He is not the doctor of my body any more.

Susan, there is the Chief Doctor, high above these doctors. When the time comes, instead of collecting fees, he collects the whole human being.

— Ammiji, let me wake up Didi.

— Let her catch some sleep. A big task awaits her. It'll be good if she can have some rest.

Bring me the soap you are going to use and show it to me.

— Here it is, Ammiji.

— No. Not this. There's a box in my cabinet, take out a cake from it. That soap doesn't make the skin dry. It's specially meant for children.

The daughter stands close by and looks on anxiously.

— Ammu, why not have some breakfast before you take your bath?

— As you please. What are you going to give me for breakfast today?

— Whatever you like. Mango juice, toast, egg, parathas, yogurt, butter . . .

Ammu smiles —

— You're fattening me before sending me up? What hard labour awaits me there? Ladki, it's only in this world, here, that one can use one's hands to create beauty and order. Up there, people don't have separate individual hearths. Nor does a fire kindle in one's body. Who has seen Heaven with his own eyes? Places of pilgrimage for the living all lie here, in this world. Nowhere else.

Night.

Ammu, in unconscious sleep, fearfully —

— What has happened to you people? Both of you are sleeping unmindful of me. Get up and attend to me.

The daughter bends close to her —

— Ammu, what's the matter?

— Crows are making such a lot of noise — caw-caw-caw . . . I can't bear the beating of their wings. Scare them away. Drive them far away. Beyond my hearing.

The daughter opens the window and makes noises as though driving away the crows. Then she closes the window and by way of reassuring her mother —

— Ammu, go to sleep now. All of them have flown away.

— Who, daughter?

— Pigeons, Ammu.

— Were they only pigeons?

— Yes.

— There must be a cat lurking outside to pounce on them.

— No, Ammu, there's nothing outside.

– You don't know, daughter. There is a lion crouching there. He will eat them up.

Susan spoons water into Ammu's mouth.

Who has placed the earthen lamp under the tree? There is a wind blowing. The lamp will be extinguished.

There are cracks in my body. See, my limbs are falling apart.

Who's this man with a bright blue face? Has he come to fetch me?

Call my son quickly . . .

Come close to me, son . . . bid me farewell.

Susan, why is it so dark? Don't remove the ladder from under my feet. I'll climb the ladder myself.

Bring me my white shoes.

I have to go up to Mashobra.

Ladki, tell your father to wait for me. I'm coming.

Why are we going via Kali-bari? They must be sacrificing goats and buffaloes there.

Away, away . . .

A copper-coloured monster is after me.

How can I slip past her?

She'll lift me by her horns.

Where are these clouds of darkness coming from?

Why are you covering me?

Don't touch my eyes.

Ladki, call your brother.

Call him quickly.

He will untether my horse.

I'll ride it across the sea!

The daughter, touching her mother's hand –

– Ammu, pour water over your head and bathe. Everything will be all right.

A deep sigh, a shudder and then there is silence in the room.

URDU

Sadat Hasan Manto (1912–55)

Sadat Hasan Manto was born on 11 May 1912 in Jalandhar, and grew up in Amritsar. For many years he lived in Bombay, writing stories, working in and around the Hindi film industry, both as a journalist and as a script-writer for not a few notable films. He was also, by then, one of the most remarkable short story writers in the Urdu language; but, in their melancholy and humour, his stories went against the robust programme of the Progressive Writers Movement that dominated the Urdu cultural ethos at the time, and which demanded from the writer an explicit form of social engagement. However, the company Manto kept was eclectic: it comprised not only poets and writers, but also actors, film directors, and prostitutes. Manto himself was a writer who was more comfortable wearing masks and planning subterfuges, so that we never know quite who, or where, he is; it is no accident, then, that both stories below, while dealing with the pressure of human emotion, are also about deceit, dissimulation, and absences. And it is no surprise, too, that the brutal clarity Partition forced upon this man who liked most to be in between things – between professions in life, and personae and voices in his stories – should prove to be traumatic. After leaving his beloved Bombay for Pakistan, he was miserable for the last eight years of his life, but also wrote some of his most powerful stories about Partition before his death in 1955. But it is also the vitality that Bombay, or an idea of Bombay, with its perpetual air of Mediterranean sanguinity, imparts to some of his stories that gives them, in spite of their dark echoes, their special bubbliness – and foreshadows how that city, with its films, magazines, low-life, and magnates, will provide metaphors for life and continuance to other, later writers in other languages.

* * *

'Peerun' (1950)

translated from the Urdu by Tahira Naqvi

The events surrounding my story took place at a time when I was impoverished and living in Bombay in dingy accommodations where there was neither water nor electricity. The place was filthy, infested with flying bugs that rained from the ceiling, and rats so big they scared away the cats. And I was paying nine rupees for this place.

The latch on the door of the only bathroom in the building was broken. Early in the morning the women gathered here to fill their earthen pots and buckets with water. Jewish, Marathi, Gujarati, Christian – all kinds of women came.

It was my custom to take a bath before the women assembled. One morning I overslept and arrived at the bathroom a little later than usual. I had barely begun my ablutions when the door opened suddenly and in walked a woman whom I recognized as my neighbour. Her arm clasped about her water pot, she stared at me for a few seconds for some reason and then dropped her pot and fled as if being pursued by a lion. I burst into laughter, shut the door and resumed my bathing.

After a short while the door opened again and my room-mate, Brij Mohan, came in. Having already completed my bath I was dressing.

'Listen Manto,' he said, 'it's Sunday today.'

I remembered that Brij Mohan had to go to Bandra to meet Peerun. Peerun was a homely-looking woman with whom Brij Mohan had been involved for nearly three years. Every Sunday he borrowed eight annas from me for the train fare and went to Peerun's house where the two chatted for half an hour or so. Then Brij Mohan gave her the answers to the crossword puzzle from the *Illustrated Weekly* and left. He used to spend most of his time, of which he had plenty because he was unemployed, poring over the crossword puzzle for her. Peerun often won small sums of money as prizes for these, but Brij Mohan never demanded a single paisa from her.

Brij Mohan had innumerable photographs of Peerun. There must be at least a hundred of them showing Peerun dressed in a trouser and tunic, tight paijama, sari, swimsuit and fancy dresses. Peerun was not beautiful.

As a matter of fact she was really quite plain, but I never voiced that opinion openly. I had never asked Brij Mohan about her – where she lived, who she was and what she did, how the two of them met, when their romance began, and if he intended to marry her. Brij Mohan had also never volunteered any information regarding his association with her. All he did was borrow eight annas from me after breakfast on Sunday mornings, leave for Bandra and return in the afternoon.

We went up to the room, I gave him the money and he left. When he came back in the afternoon he told me it was all over. This was an unusual communication since he had not taken me into confidence before.

'What's all over?' I asked, not quite sure what he was referring to.

'Well, Peerun and I came to an agreement today,' he answered in a tone that indicated a great burden had been lifted from his chest. 'I told her that while I was seeing her I had failed to find work and that she was bad luck for me. She said I was a good-for-nothing guy and if she was bad luck I was just pure sloth. So it's all over and I'm sure I'll get a job tomorrow, God willing. You must lend me four annas in the morning and I'll go and see Seth Nanoo Bhai. He is sure to employ me as his assistant.'

Seth Nanoo Bhai, who was a film director, had refused to give Brij Mohan work several times in the past and like Peerun he believed that the man was lazy and incompetent. But when Brij Mohan returned the next afternoon he imparted the good news that he had been hired by Seth Nanoo on a one-year contract and had been given a hundred rupees in advance.

'Here's the hundred rupees,' he said, showing me the money. 'Do you know what I want to do? I want to go to Bandra this minute and tell Peerun I have a job. But I'm afraid if I do that I will lose the job. It has happened before. I found work, went to Peerun, and for some reason or another I was thrown out of the job. God alone knows why this girl is such bad luck for me. Well, I'm not going to see her face for a whole year. I have very few clothes left and I plan to replenish my wardrobe. When I have sufficient clothes I will think of what I should do next.'

Six months passed. Brij Mohan went to work regularly and now possessed a decent supply of clothing. He also had a dozen handkerchiefs and now owned all the things that a bachelor requires for comfortable living.

One morning a letter arrived for him in the mail. He was at the studio and when he came home in the afternoon I had forgotten the letter. Early next morning I remembered it as we were having breakfast. He became agitated when he saw the envelope.

'Damn!' he shouted.

'What's the matter?' I asked.

'Peerun,' he mumbled angrily as he opened the envelope with the handle of his spoon. 'Life is going on so smoothly and she has to come barging in.'

He now had the letter in his hand.

'Yes, it's Peerun, I can never forget her handwriting.'

'What does she say?'

'Rubbish, what else? She wants me to meet her next Sunday. Well, Manto, God willing, I will be turned out of my job now.'

'Don't be ridiculous,' I said.

'No, Manto, you'll see,' he reiterated with great conviction. 'Tomorrow it's Sunday, but the day after that Seth Nanoo will find something wrong with the way I'm doing my work and I'll be fired.'

'But if you are so sure that a meeting with her will deprive you of your job then just don't go to see her,' I suggested.

'That's impossible. I have to go when she sends for me.'

'Why?'

'Actually I'm tired of working. It's been more than six months, you know.' He smiled and left.

The next morning he went to Bandra after breakfast, but on his return he didn't volunteer any information about his meeting with Peerun.

'Well, did you meet your star of ill fortune?' I asked him.

'Yes, and I told her I would be out of work soon,' he said, getting up from the floor mat.

'Let's eat.'

We ate at Raj's hotel and there was no conversation about Peerun during the course of the meal. Just before retiring that night he said:

'Let's see what happens now.'

I did not believe that he would lose the job. But the next afternoon he returned from work earlier than usual and when he saw me he burst into laughter.

'Well, I've been fired,' he admitted with a grin.

'Come, you're not serious.' I was certain that he was joking.

'Seth Nanoo Bhai has fallen on hard times and it's all my fault,' he said, continuing to smile. 'His studio has been sealed.'

He laughed again.

'This is all very strange,' was all I could come up with.

'Well, I didn't make it up,' he said, and slinging his camera over his shoulder, he left for a walk in the park.

Brij Mohan was unemployed once again. His savings were depleted in a short time and he began borrowing eight annas from me every Sunday so that he could go and see Peerun. I still didn't know what he and Peerun talked about in just half an hour although I was well aware of Brij Mohan's abilities as a good conversationalist. Nevertheless, I couldn't figure out what he said to a woman who represented bad luck to him. One day I asked him if Peerun was also in love with him.

'No,' he answered. 'She's in love with another man.'

'Why does she see you then?' I enquired.

'Because I'm intelligent, because I transform her ugliness into beauty in the photographs I take of her, and because I solve crossword puzzles for her. Manto, you don't know women the way I know them. Peerun looks for and finds in me what she misses in her boyfriend. She's a clever woman.' Brij Mohan was smiling.

'But why do you go to her?' I asked, somewhat perturbed by his logic.

Brij Mohan burst into a laugh.

'I enjoy it,' he explained, his eyes squinting behind his glasses.

'Enjoy what?' I still failed to grasp his meaning.

'Enjoy her being unlucky for me,' he said. 'I'm testing her, I've been testing her for a long time and so far she has passed all the tests. But now I want to beat that ill fortune. It is my wish that I approach my boss before he dismisses me and tell him I'm leaving. Then I would like to say that it was not he who was responsible for driving me out of my job but Peerun whose nose enters the camera like an arrow!' Brij Mohan was grinning broadly. 'This is just a small wish of mine,' he added. 'We'll see if it comes true.'

'What a strange wish,' I said.

'Well, I do strange things,' he declared. 'Just last week I took a photograph of Peerun specially for her boyfriend. He's going to submit the picture in a contest and will undoubtedly win a prize for it.' The smile never left his face.

Brij Mohan was a strange man indeed. He photographed Peerun several times for her boyfriend, who sent the photographs to the *Illustrated Weekly* where they appeared with his name. It amused Brij Mohan to see these pictures. He had never seen his rival. But Peerun had told him that he was extremely good looking and worked in a factory.

Then one afternoon Brij Mohan returned from Bandra and told me everything was over.

'Peerun, you mean?' I asked.

'Yes. I'm running short on clothes and I've decided to work again. Something should turn up soon, God willing. I think I'll see Seth Niaz Ali tomorrow, he's planning to produce a new film. Find out his address for me, will you.'

I located the new phone number and Brij Mohan paid him a visit. Later that day he returned beaming and threw some typewritten sheets in my lap.

'Here's a contract for a film,' he said. 'Right now it is only two hundred rupees a month, but Seth Niaz Ali has promised to increase my pay soon. Well, what do you think?'

I laughed.

'When are you going to see Peerun again?' I ventured to ask.

'I've been thinking of that too,' he replied with a grin. 'Manto, my friend, remember I told you I had a small wish? Well, I don't think I'll be hasty. I need some new clothes. I have fifty rupees, here, you keep twenty-five.'

With the twenty-five we paid the hotel-wallah's bill and things began to look up for us. My one hundred a month coupled with Brij Mohan's two hundred brought luxury into our lives. We continued thus for five months.

Then, quite suddenly and without warning, a letter from Peerun appeared, leaving us both a little shaken. An unnamed fear arose at the back of my mind, but Brij Mohan began smiling as he read the letter.

'What does she say?' I asked sarcastically.

'She says she wants me to come and see her this Sunday. It's very important, she says.'

'So, you're going then?'

'I have to go,' he said, stuffing the letter into his pocket. He began humming a line from a film song.

'*Forget not traveller, you have to go one day.*'

'Please don't go, Brij,' I pleaded. 'We're living a good life. You don't know how difficult it was for me to give you the eight annas for the train fare.'

'I know, but I'm sorry to inform you that those days are about to make a comeback, the days when you gave me the eight annas with such difficulty.' A relaxed smile hovered over his face.

That Sunday Brij went to see Peerun. When he returned he said:

'I told her I would be losing a job for the twelfth time because of her and I also cursed her.'

'What was her reaction to your remarks?' I asked.

'She said, "You silly idiot."'

'Are you a silly idiot then?'

'Absolutely!' Brij exclaimed happily. 'Now tomorrow I'm presenting my resignation. I wrote the letter at Peerun's house.'

The next morning he left early for work. But he came home in the evening with a long face. He would not talk to me or tell me anything. Finally I approached him myself.

'Well, what happened, Brij?'

'Nothing, friend,' he said, shaking his head dejectedly. 'It's all over.'

'What do you mean?'

'I handed my letter of resignation to Seth Niaz Ali and he gave me an official letter which stated that my salary had been increased to three hundred a month.'

One day he said sadly, 'Peerun's gone along with her bad luck. And one of my most interesting activities has come to an end. What excuse will I now have to stay out of work?'

* * *

'The Black Shalwar' (1942)

translated from the Urdu by Tahira Naqvi

Before she came to Delhi she was living in Ambala Cantonment where most of her clients were British soldiers, *goras*. Because of her association with these men she had succeeded in picking up a smattering of English which she did not use in the normal course of conversation. However, when she arrived in Delhi and her business failed to pick up, she was forced to exclaim in English to her friend Tamancha Jaan, 'This life, very bad,' and added in Urdu 'that is, this life is terrible. One doesn't have enough to eat!'

She had a flourishing business in Ambala. The British soldiers from the cantonment came to her quite drunk, and she was able to entertain eight or ten of them in about four hours, easily making thirty rupees or more in that time.

These soldiers were better than Sultana's own countrymen. It was true they spoke a language she didn't understand much, but her ignorance worked in her favour. If the men wanted a reduction in her fees she simply shook her head and said, 'Sahib, I don't understand what you're saying.' And if one of them attempted to take too many liberties with her, she would swear at him in Urdu. When he stared at her in stupefaction she would say, 'Sahib, you're a son of a bitch, a bastard – understand?'

assuming a sugary tone all the while. The soldier laughed as she continued to curse him. He's an idiot, Sultana would tell herself.

But since her arrival in Delhi she had not seen a single white client. She had been in this well-known city for over three months without having encountered any of those great sahibs who lived here and travelled to Simla for the summer. So far she had had only six customers and that in two months. And all she had been able to make was a meagre sum of eighteen rupees and eight annas. None of the men wanted to pay more than three rupees. Of the six, the first five had been firmly informed, at the outset, that her rate was ten rupees. They refused to give her more than three. She was surprised they considered her worth so little. When the sixth client arrived, she told him, quite emphatically, that she would not accept anything less than three rupees for each time.

'I won't take a paisa less,' she reiterated. 'If you're ready to give me three, you can stay, if not, you may go. It's up to you.'

The sixth client didn't argue and stayed. When he was in the other room taking off his coat, Sultana asked him for a rupee for milk. He didn't give her the rupee, but handed her the King's new eight-anna coin instead. Sultana took it without a word of protest, telling herself she ought to be grateful for whatever she received.

Eighteen rupees and eight annas in three months – the rent for the *kotha* alone was twenty rupees. The landlord referred to the place as a 'flat'. Her toilet had a chain which, when pulled, created pressure in the water and caused all the filth to disappear instantly and noisily into an underground pipe. When Sultana used the bathroom for the first time she had been suffering from a gruelling backache. After she was done she decided to hang on to the chain for support as she was getting up from the toilet. She had supposed that since the flats had been specially designed for people like herself, the chains had been installed so they could be used for support. But the moment she grabbed the chain, there was a gurgling sound followed by a sudden onrush of water under her, and, frightened out of her wits, she screamed loudly.

Khuda Baksh had been putting away his photographic gear and was at the time pouring some hydrochloride into a clean bottle. He came out immediately when he heard Sultana scream.

'What's the matter?' he asked her.

Sultana's heart was pounding in her chest.

'This cursed toilet,' she grumbled agitatedly. 'What's wrong with it? I had a backache and I thought it would help to hang on the chain. Why is there a chain in here anyway, like the ones we see in trains? The minute I touched the bloody thing there was a loud and terrible noise, just terrible!'

Khuda Baksh burst into loud, boisterous laughter. Then he proceeded to explain the workings of the toilet to Sultana. He told her it was something new, an ingenious mechanism that enabled all the filth to travel underground with a mere tug at the chain.

How Khuda Baksh and Sultana came together is a long story. Khuda Baksh had been living in Rawalpindi. After he passed his Intermediate exam he learned to drive a lorry and for four years he drove a lorry between Rawalpindi and Kashmir. In Kashmir he formed a liaison with a woman who eventually went with him to Lahore. When efforts to find work failed, he put her to work and continued to live off her earnings for a couple of years. Then she ran off with someone else. He heard rumours that she was in Ambala. He went there looking for her and found Sultana instead. Sultana liked him and before long the two were living together.

Sultana's business flourished after Khuda Baksh came into her life, and being old-fashioned, she imagined that her association with him was the cause of her good fortune. She began to view him with special favour.

Khuda Baksh was a hard-working man. He didn't like staying idle. Soon he became friendly with a photographer who took pictures at the railway station with his minute-camera, and began taking lessons in photography from him. A short while later, with thirty rupees from Sultana, he bought his own camera and a curtain. His next purchases were two chairs and photo-developing materials. Not long afterwards, Khuda Baksh was in business for himself.

His work flourished and he was able to move to Ambala Cantonment and establish himself there. He took pictures of the British soldiers and within a month had become well acquainted with many of them. Then he brought Sultana to Ambala. Because of his dealings with the soldiers he was able to provide Sultana with a steady flow of customers, many of whom became permanent clients.

Sultana bought a pair of gold earrings, eight bangles that weighed eight and a half tolas altogether, fifteen saris, and also had the house furnished. In short she had a good life there. But suddenly, and for no apparent reason, Khuda Baksh decided to move to Delhi. Sultana couldn't refuse to accompany him since she considered his presence lucky. As a result she agreed to go with him. Delhi is a big city, she told herself, there are plenty of wealthy people there and business is sure to do well. She had heard great stories about the fabulous city. Also Hazrat Nizamuddin Aulia's mausoleum was in Delhi and she was an earnest devotee of the saint. She sold most of her household goods and arrived in Delhi with Khuda Baksh. He found a flat for which the rent was twenty rupees a month and soon the two were settled in.

Houses stood side by side in a long row on the street. Each unit had two floors, with shops on the ground level and flats on the upper floors. The Municipal Committee had allotted these flats to prostitutes so that they would not set up shop all over town. Because the buildings looked the same, Sultana initially experienced a great deal of difficulty recognizing her own when she was out front. But when the laundry-wallah put up his sign saying 'Dirty Clothes Washed Here,' she used it as a landmark to identify her own place. She singled out other landmarks as well to seek out some of the other flats. For example a large board with 'Coal Shop' written on it marked the place where her friend Heera Bai (who sang on the radio constantly) lived; her friend Mukhtar lived in the flat under which, on a shop front, hung the sign 'Special Eat-in for the Gentry.' Over the *nawar* factory was her friend Anwari's house; Anwari worked for the businessman who ran the factory and since he had to keep an eye on the factory at night, he had moved in with her.

Customers don't start arriving as soon as you open shop, Sultana told herself as she tried to allay her fears and justify a whole month of idleness. But when another month passed and there was still no sign of a client she began to worry.

'What do you think it is, Khuda Baksh?' she asked him one day. 'It's been two months now and not a single customer has stepped over my threshold. I know the market is bad these days, but it's not so bad that I shouldn't have any customers at all.'

Khuda Baksh had been worried too, but hadn't said anything to Sultana. However, now that Sultana had broached the subject herself, he ventured an explanation.

'I've been thinking about this for a long time and I've come to the conclusion that this is because of the war. People are too preoccupied about other matters to think of coming this way. Or . . .' He was interrupted by the sound of steps on the stairs. Someone was coming up. After a few seconds there was a knock on the door. Khuda Baksh ran to open it. It was the first of the six customers, the one who would not pay more than three rupees. Five other men came after that – six customers in three months, that is, and all she earned was a poor sum of eighteen rupees and eight annas in all.

The rent for the flat alone was twenty rupees; water and electricity bills were extra and there were other expenses like food, clothing and medicine. Eighteen rupees and eight annas in three months could, under no circumstances, be considered an income. Sultana grew perturbed. In time she was forced to sell the eight-tola bangles she had bought in Ambala. When she was down to the last one she told Khuda Baksh they had better return to Ambala.

'Listen to me, let's go back. What does this place have anyway? I know it must be something, but there's nothing for us here. The city doesn't suit us at all. You did well in Ambala, please let's return. Consider whatever losses we've suffered here a sacrifice for our future good fortune. Here, take this bangle and sell it. I'll pack and we can leave by the night train.'

Khuda Baksh took the bangle from her. 'No, my dearest,' he said, 'we cannot go back now. We'll stay here and earn our living in this city. God will help us, we must trust Him. Something is sure to turn up, by His grace.'

Sultana didn't say anything. She had now lost her last bangle and it upset her to see her unadorned wrists. But what was there to be done? They had to eat.

After five months during which her expenses far exceeded her income, Sultana's anxiety began to mount, aggravated by Khuda Baksh's frequent and long absences from home. It was true she had friends in the neighbourhood in whose company she could while away the time, but she felt uneasy about visiting them too often or spending too much time with them. Gradually she stopped going out altogether. Alone all day, she occupied herself with cutting betel nuts or mending clothes, and if there wasn't anything else to do she went out on the balcony, leaned against the railing, and watched stationary and moving trains in the railway shed across the road.

There was also a large godown nearby that occupied an extensive area. To its left, under the covering of a corrugated iron roof, lay stacks of bales containing wares of every kind. On the right was an open ground crisscrossed with railway tracks. When the rails shone in the sun they reminded Sultana of her hand on the back of which blue veins stood out just like the rails. Railway engines and carriages went by constantly, in one direction or the other. The noise of moving trains remained constant. If Sultana came out on the balcony early in the morning she could see thick clouds of smoke emerging from the vents of engines, clouds that rose slowly, like fat and heavy men, toward the murky sky. From the rails seemed to issue rolling bundles of steam that quickly evaporated into the air. Whenever she saw a carriage propelled by an engine and then left to advance on its own, Sultana was reminded of her life. Like that lone carriage she had been pushed once on the tracks of life and then abandoned. Other people were changing tracks, but she continued to move in the same direction. Where she was headed, she didn't know. And then, one day, she would lose the impetus that had pushed her and she would stop somewhere at a place of which she knew nothing.

She watched the stationary and moving trains all day long, her mind becoming more and more muddled as time went on. She had lived near a railway station before, when she was in Ambala, but never had she been so moved by the sight of trains. It often seemed to her that the mesh of rails and the clouds of smoke and steam were all part of the layout of a brothel, the engines reminding her of the rich businessmen who came to her when she was in Ambala. Sometimes, when she observed an engine advancing slowly alongside a standing carriage, she envisioned in her mind a man walking past a brothel, casting surreptitious glances at the *kothas* as he went his way.

Realizing that her present state of mind might lead to madness, Sultana decided she would no longer go out on the balcony. She begged Khuda Baksh to spend some time at home with her.

'For God's sake, have pity on me, stay with me for a while,' she pleaded. 'I'm alone all day, lying around in this empty house like a sick person.'

'My dearest,' Khuda Baksh said, 'I'm trying very hard to find work. God willing, something is sure to come up in a few days and then all our troubles will be over.'

But it had been five months already and there were no signs indicating that their troubles would be over soon.

The month of Moharram was fast approaching and Sultana had no money with which to have black clothes made for herself. Mukhtar had a Lady Hamilton kameez stitched in the latest style with black georgette sleeves, and to match the kameez she already possessed a black satin shalwar that glistened like kohl. Anwari had bought a fine georgette sari, under which, in keeping with the latest fashion, she was going to wear a white silk petticoat. To go with the sari Anwari had also purchased a pair of black velvet sandals. When Sultana saw all this, she became even more conscious of her own inability to be properly dressed for Moharram, and her anguish grew.

The sight of all the finery Mukhtar and Anwari had readied for themselves filled Sultana's heart with an immense sadness. She felt that a tumour had begun to mushroom inside her. The house was empty and Khuda Baksh was out as usual. For a long time she lay on the durrie with a pillow under her head. Then, tired of lying down, she got up and went out on the balcony, hoping to get some relief from her agonizing thoughts.

There were several carriages on the tracks, but no engines today. The sun had set, water had already been sprinkled on the ground and the dust had settled. Slowly the bazaar was coming alive with the presence of men who slunk by the *kothas*, looking up stealthily as they went their way. Sultana happened to catch the eye of one such man; he had been staring at her. She waved to him involuntarily and forgot all about him a few seconds later as her gaze returned to the railway tracks. She surveyed the engine pensively until it seemed to her that the engine was draped in black. To shrug off this strange thought she allowed her attention to return to the bazaar. The man who had been leering at her only a few minutes ago, and to whom she had waved, was still there. She waved to him once more. He gestured enquiringly, as if asking how he could get to her flat. She pointed toward the entrance. He paused for a moment, then came up quickly. Sultana opened the door. He came in and sat down on the settee.

'Why were you so afraid to come up?' Sultana asked.

'What makes you think I was afraid?' The man was smiling. 'What's there to be afraid of?'

'Well, you did stand around uncertainly for a few minutes before you came up.'

He smiled again. 'You're mistaken. Actually I was looking at a woman in the flat above yours. She was sticking her tongue out at a man in the street — I was enjoying watching her. And there was a green light in her balcony. I like green light, it feels good to the eyes.'

He studied the room while he talked then rose from the durrie.

'Are you leaving?' Sultana asked.

'No,' he replied. 'I want to see the rest of your house. Show me the other rooms.'

Sultana took him on a round of the house and showed him all three rooms. He observed everything in total silence.

'My name is Shankar,' he finally said after they had returned to the room with the durrie.

Sultana studied him closely for the first time. He was of medium height and quite ordinary-looking. But his eyes were clear and occasionally shone with a special light. He was lean, his hair had begun to grey at the temples, and he wore brown trousers and a white shirt with the collar turned up.

He sat on the durrie as if it was Sultana who was the client and not he. This made her feel uncomfortable.

'Well, what can I do for you?'

Shankar eased his body into a reclining position.

'Well, what can I do for *you*?' he asked. 'You're the one who called me up.'

Sultana chose to remain silent.

'I see,' he said, sitting up. 'Now listen, you have misunderstood completely. I'm not one of those who pay. I have a fee just as doctors do, and if I'm called my fees will have to be paid.'

Sultana was confused and somewhat nervous at his attitude, but what he said amused her and she began to laugh.

'What do you do?' she queried.

'Whatever you people do,' he said.

'What?'

'What do you do?'

'I ... I ... I don't do anything.'

'I don't do anything either.'

'This is ridiculous!' Sultana became irritated. 'There must be something that you do.'

'And you must also do something,' Shankar said calmly.

'I waste my time!'

'I do the same.'

'In that case, let's do it together.'

'I'm ready, but I never pay money for wasting time.'

'You must be out of your mind!' Sultana was becoming angry. 'This is not a freeloader's place.'

'And I'm no volunteer.'

'Volunteer? What's that?' Sultana forgot her anger for a moment.

'A son of a bitch.'

'I'm not one.'

'But that fellow Khuda Baksh who lives with you is.'

'Why?'

'Because for weeks now he's been wasting his time in the company of an old fakir in the hope of having his luck changed. He doesn't know that the old man's own luck abandoned him a long time ago – what can *he* do for him!' Shankar laughed.

'You're making fun of him because you're a Hindu,' Sultana protested. 'That's why you make fun of his reverence for a holy sage.'

'In a place like this the question of Hindu or Muslim doesn't arise. The holiest of pandits and maulvis would become respectable if they came here.' A smile lingered on Shankar's face.

'God only knows what nonsense this is! Tell, are you staying or not?' Sultana was exasperated now.

'On the condition I mentioned earlier.'

Sultana got up from the durrie. 'You can leave now,' she told him.

Shankar rose slowly, thrust his hands in the pockets of his trousers, and walked toward the door.

'I come here often. If you ever need me, don't hesitate to send for me. I'm a useful man.'

Shankar left, and the black clothes forgotten, Sultana continued to think about him for a long time afterward. His conversation had somehow lightened her sorrow. If he had come to her in Ambala, where she had been prosperous, she would have viewed this man differently. She might even have thrown him out of her house. But the situation was not the same here. Since she was so unhappy, Shankar's visit appealed to her in some strange way.

When Khuda Baksh came home that evening, Sultana asked him where he had been all day.

'I was at the Old Fortress,' he told her. He looked tired and worn out. 'An old fakir is staying there and I've been attending him in the hope that he will help us see better days.'

'Did he say anything yet?'

'No, he hasn't turned his attention to me as yet. But Sultana, believe me, the hard work I'm doing for him will touch his heart and, by God's grace, our lives will change.'

Sultana could only think of Moharram.

'You're out all day,' she complained, 'I'm alone in this empty house where I feel like a prisoner – I can't even go anywhere. Moharram is upon us and you haven't given a single thought to the fact that I need black clothes. There isn't an anna in the house, the bangles are all gone. Tell me, what are we going to do?' She was in tears now. 'How long are you going to run after fakirs? I think Allah too has abandoned us. Why don't you start your business again? We'll have something at least.'

'But I need some capital to start over again,' Khuda Baksh said, reclining on the durrie. 'Please, for God's sake, don't be so unhappy, I can't bear it any more. I know we made a mistake in coming here, but it's all up to Allah and what He does is always for the best. Who knows, after suffering the way we have...'

'For God's sake, do something!' Sultana interrupted him. 'I don't care if you steal or plunder, you have to get me black fabric for a shalwar. I have a white silk sari and a white chiffon *dupatta*, the one you gave me at

Diwali, and I'll have those dyed black. But I need a shalwar. You have to get me the fabric at any cost. I'll die if you don't.'

Khuda Baksh sat up. 'This is not fair. How can I get you the fabric when I don't even have money to buy my fix?'

'I don't care what you do, you have to get me four and a half yards of black satin.'

'Pray that Allah sends you three or four customers tonight.'

'But you won't do anything, will you? If you really wanted to, you could get the fabric. Before the war, satin was only fourteen annas a yard, now it's one rupee and four annas a yard. How much money will you need?'

'I'll try, I'll see what I can do,' Khuda Baksh conceded. 'Here, calm down now. I'm going to get some food from the hotel.'

He brought over food from the hotel, they both ate dejectedly, and the next morning Khuda Baksh left for the Old Fortress to be with the fakir. Sultana was alone again. She spent some time in bed, then walked around aimlessly in the rooms. After lunch she went down to the laundry with her white chiffon *dupatta* and white silk shirt. The place specialized in washing and dyeing. On returning to the house she occupied herself for a while with film magazines that contained stories and songs of the films she had seen, and then she dozed off. When she awoke, it was four in the evening. She could tell because the afternoon sun was casting its light on the gutter in the courtyard. Sultana bathed, changed, put on a warm shawl and came out on the balcony. She stood here for nearly an hour. The sun had set and it was getting dark. Street lights shone brightly and down below the street was buzzing with activity. The air was chilly, but Sultana seemed not to mind. She had been watching people, cars and tongas come and go on the road. Then she saw Shankar. As he approached, he looked up at her and smiled. Sultana raised her hand and waved involuntarily. She regretted her action immediately, but Shankar was already on his way up. She didn't know what to say when he arrived at her doorstep. He came in and calmly made himself comfortable on the durrie, as if he owned the place.

'You can tell me to come and you can tell me to leave as often as you wish, I won't be offended,' he said when he noticed how quiet Sultana was.

'No, no, please stay,' Sultana said hastily, 'I don't want you to leave.' She was feeling awkward, unsure of what to make of his remark.

'So you've decided to agree to my terms?' He smiled at her.

'What terms?' Sultana asked with an embarrassed laugh. 'Are you planning to marry me?'

'Nikkah and marriage – neither you nor I will ever get married. These rituals are not for the likes of us. Let's drop this nonsense and talk of something worthwhile.'

'What do you want me to say?'

'You're a woman, say something to comfort the heart. There's more in life than just business.'

By now Sultana had accepted Shankar intellectually.

'Why don't you tell me frankly what you want from me?' she asked.

'What the others have wanted.'

'What's the difference between you and those others then?'

'You and I are alike, but there's a great deal of difference between me and them. There are some things you should be able to sense and not feel obliged to ask about.'

Sultana gave his remark some thought.

'I know what you mean,' she said after a moment's silence.

'All right. What do you want?'

'You win, I lose. I'm sure no one has ever accepted a proposition such as this.'

'You're wrong. There are many simple-minded women in this neighbourhood who will never believe that a woman can tolerate the kind of degradation that you're accustomed to tolerating, but despite what these people think there are hundreds of Sultanas. Your name is Sultana, isn't it?'

'Yes, it's Sultana.'

Shankar burst out laughing.

'Mine is Shankar – names can be so absurd sometimes.' He rose. 'Come, let's go inside.

When Shankar and Sultana returned to the room with the durrie, they were both laughing.

'Shankar, will you do something for me?' Sultana asked him as he was about to leave.

'Tell me what it is first,' Shankar said.

'You might think I'm asking for payment, but … but …' Sultana stammered.

'Yes, yes, come on, why did you stop?'

Sultana mustered up all her courage.

'Well, the thing is that Moharram is almost here and I don't have enough money to have a black shalwar made. You've already heard about our problems. I had a shirt and *dupatta* which I gave in to be dyed this morning.'

'So you want me to give you some money for a black shalwar?' Shankar asked.

'No,' Sultana replied hastily. 'I just want you to get me a black shalwar.'

'I rarely have any money,' Shankar declared with a smile. 'But I'll certainly try to get the shalwar to you on the morning of the first day of Moharram. Happy now?' Then he pointed to her earrings. 'Can you give me these?'

'What will you do with them?' Sultana laughed. 'They're silver and worth very little, five rupees at the most.'

'I'm asking for the earrings not the price,' Shankar said. 'Will you give them to me?'

'Take them,' Sultana said, and taking off the earrings she handed them to Shankar. Later she felt sorry she had parted with them. But Shankar had left already.

Sultana was quite sure that Shankar would not keep his promise. But eight days later, on the first day of Moharram, early in the morning, there was a knock on her door. When she opened it she found Shankar standing there with a package wrapped in newspaper.

'It's a black shalwar, might be slightly long for you,' he said. 'I have to go now.'

She took the package from him and he left without another word. His hair was tousled, his trousers heavily creased; it seemed he had just got out of bed.

Sultana opened the package. Inside was a black satin shalwar, just like the one Mukhtar had. Sultana felt exhilarated, and whatever disappointment she had experienced at the loss of the earrings and whatever misgivings she had experienced about Shankar, vanished. He had kept his promise. She was now in possession of a black shalwar.

In the afternoon she went down to the laundry and brought back her shirt and *dupatta* which had been dyed black. She had just donned these three items when there was a knock on the door. It was Mukhtar. She examined Sultana's attire when she came in.

'The shirt and kameez are obviously dyed, but the shalwar looks new. When did you have it made?'

'The tailor brought it by today,' Sultana answered. Her eyes fell on Mukhtar's ears.

'When did you get these earrings?'

'I got them today,' Mukhtar replied.

They both remained silent for a long time afterward.

Qurratulain Hyder (b. 1927)

Qurratulain Hyder is one of the greatest living writers in Urdu. She made a precocious debut as a short-story writer when she was a teenager; since then, she has written five novels, including *River of Fire* (*Aag Ka Dariya*), and several short stories, which now, together, form one of the most important oeuvres of modern Urdu literature. Yet, because she belonged to the Muslim upper middle class (the 'Muslim *bhadralok*', as she calls it), a society itself constantly in flux and in the midst of redefinition, and because she has not infrequently written about that ambivalently regarded milieu, she once antagonized an Urdu intelligentsia that was dominated by the left-leaning Progressive Writers Movement, with its insistence on social and political commitment from the creative writer. Thus, Ismat Chughtai, an older, equally important writer, had once contemptuously called Hyder 'Pom Pom Darling.'

Hyder has survived literary movements and history. She was born into a family of pioneering writers who came from a wealthy, aristocratic lineage; and the story of that family's transition from feudal aristocracy to bourgeois progressiveness is an allegory of how that society, like others in India, passed from a feudal to a modern reality at the turn of the nineteenth century – in this, the resemblance to the earlier trajectory of Tagore's family, and the similar movement it signifies about Bengali society in the middle of the nineteenth century, is striking. Hyder's life has been characterized by movement; from Lucknow to London, where she worked at, among other places, the BBC, a few years in Pakistan, and then back to India, where she now lives in New Delhi. She belongs to a generation that was divided by Partition, and to a class within a community that had to make, at one point in its history, a difficult and seemingly irrevocable choice. It is the responsibility of choice, located in the generation and political history she comes from, that perhaps occasionally gives her writing its haunting, existential quality. The restlessness and movement that have marked her itineraries in life have characterized her narratives as well; she is never happy inhabiting one point of view, or one voice, for any length of time, but must flit startlingly from point to point and make transitions that we did not know the narrative was capable of; she is an emigrant and gypsy of narrative structure, which for her is always a point of departure rather than a resting place. She has exploited the 'Pom Pom Darling' voice well: detached, quirky, fragile, nervous, by turns melancholy and extremely funny, pretending to hold a social conversation with the life whose passing and often tragic spectacles it has no real control over.

* * *

'Memories of an Indian Childhood' (1965)

translated from the Urdu by the author

The emaciated old man in the threadbare, shiny black suit arrived punctually at three in the afternoon. With his walking stick he gently tapped the gravel in the front porch till a passing servant – usually Faquira – heard the familiar sound and went inside.

'Master Sahib has come,' Baji was informed.

The old man walked down the poplar-lined drive and reached the side veranda. Feeling each step with his cane he carefully claimed the wide flight of stairs and softly called, 'Resham, Resham.'

Resham came running, followed by Baji who gracefully carried the sitar. The way my fabulous Rehana Baji handled the sitar could teach a thing or two to Ravi Verma – were he alive – or to any Bengal School artist worth his watercolours who painted dark-eyed, sitar-playing damsels. Graciously she said 'Adaab', sat down on the edge of the settee and took the instrument out of its *kamkhwab* cover. The music lesson began ...

After a light shower of rain a magical fragrance filled the air. A lone bird whistled through the leafy silence. Or a mountain wind rose and made the trees shed their unripe fruit. Often a dim, cold sun trickled through the orchard and the garden turned to gold. On his way out through the orchard the old man sometimes found a peach – partly eaten by a parrot – lying in the wet, intensely green, cool grass. He picked it up, cleaned it carefully with is handkerchief and shoved it in his pocket.

Doglike, Resham always followed him to the gate. Often she vanished in a rose bush looking for prey or deftly climbed a tree. The old man looked up, briefly watched the trembling bough, bent his head again and went out of the gate.

Ever since Jogmaya Chatterjee of Calcutta took up abode in the bungalow next door, the inhabitants of picturesque, complacent Dalanwalla had suddenly realized the acute lack of culture in their lives. Every drawing-room had its massive gramophone and its Kamla Jharia-Kallu Qawwal records. Wireless sets were still rare and tape recorders had not even been invented. The status symbols consisted mainly of bungalows, car, 'English' cook and trained bearer. (There was many an eminent cook and bearer who considered it beneath their dignity to work for *kala log*.*) Refrigerators, too, were unknown. There used to be an ice-box and a hot-case in the pantry.

But the strains of Rabindra Sangeet emanating from Mrs Jogmaya Chatterjee's house changed all that. Mrs Goswami, wife of a high-ranking (Survey of India) official, said to Begum Faruqui, wife of another high-ranking (Department of Forests) official, 'Behenji, we are really backward. Look at these Bengalis. So advanced in everything.'

'I have even heard it said, Behenji, that their daughters cannot get married unless they know music,' said Mrs Jaswant Singh, wife of a high-ranking (Royal Military Academy) officer.

'We Muslims disapprove of decent girls singing and dancing. But times have changed. I said to "him" the other day, "Our Rashida must learn how to play the harmonium",' Begum Faruqui firmly announced.

This was how the winds of Art and Culture began to blow across Dalanwalla. A seedy, *beedi*-smoking guruji was acquired from somewhere and Dr Sinha's daughters dutifully learned the Kathak. Sardar Amarjit Singh, whose father owned a large business in Batavia, Dutch East Indies, took up the violin.

The young Sardar also bought from Mr Peter Robert Fazal Masih, the pheri-wallah, yards and yards of printed georgette for his turbans. With one of his colourful turbans on his head, his jet black beard rolled with enormous finesse, the Sardar sallied forth, armed with his violin, and headed straight for the Rispana. Rumour had it that he went every evening to meet Mrs Feroza Khan, the lovely Afghan widow who lived in a Christmas card cottage by the stream. Evening after evening he informed his young Sardarni, Bibi Charanjit Kaur, that he was going for his violin lessons. But Mrs Goswami, Mrs Jaswant Singh, Begum Faruqui and my mother *knew*.

Such were the stirring times when my cousin, too, decided to take up music – partly because a sitar was handy, lying in its dusty cover in the store room. (My pioneering mother had learned and forgotten how to play it several years ago.)

---

* Editor's note: black folk.

A lot of things happened that winter. Resham broke her leg. Miss Zohra Derby, the Daredevil, arrived in town. Diana Becket was declared the Ravishing Beauty of London. Dr (Miss) Zubeida Siddiqui saw a black dog the size of a donkey at two in the morning. And Faquira's sister-in-law became a sparrow.

I must tell you about these important events in their chronological order.

My beautiful and brilliant cousin Rehana Khatoon had passed her BA that year, breaking a lot of records at Aligarh Muslim University – and was spending a few months with us. One afternoon as she sat drinking coffee with Mother and Mrs Goswami in the front veranda, somebody tapped the pebbles in the portico and a feeble voice asked, 'Excuse me, I am told that a lady here wishes to learn the sitar.'

He was Mr Simon. He said that Mr Peter Robert Fazal Masih, the pheri-wallah (he grandly called himself a travelling salesman who traded in cloth and gossip), had told him about Baji's musical intentions. He said that he lived alone in the outhouse of the late Rev. Scott's empty bunglow, and earned ten to twenty rupees a month if he was lucky enough to get one or two pupils. That was all he told us about himself, but being an ardent left-wing intellectual, Baji was greatly dismayed. Mr Simon, however, never accepted any help beyond his fees; he had that kind of dignity.

Mr Simon always wore a waistcoat – complete with an ancient watch-and-chain, a round black cap and round thick glasses.

He never entered the house (people like tradesmen and tutors were supposed to stay in the veranda) except on the first day of his employment when Baji asked Faquira to send him down to the back garden where she sat in the sun. It was a bitterly cold day. Led by Faquira Mr Simon passed through my room where I played by the fireplace. He hesitated and stopped for a few seconds, for a brief moment spread his hands towards the fire and quickly went out.

Resham, our otherwise arrogant Persian, became his friend. 'Funny, how a snob like Resham has befriended poor Master Sahib,' Baji remarked and added the observation in a typically feminine P.S. in her letter to Muzzaffer Bhai. She was allowed, as a gesture of modernity, to correspond with our cousin and her fiancé Muzzaffer, who was at that time, engaged in the pursuit of knowledge at the University of Bombay.

While Baji wrote her letters, Ghafoor Begum, her loyal anna,* sat by her

---

* Editor's note: wet nurse.

chair on the grass with her inseparable *pandan*.* When Baji went inside, Ghaffoor Begum strolled down to the servants' quarters to chat with Faquira's sister-in-law, or returned to her prayer settee in the back veranda.

A good-natured Garhwali lad, Faquira had been discovered by Abdul, the cook, who found him in rags, knitting a sweater, by the Eastern Canal. For a few days he slogged as Abdul's *masalchi* but was soon promoted to the rank of houseboy and worked under our very superior bearer (customarily called Sarder because he was the doyen of servants). A few months ago Faquira had informed Mother that both his elder brothers had 'turned to dust' in a ghastly accident and that he was going to fetch their widow from the mountains.

Tattooed and fair-skinned Jaldhara was an attractive, smiling woman of forty; she wore a golden nosering and nose-flower and a necklace of Malka Tooria (Queen Victoria to us) coins. Both her coolie husbands had fallen together to their death carrying the luggage of Badrinath pilgrims. Jaldhara suffered from some incurable disease and Faquira endlessly worried abut her health. The day Jaldhara arrived in the outhouse Rehana Baji very knowledgeably discussed, at the lunch table, the institution of polyandry in the Hills. Baji had obtained a first-class first and my father was immensely proud of her.

In the afternoon I dashed off to my friends Kamla and Vimala, to tell them about Faquira's sister-in-law who was so rich that she wore coins round her neck. Resham followed me to the avenue. Afraid that she might get run over by a car, I picked her up, threw her across the hedge and pedalled off on my little bicycle.

Instead of falling in the garden, poor Resham got entangled in the barbed wire concealed in the tall hedge. Badly bruised and bleeding, she miaowed and miaowed till Faquira, who had come out to pluck chillies for the cook, heard her desperate cries.

I returned to a sorrowing household. 'Resham is dying,' Baji told me tearfully, 'I still don't understand how she got herself entangled in those wires. Must have gone there looking for birds. The vet has just left.'

It was a dreadful realization that I was responsible for Resham's terrible pain and possible death. Trying to hide my guilt from the world I hid myself in a cluster of *leechis* in the back garden. In woodpecker-like Mrs Warbrook's house, the wireless set broadcast music from distant BBC. In the servants' quarters Ghafoor Begum was talking to Jaldhara and Abdul's wife. Baji was in her room writing to Muzaffer Bhai – probably about

---

*   Editor's note: Box in which betel leaves are stored.

Resham's accident. The Persian lay bandaged in her frilled basket in the
side veranda.

I lurked among the trees like a criminal and did not quite know what
to do next. Finally I sauntered down toward my father's room and peeped
in through the bay window. Father sat in his armchair reading *The Pioneer*.
I tiptoed in and stood behind his chair.

He heard my sobs and turned round. 'What is the matter, child?' He
asked. I told him all, flopped on the floor and howled and howled till I felt
a little better.

Every morning Resham was dressed and bandaged by Faquira and was
sent down, once a week, to see the 'horse doctor' at the '*gora** hospital'.
Her leg had been shaved. Shorn of her glorious long hair she was now a
humble, subdued and very unhappy cat. A few weeks later she limped all
the way down to the gate to see off Mr Simon.

That was when, one Sunday morning, as I played hopscotch on the drive,
Mr George Becket's head appeared over the *mehandi* hedge. A little hesi-
tantly he beckoned to me and said, 'Good morning to you, young lady.'

'Good morning, Pil— Mr Becket,' I said politely and almost bit my
tongue.

'How is your beautiful pussy cat? Mr Fazal Masih told me that she had
had a bad accident.'

This was the first time that Mr George Becket had actually spoken to
anyone in the neighbourhood. I thanked him for enquiring after poor
Resham. He nodded, shoved his thumbs into the half-torn pockets of his
shabby coat and shuffled off.

Mr George Becket was a destitute Anglo-Indian, generally known as
Pilpili[†] sahib. He lived down the avenue in a broken down cottage and was
so poor that he went to the municipal water tap himself to fetch water. His
only daughter, Diana Rose, sold tickets at an English cinema hall at the
Parade Grounds, and often passed by our house on her bicycle. She had
golden, windswept hair and four dresses which she washed at night at the
water tap and wore with extreme care. But Mrs Goswami, Mrs Jaswant
Singh and Begum Faruqui firmly maintained that Diana gadded about in
such fineries because the Tommies gave her money. But if the Tommies
gave her money (and I saw no reason why they should), why didn't her
poor papa engage a *bhishti*?[‡]

---

*   Editor's note: White or European hospital.
†   Editor's note: Soft-textured surface; a not uncommon Urdu nickname for Europeans.
‡   Editor's note: water carrier.

Dalanwalla was mostly inhabited by well-to-do, retired Englishmen who lived quietly in their secluded, exquisitely furnished bungalows. Inside the peaceful houses walnut tables displayed piles of *Illustrated London News, Tatler, Country Life* and *Punch.* Bundles of *The Times* and *The Daily Telegraph* arrived by sea mail. In the mornings the ladies sat in their 'morning rooms', writing home. In the afternoons they had their high tea in the verandas. The mantelpieces were crowded with silver-framed portraits of sons who were engaged in further brightening up the Empire's sun over such places as Kenya, Ceylon, Malaya and so forth.

Although these dear old people belonged to the twilight world of *koi hai* and *chhota hazri,* there were some dedicated, self-effacing orientalists and scholars, too, among them. Mr Hardcastle was an expert on Tibeto-Burman dialects. Mr Green wrote learned papers on the Khasi tribes of Assam. Colonel Whitehead, who had lost a leg fighting the Pathans on the Frontier, was quite an authority on Pushtu poetry. Apart from these, Major Shelton wrote *shikar* notes in upcountry newspapers. Mr Marchman was a chess fiend. Horsy Miss Drinkwater called spirits on the planchette, and woodpecker-like Mrs Warbrook painted lovely watercolours.

One of the bungalows housed the 'British Stores'. Owned and run by a tall, hawk-nosed and very ancient Parsi, this was the historic place where the ladies met for shopping and gossip while their children hung about its toy, toffee and lemonade counters (Coca-Cola had not been invented).

In this comfortably smug and very English locality (Indians were accepted as 'upper class' and civilized enough to live in bungalows), Mr George Becket of the pale blue eyes was the only Anglo-Indian. Nevertheless, he considered himself a proper Englishman and it was said that when some years ago, Georve V, King Emperor, died, Mr Becket solemnly wore a black armband and attended the Slow March Past at Kolagarh along with the mourning English gentry.

But with the characteristic heartlessness of children, we referred to him as Pilpili Sahib and Vimala's teenage, Doon School-going brother, Swarn, had devised a novel way of teasing poor Diana. When she passed by his house he placed the gramophone in the front window of his room and it blared out the nineteenth-century English musical song

> There was a rich merchant in London did stay,
> Who had for his daughter an uncommon liking.
> Her name, it was Diana, she was sixteen years old,
> And had a large fortune in silver and gold.

As Diana was walking in the garden one day,
Her father came to her and thus did he say:
'Go dress yourself up in gorgeous array,
For you will have a husband both gallant and gay.'
'O father, dear father, I have made up my mind,
To marry at present I don't feel inclined,
And all my large fortune every day adore,
If you let me live single a year or two more.'
Then gave the father a gallant reply:
'If you don't be this young man's bride,
I'll leave all your fortune to the fearest of things.'
As Wilikins was walking in the garden one day,
He found his dear Diana lying dead on the way.
A cup so fearful that lay by her side,
And Wilikins doth fainteth with a cry in his eye.

As soon as the song started poor Diana flushed deeply and bicycled away as fast as she could.

The winter's second important event was the arrival of the Great East India Circus and the Carnival Company Ltd., which pitched its Big Top at the parade ground. The handbill announced:

The Greatest Marvel of the Century
The Lion-hearted Beauty
Miss Zohra Derby
In the Well of Death
Tonight and Every Night.

Faquira took Jaldhara to see the circus and came back in raptures. 'Begum sahib, Bitya, Bibi,' he said, thrilled, 'this *zenani* who rides the *phatphati* in the death of well ... Harey Ram, Harey Ram ...!'

Next evening we, too, saw her as she sat in front of the Well of Death looking bored, chain-smoking Scissors cigarettes. She wore a *birjis* of shining blue satin, and her heavily painted face looked weirdly blue in the bright lights. (But those who knew declared that Miss Nadia of Hunterwali fame was not a patch on Miss Zohra Derby, the Female Desperado.) A ferocious-looking man, also in blue satin *birjis* sat next to her, twirling his waxed moustaches. A motorbike roared at the back.

After some minutes Miss Zohra Derby and her ferocious companion entered the Well of Death on their motorbikes and went roaring round and round. The well shook and wavered and it was all very frightening.

A week later Faquira brought the sensational news that Master

Gulquand and Master Muchchander, two stalwarts of the Circus and its star performers, had a fight over Miss Zohra Derby; she was knifed and slashed well and proper by Master Muchchander and was now in hospital.

But as was expected of him, Mr Peter Robert Fazal Masih brought the real scoop: Diana Becket had joined the Circus.

'Diana Becket?' Baji asked, wide-eyed.

'Yes, bitya,' Faquira put in enthusiastically. 'I too heard, at the water tap. In the circus Pilpili sahib's Missya, she will get a big fat salary and free tiffin, *chhota hazri*, everything. She says she could no more bear to see her old papa carrying heavy buckets, he being so poor and all. And she says, as for the world, it harasses her anyway.'

All this was very saddening. Then I remembered something and asked brightly, 'But the Tommies gave her money, didn't they?'

Ghafoor Begum glared at me. 'Run along,' she said. So I ran along.

A few days later the posters announced:

> Sensational European Belle
> The Ravishing Beauty of London
> Miss Diana Rose
> In the Well of Death
> Tonight and Every Night

In the midst of these fabulous goings-on the cinema also claimed my attention:

> The Greatest Film of the Year
> Starring Miss Sardar Akhtar
> At Palladium Cinema
> Tonight and Every Night

> The Greatest Film of the Year
> Starring Miss Sardar Akhtar
> At Roxy Cinema
> Tonight and Every Night

How could Miss Sardar Akhtar 'star' at two places the same evening? It worried me no end. But the problem was solved when my parents allowed Baji to go with Mrs Goswami and see *Achhut Kanya*. I was allowed to tag along with Baji. (About *Achhut Kanya* Mrs Jogmaya Chatterjee had informed Mrs Goswami that India had at last entered the era of cultural revolution because Gurudev's* own niece had become a cinema actress.)

---

*   Editor's note: Tagore.

This was also the time when Mrs Chatterjee's daughters began singing the latest film songs like *Tum aur main aur Munna piyara, Gharwa hoga swarg hamara.** The breeze wafted these ditties over to our garden. Ghafoor Begum shuddered, placed her hands on her waist or a forefinger on her nose, indicating censure, and said, 'What our elders used to say is coming true: A sure sign of the Day of Judgement would be when cows eat goat-droppings and virgins themselves would demand husbands ... This is *Kaljug ... Kaljug.*'

Faquira, of course, took Jaldhara to see all these films. When she returned from a visit to what is now known as a 'New Theatres classic', Jaldhara developed high fever. The doctor said she was critically ill.

Now she lay day long in the sun. One afternoon she said to Ghafoor Begum, 'My *samai* has come, Annaji. One of these days I'll give up my *praan.*' Ghafoor Begum tried to cheer her up and said good-humouredly, 'Nonsense, Jaldharia. You are going to be a doddering old woman. But tell me, Jaldharia, what is this spell you've cast over poor Faquira? Give me some *mantra* too for my faithless fellow. I am told you hill people know a lot of sorcery. Look, how Faquira dotes on you, and you old enough to be his mother!'

Upon which Jaldhara seemed to forget her illness and laughed happily and said, 'Don't you know, Annaji, old rice is always better?'

'Old rice?' I repeated.

Ghafoor Begum turned round and glared at me again. 'What are you doing here?' she said sternly. 'Run along and play.' So I returned gloomily to my hopscotch 'field' on the drive.

Bored with life, I decided to visit Kamala and Vimala. On the way to their house, I saw Mr George Becket frantically running down the avenue. Just then Major Shelton emerged from his gate in his battered Model T Ford, and asked Mr Becket to hop in, which he did, and drove away in the direction of the European Hospital.

At Vimala's place a sad-faced Swarn told me that Diana Becket had had a serious accident. She was terrified every time she sat in Master Much-chander's arms as he went roaring round and round on his motorbike. So the circus manager, 'Professor' Shahbaz, told her to start practising solo. That's how she bashed up both her legs. 'And I heard at the Parade Ground that she will have to spend the rest of her life in a wheelchair,' Swarn added.

We were too sad to play hopscotch or anything. Swarn looked shame-

---

*   You and lord baby dearest, / Homely will be our little heaven.

faced and guilty. For some time he sat dangling his long legs from the bough of our favourite *leechi* tree. Then he jumped down and went off to play football with his cronies.

Chinaman John passed by, on his bicycle, carrying his usual load of household linen. We patiently waited for Mr Fazal Masih.

Mr Fazal Masih came round late next evening. He told us that 'Professor' Shahbaz was being interrogated by the police. The circus had quietly left down. Miss Zohra Derby had also vanished from the hospital.

Dr (Miss) Zubeida Siddiqui, a family friend, arrived to spend the holidays. Lean and in her thirties Dr (Miss) Siddiqui stooped a little, inclined her head to one side like a bird and spoke in brief, abrupt sentences. She wore white, long-sleeved blouses and kept her head fully covered with her white cotton sari. She had studied in England and worked as the principal of some obscure girls' college somewhere in eastern India.

Dr Siddiqui said her prayers five times a day and was also fasting, although it was not the month of Ramzan. The ladies of Dalanwalla were deeply impressed by her piety. 'England returned and all, and yet to modest and spiritual,' Begum Faruqui commented with admiration. 'And such a strict follower of God and the Prophet – peace be on him!' said Begum Ansari. Begum Qureshi nodded.

Dr Siddiqui was forever telling Baji some seemingly endless tale in undertones. One day she went down to see Jaldhara and uttered, 'What a fortunate woman!'

One evening Dr Siddiqui was especially morose, so Baji asked me to come along and entertain her (as though I were a dancing bear). She said, 'Let's hear that funny music hall song of yours.'

Obediently I began:

> There was a rich merchant in London did stay,
> Who had for his daughter an uncommon liking.
> Her name, it was Diana, she was sixteen years old
> And had a large fortune in ...

Suddenly a lump rose in my throat and I ran away. Dr Siddiqui's expression changed from moroseness to surprise.

One could not associate any kind of mystery with a dull and prosaic person like Dr Siddiqui. Suddenly she became a figure of high romance.

One foggy morning as Vimala and I haunted the toffee counter in the British Stores, we happened to overhear Mrs Goswami at Tinned Food telling Mrs Jaswant Singh, Begum Faruqui, and Mrs Sinha:

'This lady doctor, poor thing [somehow they could never remember

that Zubeida Siddiqui was a scientist and not a lady doctor], she has been
jilted. And he is going to marry her own niece who is very pretty and
seventeen.'

'Men are like that, Behenji,' Mrs Jaswant Singh replied. 'Look at our
Amarjit.'

And Begum Faruqui said, 'The lady doctor is so God-fearing and pious.
Always praying and fasting.'

'For a woman all depends on this,' Mrs Sinha tapped her forehead with
a forefinger.

'Let's hope Bhagwan listens to her prayers,' said Mrs Goswami.

As two o'clock that night a dreadful scream rose from the guest room.
Everybody jumped out of their quilts and rushed to the scientist's rescue.

Lying prostrate on the prayer rug Zubeida Siddiqui was whimpering
hysterically. I was promptly shooed away to my room but in the morning I
'happened' to overhear her talking to Baji in her usual drab undertone (very
cleverly I had hung about the breakfast table after everybody had left).

'I hadn't told anyone,' Dr Siddiqui was saying. 'The *pirji* had ordered
that I must recite this *jalali wazifa* for forty nights. Last night was the
fortieth. The *pirji* had said, come what may, I must never look up or
sideways and must concentrate fully or else the *wazifa* would have no
effect. Last night, like a damn fool, I looked in front and saw a black dog
the size of a donkey sitting over there. Snarling. So I screamed. The
dog vanished. My *chilla* was broken. Now nothing will happen. The time
is up. Only a week. From now, nothing.' She took off her glasses and began
to cry.

Baji looked horrified.

'But Zubeida Apa,' she said mildly, 'you are a scientist. Do you really
believe in this – this hocus-pocus? You merely had a hallucination. A
black dog the size of a donkey!' And she broke into merry laughter.

I have mentioned earlier that my Baji was a left-wing intellectual (one
of the first crop).

'Rehana Khatoon,' Dr Zubeida Siddiqui said evenly, drying her tears.
'You are only twenty-one. You have doting parents. Doting uncles. Aunts.
Safe and secure. Happy family. [It reminded me of the Happy Family cards
we used to play in the nursery]. A splendid young man. About to be
married to him. You do not know the meaning of loneliness. Don't. Don't
ever laugh at somebody's loneliness.'

Suddenly Baji noticed my presence and with the flicker of her eyelashes
asked me to get lost. So I got lost.

The same evening Dr Siddiqui left for Calcutta.

In the first week of December Jaldhara was removed to the hospital where she died the following evening.

Faquira went about howling like a child.

'Accept it, son,' Ghafoor Begum tried to console him. 'Accept it as Allah's will.'

'How can I, Annaji. She was mother, *bhabi*, wife, everything to me.' He howled some more.

But, on the third day when he returned from the cremation ground, he looked strangely happy and at peace. He carried a clay pot full of poor Jaldhara's ashes. He said he was going to place the pot at the head of his cot at night and in her new form Jaldhara would leave her footprints on the ashes. Baji said she was greatly moved by Faquira's simple faith. At dinner table that night she discussed with Father the theory of transmigration of souls.

Early next morning Faquira came rushing into Mother's room.

'Begum sahib, Bitya, Bibi,' he addressed the three of us excitedly, 'My Jaldhara has become a sparrow.'

'Jaldhara has become a sparrow?' Baji repeated. Both of us went hotfoot across the dewy lawn to Faquira's quarters.

He brought out the clay pot and showed us the tiny footprints of a bird. Obviously a sparrow had entered Faquira's room at night. They did, all the time.

'It's a sparrow, Bitya,' Faquira said simply and carried the pot back into his room.

Faquira began feeding the sparrow and placed cups full of water all over the garden. Whenever a sparrow entered a room through the skylight or a window, he stopped all work, offered it millet seeds, uttering such cries as 'che che che ah ah ah leh leh leh leh' or stood motionless with breadcrumbs on his palm. He also worried that Resham might catch a sparrow.

A few days before Christmas, Baji received a letter from Zubeida Apa:

The day I reached here my niece was married to him. Posh society wedding. Photo appeared in the *Onlooker*.

I have gone on strike against God. Married Dr Uppal the other day. Teaches in Burdwan.

P.S.: Dr U. is a H. Convey news to the Begums Faruqui, Qureshi and Ansari.

Yours
    Z. Uppal

It was an exceptionally severe winter. Diana Rose was still in plaster in the hospital. Mr Becket was not seen at the water tap. He dozed all day on a bench at the Parade Ground. His upturned hat, lying near him, looked like a beggar's empty bowl. Yellow leaves floated down from the trees and filled it to the brim.

Carol singers went round the quiet roads of Dalanwalla, singing 'Silent Night' and 'O Come Let Us Adore Him'. As the night deepened the haunting notes of some lone Garhwali's flute were heard in the distance. The water in the 'sparrow-cups' was frozen. Early in the morning ragged hillmen went about hawking coal. As the mist lifted, the snow-covered Himalayas were lit up by a weak sun. All day long blazing log fires roared in the grates.

On Christmas Eve Mr Simon told us that every Christmas morning he made plum pudding before going to church and spent the rest of the day reading the Good Book. On Boxing Day he promised to bring us some of his plum pudding. As Christmas presents he had brought a touchingly cheap Japanese trinket for Baji, a green ribbon for myself and a tiny rubber ball for Resham. Mother gave him a ten-rupee note. It was absolute wealth for him. He looked at it for some moments and carefully tucked it away in his waistcoat pocket.

Mr Simon did not come on Boxing Day nor the day after. Faquira was, therefore, dispatched to Rev. Scott's bungalow. He came back and hung down his head. Then he said slowly, 'Simon sahib had become dust. Padri sahib's gardener told me on Burra Din when he opened Simon sahib's room he was lying dead and frozen on his cot. The winter killed him.'

'He had only one blanket, Begum sahib. And so he always slept in his suit.'

'It's very cold outside, Bitya. In our Garhwal people often freeze to death. Can't be helped. How can one get so much warm clothing? Winter comes every year, anyway.'

For a week Resham had been sitting on the warm cushions of her cosy basket. That afternoon it was less cold, so she limped down to the gate and posted herself at the little Chinese bridge. There she began to wait for Mr Simon.

The sun went down. Bored, she decided to have a go at a sparrow before coming inside.

The sparrow flew off and perched itself on the branch of a silver oak. Resham tried to climb the tree, but with her broken leg came sliding down. The sparrow hopped onto a higher branch. Resham lifted her face and uttered a faint, helpless miaow. The sparrow spread its wings and flew away towards the wide, blue skies.

All this happened during that winter in Dehra Dun.

After which I grew up.

Naiyer Masud (b. 1936)

Naiyer Masud was born in Lucknow on 16 December 1936. As in the case of many other writers in this anthology, the story of his family lineage becomes a metaphor for the narrative of a society moving from a pre-colonial feudal world to modernity. His ancestors were hakeems, or traditional doctors, but the family calling ended, more or less, with his grandfather's generation: his own father was a Professor of Persian at Lucknow University, and was a scholar of repute in Persian and Urdu. Masud himself has doctorates in these languages, and has been a Professor of Persian at the same university. He is now retired; he lives with his wife, three daughters, and son, in the large mansion his father built and named 'Adabistan', or 'Abode of Literature'.

The appearance of some of Masud's stories (he is principally a short-story writer, and has three collections of stories) in English translation in a single volume (Katha) in 1998 was an extraordinary event, less remarked upon, thankfully, than some of the other 'literary' events that have taken place in the recent past. But those who have encountered these stories have been left with the impress of their artistry and strangeness; they are not quite like anything one has read before. Their strangeness emanates from a background that negotiates the Persian, Urdu, and English languages; writers like Kafka (whom he has translated) and Poe; and the city of Lucknow. Indeed, Lucknow is the setting of many of his stories, but it is not a Lucknow to be found, I think, anywhere outside of the stories; instead, his stories link Lucknow to the invisible cities of Calvino, but with a greater humour and more puzzling purpose than Calvino possessed. Masud has said that 'words should signify, and signify without equivocation'; and that he 'had to struggle the most on language, on how to write precisely, on selecting words that would communicate my intent most accurately . . .' Since his stories are all directness and equivocation, Masud, here, seems to have something of the seriousness and irony of his characters, who labour so hard at tasks without definition. His stories are full of craftsmen of little-known crafts, tradesmen, houses, unnamed streets, large families in transit, and fathers who seem to have no function, the latter probably a joking reference to Kafka – unlike the authoritarian Kafkaesque father, though, Masud's fathers are more like Kafka's doorkeepers, who don't quite know who they're keeping out and what they're waiting for. His comment on language and precision reminds us that Masud is, above all, an extraordinary realist, but a realist of the unreal and imprecise states of mind that our destinies are based, and founder, on.

* * *

'Sheesha Ghat' (1996)[1]

translated from the Urdu by Moazzam Sheikh and Elizabeth Bell

> *Sad mauj ra ze raftan-e khud muztarib kunad*
> *Mauji keh bar-kinar ravad az miyan-e ma*
> *(Each wave that strikes out to embrace the shore*
> *Rolls up a hundred more when it departs.)*

Nazeeri Neeshapuri

> *And with such luck and loss*
> *I shall content myself*
> *Till tides of turning time may toss*
> *Such fishers on the shelf*

George Gascoigne

After keeping me with him with the greatest of love for eight years, my father, my *moohbola baap*, was finally forced to find another place for me.[2] It was not his fault, nor was it mine.

He had believed, as had I, that my stuttering would stop after a few relaxed days with him. Neither he nor I had expected that the people here would turn me into a sideshow, the way they do a madman. In the bazaars, people listened to my words with a curiosity greater than that displayed toward others, and whether what I said was funny or not, they always

1. Sheesha Ghat: The name of the place. Literally, the glass wharf.
2. *Moohbola baap*: Literally, 'by-word-of-mouth father,' these words have been retained here – where they appear for the first time – since neither 'foster father' nor 'adoptive father' conveys the sense of the original adequately.

laughed. Within just a few days my condition worsened so much that when I tried to say anything at all, not only in the bazaar but even at home, the words collided with my teeth and lips and palate and bounced back the way waves retreat on touching shore. I would get so tongue-tied that the veins in my neck would swell and a terrible pressure would invade my throat and chest, leaving me breathless and threatening to suffocate me. Beginning to pant I would be forced to leave my sentence incomplete, and then start all over again after I had recovered my breath. At this my father would say, 'You've said that. I heard you. Now go on.' If he ever scolded me, it was for this. But my problem was that I just couldn't resume my account from where I had left off, I had to start all over again. Sometimes he would listen to me patiently and at others he would lift his hand and say, 'All right, you may stop.'

But if I couldn't begin my account from the middle, I couldn't leave it unfinished either. I would grow agitated. Finally, he would walk away, leaving me still stuttering, talking to myself. Had anyone seen me then, I would have been thought insane.

I was fond of wandering through the bazaars, and enjoyed sitting there among the groups of people. Though I could not comprehensibly put thoughts into words, I made up for this by listening closely to what others said and silently repeating it to myself. Sometimes I felt uncomfortable, yet I was happy enough. The people here did not dislike me, and above all, my father held me dear and looked after my every need.

For some days, though, he had seemed worried. He had begun talking to me for long stretches of time, a new development. He would come up with questions that required long answers, and then listen attentively without interrupting me. When I would grow tired and begin to pant, he would wait for me to resume my account, listening all the while with the same concentration. I'd think he was about to scold me, and my tongue would start to tie itself in knots, but he would just gaze at me, saying nothing.

In only three days my tongue began to feel as if it were unknotting a little. It was as if a weight were being lifted off my chest, and I began to dream of the day when I would be able to speak as others did, with ease and clarity. I started to collect in my heart all the things I had wanted to share with others. But on the fourth day, my father called me over and had me sit very close to him. For a long time his talk rambled aimlessly, then he fell silent. I waited for him to pose one of his questions, but he said abruptly, 'Your new mother is arriving the day after tomorrow.'

Seeing the joy dawning on my face, he grew troubled, then said slowly, 'She'll go crazy if she hears you speak. She'll die.'

The next day my luggage was all packed. Before I could ask any questions, my father took my hand and said, 'Let's go.'

He didn't say a word to me during the journey. But on our way, he told a man who chanced to enquire, 'Jahaaz has asked for him.' Then they both started talking about Jahaaz.

I knew Jahaaz, too. When I had first come to live with my father, Jahaaz earned his livelihood by performing clownish imitations at fairs and bazaars. He would wear a small pink sail tied to his back. Perhaps that's why he was called Jahaaz, a ship. Or perhaps he wore the sail because his name was Jahaaz. The pink sail would billow when the wind blew hard and Jahaaz would look like he was moving forward under its power. He could mimic to perfection a ship caught in a storm, convincing you that angry winds, raging waves, and fast-spinning whirlpools were bent on sinking the ship. The sounds of the wind howling, the waves slapping, the whirlpool's ringing emptiness, even the sails fluttering, would emerge distinctly from the mimic's mouth. Finally, the ship would sink. This routine was very popular with children and older boys, but was performed only when the wind was high. If the wind halted, however, the young spectators were even more delighted, and called out: 'Tobacco, tobacco!'

I had never seen anyone smoke tobacco the way Jahaaz did. He used every kind of tobacco, in every way it was possible to smoke it, and when the air was still he would perform such astounding tricks with clouds of smoke that the spectators couldn't believe their eyes. After producing several smoke rings, he would take a step back, then twist his hands and wrists in the air as though sculpting a figure in soft clay. And sure enough, the rings would take on a shape, just like a sculpture, and stand suspended in the air for some time. The boys were not allowed to watch some of his mimic acts. For these he would hide inside a rapidly closing circle, two or three spectators deep, and the only way those standing at a distance knew that Jahaaz was performing was by a glimpse of the fluttering sail and the sound of the spectators' laughter.

A year after I had come to my father's, Jahaaz almost lost his voice. He also acquired a severe cough. For his acts he had used many different voices, but now if he opened his mouth a coughing fit would seize him, and at times it took him nearly as long to finish his sentence as it would have taken me. Not only did he cease to perform his mimic routines, he stopped coming to our village altogether, and after the first year I did not see him again.

*

We passed many settlements and ghats on our way. Everywhere we went, there were people who knew my father, and he would tell them that Jahaaz had asked for me. I didn't understand what this meant, but asked no questions. In my heart I was angry with my father. I wasn't the least bit happy about living apart from him. But my father didn't seem happy either. At least he didn't look like someone who was about to bring home a new wife.

Finally we arrived at a grimy settlement. The people here were glass-workers. There were few houses, but each one had a glass furnace, and ugly chimneys belching smoke protruded from the straw thatch of the roofs. Layers of soot had settled on the walls, the lanes, the trees. People's clothes and the coats of stray dogs and cats were black from the smoke. Here, too, a few people knew my father. One of them asked us to eat and drink with him.

An oppressive feeling stole over me. My father looked at my face carefully, then he spoke to me for the first time on that journey.

'People don't get old here,' he said.

I didn't understand him. I looked at the people strolling by and, indeed, none among them was elderly. 'The smoke eats them away,' he said.

'Then why do they live here?' I wanted to ask, but the question seemed futile, so I simply stared in my father's direction.

'Jahaaz knows glassworking, too,' he said after a while. 'This is his home.'

I stood up with a start. My tongue was in many knots all at once, but I couldn't stay silent now. Would I have to live with a smoke belching bazaari clown like Jahaaz, in this settlement where a dark barbarity seemed to pour over everything? This question had to be asked, no matter how long it took. However, with a reassuring gesture, my father beckoned me over to sit by him, and said, 'But Jahaaz moved away long ago.'

I was relieved. As long as Jahaaz doesn't live in this settlement, I said to myself, I can live with him anywhere. Then my father said:

'He lives on the ghat now.' He pointed in its direction. 'On Sheesha Ghat.'

The oppressive feeling returned. My father did not know perhaps that I had already heard of Sheesha Ghat from visitors to his house. I knew that it was the most widely known and least inhabited ghat of the big lake, and that a terrifying woman by the name of Bibi was its sole owner. She had been the lover of a notorious dacoit – or maybe he was a rebel – and she later became his wife. In fact, it was during one of his visits to Sheesha Ghat that his whereabouts had been betrayed by informers to the government people and he had died, at their hands, on this very ghat. A strange development altered the situation completely; the entire ghat was given over to Bibi. She had made her home in a huge boat that now lay anchored in the lake. She ran some sort of business, in connection with which people were allowed to come to the ghat now and then. Otherwise it was forbidden to go there. Nor had anyone the courage to do so. Everyone was frightened of Bibi.

How had Jahaaz come to live on Sheesha Ghat? Would I have to meet Bibi as well? Would she speak to me? Would I have to answer her questions? Would she lose her temper when she heard me speak? I had grown so absorbed in these questions and their imagined answers that I didn't even realize we had left the settlement of the glassworkers. I was startled when I heard father's voice in my ear, 'We're here.'

*

This was perhaps the most deserted area around the big lake. An expanse of muddy water began at the end of the barren plain, its far shore invisible in the distance. On our left, set back from the water, a big boat obscured the view of the lake. Perhaps at one time it had been used to transport logs. Some of those logs seemed to have been used later to build many rooms on the deck, quite a few of them – large and small. The planks on the boat were all loose, and a light creaking sound issued from them, as of some giant object slowly breaking apart. On the shore of the lake a low, long retaining wall lay face down on the ground. Near it stood four or five rickety platforms with huge cracks in them, and close by was a mouldy length of bamboo, nearly claimed by the soil.

I sensed that this must have been a bustling place once. It was called a ghat, but all that was left now was a roofed shelter extending from a building toward the shore, the front of it overhanging a little pool of lake water that had sloughed over into a depression in the ground. At the rear of the shelter, on a little rise, sat a shapeless building of logs and clay which looked as though its builder had been unable to decide whether to construct it of wood or earth and, during these contemplations, the building had reached its completion. The roof, however, was all of wood. A small pink sail, perched on a projection in the centre of the roof, was fluttering in the wind.

My father must have been here before. Grabbing my hand, he quickly walked down the slope and up the five earthen steps that led to the doorway of the building. There was Jahaaz, sitting on the floor smoking. We went in and sat down too.

'So you're here, are you?' he asked my father, and began coughing.

He seemed to have aged quite a bit in eight years. The extreme paleness of his eyes and darkness of his lips made it seem as though they had been dyed in different vats. From time to time his head would move as if he were admitting something. During one of these motions he caught a glimpse of me with his pale eyes and said, 'He's grown up!'

'It's been eight years,' my father told him.

We sat silently for a long time. I would have suspected that the two were talking in signals, but they weren't looking at each other. Suddenly my father stood up. I rose with him. Jahaaz raised his head, looked up at him, and asked, 'Won't you stay a little?'

'There's a lot to be done,' my father said. 'Nothing's ready yet.'

Jahaaz nodded his head, as though agreeing. My father walked out and was down the earthen steps before he turned, came over and took me in his arms.

We stood there silently for a long time, then he said, 'If you don't like it here, tell Jahaaz. I'll come and get you.'

Jahaaz's head moved in that way of his, and my father went down the steps and away.

I heard Jahaaz cough and turned toward him. He took a few quick drags of his tobacco, made an effort to even out his breathing, then got up, took my hand and walked out under the shelter. We just stood there quietly, Jahaaz running his eyes over the lake. Then we returned to the earthen steps, but Jahaaz stopped at the first step. 'No,' he said. 'First, Bibi.'

We walked along the shore of the lake until we came to the big boat. Carefully balancing on the gangplank made by joining two boards, we reached the ladder at the other end, then climbed onto the boat. There was a curtain of coarse cloth over the door of the small front room. The two-coloured cat dozing before it peered at us through half-open eyes. Jahaaz halted as he neared the curtain. I stopped many steps behind him.

At Jahaaz's first cough the curtain slid aside and Bibi appeared. The sight of her filled me with fear, but more than that with amazement at the thought that this shapeless woman had once been someone's lover. She looked at Jahaaz, then at me.

'Your son's here?' she asked him.

'Just got here,' Jahaaz replied.

Bibi looked me up and down a few times, then said, 'He looks sad.'

Jahaaz didn't say anything. Neither did I. The silence lingered for some time. I kept looking at Bibi. 'Do you know how to swim?' she asked.

I shook my head.

'Afraid of the water?'

I nodded.

'A lot?'

'Yes, a lot,' I indicated.

'You should be,' she replied, as if I had said what was in her heart.

I viewed the expanse of the lake. In the still air, the muddy water seemed completely at rest; the lake could have been mistaken for a deserted plain. I shifted my gaze to Bibi. She was still looking at me. Then she turned toward Jahaaz, who was handing her the tobacco-smoking paraphernalia. For some time they smoked and discussed something to do with finances. Meanwhile, a brown dog appeared from somewhere, sniffed at me and went away. The cat, which had been dozing all this time, raised its tail on seeing the dog, arched its back, then retreated behind the curtain.

I peeked at Bibi from time to time. She was a strongly built woman and seemed bigger than her boat, but it also seemed as if she, like her boat, were slowly disintegrating. At least, that was my impression from looking at her, and from her words, which I couldn't hear very well. Suddenly she stopped in the middle of what she was saying, raised her head and called loudly, 'Parya!'[3]

The sound of a girl's laughter came toward us, as though floating on water. Jahaaz took my hand and led me back to the gangplank. I heard Bibi's voice, 'Take good care of him, Jahaaz.' And she repeated, 'He looks so sad.'

The way she said this, even I began to think I was sad.

*

Yet there was no reason for me to be sad. When Jahaaz showed me my quarters, I couldn't believe this was part of the shapeless house on the deserted ghat, between the muddy lake water and the barren plain. All efforts had been made to ensure my comfort. The rooms were lavishly decorated, mostly with glass objects. Glass was also inlaid in the doors and

---

3. Parya: Given Urdu orthography, it is significant that although the most likely reading of this name is 'Priya' (beloved), it can also be read as 'Pariya' (fairies).

the vents in the walls. I was surprised that Jahaaz could create a place like this. He must have had help from someone, or else had been trained in the art of decoration, I thought. A lot of the items seemed to have been brought there that very day. I suspected that other things had been removed, and that before me, perhaps long ago, someone else had lived here.

After I had seen the place where I was to live, I thought I had seen the whole of Sheesha Ghat. But on the second day I saw Parya.

I am amazed to this day that during the many times people at my father's house spoke about Sheesha Ghat, no one had ever mentioned Bibi's daughter. I first heard her name the day I arrived at Sheesha Ghat, when Bibi called her from the boat. I was so overwhelmed by the day's confusion, it didn't even occur to me to wonder who Parya was. The next morning, I heard the sound of someone laughing. Then a voice said, 'Jahaaz, let's see your son.'

Jahaaz jumped up and grabbed my hand.

'Bibi's daughter,' he told me as he led me out to the shelter.

About twenty-five yards away I saw Parya, standing tall and perfectly erect at the far end of a narrow, slowly swaying boat in the lake. With a light shimmy of her body she advanced the boat toward the shelter. Another little twist brought the boat nearer. Advancing and stopping, she pulled right up to the shelter.

'Him?' she asked, with a questioning glance at Jahaaz.

I was as wonderstruck that this girl was Bibi's daughter as I had been at the thought that Bibi had once been someone's lover. I tried to look at her closely, but now she was inspecting me from head to toe.

'He doesn't look so sad,' she said to Jahaaz.

Then turning to me, she said, 'You don't look sad.'

'When did I say I looked sad?' I tried to say, feeling a little irritated. But all I could do was stutter.

Parya laughed and said, 'Jahaaz, he's really ...' Then she began laughing louder and louder, until Bibi's voice boomed from the boat,

'Parya, don't bother him.'

'Why,' Parya asked loudly, 'because he's sad?'

'Parya,' Jahaaz said encouragingly, 'you'll have fun with him.'

'Who needs fun?' she said and started to laugh again.

I began to feel uneasy, as though trapped, but then she asked, 'Have you seen your new mother?'

'No, I haven't,' I told her with a shake of my head.

'Don't you want to?'

I didn't answer and looked the other way.

'You don't?' she asked again.

This time my head moved in a way that could mean yes or no. It occurred to me that my new mother was to arrive at my former house today, or perhaps had already arrived.

My father had said that she would go crazy if she heard me speak. I tried to envision myself talking and her slowly going crazy. I tried to imagine what it would be like to live with a woman who would go crazy because of me. I also reflected that at this time yesterday I had been at my old house, and the memory seemed to come from the distant past. I relived my eight years there in eight seconds. Then I thought of my father's embrace before leaving me in Jahaaz's custody. I believed now, even more than before, that he loved me deeply.

'Jahaaz will love you deeply, too.' Parya's voice startled me.

I had forgotten about her, but she had been watching me all this time. She moved to the other end of the boat, balancing herself as she walked. With a little spin of her body, her back was toward the shelter. A light swing of her torso nudged the boat forward and slowly she slid away from us. I felt as if a wonder had taken place before my eyes.

'If Bibi had not called to her,' I said to myself, 'I would have thought she was the spirit of the lake.' If not the spirit of the lake, she was indeed a wonder, because she had been born underwater, and her feet had never touched the earth.

*

Bibi had recieved her boat from her forefathers, Jahaaz told me that day after Parya left. No one could say how long it had been in the big lake. But Bibi had lived far away from the lake where her husband, the dacoit, or whatever he was, came to meet her clandestinely. When Parya was about to be born, her husband had Bibi sent to the boat along with a midwife. One day, Jahaaz had heard Bibi crying in pain. Suddenly, the voices changed. Some government people had arrived and were questioning Bibi as to the whereabouts of her husband. Bibi would not tell them anything at all, so they took to repeatedly holding her underwater and in the midst of one of the longer episodes, Parya was born.

'I could clearly see bubbles coming from Bibi under the water,' Jahaaz said, 'then amid the bubbles Parya's little head emerged. And you could hear her cry.'

The government people realized that Bibi hadn't been lying about the pain. They left, but continued their surveillance. And one day, Parya's father came to the ghat, just as they had thought he would. They surrounded him on the boat. He tried to escape, but was injured, fell into the lake and drowned.

Since that day Bibi had made the boat an abode for Parya and herself. She sometimes ventured out, but never let Parya set foot on land. She would roam around the lake in her small craft, or would return to her mother on the big boat. Why? Had Bibi made a vow of some kind? Was it the condition of some pact? No one knew how long Parya would continue circling the lake, and whether her feet would ever touch earth.

I spent a year at Sheesha Ghat, and during that year I witnessed the passing of every season, and in each season I watched Parya's boat roam the waters. She was my only means of diversion. The outer door of my abode opened on to the barren field, which led only to the fishing settlements at its nearest outskirts, past the smoky dwellings of the glassworkers. I stayed away from these habitats because of the drying fish. The fishermen were always immersed in their work and were of no use to me, just as I was of no use to them.

There were many ghats at the far ends of the field, including some large fishing settlements. A few ghats were alive with activity, but once or twice when I went to them I realized that the news of Jahaaz's foster son had preceded me. So, except for roaming the abandoned field and amusing myself with a few stray objects, I mostly sat underneath the shelter. Jahaaz, too, after running around all over to complete his errands, would come and sit here with his tobacco supplies and recount all sorts of tales. They were tales worth remembering, but I forgot them anyhow. But, I do remember that when a story of his failed to hold my attention, he would become agitated, even frenzied, and narrate it the way he used to perform his imitations. He would then suffer a bout of coughing and ruin what little interest there had been in the story.

In the beginning, I thought that Sheesha Ghat was completely cut off from the rest of the world, and that this part of the lake had always been a wasteland. That was not the case. It was true, however, as I had heard before, that no one could set foot here without Bibi's consent. I had assumed that Bibi never let anyone come here, but once, at Jahaaz's, I noticed that on certain special days the fishermen gathered here, bringing their nets and boats. Sometimes, they came in such large numbers that the scene looked like a little fair set up on the water. Sitting at my post under the shelter, I would hear the fishermen calling to each other and shouting directions. Filtering through their voices here and there came the sound of Parya's laughter. At times they seemed to be forbidding Parya from doing something. Occasionally, the voice of one of the older fishermen would be heard scolding Parya, yet laughing heartily at the same time. Then Bibi's voice would come from the boat: 'Parya, let them work!' Parya would laugh in reply, and the fishermen would tell Bibi not to say anything to Parya.

On those days, and other days too, Parya would come to the ghat early in the morning. Standing in front of the shelter in her boat, she'd chat with Jahaaz for some time, then call me out to the shelter as well. If Jahaaz went away, she would talk to me. Her conversations were a bit childish. She would tell me stories about her dogs and cats, or why Bibi had scolded her the day before.

Sometimes she would ask me a question so suddenly that I'd start to answer with my tongue instead of the bobbings of my head. She would laugh wildly at these attempts only to get a scolding from Bibi that made her push out to the far reaches of the lake. In the afternoon, Bibi would call out to her in a loud voice and Parya's tiny craft would be seen advancing toward the boat. Then the sounds of Parya laughing and Bibi getting angry would emanate from the boat. Late in the afternoon, she would set out again and stop in front of the ghat. If Jahaaz were not there, she would talk to me about him. She found something to laugh at in everything about Jahaaz, whether it was his smoking, his disorderly dress or the sail on top of his house.

As she was talking to me one day, I began to suspect, and was soon convinced, that she had never seen the clown routines Jahaaz used to perform in the bazaars years before, and neither did she know about them. That day, for the first time, I tried to speak somewhat calmly, so that I could tell her about Jahaaz's mimic routines. She listened to me very attentively for a long while, without laughing, the way my father had begun to listen to me in the end.

Then Jahaaz walked out underneath the shelter, smoking, and relieved me of my efforts by telling Parya all that I had been trying to recount. He even performed two or three of his minor routines. To me they seemed pathetic imitations of his old ones, but Parya laughed so hard her boat began to rock. She wanted more, but Jahaaz was overcome with a coughing fit. Parya waited for it to stop, but he gestured to her to go away. As she turned her boat around she said, 'Jahaaz, Jahaaz, you would make even Bibi laugh.'

*

The next morning she arrived at the shelter earlier than ever, but Jahaaz had slipped away somewhere. She began talking to me about Jahaaz and described the mimicking as though I hadn't seen Jahaaz performing his routines the day before, indeed, as though I'd never known about them. I listened to her for a while, then tried to tell her that Jahaaz used to walk through the bazaars with the sail tied on his back, and mimic sinking ships before the crowds. But I could not tell her, by tongue or by gesture. Finally, I fell silent.

'Tomorrow,' I said in my heart, 'somehow, I will tell you.'

I watched her as she retreated from sight.

'Tomorrow,' I said again in my heart, 'somehow.'

My father arrived at the ghat the same evening. In one year he seemed to have aged more than Jahaaz had in the eight-year period before my arrival. His step was halting. Jahaaz walked by his side, supporting him, almost carrying him.

As soon as my father saw me he drew me into his arms. Finally, Jahaaz separated him from me, and made him sit down.

Turning to me, Jahaaz said, 'Your new mother has died,' before the coughing overtook him again.

There was no conversation between my father and me. Shortly after he arrived, Jahaaz took him off somewhere and returned late at night, alone. I had just lain down. Jahaaz fell asleep after smoking his nightly tobacco, but I kept wondering how my father could have grown so old so quickly. I thought of my new mother who had died without seeing me, and perhaps without going crazy. Then I went over the year I had spent at Sheesha Ghat, remembering how I had been bored at first by the extended, nearly unbreakable silence. Now I felt that the place was always full of sounds. Faint calls would come from the glassworkers, fishermen and the other ghats. Waterbirds would call over the lake. But I had never paid attention to them. Now, when I tuned my ears a little, I heard the halting sound of waves coming in and turning back after touching shore, and the faint creaking of the planks of Bibi's boat.

I decided that Sheesha Ghat was the only place for me, and that I had been born to live here.

'Tomorrow morning, I'll tell Jahaaz,' I told myself, and fell asleep.

*

In the morning my eyes opened, as usual, to the sound of Jahaaz's coughing. Then I heard Parya's voice, too. They were talking, as on any other day. Jahaaz was inside and since he was unable to see Parya's boat from where he sat, he spoke loudly, coughing again and again.

I got up and went out to the shelter. There was Parya, standing in the middle of her boat. After chatting with Jahaaz a little more, partly about Bibi, she walked to the other end of the boat. The boat made a half-circle from the light movement of her feet and then Parya's back was toward the shelter.

For the first time I took a good look at Parya, and found myself more amazed than ever that a woman like Bibi could be her mother. At that instant Parya's body twirled and the boat moved away from the shelter. It swayed a moment and stopped. Parya scanned the expanse of lake before her. Again the boat rocked lightly but Parya, straightening her body, adjusted its balance. She made another barely perceptible motion with her feet. The boat made a very slow half-circle.

I viewed Parya from head to foot as she stood in the bow. I was afraid she might not like the way I was staring at her, but she wasn't looking in my direction. She was gazing intently at the ghat's still water, as if seeing it for the first time. Then, measuring her steps, she walked to the end of the boat nearer the shelter. Leaning over the water, she looked into it once again, stood up, shook her body into alignment, and very calmly placed a foot on the water's surface as one steps on dry earth. Then her other foot left the boat. She took one step forward, then another.

'She's walking on the water!' I exclaimed to myself, my surprise tinged with fear. I turned my head toward Jahaaz, who was smoking a little distance away, then looked back to the lake. Between Parya's empty boat and the shelter there was only water, concentric circles of waves spreading on its surface. A few moments later Parya's head emerged from the circles. She slapped the water with her palms over and over as though trying to clutch the surface of the lake. The water splashed and I heard Jahaaz's voice, 'Parya, don't fool around with water.'

Then a noose of smoke tightened at his throat and he doubled up, coughing wildly. My eyes turned to him for an instant. He was having a fit and needed help. I looked back at the lake. New circles were spreading on the bare water.

Parya rose again, then began to sink. My eyes met hers.

I jumped up shouting, 'Jahaaz!' my tongue beginning to knot.

I leapt toward the old man. His coughing had stopped, but his breath was gurgling. He was rubbing his chest with one hand and his eyes with the other. Dashing up the steps, I grabbed both his hands and shook him with force.

'Parya . . .' my mouth said.

He looked into my eyes with his pale irises, then lightning flashed in his eyes and I felt as though a bird of prey had escaped from my grip. Dust was dancing on the steps to the shelter and Jahaaz was standing at the shore.

Parya's boat completed a full circle. Jahaaz looked at the boat, then at the water. Then, with full force, he let out a call in a strange language. I heard Bibi match his cry from her boat. Then from far, far away the same voice returned. Bibi's asked, 'The sad one?'

'Parya!' Jahaaz said with such force that the water before him trembled. Other voices, far and near, repeated Jahaaz's cries over and over. Fishermen, some with nets, some empty-handed, began running toward the ghat from all directions. Even before they got to the shelter, some of them had plunged into the water. Jahaaz was signalling to them with his hands when a splashing sound came from the left. I saw a barking dog running helter-skelter on the big boat and the two-coloured cat, its back raised, looking at the dog from a corner of the roof. Then I saw Bibi, almost naked, like some prickly man-eating fish, as she cut through the water. Her body collided with Parya's boat, sending it spinning like a top. Bibi dived and came up on the other side of the boat. She signalled to some of the fishermen and dived again.

Fishermen from other ghats were seen rowing toward us. Some had jumped overboard and were swimming in front of their boats.

Heads bobbed everywhere in the water between the shelter and Parya's boat. The crowd grew, collecting along the shore as well. There was din and commotion everywhere. Everyone was talking, but it was hard to tell what was being said by whom. The loudest noise, of splashing water, obscured all sense of the passage of time. Finally, a loud voice rang out. The clatter peaked and suddenly died to nothing. The bodies in the water, swimming soundlessly, slowly gathered at one spot. All were silent now except for the dog barking from the boat. At that moment I felt my hand clamped as though in a vise. Jahaaz was standing next to me.

'Go,' he said, giving my hand a shake.

*

I couldn't understand where Jahaaz wanted me to go. Now he was pulling me into the house. Turning back, I tried to look toward the lake, but he tugged my hand. I looked at him. His eyes were glued to my face. 'Go,' he said again.

We had come to the back door of the house. Jahaaz opened it. In front was the barren plain. 'They've found her,' he told me, then pointed across the plain and said hurriedly, 'You'll reach the glassworkers' settlement in a short time. There you'll find someone to take you out of here. If not, just mention my name to anyone.'

He put some money, tied in a handkerchief, in my pocket. I wanted to ask him many things and didn't want to leave, but he said, 'Only you saw her drown. Everyone will ask you questions. Bibi more than anyone. Will you be able to answer?'

The scene rose before my eyes – the people, fishermen with rings in their ears, rowers with bangles on their wrists, visitors from different ghats – all forming a ring around me, two or three deep, questions flying from every direction, Bibi fixing me with her intent stare. They all fall silent as Bibi approaches me ...

Jahaaz noticed me trembling and said, 'Tell me what happened. Anything ... Did she fall into the water?'

'No ...' I managed somehow.

'How did it happen, then?' Jahaaz asked. 'Did she jump?'

'No,' I said, and followed it with a shake of my head.

Jahaaz shook me, 'Say something, hurry!'

I knew I wouldn't be able to say anything with my tongue, so I tried to communicate through hand gestures that she had been trying to walk on the water. Yet my hands halted again and again. I felt that even my signals were beginning to stutter, and that they too were incomprehensible.

Jahaaz asked in a constricted voice, 'Was she walking on the water?'

'Yes,' I said again with some difficulty.

'And she went under?'

'Yes.'

'She was heading toward Bibi?'

'No.'

'Where then?' he asked. 'Was she coming toward us?'

'Yes,' I gestured with my head.

Jahaaz lowered his head and grew a bit older before my eyes.

'I've seen her every day,' he said at last, 'from the day her tiny head popped out of the water' – he was nearly coughing the words – 'but I hadn't noticed how grown-up she'd come to look.'

I stood silently, watching him grow even older.

'All right, go!' he said, putting his hand on my shoulder. 'I'll find something to tell them. Don't you tell anybody anything.'

What could *I* tell anybody? I thought. And my attention, which had meanwhile strayed from the ghat, returned to it. But Jahaaz gently turned me around and nudged me in the direction of the open field.

When I reached the edge of the field, I turned toward him and he said,

'Your father came to take you back yesterday. I told him to wait a few days.'

Again he coughed a little. He grabbed both panels of the door and slowly began to back away.

Before the door closed, I had already started on my journey. But I'd only gone some fifteen steps when Jahaaz called out to me. I turned around and saw him walk toward me haltingly. He looked as though he were imitating a ship whose sails had been torn off by the winds. He came up to me and embraced me. He held me to him for a long time. Then he released me and stepped back.

'Jahaaz!' Bibi's wail was heard from the ghat.

The pale eyes of the old clown looked at me for the last time. He nodded, as though in affirmation, and I turned and walked on.

THE SOUTH

U. R. Anantha Murthy (b. 1932)

U. R. Anantha Murthy was born into a Brahmin family on 21 December 1932, in a village in Karnataka. He studied at Mysore, and was awarded a Gold Medal by the University upon passing his MA. He was appointed a lecturer at the same university, and has continued to be a teacher of English literature for the greater part of his working life. In 1963, he left for England, and was supervised by Malcolm Bradbury when a doctoral student at the University of Birmingham. It was here he began to write and revise his first novel, *Samskara* (1965), a story about a Brahmin priest faced with an existential choice after the death of a fellow Brahmin. At the time he was revising the first draft, Bradbury took him to see Bergman's *The Seventh Seal*, which was being shown without subtitles; seeing the film as a series of dark images and in snatches of untranslated dialogue crystallized, for Anantha Murthy, the nature of the subject matter – a South Indian village; death and its aftermath; sex, metaphysics, and individual choice – that he was working on, and pointed out a way as to how he should revise it. The late D. R. Nagaraj, distinguished critic and commentator, divided Anantha Murthy's fiction into two phases. To the early, 'radical' phase belonged, according to him, the portrayal of rebels who transgress a boundary – of caste, community, society. The second phase, to which the story below belongs, is characterized by self-doubt, and by a critique of what was dramatized in the earlier work. While this is pertinent, one also sees a continuity between an early work such as *Samskara*, and a relatively late one, such as 'A Horse For The Sun', the story below. Both narratives are a record of the duress that the rational and high-minded values of the protagonist – an unusually individualistic Brahmin in the first case; an educated Marxist writer in the second – undergo when confronted with the life of another man who has unashamedly absconded from a style of existence that might adhere to some idea of progress or, at least, propriety. In the novel, it is the dead Brahmin, Naranappa, who has led an irresponsible life, leading to an embarrassing and unpleasant situation after his death, with none of the priests, except the protagonist, wishing to perform his death-rites; in the story, it is Anantha's friend, who, by not having changed or evolved with modernity, presents an equally

exasperating dilemma to the narrator. These texts seem to allegorize
Anantha Murthy's own dilemma and ambivalences as a writer; the fact
that he must write in a style that is rational, individualistic, even progressive, while the material from which he derives his vitality and inspiration
can be seen to represent a retrograde form of existence – erotic, centred in
community, and the vernacular. Like Ramanujan and many other writers
in this volume, Anantha Murthy has said that his more rational and
intellectual mental processes belong to the English language, which is why
he often writes his essays in English; but that it is his intention, in his
stories, to let in the unrecognized, local traditions through the back door.
In the story below, Anantha's friend Venkata is that 'back door', and while
opening that door is necessary and enriching, it must also result in a
psychological crisis for the writer, a crisis that the story below dramatizes
in a familial and domestic setting.

* * *

'A Horse for the Sun'* (1984)

translated from the Kannada by Manu Shetty and A. K. Ramanujan

I am writing this about Good-for-nothing Venkata – his real name is
Venkata Krishna Joisa – who suddenly appeared before me one day in the
market place after fourteen years. He didn't recognize me, I had left
the village and gone away, but how could I possibly forget him? There he
stood, my boyhood chum, a spot of kumkum between his eyebrows, his
head a shaven crescent, an open-mouthed laugh with teeth fallen off here
and there, and a jaw that moved round and round like an *arati* platter.
How can I forget such a Venkata? There was a *khadi* bag under his arm.
He was standing there, his mouth open, gaping at the vegetable shop as if
it were a toy shop. I stood there in front of him, like someone who had
come upon a river in the sweltering heat. Shifting his gaze from the heap
of lentils to the bunch of bananas, from the bunch of bananas to the
beans, from there to the bright-coloured cucumbers ripening through the
year, and then to the one-eyed Konkani shopkeeper who was looking at

---

* The Sun's horse (or a horse for the sun) is a translation of the common Kannada name
  for a grasshopper (*Suryana Kudure*).

him without any expectations as if he were looking at the stray cows in front of him, Venkata finally looked at me. But – he just looked. Around there, he and I were the only ones without an umbrella under their arms – just the two of us. Although it was the month of July, being an astrologer he was confident that it wouldn't rain. The presence of umbrellas by everyone's side, in spite of the cloudless sky, proclaimed their hopes and anxieties. That I, who had left the village long ago, lived abroad and was now a city-ape in Mysore and had come to the village without an umbrella would not have surprised anyone who saw my crisp trousers. But as he stood there without his dhoti tucked up, without even an umbrella, a bag by his side, looking at the vegetables that had come to the market place either from the Kanara coast or Shimoga as if they were not edible matter, the smile on his face seemed to indicate that he was the only one who knew the secrets of the heavens. But would my thrill at seeing Simple Venkata so unexpectedly be muted by the disappointment of his not recognizing me? How could memories stay green in a land where the rains had failed?

He was at least five or six years older than me – this Venkata. Yet he was the bosom pal of my boyhood. Someone who had time and again freed up my mind and body. One incident flashes across my mind: I was scared of the river. I must have been around eight or nine then. Without my mother's knowledge, he coaxed me to go with him to the river. He grabbed me and, as I was flailing and screaming, jumped with me from a rock into the water. I coughed, gulped water, fainted, and then in his firm grasp floated gently into the depths of the water, rose to the surface, learned to open my eyes in the water, watched with delight my palms getting smaller under the water, my crotch tickled by the tiny little fishes; my palms bloated under the water. Neck, mouth, nose, head – step by step I descended into the depths of the water. I just had to press down with my fingers and the water would buoy me up like a cork. When I got out of the cool water and lay down on the cool sand, the sun would dry me ... The village stream must have dried up now. Although Venkata did not recognize me as I stood there reminiscing, I stood on tiptoe and reached out with my hands like one about to dive into the water, and said, 'What's up?'

'Ripe cucumbers have become so expensive.'

I didn't give up. Locking my eyes with his, I tried to rush him.

'Did what's under my arm look like a rooster to you?' said he, opening his gap-toothed mouth.

'I say, *budaan saabi*, why is your rooster's head dangling like a Brahmin's empty bag?'

'My rooster crushed and killed this one in a battle, sir.' He raised the bag, as if he were holding a rooster by its feet and held it out to me.

'Having lost so many teeth, without having shaved that scraggly grey beard, on this full moon day, in this daylight, with that cock under thine arm, to be running around like this in an alien land, what ill fate has befallen thee, O Prince?'

Listening to the cadence of my speech, delivered in the style of the *Yakshagana* plays that we used to watch together, he lifted his dhoti to tie it up, and sprang back. His buttocks hit the horns of an old cow that was chewing a banana peel. Rubbing his bottom, he said, 'Anantha, aren't you?' He turned round and addressed the cow that had its muzzle in the gutter rummaging for banana peels: 'Mother, *Mahalakshmi*, why did you make me think that this Ananthu might be an *amaldar*? Or are you the sorceress who always plays tricks on me?'

The cow lifted a banana peel out of the gutter and devoured it with its eyes half closed and mouth askew. The one-eyed *Konkani* in the shop asked me: 'How much lentils shall I give?' I took Venkata's bag and filled it to the brim with lentils, *tondekayi*, cucumbers, beans, potatoes and onions. I said to Venkata, 'Let's go to your house.'

'Come home, I'll give you an oil bath and make you see the moonlight. There'll be hot water in any case.'

Then he hurried on purposefully, like someone taking things home for a feast, gently pushing aside the people with his hands.

'Then I'll buy *bhrngamalaka* oil.'

I climbed up the stone steps of Prabhu's shop that reeked with the stench of tobacco.

'How come you are paying such a rare visit to the village, Mr Murthy? Your brothers too have an account here, just like it's been since your father's days. Come in, come in, shall I get you something to drink?'

Prabhu, who was sitting with a pencil stuck behind his ear, showed me a stool between the bins.

'I keep coming to the village. I haven't been to the market place – that's all. All's well?' I said. The stench of tobacco blended with the smell of jaggery that he was weighing on the balance.

'What's well? No rains. Won't be able to collect my dues. My eldest son died last year after just three days of illness. Don't have a paisa of profit in business. I sit here because this is the trade my father taught me – that's all. My children haven't the good fortune of going to England and studying there like you. They sat here saying that our tobacco and gram business was good enough. Look, he's the second one, he the fourth, the other two have opened a cloth shop. I married off three of my daughters to lawyers. My eldest son's children are going to high school. How many children do you have – now – where are you . . .' he spoke, swatting the flies and cutting jaggery pieces to balance it to the right weight. I had a sense of déjà vu; it had happened just like this way, right here, a long time ago.

'In Mysore. Two children. A boy and a girl. Do you have *bhrngamalaka* oil?'

'What, Mr Venkata Jois's oil bath, eh? When he was in prison wasn't he the one who gave an oil bath to K. T. Bhashyam? The number of ministers he knows! All the old timers. In this entire state of Karnataka, there's no one who hasn't had his head massaged by him. But yet I wonder why he hasn't received his pension for two years. I say Jois-*re* – why don't you ask Mr Murthy to put in a word? If you receive your pension I might even get some of my old dues back. On the whole, this Jois here is an ill-fated man like me. He has a son – only in name. An utter rascal. Didn't study, didn't pass an exam. Hangs out in the coffee shop. In all, our times were better. Now things have all degenerated.'

Venkata opened his mouth wide and smiled and put the bag down, leaning it against his limp leg. He took the snuff out of his pocket and sniffed it. He took the dust-covered bottle from the hands of the boy who had brought it and said, 'B. V. Pandit's brand, I hope? That's the best. It really cools the body.'

'Yes, Jois-*re*, fresh stuff. I am the only stale thing here,' he said, as he took the money from me. 'This is the day's first cash transaction. Look at the state we are in.'

Venkata reached out his hand over the boxes and held Prabhu's hand that was on the balance. Then he meditated.

'Prabhu, I thought as much the moment I saw you. You have excessive heat in your system. You need an oil bath. I'll come tomorrow and massage your head – OK?'

Prabhu who had let his hand lie limp in Venkata's as if it were a bunch of greens, let out a tired sigh and said: 'Do you think there's a single head left in the village that has not been massaged by this Jois, Mr Murthy? How such a son was ever born to such a man, God only knows. I heard that the other night the boy accosted the College Principal, beat him up and took his money.'

Venkata drew a line across his forehead to suggest what fate had written there and laughed. And then, as if to manifest the line, he raised his eyebrows. When Prabhu too raised his eyebrows, lines formed on his forehead. He said, wiping the jaggery sticking to his hands: 'Will it mean jail, Jois-*re*?'

Venkata lowered his eyebrows, picked up the bag and, getting ready to move, said: 'What's written on his forehead has to happen. I've got him out on bail. I gave the Inspector a good oil bath. The Principal too. Now I've to do it to the Judge . . .'

Venkata's laughter embarrassed me. But Prabhu was not embarrassed. Just as ever – this Venkata was the laughing-stock of the village. A shameless man.

We walked towards Kerekoppa. Only the footpath didn't seem to have changed in all these fourteen years. I began to scold Venkata. He's always been a clown like this. The way this sage had put us in a fix during the Quit India movement. We were in the high school then; he woke us up in the middle of the night one day and led us, saying 'Come on you guys, let's hide the post box.' In the darkness of the new moon night we stole the post box, buried it six feet deep in the sand by the river bank and came back. Next morning there was such a commotion in the village. But we went about our business as usual as if we had nothing to do with it. We sang: 'Oh Kamala Bai, Oh Kasturi Bai, we too shall fight,' and such other songs. We lay down in front of the toddy shop. We went to the school and lay down and picketed it. Venkata was our leader. But how could he ever hold his tongue? They say some stranger stopped him by the roadside. He's supposed to have asked: 'I'm an outsider, where can I get some good coffee?' This do-gooder Venkata took him to Shinappayya's coffee shop. This idiot didn't realise the man was a CID. 'What good-for-nothing boys you are, do you know what the students in Shimoga have done?' and so on, that scoundrel of a CID taunted him, sipping hot coffee. Venkata let his tongue loose: 'Come on, come on, we are no less than the Shimoga students.' 'Where do you boys have the guts to hit at the Government directly?' the CID dared him. And then Venkata bragged on and on about our night's adventure. The result: the police marched us along with Venkata in a procession to the river bank.

Then, sure enough, the whole village assembled by the river bank and the police handed us shovels and said 'You bastards, dig it up yourselves.' In the blistering sun we dug and dug and took out the post box we had buried. In front of everybody's eyes, we carried it in a procession to the post office and put it back. Did it stop at that? The police herded us into a lorry and left us in the Sakkarebailu forest. We walked and we walked,

chanting Hari Hari, eating berries on the way and reached our village the
next day.

Although I tried to remember all this in anger, I couldn't help laughing.
Venkata put down the bag and laughed with me, clapping his hands and
dancing. 'You are an eternal sucker,' I said. He had failed year after year
and ended up as my classmate. By then he had already acquired a
quarrelsome wife. If an occasion ever arose to bring her from the village
for some function or ceremony, on his way to school he would walk
briskly ahead of her in the street as if she were someone unknown to him.
She would run after him, saying, 'Listen, listen.' That's how we all came to
know when we were in lower school – that he even had a wife. Once when
our maths teacher started to cane him saying, 'You overgrown buffalo,' he
made a pathetic face and said, 'Sir, sir, I'm a married man. Please don't beat
me.' The teacher burst out laughing, carefully removed his turban, placed
it on the table and continued to laugh as he wiped his face and smeared it
all over with chalk powder. Seeing the dark face of our teacher smeared
with chalk and turn grotesque, we began to laugh. Venkata went up to the
teacher to wipe his face with a duster and made us laugh even more.
When the teacher went at him again with the cane he crawled under
the table and prayed with folded hands: 'Please don't. If I have welts, my
wife will find out.' The teacher who suffered from chronic backache and
couldn't bend down, kicked Venkata's bottom and said, 'Get out, you
madcap, you widow's husband.'

Yet even as this Venkata made me laugh, making it impossible to get
angry with him, I realized he had brought up his own son without any
sense of responsibility. I turned serious and tried to scold him: 'You are an
escapist, a characterless fellow, a spineless eunuch.' He said, 'Tell me, who
has achieved anything through tenacity? Come – I'll give you an oil bath
and drain you of all your conceit.'

Venkata then began to strut – like a schoolboy saying, come, I'll show
you.

*

'Wait,' I said. I had to talk to him honestly and say: I had ignored you.
Although I came to the village every now and then, I never came to see
you. You met me accidentally today and are opening me up like this. Yet I
know that this game is only momentary. I am drying up. This clowning of
yours may be a habit with you. But in me there's been born a disquiet that
I cannot understand. I desire nothing. Of late I can't think of anything to

write. The moment I open my mouth, big fat words tumble out – the heads in front of me nod in appreciation. The moment the play is over I feel empty. Why don't I see anything? Do you see, or are you merely pretending that you see? Isn't even your humility a posture? Or is it that I who had spent my childhood with you didn't write about you, but instead went on to write about highfalutin things and ended up being an empty drum like this?

'The smell of *kedige*,' said Venkata. He flared his nostrils and sniffed the air around – the way the demons in stories sniffed – and said, 'The smell of humans.' I kept my mouth shut. And that kept him quiet too. He put the bag down and vanished into the bushes saying, 'My daughter Ganga loves to braid her hair with *kedige*.' I didn't know it was the season for *kedige*. After a while he reappeared empty-handed. He swore, 'Don't know where the damn things are hidden. Let's go,' he said.

Someone met us on the way and stopped us. He wore gold earrings and carried a cloth bundle on his head. He spat out betel juice and spoke:

'What, Joisa, I came by your house. Your wife stopped me and told me an earful. I believe you have been absconding since morning. Went to the market place and hasn't returned yet, she said and then she started to recite your thousand names . . .'

Venkata lowered the bundle down from his head and asked:

'Did you see her in the backyard? Or in the front door? Will you enlighten me regarding the exact location of your encounter with my consort, O Sage Narada?'*

'Why, in the backyard.' He spat out all the betel juice from his mouth, wiped his mouth with his hand towel and started to laugh – showing the few red teeth that remained here and there.

'Then she's made a curry out of the *chagathe* leaf that grows in the backyard. My wife is a noble soul who can cook cattle feed and make it taste delicious. We are beholden to you for these auspicious tidings, O great sage.'

'But her tongue is something else,' he said as he went ahead and then he turned around to say:

'But, Joisa. But why does your son Subba keep hissing like that? I tried to talk – "You mind your business and go, go away," he said. Although the words, "All right, Subba, you red-faced firebrand" were on the tip of my

---

* Editor's note: Sage in Hindu mythology who delights in instigating quarrels.

tongue, I swallowed them and walked away thinking why should I meddle in others' affairs. We think we're all a family in our village, but that son of yours ... It's the fate of all those who go to college.'

Narada went away, balancing the bundle on his head and swinging his arms. Venkata said, 'Ha, OK,' and came and joined me. He behaved as if nothing had happened. This man is swan-footed, water doesn't wet him. Oh, you scoundrel, I thought to myself. I was certain his worldly affairs were in chaos. But he is untouched by all this – is he a madcap or a hypocrite or a scraggly-bearded saint?

'How many children?' I asked.

'Four. The first is my illustrious son. Don't ask, the girls aren't married yet. Hence my wife, who was fierce as Chamandi to begin with has now become Kali, no less. But then, am I not a devotee of the Mother? I accept the scoldings of Mahakali as her gift and am still thrilled by the smell of this world.'

I was irritated by the reply that he delivered in the *Yakshagana* style. Why should someone like him father four children? Live as the butt of every passer-by's joke? I began to think: the village idiocy that Marx spoke of, which is the cause of this country remaining backward ... and so on. Venkata seemed to symbolize for me everything that lived in a state of inertia. I tried as seriously as possible to expound to Venkata my anxieties about the stagnation in this country that I had been sharing of late with my friends. But is he the kind who would listen?

'No rains at all.

'Should see this coming December whether the mango tree will blossom at all.

'Last year it didn't yield a single bud-mango for pickles.

'Look, flocks of parrots come to that tree.

'There is Peacock Hill, there's a cave, I'll go live there the moment my children are married ...

'Do you know how beautiful everything around looks from there? I'll give my pension to my wife – and then I'll stay there.'

He blabbered like this all along the way, yet he heard me through. In the spaces between Venkata's various responses, I said:

'What is politics but changing the quality of life?

'But then, change in which direction? In that of the haves? Or the have-nots? But why does one need determination to bring it about?

'The determination to change nature and the rest of the world to suit our goals and desires, is the foundation of all politics. It is also the foundation of science.

'It is the root of all religious acts. That too is politics – the politics of the eternal . . .

'Don't you wish that your wife and children should live in the way you think is right? To say that things should not change but go on the way it is, is also politics.

'Do you know why? To change is the way of nature. Some try to stop it for their benefit, but that doesn't work for long.

'Everything cracks, explodes, nothing remains the same. That's why we have to keep striving towards an order that we think is right.'

I walked on, saying these things.

'What counts is what each one is born with.'

Saying this, Venkata put the bag down, joined his hands, looked up at the sky and prayed:

'I bow, I bow to heroes like you. Let people like you forgive this Clown Venkata. But then when your head is all heated up, you will certainly need the services of someone like me to give you an oil bath,' and he pretended to massage briskly an imaginary head in front of him.

'*Thoo*, you!' I said. Venkata took my anger to be real and said:

'But, tell me, Ananthu. I couldn't change even the wife I married. Can I change the world? I am here now, what guarantee is there that I'll be here the next moment?' We had to cross a log bridge made of three areca stems placed together. He stood behind, saying, 'Careful. You go first.' I walked nervously on the bridge, crossed over and stood waiting for Venkata. Thinking that I had finally cornered him in an argument, I said:

'Venkata, we may die the next moment. Or we may not die. But even if we do die, there'll be others who'll remain.'

I forced Venkata to give the bag to me. Walking along the edge of the field, Venkata said:

'You know, we were in Panjurli's grove before we crossed the bridge, Ananthu. They say this Panjurli spirit has his temper at the tip of his nose! Once, long ago, I was coming through the grove singing to myself. It was evening. I heard a rustling sound behind me, like someone stepping on dry grass. I turned around to see what it was. It was a tiger. I blacked out and collapsed. I come around and find that I had peed in my dhoti.'

'Why are you telling me this?'

'*Che, che*, just like that. I am a sissy, Ananthu. I didn't know what to say when you started to talk as if that demon Panjurli had possessed you. I keep telling my wife, Look. I am like this. Tell me, what can I do? She has a foul mouth, that's all. If I ever have a stomach ache, even if she has her period, she'll walk all over and bring this herb and that herb and make a concoction for me ... I was frightened by the tiger – do you know why? Because I don't know how to catch it and make it sit down and give it an oil bath. If only I knew, I'd hold it by its whiskers, make it sit down, and gently massage its forehead...'

Venkata clutched his belly and started to laugh. I laughed too, reminded of all the kicks that he used to receive when we were kids. But then thinking that all his unsaid words were there in his laughter, I was terrified that I might give in to him. 'Hey, you fool. Can you live without an ego? Even a saint needs an ego.' Saying this, I thought – without destroying the likes of Venkata, there is no electricity, no dams, no penicillin, no dignity, no respect, no joy of sex, no woman won, no peaks, no aircraft, no evolution, no memory, no passion, no joy. As I was thinking all this, I saw Venkata standing barefoot by the edge of the field, bubbling with joy, and I was flabbergasted. Was he laughing at me out of pity?

'You say you haven't married off your daughters who have come of age. What if they go astray?'

I felt like hurting this Venkata who could look upon me with pity. 'Why don't you find a groom? Where will I get the dowry from? Those girls are like pearls. Why would they go astray? If they do go astray, then it's their destiny. How can I possibly change it?'

Venkata's guileless manner silenced me. Shall I ask him to make money by any means? Shall I ask him to make a revolution to change society? Then Venkata said, smiling, dropping his playfulness:

'I am a priest, a worshipper. To worship is what I was born for. I worship everything I see. Worship every head that I find. Spirits like Panjurli, Bobbarya, Jattiga, and the School Inspector, the policeman, the district officer, now you, once K. T. Bhashyam – this way I worship the Mother. If you try to butt back at what comes butting at you, do you know what happens? You bruise your head. The goddess, my Mother, fills my belly with food – my wife Rukku makes cups out of banana leaves. I carry them on my head to the market place and sell them. Now, soon, I'll receive my pension. The other day I gave our MLA a grand oil bath. I told him how I had made K. T. Bhashyam see the moonlight when we were in jail ... Just look how these trees and plants let the gods into them. Just like them we too should let the gods into us. But then, there must still be some rancour left within me. Otherwise my son Subba wouldn't be such a hothead, burning away like this.'

Venkata snatched the bag from my hand and asked me to walk comfortably. He pointed out all his favourite birds.

'Look, they don't like to be seen by us. They don't need your political change, they don't even need my oil bath. They shit *pichak* on the heads of the most fearsome devils and *whrrrr* they fly away. To live they don't have to be clowns like me; they don't even have to be heroes. Isn't it so, Ananthu?'

I was beginning to feel hungry. I started to walk briskly. Venkata walked behind me, mocking my gait – just as he used to mock me during our schooldays. Do I still walk like that immature boy of days gone by? I felt embarrassed.

The people of the village who were sitting idly here and there were worried about the rain. 'Jois-*re*, when will it rain?' To this idle query Venkata replied with mock gravity, 'Wait for a week more.'

'There aren't even banana leaves for you to make your cups. So your mantras and tantras are good for nothing, eh?' said a young man from the village wearing trousers, trying to taunt him. Venkata replied, 'Of late I've been bringing *muthuga* leaves from the forest and making cups. Life has to go on somehow, you see,' and he bowed to the young man with folded hands and walked on. He called out to the boy grazing the cows, 'What, Chikka, I heard your master's cow ran away. He had come to me for divination. I gave him a talisman. Did the cow come back?'

'It came back, Jois-*re*,' said Chikka and continued to sit and play with the stones all by himself. I thought to myself, this must be Venkata's daily routine. The open life of feckless Good-for-nothing Venkata. Doesn't sprout. Doesn't rot. Laughs, makes others laugh. Dreams of living all by himself in the cave on Peacock Hill. When something comes butting at him, he steps aside and makes way. Gets scolded by his wife. Has no secrets, hides nothing. Only when there's a gem in the hood of the cobra, can there be venom in the belly. This one has neither gem nor venom. He's an idiot, devoid of anger, fury and jealousy. I shouldn't give in to him, just because my raised fist has withered.

Venkata pointed out a tree to me. It was a huge, massive tree. 'There's something special about this tree. It has a hand, do you see? It is pointing to the ground. They say it means there is a treasure there,' he said. I laughed. 'Some greedy people have tried to dig it up. But the treasure belongs to a spirit of the place called Jattiga. How could anyone else get it?' This childhood friend of mine was able to expound every square foot of this land. And not just that, he had a personal philosophy too, shaped in the presence of the various spirits of the land.

*

This is how I got to know of it. Venkata, who knew the by-ways within by-ways of Kerekoppa, took me round and round, and as he took me around he wove every secret path we walked on into the story of Sri Rama's exile. In the pathetic story of exile which began with 'Once, Mother Sita . . .', the thick leaf that he pointed out to me became the wick of the lamp that Sita had lit. Rama had once adorned his wife's hair with the *sitaladanda* flower he had plucked from the tree that was in front of us now. Over there, Lakshmana had shot an arrow into the rock and released the underground waters. On the rock, he showed me a pit as big as cupped palms and said, 'Drain it, let's see.' It filled up as soon as I drained it. 'Drink,' he said. The water was cool and sweet. He showed me a stone protruding on the rock and said, 'This is the *udbhava linga* that rose out of the earth, which Sri Rama had worshipped.' He scooped the water in the cup of his hands and poured a libation on the *linga*. Then he closed his eyes and stood with his legs bent like Shiva's nandi bull and said something like this:

'The Supreme Soul is Father to some, Mother to some. Those who think of it as Mother always have their eyes on Mother's breast. It is a breast ever flowing with milk. Those who drink it can't take their mouth off that breast. They don't ask for other breasts. Those who think of it as Father, raise their heads and look at the Lord in his eye, and they are roused. They want to look and they want to see; they want to swallow the whole world. Can the hunger of the eye ever be quenched? The infant at the breast falls asleep; it wakes up and again drinks the milk. I am one of those who drinks. You are one of those who see . . .

'I wonder why in someone like Sage Shankara who aspired to see and conquer the world, the desire to become the infant Shanmukha and drink of the breast was ever born. Even if you do not understand, it's all right. There is no problem with drinking at Her breast. See how the earthworm keeps drinking. How the tree drinks and blossoms . . .

'If Mother says, on her own, "How much do you drink?" and puts you down, you might open the eyes and see and know. That's Mother's wish. Sometimes Mother takes you off one breast and puts you on to the other. Then it is terrifying. If this breast is life, that breast is death. There are some fortunate souls who have even seen her eyes between the two of them. That is, if they didn't scream out.

'Moustache-twirling heroism is not for the likes of me. Take it that my service to this world is that of a clown. I just have the desire to eat and sleep. In sleep, you too drink. When children drink they kick their mothers. But before your heroic passion to bend the world to your desires is born,

should or shouldn't your belly be soothed a little first? Where do you find
that soothing thing? In Mother's milk, in my oil bath . . .'

Venkata who had delivered these words like a *bhagavata* in a mytho-
logical play, stood enchanted by the flow of his own words. He snorted
some snuff and said, 'This is a habit I've acquired since I quit *beedis*.' Then
he said, 'The sight of you will be like putting a lock on my wife's mouth,'
and laughed happily. And nodding his head approvingly at his own words
he walked, splaying his crooked legs here and there. His legs are knock-
kneed, so he walks with his feet spread out.

*

There was a house in front of us. A country-tiled, leaky house. Unwhite-
washed, unswept, a barren house without *rangoli* designs in front of it.
'Sheshanna's. He is very ill. Let's see him – come.' Saying this, Venkata put
the bag down at the door, held my hand and led me into the darkness of
the inner rooms. 'Ananthu has come – Acharya's son Ananthu – Professor,
at Mysore, you know him, right?' he said. Adjusting my eyes to the
darkness, I thought: *Arre*, Venkata. This guy is a philosopher too. How
shall I answer him? I need English words to do that. Or translations of
them that Venkata doesn't understand.

Like these:

The bravado that becomes insensitive to suffering . . . the philosophical
resignation of a coward . . . inauthentic character . . . escapism . . . acquiescence born of superstition . . . the innocence of village idiocy . . . and so on.

If he reads what I write he will read only himself. Since he is a simpleton
to begin with even my irony won't touch him. But what began as an object
is now confronting me as a consciousness. For one without desire, the
incessant movement of the world, its flux, and its change are of no interest.
In the presence of such a non-political being all my knowledge is a waste.
This man is the exact opposite of a Kissinger. But in Gandhi, along with an
aspiration there was a quietude too . . . *Arre* Venkata, you came in as a
story, now you are growing into an essay!

'This is Sheshanna. His son is in Bombay. You know Bombay where
they make atom bombs – there. Like you, a red-eyed fellow. My illustrious
son wants to be like him. He has a white woman for a wife. If she wears
sari and puts on kumkum, she looks just like our Mother Goddess . . . She
had come here. She asked her father-in-law to go stay with them. Where
will he go? He is hooked on his onion-potato sour curry. On top of it he
likes to boss around. Everything should be as he says. Why should his
educated son listen to it?'

Venkata continued to chat, slicing the betel nut fine with the cutter. Sheshanna started to cough. The kind of coughing that seemed to choke him. Venkata lifted him and made him sit, leaning against himself. He held a plate in front of him, rubbing his back all the while. I thought this was the end of Sheshanna. He coughed, coughed and coughed, threw back his head and groaned, struggling to breathe. Venkata bent his head forward and said 'Spit, spit.' Sheshanna must have spat blood. Venkata made him lie down and went to the backyard to wash the plate and came back. He said 'I'll heat some coffee on the stove,' and went in. Sheshanna had his mouth open and was heaving heavy sighs. His breath came and went *Ha Ho* noisily, his eyes opened and shut mechanically. From a glass tile in the roof and a high window, light dimly floated into the inner quarters. I counted the bright-coloured cucumbers that were hanging from a rafter. I sat shrinking into myself, moment by moment. In one corner Sheshanna was lying on a rough-hewn bed like a ghost covered by a thin blanket. Suffering from tuberculosis. Must be under Venkata's medical care. Venkata has always been a do-gooder like this. His school bag would contain scores of cork-stoppered bottles, medicines from the town for all and sundry. Little wooden caskets of snuff for the women who had cultivated the habit on the sly. Ribbons and double-edged combs for de-lousing the girls, silk thread for the *anantha* ritual, palm leaf, cotton and silver paper for the gowri festival. Candy from the muslim's shop, for who knows whose children. Except for the books that were supposed to be there, his school bag contained all these and god knows what else. Along with his umbrella, there would be two other faded ones that were brought along for repairs. Wearing a patched-up shirt, a tulsi leaf tucked in the knot of his hair, Venkata would swagger down the market place as if the whole street belonged to him. He would bring *amte* fruit for us to eat.

Venkata brought hot coffee and made Sheshanna drink it. Sheshanna drank it noisily in small gulps, saying, 'When will I close my eyes, tell me.' Venkata replied, as he blew into the tumbler to cool the coffee and kept putting it to Sheshanna's mouth, 'Why will you close your eyes so soon? If Yama* ever comes to your doorstep riding his buffalo, you are the kind who will say, "Wait a moment Sir, I've made onion-potato sour curry; I'll finish it off and come." If Yama says, "Let me see what kind of a sour curry this is" and tastes it, he'll leave you here in this world and go back saying – it's best not to transfer this man from here, should we be hungry on our way it's good to have a place like this where we can get such superb sour

---

* Editor's note: The god of death.

curry. But then – why will Yama who has come all the way go back empty-handed? Since he won't want to waste his TA and DA he'll ask you to show him another client. Then you'll say, "In this village there's a man called Good-for-nothing Venkata. He's younger than me, but now his clowning has all gone stale – take him along." If Yama is scared off by my wife's tongue then I am saved. Otherwise that'll be the end of me.'

Sheshanna's face seemed to come alive a bit. Venkata placed his head on the pillow and got up. He made signs at me to get going, and started to go, saying, 'Sheshanna, I'll send seasoned rice mixed with *saru* – my daughter will bring it for you.'

Sheshanna turned to me and said, 'Your son might know my son, Dr Subramanya Shastri. Studied in London. He's an engineer in Bombay. You know the place where they make the atom bomb – there. They say he gets something like three thousand as salary. A big bungalow . . .' Saying this, he tried to sit up. Venkata said 'Lie down, lie down.' I said namaskar and got out.

*

Venkata took the pole off the stile and let me in first. 'Say, come look who's here,' he shouted, joyfully announcing the weapon of his self-protection. Rukku who came out fuming, cooled off as soon as she saw me, like a burning log doused by water. She wiped her hands on her sari and beamed. 'He wouldn't listen to me, Ananthu bought this for you,' said Venkata, putting the bag of vegetables into her hands. The wrinkles on her face that had been etched by a thousand worries, crinkled around her eyes in a smile of gratitude.

A big elongated spot of *kumkum* was prominent on her forehead. A *sampige* flower in her thin grey braid, Rukku looked short and frail. Eyes that had dimmed, with the smoke of the stoves. Shakuntala, Gowri and Ganga appeared. The elder two girls were wearing saris. They had come of age. Their black hair was braided tight. Glass bangles, earrings, and fragrant *sampige* in their hair; that was all their adornment. Seeing me they beamed bashfully. One of them brought hot water for me to wash my feet with. The other one brought the towel. The youngest wearing a patched-up frock stood peeping from behind her mother. In the hands of the youngest one I saw the jasmine garland that she was stringing with banana fibre. I looked around as I was washing my feet: the garden in front of the house was beautiful. Flowering plants that I hadn't seen for years were all there. Round jasmine, needle jasmine, rose, *nandi battalu*, chrysanthemum, *kumkumajaji*, *rathnagandhi*, evening jasmine, canna, *sampige*, various kinds of *tumbe*, conch flowers of various colours, *chendu, parijatha* – a garden that had drunk water and was green. Though there were no rains, Venkata's well hadn't dried up.

The house was equally kept cool. A cool mud floor that had been scrubbed and shined into a dark smooth surface. On it was a *rangoli* design drawn with white flour. Walls whitewashed. Bright-coloured ripe cucumbers hanging from the rafter. On the nail on the wall was an almanac. Venkata took off his shirt and hooked it on another nail. In a corner, mattresses neatly rolled. On the door-frame, a garland made of bangle pieces, and a cotton garland – must be from last year's *Gowri* festival. The copper vessel I had used to wash my feet with was sparkling. Shakuntala placed in front of me a bronze tumbler with a cool drink made of rice water, milk, jaggery and cardamom. 'I too have two children,' I said. 'Is everybody well at home?' asked Rukku. As she hurriedly ran from the kitchen to the inner quarters and from there to the kitchen, a dispute arose between her and Venkata. 'Oil bath, right away,' he insisted. 'Let him bathe and eat. You can give him an oil bath at night,' she said. Rukku won. Venkata followed me to the bath house. 'Thanks to your visit I wasn't greeted with the sixteen-course ceremonial reception,' he said.

I laughed and poured the hot bath-water on myself. In the bath house was a large pot meant specially for the oil bath. A trough of black stone. On either side were large cauldrons. In a big vessel there was cool *matti*. Soapnut powder in tins. Seeing all this paraphernalia, I dreaded to think of the night.

'Why do you make your wife angry?' I said.

'Why should I make her angry? It happens by itself. It's a weapon that the Mother has granted her in order to protect me. This clown has to be kept within bounds, you see. Children's hair shouldn't be dishevelled. Firewood should be dry. I shouldn't be chattering with everyone I meet. People riding on this clown's back should be gotten off, you see ... She protects me with her tongue.' Venkata said this as he pushed a burning log of wood into the stove.

'Where is your son?' I asked.

'He is addicted to cards. None of my weapons work on him. He flares up when he sees me.'

I didn't tell him that the failure of his philosophy confronted him in the person of his son. But as I poured the water on myself, I looked at him as if I were making that criticism. Venkata spoke as if he didn't understand any of this:

'Subba gnashes his teeth saying that his father is worthless. But will my nature change? I believe his Principal didn't let him sit for his exam because he did not come to class regularly. So he accosts him at night and beats him up. They say my son even took his money. He pesters me for money, he wants to start a flour mill in the town. I am bankrupt. Where can I get that kind of money from?'

Don't you understand evil at all, you fool. You are like the lotus that blossoms only in stagnant water. I couldn't stand you for more than two days. Doesn't time move at all for you, O Sage, O *Raikva*. You live breezily, scratching your sores and sunning yourself – playing the same clowning game over and over again. Swallowing these thoughts, feeling both affection and disgust, I finished my bath. Venkata prayed loudly to all the holy rivers: '*gangecha yamunechaiva godavari saraswati narmade sindhu kaveri jalesmin sanidhi kuru*', and he channelled the water he had ritually poured on himself on to the yam that had grown in the dirty water. Seeing me look at the yam, he said 'We'll pluck those leaves. My wife will make *pathrode* tonight.'

Shakuntala dried a tender leaf on the fire, laid it out for me, and drew a *rangoli* around it. She placed a plank for me to sit on. Pickle made out of mangoes that still had the sap in them, jack-fruit *pappads*, long chillies, lime pickle that was still tender, lemon pickle that had been dried for so many years, rice flour fries, another kind of flat, spicy fry – I was too shy to ask its name – and rice *payasa* at the corner of the leaf.

'I haven't made anything special. It was made in a hurry,' said Rukku, playing the hostess and pouring the sauce on the hot rice. Two other kinds of *tambuli*, and, just as Venkata had guessed, the *chagathe* leaf curry. Buttermilk, with coriander and fresh ginger in it. Venkata sat resting on his hand, relishing the meal with his eyes closed. It was a long time ago, as a child, I had had that soup of seasoned rice water and sour curds. I had even forgotten its name. It was a tasty, light meal that filled every corner of the stomach.

Before I could lie down on the mattress that Shakuntala and Gowri had spread out for me, I heard Rukku stand by the door step and call out,

'*Ayye*, Subba, Subba, come eat,' The strained voice of a mother, that called out half in anger, half in anguish: 'Listen, listen. Call Subba.'

I came out with Venkata and looked. I only saw the back of someone wearing a shirt and a pair of pants. Hippie-style hair covered the neck. He was walking briskly without looking back. His gait was just like his father's. But he was taller than his father, and slimmer. Venkata ran after him, without his shirt, in his dhoti. Subba stopped, turned around, and swung his hands violently; he was shouting something. As he stood pleading with his son, Venkata looked like Ashtavakra, the mythical Brahmin who was crooked in eight limbs. Subba suddenly bent down. He looked around and picked up a stone. Venkata covered his face with his arms and continued to plead as he stepped back. Subba walked away. I couldn't stand the sight of Rukku standing on tiptoe, agonizing over her son. Venkata who returned looking foolish, saw me and said,

'Subba's head is heated up. He was about to pounce on me like a tiger,' and shivered in mock terror.

'Can't you stop your clowning at least now? I don't know what kind of a father you are who can't slap the boy and drag him in,' said Rukku and went in, wiping her tears with the end of her sari.

'You go in and eat. Set aside Subba's food. He'll come home the moment he is hungry. Where will he go?' said Venkata and went after his wife. I went in and lay down. The little girl Ganga sat playing with the shells all by herself.

*

Rukku was viciously telling her husband, all that I had ever wanted to tell him:

'Just because you rot here in this village, will your son rot too? The whole village mocks his father; you don't have a paisa's respect. Why will your son respect you, tell me. You come and go grinning and giggling *he he he*. What will the children learn from someone like you? Tell me, why does someone like you have a family? How many years has it been since you received your pension? I have to do everything. I make leaf cups, look after the house, keep the children in control. Cook three times a day and feed that miser Sheshanna who doesn't part with a paisa. When I sent him seasoned rice and curry, I believe he said, Couldn't she send some mango pickle? Why is your mother so tight-fisted? In addition to slaving for him, do I have to listen to this too from him? The children and I are cooped up in this village. A carnival, a movie, a town – tell me what have we seen? Poor Subba. He is so fond of rice and black gram *payasa*. He is roaming in the sun on an empty stomach. He has gone so far astray that he assaults his own father. Someone who doesn't like us has put a spell on him. You don't understand anything bad. You are a perfect fool . . .'

Her scoldings that kept rapping like the falling rain made me drowsy and I don't know how long it lasted. It was only when I opened my eyes that I realized that Venkata was fluttering around me with a bottle of *bhrngamalaka* oil in his hand. I sat up, saying 'What's this?' He smiled with his mouth full of betel juice and said, 'Come, come with me.' I got up and followed him to the bath house. He made me tie a string round my waist and wear a loincloth and asked me to strip. There was a fire raging in the stove. He had filled up all the pots with cold water. He shut the door of the bath house and made me sit on a plank. He dipped a blade of *durba* grass in oil and touched it to my forehead and the crown of my head and then, turning up his mouth full of betel juice, muttered some mantras and performed the oil ritual. He poured some oil in his palm and smelled it. He lifted his dhoti and tied it up like someone about to dig a pond, and tied another towel round his head. He spat out the betel juice and came back and started massaging my feet. After he had applied oil all over my body, he poured castor oil into a plate, made me sit on a stool and placed my feet in the plate. 'Its coolness will gradually rise to the crown of your head,' he expounded. He moved his hands up and down, hollowed his palm into a spoon, poured *bhrngamalaka* oil into it, and dripped it on to my head. Saying 'Mother, Great Goddess,' he started to beat my head like a *maddale* drum. Changing the beat and rhythm of his drumming, he said, 'I am now talking to your head. How does it sound? Now it sounds like the *mridanga* drum, right?' I said *hm*, out of politeness. This ritual was beginning to embarrass me. From the way he was beating out a rhythm, I suspected he was dancing behind me. But I couldn't turn around. 'Through your head this rhythm will flow right down to your navel,' he said. 'They say this rhythm massages the six nodes of the body, the *Kundalini* centres. I don't have any special knowledge of it. But I know the job,' he drawled. Surely, he must be dancing. He sounded like the drummer who plays on the earthen pitcher during the drum passage in a concert.

After the drum session was over, the procedures that followed were intended to produce various kinds of vibrations. Venkata's heaving, gently trembling voice which provided a running commentary was directed towards this vibratory activity. My back was being roasted by the fire that was way behind me. Venkata now circumambulated me and worshipped my head with oil as he devoted himself to the various parts of my head in complex compositions of tickling, teasing, pinching, squeezing, scratching, caressing, pushing and pulling. 'I was now talking to your head,' he said and wiped off his sweat with the towel and readied himself to commence the second stage of the oil worship. As I wondered whether he had twenty fingers or a hundred, his running commentary appropriately changed its rhythm and melody and took the form of a mantra-like chant. It went like this.

'Ananthu, Ananthu, you have now entered the forest. Entered the forest ... in the forest, tree, tree, tree ... on the tree ... a parrot, a parrot. Green parrot ... between the leaves, a green, green parrot ... a green parrot with a hooked beak, in the hooked beak, in the hooked beak a red fruit, red, red, fruit ...

'It's cool below, cool, in the cool place a bush. From the bush a fragrance, a fragrance ... it's a yellow-hued *kedige*. Look ... look ... look through the crack, how it is splitting – look ... long, rough, thorny, green leaf, inside the green soft yellow ... gentle yellow, fragrant, fragrant yellow ... powdery, powdery yellow ... slippery yellow ... mysterious yellow ...

'Walk on, gently walk ... walk softly, softly and look ... this is *basari*, this is jack-fruit, this *nandi*, this *muthuga*, this banyan, this *ranja*. Look at the root of the banyan ... look at the tip of the roots ... it has nails at the tips ... This is a sage, a sage with matted hair ...

'All over here the sky is splintered, splintered blue. Lurking blue, provoking blue. Irritating blue, exasperating blue. Walk on. Walk on ... stop ... now an open space. An open open space, a wide open space, look ...

'In front of you a tiny plant. On the plant a leaf, on the leaf something is springing and leaping. Springing and leaping, springing and leaping ... bursting ... like this.

'... like this one day, long long ago, as you were coming from school it sprang – didn't it? You threw away your bag and stood watching. Stood watching. Watching ...

'You stood watching the sun's horse. You stood watching its crooked legs. You stood watching its humped back. You stood watching its whirling whiskers. Here, then there. Here, then there. There. There ... ohohoh then here ...

'Tiny horse, teeny horse ... You stood watching wondering how the sun rides on its back ...

'On the green, oh how the sun rides – he's the rider ... this the little horse. Teeny green horse. Horse who springs lightly and flies. On its humped back the big sun lightly sat, gently sat, sat lightly, sat unseen, sat flashing between the cracks ...

'Look where he flashes. He flashes on the roof. He flashes on the green. He flashes in the pupil of the eye, he flashes in the fringe of the cloud. He thunders and rolls. He glides in the water. He glides, falls and shatters. He was whole but now he breaks into a thousand splinters. He becomes the shadow, he becomes the hue, he becomes the night, he becomes the light. He glides, he shimmers ...

'Look, now an open space. A wide open space. Up above, the sun pouring down. And in all this open space, there's only this sun's horse, lightly carrying the sun on his back and springing and leaping and springing and leaping around. Look at his unharnessed back, his unbridled pride. Look at his crooked legs ... Look at his erect tail ... Look at how his whiskers explore the world.

'It is leaping from leaf to leaf. Look at it whole. Look at it piece by piece. Cream of green on a pile of green. Even the eyes are green. Listen to what it has to say. Listen to what the sun's horse has to say.

'What kind of a horse am I, what kind of a man are you. You are me and I am you.'

'Ananthanna, Ananthanna, Springing leaping Ananthanna. Ananthanna carrying the sun on his back.

'Now it's gone. It's gone, it's gone, it's gone. Anger's gone, arrogance's gone. Fury's gone. Fire's gone. Love of money's gone. Pride of name's gone. Everything's gone.

'All the evil spells have gone – father's spell, mother's spell, minister's spell, magician's spell, whore's spell, widow's spell, tomb's spell, womb's spell, old spell, broken spell, spell of all the books you've read, it's gone, it's gone, it's gone. All the evil spells are gone.

'Only the sun's horse remains. You are the horse, you are the horse ...'

And as the tempo of his speech changed the rhythm of his massage too changed, and a thousand fingers were dancing on my head. The oil dripped into my eye and it began to smart. Venkata who noticed it let out a sigh and wiped my eye with the towel that was wrapped round his head. He enquired anxiously:

'Ananthu, did you begin to see the moonlight?'

I didn't have the heart to say no. I said *hm*. Venkata was drenched in sweat as if he had poured water on himself. Sitting limply in front of him I felt ashamed of my nudity.

'No – you've only seen something like the moonlight. One more oil bath and you'll see the real moonlight,' said Venkata drawing in the snuff.

I was wrong: this Simple Venkata too is a scheming politician. What a manipulator! He planned to alter my very being.

He made me sit in a trough filled with hot water. He asked me to rub my armpits. He poured the cool of *matti* on my head and rubbed it briskly with soap-nut powder. He kept filling the bowl with water and splashed it at me from above. I was stewed and cooked and had turned red all over. There was no strength left in my arms anymore. He wiped my body himself. He made me drink jaggery syrup, put a spot of soot from the cauldron on my forehead and made me lie down on a mattress and covered me with all the blankets he could find in the house and said,

'Should sweat well.' In a short while I was soaked in sweat as if I had had another bath. He wiped me again and made me lie down on a mat. He brought me some steaming coffee. I felt drowsy as I drank the coffee. Rukku who continued to cry, started to make *pathrode*.

When I woke up, Venkata was pleading with his wife, 'Make some rice gruel for Sheshanna. I'll go feed him myself and come back soon.' Rukku grumbled, 'I believe his son sends him five hundred rupees a month. He doesn't give you a paisa. You are not worried about the son who was born to you. Why should I cater to that miser? What is it to us if that old fogey lives or dies?' Yet, Venkata got Shakuntala to make the gruel and left. As I sat up, Rukku came and stood in front of me and started to cry. According to her the trouble was with Subba's stars. He wanted to go to either Bangalore or Mysore and learn 'engine-work'. Why shouldn't he come up in life like Sheshanna's son? What does he lack? At least out of consideration for my friend, I should take him to Mysore with me and find a job for him.

I was scared. If I took him to Mysore and kept him in my house, my wife wouldn't put up with his pranks. Yet I promised. I'll rent a place for him to stay, I thought to myself. This made Rukku so happy that the whole house glowed with her happiness. Shakuntala, Gowri and the little girl Ganga too ran around with joy. Venkata who returned and noticed the changed atmosphere in the house puffed up like a pumpkin. He didn't know the promise that I had made. Then without a trace of sarcasm, he enacted Sheshanna's stinginess as if it were a scene in a play. This happened long ago: Venkata had brought him medicine. Sheshanna counted the change that he returned. Then he counted again. (Seeing Venkata cough and count out the coins one by one with trembling hands, even Rukku couldn't help laughing.) When he counted again, Venkata asked, 'What's the matter, Sheshanna?' 'This coin is worn out,' said Sheshanna. 'It'll pass,' replied Venkata. 'Pass this off and get me another one.' (Venkata opened his mouth and groaned like Sheshanna.) Venkata who had just walked three miles from the market place, enquired, 'Do you want me to bring it right now from town, Sheshanna?' 'If you have occasion to go back to town again today...' 'Thinking that he'll lose sleep over it, I gave him the coin that I had with me. What else could I do?' said Venkata and took out from his pocket and showed us a coin that he hadn't been able to pass off after all these days. 'Throw it on his corpse when he dies,' said Rukku and walked away to lay out the leaves for the night meal.

*

Then an incident took place that made it impossible for me to eat *pathrode*, that favourite dish of my childhood. Although Venkata and Shakuntala tried to persuade me, how could I possibly ignore the relentless weeping of Rukku? This is what had happened: Wishing to serve me cream in a silver tumbler, Rukku had opened the big bronze trunk in which she kept all the silver and jewellery that she had brought with her as a bride. What did she find there? Medicines that she had saved for her grandchildren, berries, dried ginger, *kasturi* tablets, *rudrakshi*, dried pomegranate seeds, sandalwood bark, and soapnuts for cleaning the jewellery – there was nothing else. All that Rukku had preserved for her daughter's wedding, making sure that they were not pawned even in the worst of times – earrings, gold chains, a four-stranded necklace, four bangles, a waist band, ear screws, nose ring, anklets, a pearl necklace, two silver plates, three silver vessels, a silver prayer tray, a silver bowl, a silver plate for the unguents – all of this, all these that had been carefully wrapped in a torn silk sari after the last *Gowri* festival, everything was gone. Although Venkata pretended as if nothing had happened and kept persuading me to eat the *pathrode*, the little girl Ganga came running and blurted out:

'Mother's crying. Subba has stolen all the jewellery. Everything was there on Friday, when mother opened the trunk. She had opened it to take the pomegranate peel for your stomach ache. The day before, Mother had gone to the tank to wash the clothes, no? Even Shaku and Gowri had gone with her, no? The same day, Subba gave me a wet piece of banana fibre and said, "Make a jasmine garland, I'll sell it in the town and bring you the money." I wondered why he was being so nice to me that day and went to the bathroom. Subba was doing something in the room. I thought he had closed the door to smoke a *beedi*...'

Neither Venkata, nor Shaku, nor Gowri spoke. Shaku went in to console her mother. 'We'll get it. Where will it go? Must have pawned it somewhere. Eat your meal,' said Venkata and quickly finished his own meal. I went through the motions of eating and got up. I went out and sat on the platform in front of the house. Thinking why a harmless soul like Venkata had been cursed like this, I sat trying to catch a glimpse of Subba. Far away there were a couple of houses and a temple. A path that had been worn down by walking feet. At a distance, the green hill. The footpath that leads to the market place goes by this way. There was a coral tree near where I sat, exuding a gentle smell. The yard was full of flowering plants. The moonlight that I had failed to see in spite of Venkata's oil bath, flooded the garden now. I could hear Rukku weeping and moaning: 'How shall I marry off my daughters now? Why do you torture your mother so?'

'Aha! The moonlight,' said Venkata approaching me. He must have come with the hope that my proximity would soften his wife's wrath. He must be embarrassed to see me in the midst of all this. I felt bad seeing my friend in such a state. I said, 'Come, sit down.' He replied, 'The smell of coral is lovely, isn't it?' I laughed and made a sign to him to keep his mouth shut. I am no good at words of solace. Yet I went in and said, 'Rukkamma, you eat your meal now.' She burst out weeping in front of me. When I came out, Venkata who was going round and round in the moonlit garden said, 'The garden is our Ganga's life.'

Nobody slept that night. I felt that Subba was in a situation anyone could find himself in – anyone other than a totally unambitious person like Venkata. What would I have become if I had had to rot in the village all my life? It is only because I had stood up to my father and rejected the ways of my family that I could grow and become what I am now. But why did the same impulse erupt even in this house? Venkata seemed stunned by his son. His clowning, his oil bath, his servility – nothing seemed to work in this case. This moon, this plant, this tree, these birds – people like Venkata exist in their midst, but so do the likes of Subba, with their causeless cruelty. Will a state of mind like Venkata's swallow it and digest it, or just spit it out? If so, the clowning of an escapist is pitiable and embarrassing. But my mind wouldn't let me brush aside this childhood friend of mine who had begun to kindle in me the simple human love that I seemed to have lost of late. The picture of Venkata cowering, twisted and curled up like Ashtavakra, when his son came to assault him, haunted me. Subba with a stone in his raised hand had appeared like a barbarian embodying fierce energy. It seemed that his barbaric rejection and nihilism contained in them the same life force that created nuclear weapons and poison gas. It had spurned the limited shell of Venkata's acquiescence and come into being. How else? I too had kicked my parents. In Venkata's state, there is only the blossoming and the withering, like the *parijatha* tree; but there is no movement.

While lying down, I might have exaggerated the image of Subba embodying the movement. What was so unusual about his stealing the jewellery? I tried to console myself later. But what I saw – at a time when everyone was asleep, before the crack of dawn, when the earth and the plants were being drenched with dew, and Venus was sparkling like a crystal in the sky – what I saw then weighs me down to this moment.

Hearing some noise in the garden, I got up and went out to see – it was the sound of trees being felled. 'Who's it?' I said and started to go down the steps. 'If you come near, I'll chop you down,' cried out Subba with a

knife raised, in the haze of darkness. I froze. In the dim light of daybreak,
Subba was hacking down the *parijatha* tree with his teeth clenched and
hair flying. He looked like a demon. All the softer flowering plants had
already been felled by him. Only the knotted and twisted *parijatha* tree
withstood the strokes of his sickle and still stood in its place. Venkata who
came behind me ran up to Subba. When Subba raised the knife to hack
down his father, Venkata sprang to the side crying, '*Amma*, mother!' and
came running back. Although I tried to restrain her, Rukku blurted out by
my side, 'Cut me down, cut me down. Hack me. I'll drink the poison that
was born in my womb and die.' She broke free of her daughters who were
trying to hold her back and ran and stood in front of Subba. 'Don't, don't.
Don't provoke me. I'll split your head open,' cried out Subba raising the
knife. All of us stood still with our eyes closed. When I fearfully opened
my eyes, Subba had crossed the stile and was walking away with the knife
in his hand, cursing. Walking swiftly, he disappeared down the road that
led to the market place. Rukku stood still with her eyes closed, as if waiting
for the knife to fall. Venkata dragged her by her hand and took her in.
Seeing Ganga weep at the sight of her ravaged garden, her sisters wept
with her. I sat stunned on the mud bench. There were no words of solace
left in me. I thought that Venkata would be broken by all that had
happened. But a surprise awaited me that morning.

*

No matter who dies, no matter how dear the person, life's daily routines
go on, don't they? Even in Venkata's house, which looked as if there had
been a death in the family. Shakuntala prepared the morning coffee. I
brushed my teeth with ash of the paddy husk. Venkata finished his bath
and sat grinding the sandal paste for the morning worship at the temple
by the riverside. Rukku lay in bed. When the cow herd came to graze the
cows, Gowri quickly milked the cows and sent them away. I thought
something must have died inside Venkata and did not want to meet his
eyes. So I sat on the bench outside. But unable to bear the sight of the
ravaged garden I went round the house to the backyard and stood under
the pomegranate tree.

Venkata was standing by the fence, quite limp, on his bandy legs. He
was wearing only a loin cloth. I was surprised: *Arre*, Venkata, what's he
doing here, standing by the fence and looking so engrossed? He couldn't
have gone out to relieve himself; he had already finished his ablutions and
morning prayers; his sacred thread was not twined around his ear. He
stood absolutely motionless, unaware of my presence. I stood watching

him. In front of a *rathnagandi* fence stood Venkata, crooked, bare bodied, motionless and totally entranced. Except for the tall green fence in front of him nothing else was visible. I softly walked up to him, not making a sound. I stood behind him. Yet he was not aware of me. *Arre*, I thought and curiously looked at the *rathnagandi* fence. Bunches of yellow flowers, here and there. Green leaves. I examined them, leaf by leaf. Curious as to what his gaze was aimed at, I closely scrutinized everything that fell within my view. Then I saw it: a sun's horse. Seeing this innocent friend of mine watch with such rapture this insect with its raised crooked legs, a light body, a green geometrical angular Ashtavakra form, I was amused for a moment. But only for a moment. The sun's horse sprang; and as it sprang, Venkata's intent head with its crop of hair sprang with it in sympathy. I felt happy. Venkata turned around and, looking at me, said with such innocent ecstasy: 'The sun's horse.' My eyes locked into those wonder-struck eyes of his that had seen the sun's horse and my mouth fell open: 'The sun's horse,' I said.

Vaikom Muhammad Basheer (c. 1908–94)

Vaikom Muhammad Basheer was born in a small village in Southern Kerala, circa 1908; he died in 1994. He belonged to the Keralite Muslim community, which claims that Islam had been brought to the Malabar Coast in the lifetime of the Prophet Muhammad. He was the eldest of six children, and his father was a prosperous timber merchant. After attending a primary Malayalam school, he went to Vaikom English School. 'This suggests,' says M. N. Vijayan, 'a rather progressive attitude on the part of his parents . . . since orthodox Kerala Muslims considered Malayalam and English to be languages of the Kafirs.' Travelling the length and breadth of India, he worked as a seaman, journalist, apothecary, and was also touched by Gandhian politics.

Basheer set most of his works – mainly novellas and stories – in the theatre of his community, and many of them are unmistakably autobiographical. The autobiographical element does not only have to do with the recounting and transformation of personal memory; it has something to do with the fact that Basheer makes himself an actor in his works, even when he is not visibly present in them, or even when he is, as in the story below, in which a writer called 'Basheer' is incarcerated in a prison during the Freedom movement. His world is both mystical and subtly political, populated with charlatans, thieves, childhood sweethearts, soldiers, policemen, innocents, and informed by the presence of a writer who, in the excitement of discovering material which, till then, might not have been considered fit for literature, no longer finds it useful to distinguish between fiction and 'real' life; his fictions tell us that the principal characteristic of life is its narrativity, and absolute veracity that of the imaginary world. Thus, his works remain poised between magic and scepticism, a backward-looking regret and a perpetual, humorous flux, the immutable order of art and the anarchy and makeshiftness of the present.

* * *

'Walls' (1965)

translated from the Malayalam by Nivedita Menon

Have you heard a little love story called 'Walls?' I don't think I have narrated it ever before. I had thought of calling it 'A Woman's Fragrance' or 'The Scent of a Woman' or some such thing. You know how we talk of Fate, Time and things like that. Well, this incident comes from the far side of that great Time – only, I am on this side now, a lonely heart. This is a song of grief from the vast shores of that heart.

*

High stone walls that seem to touch the sky, circle me. There are several buildings within the boundary of the Central Jail. And numerous people. All the prisoners have been locked up. No particular sounds can be heard. Some prisoners are to be hanged at dawn. Some have completed their terms and will be released into the world of freedom tomorrow. Yet, a sort of calm prevails.

We are walking. Somewhat close to the gallows. On a very narrow path. All around us, stretching into the distance, are the walls. Ahead of me walks the warder. It has been only minutes since they put me into prison clothes and transformed me into a number. A white cap striped in black, a white shirt, white *mundu*. A rug to sleep on, a blanket to cover myself with, dishes to eat and drink from ... Each one of these is numbered. I am not new to all this. Several times have I been in jail and become a number.

Long ago I had read a book called *Numerology*. Remembering it, I looked at my new number. Added the digits. Nine. Good. What is the significance of nine? What will I go through in this jail? My thoughts wandered. My pace slackened.

'Walk a little faster, can't you?' the warder ordered. That made me laugh. I never waste an opportunity to laugh. God's greatest gift to humanity – laughter.

I asked, 'Where are you off to in such a hurry – are you off from this earth itself?'

The warder was silent. He kept walking. I said, 'I suppose you have to rush off to some important business after you have locked me up?'

The charge against me *was* a little serious. Some reserve policemen had threatened to crush my right hand into cotton-fluff, from the tip of the middle finger to my shoulder. Of course, my parents, brothers and sisters were not actually informed by the police. They were told by the magistrate – the cheek of the police! And then the police had laid siege to my house. To arrest me. I was not there. I was caught later. But no one beat me. I was put into a major police lock-up in a town some fifty-sixty miles away. For fourteen months or so, the case did not come up for a hearing. I was just locked up! Following the advice of a police inspector, I made an issue of it. I fasted. That is, I went on a hunger strike, a satyagraha! Which is how I managed to get the case to court and was awarded a sentence.

In the lock-up, I had spent my days as a member of the family, under the benevolent gaze of a few hundred constables and inspectors. Many of them had become my disciples. I had the status of a head constable there. I also wrote several police stories about my stay in the lock-up. The Inspector had provided me with paper and pencils. I bid farewell to everyone and set out, escorted by two policemen carrying guns and handcuffs. They brought me here, to the Central Jail. But all this is besides the point.

The two policemen had given me two packets of *beedis*, matches and a brand-new blade. With the grand announcement that, 'This kind of thing is forbidden in jail,' this warder took it all away. He removed his high headgear, put my things into it, covered them with a piece of old cloth, and replaced it on his head. And now, there he was, walking along as if nothing had happened. Let him. The beast!

What was the blade for, you ask. Nothing that you could possibly imagine. One can split a match stick into four with it. Why, these eyes have seen artists who have split one match into six. It is not easy to come by matches in the jail. After all, that requires money. And money is something one does not have. At such times, the blade can be quite a useful little implement. Not all by itself, but to make what I call a *chakki*. This is how the *chakki* is born. From the rug provided by the government, pull out some threads, each as long as your palm, till you have them to a thickness of two fingers. Tie the threads together, leaving a head of two inches or so. Set fire to this head and burn it well. What true artists do is to wrap up the burnt ends in a piece of leather folded several times. But poor people like me have to make do with the thick leaf of a jack-fruit.

Now if you have a small piece of steel, you can rub it on cement or stone at any time to produce a spark. You can introduce this spark to the charred ends of the *chakki*, and there it is – fire! But where would one get steel? Almost everything else is, of course, available in the jail – not just wax but *beedis*, matches, ganja, booze, jaggery. If you have the money. But if you have a blade, you have steel! You must preserve the blade by pushing it deep into a piece of wood. Such were the marvels secreted away in the noble warder's cap!

I remarked, 'Policemen are not bad!'

Hadn't he heard? He walked on silently. He would sell anything for a profit. The so-and-so must have made enough to feed his children and his grandchildren and even get the moon and the stars for them.

I asked him, 'How many children do you have?'

Awakened from his musings, he replied, 'Six. Five girls and a boy.'

Poor warder! Five girls!

'And are the children and their mother well?'

'Yes, yes,' he said impatiently. 'Walk faster.'

The reason for his hurry was suddenly clear to me.

'What will happen to them if you die?' I asked then.

'God will provide for them.'

'I doubt that.'

The warder asked, 'Why?'

'Divine knowledge!' I replied. 'I was a sannyasi once. There is not a single holy mosque or temple in India that I haven't visited. Not one sacred river I haven't bathed in. Mountain peaks, valleys, forests, deserts, seacoasts, ruined temples . . .'

'So what?'

'God will not leave you unpunished!'

'But I haven't done anything wrong.'

'What about the daylight robbery you committed today?'

He seemed surprised. 'What robbery?'

'One day, you die and your soul appears before the divine presence. God asks then, O you wretched jail-warder, where are the matches, the blade and the two packets of *beedis* you took from poor Basheer?'

The warder stood silent and still. 'Come, come. Don't you have to rush off to your business after locking me up?' I asked.

He did not move. Then, shaking with silent laughter, he removed his cap and returned my treasures.

'Good fellow!' I said. 'The Inspector told me this morning that Gandhiji is on a fast. Have you heard anything about it?'

He replied, 'He has ended his fast by drinking lime juice.' Good. Mohandas Karamchand Gandhi *zindabad*! *Zindabad*, all humanity!

We walked on, passing many iron doors. Walls! Walls!

'How many political prisoners does this jail have?'

'There are seventeen where you are going to be kept. Counting you, there would be eighteen.'

So, we were going to a special place. The government was taking this fellow seriously! Good.

*

As we walked on, I was overcome by the most maddening scent in the world. The scent of a woman! Female fragrance!

I was shaken. Every little atom of my being was aroused. My nostrils expanded. I inhaled and drew into myself ... everything in this world.

Where was she? I looked around. Nobody! Nothing!

And as we continued, my ears heard the most beautiful sound in the world. A woman's laughter.

Had this sound and this fragrance come together? Or had I imagined one in the wake of the other?

I had almost forgotten that marvellous creature – Woman!

It was real, the laugh I heard, and the fragrance that came to me – real!

This fragrance was not of soap. Nor of oils. Nor was it the smell of powder mingling with sweat. But the amazing fragrance of Woman Incarnate!

I tried to evoke that fragrance ... I could hardly breathe. My nostrils expanded again and yet again. As if they would burst with desire. Where are you, woman?

I asked, 'Where did it come from, that woman's laugh?'

The warder asked mockingly, 'Not married, are you?'

'No, but what does that have to do with my question?'

'Why else would you pay attention to things like that?'

'In this terrifying Central Jail, close to the gallows, I hear a woman's laugh. Now should I get married immediately, just to have the right to ask where it came from?'

The warder laughed. 'From the women's jail. You are going to be kept next to it.'

Just one wall in between!

And my sentence – two years of rigorous imprisonment and a fine of one thousand rupees. And if the fine was not paid, lift loads for six more months. And between me and the women's jail, just a wall, right?

A wall ... the woman's jail. Oh, my precious ones!

I hugged the blanket and rug to my heart as we walked on. Opening an iron-barred door, we entered a walled complex. Lots of trees, mostly jack-fruit. Several cottages. In the distant east, on either sides, were two massive walls. Beyond the right wall was the wide, wide world of freedom. Across the wall on the left ... was the women's jail.

The cottages, encircled by small walls, were the lock-ups. There, the lock-up warder took over. I folded my hands in a namaste to the warder who had accompanied me. He returned my greeting and left. A good man. May God protect him!

The new warder took me to a cottage. He opened its iron door. A very small room. Outside the room, at a distance, was the toilet. Near the door was a tap. I turned the tap and washed my hands and feet and face. After drinking a lot of water and filling a bowl with some more, I uttered the name of God and entered the mini-jail with my right foot.

Walls, walls! Many, many walls enclosed me.

The warder shut the iron-barred door and locked it.

I said, 'This new dependent of our beloved *sarkar* has not been given any dinner.'

'You did not fall into today's quota officially. You will be fed from tomorrow.'

'Then let me go. I'll come back in tomorrow's quota.'

He asked me, 'What is the case?'

'Writing ... sedition.'

As if frightened out of his wits, he exclaimed, 'Sedition! Shri Padman-abha! Protect me!'

A true patriot!

Outside and above the iron bars of the lock-up, an unbearably bright bulb came on. I was alone in this little prison within the vast prison of the universe. Eternity and myself.

I straightened the rug. Arranged the vessels in a corner. Dusk was falling. The interior of the lock-up, including me, was brightly lit. And I did not even fall in today's quota! That meant going to sleep hungry. I knew very well how to get some food. I could shake the iron bars, yell for the warder and create a terrible racket. The superintendent, the jailer and everyone else would turn up. And I would be fed.

But I decided against it. One must make some small sacrifice for the

Author's note: I was brought to the Thiruvananthapuram Central Jail from the Kollam Kasba lockup. This was when Maharaja Sri Chitra Tirunal ruled over Travancore.

Translator's note: Shri Padmanabha Swami (Vishnu) is the presiding deity of the Travancore royal family. The author's note contextualizes the warder's exclamation, identifying him as a native of Travancore.

sake of Literature. In the cause of the country's freedom, I have been beaten up several times. With great tenderness, I have been pushed to the ground by rifle butts in my chest and dragged through the streets. And several times I have landed in jail. But this time? This time, a prison sentence for Literature itself! ... And politics too. When I thought about it, I felt some pride.

I drank a lot of water. Then, in royal style, forgetting to split the match stick into two, I used a whole stick to light a *beedi*. After a few puffs, I stubbed it out and put it away. I must not be greedy.

Sitting there, I listened. I could no longer hear the woman's laugh. Could not sense that woman's smell. And here I was, near the women's jail. Woman, where are you?

That primeval smell of woman – could I have imagined it? Long, long ago ... aeons ago, before the age of Manu ... walking in the Garden of Eden as Adam, I had experienced that mysterious fragrance of Hauwa! The scent may have remained, stored in my soul ... a mere mirage, like the pool of clear water an exhausted wanderer sees in the desert ... And like a mirage it had vanished ... But my awakened soul, widening nostrils, my heart which was about to break ... Oh woman!

Where was that lovely sound? And where, where was that maddening fragrance?

I looked out through the iron bars. The light was so dazzling that I could not see at all. The world was covered with darkness. But it was a darkness I could not clearly see. One thing I came to understand then – I had never seen darkness. O primeval, deep, amazing darkness! O millions of stars that twinkle and flash in the endless vastness of the skies! O glorious, glorious, moon-drenched night! Why have I never seen you?

But that was not correct. I had seen it. I had seen it all. But I had never paid enough attention. Yamini! Night herself! I remembered another lovely night long ago. A little village. Beyond it, thousands of miles of desert filled with sand, stretching to the farthest horizon. A dusk like this one. I had gone into that desert. I must have walked a mile or so. White silk lay spread all around ... an endless expanse of sand. And I, in the centre of that vast universe ... Alone. Above my head, so close that I could have plucked it, hung the full moon, radiant. The deep blue sky, as if swept and scoured clean. The full moon and the stars. Stars sharply defined in their brightness. Crores ... endless crores ... impossible to count. The perfect circle of the moon. The perfect silence of the universe ... and yet, some kind of celestial, silent music ... the music of the spheres in their eternal orbits ... everything was steeped in it.

I stood in joyous amazement. My happiness and surprise turned to tears. I cried. Unable to bear it any more, I ran back, sobbing, to the world of humans.

Creator of the worlds, protect me. It is impossible for me to contain this within myself. This blinding brightness of yours, this grand miracle. I am but a small creature. I cannot bear it. Save me!

*

The next thing I remember is the jail warder unlocking the door in the morning and shaking the bars to wake me.

Salaam, world! I got up. Lighting a *beedi*, I started my morning ablutions in style. I cleaned my teeth with a neem twig. Long ago, in the valleys of the Himalayas, I had used neem twigs like this. Standing under the pipe, I bathed luxuriously. Then I put on my jail clothes, picked up the bowl for food after washing it, and set off to meet the leaders. Everybody there was a leader.

After I had met the leaders, a large bowl of *kanji* arrived. I ate my portion with substantial helpings of chutney. Actually, it was more like '*kanjo*'. Let me tell you what this *kanjo* is. First swallow the watery portion of the *kanji*. Then mix the remaining rice with chutney and feed on that to your heart's content. After that you must wash your hands, mouth, and the bowl. Drink some water . . . What bliss!

After working up this euphoria, I slit a match stick into two, lit a *beedi*, and took a drag. Then stubbing it, I went out to explore the world. That is, I made a tour of the jail. In search of tea-leaves and sugar. Even though I was in jail, I needed my tea. Black tea would do.

The leaders had neither tea-leaves nor sugar. One of these great souls had hidden away a bottle of Eno's Fruit Salt in his cell. Without it, he could not even begin his usual routine in the morning. Another had managed to secrete Karl Marx's magnum opus, *Das Kapital*. Another interesting leader possessed two packs of cards, and even promised to teach me the amazing game of bridge.

I avoided the leaders.

*

After a month, there was I, leading a 'deluxe life'.

In a corner of my cage were two bricks. Next to them was a bundle of twigs almost as thick as the trunk of a jack-fruit tree. Also, a small vessel to make tea in. Tea and sugar in two paper packets reposed in all their glory under my mattress, like two tiny pillows. Then a deluxe *chakki*.

Plenty of *beedis*. Paper to write on. Pencils. A big knife, a special concession from the jail superintendent ... for grafting mango trees. He had realized that I was adept at gardening. In front of the lock-up, my mini-jail, I have made a rectangular patch fringed by rose plants in full bloom, spreading their fragrance.

Fried fish for lunch, eggs, liver, a special chutney ... A day in this life of lordly prosperity begins with a worthy soul bringing in my *kanji* in the morning. He happens to be a red-cap. That is, he has killed someone. He wasn't hanged, but was awarded rigorous imprisonment for life. He is a stout, fair, round-faced man with smiling eyes.

I perform a few exercises in the morning. After all, I am a wrestler of some repute. Next to my rose garden is a tall jack-fruit tree. Its lower branch is as thick as my thigh. I use that as an exercise bar. By the time I emerge from my exercises and a bath, the red-cap with smiling eyes has left my daily quota of *kanji* and special chutney in a covered dish in the lock-up. This repast is not exactly in the *kanji* department. But more like rice. Then again, is it really rice? The stuff is a little watery.

The first time the red-cap poured out the *kanji* for me, he suggested softly, 'Go and see the hospital orderly. He will arrange for tea!'

I went. I saw. A thin, dark man with a stylish moustache. Dazzling white teeth. A beautiful smile. He turned out to be an old friend of mine. I had once visited his hometown. He was implicated in a case of arson. Two people had been killed. Again, a red-cap. Sentenced to rigorous imprisonment for life. He had been made a hospital orderly for good behaviour, also because he was educated. No further need to worry about procuring tea-leaves, sugar, eggs, liver, bread, milk, *beedis* and other such etceteras.

As I walked back, I saw rose plants blooming riotously behind the hospital. I had pulled out some plants from there and gently transplanted them in the patch in front of my little jail. Seeing my garden, all the leaders wanted one each. I made gardens for all of them.

The leaders kept in touch with the world outside. The jail warders would carry letters in and out for a price. At night, various packets would be thrown in from over the high walls. The leaders would collect them in the morning. Banana chips – the salty kind as well as *sharkara upperi*, the jaggery-coated ones – lemon pickle, and other eatables. Sometimes I would join them in picking up small tins and containers. One day, a leader gave me some lemon pickle. Oh how tasty it was! The look on his face as he gave it to me ... even if I were to write an epic poem on that expression, I would not be able to repay my debt.

And so there I was, with my comrades and disciples, the red-caps. A life free of stress and strain.

*

Sometimes I would look towards the women's jail. Those frightening, fiendish walls! I would remember the laugh I had heard. And the smell. At other times, I would climb the jack-fruit tree. This was usually in the afternoon when, after lunch, the leaders and others would doze for a while. I would stand on the topmost branch of the tree and gaze at the free world far beyond.

'The free world!' But what free world? The entire globe is a prison after all. Over the brick walls ... far away in the distance ... on the road ... men and women walk, completely unaware of the existence of this jail. Comrades, turn your heads just a little. I address the women. Please, turn your heads a little. Let me refresh my eyes with a glimpse of womankind!

These were the sentiments of each man in the jail. Every thought and feeling I express would be echoed by each one of the inmates. Our lonely nights, our lonely thoughts, our sexual fantasies ... It would be better not to delve too deep into our hearts.

After long musings, I would climb down and just stand in the middle of my rose garden. All around me, flowers spread their fragrance. There was beauty. There was fragrance. Yet I felt the lack of someone or something. What could it be? No, stop it! These thoughts were dangerous. They all led to Woman.

I went for a walk. There were several walls. Several doors. Warders everywhere. It was impossible to do anything in jail without their knowledge. There were large towers too, to keep an eye from above.

I was walking around the towers. Suddenly I saw something. And burst out laughing. Such a funny sight! A mad elephant in fetters. No, it was a man. A black-cap. Fair, tall, well-built. Radiant eyes. As he approached, he staggered, his head pulled back and his body arched backwards. His strange gait was because of the two chains that went over his back to fetter his feet to his neck. I wondered if he was a convict who had attempted a jail break.

When I reached him, I was shocked to find that he was an old classmate of mine. Our eyes met. Our minds remembered. We laughed. Spoke of many things. Laughed again. Our man had set forth to somehow meet me. Secretly!

I asked him, 'Couldn't you have just sent someone?'

'Wouldn't it have been embarrassing for you if people found out that I know you?'

'Know me? Say that I am your friend, you old rascal, you idiot!'

I hugged him and gave him a kiss on the cheek. I might as well have kissed every single person in jail. The story of the kiss spread, the entire jail was thrilled by it!

The chap, a thief, had been sentenced to one-and-a-half years of imprisonment. He had started a flourishing business in *beedis*, sugar and dried fish in the jail. Soon, he of the radiant eyes, now in chains, had become a living legend in this jail. A martyr because of a small incident that took place six months after he came to the jail. One of the warders did something terrible. No other warder had ever done such a thing before. Let us call him the 'Terrible Warder.'

Almost all the warders have a share in the business conducted in jail. Many prisoners are taken out, far from the jail, to break rocks and do similar jobs. In those places, there are many inhabited huts. That is where the major business takes place. And so, my classmate became one of the big businessmen in jail. Most things come into jail via the *langoti*. An inspection is carried out at the gate. The cap, shirt, *mundu*, towel are provided by the jail. All these are checked thoroughly. Nothing there. Clean! But the *langoti*, the underwear which is almost a part of the human body, is not given by the authorities. So it is slipped off just a little. A quarter of a minute will do. And so the tale proceeds.

All this is immaterial, really. Didn't I say that our Terrible Warder did something terrible, almost unspeakable? Well, my classmate planted two hefty blows on his pate for it! The news spread. Not just in the men's jail, but also in the women's jail. There was much excitement in both places. My classmate was tied to the flogging frame and given twelve lashes. His sentence was increased to three years. His wounds healed. He wanted to go back to breaking rocks. But the Terrible Warder was against it.

'You don't know me. And you don't know where I come from. Here, take this!' With this spirited introduction, my classmate again administered the Terrible Warder two solid ones on his throat. And as a finishing touch, a hefty kick on the navel. There was nothing wrong with such behaviour. Outside the jail, the Terrible Warder would have been lynched for his deed! That should tell you how hideous his act was.

My classmate got another twenty-four lashes. He bore it all stoically. Didn't faint. His sentence was extended to six years. The Terrible Warder was boycotted by the entire jail. He became the target of the prisoners' collective wrath. He could see the lust for blood gleam in each eye. What if he were strangled to death? Realizing the gravity of the situation, he claimed to have urgent business outside and resigned his job.

You know the common saying, 'Unity is strength'. Well, in jail, we did stand united! Even though he was no longer allowed to go out to break stones, my classmate continued to run the business in jail.

*

So I live, in supreme happiness. I have everything I need.

Sometimes the assistant jailer comes to my lock-up. He is a fair young man with a sense of humour, dressed in khaki trousers and khaki shirt. He sports a hat! All the prisoners call him Anian Jailor.* He comes not to inspect my lock-up, but to chat. He has a young Alsatian dog called Joker. We discuss Joker's training, exercise and food habits. Anian loves to hear my dog stories. I make him black tea.

Most people know that I have tea-leaves and sugar. Sometimes men who are to be hanged at five in the morning feel like a little tea the night before. The warder wakes me up and I send them some black tea. Along with a couple of *beedis* and matches. I also send a message that they should be brave. There are two ways of facing death, laughing or crying ... either way one dies. In that case, why not face death laughing!

On such occasions I stay awake. Only after the hanging at five do I go to sleep. Just as I am about to drop off, one of the leaders comes and wakes me up. Not out of spite. After all, the others don't know that I have been keeping a death vigil!

Altogether, the jail is like a small town. Debates and discussions. Bursts of laughter. Arguments. Noise, bustle, more laughter.

Sometimes the jail superintendent accompanies Anian Jailor. After talking to the leaders, they come to my garden. I am very fond of trees and plants. To the extent that I believe they understand me when I speak to them. The jail superintendent shares my sentiments. We stroll around, chatting about what fertilizers to use, how to tend to the plants.

The superintendent has six potted rose plants at home. All of them have been sent by yours truly. Some of my red-cap friends do not approve of my friendship with the jail superintendent. They ask me all sorts of questions. Can't you live here without his patronage? Wasn't it he who sentenced your classmate to be lashed two dozen times? That Anian Jailor is a much nicer fellow!

---

*   Anian: Younger brother.

Do you see where all this is leading to? You have to affiliate yourself to one party or the other. It is impossible to stay detached and independent and love everyone.

*

Most of the time I was in my cage. At times I strolled in my garden, talking to plants and trees. One day, at such a time, Anian Jailor came and told me that all political prisoners were to be freed!

Everybody was jubilant. Everybody had a haircut and a shave. Including yours truly who got the sparse hair on his bald pate trimmed. But I didn't have my moustache shaved. I was happy in the belief that I looked good with it. There was laughter and bustle all around. Anian Jailor had everyone's clothes brought to them. We got them washed and ironed, and kept them ready wrapped in paper.

I bid farewell to my friends who were thieves and murderers. I said that I would write to all of them and promised to send them books. We waited impatiently for our release.

The release order arrived.

Release! Except for one person! There was no order for the release of this poor chap. It must be a mistake! Anian Jailor rushed to find out. He got the superintendent to make a special phone call for me.

There was no mistake. This man was not to be released. Good. That meant I had not yet attained the level of maturity they wanted.

The leaders left, rejoicing. And there I was, the sole heir to Eno's Fruit Salt, Karl Marx's tome, two packs of cards, a small bottle of lemon pickle, a sweet-tin full of banana chips, a large palm-leaf bundle of *sharkara upperi*, lots of pounded tobacco, betel leaves, supari, lime.

The leaders all left with smiles . . . Nothing stirred anywhere. It was as if I was alone in a deserted town. In any case one is alone in this wide world. From the entire flock sent out to graze, just one old goat had been kept back. For what? To be butchered, certainly. A disaster loomed ahead, I felt. No happiness, no smiles, no nothing. Altogether, there was a sort of twilight in my heart.

I gave Karl Marx's *Das Kapital* to Anian Jailor. And the *sharkara upperi* to the hospital to be distributed among my fellow inmates. I gave the packs of cards as a special gift to my classmate. The betel leaves and all that went with it were donated to my disciple, the red-cap who brings my *kanji*. By and by, I distributed most of the banana chips. Only half a tin was left. The lemon pickle and Eno's Fruit Salt remained in my room. After a couple of days, I threw the Eno's Fruit Salt over the wall of the jail. And I lived on, in fear and foreboding.

*

I had no peace of mind. What was to happen to me? It is easy to advise others. Face death bravely, and so on. About laughing and crying. Now face it laughing! God, I cannot even smile. I am such a completely insignificant person, utterly helpless. Save me. What am I to do?

Escape! I decided to break out of jail. There were just two walls between me and the world outside. I must tunnel my way through one and climb over the other. The jail warder would be asleep at night. Let night come, a night of rain and wind and lightning, a deep dark night.

I planned the minutest details. The walls of my small lock-up are not very thick. I have an instrument with which to bore through them. In the quiet of the night, I will get out. And there will only be the high old stone wall of the jail. Between the ancient stones, there is just gravel.

I need some ten or twelve large nails. These have to be hammered into the wall with a stone wrapped in cloth to avoid making any noise. I will climb them to reach the top of the wall. With the rug, blanket, *mundu*, towel, I will make a rope, tie one end of it to a nail, then lower the rope carefully over the other side, climb down and escape. The plan should work.

But the nails? In a corner, next to the wall, lie several rusty iron buckets. They are falling apart, but the handles are undamaged. I hammered them straight, shaping them into the nails I wanted, and carefully hid them away. About thirty nails. Then I waited. I waited for a night of rain and lightning and howling wind.

And so arrived another dawn. A number of the red-caps who are my friends and disciples arrived with a warder. They were going to make a vegetable garden near the women's jail. Would I like to come?

No. I'm not interested in anything. All the warmth and light has gone from my life. Just go away, all of you. Who wants your vegetables? All I'm waiting for is a night of wind and rain and the rumbling of thunder. Stop bothering me!

But they wouldn't let me alone. Why should you withdraw from society like some sage?

Well, that's what I am, a muni who meditated with his guru in a dark cave long ago!

I went along. We made a garden. And then a friend showed me

something interesting. At the bottom of the reddish wall was a large black, poppadom-like circle, blocked with cement. Earlier it had been a large hole. Born of many moments, many hours, many days, many months of love-inspired hard labour by many men. And there it had stayed. For days, months, years.

Meanwhile, the prisoners became decent and obedient. Through that hole the men's jail and the women's jail had seen faces and things . . . faces and things. Had heard sounds. Had taken in the scent. Good! Through that hole, the smell of woman had spread in the men's jail. Marvellous! Not that this had been some well-kept secret. The business had been conducted under the benign, neglectful eyes of the authorities.

At this point you might want to set yourself on some high pedestal and deliver a fantastic lecture on morality and culture. Oh, go away! You of the great soul and perfect qualities, we are mere human beings, full of lust and anger. We have many a weakness. Show us some pity. This attraction between man and woman is a gift of God, right? Attraction! Don't forget that. You must look upon us with the gaze of divine understanding.

They used the hole. Looked through it. Everyone looked. But the Terrible Warder had seen a nice little business there. He levied a small tax on looking through the hole. One anna per person. The prison had both rich and poor inmates. Their sexual desires are the same. What were the poor to do? Was it to be the death of their lust?

My classmate said, 'Warder, this isn't fair.'

'If it isn't fair, I'll just plug the hole!' threatened the Terrible Warder. This was how my classmate received four and a half years and thirty-six lashes. And then he got the hole closed with cement. That cement wasn't mixed with the blood of men and women! Yet I bent my head and sniffed at the cemented portion. Was there a hint of a female fragrance still?

*

We reared our vegetable garden with great zest. The area around my lock-up was deserted. Just me and a sleepy warder. I was alone inside a large, walled structure!

Two or three fellows would come in the morning to water the vegetable garden. I would just stroll around with a warder in tow. It was as if I was walking the streets of a ruined, deserted city. Gloom, silence everywhere. I would suddenly stop while walking. Was the silence going to deepen? I would whistle. Speak to the trees and plants. There were lots of squirrels. I caught one. Decided to tame it. Made it run up a tree. Then tried to make it fall.

One day, as I walked along the wall of the women's prison, whistling to myself, I heard a heavenly melody. It was the most beautiful sound in all the world. It came from the other side of the wall ... And then, came a question, 'Who's whistling like that?'

It was like a sudden burst of light and fragrance. A miracle! My hair stood on end. I looked around. Then summoning up courage, I said, 'It is me!'

I shivered. Ah, Woman!

The conversation had to be quite loud. She, on one side of the wall. I, on the other.

She asked me, 'What's your name?'

I told her about my education, my job, my seditious writings, everything. She too told me about herself, the mistakes she had made in her life.

Her lovely name, Narayani.

Her lovely age, twenty-two.

She knew how to read and write. She had had a little education. Sentenced to fourteen years of rigorous imprisonment, it had been a year since she arrived here. One year of no happiness!

I said, 'Narayani, we seem to have come to this jail at about the same time.'

'Is that so?' There was silence for a while from the other side. Then she asked, 'Will you give me a rose plant?'

I was surprised. 'How did you know about the rose plants here?'

'This is a jail. Everyone knows everything. There are no secrets here.'

Did you hear what she said? No secrets here! But what do I know about the women's jail? About the women there?

Narayani asked again, 'Won't you give me a rose plant?'

'Narayani!' I said with all my strength, as if my heart was being plucked out. 'I will give you all the rose plants in this entire world!'

Narayani laughed. The sound was like the tinkling of a thousand little golden bells. As I heard the sound, my heart felt as if it had been shattered into millions of tiny pieces.

'One will do. Just one. Will you give it to me?'

Listen to her! She asks me if I will give her one rose plant! What am I to do with this Narayani? Hold her tightly and kiss her so hard that she becomes breathless, what else!

'Narayani!' I called out, 'Wait. I'll go and get one right away!'

'All right.'

I rushed to my garden. Seeing me, all the squirrels ran away and climbed up the trees! I scolded them, 'What's the matter with you, you stupid creatures! Clambering up trees like this? Just get down and walk around, you hear!'

I reached my rose garden. All the bushes were in bloom, smiling, bathed in sunlight ... I uprooted the most beautiful one, with the maximum number of branches, taking care to protect its roots with a large yam-like covering of mud. Covered this up with a piece of sacking. Smoothed all the twigs and tied them together. Then I ran to the wall.

'Narayani!'

No answer. Had she left?

'Narayani!' I called again.

The sound of laughter.

Then, a voice. 'What?'

'Where were you when I first called?'

'I was right here!'

'Well, why didn't you answer then?'

'I was hiding!'

'You little rogue!'

She laughed and asked, 'Have you brought the rose plant?'

I was silent. Soundlessly, I was planting kisses. On each rose, on each bud, on each shoot.

Narayani called out to me by name.

I didn't answer. I was busy planting kisses. On each thorn, each branch. Again Narayani called out my name with anxiety. This time I answered.

Perplexed at that, she said, 'If I had called upon God with such love ...'

'And if you had?'

She snapped, 'If I had called out to God with such love ... that is what I said!'

'And if you had called out to God with such love?'

'God would have become visible to me!'

'Is that so? ... But Narayani, God does not become visible to anybody! God is with us always. In the universe, in the light of the universe, its radiance ... Narayani! Isn't it I who have to become visible?'

'Then why didn't you answer?'

'I was kissing ...'

'The wall?'

'No.'

'Then?'

'Each rose and each branch and each leaf.'

Narayani said, 'Oh! I feel like crying.'

I called, 'Narayani!'

'What?'

'You must not remove the sacking. Dig a hole and place it inside, taking the name of God. Then fill the hole and water it.'

'Hmm.'

'OK, here it comes!' Holding the bundle by the top, I threw it over the wall with all my strength. 'Have you got it?'

'Oh my God!' exclaimed Narayani, and in her voice was the happiness of having gained an empire.

I said, 'Untie the branches.'

'I'll do that. I'm going to pluck out all the flowers and put them away.'

'Where? In your hair?'

'No.'

'Then?'

'In my heart. Inside my blouse.'

And they had my kisses! I leaned weakly against the wall. I stroked it gently.

Narayani said, 'I'll go and plant this and water it. You must always look towards the wall. Whenever I am here, you will find a dry twig above the wall. When you see it, will you come?'

'I will!'

It sounded like she was sobbing.

'Ohh ... my God!'

'What is it, Narayani?'

She replied, 'I feel like crying!'

I asked, 'But why?'

Narayani said, 'I don't know!'

I said, 'Go, plant it and come back.'

'I'll throw up a dry twig!'

'And I'll look out for it.'

'When you see it, will you come?'

'I will!'

*

I went back to my lock-up. What a mess it was in! I cleaned it. It had been ages since I had shaken out my mattress and made my bed. Then, with my gaze fixed on the sky above the wall in the distance, I began to wait. I saw no twig. Had she forgotten about me? That dry twig would never rise against the sky ... Just as I had begun to despair – O celestial world! A beautiful sight! A twig rose against the sky! I didn't stir. Again it flashed.

I dashed as fast as I could to the wall. Several squirrels fled for their lives up trees, and cursed me roundly.

'Narayani!'

Silence on the other side of the wall! I called again. Finally, she answered angrily, 'What is it? What do you want?'

'Oh!'

'My arm has almost fallen off from flinging twigs!'

'Come, I'll stroke and make it better.'

'Here's my arm. Stroke it! I've put it close against the wall.'

'I'm stroking it now. And kissing it.'

'I'm pressing my breast against the wall . . . and kissing you!' she said.

'Narayani, how many women are there in the jail?'

She laughed. 'Just me!'

'Little liar! Seriously, how many?'

'Lots. All of them are old hags!'

'How many?'

'Eighty-seven.'

'How many beauties, how many hags?'

'One beauty and eighty-six hags!'

I gave up. I asked, 'Aren't there rose plants in your jail?'

'No,' said Narayani. 'You know, I . . . are you listening?'

'Yes.'

'Tomorrow I'll toss you a bag of roasted and powdered *bajra*. You must eat it with jaggery. Will you?'

'Of course!'

'No!' she said with certainty. 'You'll throw it away!'

'I won't waste even a grain!'

'What is your face like?'

'It is longish. Fair. My hair is cropped. I'm a little bald.'

'Eyes?'

'Rather small, elephant eyes.'

'Mine are large elephant eyes. Chest?'

'Somewhat broad.'

'My chest is full too. Waist?'

'My waist is trim.'

'And my waist? Well, I don't feel like telling you!'

'Must be like a barrel!'

'I could scratch you and tear you to pieces!' she growled.

'Narayani!'

'What?'

'What colour are you?'

'Where?'

'On your beautiful face.'

'Sort of fair.'

'Narayani!'

'Yes?'

'I could get the smell of a woman!'

'Right now? Oh my god!'

'No, when I came into this jail and was walking here!'

'Could it have been mine?'

'I don't know.'

'The smell of male bodies . . . the smell there, what is it like?'

'I don't know. Narayani! The smell of your body!'

I widened my nostrils and inhaled deeply. Had she heard the intake of my breath?

She asked, 'Can you get the smell?'

'No.'

'Nor can I. This damned wall.'

'Narayani, there used to be a hole in this wall. Have you seen it?'

'I have seen the part that has been blocked with cement. I have even touched it. It was closed before I came here.'

'I tried smelling there!'

'The warder who closed it was beaten up by someone. I heard that the man who beat him was tied to the frame and lashed. Each stroke was painfully counted by the women here!'

'It's a shame.'

'The man who was thrashed is from my hometown. He was my classmate.'

'Really?'

'Really.'

And over the wall appeared a long, rounded, white cloth-bag. In it was roasted and powdered *bajra*. Chillies, fried and salted, also arrived. Lemon pickle went over to the other side. And the tin of banana chips.

Narayani asked, 'Can I . . . distribute . . . these chips?'

'Yes, do give them to everyone. From both of us.'

'Will you love me . . . and me only?'

'Why, do you doubt it?'

'Here,' said Narayani with some pain, 'there are many who are more beautiful than me. I'm not very beautiful.'

'Nor am I very handsome.'

She said, 'I want to see you.'
I said, 'And I want to see you.'
'Oh my God! I'll cry all night.'

＊

The night of wind and rain and thunder is here! I'm sitting in the iron-barred cage, bathed in light. The rain falls like rods of glass. Like showers of gravel. The blessing of God. Let it rain! Blow, stormy wind. But please don't pluck out any trees! Clouds, thunder softly, softly. This rude roaring of yours might frighten the poor women! So, softly . . .

With morning, the warder arrived, switched off the lights and unlocked my door. I stepped outside. The world was washed clean.

I felt suddenly that it was not such a good idea to escape from jail! What was I going to do outside? After all, what is called the free world is only a larger jail. There would be more nights of rain and thunder and wind and lightning. I put out of my mind the memory of where I had hidden the big nails. In short, I was convinced it was *adharma* to contemplate escaping from prison!

The wall may not be flesh and blood. But I was beginning to wonder if it did not have a soul. These walls had seen much. Heard much.

One day, I saw a large squirrel sitting on top of the wall. He was glaring at me! I said, 'Get down, you scoundrel. Have you no shame?'

Narayani asked, 'Whom are you scolding?'

'A squirrel. He's sitting on the wall and listening to us. The rogue!'

'Let him be,' said Narayani.

'He has come to laugh at me. I have often given him and his friends the chase of their lives!'

I threw gravel at him. The squirrel ran away.

Narayani complained, as if in pain, 'That stone hit my breast!'

'Did it hurt?'

'Is there no way we can get to see each other?'

'I don't really see any way.'

'I'll cry tonight, thinking of you!'

I too thought of her that night and dreamed my dreams.

＊

So the nights and days passed.

'I'll try to come to the hospital!' said Narayani one day. 'If you can . . . will you come to the hospital to see me? I want to see you, even if from a distance!'

'I'll come running up to you and hold you tight and kiss you. On your face, and your neck, and your breasts, your navel . . .'

'How will you recognize me?'

'I'll know you by your face!'

Narayani said, 'On my right cheek I have a black mole. Will you look out for it?'

'That black mole! I want to shower kisses on it!'

'You must come. Don't let me down. There will be other women with me.'

'I will be alone. I won't be wearing my cap. I am a little bald. And I'll be carrying a red rose in my hand.'

'I'll look out for that!'

'The orderly at the hospital is an old friend of mine.'

'I guessed as much.'

'Why?'

'How else would you get eggs, liver, bread? If I die will you think of me?'

'Do you want any more rose plants? There are many here.'

'No. From what you gave me, I have started making a garden . . . Will you remember me when I am dead?'

'My dear Narayani! It isn't possible to say anything about death. Who will die, when, how – only God knows these things. It could be me who dies first.'

'No. It will be me. Will you remember me?'

'I will.'

'How? Oh God! How will you remember me? You haven't seen me, touched me.'

'Narayani, your image is everywhere in this world!'

She asked sorrowfully, 'Everywhere in this world? Why do you flatter me?'

'I'm not flattering you. I swear! Walls, walls!'

I stood looking at the walls. A long silence came from the other side.

Then Narayani said, 'Can I cry to my heart's content?'

'Not now. You can cry at night, remembering.'

Silence. Then she said, 'I'll tell you tomorrow when we can meet at the hospital.'

We parted, with longing in our hearts.

*

Night fell. The light came on. The warder came. The light was switched off. The door opened. I stepped out. Quickly finished brushing my teeth, exercising, bathing. Managed to eat a bit. Lit a *beedi*. And so waited, smoking. Anian Jailor arrived to ask after me. It was then that a dry twig rose against the blue sky over the wall.

I broke into a sweat. I could hardly breathe. What was I to do?

At last! Anian Jailor left. I ran.

'Narayani!'

'What?'

'When?'

Narayani said, 'Today's Monday. On Thursday morning, at eleven. I will be at the hospital. A black mole on the right cheek. Don't forget!'

'I'll remember. And in my hand, a red rose.'

'I'll remember!'

Monday, Tuesday, Wednesday . . . I dozed off a little after lunch. Awoke and took a bath. And as I was sitting around, Anian Jailor walked smiling into my rose garden, plucked several blooms, and coming into my lock-up, sat on my bed. 'Do you want some flowers?' he asked.

I was amused. I said, 'I am the garden. And the flower.'

'Not the fruit?'

'The fruit too!'

And suddenly I spotted the dry twig flash above the wall, against the blue sky!

Anian Jailor said, 'I haven't ever seen you in ordinary dress.'

'You mean a kurta and *mundu*.'

Anian Jailor took out the packet in which my laundered clothes were kept.

'Please put them on. I want to see how you look.'

'But they will get soiled.'

'So what? Can't you get them washed?'

'All right.' I put on my clothes. 'What do you say?' I asked.

'Fine!' said Anian Jailor happily.

Then in a dramatic manner, in English, he announced, 'You can go, Mr Basheer. You are free!'

I was stunned. My eyes stopped seeing. My ears stopped hearing. I was dazed. 'Why should I be free . . . who wants freedom?'

Anian Jailor laughed. 'The order for your release has arrived. You are free from this moment. You can go out into the free world.'

'The free world . . . which free world? I'd just be going into a bigger jail. Who wants this great freedom?'

Anian Jailor said, 'You can collect the money to go home and leave. Do you have anything else to take?'

He folded up the mattress. Under it was the story I was writing for the lifers, called 'Love Letter'. He put it inside my pocket. Many other stories of mine were with the lifers still. It did not matter! Anian Jailor happily took me by the hand and led me out of the lock-up.

I stood for a little while in my rose garden. As if in a dream, I broke off a flower and, kissing it, looked around. Above the wall was a dry twig! It rose. And rose ... Oh God!

Anian Jailor locked my room.

Well, Narayani, God be with you!

I stepped out of the large gates of the jail with the money to go home in my pocket. The monstrous gates clanged shut behind me, making a hideous noise.

I was alone. Looking at the fragrant rose I held in my hand, I stood on the road for a long while, stunned.

God be with all of us!

O. V. Vijayan (b. 1930)

O. V. Vijayan, born in Palghat, Kerala, has been many things, often seeming to pursue what appear to be radically incompatible positions and professions. He has been a Marxist who later grew disenchanted with Marxism, lately appearing to move towards a politics very distant from socialism; he has been an atheist who was always susceptible to the terror and grandeur of divinity, so that his position moved gradually towards belief; he has been one of the great modern writers of the Malayalam language, and also a political cartoonist of repute for some of the major English-language newspapers in India. When he was 26, a young Marxist with a Master's degree in English Literature from Madras University, he became a school-teacher in an obscure village in Kerala, as 'part of a State scheme to send barefoot graduates to man single-teacher schools in backward villages'. His encounter with the culture of that village changed him, and transformed him as a writer; and from that experience came his first novel, the surreal and poetic *The Legends of Khasak* in 1969, breaking realist conventions and taking the literary world in Kerala by surprise. He has since written other novels and many short stories; with their translation into English, there have been occasional attempts to reinvent him as an early postmodernist and an unacknowledged precursor of 'magic realism'. This analogy seems mistaken, however; the strangeness of Vijayan's work has less to do with ludic self-consciousness, and more to do with the implicit Rilkean premise that Art can change your life. Vijayan does not utter this prophecy in so many words, but it informs his fiction. A comparison with the film-maker Tarkovsky would probably be more apposite; both artists explore the conflicting landscapes of antique traditions, futuristic technology, tender reminiscence, and apocalypse; both, probably believing themselves to exist in a transitional moment in their respective cultures in particular, and in history in general, pursue hybrid genres that owe something to both science fiction and poetry. And both convey to us the substance of their artistic universe with the ardour and agonized self-doubt of a preacher, but without the preacher's didacticism.

* * *

'The Rocks' (1969)

translated from the Malayalam by the author

Mrganga remembered many things: walking over the rocks warm with sunset he saw the temple of the goddess on the hill beyond the valley. And tugging at Father's little finger he asked, 'Father, may I go to that temple?'

'Why do you want to go?' asked Father.

Mrganga said nothing but trotted along behind Father. The birds shot overhead like the little silver fish of the river. There was the scent of dung in the dust, and the scent of tulsi.

'Mrganga,' said Father, 'you have not answered me.'

Mrganga said guiltily, 'I want to see that goddess.'

'It is a thing cut out of rock,' said Father. 'I see no sense in going all that way to see it.'

It was difficult to make Father understand. All courage left Mrganga as he thought of Father's face growing sombre forbidding him to go. He felt repudiated. Presently he snuggled against Father again for reassurance. There was something more he wanted to tell Father, but it so overwhelmed him that he could no longer articulate it. It was that as he walked over the rocks at sundown, the goddess on the hill made him think of his dead mother.

He had to cross the valley to get to the temple, but the girl next door could have taken him. So he ventured again, 'Father, may I go with Sunanda?'

'There is no need to go with anyone,' Father said.

There was nothing more to say, and father and son walked on in silence. The rocks were gentle and warm, and their feel on the boy's feet grew vibrant. In his noontide strolls, stalking the hillsides, Mrganga would come upon the statues of serpent gods beside the foot tracks under the strange trees sacred to the serpents. He would kneel before them, and caressing their granite hoods, ask, 'O serpent gods, will you bite me?'

'In you we are well pleased,' they would tell him. And they would call him to play in their caverns where the lilies blossomed over the deep water and the blue fish, and where the crypts were full of jewels from the serpents' diadems. There were beds for the child to sleep on, cut in rock and smoothed with the warmth of setting suns.

*

It was just that Mrganga remembered his childhood. For again, the rocks were warm under his bare feet. Far away the forest stood charred. Beyond the forest the poison churned in the seas, the clouds changed colour and the wind swept on with the myriad voices of the dead. Mrganga scanned the forest with his spyglass. He saw her crouching in the charred tangle. He put his spear down, and as he did so, the palm of his hand was on the rocks. Their touch grew into him and filled him as it did in his childhood.

'Mrganga,' said the rocks, 'why did you bear the weapon in your hands? You did not want to partake of our peace?'

Mrganga was filled with remorse. He wanted to be the child again, in whom they were well pleased. And he remembered the goddess of the hill. He never saw her, never touched her granite breasts and anointed thighs, and so was his innocence wasted away. He wondered if the temple still stood on the hilltop and if the sun set over the hill. No, the radiation must have worn the temple and the hill to dust. Goddess, mother, said Mrganga, why didn't I come to you with Sunanda? While Father slept or was out hunting the little beasts, I could have slipped away.

Mrganga stirred himself out of his remembering. Now the deep experience of the rocks was gone. He yanked a charred twig and tied a strip of white cloth to it to make the flag of peace. He walked down towards the forest.

The forest was a giant carcass of gesturing cinders. He stood on its edge and raised his white flag.

'I have come without my spear,' he called out. 'Can you see my white flag?'

He had to wait a while for the thin voice which replied, 'Wait there. I am coming.'

She came out of the forest. Mrganga exclaimed in spite of himself. 'How terrible! You're burnt all over.'

She smiled.

'Why do you grieve over me?' she asked. 'Am I not your enemy?'

He caught himself reasoning. He was reasoning like Father would have. This woman is my enemy, he reasoned. 'These are not burns,' she said laughing, 'but ash and soot I smeared on myself.'

She dusted herself clean. Now her skin showed the pallor of the yellow people. She stood before him in her tiny undergarment which sagged below her navel.

'Where are your clothes?' he asked.

'I have lost them all in battle,' she said. 'No one shall spin and weave anymore.'

He moved closer to her.

'Tan Wan,' he said, 'can I call you Sunanda?'

'Why?' she said. 'Tan Wan is a beautiful name. Do you know what it means in our language?'

'I do not want to know what anything means in your language,' he said. 'The fathers of my people would have been disappointed in me if I knew.'

'Mrganga,' she said, gazing with satisfaction at the colours playing on the clouds, 'those fathers of the people are all dead.'

She stood there and with a sweep of her hand turned his gaze to the far horizon. All the way to the burning rim lay the pollen of death, soft and golden like the dust of moths' wings.

'It is just you and me now,' she said. 'All that is left of the two great armies. We are the last surviving enemies.'

Tan Wan pulled off her undergarment. She stood yellow and naked.

'Look at me,' she said.

'You are beautiful,' he said.

She gazed down her breasts at her own body. She gazed down below her navel.

'Can you see me bleed here?' she asked.

'Yes, I see the blood,' he said.

'It is my womb crying,' she said.

The cry of the womb went out over the wilderness, of the pollen. Mrganga could not hear it, but stood beside her contemplating the far sweep of the dust.

'It is into this pollen,' said Tan Wan, 'that my son had integrated. Your spear killed him, Mrganga. And death flamed up his limbs, my little Chen cried, "Mother, I am in pain."'

She stood a while in that memory.

'Mother, I am in pain,' she said, 'Sorrow goes no deeper than these words. Dying, he stretched his hand towards me. He was afraid and wanted to hold mine. I did not touch him. I was a soldier and my duty forbade it. I could not let my hands catch fire. My Chen, who never went out anywhere without clutching my little finger, went alone.'

'If you had caught fire,' he said, suddenly triumphant, 'and I stayed alive, your country would have lost the war!'

'True,' she said. 'But the nations are dead. And no one walks the earth anymore save you and me. So the computers tell us. Just the two of us.'

He peeled the rag off from around his waist. Like her he too stood naked. Naked, they held hands. Then hands round each other's naked waists, they walked over the rocks. All around them lay the primordial nothingness. The sunset darkened over the dust of plants and insects and machines and fortresses.

'Tan Wan,' Mrganga said abruptly, 'my daughter was three years old. She would half wake in the middle of the night and if she found me at the other end of the bed, would roll over to me, and reassuring herself, go off to sleep again. She would smile in her sleep knowing, as one knows in sleep, that I was near. Her name was Sita. Once a girl asked her if her name was Gita. Tears came to Sita's eyes, her lips twitched. I scooped up Sita and smothered her on my bosom and laughed. But as the fire spread over her, again I saw her lips twitch.'

A scalding wind blew over the pollen of the dead children. The pollen rose. The pollen fell and was quiet again. Tan Wan caressed Mrganga below the navel.

'No!' he said. Yet he let her hand be.

'Are you not my enemy?' he said.

'The sun is setting,' she said.

Under the darkening sky the pools of lava gleamed. The pollen gleamed.

'I remember how the dark used to scare him,' she said. 'He would cling to me in the dark. Yet I did not touch him.'

She turned her face away.

'Tan Wan!' Mrganga said. 'Are you crying?'

He was holding her in his arms. She laid her wet cheek on his shoulder. She pressed her wet lips on his bosom.

'I like your breasts,' he said.

Her sobbing ceased.

'They are small,' she said apologetically.

He let them spill into his palms and felt their heaviness. He wiped the lingering soot from them.

'I have seen your women and the goddesses in your temples,' she said. 'I wish I had their large round breasts.'

'Oh,' he said. 'What if you had them?'

She said shyly, 'I might have pleased you better.'

They walked on over the rocks.

'The cry of my womb envelops me now,' she said.

'Mythili,' he called her.

'Oh, my lover,' she said, 'may I kneel before you?'

Tan Wan kneeled. Mrganga towered over her, sorrowing like a king, looking down on her fullness as she kneeled.

The machines that survived over the earth clattered to one another, communicating passionlessly. An occasional spacecraft strayed back home bearing the body of its navigator.

Tan Wan and Mrganga came upon a patch of soft grass.

'It is not contaminated here,' she said.

'The grass is growing,' he said.

'Look,' she said. 'Flowers in the grass!'

They lay down on the flowers.

'Look at the stars, Mrganga,' she said. 'So many of them like the seeds of men wasted in the dark. And just as futile. They spin out through the emptiness, fleeing from the emptiness within. So does the child, as he seeks love, relentlessly feed on the mouldering ancestor molecule, chasing molecule, in a metabolism which knows no mercy. There is desolation within every created thing.'

'Do not remind me,' he said.

The grass rose around them like incense and roused them. He caressed her all over. He kissed her thighs and her breasts and the slight slits that were her eyes. He kissed her beneath the navel and on the sacrificial blood.

*

They woke. Their joy had left their limbs weary. Tan Wan rose and started to walk down towards the forest.

'Tan Wan,' he said, 'where are you going?'

'I am going to get my spear,' she said.

'Why,' he said, 'it is not day yet.'

She did not reply, but walked on. He made no attempt to stop her. Presently she was back with her spear. She put the spear on the grass and sat down beside him. She caressed his limpness with gratitude.

'Mrganga,' she said, 'your seeds are within me. If you so desire, I will wait for them to sprout again and people this garden. They will become multitudes, great nations. What is your desire, my love?'

'Burn down the garden,' he said.

Tan Wan's face shone. She lit the grass and flowers with her spear.

'God of the Vanity of Creation,' she said, 'we will no more be your accomplices!'

'Love me, my beloved,' he said.

She lay on him again for the last act of love. When it was over she wept disconsolately and long.

'My love, my love,' she said, 'the wars are ending within us.'

In infinite compassion she raised her spear and touched him where her tears had fallen. Then she put it in his hand. Gently he touched her breasts with it. The fires began swirling through their flesh.

'Peace, my love.'

'Farewell.'

When it was over, all that remained was the fine dust of gold.

*

A wind blew over the rocks, and the rocks awoke to an ancient memory. The memory of salt waves lashing on them, the memory of incipient life. They remembered it unfolding through the ages in death and slaughter, those ages a mere instant in Time. The instant had passed. The wrong had been undone.

The rocks had waited for this knowledge. Once again they were lost in their slumber.

Ambai (C. S. Lakshmi) (b. 1945)

Ambai is the pen-name of C. S. Lakshmi. Her first collection of Tamil stories appeared in 1976, and in 1986 she published a critical study in English. In 1988, a second collection of stories was published, and, with a good English translation of her work coming into existence in the early nineties, her reputation as one of the most considerable of living Indian writers, and of women writers, was established. She has been an academic by profession, and her concerns have been both scholarly and political; much of her academic work is situated in the field of women's studies, just as her fiction is, among other things, located in feminine, and feminist, experience. She narrates, in her fiction, of how individual belief, political conviction, social and gender roles, and human destiny – in landscapes that range from South Indian small towns (as in the story below) to Bombay to other countries – are interconnected in bewildering ways; that bewildering interconnection is often the plot, the narrative. Here, yet again, is an Indian writer whose creative energies are channelled into the vernacular, and whose conceptual formulations and intellectual enquiries belong to English; and this dichotomy, which might be called a sexual one, the vernacular possessing feminine resonances, and English, the colonial tongue, masculine ones, is dramatized, interrogated, and overturned in Ambai's aesthetic, with sexual difference becoming a metaphor for cultural difference, and vice versa, so that the dichotomy is always being reinterpreted. The violence and immediacy with which words, in her stories, apprehend and transmit the sensory dimensions of the universe, as in the story selected here, remind us that physicality, rather than psychology, is the agent of the political in Ambai's stories. The story is reminiscent of Anantha Murthy's; as in the earlier story, a middle-class narrator records the discomfiture she feels when confronted with a value-system she considers regressive; but, once more, the discomfiture is ambivalent, because that value-system, while appearing to be oppressive in the traditions and hierarchies it perpetuates, also hints at an eroticism that is deeply alluring and, thus, vaguely threatening.

* * *

'Gifts' (1988)

translated from the Tamil by Lakshmi Holmström

She wanted to hold that bus terminus in her memory. To lodge its sounds and images deep in her mind so that she might recall them at will later. A Tamil film song, full of murmuring, heaving and moaning. Ringing invitations of video coaches. Announcements. Against these reverberating background noises, a breast emerging from a folded back choli. The nipple ripe and full. Tiny lips seizing it with little sucking movements. A clashing red and blue silk sari, damp at the neck. Jasmine and *kadambam* flowers squeezed into sleekly oiled, tightly bound hair. Dark haunches of a man squatting outside the town lavatory, preferring to spray its outside walls. A girl with stick-like plaits, arrested at midpoint of a shrill call, mouth gaping open to reveal the deep throat.

He – Chidambaram – was trying to get her a ticket, standing among the crowd jostling about the conductor. It seemed to her that he never let his *veshti* down to its full length. It must have stayed folded and doubled since the morning when she first saw him. A half-sleeved shirt. Worn sandals on his feet. It was in just those clothes that he had come to meet her at the railway station, in the early morning. He had recognized her immediately. At once he had relieved her of her small suitcase. He had evidently decided she couldn't cope with such things as carrying her own case, or buying her own ticket. As they came out of the station, he had remarked with some surprise, 'My goodness, you walk at quite a pace,' and had led the way out.

'Where are we going?'

'Look there, just to the corner street. To the Tamaraparni. We'll bathe in the river and then carry on.'

'Oh no, I couldn't possibly do that.'

'Nothing to worry about. Look at the number of people bathing out there.'

One end of a sari was held against the chest while the other end went slap-slap against a stone. Water splashed against turmeric-stained cheeks and feet; wet thighs. Wet hair fell upon shoulders. Sari ends were held up by the teeth while cholis were slipped on in seconds.

Lightning glimpse of waist and back; then magically the sari was securely in place.

Not she. She wore too many bits and pieces. Nor were these simple enough garments to manage with such ease: to remove, to put on in full view of all.

'Do you not want to bathe?'

'No. I am not accustomed to the river.'

'It's a shame to come here and not bathe in the Tamaraparni.'

'No, no, no. I can't manage it.'

He was a bit taken aback by her obstinate refusal.

'Can't see why you have to fuss about bathing in a river,' he muttered. Then, 'Well, in that case let's go.'

He stopped before a wooden door and called, 'Anni'. The door opened. He said to the man who held the door open, 'This is the lady I told you about. It seems she is writing some sort of report. Krishnamurti wrote, asking us to assist her. Ganapati is not in town, though. At first I thought we'd book her a room in the Hotel, but she doesn't want that as she is here for only half a day. So I've brought her along.'

'Please come in. Why take a room when my house is at your disposal?'

Inside, a face peeped out of the kitchen.

'She says she'd like a bath,' he announced, as if it were news.

'What?'

'She wants a bath, she says.'

'Didn't you bring her along the river?'

'Of course. But she says she is not accustomed.'

'It doesn't matter. She can bath here.'

There was coffee in a minute. Then, 'Come,' the woman invited her.

She pointed to the washing area inside the kitchen. 'I've put water for you in a bucket. Help yourself. No need to shut the door: nobody comes here.'

At the hearth, there was daal cooking, fragrant with turmeric. Next to it stood the *dosai* griddle.

'You'll find a piece of turmeric on the shelf,' she said, coming into the kitchen with a swift movement, to sit in front of the griddle. And before her visitor could quite take in the casualness, the utter lack of self-consciousness of that entry, she had started pouring out the *dosai* batter.

Hunger tore at her insides. The very first green chilli coming apart under the grindstone tickled her nostrils and went straight to her head.

'Do you want me to scrub your back for you?'

'No, no. Thank you.'

'Are you shy? No need to be shy; we're both women.'

The very first *dosai* fell on the waiting banana leaf, crisply gold. Another sizzle. Under the quick strokes of the ladle, the batter spread again to a perfect round.

'Don't you ever put oil on your hair?'

'Of course I do.'

'Then why has it become so dry? No reason why you shouldn't have a healthy head of hair if you rub in a couple of handfuls of oil and then wash your hair with *shikakai* paste in the Tamaraparni.'

Her own hair was shining black, tight and sleek as a bronze pot.

'Are you looking at my hair? I'm fifty years old. You won't find a single grey hair on my head. I still get my periods.'

Is there nothing you want to hide? You too must have been reared as I was ... Why is your sari hanging off your shoulder? Tuck it in properly at the waist. What are you doing in the front veranda? Shut up. I don't want to hear your voice. Put those books away. Chop these vegetables for me. Churn the curds later ... Regulated. Repressed. Then from what source of strength does such innocence spring? Such a smile?

'I was married at fourteen. He was twenty at the time. Not that he was unknown to us or anything; he is my own uncle's son. What else was there after that? My realm has been to feed them all: two girls I have; one son. We've married them all off now. Can you imagine, I have a grandson?'

And is that the sum total of your life story? In four lines?

Meanwhile she was wondering how she was going to put on her underclothes.

'I'll go and serve him now. I have to serve him a fresh *dosai* the second he has finished the last. He can't stand it otherwise. If he gives a single blow ...' She smiled and hastened, leaf in hand.

She drew on her clothes quickly. The choli was difficult to pull on over her still wet body; it caught at the elbow.

'Will you come and eat? I'm hungry.'

'Would you like me to do the *dosais*?'

'Do you really know how?'

'I can manage. They won't be as perfect as yours. But they'll do.'

'When you say that you forget the difference in age between us. How old are you and how old am I? And I've been cooking *dosais* since I was ten. Enough to feed twenty people a day, for forty years. How many does that make?'

Seven thousand and three hundred *dosais* a year. Two lakh and ninety-two thousand *dosais* in forty years. Besides *idlis*, *vadais*, *appams*, vegetable curries and sambars. How many times has she drained the rice? How many kilos of rice has she cooked? And she smiles.

'What is this report you are writing?'

'About women.'

'What is there to write about women?'

'How they live. What work they do. What they think about their lives.'

'What do they think? We bore our children. We fed them.'

'But you didn't bear children all the time. You must have had other thoughts in between. Mustn't you?'

'Yes. So we had our thoughts. Go on with you.'

They continued to eat silently.

She dipped a fragment of *dosai* in chutney, but paused before eating it.

'There was a book in our house, when I was a small child. It had many photographs. Of the sea. With waves, covered in foam. In some photos the sea was still as a mirror. But I've seen the sea at Tiruchendur. Once when I was very ill I kept calling for the sea in my delirium. He was furious; called me a mad woman. I don't know what that disease is. It was like a spell, a curse of the sea. I used to start up from my bed saying, "I want to go to the seaside. I want to see the sea". Then he'd give me such a slap across the face ... I'd quieten down. He's a great devotee of Muruga, he is.'

*

In another city there was a little girl. On the street she lived in, there was a small bookstore, glass-fronted. If she stood on her toes, her eyes and nose alone would reach the glass window. It stood behind a swivelling bookcase. A small patch of the blue sky, the moonlight threading through it like embroidery. A boat. The sea and boat and moonlight blended together in a mass of blueness. She loved blue. Very much. Every time she reached the street corner, her eyes and nose would press against the glass. The shopkeeper noticed her one day.

'What is it, child?'

'The sea.' She pointed.

'Come in.'

He took it down and gave it to her to look at. It was a painting from Europe. Could it have been a Monet? Can't remember now. One day he actually gave it to her. A gentle moment from her own childhood. The painted sea.

*

'What is the conversation about, Teacher? She doesn't know much, but she can make you a good fish curry.' He was laughing.

The visitor watched her. She returned that glance for half a second and then stood up with her leaf to walk past her husband.

As they left, she said, 'Next time you come, you must plan to spend a couple of days. We could make a trip to Tiruchendur.'

'Oh yes, certainly. We will take a picnic. The Murugan temple there is a very fine one, Teacher,' he added.

She wanted to stroke that cheek. To take down the tightly plaited hair and see it spilling down, free. To touch the dark neck where the heavy gold chains lay. But what they had shared in material terms were the *dosais* alone. So, 'I will certainly come again to eat the *dosais* made by your hand,' she said.

Chidambaram brought her her bus ticket. 'You will be all right, won't you? Ganapati will certainly meet you there. He'll take you home as soon as your work is finished. He's not here at the moment ... That's why ... You'll reach there safely, won't you?'

'I got to this place from Delhi, didn't I? Of course I'll be all right.'

'But alone ...'

'Don't worry. I'll be fine.'

Before the bus finally got going, he said to the conductor, 'She's new here. Please make sure she gets off at the right place.'

She could hardly breathe. Protection is a form of repression too. I can only protect you if you stay at home. As soon as you come out and breathe the air that I breathe, danger surrounds you. Terrifying dangers stand at all eight points of the compass, mouths open, ready to devour you. Look how much I care about you, how concerned I am.

She longed for the sea. The tossing, insulting sea.

Ganapati had indeed come to meet her. After her work was done, they took a bus to his home. By that time it was one o'clock at night. They crossed a gravelled veranda, then the outer courtyard, and came to the door. He called softly, 'Chandra, Chandra,' without knocking. Immediately, a young girl of about twenty came to the door, a wooden one with an iron grille, and opened it with a smile.

'Come in,' she said, tidying her loosened hair. 'Anni is asleep upstairs,' she added.

'My sister,' he introduced.

The girl smiled again. She spread a small mat in the main room, next to the kitchen. 'Please sit down.'

She lit the portable stove and placed the griddle upon it. Inside the kitchen there was an old-fashioned hearth with firewood stacked under it and *kolams* upon it. She brought two banana leaves. Fresh *dosais* fell upon them. Spices. Ghee. And hot milk arrived in tumblers before they had finished eating.

In the morning, she came with tea.

'How did you guess that I drink tea?'

'My brother told me. He said that people from Delhi only like tea.'

'What else did he say?'

'That you walk terribly fast. That you go everywhere on your own.'

'How would you like to come with me?'

'How is that possible? They won't allow me to go anywhere outside the house.'

'Don't you ever go out?'

'Once in a while. To the temple. Sometimes to the festivals. To the cinema, if my brother and sister-in-law take me.'

'Then what do you do at home?'

'Oh, I've got masses to do. How can Amma do all the work by herself? Anni and I help her. We have to feed the cows, grind the rice for *dosais*, make the chutney. Then there is the washing to do. My brother likes to have his shirts and trousers starched and ironed. Otherwise he can get very angry. If I have time, I'll read a magazine in the afternoon. I like the serials . . .'

'The tea is delicious.'

'In that story from *Surabi* magazine, this girl has just gone off with this man just because he asked her. "To be continued," it says. I'm afraid he'll ruin her. She shouldn't have gone to him, should she?'

'Don't you ever want to go out?'

'Of course I do. But I will be able to, won't I, when I marry? I could go with "him" anywhere I want – shops, cinemas, other places, other towns . . . They are looking for a bridegroom for me, but so far things haven't worked out.'

'What sort of husband do you fancy?'

'Why do you ask? Are you going to look out a bridegroom for me, then?' Mischief in her eyes.

'Why don't I look out a bridegroom for you in Delhi? How do you fancy a fair, light-skinned Punjabi?'

'You are laughing at me.'

'No, really. You tell me.'

'Are you asking me what sort of man he should be? Well, he should be a good man.'

'Meaning? That he shouldn't drink or smoke? Or what?'

'He mustn't get angry. He mustn't threaten me.'

'Rich or poor?'

'He must be good-natured. If he is educated, he'll get a good enough salary, won't he? He should look after me well.'

She reached for a piece of paper. 'What do you really want after you are married? Come on, let me make a list.'

'Are you teasing me?'

'No, honestly, I want to know. Tell me.'

The girl stood leaning her head against the heavy chains of the indoor swing, bent knee resting on the plank. Her hair fell in waves upon her forehead, the eyelashes dropped slowly like sails, letting the boat eyes drift. She had her list, sure enough:

I want to walk along the streets outside, every day.

I want to eat a plate of snacks in a restaurant.

I want to walk into a shop and choose my own sari.

I want to go to the cinema.

I want to see lots of places.

She walked about with firmness in the world of her own backyard. She restrained the buffalo. She fed it. She showed the visitor the bath house that was used during menstrual pollution, dark as a cave. Whenever one peeped in, she was found by the kitchen hearth ... *Shall I cook the* dosais *now? Would you like me to pour the* idli *batter?* ... At night she folded her legs quietly and modestly and fell asleep, her sari neatly tucked about her. At the slightest sound of a sneeze she was up, as if she were switched on, to make a soothing drink of pepper and *jeera* in hot water. When she put her hands to her face, they smelt of food. The smell of food which had been cooked for generations.

As the suitcase was closed, she said, 'I shall really miss you.'

'You'll send me a wedding invitation, won't you?'

'Of course. How can I not?'

Ganapati took the case from her. She came to the front door of the house. 'Won't you see me to the gate?' But she signalled, no. She smiled. She wore a purple sari, the colour of aubergine flowers. As they reached the gate, her voice alone followed, 'Don't forget to buy some of the special halva of this town for *akka*.'

When she turned around she caught only the tail-end of that purple sari. She let that purple cloth spread out across her mind. It seemed to unfold, then gather itself and swirl in waves. A purple sea. Gradually it seemed to turn into a poisonous blue, rising higher and higher. She could hear the sound of a sharp slap across a face. From the hand of the devotee of Murugan.

Chidambaram, waiting for her at the bus stand, handed her a package.

'What's this?'

'I told Anni you were leaving. She sent you *dosais* for the journey.'

And Ganapati brought her the halva just as Chandra had wished. Halva nestling upon a banana leaf, glistening with ghee.

PAGES FROM
AUTOBIOGRAPHIES

Fakir Mohan Senapati (1843–1918)

Some of the most important and creative work in modern Indian writing has been done in the genre of the autobiography. Autobiography has not, for these writers, been only a form of confession, or revelation, but an act of distancing and interpretation; it has been shaped not only by the personal, but has been an examination of what the personal is in relationship to the national, and to the historical. Among the notable Indian autobiographies is *Story of My Life* by Fakir Mohan Senapati, which, published posthumously in 1927 (although extracts from it appeared in journals during his lifetime), is also, as it happens, the first Oriya autobiography. Senapati, his translators tell us, 'was born in a poor peasant family in the coastal district of Balasore ... It is important to note that the period in which Senapati lived and wrote was one of the darkest in Oriya history. The Oriyas had no state of their own (Orissa became a separate province in 1936) and they lived scattered in Bengal, Madhya Pradesh and Madras. As a result, they were economically neglected ... Some influential Bengalis, interestingly, claimed that Oriya was not a language but a dialect of Bengali, and hence demanded that Oriya should be replaced by Bengali in Orissan schools.' Senapati, the first major writer of Oriya fiction, was a late-flowering writer, and wrote no prose before he retired from the administrative service. In his autobiography, he had to define himself not only against the British, but, as it turns out, the hegemony of the Bengali language, with which he must have had a profound, but also fraught, relationship. The haunting account of the famine in 1866 in Orissa reminds us of the floods and devastation in that state as recently as 1999, and of the continuing complicity between the tyranny of nature and the wrong-headedness of human agency in this part of the world; we are also reminded of how long, crucially, writers in this part of the world have borne witness.

* * *

Fakir Mohan Senapati

from *Story of My Life* (1918, published 1927)

translated from the Oriya by Jatindra K. Nayak and Prodeepta Das

CHILDHOOD

I was born on a Friday in January 1843 in a village called Mallikashpur, which was a part of the town of Balasore. My mother's name was Tulsi Dei and my father's, Lakshman Charan Senapati.

I am told that as soon as I was born the upper lobe of my left ear was pierced and a gold earring was put on. I had an elder brother whose name was Chaitanya Charan; he died before I was born. There was then current superstition among our people that if the ear of the child born after the death of an elder brother was pierced, he would be spared by Yama, the god of death. In my childhood I saw hundreds of such cases.

When I was only a year and five months old my father set out for Puri to witness the Car Festival. On the way home, he had an attack of cholera at Bhubaneswar. It claimed his life. With him on the pilgrimage were a few people from the village including his mother (my Thakurma). From her I came to know that my father breathed his last on the stone steps of the Bindusagar tank near the Bhubaneswar temple. People in our village burst into tears when they heard the news of his death. A pet dog of my father's also started wailing along with the village people. Even when the people stopped, the dog continued wailing. It would sniff at places which my father frequented, where he used to sit. It died eight days later, not having touched food since his death.

My mother took to her bed after receiving the news of my father's death, and never got up again. She died on the eighth day of the month of Bhadra, after going through intense physical and mental suffering for fourteen months.

I felt utterly helpless on that day. Many of my contemporaries, who were more fortunate and healthier and stronger than I, have left the world long since. And here I am, orphaned as a child, plagued by diseases, and having survived terrible threats to my life, writing down with this feeble hand the story of a long, yet worthless life. Why? The creation of even a blade of grass is not pointless. Why has God kept me alive for so long, to serve what purpose?

As if by God's will, Kuchila Dei, my Thakurma, took me under her wing after I lost my parents. We have a saying: an orphan has only one hope – his mother's mother, or his father's mother. It breaks my heart to think of Thakurma's loving care, the great suffering she endured to save my life. Alas, in return, I have given her nothing.

After my mother's death, I lay bedridden for about seven or eight years, suffering from diseases like diarrhoea and piles. Thakurma would sit by the bed day in and day out. Month after month, year after year passed this way. Thakurma would go without sleep and food for days. It was as if she was locked in a desperate struggle with death. At last, Thakurma won, and I grew better.

During my sickness Thakurma would pray by my sickbed to all manner of gods and goddesses to save my life. At that time there were two pirs in Balasore; at last Thakurma turned to them for support. She pledged, 'If my child recovers, I will offer him to you as a fakir.' The name originally given to me was Brajamohan. Thakurma now called me Fakir: the purpose of this Muslim name was to please the pirs.

The illness was over – I survived. But Thakurma could never bring herself to offer me up to the pirs, which would mean giving up all she had in this world. Instead, I was made a fakir for eight days every Mohurrum. I would wear the outfit of a fakir for these days – shorts which would reach down to my knees, a multicoloured shirt, a fakir cap, a patchwork shoulder bag, a red walking-stick. Dressed in this manner and with my face smeared with chalk I would go from house to house in the afternoon for alms. In the evening the alms collected would be sold and the money spent on *sirni* for the pirs.

EDUCATION (1852)

I was nine when I started school. Each large village in the town had a school; if the villages were small, they would have one school between two or three of them. People of means employed private tutors for their children. Children of the untouchables had to do their lesson sitting at a little distance from those of the higher castes.

In those times, schoolteachers came from Cuttack district, mainly from the Jhankad sub-division. The month of Chaitra was the time when *abadhans* were recruited. You could easily tell from the way he dressed that he was after a teacher's job: a loincloth that would barely reach the knees, a dirty towel on his head, a cane on his shoulder balanced by a small brass pot for cooking on one end, a light tumbler, two or three palm leaf manuscripts, and a piece of cloth about three yards long on the other. From the middle of Phalgun to the end of Chaitra these teachers would be seen wandering about the village streets.

Most of them were of the *karana* caste, only a few were *matibansha ojhas*. Those who came from Balasore were astrologers by caste. The *matibansha ojhas* were known for their arithmetic skills. People believed that they were well-versed in the *Lilabati Sutras*. It is said that, with their special skills, these *ojhas* could count the feathers of a bird in flight.

It is not that these village teachers ran schools only in Balasore; they had spread out to neighbouring feudatory states, and places like Dantun, Pataspur, Mahishadal, Kanthi and Haripur in the Midnapore district.

Midnapore district comprised almost 5,200 square miles, of these about 2,200 in the south were inhabited by Oriya speakers. In their conversations, letters, in maintaining accounts, and in the moneylenders' offices as well as in the writing of legal documents they used the Oriya language. Previously, the court language of Midnapore had been partly Oriya. It was from the Balasore cutchery that officials were sent there. Nowadays this is no longer so.

Even now religious scriptures in Oriya such as the *Bhagabat* by Jagannath Das, the *Mahabharat* by Sarala Das, and the *Ramayan* by Balaram Das are read out every evening in important households in these parts. The Sanskrit text of the *Bhagabat* was rendered into Oriya verses by a high-ranking lady from Pataspur. This text is still in use in certain parts, and by reciting this and other texts, hundreds of Brahmins from Balasore and Cuttack make a living and find employment in the households of a number of zemindars and moneylenders. In these modern times, English-educated babus in this area find it rather embarrassing to speak Oriya. However, Oriya still reigns in their households as their wives would not have it otherwise.

The disappearance of Oriya medium schools from southern Midnapore is very unfortunate and remains a mystery. In 1865–70 a Bengali sub-inspector was appointed to set up schools in this area. He tried to start Bengali medium schools but people were not willing to allow their children to be taught in Bengali. He tried very hard but did not succeed. His special appointment was to start schools in this part; if he failed, he would lose his job. How could he give away such a lucrative job by admitting his defeat to his superiors?

There seemed a way out. The babu's brain was prompt in producing a brilliant idea: he would go to a police station and get the daroga to round up all the village teachers on a fixed day. He would then produce a fake warrant in English complete with the official seal and say, 'Look at this. It is the order of the Collector sahib of Balasore. All the schools in the area under this police station are to be closed down, and all the *abadhans* must leave within seven days of hearing this warrant. If any *abadhan* is seen after this time, he would be arrested, sent to he cutcherry and would be fined and jailed.' The sub-inspector went round the police station to make this known to the *abadhans*. It was but natural that the poor *abadhans* panicked. The order came straight from the Collector. They did not waste any time and headed home.

I need hardly say that the sub-inspector now had little difficulty in founding Bengali medium schools. I was quite close to the Headmaster of Balasore District School, who also was the elder brother of this sub-inspector. He told me this incident to make a point of his brother's great intelligence and application.

Although Bengali became the medium of instruction in southern Midnapore, Oriya continued to be spoken at home. It is hard to give up one's mother tongue; the Oriya *Bhagabat* and a few other Oriya texts have been printed in the Bengali alphabet and are still read in almost every house there.

At the village schools, whoever stepped out of the rules, was punished. Every movement of the pupils had to have the approval of the *abadhan*. If your legs went to sleep, you had to fold your hands and say 'One, Sir', which meant you wanted to go out to pass water. 'Two, Sir' meant that you wanted to go out to answer the call of nature, 'Five, Sir' meant you wanted a drink of water.

The following were some of the standard punishments in the penal code of the school.

1 being caned.
2 having to stand on one leg.
3 having to stand with one hand clutching the hair and the other touching the nose.
4 having to kneel down, left hand on the head, a piece of chalk on the outstretched right hand.
5 having a rope formed of shredded palm leaf slung across your neck and tied to your toes.

At the end of every day the pupils were given what was known as *sunyachati*. Both the teacher and monitor, the cleverest boy of his class, remembered which pupil came at what time to the school. Before leaving school for home you had to stand in a row stretching your joined palms. The teacher would touch the palm of the pupil who arrived earliest with the tip of his cane: that meant zero. After that the next to arrive was to get two strokes, and so on. The force of the stroke was not the same throughout: sometimes it was heavy, sometimes it was light. While giving the stroke the teacher would look into the face of the pupil, and any sign of protest would weaken the force of the stroke; with the others, the swish of the cane would be much louder.

If a pupil woke up late, the fright of the *sunyachati* made him seek a safe retreat near the hearth, where he would sit clutching an earthen pot. But it was no use. Three or four boys of his own caste would take off their clothes, follow him there, frogmarch him to the school, where the teacher would promptly land a few strokes on his back.

I went to one such school, where we were taught arithmetic in the morning and scripture and astrology in the afternoon. The lessons over, other boys went home, but I had to stay back at the school to wait upon the teacher and help with cooking. The name of our teacher was Baishnab Mohanty, and he came from Cuttack district.

My uncle, Purusottam Senapati, was very cruel to me. At the end of every month, when the teacher asked for his fees he would reply, 'You teach him nothing. Why do you ask for money?' The teacher would say, 'I watch over him night and day; I don't allow him to go out even for a minute to play.' My uncle would retort, 'But I see no signs of it on his back.' The teacher would thus get my uncle's message; for no reason he would come and hit me hard with his cane ten or twelve times. The crack of the cane and my screams would make my uncle and his wife very pleased indeed. But Thakurma would come rushing in and demand, 'Teacher! Haven't you got children of your own?' Every time the teacher came to ask for his tuition fee this drama would recur.

Later, however, Baishnab Mohanty went back to his village. I was taken to the other school in our village at the Landa Gosain monastery. On some auspicious day – the first, the eighth, the fourteenth and the last days of the lunar month – the women of the village gave us alms for singing to them. The rice we thus collected would do for our teacher. He might occasionally sell the surplus, if any, and save a little money. There were other sources from which he also received rice. A new pupil brought the following gifts to the school: a seer of rice, an areca nut, a pinch of molasses, sweetened puffed rice, and flowers.

At the time there was a free Parsi School at Balasore. After the village

school I went on my own there, and got myself admitted. The school had
on its staff three Muslim teachers and an Oriya pundit, whose name was
Banamali Bachaspati. His job was confined to teaching students how to
write letters to their relatives and letters to the court.

No printed books other than the Bible were available in Oriya in those
days. The Mission Press at Cuttack were the only printers in Orissa. The
missionaries ran a school in Balasore, but only the Bible was taught there.
No Hindu student went there for fear of 'losing caste' by reading printed
books.

SAILS AND SALT

In the days of my childhood, Balasore was the centre of much shipping
business. About five to six hundred ships were at sea, 75 per cent of these
carrying salt, and the rest carrying cargo, to places such as Rangoon,
Madras, Colombo and islands in the sea. No one in Balasore in those days
had heard of steamers.

The ships needed sails. Depending on its size, a ship might need six to
twelve sails of varying shapes and measurements. These sails were known
by names such as *karaju, sabar, tavar, kalami, jivi, daria, pela*, etc. These
sails came in rectangular, triangular or irregular shapes. The sails had to
fit the ships: if the sail was too large, a strong wind might overturn the
ship; if it was too small, it would not pull the ship. It needed a lot of
experience to cut sails of the right size.

My father and my uncle took contracts for most of the ships. Many in
the shipping business gave them advances to make sails. Hundreds of
tailors were employed at our house to make these sails. It was a highly
profitable business. We had our own office to keep the accounts. My uncle
got me to work under the manager as an apprentice. In the morning and
in the afternoon I would walk along the river bank and note which sails
were made for which ship, which tailor was responsible for which work,
and report to the manager. I would still have a lot of time after finishing
all this work. During the spare time, my uncle would engage me to stitch
sails.

Every year, the shipping business in Balasore lasted from the month of
Kartik to the month of Chaitra. With a strong south wind blowing, ships
would not move out of the mouth of the river; they anchored there until
the month of Kartik. Till then all work stopped here. And yet traders,
craftsmen, contractors, the crew, the porters and other employees could

live off their earnings for the rest of the year. The rainy season put paid to sailings, and so all who worked in this line had to sit idle at home.

When the shipyard was closed down for good, my uncle took me to Biswanath Das, who lived in a neighbouring village and was officer-in-charge of a salt-making unit. Every day I would go with him to his office to learn the working of the salt division.

Of all the departments in the cutchery, the salt division was the most important; several clerks were employed there. The division was divided into two sections: the *sirasta* section and the *dewani* section. The former kept the accounts of the mofussils, the latter looked after the accounts of the towns.

In those days, Balasore owed all its flourishing prosperity to the making of salt. *Ponga* salt was raised in the area between the mouth of Subarna-rekha in the north and that of Dhamra in the south. After the needs of Balasore were met the surplus salt was shipped off to the Shalimar depot near Calcutta. From there salt would then be sent to villages in Bengal for sale. At that time many people in Bengal dealt in *ponga* salt from Balasore. Making salt was almost the only source of living for the natives of Balasore.

To ensure the safe sailing of ships all the deities of the town had to be appeased, and for this reason hundreds of Brahmin pundits were put on the payroll. Every year, before the making of salt would begin, worship was offered to Lord Mahadev at the temple near the cutchery by the government to make sure the raising of salt ran into no difficulty. All the expenses were paid out of the government treasury. Since all those who worked in the salt division were Hindus, the government had to do this in order to please them.

I began to learn work at the office for salt manufacture. Oriya, Bengali and Parsi were the languages used in the office. Unfortunately, the goddess of wealth moved to Liverpool and other such places. The salt division was wound up. The Bengali clerks went back to Bengal, and the Oriya clerks found employment in other departments and sections.

As an important port and centre of trade and commerce, Balasore was famous not only in India but in Europe as well. Even before setting up in Bengal, Dutch, Danish, French and English merchants set up trading stations here. But time does not run even; every rise has a fall. For countless years, the river banks in Balasore teemed with people. Today the same place is deserted like a sepulchre, almost a wilderness. The river, too, is silted up. Trade in Balasore is now in the hands of foreigners.

MISSION SCHOOL AT BALASORE (1864–71)

The post of Headmistress at Balasore Mission School fell vacant. It carried a salary of ten rupees a month. Rev. A. Miller, the Secretary of the school, appointed me to this position in 1864. The post of the second teacher, too, fell vacant. Gobind Chandra Pattnaik, a good friend of mine, was appointed. His salary was seven rupees.

Miller sahib was tall, handsome, well-built, and a little on the heavy side. You could count an irascible temper among his faults: he would not try and understand anything, he would do whatever he wanted. He had to employ Hindu teachers like us because Christian teachers were not around, but he would not trust Hindus. In his eyes Hindus were idol-worshippers, incarnations of the devil, liars, unreliable and wicked. I was a Hindu; therefore, I was wicked and unworthy of trust. He knew little Oriya and even less of how to run a school. If I made any suggestion about the school, he would fly into a rage and do the exact opposite of what I had suggested. His unnecessary anger never scared me. On the other hand, his funny Oriya and his gestures amused me. I would quietly go away.

There was a pundit at the Mission Girls' School. His name was Biswanath Satpathy. He was a versatile man who could compose impromptu poems in Oriya as well as in Sanskrit and was good at music, embroidery and many other arts. He was a very amusing man, to whom I was very close. I would like to give an example of his ability to compose a poem in no time. The Mission School and the Girls' School were housed in a large bungalow, and were separated by a wall. Only Christians studied in the Girls' School. The fear of losing caste was so great among the Hindus that they would not send their daughters to school. There was a big girl called Sharada in the Girls' School. Once I wanted to send for Sharada, and so I scribbled a note to Biswanath. He wrote back in Sanskrit, 'The coy girl does not want to go there.' I carried the piece of paper, went up to the veranda and called out to Biswanath, 'Give me the full poem right now. If you are a good poet, one line will not do.' Biswanath stood there and reeled out these lines:

> With heaving breasts and rounded buttocks
> Fresh thin lips and beautiful tresses
> Always smiling
> The coy one does not want to go there.

One day pundit Biswanath happened to be absent from school. It was also the day of the Moharrum festival. Miller sahib sent for him and demanded, 'Biswanath pundit, why weren't you at school yesterday?'

 Biswanath: I was ill. So I could not come.
 Miller: You are lying. You stayed away to celebrate Moharrum
  yesterday. I fine you one rupee.
 Biswanath: Sahib. I am a Hindu Brahmin. How could I celebrate a
  Muslim festival like Moharrum?
 Miller: Oh, you idol-worshippers are all alike.

Although he had to pay the fine, we had a good laugh about the sahib's ignorance. For a month our friends would joke and laugh about this.

The sahib used to visit distant villages with his fellow preachers to spread the gospel in markets and other important places. As soon as they came back, criminal charges would be brought against them. The sahib, accompanied by his fellow-preachers, would stand at the market place and break into a high-pitched song in English. This would attract a crowd. The educated people, let alone the villagers, would not be able to make head nor tail of this song. Having finished his song, the sahib would begin a lecture in broken Oriya: 'O brothers. Your Lord Jagannath is only a piece of wood or stone. If you worship him you will go to hell. Lord Jesus is your saviour. Worship him, find light and inherit the kingdom of heaven.'

If by chance someone from the assembled crowd answered back, 'No sahib. Our Jagannath is good, your Jesus Christ is not good,' the sahib would fly into an impatient rage and scream, 'You idol-worshipping wicked Hindu! How dare you speak ill of our Lord?' He carried a whip. He would then lash out at whoever came in front. As a result, criminal charges were preferred against him.

The sahib was confident that he knew Oriya very well. He had worked hard for a few days on an Oriya translation of a slim volume in English. It was decided that first I would go through the translation and correct errors, if any, then the principal preacher, Bhikari Bhai, would again read it from start to finish. If it was all right it would go to the press. As soon as I received the manuscript I started correcting it. The very opening sentence suffered from absurd syntax. When I rewrote it, it read, 'There are many in the world who do not believe in the existence of God.' The sound of the Oriya word for 'existence' is similar to that of the word for 'bone'. I took the manuscript after correction, and read it out to Bhikari Bhai as he found it hard to read manuscripts. The very first line made him explode with anger and he shouted, 'What! What have you written, pundit? The bone of

God? Is he an idol that he would have bones?' I did not understand what
was happening and just stared at him. Bhikari Bhai tried very hard to make
me understand that God did not have bones. I asked him humbly, 'Bhikari
Bhai, where have I mentioned the bone?' Bhikari Bhai pointed at the word
'existence' and said, 'Here. Can't you see?' Having said this he went to the
sahib and shouted furiously, 'Sahib. This pundit has sacrileged your book.'
In the sahib's opinion, Bhikari Bhai was a learned man, although he could
read a printed version of the Bible with some difficulty. But he was a
Christian, therefore reliable. I was a wicked, idolatrous Hindu, therefore
untrustworthy. The sahib did not say a word to me, but he seethed in
anger. For many days afterwards he would not talk properly to me. I
cannot tell what became of his book. As criminal cases against him piled
up, the American mission disowned Rev. Miller. But he did not have to sit
idle in his bungalow for long: the Collector of Balasore, Bignold sahib,
wrote to the government and got him a job as a deputy collector. A few
months later he died in harness.

R. H. Pusey, the acting Collector of Balasore, and Myers, the Joint
Magistrate, shared the same bungalow. I was giving them lessons in
Bengali. As I wanted to better myself I requested them to find me a
government job. Collector Pusey made me a *munshi* in his office for the
time being. When Rev. E. C. B. Hallam was appointed as the Secretary of
the Mission School, I came back to my earlier job.

Rev. Hallam was as handsome as he was learned and virtuous. He was
soft-spoken and sweet-tempered and had a good command of Oriya
language. His voice and accent were not different from those of native
speakers. He compiled a grammar of Oriya language in order to help the
British with their learning of Oriya. I helped him on the book and my help
was acknowledged. I was in agreement with him on all points of grammar
except a minor one relating to the dative case. He was of the view that
there was no need for a separate dative case in Oriya. He left it out of his
book.

Those who were successful in the final examinations of the maintained
schools were awarded four scholarships of four rupees a month each to
enable them to study English. In the first year of the award, four from
Balasore Mission School were successful. Among them was Raghunath
Choudhury, who was later to be my son-in-law. Balasore Mission School
outdid all schools in the state. Rev. Hallam appreciated this and increased
my salary to twenty-five rupees.

John Beames, the then Collector of Balasore, was regarded as a great
scholar among the British civilians and educated natives alike. He was

well-versed in as many as eleven languages. At the time he was engaged
in writing his *Comparative Grammar of the Indian Languages.* He needed
someone who was knowledgeable in Sanskrit, Bengali and Oriya. My well-
wisher, Hallam sahib, introduced me to Beames. During our first meeting
Beames asked me a few questions on grammar, and as my answers were to
his satisfaction he put them into his book. I quickly gained a reputation
among the sahibs as a pundit. It is said, a small bush is a big tree in a
treeless country. The sahib asked me to see him at least once a week. If I
was delayed by a day or two for some reason or other, he would immediately enquire, 'Babu. Why did you take so long to come?' Whenever we
met we discussed linguistics. On some days we discussed Sanskrit hymns,
on others Bengali verses, the Oriya poem *Rasakallol*, the snakecharmers'
chants.

There was then a lot of ill-feeling between the Bengalis and Oriyas in
Balasore. Because the sahibs were on my side, Bengali officials and powerful Bengali clerks did not dare do me any harm. In those days in Balasore
nearly all the officers, petty as well as the highly paid, were Bengalis.

I received much help from Beames sahib in my campaign for women's
education, introduction of the Oriya language, and better nutrition. On
many an occasion Beames sahib came to my rescue. All my worldly
prosperity I owe only to John Beames. I shall remember his holy name to
my dying day. He used to tell everyone that I was a patriot and I would
contribute a lot to the country.

R. L. Martin, the inspector of schools for the south-western part of
Bengal, had his headquarters in Mindapore. Once he came to Cuttack to
inspect schools in Orissa. At the time the post of second teacher in Cuttack
Normal School lay vacant – the monthly salary was thirty rupees. The
sahib wrote asking if I would be interested. However, a postscript made it
clear that if I accepted the job I would have to move to Cuttack and would
not be allowed to change my mind. At that time Hallam sahib was touring
Jaleswar in northern Balasore. I went to him to discuss this matter. The
sahib increased my salary to thirty rupees and asked me not to go to
Cuttack.

On my way home, as I reached Basta, some eight miles north of
Balasore, I went down with a fever in the evening. By morning my whole
body was covered with smallpox. I hired a palanquin and came to Balasore.
It was evening when I reached home. As I sat down on the doorstep, I
burst into tears. Thakurma came near me and with tears in her eyes said,
'You need not go to Cuttack. Why did the sahib beat you?' I explained,
'The sahib did not beat me. I have smallpox. I can't even sit down. Make

my bed quickly. I want to lie down.' Later, when I asked her why she talked like that, she said, 'I dreamt yesterday that the sahib had beaten you up. Your body was swollen and you were sitting on the doorstep and crying.'

THE FAMINE (1866)

Hallam sahib's encouragement made me work with a lot of enthusiasm. After school we often discussed literature. Although I was his subordinate, he treated me as if I was a close relative.

During this period more and more people were becoming Christians. The main reason for this was the famine. This catastrophic event took place in 1866. To this day people have not been able to forget this terrible famine; as many as three million people died in the space of one year. Nearly six million people became homeless. Many died, many others got displaced. I was twenty-three at the time and working as the Headmaster of Mission School. Fifty years have gone by since, but those events remain engraved in my mind. It rained heavily for about four days in the month of Bhadra, and then it was dry. As Bhadra passed into Ashwin, people anxiously looked up to the sky. The only thing they now talked about was water. From the start of the month of Kartik, people began to despair. Even if the rains came, it would be too late now; the rice saplings had started dying out. Rice was the only crop in Balasore; people's lives depended on this crop. The dried-up rice saplings were straw now. Ears of rice, some fully grown, others less so, tossed in the air like tufts of white hair. The cattle were left to graze freely among the paddies. But only one sniff at the dying rice stalks, and they would turn away.

The town stopped half a mile south of my house. From there rice fields stretched endlessly to the horizon. Scattered hamlets lay in between like islands. In those days I would have my bath at nine in the morning and go out carrying a rug, which I would spread out in the middle of a rice field, and sitting on it, pray to God to save my people.

The daily labourers scraped a living for a few days by selling off whatever utensils they had. Towards the end of the month of Kartik, they abandoned their homes and went wherever they could. Husbands and wives, fathers and sons all were separated. They would go from house to house begging for alms. But who had a handful of rice to spare?

The peasants could manage to stick to their homesteads until the months of Magh and Phalgun by selling off whatever utensils, cattle, or ornaments they had. An ox fetched five measures of rice, a cow, two measures. There were no scales; nor was there the time to find one. Who cared what the right price was? People took whatever they got. Some of the better-off people went from village to village with ready cash on them to buy rice. There was none to be found; whoever had any kept it hidden.

By the end of the month of Phalgun, many peasants and nearly all artisans had started devouring whatever they could find. As the tamarind trees put out tender leaves, you would find ten to twenty people clambering like monkeys to chew the leaves. Everyone you saw had been reduced to skin and bones, the eyes sunken into their sockets. Many women from good families were seen wandering about the streets with rags wrapped around their waist. The breasts were now two shrivelled stretches of skin dangling nakedly. Some had in their arms withered babies sucking at their emaciated breasts. It was hard to tell whether the child was alive or dead. The death toll began to rise from the month of Chaitra. The village streets, the bathing ghats, the jungle – all were strewn with dead bodies.

If I remember right, Ravenshaw sahib had just taken over as the new Commissioner of Orissa. He was a great benefactor of the state. The government wrote to Ravenshaw in September, or maybe in October, suggesting that Orissa was most likely to face famine as a result of the drought. They wanted to find out what precautions had been taken. In order to give a reply, the Commissioner sahib sent for all the officials and asked for their advice. Two departmental officers said, 'If there is going to be a famine, we need not worry at all. The mofussil zemindars have plenty of rice. That will last us out a whole year.' Since the departmental officers said this, the court officers deemed it proper to exaggerate the matter somewhat in order to please the Commissioner. One of them said, 'The zemindar of Gopalpur has a reserve of fifty thousand bags of rice in ten granaries. You could get another forty thousand from Sam Sahu of Bhimpur. Besides, smaller merchants have depots full of rice. Orissa could be fed easily for two months on rice from these.' The court officer for the political department went a step further and spoke of lakhs of bags, not thousands. From all accounts it seemed Orissa had unlimited reserves of rice, and that there was no problem for at least a year. The Commissioner sahib wrote back to the government saying famine in Orissa might be imminent, but what reserve of rice there was would last at least a year.

It was a big blunder. The Commissioner should have found out whether Orissa truly had so much rice and whether people who had the rice would sell or donate it when famine struck. But it seems the Commissioner had no idea that fate had decreed the death of three million people in Orissa.

People started dying from the month of Phalgun. The number of deaths increased daily. The roads, the bathing ghats, the fields, the jungle – wherever you went you saw dead bodies; it was as if death was spreading all over the land.

Rice was now sold at ten seers a rupee, but only for three or four days. Then it was sold at three seers a rupee. Then it was hard to come by. But when supplies of rice arrived from Rangoon, the price dropped back to one rupee for ten seers. In the year before the famine the price of unhusked rice was one rupee for 150 seers, and the price of husked rice was one rupee for a maund and a half. The same rice sold at ten seers a rupee in the famine year. You could somehow get to buy rice in the towns; in the villages it was impossible to get any. There, people who had rice kept it from others; some even hid it in holes dug in their courtyards.

Towards April, the Commissioner sahib wrote to the government about the real condition of Orissa and pleaded for adequate supplies of food grains. The government, possibly with the Commissioner's earlier letter in mind, wired back: *you have asked for food grains, but food supplies cannot be sent by wire.*

The fine trunk road of today that connects Puri with Calcutta was something of a ravine in those days. It was overgrown and much frequented by thieves and bandits. For this reason, food supplies in no way could be transported by land. With the abolition of the salt division, ships no longer put in at the Balasore port. The people of Balasore had only heard about steamships but had never seen even one. The government requisitioned a big luxury liner from Calcutta to bring rice from Rangoon and Bengal. They also opened mercy camps in many towns.

As soon as the word got around starving millions flocked to the towns. For days they had not had a proper meal. They had survived on tender leaves and barely edible roots. Now that there were mercy camps, they ran to the towns. But how could they survive such a long journey? 75 per cent perished on the way. Of those who reached the mercy camps some died of dysentery and diarrhoea after eating only one or two meals. Their stomachs had been empty for such a long time; they were tempted to eat as much as they could. But they had lost all power to digest.

Doctors were brought in to treat them. The government had stockpiled sacks of sago specially brought over from Calcutta. In the mercy camps, the starving were given sago for the first few days. But that was no use. Nearly everyone died.

Every morning, the sweepers brought their carts and carried off dead bodies lying all around the mercy camps and elsewhere in the town and threw them in the river. I have seen with my own eyes sweepers daily taking corpse-laden carts towards the river.

After the needs of the mercy camps were met, the surplus rice was sold at the open market at ten seers a rupee. Of course, you could not buy as much as you wanted. The members of the relief committees issued ration tickets and you could get rice only on showing these tickets.

Nothing in this world lasts for ever. The famine came and went. The year after the famine, many children and grown-ups were seen wandering around. Their Hindu society did not accept them any longer because they had been feeding at mercy camps. But the Christian missionaries accepted them with love, and brought them up like their own children and gave them education. Is Hinduism not to blame for deserting them? According to Hindu scriptures there is nothing wrong in accepting food from the untouchables in a life and death situation. The *Mahabharat* mentions the hermit Viswamitra, who did not have to lose his place among the sages for having eaten dog-meat cooked by a *chandala*.

THE FIRST PRINTING PRESS IN BALASORE (1868)

While teaching at Mission School I was doing all I could for the development of Oriya literature. I wrote a history of the Rajputs. The mission press at Cuttack was then the only printing press in Orissa. I found out that it would cost me four hundred rupees to get my book printed there. I did not have the money, so I gave up the idea. Later on, Iswar Chandra Vidyasagar allowed me to translate his book *Jeevan Charita* into Oriya, and it was printed by the Baptist Mission Press of Calcutta. This was recommended as a textbook for scholarship examinations. Afterwards, I wrote a book on Oriya grammar, and another on arithmetic, both of which became school textbooks.

We founded an association for the development of Oriya literature. The members were:

>   Babu Jayakrushna Choudhury
>   Babu Bholanath Samantray
>   Babu Gobind Prasad Das
>   Babu Damodar Prasad Das (Secretary and Treasurer)
>   Babu Fakir Mohan Senapati
>   Babu Radhanath Ray

It was decided in the first meeting that all the old Oriya manuscripts should be printed. *Rasakallol* should be printed first. The proceeds from the sales would then finance the printing of other texts. A company would be set up to find the capital needed for printing the first book; each share would go for two rupees. By working hard for three or four months we could collect a working capital of 250 rupees. Then we set to work on annotating the text of *Rasakallol*, spending two hours every evening on this work. Before this was complete, the association realized that without a press of our own we would have to wait until all the copies of *Rasakallol* were sold to find the money needed for printing another book; but with a press of our own, we could print a number of books at the same time. A few days earlier, a printing company had been established at Cuttack. We decided that we could set up a similar company in Balasore, too. The annotation of *Rasakallol* was discontinued. The money we had collected for its printing is yet to be recovered from the Treasurer.

At last, in 1868, a printing house was set up at Balasore. It was named 'P. M. Senapati and Co. Utkal Press.' The value of each share was five rupees. Four members of the association went out to collect the fixed capital for the company. Some bought shares because they realized the benefits of such a press, while others were guided by the love of profit. Some others bought shares because they found our repeated appeals too much to resist. Thus, in four or five months, we collected twelve hundred rupees and put it in the care of the Treasurer.

Nobody in Balasore in those days had any idea what a printing press looked like. We did not have the money to hire printers from Calcutta. I sent my cousin Jagannath to Calcutta to learn printing. I sent him a monthly allowance of fifteen rupees for a year. This I paid from my own pocket. We asked him to find out what we needed for the press and how much it would cost.

Gradually, the parts arrived by ship. Depending on the wind, ships from Calcutta took anything from ten to twenty days to reach Balasore. Finally, Jagannath came carrying the typefaces. All this cost us eight hundred rupees, leaving us a balance of only four hundred. All that was needed now was the printing machine itself, which would cost us at least seven to eight hundred. Was all our labour in vain? The missionaries in Midnapore had a printing press. I wrote to them enquiring if they would sell us a cheap printing press. Before their reply, a printing press arrived on a bullock cart. If I remember right, we had to pay only 150 rupees or so.

Our family owned a pukka house in the Motigani bazar. It used to be rented out. I took it on rent from my uncle. The printing press was to be housed here. Jagannath, who was now our printer, assembled the press. Some six more workers were hired. The plan was that Jagannath would train them. We joyfully announced that printing would begin. Half of the shops in Motigani were closed on this auspicious day. Many distinguished people came to see the machine at work. The street outside was full of people, and the traffic came to a stop. The types were set and put on the machine; a wooden ruler dabbed with ink was rolled on the typeface; then paper was pressed on to it. Hundreds of people were waiting with baited breath: the printed paper would now come out of the press. But what happened? Not a single letter was printed. The paper was only smudged with ink here and there. Full of embarrassment, the printer stood, pulling a long face. We felt as if the earth slipped from under our feet. We were speechless with shame and disappointment; we were in a terrible predicament. Then a barrage of questions came from the people. With difficulty I replied, 'Today we only put ink on the paper; later this ink will turn into letters.'

We learnt later that the mission press got rid of this machine because it was not working. We needed to bring a new machine from Calcutta, or else a year's hard work would go down the drain. The new machine would cost eight hundred rupees. Where would the money come from?

One misfortune leads to another. It was the middle of summer – the heat was intense; a lot of running around, worries, irregular meals and lack of sleep gave me blood dysentery. One day, while I was working at the machine for several hours, I became drenched in sweat, and because of dysentery blood ran through my clothes and dripped on the floor. On coming home, I fainted. During this time I passed out at home a lot of times following long hours at the press. But I kept it from everybody. I put on a brave face when I talked about the press to others. Faced with such misfortunes, I resolved: it is either the press or my life.

If you are committed to some good deed selflessly, God always comes to your aid. Kishore Mohan Das, younger brother of the zemindar and merchant, Babu Manmohan Das, was a close friend of mine. As soon as I asked, he gave me a loan of eight hundred rupees without question. I purchased a Super Royal Albino printing machine from Calcutta. It was the monsoon, so no ships could come to Balasore. The printing machine had to be carried by a bullock cart. Nowadays, we have a fine road from Calcutta to Balasore, but at the time it was a dust track. The rainy season made it impassable: the cart wheels would often get stuck in the mud, and labourers from nearby villages had to be hired to pull it free. The cart carrying our printing machine got stuck in the middle of Dantan bazaar.

We had to get fifteen to twenty coolies, who took eight days to clear the way for the cart. Anyway, the printing machine reached Balasore after twenty-two days.

At last, our ordeal was over. The workers had learnt printing by now. The machine could print in Oriya and English beautifully. One day, Bignold sahib, the Collector of Balasore, sent for me and congratulated me heartily on our success, and, to further encourage us, gave us a contract to print several forms for the cutcherry. We made a handsome profit out of this work.

People from afar kept coming for two or three months to see the printing as if it was as exciting as the Car Festival. Zemindars came in palanquins from remote villages to see our press. For months, the towns-folk came to watch our work. In these days, when printing presses are common, people might find this hard to believe. But, when the first printing press was established in London, the King and Queen came in person to witness this novel event.

Six months later, Ravenshaw sahib, accompanied by Bignold sahib, and his successor, John Beames, arrived one morning. We told him briefly how the press came to be. He looked around and gave us ten rupees. But instead of keeping it for ourselves, we bought two shares in his name with the money. When the company broke up, we gave him thirty rupees, which included his money and his share of the profits.

On the occasion of the Parvana festival, Babu Madan Mohan Das, a distinguished businessman of Balasore, invited many people to his house. Among others were Babu Radhanath Ray and myself. Radhanath babu looked in my direction and said, 'History will record in letters of gold the hardships you endured in order to found the printing company.'

The press ran smoothly. We made a lot of profit. Previously Cuttack Printing Company used to publish a weekly called *Utkal Dipika*. The executive committee of our company suggested that we bring out a fortnightly. It would be called *Bodhadayni ebam Balasore Sambadbahika*. The former part would be literary and the latter would carry news. The magazine came out on time, but contributors were hard to find. Teaching all day at school and looking after the press used to tire me out. There was no energy left to do work in the evenings. So the magazine became irregular. About forty or fifty were on the subscribers' list, but only eight or ten paid their subscriptions.

DEATH OF THAKURMA (1867)

One April afternoon in 1867, my Thakurma, Kuchila Dei, who had brought me up, passed away. I have a feeling that God had kept her alive so long to look after me. Now that I was able to look after myself it was no longer necessary for her to linger in this careworn world.

My grandfather, Kusha Senapati, worked for the Nawab of Murshidabad as a durwan or jamadar or in some such menial position. He died there, away from home. My grandmother had no one left to lean on. She had two young sons to support.

She was of medium build, fair-complexioned, good-looking and hardy. She was hardly ever ill. She had all her teeth when she died. Even half her hair was black. She was simple-hearted, and had an even temper. No one ever heard her raise her voice. There were a number of quarrelsome widows in our village. Whenever they squabbled among themselves, Thakurma would shut herself in the house. My aunt, that is her elder daughter-in-law, was somewhat vain and foul-mouthed. Whenever she turned abusive, Thakurma would leave at once; if it hurt deeply, she would sit in a dark corner of the house and cry. No one ever heard her laugh aloud. It seemed as if she was always overshadowed by melancholy. She was very devout and pious. She would observe all religious rituals. She used to spend a good part of the year fasting or living on a strict diet. She considered it a sin to ride a bullock cart; she therefore travelled to several holy places on foot. The only illness I have ever seen her with was an attack of filaria every three or four months.

She would get up well before dawn and bury herself in domestic chores till midnight. She would not utter a word to anyone unless there was a need. She would take a break at midday for a bath and worshipping and in the evening to listen to the scriptures. About midnight when everybody had eaten and gone to sleep she would have a meal and go to bed. She hardly had four hours' sleep a day, but her sleep was so light that the slightest noise in the house would wake her up.

Her worldly goods consisted of three bamboo chests. The first was full of all sorts of herbs and roots; the second contained various types of seeds of seasonal plants for the garden; the third, which was the biggest, contained bric-a-brac. She would not throw anything away. If a child in the house or in the village took ill she would take it upon herself to treat him. At the back of the house lay a grove where she would retire with her beads whenever she had a break from household work. All the year round it would be full of seasonal vegetables. We did not have to get vegetables from outside. Thakurma is gone, but the mango trees she had planted are flourishing.

To look after others, not bothering about her own comforts, was her life's sole purpose. My father's death caused her great sorrow. It pains me a great deal when I think of how much she sacrificed for me. She would spend sleepless nights when I was ill. Like a cow watching over her calf, Thakurma always kept an eye on me. I was twenty-two when I went to Calcutta for the first time. When I returned, Thakurma, who was worrying about me, had just one look at me, and suddenly paced about the courtyard restlessly. She was the only support of my life and everything I have gained was a result of Thakurma's piety. Her death was a specially terrible blow to my life.

Nirad C. Chaudhuri (1897–1998)

Nirad C. Chaudhuri (1897–1998) published, in 1951, when a little more than half his long life was over, what is probably the greatest autobiography written in the English language in the twentieth century. Born in Kishorganj, a small rural town – 'one among a score of collection of tin-and-mat huts or sheds, comprising courts, offices, schools, shops, and residential dwellings which British administration had raised up in the green and brown spaces of East Bengal' – he came from an educated but not particularly affluent *bhadralok*, or middle-class, family. He studied at the Scottish Church College in Calcutta, and stood first in History in the University in his BA exams; and then duly failed his MA. He then set about leading the life of an 'unknown Indian' in earnest, working as secretary to the nationalist Sarat Bose and also at All India Radio, a brilliant, if somewhat perverse, man, largely hidden from his contemporaries. Chaudhuri is what he is because of his location in, and rejection of, the Bengali middle class; all his life he remained a Bengali, wearing a dhoti (the traditional apparel worn by Bengali men) to the end of his days, but couldn't bear to live with Bengalis, and escaped to England, where he lived in Oxford for roughly the last thirty years of his life. His autobiography, too, is marked by its rejection, as well as articulation, of middle-class Bengaliness; the rejection begins with the book's lapidary and impudent dedication to the British Empire; its articulation of Bengaliness imbues its every sentence. The 'unknown' in *Unknown Indian* is truthful but ironical, inserted by a man who is intent upon making a lasting impression upon the world stage, and is a rebuff to his compratriots who so excel at ignoring brilliance in their compatriots when they encounter it. The act of writing the book in English, extremely unusual in the nationalistic, post-Renaissance Bengal of his time, is also meant to be a calculated escape from Bengaliness, although it is the revelation of a certain kind of Bengaliness that the book escapes into. Chaudhuri's decision to write the work in English was frankly connected to his aim to speak to a worldwide audience; these are, in a sense, 'private words addressed in public'. His achievement makes nonsense of the sanctimonious and lazy claim that explaining or interpreting your culture to the

West is necessarily incompatible with exploring, and giving expression to, its subtlest, truest, and most recondite features.

* * *

from *The Autobiography of an*
Unknown Indian (1951)

THE SONS OF CALCUTTA

The Bengalis native to Calcutta fell perceptibly into three classes: the upper and the wealthy, the lower-middle, and the intermediate, whose members rose or fell to the two other classes wholly on the strength (or weakness) of their monetary position. In recent times a class of new rich people have sprung up, who have all the repellent characteristics of this class and can be clearly distinguished from the older rich (and the new poor) of the city. But in the first years of the twentieth century the rich of Calcutta were a fairly homogeneous set. By that time they had outgrown their caterpillarish new-rich stage of the late eighteenth and early nineteenth century and become imagos with all the mellowed attributes of wealth.

To begin with, they possessed a very distinctive physical appearance which marked them out for special notice among all other Bengalis and even more conspicuously from the Bengalis of East Bengal. These features were developed in the first instance by very careful selective breeding and, after that, they were favoured by the easy and comfortable life of the whole class. In trying to give an idea of this physical type, perhaps I could do no better than begin with the women, although this would necessitate a preliminary reference to an older type of Bengali beauty.

The traditional type of female beauty, accepted as the ideal all over rural Bengal, was derived from the iconography of Mahayana Buddhism and Puranic Hinduism. By this criterion a Bengali beauty was likened to a goddess, which meant that she had an oval face, wide at the forehead and pointed at the chin, long and rather narrow eyes with a perceptible slant, thin but fully modelled lips, and a complexion pronouncedly yellow with no tinge of rose, rather like beaten pure gold. Even now one can pick out Bengali girls who are exactly true to this type.

But the Calcutta type was different. It was rounder, fleshier, and rosier. Faces of this cast are very common in the Bengali drawings of the nineteenth century known as the *pats* of Kalighat, on which the well-known and fashionable contemporary Bengali painter, Mr Jamini Roy, has based his linear technique. Nothing in the English tradition of the charming in women resembled these faces and figures, not even the bare-bosomed beauties of the Restoration, but the heavier French beauties at the court of Louis XIV offered quite close parallels to the Calcutta type. The contours of these women were distinguished by an almost cloying abundance of curves, large curves enclosing small curves, one curve melting into another, so that it was impossible to determine the origins or ends of these lines. These women harmonized with no furniture of the Western type, but were most successfully camouflaged by a bed of highly piled mattresses covered with a snow-white sheet and amply provided with bolsters. In such surroundings theirs was a protective configuration.

Since at least one half of every mother's son is woman, the men of Calcutta also tended to approximate to this type. In any case, among the natives of the city, bones and bony effects were considered to be very unbecoming in a man. To have such an appearance was, in their eyes, equivalent to being Chuars, a tribe of low-caste and wild men of the western borders of Bengal whose tribal name came ultimately to mean any ruffianly fellow. Whenever a Bengali of Calcutta saw a young man with rounded limbs, a round face, and large liquid eyes,, he cried out in ecstasy, 'A prince!' or 'The scion of a noble house!' A fair complexion was an asset to a man; it was not, however, a *sine qua non* as in a woman with pretensions to beauty; but neither man nor woman could advance the slightest claim to physical attractiveness without sleekness.

Of course, every individual in this class did not breed true to type, but it was really surprising to see how many did. The less wealthy were a more mixed lot. Still, they too were more plump and chubby than could be presupposed from their less adequate means of nourishing their fatty tissues. The Bengalis of Calcutta, irrespective of wealth, took great care of their body, and more particularly of their hair and skin. The afternoon toilet of the women was a most elaborate affair, and, whether married or unmarried, a young girl would feel extremely humiliated not to appear at her best in the evenings. These men and women presented a very striking and pleasing contrast to the generally untidy and scraggy persons from East Bengal, and this was noted with ungrudging admiration by the lesser Bengali. When I first came to Calcutta the purdah used to be very strictly observed there, but whenever an East Bengal man found an opportunity to spy he breathed a rather wistful sigh.

In appearance and manner the people of Calcutta were placid and quiet. They were soft-spoken and generally courteous. That earned for them a bad reputation among the immigrants or sojourners from East Bengal. They said that the people of Calcutta had honey on their lips and poison in their hearts. I used to remonstrate that it was after all not so very bad to have honey somewhere, even if not everywhere, since we of East Bengal had poison both in our hearts and on our lips. This argument never convinced my fellow East Bengalis, for what they were mortally afraid of in the man of Calcutta was that the polished and plausible fellow would cheat them of money or wheedle them into some imprudent course by the power of his glib tongue.

The natives of Calcutta had also a very quick sense of humour. The slightest suggestion of the comic in any person or situation never escaped them, and no sly dig was lost on them. They would be ready with their laugh or come forward pat with a counterthrust. In this they too differed from us East Bengal men. To joke with the latter is always dangerous, almost as dangerous as playing with fire. There is no knowing how they will react. Therefore the Calcutta man's sense of humour, too, discredited him in the eyes of the easterner, who attributed his rival's easy smiles and careless banter to incorrigible frivolity and light-headedness. I, however, found the westerner's easier manners very agreeable, and if I have any criticism to make of his wit it is only this: that it was not very wide in range, for it was identified too often with the perpetration of a salacious innuendo.

The real shortcoming of the true native of Calcutta, as I saw it, was a pronounced lack of magnanimity and passion. His urbanity had no charity in it. After the departure of a person with whom he had talked with impeccable politeness he would make a malicious remark which revealed all the smallness of his heart. Even the greatest sons of Calcutta, some of whom were the greatest of modern Indians, were not free from this unlovable trait. But the lack of charity was shown most blatantly in the conduct of the aristocracy of Calcutta towards those whom they did not consider their equals. They would not be exactly rude, but would stare and remain silent as if they were in the presence of some strange animal. This was worse than being rude, it was being reptilian, and if the man so treated was of a sensitive nature he came away with unforgiving wrath in his heart and with the resolve to hit the serpent on the head if ever he found it at a disadvantage.

Even of one another, the members of the Bengali aristocracy of Calcutta spoke with amazing malice, although accompanied by every mark of outward cordiality. The people of Calcutta in general, if all that they said was meant to be taken seriously, seemed to entertain very odd notions about the role of the servants in relation to the women of the family. The reproach which came very readily to their lips when they were angry with a certain person was that he was not the son of his reputed father but of a servant or groom. I have read a letter published in a Bengali newspaper of 1831, in which the correspondent related that in a very respected household the master and the sons came out of the zenana in the evening and the servants went in. The motive of this particular letter was unexceptionable. It was written in the interest of 'female education', for the writer attributed the looseness in question to the prevailing ignorance and to the narrowness of those who, instead of giving a good education to their womenfolk, kept them confined to the kitchen. But I have also read another letter of a slightly later date, which was plain blackmail. It purported to be an eyewitness's account from a maidservant of the misconduct of her mistress with a manservant, and the amazing part of the communication was that the incident was attributed to an actual Calcutta family mentioned by name. The restrictions on the vernacular Press imposed by the English Government and the laws of libel ultimately eliminated these crude scandals from the newspapers. But the whispering campaign went on for a long time. I have myself heard a number of stories of this kind. One of them was that a certain well-known person of north-eastern Calcutta, after whom the Calcutta Corporation has named a thoroughfare, was actually the son of his father's syce. Another was that a certain notability of the last quarter of the nineteenth century was only too ready to oblige an amorous English lieutenant-governor with a widowed sister. An acquaintance of mine even offered to produce an eyewitness to the misbehaviour of an eminent contemporary for whom he had no love, and at the time the offer was made to me, the alleged misbehaviour was at least fifty years old! This queer scandal-mongering formed the undertone of social gossip in Calcutta.

With this proneness to take the worst view of human motives and character there went an obstinate disbelief in high purpose, both exemplified in such favourite quips as 'Every fellow is a thief, although I am the only one to be caught'. Of this side of their nature the natives of Calcutta were perfectly conscious. In fits of self-abasement, of which too they were capable, they admitted that, compared with the Bengali from East Bengal, they lacked 'sincerity', by which they really meant idealism. But in normal moods they were more disposed to be proud of their idealism. Tagore has referred to the contrast in one of his short stories written in 1892. He makes the hero of the story say: 'We were from the country, and had not learnt to scoff at everything with the precocious levity of the boys of Calcutta, and therefore our faith was unshakable: The patrons of our association delivered speeches, and we begged for subscriptions from door to door, caring neither for the midday sun nor for meals, distributed handbills in the streets, arranged chairs and benches for the meetings, and rolling up our shirtsleeves got ready to fight it out with anybody who said a word against our leaders. The city boys duly noted these characteristics and ragged us as East Bengal fools.' On account of this absence of idealism and respect for causes the Bengalis of Calcutta, taken as a collective mass, could be moved to action only through their gross worldliness or what was its counterpart in them, a frothy sentimentality. During the years of my stay in Calcutta the sentimentality rather tended to gain the upper hand, but even in his most abandoned moments the true native of Calcutta was never worked up to such a pitch of emotional disturbance as to be wholly forgetful of his personal safety and interest.

Such shallow worldliness could not, of course, exist at all without finding some visible expression somewhere, and it did in the faces of the men and women of Calcutta. In spite of their sleekness, smooth outlines, and quick responsiveness to the humorous, these faces were extraordinarily hard, and the hardness was further accentuated by the universal habit of chewing the *paan* or betel leaf. A small bulge was always to be seen under one of the cheeks of the men and women of Calcutta, appearing now under the right cheek and now under the left, and on account of this perpetual grinding exercise the jaws acquired a strength and prominence which was quite unexpected in visages otherwise so placid, self-satisfied, and devoid of features denoting strength of character. The eyes more particularly, when not lit up by some giddy fancy or humorous conceit, were expressionless. It was in repose that these faces showed themselves at the greatest disadvantage. Many of them were faultless in features and proportions, and should normally have pleased by reason of their symmetry, but a thin and hard enamel appeared to have vitrified all quality of being live in them. These countenances looked like cloisonné vases. Even haughtiness, which sat most easily on them, was not present in a majority of cases.

THE MANSIONS

The houses in which these people lived could be divided, like themselves, into three classes, the higher, the lower, and the intermediate. The intermediate is a very important category in Bengali society, which is divisible in the first instance into two classes, the gentlefolk and those who are not gentlefolk. There is even now no easy passage from the one to the other. But among those who are admitted to be gentlefolk or, as we say in Bengali, *bhadralok* – a class based equally on occupation and on birth, there is complete elasticity in spite of the infinite gradations of wealth and standard of living which are to be found within the order and which often range from extreme poverty to extreme luxury. The intermediate group constitutes the bridge of this continuous transition. It is the middle class within the middle class, without which the influential and stable Bengali *bhadralok* could not have maintained the health, hold, and power of their order. It is curious to note how the social fact found recognition in the sphere of transport. The railway companies in India, which began their activities in Bengal, felt compelled, in contradistinction to the practice all over the world, to provide an 'intermediate' or 'inter' class between the first and second on the one hand and the third on the other.

But their medial position makes any description of the houses and ways of the intermediate social class unnecessary. Both can be reconstructed in imagination by bringing together in varying proportions a number of features from the two extreme wings. On the other hand, the houses and ways of life of the wealthy in Calcutta, and in no less degree those of the poor, presented very strongly marked characteristics, which to an observer unaffiliated to either seemed to possess, each in its way, a physical power to clutch and grip. The great mansions of Calcutta, leaving out of the reckoning some half a dozen which looked like modest imitations of Buckingham Palace, were inconspicuous from the outside. They hardly ever presented a front. In most cases they lay ensconced in the familiar mass of shabby brickwork, distinguishable only by their larger proportions and more extensive dimensions, like a pyramid among mastabas.

The front entrance, as usual, was unimpressive. Even where there was a generous porch, the entrance was often no better than a mere gap between two suites of rooms, giving access to very ordinary passages and to a large quadrangle, which too was very ordinary and drab in appearance except for a hall with high arches at one end, used as the worship hall. But following one of the corridors one would come upon a door which led into a handsome entrance hall, the real entrance hall, either paved with marble or parqueted, with a flight of wide stairs in veined marble or wood covered with the usual carpet. The walls would be papered or richly painted. At the corners there would be jardinières and tall vases of Chinese design but not always of genuine Chinese manufacture, and on or near the newel post there would be at least one bronze nude holding an electric lamp. The most ambitious *pièce* in these houses was always the drawing-room. These rooms were immense, hardly ever less than fifty feet by twenty-five feet, and in some cases very much bigger. In the older houses they were built, not as drawing-rooms, but for the exhibition of nautch or Indian ballet dance. During the latter part of the nineteenth century, however, nearly all of them were converted into drawing-rooms in the European style. In these rooms, too, there were echoes of Buckingham Palace, for with their rugs and carpets, wall and ceiling decorations, screens, mirrors, chandeliers, vases, statuettes, and carved mahogany or gilt Louis Quinze furniture they looked like copies of one or other of the drawing-rooms of the Palace. But the general effect, though patently imitative, was never crude or tawdry. It was in very few instances, indeed, that these rooms revealed any personal taste or even idiosyncrasy, but all were dignified and respectable. Some had pictures, usually heavily framed oil paintings, and mostly family portraits. When they dated from the early nineteenth century or before they showed considerable mastery of technique.

Very few of the houses had a regular dining-room matching the drawing-room, but some had a second sitting-room furnished in the Indian style, with carpets covered with a snow-white sheet and strewn with pillows, cushions, and bolsters. But these rooms also had some European furniture – console tables with marble tops, chandeliers and wall brackets, Venetian mirrors, overmantels without mantelpieces, and a number of divans and pouffes at the corners. The piano, most often an upright and only rarely a grand, would be in either of the two rooms.

No gracious or brilliant hostess presided over these rooms, and they never hummed with conversation – either sapient or frivolous or even flirtatious. The aristocracy of Calcutta was not given to an animated or enterprising social life, and even where it was social in a lackadaisical fashion there was no place for women in the drawing-rooms. They kept themselves within the zenana, which comprised a second quadrangle behind the main one in front, and there they had unisexual small talk of their own. The outer rooms were reserved for the master of the house and his friends, but even they for the most part would only loll and lounge in them, enjoying an easy and luxurious gregariousness, and displaying some adumbration of sociability only in languid card parties. The rich of Calcutta, when they were inclined that way, kept their high spirits for their garden houses or houses of ill-fame. In my time even the garden houses were growing respectable, although they had not wholly outlived their saturnalian or satyric reputation dating from the nineteenth century.

Thus these big houses were preternaturally silent. The silence was not disturbed even by the young people, in whom these homes, though not as abundantly provided as those of the less wealthy, were not lacking. The *jeunesse dorée* of Calcutta showed a tendency to get out of hand when away from home, but in their houses they were as a rule quiet. Even the depraved preferred an obstinately silent viciousness to a rowdy and obstreperous viciousness. What was true of the *jeunesse dorée* was truer of the *enfance dorée*. The children of the wealthy in Calcutta appeared to be unendowed even with boyish playfulness. They were extremely solemn, and whenever they made their public appearance they looked like exact, though diminutive, replicas of their elders. Occasionally, passing before these houses, one would see at the gate, among the liveried servants and doorkeepers carrying swords or muskets, who stood admiringly contemplating him, a handsome little boy in a fine crinkled dhoti and a starched shirt, or a silk suit, or even in kilt complete with sporran and plaid. He would stand still, staring at the crowds in the street with wide uncomprehending eyes. The older boys usually kept indoors. They always had a large room to themselves, generously furnished as a schoolroom, in which they sat with their tutors, listening with quiet gravity to the lessons but never giving any indication that they were taking in anything. Most often they looked more unintelligent than they really were. Of course, they never went out of their houses, even for a distance of one hundred yards, except in their carriages, which were landaus or broughams, and, later, in big limousines or sports cars.

I have never seen the zenana of any of these houses, and thus have no means of describing them from direct observation. But I can imagine them as a suite of bedrooms, fitted up in very eclectic style, rather cluttered up, but lacking nothing in the Indian manner, and latterly in the European as well, that could conduce to laziness. They were never on the same plane of luxury and stateliness as the outer rooms. This part of the houses invariably had a very large establishment of abigails who were an incorrigibly fussy, raucous, and intriguing set. It was rather a surprise that their placid mistresses were able to endure them. But among themselves the

women of Calcutta, irrespective of class, are very loquacious, and that may
have supplied the connecting link.

One other feature of these houses must also be mentioned. The larger
of them had a back garden, forming a third quadrangle behind the second
or zenana quadrangle. These gardens never received the care which was
usually bestowed on the gardens of the suburban villas of the same
owners, nor did they have the *magnolia grandiflora* with which of all
flowers the Calcutta aristocracy was *engoué*, but they had a homely and in
some cases a subtle appeal. Tagore in his reminiscences has described the
back garden of his ancestral Calcutta house. 'It would be too much,' he
writes, 'to claim for the garden at the back of our house the status of a
garden. Its mainstay was one pomelo, one round plum, and one Otaheite
apple tree, with a row of coconut palms. At the centre was a round platform
of brickwork, in whose cracks grass and a variety of wild creepers had
planted the intruding banner of their usurpation. Among flower plants,
only such as never died of neglect, continued to discharge an unaggrieved
duty to the best of their power, without bringing any accusation against
the gardener ... I do not believe that the Garden of Eden of the First Man,
Adam, was any the better laid out than this garden of ours, for it was like
him unapparelled – it had not smothered itself under a load of display. For
man, the exigency of display is ever on the increase. It began on the day
he tasted the fruit of knowledge and will go on augmenting until the fruit
is digested. The back garden of our house was my Garden of Eden, and
that was enough.' Not every well-to-do person in Calcutta had the boy
Tagore's sensibility. That was why they never frequented these gardens
and these remained as exclusive preserves for the women and young
people of the family, who ordinarily went into them when in search of
sour fruits. But if they had, they might have found in them that leisure for
introductions to themselves which they never had elsewhere, not even in
their large and silent drawing-rooms.

THE HUMAN HIVES

To pass from these mansions to typical middle-class houses was to pass
apparently into dwellings of a different species altogether. At first sight,
it was the dissimilarity between the mud-walled and tiled *bustees* of
the working class and the brick-built houses of the gentlefolk which
struck the observer as an unbridgeable hiatus, both in its visual and its

sociological aspect. But internally examined, a typical middle-class house was as far removed from the great mansions as they themselves were from working-class tenements. Perhaps the difference was greater, for its measure is not fully given even by confronting the peacock with the crow, which becomes all the more surprising when one considers the social and mental solidarity of the whole gentlefolk class. This leads me to define the difference between the two classes of houses of the gentlefolk as the difference between the grub and the butterfly of the same insect, rather than as the difference between two species of animals.

The middle-class house was small, sometimes even as small as twenty-five feet square. The interior showed only two colours, the grey of the cemented floors and the white of the walls and the ceilings. If any patterns were to be seen anywhere they were only pencilled scribblings by the children and marks of a deep burnt sienna tint from betel-stained fingers. After taking betel the men and women of Calcutta were given to wiping their soiled fingers on the nearest wall. There was also an impression of bareness, for these households possessed only a minimum of furniture. Most often there were only an almirah or two and a number of wooden beds, and these latter too were mere frameworks of lath on four weak legs. Those whose means permitted added some tables and chairs, and the rear was brought up by immense piles of bedding and rolls of mats and a vast assortment of earthen pots and pitchers, empty tins of all sizes and shapes, bottles and jars, and sacks for the storeroom, and iron, brass, and earthen pots and pans for the kitchen.

None of these houses had proper living-rooms. In some instances one outer room on the ground floor, provided either with a bed, or a table with some chairs, or both, was set apart as a reception room for visitors. If the servant lived in the house instead of going away at night to his *bustee* he usually slept in this room, and during the day his rolled-up bed and mat would occupy a part of the floor near one of the walls. The rest of the habitable rooms were bedrooms. Their typical assignment was: one to the master and mistress and the younger children, one to the grown-up girls and the widowed mother, and one to the older boys. But when a joint family lived in the same house, as often was the case, the married brothers with their young children took one each of the best rooms, and the indifferent ones were occupied by the rest of the family, the widowed mother and the marriageable girls, the older boys, and the dependants. The rooms which were not fit to sleep in, and there always were a number of them on the ground floor of every house, were used as a kitchen, storeroom, and lumber-room.

In very few houses were there separate dining-rooms. The meals were taken in the kitchen, or in any odd strip of superfluous space, or even in bedrooms. In joint families past their prime the taking of meals in bedrooms was quite common, because those brothers or cousins who earned more money than the others were not willing to raise their contribution to the common household fund and yet were not ready to forgo the luxuries to which they thought their better means entitled them. So they had the standard common meal requisitioned upstairs, added to it sweets and other delicacies bought with their own money, and ate the food in the privacy of their bedrooms with their own children. Even in families which were not joint the master often took his meals privately, for as the earning member of the family he felt that he had a right to specialities which he could not and would not share with his children and wife.

The visitors, all in the case of women, and relatives in the case of men, made straight for the bedrooms, sat on the beds there and chatted. Sometimes even the intimate friends of the master of the family would come into the bedrooms. The other visitors were kept at a distance. In those houses which had no outer parlour the master often went out to talk with callers on the footpath or lane, and occasionally even carried on a shouted conversation from an upper-storey window. Many of the houses had a strip of open veranda in front, which was called a *ro'k*. The elders and the young men sat cross-legged on them in the mornings and evenings, either reading their newspaper and discussing it or merely gossiping. At night beggars, vagrants, and other waifs and strays slept there. Sometimes even wandering goats appropriated them.

It must not be imagined from this description that these interiors presented a chaotic appearance. On the contrary, they were always extremely tidy. The mistress or the mistresses never permitted the slightest displacement of any object from its place. It was in no wise unusual, when a family had lived in a house for a long time, to find a bottle or a book or a bundle remaining in its place on a ledge or rack out of reach of the children for twenty years. In fact, tidiness was the forte of these interiors and inelegance the foible. Every touch of added orderliness seemed to lay an extra coat of housewifely plainness on them.

A typical bedroom would have two beds occupying half or one-third of its space, of which at least one would be a carved fourposter received by the occupant of the room at the time of his marriage as a wedding present from his father-in-law. If the second bed had legs shorter than those of the fourposter, it would be raised by putting one or two bricks under each of the legs. Along one wall would be a long row of trunks, sometimes on the ground and sometimes on a bench. Most often a second tier of trunks would be placed on top of the first tier, and on the second tier of trunks there would be piled all the spare bedding and bedclothes appertaining to the room, so that in order to get at the contents of a trunk of the lower row the trunk resting on it, together with the bedclothes on the top, would in every case have to be taken down. The mistresses of these houses thought nothing of lifting and lowering fully loaded trunks. Another section of the wall would have one or more clothes-horses pushed against it, and at the end of a blind alley formed by the narrow space left between the lower ends of the beds and the wall opposite them there would be, where the householder could afford it, a chest of drawers or a dressing-table.

In this manner all the sides of the wall would be neatly and fully occupied, and in the most conspicuous position there would be a glazed almirah, about five and a half feet high, four feet wide, and over eighteen inches in depth, containing an overcrowded array of china, wax, and celluloid dolls, toys, and gewgaws of every kind. In certain respects the women of Calcutta were like bower birds. They could never resist gaudy trifles. At the time of their marriage they were presented with dolls and similar toys, which they brought with them with their trousseau, which in fact formed a part of their trousseau, and from year to year they went on adding to their collection. They were always buying new trifles for themselves, for example, doll's house furniture, and seizing, over and above, the toys of the children, who in the ordinary course were not allowed to play with them. They put the whole lot in the glass-fronted cupboards in their bedrooms, to be admired by other women and even by the men.

Anything in the nature of pictures in these rooms, if within the lower reaches of the walls, was sure to be calendars with brightly coloured pictures or small photographs. The bigger framed pictures, where there were any, were hung high, above the doors and windows, and in order to be seen without the discomfort of kinking the neck they were inclined at an angle of about forty-five degrees towards the floor. These were mostly coloured pictures of the gods and goddesses, very alluringly amatory if of Krishna and Radha, and if of Kali very minatory and blood-curdling, in spite of her nudity. There usually would also be another picture, a large photographic enlargement, which stood out from the rest by reason of its more prominent position as well as by having a jasmine garland hanging in a half loop from the two upper corners of its frame. It would be the portrait of the departed father or mother.

If the keynote of the large mansions was repose, that of these houses was bustle, not confused scuttling about or noise, but a methodical organization of movement and sound which created the impression of a running machine. The metabolism of these homes was quick. The mistress, the other women, and the young girls were to be seen in purposive motion from upstairs to downstairs and again from downstairs to upstairs: now putting off their saris and chemises to wrap only a red loom-made towel round the waist in order to bathe, do some washing, or perform some other connected task, for which immemorial custom and inexorable taboo required a clearing of the decks; now getting back into their saris and chemises; now rushing into the kitchen to stir or turn some dish; now setting down the pan on the floor and running to the storeroom to bring a fresh supply of oil or ghee; now soaping the dirty linen with energetic jerks of the forearms; and, after that, wringing it with supple twists of the wrists; in a word, seeing the household tasks through with precision and celerity and at the same time scattering all around them the charms of their throbbing fullness.

The flagstone under the tap, called the Foot of the Tap in Bengali, was in one sense the heart of the machine, surpassing even the kitchen in importance. It was almost like an altar, corresponding to the hearth of the colder countries. To this place every domestic task found its way, because every task either began or ended with a washing up of human beings as well as inanimate objects. The women would not enter the kitchen without an early-morning bath, sometimes under the tap, at others with water taken from the cistern adjoining the tap and poured over the head from a mug. These cisterns, built of brick and cement-plastered, were to be found in every house, and they received their water from the tap through a split bamboo or a tin pipe, which formed a sort of umbilical cord between the city's water supply and the domestic stock of water. If we had had Vestal Virgins we would have employed them, not to tend the fire, but the cistern.

Above everything else, the Foot of the Tap symbolized release from work. To it everybody rushed to clinch the conclusion of domestic tasks. Once the hands and feet were washed there, a human being could relax. The maidservant scrubbing utensils under the tap and taking the water she needed through a long piece of rag which she always tied round the tap's spout in order to prevent the water from splashing on her, looked forward to the moment when she would whisk away the rag and, washing her arms up to the elbows and the legs up to the knees, also wash her hands of the back-breaking task. The master went there after his return from the office, the mistress almost every half-hour, the others when they were let off.

The domestic bustle produced continuous and consistent sound effects. In the kitchen there was a succession of bubbling, fizzling, hissing, and crackling sounds. It was punctuated intermittently by a metallic sound like that of the triangle in an orchestra, which was produced when the energetically manipulated iron or brass ladles and turners struck against the pots and pans. The scrubbing of the utensils gave out a low abrasive sound, which became gritty at times and set the teeth on edge, but was generally smooth like the process of lens grinding. When clothes were being washed the sound was now like that of bass drums and now like that of castanets, depending on the volume of the washing undertaken. Dominating every other sound was the sound of falling water. The day began with the sound of the old water rushing out through the hole at the bottom of the cistern, followed by the patter of the new water falling on its floor. A whole gamut of watery sounds continued throughout the day, and sometimes into the night when the tap was left open.

The only time of the day when there was relaxation and quiet, and even stillness, in these houses was between the end of the midday meal of the women at about one o'clock and four o'clock in the afternoon. It was the time when the hawkers of dress fabrics – chintzes, muslins, organdies, and silks; of laces, ribbons, hairpins, and combs; of toilet goods, glass bangles, toys, and, as we used to say in those days in Bengali, all the 'heart-stealing goods', contributed by their cries more to the stillness of the noontide than to the noises of the great city. This was the time they chose to tempt Eve, knowing very well that Adam would be safely away in his office. The women crowded into the narrow entrance passage to make their purchases, and while the hawker displayed his goods, lectured and protested, they haggled. When not engaged with the hawkers the women spread themselves and their long and moist hair on the cool floor of their bedrooms, usually with the baby at the breast and a novel in hand. But very soon the novel dropped from the hand, and, though the baby stuck fast, making ceaseless sucking movements of its lips and cheeks, the mother slept on unmindful. She woke up only when the maidservant rattled the knocker on the front door or water began to fall again from the tap after the midday cut-off. The nights on the other hand were not very peaceful, for the babies had a habit of waking up and crying from hour to hour as our common mynah does at night.

Twice a day these houses gave out characteristic exhalations. These were nothing but the smoke from the cooking ovens, which were mere things of half a dozen bricks, some mud, and a gridiron for each. These ovens had no flues, burnt coke of a very bad quality, and were kindled with cow-dung cakes soaked in kerosene, and generated a kind of smoke whose grey density had to be breathed in order to be believed possible. This thick and strongly smelling mixture of gaseous products rose from the oven in a solid column, and met the ceiling like a waterspout. Deflected therefrom, it came down and made its way out through the doors and windows in whirling clouds. Then progressively diluting itself with the air it floated in blue wisps until it pervaded every nook and cranny of the house. There was no means of resisting it, no means of escaping from it or of blowing the rooms free of it. The wind bloweth where it listeth. So did this smoke, wind's junior partner, in Calcutta. I had to breathe this smoke for thirty-two years and know what it is. But the true native of Calcutta appeared to have his lungs enamelled against its corrosive contact. He did not mind it at all.

*

These houses had sprung up like mushrooms on account of the absurd value that was set in Calcutta on the possession of a house. No true son of the city would willingly marry into or give in marriage to a family which did not live in a house owned by itself. To do so was to the native of Calcutta equivalent to losing caste by marrying gypsies and their like. I was once insulted in the most atrocious manner by an old virago of a washerwoman, not a mere washerwoman by caste, but a real, practising washerwoman, because I was living in rented apartments whereas she had a brick-built house of sorts of her own. I also knew a barber, a very dignified barber he was, who owned a house in a very respectable locality and showed no alacrity to set his razor to the chin of anybody whose house did not cover something like an acre of roof-space. The natives of Calcutta were resolved to disprove the biblical saying and have, not only houses to lay their heads in, but also a Permanent Settlement in housing supplementing the Permanent Settlement in land tenure.

After they had provided houses for themselves the natives went in for house property, which, next to gilt-edged securities, was their favourite investment. They let these houses to those who did not possess houses of their own. These tenants were mostly people whom the true native of Calcutta regarded only as resident aliens. But there were also true but poor natives who did not own their own houses. Their standing in the eyes of their fellow-natives and of their own was mud. They could never console

themselves for this deprivation, nor formulate a philosophy of life independent of house property in Calcutta. Thus they were always saving every
pice they could by scrimping and screwing, until they had saved enough
to die as a houseowner. But even those who lived in rented houses
disdained to live in flats. They would live only in independent, self-
contained houses. But as it was impossible to combine independence,
spaciousness, and economy, the typical middle-class house in Calcutta, in
spite of being the proud citizen's castle, looked a mean castle in every
instance.

Aubrey Menen (1912–89)

Aubrey Menen was born in 1912 in London of Indo-Irish parentage. Being what is loosely called 'Anglo-Indian', or what was once termed 'Eurasian', meant that he would never fit in easily with the self-definition of being Indian in pre- or post-Independence India. Both an inward, and a physical, restlessness, thus, shaped his life; often a savage satirist in his novels, he nevertheless read widely in philosophy and religion, and attempted to translate the metaphysical question, 'Who am I?' into a cultural one. Again, he travelled widely, especially in Italy, where he lived for many years, and travelling, too, for him, was an interrogation of identity. In addition to the tension of being of mixed-race parentage was the tension of being homo-sexual at a time when such a fact would require concealment; and this concealment certainly lends its particular resonance to the search he was engaged in, between the two cultures he belonged to, one of them, on a certain level, more fluid and androgynous than the other. Reflecting on Menen and some of the other writers in this section, one begins to wonder if the autobiography or the memoir has not been, in India, a genre preferred by those who don't quite belong, and a means of mapping that position of not-quite-belonging; while writing novels in this country has become, especially in the English language, an increasingly respectable profession, like dentistry. The immeasurably light touch of Menen's prose, and its sly humour, is meant to test the limits of that respectability. He died in Trivandrum, Kerala, in 1989.

* * *

from *Dead Man in the Silver Market* (1954)

MY GRANDMOTHER AND THE DIRTY ENGLISH

My grandmother, like Michelangelo, had *terribilità*. She had a driving will; she would not be baulked and whatever she did was designed to strike the spectator with awe. She was also something of a stick. She rarely spoke to anyone who was not of her own social station and she received them formally: that is to say, with her breasts completely bare. Even in her time women were growing lax about this custom in Malabar. But my grand-mother insisted on it. She thought that married women who wore blouses and pretty saris were Jezebels; in her view, a wife who dressed herself above her waist could only be aiming at adultery.

When I was twelve she demanded that I be brought and shown to her. I was incontinently taken half across the earth, from London to south of the town of Calicut. My mother came with me.

The last part of the journey was made by dug-out canoe (there being no railways and no good roads near our family estate) and in this we were poled on a moonlit night up the Ponani River. The river was lined with palm trees and crocodiles.

My mother taking fright at these beasts, I sang to keep them away from the boat. I sang a song I had been taught at school called *Drake's Drum*. This had been written in the reign of Queen Victoria and told how, if the Spaniards should embark on the unlikely project of attacking nineteenth-century England, Drake would come back to life and drum them up the Channel 'as he drummed them long ago'. I had been taught many songs with similar sentiments but this was the noisiest. I sang it with a will because my young heart (especially in such very foreign parts) glowed with the sentiment. The crocodiles yawned and, like the Spaniards in the Victorian age, showed no signs of attacking.

This singing marked a stage in my life. Shortly afterwards I lost my innocence. My grandmother took me in hand and I never thought the English were perfect again.

When our boat journey was done, servants with flaming torches led us along narrow paths between tall trees, and finally conducted us to a house. This house was large and smelt of paint. It was (my father said) not my ancestral roof.

*

When my grandmother had heard that my mother intended to make the visit as well as myself, she had given orders for a special house to be put in repair for my mother's accommodation. It was on the furthest confines of the family property. This was her solution of a difficult problem. My mother was ritually unclean, and therefore whenever she entered my family house, she would defile it. The house would have to be purified and so would every caste Hindu in it. It followed logically that if my mother stayed in the house, it would be permanently in a state of defilement and permanently in a state of being ritually cleaned. Since this ceremony involved drums and conch shells, my mother's visit foreshadowed a prolonged uproar. All this was avoided by my grandmother's decision to put her up in a separate building.

I cannot say that my grandmother was ever rude to my mother. She never referred to her by name but always as 'the Englishwoman'. This was not necessarily an insulting expression, but my mother had Irish blood and what with this, and the house, and some other pinpricks, her temper rose. She ordered a quantity of medical stores from Calicut, and when they arrived she set up a free dispensary on the veranda, to which the peasants flocked. It was an admirably devised answer. My grandmother had shut the door in my mother's face. She now had the galling experience of seeing my mother industriously cleaning up the doorstep. As my mother well knew, each drop of iodine that she dispensed stung not only the grateful patient, but also my grandmother's conscience.

My grandmother brooded on this for a while and then sent my mother a bag of golden sovereigns. My mother, taking this to be a bribe at the worst, or at the best, a tip, sent it back. But she was wrong. It was a peace offering. It was sent again next day, accompanied by the family goldsmith who sat, slept and ate on the veranda for one week while he made the sovereigns (with tweezers and a charcoal fire) into a great gold collar which my mother still, on occasion, wears.

When, fourteen years before my trip, my father had written from England to say that he was getting married to a white woman, my grandmother had been far from giving the union her blessing. But it would be wrong to say that she had objected to it. If an English boy of twenty-two wrote home from foreign parts to say that he had taken to cannibalism, his parents would not object. They would be so revolted that a mere objection would never meet the case. So with my grandmother.

She had never met the English but she knew all about them. She knew they were tall, fair, given to strong drink, good soldiers and that they had conquered her native country. She also knew that they were incurably dirty in their personal habits. She respected them but wished they would keep their distance. It was very much the way that a Roman matron looked upon the Goths.

My eldest uncle had been to England for two years and he spoke up for the English. He said that while the Hindus were undoubtedly the most civilized race on earth and had been civilized a thousand years before the English, nevertheless, the English were now the masters of the Hindus. My grandmother's reply to this was that the English were masters of the

Hindus only because 'nobody would listen to *us*'. By this she meant that
our family, along with others of the same caste, had strongly objected to
Vasco da Gama being allowed to land in Calicut. They had, in fact, done
their best to get him and his sailors massacred. But the country was not
behind them and he escaped. Everything, my grandmother argued (and
not without some reason), had started with that.

But her chief complaint was that the English were so dirty, and this was
rather a poser for my uncle. When my grandmother asked if, like decent
people, they took a minimum of two baths a day, my uncle, who could not
lie to his mother without committing a disgraceful sin, said that, well,
no; but a few took one bath and the habit was spreading. He could go no
further than that. But he added that my grandmother should remember
that England had a cold climate. This she loyally did, and when she
discussed the matter with me she was able to treat the matter lightly, as
one does the disgusting but rational liking of the Eskimos for eating
blubber.

As for the question of eating, she did not have the expected prejudices.
She did not think it strange that the English ate ham and beef. The outcast
hill-tribes (called *Todas*) who made the family straw mats and cleaned the
latrines, ate anything. She was not disturbed, either, about their religion,
because my uncle assured her that they had practically none. Their
manners, however, she abominated. If she did not mind them eating meat,
she considered their way of eating it beyond the pale of decent society. In
my family home, each person eats his meal separately, preferably in a
secluded corner. The thought that English people could sit opposite each
other and watch each other thrust food into their mouths, masticate, and
swallow it, made her wonder if there was anything that human beings
would not do, when left to their own devices.

She was not surprised to hear, after this, that in England a woman could
have more than one husband, particularly (and this was the crowning
paradox) if she had been a widow. To the day of her death my grandmother could never understand how people could call themselves civilized
and yet allow widows to marry again. For her the very foundation-stone of
society was that a child should have one father, and obey him. Nobody
ever dared her wrath sufficiently to explain the position of women in
English society. She was intensely proud of the standards of her house and
she permitted no lewd talk to defile them – certainly never in her presence.

With this background, then, my grandmother's peace offering of a bag
of sovereigns was a considerable victory for my mother, particularly since

the gold collar which the goldsmith had been told to make from them was the characteristic jewellery of a Malabar bride.

The way was now open for me. I could go and see her. I had waited about three weeks.

*

I had many meetings with her. I used to visit her in considerable state. The distance from our home – the isolation wing, so to speak – to the main family mansion was too far for walking in the Malabar sun. I used to go by palanquin. It was a hammock of red cloth with rather worn embroidery of gold thread, and it was swung on a black pole which had silver ornaments at either end. Four virtually naked men, two in front and two behind, carried the palanquin at a swift trot. There was considerable art in this. If the four trotted just as they pleased, the hammock would swing in a growing arc until it tipped the passenger out on to the road. To prevent this, the men trotted in a complicated system that I never really understood: watching them and trying to trace it out was as difficult as trying to determine the order in which a horse puts its hoofs down. They kept their rhythm by chanting. I used to fall asleep on the way, listening to them. It must have presented an interesting spectacle – a red palanquin, the sweating men, and a sleeping schoolboy wearing an English blazer with its pocket sewn with a badge gained by infantile prowess at some sport that I do not now remember.

The family house was vast and cool and in my view, unfurnished. But to my grandmother's eyes it was very elegant. There was nothing but the floor to sit on. She disliked chairs and thought them vulgar. What use were they, except for ostentation? She approved of beds but insisted that the mattress be made of taut string – nothing else was considered clean. She also had a taste for handsome brass-bound boxes. So beds, boxes, and oil lamps were the sole furniture of the innumerable rooms of the house. There were no tables and no tablecloths. In my grandmother's house, if anybody dared eat in any fashion but off a fresh plantain leaf, his next meal would have been served in the kitchen, where the servants were allowed to eat without ceremony.

My grandmother usually received me sitting by her favourite box in her boudoir. She made an unforgettable picture. She had great black eyes, a shock of white hair, and lips as lush and curved as a girl of eighteen. The skin of her bosom, bare as I have said, was quite smooth. I used to sit on the floor in front of her in my school blazer and since my father had never taught me Malayalam (wishing me to be brought up like any other English schoolboy), we talked through one of my uncles.

The things my grandmother told me were a puzzle at the time. But I have come to understand them better. Much as she looked down on the English, I think that had she met some of them, had she overcome her well-bred fastidiousness and actually mixed with them, she would have found she and they had much in common. Her riding passion, like theirs, was racial pride. She believed – and this made her character – that she belonged to the cleverest family of the cleverest class of the cleverest people on earth. According to Lord Russell, this was also the firm faith of Mrs Beatrice Webb, who used to repeat it to herself in moments when, otherwise, she might have felt inferior, such as when she made her entry into a distinguished party. Though my grandmother never went to parties I'm sure that she, too, repeated the formula as a stiffener of her already formidable morale.

She felt that she was born of a superior race and she had all the marks of it. For instance, she deplored the plumbing of every other nation but her own. She would often say to me, through my uncle:

'Never take a bath in one of those contraptions in which you sit in dirty water like a buffalo. Always bathe in running water. If you have servants to pour it over you, that's best. But otherwise you must stand under a tap and pour the water over yourself. A really nice person does not even glance at his own bath water, much less sit in it.' Here she would laugh to herself, while my uncle translated; not an unkind laugh, but a pitying one, as she thought of the backwardness of the white man's bathroom.

Another mark – and I have met it in many nations – was that she believed that English sexual morals permitted and encouraged all sorts of abominations from which a civilized person shrank. She spoke to me with great freedom on this point: I was after all at puberty. I could not always follow the drift of her remarks, but I did gather that she felt strongly on one point. Why, if the English wanted their offspring to grow up decently and not lewdly, did they omit to marry them off when they were children? There was something sinister in the neglect. A child should grow up knowing quite well that all that side of his life was settled according to the best available advice and in the best possible manner for his welfare. When he was eighteen or twenty the marriage would be consummated. Till then, he did not have to worry his head about women – or if he did worry, he knew he was morally slipping.

History, I have discovered, is on my grandmother's side. The great majority of civilized peoples have always agreed with her. Romance and love and such things were, in antiquity, things for slaves. Respectable families arranged their marriages as my grandmother arranged those of her offspring. To take a single example, my grandmother and Brutus would fully have understood each other. She felt hurt that she had not been consulted over my father's marriage: while among the many sidelights that we have on that honourable man who assassinated Julius Caesar is a letter in which he complains at being left out of the bargaining that went on during the betrothal of 'my dear little Attica', who was nine years old.

But a grandson was a grandson, even though her permission had not been sought to bring him into the world, and she set about being a mother as well as a grandmother to me. She knew that soon I would go back among the heathen to finish my education, and she wanted me to go back knowing who and what I was. On one of my visits she gave me a small book in which was written all my duties and privileges as a member of my class. The book was written on dried palm leaves, strung together with a cord between two covers of wood. It began with a prayer to God thanking Him for creating us – our caste, that is – so much superior in every respect to the great majority of other human beings.

My grandmother explained what followed several times and with much emphasis, for she wanted to imprint it on my memory. Our family belongs to the caste – or class – called Nayars. The Nayars of Malabar are as old as Indian history and therefore, it can be assumed, a good deal older. My grandmother told me that traditionally we had two obligations to society. We were warriors when there was fighting to do: and when there was not, we had the duty, on certain holy days, of carrying flowers to the temple.

I remember that I thought this very romantic at the time and could not understand why my grandmother took it so prosaically: to me, warriors, flowers and temples conjured up a picture of some Oriental Round Table. But my grandmother was right. Our caste is a commonplace: it exists everywhere. In England it is scattered all over the countryside. The men are what is called 'Army' and the women take not only flowers, but fruit to the temple on the occasion of the Harvest Festival. It is curious, and inexplicable, that the combination of these two activities, whether in the Shires or in the coconut groves of Malabar, produces the most ferocious snobs.

My grandmother explained to me that, as a Nayar, I should always be very careful to keep my dignity when dealing with Brahmins: Brahmins are priests. The priests who have the cure of souls in my family are treated as domestic chaplains. Since their temples were on our property my grandmother had several 'livings', so to speak, at her disposal, this side of religious affairs always being left in the hands of the older women. Priests were therefore expected to make themselves agreeable, in return for which they were regularly fed. They were expected to mind their own business, which was to perform the weekly ceremonies and to direct their preaching at the lower orders, particularly the servants. The Anglican Settlement in England was much more elaborate, but reduced to what it meant to the average priest-in-the-vestry it came to much the same thing, and provides one more reason why I wish my grandmother had visited the country of my birth.

But my grandmother was quite ignorant of these striking resemblances and begged me when moving among the English to remember myself. 'They will look up to you, as a Nayar, to set an example,' she used to say. 'They know that you have two thousand years of advantage over them and they will be willing to learn. Show them this book. They will be very interested. It was written when they still went about naked. And I will give you some trinkets which you can hand out as gifts: some amulets which we use and some things made of sandalwood, which is very rare in England, so I am told, and much sought after. They will help you make friends. But remember, it is your *example* which will count more than anything.'

She gave me all the things she promised and as she had foretold, they were much admired. Some of them, I believe, are still in my school museum. She also gave me her blessing, which was what I had been brought across the world to get.

I thought over her advice but I was in some confusion. My headmaster, wishing me goodbye and good luck when I had set out on my trip, had said much the same thing. 'Let them see,' he had said, 'by your example that you have been trained in an *English* school. Wherever you go, it is for *you* to set the tone.' He did not give me any sandalwood, but I was very impressed. I was also very impressed with what my grandmother had said.

In my dilemma I remembered that I had another grandmother. She had been born, as I have said, in Killarney, but had come to England to live – briefly enough, for she had died before I was born. I asked my mother about her. She told me many things but one stood out in my mind.

'My mother,' she said, 'was never really happy among the English. She longed to go back to Killarney. Sometimes when things had become unbearably tiresome, she would heave a long, deep sigh, shake her head and gently close her eyes.'

Pankaj Mishra (b. 1969)

Pankaj Mishra was born in 1969, later than anyone else in this volume. His childhood and youth (though it's not as if he's old now) have been divided between small towns and hill-stations, including a superannuated colonial centre, Allahabad, a superannuated colonial resort, Simla, and a superannuated medieval city of pilgrimage, Benares. He was later at the Jawarharlal Nehru University in New Delhi; but, unlike most Indian writers in English of his generation, he is unusual in seeming to come from nowhere, from a small-town background situated in the void of an Uttar Pradesh that has been devastated by caste politics and the continuance of petty and violent power struggles. He came to the notice of readers with his acerbic, well-argued, often courageous polemical pieces of criticism; but his first novel, *The Romantics*, published in 2000, has little of the measured belligerence of his criticism, but is an exploration, instead, of uncertainty and a deep sense of inadequacy, of the desire to belong and the inability to do so. The story of the autodidact, reading American, English, and European classics in a small colonial town, may have been more common fifty or seventy years ago. What is unusual is that the story of the redemption that Western literature might offer, and the journey, physical and imaginary, it might provoke one to make from a small place to a greater world, should be retold and reinterpreted in the postmodern age, when both the potency of literature as a means to self-improvement, and the sanctum a small town might offer to such inward development, are increasingly threatened, if they have not altogether ceased to exist. The germ of the novel is contained in the piece below, but the piece is more than a germ of something, it is an achieved, self-contained, almost musical narrative, a sort of threnody, and possibly the best thing Mishra has written so far. The Uttar Pradesh he presents us with is not unlike the small, fictional, post-colonial African nation-states of Naipaul's novels of the seventies, where centres of power are constantly shifting, and the scent of danger, hope, and hopelessness is always in the air. In the midst of all this, Flaubert and Edmund Wilson, like the idols of some neglected religion, point to desires and destinies there are no practicable ways of talking about, let alone fulfilling.

* * *

'Edmund Wilson in Benares' (1998)

1

I spent four months in Benares in the winter of 1988. I was twenty years old, with no clear idea of my future, or indeed much of anything else. After three idle, bookish years at a provincial university in a decaying old provincial town, I had developed an aversion to the world of careers and jobs which, having no money, I was destined to join. In Benares, the holiest city of the Hindus, where people come either to ritually dissolve their accumulated 'sins' in the Ganges, or simply to die and achieve liberation from the cycle of rebirths – in Benares, with a tiny allowance, I sought nothing more than a continuation of the life I had led as an undergraduate.

I lived in the old quarter, in a half-derelict house owned by a Brahmin musician, a tiny, frail, courteous old man. Panditji had long ago cut himself off from the larger world, and lay sunk all day long in an opium-induced daze, from which he roused himself punctually at six in the evening to give sitar lessons to German and American students. It was how he maintained his expensive habit, and also stayed off penury. His estranged, asthmatic wife lived on the floor above his – she claimed to have not gone downstairs for fifteen years – and spent most of her time in a windowless kitchen full of smoke from the dung-paved hearth, conversing in a low voice with her faithful family retainer of over fifty years. The retainer, a small, reticent man in pleated khaki shorts, hinted, in that gloomy setting, at better days in the past, even a kind of feudal grandeur.

The house I lived in, the melancholy presence of Panditji and his wife, were part of the world of old Benares that was still intact in the late eighties, and of which the chess games in the alleys, the all-night concerts in temples, the dancing girls at elaborately formal weddings, the gently decadent pleasures of betel leaves and opium formed an essential component. In less than two years, most of this solid-seeming world was to vanish into thin air. The old city was to be scarred by a rash of fast-food outlets, video-game parlours, and boutiques, the most garish symbols of the entrepreneurial energies unleashed by the liberalization of the Indian economy, which would transform Benares in the way they had transformed other sleepy small towns across India.

But I didn't know this then, and I didn't listen too closely when Panditji's wife reminisced about the Benares she had known as a young woman, when she told me about the time her husband came to her family home as a starving student, when she described to me the honours bestowed on her father by the Maharajah of Benares. I was even less attentive when she complained to me about her son and his wife, more particularly the latter, who, though Brahmin, had, in her opinion, the greedy, grasping ways of the merchant castes.

I didn't pay much attention to the lives around me. I was especially indifferent to the wide-eyed Europeans drifting about on the old ghats, each attached to an ash-smeared guru. I was deep into my own world, and, though I squirmed at the word and the kinds of abject dependence it suggested, I had found my own guru, long dead, but, to me, more real than anyone I knew the winter I spent slowly making my way through his books.

*

On an earlier visit to the library at Benares Hindu University, idly browsing through the stacks, I had noticed a book called *The American Earthquake*. I read a few pages at random, standing in a dark corridor between overloaded, dusty shelves. It seemed interesting; I made a mental note to look it up on my next trip to the library. Months passed. By then I had moved to Benares, and one day while looking for something else in the same part of the stacks, I came across the book again. I took it to the reading room this time. An hour into it, I began to look at the long list under the heading 'Other books by Edmund Wilson.' Later that afternoon, I went back to the stacks, where they all were, dust-laden, termite-infested, but beautifully, miraculously, present: *The Shores of Light, Classics and Commercials, The Bit Between My Teeth, The Wound and the Bow, Europe Without Baedeker, A Window on Russia, A Piece of My Mind . . .*

It was miraculous because this was no ordinary library. Wilson's books weren't easily accessible. I had always lived in small towns where libraries and bookshops were few and far between, and did not stock anything except a few standard texts of English literature: Austen, Dickens, Kipling, Thackeray. My semi-colonial education had made me spend much of my time on minor Victorian and Edwardian writers. Some diversity was provided by writers in Hindi and the Russians, which you could buy cheaply at Communist bookstores. As for the rest, I read randomly, whatever I could find, and with the furious intensity of a small-town boy to whom books are the sole means of communicating with, and understanding, the larger world.

I had realized early on that being passionate about literature wasn't enough. You had to be resourceful; you had to be perpetually on the hunt for books. And so I was, at libraries and bookshops, at other people's houses, in letters to relatives in the West, and, most fruitfully, at the local paper recycler, where I once bought a tattered old paperback of Heinrich Mann's *Man of Straw*, which I – such were the gaps in my knowledge – dutifully read, and made notes about, without knowing anything about his more famous and distinguished brother. Among this disconnected reading, I had certain preferences, a few strong likes and dislikes, but they did not add up to coherent standards of judgement. I knew little of the social and historical underpinnings to the books I read: I had only a fleeting sense of the artistry and skill to which certain novels owed their greatness.

I had problems, too, with those books of Edmund Wilson I had found at the library, some of which I read in part that winter, others from cover to cover. They constantly referred to other books I hadn't heard of; many of them were collections of reviews of books I could not possibly read at the time. Proust, Joyce, Hemingway, Waugh, yes; Malraux and Silone, probably; but where in India could one find John Dos Passos? Wilson's books also assumed a basic knowledge of politics and history I did not have. They were a struggle for me, and the ignorance I felt before them was a secret source of shame, but it was also a better stimulus to the effort Wilson's books demanded than mere intellectual curiosity.

I was never to cease feeling this ignorance, but I also had a sense as I groped my way through his work that all those unread books and unknown writers were coming to me filtered through an extraordinary cohesive sensibility. Over the next few months, it became clear to me that his powers of summary and explication were often worth more attention than the books and writers that were his subject. There was also a certain idea that his lucid prose and confident judgements suggested, and that, at first, I found so attractive about him: the idea of a man wholly devoted to reading and thinking and writing. I thought of him at work in his various residences – Provincetown, Talcottville, Cambridge, Wellfleet – and these resonant names became attached in my imagination to a promise of wisdom and serenity.

*

The library where I had found Wilson's books had, along with the university, come out of an old, and now vanished, impulse, the desire among Hindu reformists in the freedom movement to create indigenous centres of education and culture. The fundamental idea was to train young Hindu men for the modern world: and, like many other idealisms of the freedom movement, it hadn't survived long in the chaos of independent India, where even the right to education came to be fiercely fought over under the banner of specific castes, religions, regions, and communities.

Sectarian tensions were particularly intense in North India, especially here in Uttar Pradesh, the province with the greatest population and second highest poverty rate in the country, where caste and political rivalries spread to the local universities. The main political parties,* eager to enlist the large student vote in their favour, had begun to put money into elections to the student unions. Politically ambitious students would organize themselves by caste – the Brahmin, the Thakur (the so-called warrior caste), the Backward, and the Scheduled (the government's euphemism for former untouchables). The tensions were so great that academic sessions were frequently interrupted by student strikes; arson, kidnapping, and murder among students became common features of campus life.

Miraculously, the library at Benares had remained well stocked. Subscription to foreign magazines had been renewed on time: you could find complete volumes of the *TLS, Partisan Review* and *The New York Review of Books* from the sixties in the stacks. Catalogues of university presses had been dutifully scrutinized by the library staff; the books, as though through some secluded channel untouched by the surrounding disorder, had kept flowing in.

The library was housed in an impressively large building in the style known as Hindu-Saracenic, whose attractive pastiche of Hindu and Victorian Gothic architecture had been prompted by the same Indian modernist aspirations that had created the university. But now chaos reigned in almost every department: few books were to be found in their right places; the card catalogue was in complete disarray. In the reading room, students of a distinctly criminal appearance smoked foul-smelling cigarettes and noisily played cards. Some of them chose to take their siestas on long desks; bored young women spent hours scratching their initials on table tops.

It was hardly a congenial place for long hours of reading, but since I wasn't enrolled as a student at the university, I could not take books out of the library. I was, however, allowed to sit in the reading room, and I was there almost every day from the time it opened in the morning. Since I

---

* For many years Benares was a stronghold of left-wing parties. In recent elections, however, the BJP candidate has won.

had little money, I walked the four miles to the library from my house. For lunch I had an omelette at a fly-infested stall outside the library, and then hurried back after a glass of sticky-sweet tea which effectively killed all hunger for the next few hours. In the evening, I would walk home along the river and sit until after dark on the ghats, among a mixed company of touts and drug-pushers; washermen gathering clothes that had rested on the stone steps all afternoon, white and sparkling in the sun; groups of children playing hopscotch on the chalk-marked stone floor; a few late bathers, dressing and undressing under tattered beach umbrellas; and the groups of old men, silently gazing at the darkening river.

Many of my days in Benares were spent in this way, and when I think of them they seem serenely uneventful. But what I remember best now are not so much the clear blue skies and magically still afternoons, glimpsed from my window-side perch at the library, as the peculiar factors that constantly threatened to undo that serenity. For a radically different world existed barely a few hundred metres from where I sat, reading about Santayana.

The university in those days was the scene of intense battles between students and the police. Anything could provoke them: a student who was not readmitted after being expelled, an exam that a professor refused to postpone. A peculiar frenzy periodically overtook the two sides when the students rampaged through the campus, smashing furniture and window-panes left unbroken from their last eruption of rage. Challenged by the police, they retreated to the sanctuary of their hostels and fired pistols at the baton-charging constables. In retaliation, the policemen often invaded the hostels, broke into locked rooms, dragged out their pleading, wailing occupants, and proceeded to beat them.

I once saw one of their victims, minutes after the police had left, coughing blood and broken teeth, his clothes torn, the baton marks on his exposed arms rapidly turning blue. Another time I saw a policeman with half of the flesh and bones on his back gouged out by a locally made hand grenade. Anxious colleagues watched helplessly from behind their wire mesh shields as he tottered and collapsed on the ground. Terrified bystanders like myself threw themselves to the ground in a defensive reflex we'd seen in action movies. The grenade thrower – a scrawny boy in a big-collared shirt and tight polyester pants who, I learned later, had targeted the policeman after being tortured by him in custody – stood watching on the cobblestone road, fascinated by his handiwork.

*

Such violence, extreme though it seemed, wasn't new to the university, which had long been witness to bloodier battles between student wings of Communist and Hindu nationalist organizations. These two groups tended to be allied with different ends of the caste system: the lower castes tended to be Communist; the upper castes tended to be Hindu nationalist. But frequently now, the violence came for no ideological reason, with no connections to a cause or movement. It erupted spontaneously, fuelled only by the sense of despair and hopelessness that permanently hung over North Indian universities in the eighties. It was part of a larger crisis caused by the collapse of many Indian institutions, the increasingly close alliance between crime and politics, and the growth of state-organized corruption – processes that had been speeded up during Mrs Gandhi's 'Emergency' in the mid-seventies.

For students poised to enter this world, the choices were harsh – and it didn't matter what caste you belonged to; poverty was evenly distributed across caste divisions in this region. Most of the people I knew were deeply cynical in their attitude toward their future. You could work toward becoming a member of either the state or national legislature and siphon off government funds earmarked for literacy and population-control projects; if nothing worked out, you could aspire, at the other end of the scale, to be a lowly telephone mechanic and make money by selling illegal telephone connections.

Most of the students in this traditionally backward region of India came from feudal or semi-rural families, and aspired to join the Civil Service, a colonial invention which in independent India continued to offer the easiest and quickest route to political power and affluence. But there were fewer and fewer recruitments made to the Civil Service from North India, where the decline in standards, as well as the cheap availability, of higher education had made it possible for millions to acquire university degrees while they had less and less prospect of employment. Bribery and nepotism had a major part in the disbursement of the jobs in the minor government services. Students from the lately impoverished upper castes suffered most in this respect: if poverty wasn't enough, they were further disadvantaged by the large quotas for lower-caste candidates in government jobs.

The quotas, first created by Nehru's government in the early fifties and meant as a temporary measure, were expanded and used by successive governments as an electoral ploy to attract lower-caste votes. The upper-caste students found themselves making the difficult adjustments to urban life only to confront the prospect of being sent back to the oblivion they had emerged from; and their sense of blocked futures, which they acquired early in their time at the university, was to reach a tragic culmination in 1990 in the spate of self-immolations following the central government's decision to provide even larger quotas in federal jobs for applicants from lower castes.

My own situation was little different from that of the people around me. I had recently spent three years at the nearby provincial university at Allahabad, where I was in even closer, more unsettling, proximity to the desperation I saw in Benares. I was upper-caste myself, without family wealth, and roughly in the same position as my father had been in freshly independent India when the land reform act of 1951 – another of Nehru's attempts at social equality, it was meant to turn exploited tenants into landholders – reduced his once well-to-do Brahmin family to penury. My mother's family had suffered a similar setback. Like many others in my family who laboriously worked their way into the middle classes, I had to make my own way in the world. Looking back, I can see my compulsive pursuit of books, and the calm and order it suggests, contrasting so jarringly with the rage and desperation around me, as my way of putting off a grimly foreclosed future.

So, during my months in Benares, I was able to live at a slight tangent to the chaos of the university.

2

I got to know Rajesh early in my stay in Benares. A tall, wiry, good-looking man in his mid-twenties, he had continued to live in Benares after he had finished his studies at the university. He was eccentric and moody; he would start reciting Urdu poetry one moment and then denounce its decadence the next, and start enumerating the virtues of the farming life. 'All these wine-drinkers with broken hearts,' he would say. 'You can't compare them to simple peasants who do more for humanity.' He used to say he would rather be a farmer than join government service and do the bidding of corrupt politicians. On other occasions, he would tell me about the good works honest civil servants in India could achieve, and how he himself aspired to be one of them. There was also an unexpected mystical side to him. I once saw him standing on the ghats gesturing towards the sandy expanses across the river. 'That,' he was saying to his companion, a slightly terrified young student, 'is *sunyata*, the void.' 'And this,' he pointed at the teeming conglomeration of temples and houses behind us, 'is *Maya*, illusion. Do you know what our task is? Our task is to live somewhere in between.'

He revered Gandhi, and distrusted Nehru, who he said was too 'modern' in his outlook; but then he would change his mind and say that Gandhi wasn't 'tough' enough. All of these opinions he delivered with a faraway look; they formed part of monologues about the degraded state of contemporary India. 'Where are we going?' he would say, dramatically throwing up his hands. 'What kind of nation are we becoming?' He loved Faiz, the Pakistani writer whose doom-laden poetry he knew by heart; he was also fond of Wordsworth, whom he had studied as an undergraduate; he showed me a notebook where he had copied down his favourite poems, 'The Solitary Reaper' among them. But I could never get him to talk about them. He did not listen much; and he did not like anyone interrupting his monologues. It wasn't easy to be with him.

*

He had been at the university for eight years when I met him, and at first he appeared another of the countless students who hung around the campus, mechanically accumulating useless degrees, applying for this or that job. I had come to him with an introduction from a mutual friend at my undergraduate university. This friend believed that 'studious' people like myself needed powerful 'backers' at Benares Hindu University – he used the English words – and that Rajesh was well-placed to protect me from local bullies and criminals. Rajesh himself believed so, and was more than happy to take me under his wing. 'You are here to study,' he told me at our first meeting, 'and that's what you should do. Let me know if anyone bothers you and I'll fix the bastard.'

Part of his concern for me came from an old, and now slightly melodramatic, reverence for 'studious' Brahmins. He was Brahmin himself, but considered himself unequal to what he felt to be the proper dignity of his caste. The feeling was widespread in the region, where the traditional dominance of Brahmins was beginning to collapse in the face of a serious political challenge by assertive lower castes. The decline of Brahmin prestige and authority – which was intimately linked to their diminishing political importance – was symbolized by a famous family of Benares, which was once very close to the Nehru-Gandhi dynasty, and had been pushed into irrelevance by the new, militant kind of low-caste politician. The members of the family still wore their caste marks on their foreheads; they still observed fasts, regularly bathed in the Ganges, were chief guests at temples on holy days, and would not accept food from low-caste people. But it was only this excessive concern about their public image, and an overdeveloped sense of uncleanliness and contamination, that remained of their Brahminness. No crowds of job-seekers and flunkeys gathered at their house anymore; the women in the family went around the bazaars unescorted and unrecognized; visiting journalists went elsewhere for good copy.

Rajesh felt the general change of status differently. He fasted religiously, went to offer flowers at the temple of Hanuman, the monkey god, every Tuesday. His regard for Faiz and love for Urdu poetry spoke of an older Brahminical instinct for learning and the arts. But he also gave the impression that none of the old ways or values mattered any more in a world in which Brahmins were forced to struggle to survive with everyone else. 'Yes, I am a Brahmin, too,' Rajesh would say, and then add, mysteriously, 'but I have done things no Brahmin would have ever done.'

I remember my first visit to his room, which was in one of the derelict-looking hostels with piles of broken furniture scattered on the front quad. The stairs to his room were splattered with blood-red patterns made by students spitting betel juice. In the assorted shabbiness of his room – light from a naked bulb weakly falling on scabby blue walls, unmade bed, discarded slippers, rickety table, cheap denim jeans hanging limply from a solitary nail in the wall, a bamboo bookstand tottering under the weight of old newspapers – I noticed a jute shoulder bag lying open on the ground, bulging with crude pistols. No attempt had been made to conceal the pistols, which seemed to belong as naturally to the room as the green plastic bucket next to it. It made me nervous: so did the hint of instability given by his speech and manner, the long monologue, the unconnected references to Wordsworth, to India. I began to wish I saw less of him.

But it was hard to break off contact, even harder to be indifferent to the innocent friendliness he exuded every time I saw him. He often appeared at the library, 'checking up', he said, on whether I was being my studious self, or whether I went to the library to 'ogle the girls'. I would try to avoid him by disappearing from the library at the time he was likely to be there, but he would then show up at a later hour. He also showed a surprising amount of interest in my reading; surprising, because although he had done an undergraduate course in English, I rarely saw him reading anything more than the Hindi newspapers scattered around the tea shops on the campus. 'Edmund Wilson! Again! Why,' he would ask with genuine bemusement, 'are you always reading the same man?' He listened patiently while I tried to say a few explanatory words about the particular book or essay he had pointed to. He once caught me reading *To the Finland Station*, and I had to provide a crude summary, in fewer words than used by Wilson, of Trotsky's main ideas. I couldn't, of course, refuse; the thought of Rajesh's instability, the pistols in his room, always forced me to summon up a reasonably friendly response. It could be exhausting being with him at times. Why, I would wonder, did he, who seemed to have read little beyond Faiz and the Romantics, want to know so much about people so distant from us, like Trotsky or Bakunin? (More simply, why couldn't he spend his time with other people in the university?)

*

Rajesh was well-known in student circles. There was a special respect for him among other upper-caste students from nearby villages; lonely and vulnerable in what to them was the larger, intimidating world away from home, they saw in Rajesh a sympathetic fellow provincial and older protector. Rajesh fitted the role rather well: he was physically bigger and stronger than most students on the campus; he had a certain reputation – a lot of people seemed to know about the pistols in his room; and it pleased him to be thought of as a godfather-like figure.

A small crowd instantly gathered around him whenever I went out with him to a tea stall, and eagerly hung on to every word he spoke. He often talked about politics, the latest developments in Delhi, the current gossip about the size of a minister's wealth; he would repeat colourful stories about local politicians, the imaginative ways in which they had conned the World Bank or some other development agency, the bridges that were built only on paper, the roads that existed only in files.

Indeed, I often wondered – although he seemed content simply talking about politics – if he was not planning to be a politician himself: students with a popular mass base in the university who proved themselves capable of organizing strikes and demonstrations were often handpicked by local political bosses to contest elections to the local municipal corporation. He seemed to know people off-campus as well; I once noticed in his room a couple of conspicuously affluent visitors who had driven to see him in a sinister-looking pale green Ambassador with tinted windows.

But I was preoccupied, particularly with Wilson's writings and their maze of cross-references which sent me scurrying from book to book in an effort to plug up at least some of what I felt were egregious gaps in my knowledge. One of the books I came across in this way was Flaubert's *Sentimental Education*, which I had read rather indifferently in a Penguin Classics edition some time back. Wilson's essay on the politics of Flaubert, collected in *The Triple Thinkers*, made me want to reread it. Now I found this account of an ambitious provincial's tryst with metropolitan glamour and disillusion full of the kind of subtle satisfactions that a neurotic adolescent sensibility would be especially susceptible to. I identified with Frédéric Moreau, the protagonist, with his large, passionate, but imprecise, longings, his indecisiveness, his aimlessness, his self-contempt. I cannot ever forget the sick feeling that came over me after I finished the novel late one evening at the library. I was only twenty, and much experience, and many more books, lay ahead of me. Yet I couldn't fail to recognize the intimations the novel gave me of the many stages of drift and futility I was encountering and was yet to encounter in my own life.

I recommended *Sentimental Education* to Rajesh one evening, and gave him a Xeroxed copy of Wilson's essay. I didn't expect him to read all of it; but he had been curious about Wilson, and I thought the essay was a good example of his writing. I didn't hear from him for a few weeks. My life went on as before. I left for the library early in the morning, and came back to a house reverberating with the exuberant jangling of sitars, the doleful twang of sarods, the hollow beat of tablas. I ate every evening with Panditji's wife, sitting cross-legged on the floor in her dark kitchen, awkwardly inhaling thick smoke from the wood fire, over which Shyam dextrously juggled hot chapattis from one calloused palm to another.

Later, back in my room, trying to read in the low-voltage light, I would hear the bells for evening prayers ring out from the adjacent temple. I spoke little to the Americans who, after their lessons with Panditji, came up to the roof to smoke opium. I already knew I could not share my intellectual discoveries with them. They hadn't heard of Edmund Wilson: one of them, a Princeton undergraduate, straining to recognize the name, thought I meant the biologist E. O. Wilson. The cultural figures they spoke about, and appeared to miss in the often oppressive alienness of this most ancient of Indian towns, were then unknown to me; it was to take me a few more years to find out who David Letterman was. But the Americans were, like me, whatever their reasons, refugees from the modern world of work and achievement, explorers of a world that antedated their own, and I was sympathetic to them.

*

Several weeks after I'd last seen him, Rajesh abruptly reappeared one afternoon at the library. He had been away, he said, on urgent work. Now he was on his way to visit his mother who lived in a village forty miles west of Benares. Would I come with him? I thought of making some excuse, but then I realized I needed some diversion and I said yes. Besides, I was curious about Rajesh's background, of which he had told me nothing until then. I could guess that he wasn't well-off, but one could have said the same for most students at the university.

We left one cold foggy morning on the small-gauge, steam-engined train that in those days used to run between Benares and Allahabad. A chilly wind, gritty with coal dust, blew in through the iron-barred windows as the train puffed and wheezed through an endless flat plain, stubbly fields stretching to tree-blurred horizons, coils of smoke torpid above ragged settlements of mud huts and half-built brick houses. The train was empty, and we stretched ourselves on hard wooden benches, wrapped from head to toe in coarse military blankets, and hurriedly sipped carda-mom-scented tea that seemed to turn cold the moment the vendor lifted the kettle off his tiny coal stove. We got off at a small station populated entirely, it seemed, by mangy dogs. Another half-hour tonga ride from there, the horse's hooves clattering loudly against the tarmac road. Mango groves on both sides. Here and there, a few buildings: box-shaped houses of naked brick and mud huts with large courtyards where men slumbered on string cots: cold-storage warehouses: tiny shuttered shops. At an enclave of mud huts, swarthy blouseless women swept the common yard with brooms made of leafy neem twigs that left the earth raked over with crows-feet patterns. Finally, at the end of a row of identical roadside buildings, there was Rajesh's own house, brick-walled, one room, poor – but what had I expected?

The door was opened by Rajesh's mother, a tiny shrunken woman in a widow's white sari. She looked frankly puzzled to see me at first, but suddenly grew very welcoming when Rajesh introduced me as a friend from the university. After the early morning light, it was dark and damp inside the high-ceilinged room. There was a solitary window, but it was closed. In one corner, partitioned off by a flimsy handloom sari, was the kitchen, where a few brass utensils dully gleamed in the dark, and where Rajesh's mother busied herself with breakfast. In another corner, under a sagging string cot, was a tin trunk, leprous with rust. There were religious calendars in garish colours on the walls: Shiva, Krishna, Hanuman. I recall being unsettled by that bare, lightless room, and its extreme poverty, something not immediately apparent in Rajesh's life in Benares.

Rajesh, who since the morning had become increasingly silent, left the room, and I sat in a straight-backed wicker chair and talked to his mother. Both of us had to speak very loudly to make ourselves heard above the hissing sounds from the kerosene stove. It wasn't easy to express sympathy in that high-pitched voice; and sympathy was what was increasingly required of me as she began to tell me stories from her past. She had been widowed fifteen years ago when Rajesh was still a child, and soon afterward her wealthy, feudal in-laws had started to harass her. The house in which she lived with her husband and son was taken away from her, and they refused to give back the little dowry she had brought with her. Her parents were dead, her brothers too poor to support her. There was only Rajesh, who had worked since he was thirteen, first in the maize fields, and then at a carpet factory in Benares, where he had gone to evening school and done well enough to enter the university. The years had somehow passed.

But now she was worried. Rajesh, she felt, had reached a dead end. There were no more openings for him. All the jobs these days were going to low-caste people. And not only did Rajesh have the wrong kind of caste, he had no connections anywhere for a government job. And, she added with a touch of old Brahmin pride, he had too much self-respect to work for low-caste shopkeepers and businessmen.

How little of his past I had known! I knew a bit about those carpet factories; they had been in the papers after some human rights organizations petitioned the courts to prohibit them from using child labour. There had been pictures of large-eyed, frightened-looking children in dungeon-like rooms, framed against their exquisite handiworks. I was shocked to know that Rajesh had been one of them. The tormenting private memories of childhood that he carried within himself seemed unimaginable.

On the train back to Benares, Rajesh broke his silence to say that he had read *Sentimental Education*, and that it was a story he knew well. '*Yeh meri duniya ki kahani hai. Main in logo ko janta hoon*,' he said, in Hindi. 'It is the story of my world. I know these people well.' He gave me a hard look. 'Your hero, Edmund Wilson,' he added, in English, 'he also knows them.'

What did Rajesh, a student in a provincial Indian university in the late 1980s, have in common with Frédéric Moreau or any of the doomed members of his generation in this novel of mid-nineteenth century Paris? As it happened, I didn't ask him to explain. I had already been made to feel awkward by the unexpected disclosures about his past. And then the day had been somewhat exhausting. We talked, desultorily, of other things, and parted in Benares.

*

I was in Benares again two years later, when I heard about Rajesh.

The man who told me, someone I remembered as one of Rajesh's hangers-on, appeared surprised that I didn't already know that he had been a member of a criminal gang specializing in debt collection on behalf of a group of local moneylenders and businessmen. That explains his mysterious absences from Benares, I thought, as well as the pistols in his room and the sinister-looking Ambassador with tinted windows.

It was, the man said, a good, steady business: once confronted with the possibility of violence, people paid up very quickly, without involving the police. But then Rajesh had graduated to something riskier – and here, although shocked and bewildered by what I had been told, and fully expecting the worst now, I could not take it in.

At some stage, the man said, dramatically pausing after every word, Rajesh had turned himself into a contract killer. It was an extremely well-paid profession; also, a well-connected one. You worked for small-time contractors who in turn worked for wealthy industrialists and also did favours for local political bosses who did not always rely on their own 'private armies' (the local term for loyal henchmen) for certain jobs. You got to know everyone well after a few years in the business. You worked for all these important people, yet you were always on your own. The chances of survival weren't very high. Sooner or later, the police came to hear of you. Fierce loyalties of caste and clan ensured that every murder would be avenged. It was what would one day happen to Rajesh, he said. In a typical ambush of the kind often reported in the local papers, he would be on his motorcycle when four men would surround him at a busy intersection in the old city, and shoot him dead. The prurient excitement on the man's face filled me with disgust and anger.

I never did hear what happened to Rajesh. Such stories were in the newspapers every day. But it took me a while to sort out my confused feelings. I kept seeing Rajesh at that busy crossroads, trapped in the dense swarm of scooters, cycle rickshaws, bullock carts, cars, buses, trucks, and bicycles, the four men converging upon him, producing crude pistols from their pockets ...

Rajesh had bewildered me: his self-consciousness about his Brahmin identity, the pistols in his room, his constant talk of the void. I could now see that he had been struggling to make sense of his life, to connect the disparate elements that existed in it; but so, in a different way, was I.

*

Then a few months ago I thought of writing something on Edmund Wilson. I had tried before, in 1995, the year of Wilson's centenary, but what I wrote seemed to me too much like a reprise of what a lot of other people had already said about him. But then I was trying to write about him in the way an American or European writer would have. What I had in mind was a straightforward exposition of Wilson's key books. It didn't occur to me that a separate narrative probably existed in my private discovery of Wilson's writings in a dusty old library in the ancient town of Benares.

Now I was again looking for material on Wilson in preparation for another attempt when, browsing through old papers, I came across a xeroxed copy of his essay on Flaubert's politics. It looked familiar. Idly flipping through the essay, I came to the pages on *Sentimental Education*, where I saw some passages underlined in red. As I am not in the habit of marking up a printed text, I wondered who had done this. I read the underlined sentences:

> Frédéric is only the more refined as well as the more incompetent side
> of the middle-class mediocrity of which the dubious promoter represents
> the more flashy and active aspect. And so in the case of the other
> characters, the journalists and the artists, the members of the various
> political factions, the remnants of the old nobility, Frédéric finds the
> same shoddiness and lack of principle which are gradually revealed in
> himself . . .

On another page the underlined passage read:

> Flaubert's novel plants deep in our mind an idea which we never quite
> get rid of: the suspicion that our middle-class society of manufacturers,
> businessmen, and bankers, of people who live on or deal in investments,
> so far from being redeemed by its culture, has ended by cheapening and
> invalidating all the departments of culture, political, scientific, artistic,
> and religious, as well as corrupting and weakening the ordinary human
> relations: love, friendship, and loyalty to cause – till the whole civilization
> seems to dwindle.

The passage offered a small glimpse of Wilson's way of finding the sources and effects of literature in the overlap between individual states of mind and specific historical realities. But I hadn't noticed it when I first came across it. I read it again and thought about the red underlinings. And then, after almost seven years, Rajesh strode back into my conscious-ness. I remembered the afternoon I had given *Sentimental Education* and Wilson's essay to him; I remembered his words to me on the train, words I dismissed as exaggeration, the hard, determined look on his face as he said, 'It is the story of my world. I know these people well. Your hero, Edmund Wilson, he also knows them.'

What had he meant by that?

*

The question did not leave me. And there came a time when I began to think I had understood very little, and misunderstood much, during those months in Benares. I thought of the day I went to visit Rajesh's village and I at last saw that there had been a purpose behind Rajesh's invitation to his home, his decision to so frankly reveal his life to me. Even the cryptic remarks about *Sentimental Education* and Wilson on the train: he wanted me to know that not only had he read the novel, he had drawn, with Wilson's help, his own conclusions from it.

In the hard and mean world he had lived in, first as a child labourer and then as hired criminal for politicians and businessmen, Rajesh would have come to know well the grimy underside of middle-class society. What became clearer to me now was how quick he had been to recognize that the society Flaubert and Wilson wrote about wasn't much different from the one he inhabited in Benares. 'It's the story of my world,' he had said. I couldn't see it then but in Benares I had been among people who, like Frédéric Moreau and his friends, had either disowned or, in many cases, moved away from their provincial origins in order to realize their dreams of success in the bourgeois world. Only a handful of them were able to get anywhere near to realizing their dreams while the rest saw their ambitions dwindle away over the years in successive disappointments. The degradation of bribery, sycophancy, and nepotism that people were forced into in their hunt for jobs was undermining in itself: so pervasive was the corruption around them that neither those who succeeded nor those who failed were able to escape its taint.

The small, unnoticed tragedies of thwarted hopes and ideals Flaubert wrote about in *Sentimental Education* were all around us. And this awareness – which was also mine but which I tried to evade through, ironically, the kind of obsessive reading that had led me to the novel in the first place – had been Rajesh's private key to the book. Thus, where I saw only the reflection of a personal neurosis – the character of Frédéric in particular embodying my sense of inadequacy, my severe self-image – he had discovered a social and psychological environment that was similar to the one he lived in.

The discovery did honour to both Flaubert and Wilson. The world we knew in Benares was many years away from those of the French novelist and the American critic. Yet – and this was a measure of their greatness – they seemed to have had an accurate, if bitter, knowledge of its peculiar human ordeals and futility. It was a knowledge Rajesh himself arrived at by a somewhat different route. 'To fully appreciate that book,' Wilson had written of *Sentimental Education*, 'one must have had time to see something of life.' It sounds like a general sort of adage; but Rajesh exemplified its truth even as he moved into another world, taking what in retrospect look like all the wrong turns. Rajesh had known how to connect whatever little he read to the world around himself, much in the same way Wilson had done in his essay, and in his other writings, which reveal a symbiotic relationship between life and literature that I, despite all my reading, was not fully to grasp until long after I had left Benares and thought again of that time of hopeful, confused striving when I first read Edmund Wilson.

ENGLISH

R. K. Narayan (b. 1907)

R. K. Narayan was born in 1907 in Mysore in South India; one of his younger brothers, R. K. Laxman, is India's most famous cartoonist. He studied English literature, and for a while he was a schoolteacher, writing stories in English (hardly a recognized pursuit at the time) and getting them published in local newspapers. His first novel, *Swami and Friends* (1935), came to him with an image of a train leaving a railway station, an image with which the actual novel culminates. (The way trains dominate the modern Indian imagination as a symbol of mystery and promise is notable, comparable to the image of the sea, and the ship, in English fiction and poetry, and to the car and the freeway in American writing.) The train and the railway platform appear, indeed, in the extract below, a reminiscence of the origins of Narayan's oeuvre. The story of how he embarked upon his career is part of literary history: unable to get the novel published, he sent the manuscript to a friend in Oxford, instructing him to either find the novel a publisher, or to drown the manuscript in the Cherwell. The desperate and destructive instructions left by writers to their friends regarding their work, disguised missives for help, are always interesting: Kafka told Max Brod to burn his manuscripts, instead of taking the trouble of burning them himself. Just as Kafka's friend found him an audience, so did Narayan's: he sent them to Graham Greene, who ensured the novel's publication (apparently publishers paid heed to the advice of novelists in those days), and went on to call him his favourite living writer in the English language. Indeed, Narayan has always been something of a writer's writer; his other admirers include V. S. Naipaul, John Updike, and Saul Bellow. In the past, he has been important to younger writers for being a sort of Homer of post-colonial Indian English writing, naive, originary, and sophisticated at once, or a sort of tranquil Wordsworth to Naipaul's agonized, belated Arnold, seen by the latter to possess an immediate and vivid access to his material no longer available to the younger writer. In the current climate, he is neglected, or patronized, probably because his seemingly innocent but chameleon fictions are not analysed easily by the simple chemical apparatus of post-colonial theory. In the fictional South Indian town of Malgudi, he has created a cunning pastoral, to delight the reader, but also to instruct her or him, in comic vignettes, of the evasions and ironies of colonial history. He is over ninety years old now; but, in his fiction, he has always, from the beginning, seemed old, possessing an old man's delicacy, sparseness of expression, childlike mischief, an occasional cruelty – and an 'old man's eagle mind'. *The English Teacher* (1945), the most autobiographical of his novels, is about a teacher of English in Malgudi, his wife, and their only child, a daughter; about a relatively new institution, then, in the macrocosm of India – the microcosm of the nuclear family, and how its language, dreams, tragedies, and hopes beat, unknowingly, at the centre of a vast nation. The wife dies, leaving the man preoccupied with making contact with her, through a medium, as Narayan did in real life; the first part of the novel, to which the extract below belongs, is one of the most perfect renderings in literature of the texture of happiness in married life, a happiness held, here, within the quotation marks of mortality. It is comparable, in its way, to Bibhuti Bhushan Banerjee's, and, later, Satyajit Ray's, portrait of a marriage shadowed by death in *Aparajito*.

* * *

from *The English Teacher* (1945)

The next three days I was very busy. My table was placed in the front room of the new house. All my papers and books were arranged neatly. My clothes hung on a peg. The rest of the house was swept and cleaned.

My mother arrived from the village with a sack full of vessels, and helped to make up the house for me. She was stocking the storeroom and the kitchen and spent most of her time travelling in a jutka to the market and coming back with something or other. She worked far into the night, arranging and rearranging the kitchen and the store. At night she sat down with me on the veranda and talked of her house-keeping philosophy. I liked this veranda very much. We had a cool breeze. I felt immensely satisfied with my choice of the house now. I hoped my wife too would like it. But my mother, the moment she arrived from the village, said, 'What an awful kitchen! So narrow! And the dining room would have been better if they had added at least a yard in length that side ...'

'We can't have everything our way in a house built by someone else ...' I became rather impatient if anyone criticized this house. She understood it and said: 'I'm not saying it is a bad house...' She had been used to our large, sprawling home in the village, and everything else seemed to her small and choking. I explained this fact to her and she agreed it was so: 'But do you know how hard it is to keep a huge house like ours clean? It takes me a whole lifetime to keep it tidy, but I don't grudge it. Only I want a little more cooperation. Your father is becoming rather difficult nowadays...' She explained how impatient he became when he heard the swish of a broom or the noise of scrubbing, and shouted at her to stop it all. As he was growing old, these noises got on his nerves. And so every time she wanted to clean the house, she had to wait till he went away to the fields. 'And do you know, when I delay this, how many other things get out of routine? Unless I have cleaned the house I can't go and bathe. After bathing I've to worship, and only after that can I go near the cows... And if I fail to look at the cowshed for half an hour, do you know what happens?' She was completely wrapped up in her duties. House-keeping was a grand affair for her. The essence of her existence consisted in the thrills and pangs and the satisfaction that she derived in running a well-ordered household. She was unsparing and violent where she met slovenliness. 'If a woman can't take charge of a house and run it sensibly, she must be made to get into man's dress and go out in a procession...' I thought of my wife and shuddered at the fate that might be awaiting her in the few weeks my mother was going to stay and help us run the house. My wife was the last daughter of the family and was greatly petted by her parents, in her own house, where she spent most of her time reading, knitting, embroidering or looking after a garden. In spite of it, after my marriage my mother kept her in the village and trained her up in housekeeping. My wife had picked up many sensible points in cooking and household economy, and her own parents were tremendously impressed with her attainments when she next visited them. They were thrilled beyond words and remarked when I went there, 'We are so happy, Susila has such a fine house for her training. Every girl on earth should be made to pass through your mother's hands...' which, when I conveyed it to my mother, pleased her. She said: 'I really do not mind doing it for everyone, but there are those who neither know nor learn when taught. I feel like kicking them when I come across that type.' I knew she was referring to her eldest daughter-in-law, my brother's wife, whom she detested heartily. I had half a suspicion that my eldest brother went away to seek his livelihood in Hyderabad solely for this reason, for there used to be very painful scenes at home while the first daughter-in-law was staying in our house, my mother's idiosyncrasy being what it was and the other being of a haughty disposition. She was the daughter of a retired High Court Judge, and would never allow a remark or a look from my mother to pass unchallenged, and as a result great strife existed in the household for a number of years. My mother used to declare when my elder brother was not present, 'Whatever happens, even with a ten-thousand rupee dowry, I shall never accept a girl from a High Court Judge's family again . . .'

It had always been my great anxiety that my wife should not share this fate. My mother seemed to feel that some reference of more immediate interest was due to me and said: 'Susila is a modest girl. She is not obstinate.' I was grateful for that negative compliment. That was at the beginning of our married years. They had constant contact after that, and with every effort Susila came out better burnished than before. And then came a point when my mother declared: 'Susila has learnt how to conduct herself before guests.' At this point they separated; now they were meeting again, with Susila having a home of her own to look after, and my mother ready to teach the obedient pupil her business. It was really this which I secretly dreaded.

*

On the following Friday, I was pacing the little Malgudi railway station in great agitation. I had never known such suspense before. She was certain to arrive with a lot of luggage, and the little child. How was all this to be transferred from the train to the platform? And the child must not be hurt. I made a mental note, 'Must shout as soon as the train stops: "Be careful with the baby".' This seemed to my fevered imagination the all-important thing to say on arrival, as otherwise I fancied the child's head was sure to be banged against the doorway . . . And how many infants were damaged and destroyed by careless mothers in the process of coming out of trains! Why couldn't they make these railway carriages of safer dimensions? It ought to be done in the interests of baby welfare in India. 'Mind the baby and the door.' And then the luggage! Susila was sure to bring with her a huge amount of luggage. She required four trunks for her saris alone! Women never understood the importance of travelling light. Why should they? As long as there were men to bear all the anxieties and bother and see them through their travails! It would teach them a lesson to be left to shift for themselves. Then they would know the value of economy in these matters. I wrung my hands in despair. How was she going to get out with the child and all that luggage! The train stopped for just seven minutes. I would help her down first and then throw the things out, and if there were any boxes left over they would have to be lost with the train, that was all.

No one could help it. I turned to the gnarled blue-uniformed man behind me. He was known as Number Five and I had known him for several years now. Whatever had to be done on the railway platform was done with his help. I had offered him three times his usual wages to help me today. I turned to him and asked: 'Can you manage even if there is too much luggage?'

'Yes, master, no difficulty. The train stops for seven minutes.' He seemed to have a grand notion of seven minutes; a miserable flash it seemed to me. 'We unload whole wagons within that time.'

'I will tell the pointsman to stop it at the outer signal, if necessary,' he added. It was a very strength-giving statement to me. I felt relieved. But I think I lost my head once again. I believe, in this needless anxiety, I became slightly demented. Otherwise I would not have rushed at the stationmaster the moment I set eyes on him. I saw him come out of his room and move down the platform to gaze on a far-off signal post. I ran behind him, panting: 'Good morning, stationmaster!' He bestowed an official smile and moved off to the end of the platform and looked up. I felt I had a lot of doubts to clear on railway matters and asked inanely: 'Looking at the signals?'

'Yes,' he replied, and took his eyes down, and turned to go back to his room. I asked: 'Can't they arrange to stop this train a little longer here?' 'What for? Isn't there enough trouble as it is?' I laughed sympathetically and said: 'I said so because it may not be possible for passengers to unload all their trunks.'

'I should like to see a passenger who carries luggage that will take more than six minutes. I have been here thirty years.'

I said: 'My wife is arriving today with the infant. I thought she would require a lot of time in order to get down carefully. And then she is bound to have numerous boxes. These women, you know,' I said laughing artificially, seeking his indulgence. He was a good man and laughed with me. 'Well, sometimes it has happened that the train was held up for the convenience of a second-class passenger. Are your people travelling second?' 'I can't say,' I said. I knew well she wouldn't travel second, although I implored her in every letter to do so. She wrote rather diplomatically: 'Yes, don't be anxious, I and the baby will travel down quite safely.' I even wrote to my father-in-law, but that gentleman preserved a discreet silence on the matter. I knew by temperament he disliked the extravagance of travelling second, although he could afford it and in other ways had proved himself no miser. I felt furious at the thought of him and told the stationmaster. 'Some people are born niggards ... would put up with any trouble rather than ...' But before I could finish my sentence a bell rang inside the station office and the stationmaster ran in, leaving me to face my travail and anguish alone. I turned and saw my porter standing away from me, borrowing a piece of tobacco from someone. 'Here, Number Five, don't get lost.' A small crowd was gathering unobtrusively on the platform. I feared he might get lost at the critical moment. A bell sounded. People moved about. We heard the distant puffing and whistling. The engine appeared around the bend.

A whirling blur of faces went past me as the train shot in and stopped. People were clambering up and down. Number Five followed me about, munching his tobacco casually. 'Search on that side of the mail van.' I hurried through the crowd, peering into the compartments. I saw my father-in-law struggling to get to the doorway. I ran up to his carriage. Through numerous people getting in and out, I saw her sitting serenely in her seat with the baby lying on her lap. 'Only three minutes more!' I cried. 'Come out!' My father-in-law got down. I and Number Five fought our way up, and in a moment I was beside my wife in the compartment.

'No time to be sitting down; give me the baby,' I said. She merely smiled and said: 'I will carry the baby down. You will get these boxes. That wicker box, bring it down yourself, it contains baby's bottle and milk vessels.' She picked up the child and unconcernedly moved on. She hesitated for a second at the thick of the crowd and said: 'Way please,' and they made way for her. I cried: 'Susila, mind the door and baby.' All the things I wanted to say on this occasion were muddled and gone out of mind. I looked at her apprehensively till she was safely down on the platform, helped by her father. Number Five worked wonders within a split second.

I wouldn't have cared if the train had left now. The mother and child stood beside the trunks piled up on the platform. I gazed on my wife, fresh and beautiful, her hair shining, her dress without a wrinkle on it, and her face fresh, with not a sign of fatigue. She wore her usual indigo-coloured silk sari. I looked at her and whispered: 'Once again in this sari, still so fond of it,' as my father-in-law went back to the compartment to give a final look round. 'When will she wake up?' I asked pointing at the child, whom I found enchanting, with her pink face and blue shirt.

'Father is coming down,' she said, hinting that I had neglected him and ought to welcome him with a little more ceremony. I obeyed her instantly, went up to my father-in-law and said: 'I am very happy, sir, you have come ...' He smiled and said: 'Your wife and daughter got comfortable places, they slept well.'

'Did they, how, how? I thought there was such a crowd ...' My wife answered: 'What if there are a lot of others in the compartment? Other people must also travel. I didn't mind it.' I knew she was indirectly supporting her father, anticipating my attacks on him for travelling third. 'I only thought you might find it difficult to put the child to sleep,' I said.

'Oh, everybody made way for us, and we got a whole berth to ourselves,' she said, demanding of me by every look and breath that I should be sufficiently grateful to her for it. I turned to him and said: 'I'm so happy you managed it so well, sir.' He was pleased. He said: 'People are ever so good when they see Susila and the baby.'

'I hope you will stop with us for at least a week,' I said, and looked at my wife for approval. But her father declined the invitation with profuse thanks. He was to be back in his town next day and he was returning by the evening train. He said: 'There were three Bombay men, they liked Leela so much that they tried to give her a lot of biscuits. She was only too eager to accept, but I prevented...'

'Biscuits are bad for the baby,' I said. We moved on. I stretched out my hand: 'Let me carry her,' I said. My wife declined: 'You don't know how to carry a baby yet. You will sprain her.' She clasped her closer, and walked off the platform.

A Victoria carriage waited for us outside. Our trunks were stuffed into it, and we squeezed ourselves in. I shared the narrow seat behind the driver with my father-in-law, leaving the other seat for mother and child. Between us were heaped all the trunks and I caught patches of her face through the gaps in the trunks. She talked incessantly about the habits of the infant, enquired about the plan of our house, and asked the names of buildings and streets that we passed.

My mother came down and welcomed her at the gate. She had decorated the threshold with a festoon of green mango leaves and the floor and the doorway with white flour designs. She was standing at the doorway and as soon as we got down cried: 'Let Susila and the child stay where they are.' She had a pan of vermilion solution ready at hand and circled it before the young mother and child, before allowing them to get down from the carriage. After that she held out her arms, and the baby vanished in her embrace.

A look at my mother, her eagerness as she devoured them with her look, and led them into the house, and I was moved by the extraordinary tenderness which appeared in her face. All my dread of yesterday as to how she would prove as a mother-in-law was suddenly eased.

My mother was swamped by this little daughter of mine. She found little time to talk or think of anything else. She fussed over the young

mother and the child. She felt it her primary duty to keep the young
mother happy and free to look after the little one. The child seemed to be
their meeting point; and immediately established a great understanding
and harmony between them. All day my mother compelled my wife to
stay in her own room and spent her entire time in the kitchen preparing
food and drink for her and the child. When the child cried at nights, my
mother, sleeping in the hall, sprang up and rocked the cradle, before the
young mother should be disturbed. The child still drew nourishment from
its mother, and so the latter needed all the attention she could get.

My mother stayed with us the maximum time she could spare – two
months – and then returned to the village.

*

I left the college usually at 4.30 p.m., the moment the last bell rang, and
avoiding all interruptions reached home within about twenty minutes. As
soon as I turned the street I caught a glimpse of Susila tinkering at her little
garden in our compound, or watching our child as she toddled about
picking pebbles and mud … It was not in my wife's nature to be demon-
strative, but I knew she waited there for me. So I said: 'I have taken only
twenty minutes and already you are out to look for me!' She flushed when
I said this, and covered it up with: 'I didn't come out to look for you, but
just to play with the child …' My daughter came up and hugged my knees,
and held up her hands for my books. I gave her the books. She went up
the steps and put them on the table in my room. I followed her in. I took
off my coat and shirt, picked up my towel and went to the bathroom, with
the child on my arm, as she pointed at the various articles about the house
and explained them to me in her own terms. Most of her expressions were
still monosyllables, but she made up a great deal by her vigorous gesticu-
lations. She insisted upon watching me as I put my head under the tap.
The sight of it thrilled her and she shrieked as water splashed about. I put
her safely away from the spray as I bathed, but she stealthily came nearer
step by step and tried to catch some of the drops between her fingers. 'Ay,
child, keep off water.' At this she pretended to move off, but the moment I
shut my eyes under water and opened them again, she would have come
nearer and drenched a corner of her dress, which was a signal for me to
turn off the water and dry myself. I rubbed myself, lifted her on my arm,
went to my room, and brushed my hair. I did this as a religious duty
because I felt myself to be such a contrast to them when I returned in the
evening, in my sagging grey cotton suit, with grimy face, and ink-stained

fingers, while the mother and daughter looked particularly radiant in the evenings, with their hair dressed and beflowered, faces elegantly powdered.

By the time I reached this stage my wife came out and said: 'Your coffee is getting cold. Won't you come in?'

'Yes, yes,' and we moved off to our little dining room. An alcove at the end of the dining room served for a shrine. There on a pedestal she kept a few silver images of gods, and covered them with flowers; two small lamps were lit before them every morning. I often saw her standing there with the light in her face, her eyes closed and her lips lightly moving. I was usually amused to see her thus, and often asked what exactly it was that she repeated before her gods. She never answered this question. To this day I have never learnt what magical words she uttered there with closed eyes. Even when I mildly joked about it, 'Oh! becoming a yogi!' she never tried to defend herself, but merely treated my references with the utmost indifference. She seemed to have a deep secret life. There hung about this alcove a perpetual smell of burnt camphor and faded flowers.

I sat down on the plank facing the shrine, with the child on my lap. A little plate came up with some delicacy or titbit heaped on it – my tiffin. Susila placed this in front of me and waited to see my reaction. I looked up at her standing before me and asked: 'What is this?' She replied: 'Find out for yourself, let us see if you recognize it . . .' As I gazed at it wondering what it might be, the child thrust her hand out for it. I put a little into her mouth while the mother protested: 'You are going to spoil her giving her whatever she wants . . .'

'No, just a little . . .'.

'It will make her sick, she has been eating all sorts of things lately. Don't blame me if she gets sick . . .'

'Oh, she won't, just a little won't do her any harm . . .' As Leela held up her hands for more, her mother cried: 'No, baby, it won't do. Don't trouble father, come away, come away,' and the little one stuck to me fast, avoiding her mother's gaze, and I put my left arm about her and said: 'Don't worry about her, I won't give her any more . . .' As I finished what was on the plate Susila asked: 'Do you want some more?' This was always a most embarrassing question for me. As I hesitated she asked, 'Why, is it not good?'

'It is good,' I groaned, 'but . . .'

'But smells rather smoky, doesn't it? But for the smell it would be perfect,' she said. And I couldn't but agree with her. 'I prepared such a large quantity thinking you would like it . . .' She went in and brought out a little more and pushed it on to my plate and I ate with relish just because she was so desperately eager to get me to appreciate her handiwork!

She gave me coffee. We left the kitchen, and sat down in the hall. The child went over to her box in a corner and rummaged its contents and threw them about and became quite absorbed in this activity. My wife sat in the doorway, leaning against the door and watching the street. We spent an hour or more, sitting there and gossiping. She listened eagerly to all the things I told her about my college, work and life. Though she hadn't met a single person who belonged to that world, she knew the names of most of my colleagues and the boys and all about them. She knew all about Brown and what pleased or displeased him. She took sides with me in all my discussions and partisanships, and hated everyone I hated and respected anyone I respected. She told me a great deal about our neighbours, their hopes and fears, and promises and qualities. This talk went on till darkness crept in, and the lights had to be switched on. At the same time the clattering at the toy box ceased. This was a signal that the child would demand attention. She came towards us whimpering and uttering vague complaints. My wife got up and went to light the oven and cook the dinner, while I took charge of Leela and tried to keep her engaged till her food was ready.

*

On the first of every month, I came home, with ten ten-rupee notes bulging in an envelope, my monthly salary, and placed it in her hand. She was my cash-keeper. And what a ruthless accountant she seemed to be. In her hands, a hundred rupees seemed to do the work of two hundred, and all through the month she was able to give me money when I asked. When I handled my finances independently, after making a few routine savings and payments I simply paid for whatever caught my eyes and paid off anyone who approached me, with the result that after the first ten days, I went about without money. Now it was in the hands of someone who seemed to understand perfectly where every rupee was going or should go, and managed them with a determined hand. She kept the cash in a little lacquer box, locked it up in her almirah, and kept a minute account of it in the last pages of a diary, four years old.

We sat down at my table to draw up the monthly budget and list of provisions. She tore off a sheet of notepaper, and wrote down a complete list – from rice down to mustard. 'I have written down the precise quantity, don't change anything as you did once.' This was a reference to a slight change that I once attempted to make in her list. She had written down two seers of Bengal gram, but the National Provision Stores could not supply that quantity, and so the shopman suggested he would give half of it, and to make up the purchase, he doubled the quantity of jaggery. All done with my permission. But when I returned home with these, she saw the alterations and was completely upset. I found that there was an autocratic strain in her nature in these matters, and unsuspected depths of rage. 'Why has he made this alteration?' she had asked, her face going red. 'He didn't have enough of the other stuff,' I replied, tired and fatigued by the shopping and on the point of irritability myself. 'If he hasn't got a simple thing like Bengal gram, what sort of a shop has he?'

'Come and see it for yourself, if you like,' I replied, going into my room. She muttered: 'Why should it make you angry? I wonder!' I lay down on my canvas chair, determined to ignore her, and took out a book. She came presently into my room with a paper screw full of sugar and said: 'This man has given underweight of sugar. He has cheated you.' I lowered the book, frowned at her and asked: 'What do you mean?'

'I fear to speak to you if you get angry,' she said.

'Who is angry?' I asked. 'What is the matter, tell me?'

'I wrote for two measures of sugar, and see this; he has billed for two measures and has actually given a measure and a half. I have measured it just now.' She looked at me victoriously, waiting to hear how I was going to answer this charge. I merely said: 'He wouldn't do such a thing. You must have some extraordinary measure with you at home.'

'Nothing wrong with my measure. Even your mother measured everything with it and said it was correct.' So this was a legacy from her mother-in-law. She had taught the girl even this. She had a bronze tumbler, which she always declared was a correct half measure, and she would never recognize other standards and measures. She insisted upon making all her purchases, ghee or oil or milk or salt, with the aid of this measure, and declared that all other measures, including the Government stamped ones, were incorrect, and were kept maliciously incorrect because some municipal members were business men! She used the same tumbler for weighing too, placing it for weight in the scale pan, declaring that the curious thing about the vessel was that by weight too it was exactly half seer, and she would challenge anyone to disprove it. All tradespeople somehow succumbed to this challenge and allowed her to have her own way. She carried this tumbler about wherever she went, and I now found that she had procured a similar one for her daughter-in-law, and had trained her in the use of it.

'Throw away that tumbler and use an honest measure,' I said. Susila merely looked at me and said: 'Please don't speak so loudly. The child is asleep,' and tried to go out of the room. I called her back and said: 'If you use an honest measure you will find that others have also done so.'

'This National Provisions man is a thief,' she cried, 'the sooner you change the better.' This annoyed me very much. I had known the NPS man for years and liked him. I went all the way to South Extension to patronize his shop, and I liked the man because he was fat and talkative, and Sastri the logic man always said that it was the best shop in the town. I rather prided myself on going to the shop. I liked the fat, thoughtful proprietor. I said: 'There is nothing wrong with him. He is the best shop man known. I won't change him . . .' 'I don't know why you should be so fond of him when he is giving undermeasure and rotten stuff . . .' she replied. I was by this time very angry: 'Yes, I am fond of him because he is my second cousin,' I said with a venomous grin.

Her hatred of him was not mitigated. She said: 'You would pay cart hire and go all the way to South Extension to be cheated by him rather than go to a nearer shop. And his rates!' She finished the rest of her sentence with a shiver. 'I don't care if he overcharges – I won't drop him,' I declared. 'Hush, remember the child is sleeping,' she said and left the room. I lay in my chair fretting for fifteen minutes and then tried to resume my study, but could read only for five minutes. I got up and went over to the store-room as she was putting away the provisions and articles in their respective tin or glass containers. I stood at the doorway and watched her. I felt a great pity for her; the more because I had not shown very great patience. I asked: 'I will return the jaggery if it is too much. Have you absolutely no use for it?' In answer she pushed before me a glass goblet and said: 'This can hold just half a viss of jaggery and not more; which is more than enough for our monthly use. If it is kept in any other place, ants swarm on it.' I now saw the logic of her indignation, and by the time our next shopping was done, she had induced me to change over to the Co-operative Stores.

Since then every time the monthly list was drawn up she warned me: 'Don't alter anything in it.' I followed her list with strict precision, always feeling that one could never be sure what mess any small change might entail. If there were alterations to be made, I rather erred on the side of omission and went again next day after taking her suggestion.

She was very proud of her list. It was precise. Every quantity was conceived with the correct idea as to how long it should last. There were over two dozen different articles to be indented and she listed them with foresight and calculation. She was immensely proud of this ability. She gave me twenty rupees or more for these purchases. I went out to the Co-operative Stores in the Market Road and returned home three hours later followed by a cooly carrying them all in paper bags and bundles, stuffed into a large basket. She always waited for them at the door with uncon-cealed enthusiasm. The moment I was at the gate she held out her hand for the bill, and hurriedly ran her eyes down the columns checking the figures and prices. 'Oh! you have got all the things, and the cost didn't go up above 22–8–0 total ... slightly better than it was last month. Which item is cheaper this month?' She was in raptures over it. I loved to see her so pleased, and handed her the change to the last pie. She paid the cooly three annas; she would never alter this figure whatever happened. If anyone had the hardihood to expect more she declared: 'Don't stand there and argue. Be off. Your master has offered you an anna more than you deserve. After all the market is only half a mile away!' She carried the packages to the storeroom, and put each in its container, neatly labelled and ranged along a rank. She always needed my assistance to deal with rice. It was the bulkiest bag. It was my set duty on these days to drag the gunny sack along to the store, lift it and empty it into a zinc drum. I invited her displeasure if I didn't do it carefully. If any rice scattered accidentally on the floor, she said: 'I don't know when you will learn economic ways. You are so wasteful. On the quantity you throw about another family could comfortably live.'

She watched these containers as a sort of barometer, the level of their contents indicating the progress of the month. Each had to be at a particular level on a particular date: and on the last date of the month – just enough for another day, when they would be replenished. She watched these with a keen eye like a technician watching an all-important meter at a power house.

All went very well as long as she was reigning supreme in the kitchen – till my mother sent an old lady from the village to cook for us and assist us.

*

One evening we were sitting as usual in the front veranda of the house when an old lady stood at our gate, with a small trunk under her arm, and asked: 'Is this teacher Krishnan's house?'

'Yes, who are you, come in ...' I opened the gate for her. She looked at me, wrinkling her eyes and said, 'Kittu ... I have seen you as a baby and a boy. How big you have grown!' She came up to the veranda, peered closely into my wife's face and said: 'You are our daughter-in-law. I am an old friend of Kamu,' she said, referring to my mother by her maiden name. By this time Leela, who had been playing near her box, came out on hearing a new voice. At the sight of her the old lady cried: 'So this is Kamu's grandchild!' She picked her up in her arms and fondled her. Susila's heart melted at the sight of it and she said: 'Come into the house, won't you?' The old lady went in, sat under the lamp and took out of a corner of her sari a crumpled letter and gave it to me. It was from my mother: 'I am sending this letter with an old friend of mine, who was assisting me in household work when you were a baby. She then went away to live with her son. He died last year, and she has absolutely no one to support her. She came to me a few weeks ago in search of work. But I have no need for assistance nowadays. Moreover your father grows rather irritable if he sees any extra person in the house. So I have given her her bus fare and sent her on to you. I have always felt that Susila needed an assistant in the house, the baby demanding all the attention she can give. My friend will cook and look after the child. And you can give her whatever salary you like.'

While the old lady kept fondling the child, sitting on the floor, I read the letter under the hall light and my wife read it over my shoulder. We looked at each other. There was consternation in her look. There were many questions which she was aching to ask me. I adjourned to my room and she followed me.

'What shall we do?' she asked, looking desperate.

'Why do you look so panicky? We will send her back if you do not want her.'

'No, no. How can that be? Your mother has sent her. We have got to have her.'

'I think it will be good to have her. All your time is now spent in the kitchen when you are not tending the baby. I don't like you to spend all your time cooking either tiffin or food.'

'But I like it. What is wrong in it?' she asked.

'You must spend some more time reading or stitching or singing. Man or woman is not born merely to cook and eat,' I said, and added: 'You have neglected your books. Have you finished *Ivanhoe*?' She had been trying to get through *Ivanhoe* for years now, and *Lamb's Tales from Shakespeare*. But she never went beyond the fiftieth page. Her library also contained a book of hymns by a Tamil saint, a few select stanzas of Kamba Ramayana, Palgrave's *Golden Treasury* and a leather-bound *Bhagavad-Gita* in Sanskrit. I knew how fond she was of books. She was always planning how she was going to devour all the books and become the member of some library. But it never became more than an ambition.

In the earlier years of our married life we often sat together with one or other of the books, in the single top-floor room in her father's house, and tried to read. The first half an hour would be wasted because of an irresponsible mood coming over her, which made her laugh at everything: even the most solemn poem would provoke her, especially such poems as were addressed by a lover. 'My true love hath my heart and I have his.' She would laugh till she became red in the face. 'Why can't each keep his own or her own heart instead of this exchange?' She then put out her hand and searched all my pockets saying: 'In case you should take away mine!'

'Hush, listen to the poem,' I said, and she would listen to me with suppressed mirth and shake her head in disapproval. And then another line that amused her very much was 'Oh, mistress mine, where are you roaming?' She would not allow me to progress a line beyond, saying: 'I shall die of this poem some day. What is the matter with the woman loafing all over the place except where her husband is?'

However much she might understand or not understand, she derived a curious delight in turning over the pages of a book, and the great thing was that I should sit by her side and explain. While she read the Tamil classics and Sanskrit texts without my help, she liked English to be explained by me. If I showed the slightest hesitation she would declare: 'Perhaps you don't care to explain English unless you are paid a hundred rupees a month for it?'

But all that stopped after the child was born. When the child left her alone, she had to be in the kitchen, and my argument now appealed to her. She said: 'But that will mean an extra expense. What shall we pay her?'

'About eight rupees, just what everyone pays, I think,' I said.

'Oh, too much,' she said. 'I'm sure she will waste another eight rupees' worth of things. This is an unnecessary expense,' she said. I explained: 'Very necessary and we can afford it. In addition to the provident fund, why should we send thirty-five to the savings bank? I think about twenty-five rupees a month for the bank will be more than enough. Many of my friends do not save even five rupees.'

'Why do you want to follow their example? We must live within our means, and save enough.' She often declared: 'When we are old we must never trouble others for help. And remember there is a daughter, for whose marriage we must save.'

'When we bring forth some more daughters and sons...' I began, and she covered my mouth with her fingers. 'You men! What do you care! You would think differently if God somehow made you share the bothers of bringing forth! Where is your promise?' I often reiterated and confirmed our solemn pact that Leela should be our only child. And anything I said otherwise, even in jest, worried her very much.

*

With the future so much in mind she planned all our finances. She kept a watch over every rupee as it arrived, and never let it depart lightly, and as far as possible tried to end its career in the savings bank.

But now our savings were affected to the extent of at least ten rupees – as she explained: 'Six rupees, old lady's salary' (Susila stubbornly refused more than that for a year) and 'four rupees for all her waste, putting it at a minimum . . .' She was disconsolate over it for a long time, till I appeased her by saying: 'Oh, don't worry about it. When I get some money from examination papers I will give you the whole of it for the saving bank.'

In course of time we found that we simply couldn't do without the old lady. She cooked the food for us, tended the child, gave us the necessary courage when the child had fever or stomach-ache and we became distraught; she knew a lot of tricks about children's health, she grew very fond of the child and took her out and kept her very happy. She established herself as a benign elder at home, and for us it meant a great deal. Her devotion to the child enabled me to take my wife twice or thrice a month to a picture, or a walk along the river, or out shopping. My wife grew very fond of her and called her 'Granny', so did Leela. But Susila had a price to pay for this pleasure. She lost her supremacy over the kitchen and the store. The levels in the containers at the store went down in other ways than my wife calculated. Susila protested and fought against it for some time, but the old lady had her own way of brushing aside our objections. And Susila adjusted her own outlook in the matter. 'Didn't I bargain for a waste of four rupees a month? Well, it is not so hard, because she wastes only three rupees . . .' Our provision bill fluctuated by only three rupees, and it was a small price to pay for the great company and service of the old lady, who lived on one meal a day, just a handful of cooked rice and buttermilk. It was a wonder how she found the energy for so much activity. My wife often sat down with her in order to induce her to eat well, but it was of no avail.

*

I sat in my room, at the table. It was Thursday and it was a light day for me at college – only two hours of work in the afternoon, and not much preparation for that either. *Pride and Prejudice* for a senior class, non-detailed study, which meant just reading it to the boys. And a composition class. I sat at my table as usual after morning coffee looking over the books ranged on the table and casually turning over the pages of some exercise books. 'Nothing to do. Why not write poetry? Ages since I wrote anything?' My conscience had a habit of asserting itself once in six months and reminding me that I ought to write poetry. At such moments I opened the bottom-most drawer of my table and pulled out a notebook of about five hundred pages, handsomely bound. I had spent nearly a week at a local press getting this done some years ago. Its smooth pages contained my most cherished thoughts on life and nature and humanity. In addition to shorter fragments that I wrote at various times on a miscellany of topics, it contained a long unfinished poem on an epic scale to which I added a few dozen lines whenever my conscience stirred in me. I always fancied that I was born for a poetic career and some day I hoped to take the world by storm with the publication. Some of the pieces were written in English and some in Tamil. (I hadn't yet made up my mind as to which language was to be enriched with my contributions to its literature, but the language was unimportant. The chief thing seemed to be the actual effort.) I turned over the pages looking at my previous writing. The last entry was several months ago, on nature. I felt satisfied with it but felt acute discomfort on realizing that I had hardly done anything more than that. Today I was going to make up for all lost time; I took out my pen, dipped it in ink, and sat hesitating. Everything was ready except a subject. What should I write about?

My wife had come in and was stealthily watching the pages over my shoulder. As I sat biting the end of my pen, she remarked from behind me: 'Oh, the poetry book is out; why are you staring at a blank page?' Her interruption was always welcome. I put away my book, and said: 'Sit down,' dragging a stool nearer. 'No, I'm going away. Write your poetry. I won't disturb you. You may forget what you wanted to write.' 'I have not even thought of what to write,' I said. 'Some day I want to fill all the pages of this book and then it will be published and read all over the world.' At this she turned over the leaves of the notebook briskly and laughed: 'There seem to be over a thousand pages, and you have hardly filled the first ten.'

'The trouble is I have not enough subjects to write on,' I confessed. She drew herself up and asked: 'Let me see if you can write about me.'

'A beautiful idea,' I cried. 'Let me see you.' I sat up very attentively and looked at her keenly and fixedly like an artist or a photographer viewing his subject. I said: 'Just move a little to your left please. Turn your head

right. Look at me straight here. That's right ... Now I can write about you.
Don't drop your lovely eyelashes so much. You make me forget my task.
Ah, now, don't grin please. Very good, stay as you are and see how I write
now, steady...' I drew up the notebook, ran the fountain pen hurriedly
over it and filled a whole page beginning:

> She was a phantom of delight
> When first she gleamed upon my sight:
> A lovely apparition, sent
> To be a moment's ornament.

It went on for thirty lines ending:

> And yet a spirit still, and bright
> With something of an angel-light.

I constantly paused to look at her while writing: 'Perfect. Thank you. Now
listen.'

'Oh, how fast you write!' she said admiringly.

'You will also find how well I've written. Now listen,' I said, and read as
if to my class, slowly and deliberately, pausing to explain now and then.

'I never knew you could write so well.'

'It is a pity that you should have underrated me so long; but now you
know better. Keep it up,' I said. 'And if possible don't look at the pages, say
roughly between 150 and 200, in the *Golden Treasury.* Because someone
called Wordsworth has written similar poems.' This was an invitation for
her to run in and fetch her copy of the *Golden Treasury* and turn over
precisely the forbidden pages. She scoured every title and first line and at
last pitched upon the original. She read it through, and said: 'Aren't you
ashamed to copy?'

'No,' I replied. 'Mine is entirely different. He had written about someone
entirely different from my subject.'

'I wouldn't do such a thing as copying.'

'I should be ashamed to have your memory,' I said. 'You have had the
copy of the *Golden Treasury* for years now, and yet you listened to my
reading with gaping wonder! I wouldn't give you even two out of a
hundred if you were my student.' At this point our conversation was
interrupted by my old clock. It burst in upon us all of a sudden. It purred
and bleated and made so much noise that it threw us all into confusion.
Susila picked it up and tried to stop it without success, till I snatched Taine
and smothered it.

'Now, why did it do it?' she demanded. I shook my head. 'Just for pleasure,' I replied. She gazed on its brown face and said: 'It is not even showing the correct time. It is showing two o'clock, four hours ahead! Why do you keep it on your table?' I had no answer to give. I merely said: 'It has been with me for years, poor darling!'

'I will give it away this afternoon – a man comes to buy all old things.'

'No, no, take care, don't do it . . .' I warned. She didn't answer, but merely looked at it and mumbled: 'This is not the first time. When you are away it starts bleating after I have rocked the cradle for hours and made the child sleep, and I don't know how to stop it. It won't do for our house. It is a bother . . .'

That evening when I returned home from college the first thing I noticed was that my room looked different. My table had lost its usual quality and looked tidy, with all books dusted and neatly arranged. It looked like a savage, suddenly appearing neatly trimmed and groomed. The usual corner with old newspapers and magazines piled up was clean swept. The pile was gone. So was the clock on the table. The table looked barren without it. For years it had been there. With composition books still under my arm, I searched her out. I found her in the bathroom, washing the child's hands: 'What have you done with my clock?' I asked. She looked up and asked in answer: 'How do you like your room? I have cleaned and tidied it up. What a lot of rubbish you gathered there! Hereafter on every Thursday . . .'

'Answer first, where is the clock?' I said.

'Please wait, I will finish the child's business first and then answer.'

I stood at the bathroom doorway and grimly waited. She finished the child's business and came out bearing her on her arm. While passing me she seized the child's hand and tapped me under the chin with it and passed on without a word to her room. She later met me in my room as I sat gloomily gazing at the table.

'Why have you not had your tiffin or wash?' she asked, coming up behind and gently touching my shoulder.

'I don't want any tiffin,' I snapped.

'Why are you so angry?' she asked.

'Who asked you to give away that clock?' I asked.

'I didn't give it away. That man gave me twelve annas for it – a very high price indeed.'

'Now you are a . . .' I began. I looked at the paper corner and wailed. 'You have given away those papers too! There were old answer papers there . . .'

'Yes, I saw them,' she said. 'They were four years old. Why do you want old papers?' she asked. I was too angry to answer. 'You have no business to tamper with my things,' I said. 'I don't want any tiffin or coffee.' I picked up my coat, put it on and rushed out of the house, without answering her question: 'Where are you going?'

I went straight back to the college. I had no definite plan. There was no one in the college. I peeped into the debating hall, hoping there might be somebody there. But the evening was free from all engagements. I remembered that I hadn't had my coffee. I walked about the empty corridors of the college. I saw the servant and asked him to open our common room. I sent him to fetch me coffee and tiffin from the restaurant. I opened my locker and took out a few composition books. I sat correcting them till late at night. I heard the college clock strike nine. I then got up and retraced my way home. I went about my work with a businesslike air. I took off my coat, went at great speed to the bathroom and washed. I first took a peep into my wife's room. I saw her rocking the baby in the cradle. I went into the kitchen and told the old lady: 'Have the rest dined?'

The old lady answered: 'Susila waited till eight-thirty.'

I was not interested in this. Her name enraged me. I snapped: 'All right, all right, put up my leaf and serve me. I only want to know if the child had eaten.' This was to clear any misconception anyone might entertain that I was interested in Susila.

I ate in silence. I heard steps approaching, and told myself: 'Oh, she is coming.' I trembled with anxiety, lest she should be going away elsewhere. I caught a glimpse of her as she came into the dining room. I bowed my head, and went on with my dinner unconcerned, though fully aware that she was standing before me, dutifully as ever, to see that I was served correctly. She moved off to the kitchen, spoke some words to the old lady, and came out, and softly moved back to her own room. I felt angry: 'Doesn't even care to wait and see me served. She doesn't care. If she cared, would she sell my clock? I must teach her a lesson.'

After dinner I was back in my room and sat down at my table. I had never been so studious at any time in my life. I took out some composition books. I noticed on a corner of my table a small paper packet. I found enclosed in it a few coins. On the paper was written in her handwriting:

Time-piece	12 annas
Old paper	1 rupee
Total	One rupee and twelve annas.

I felt furious at the sight of it. I took the coins and went over to her room. The light was out there. I stood in the doorway and muttered: 'Who cares for this money? I can do without it.' I flung it on her bed and returned to my room.

Later, as I sat in my room working, I heard the silent night punctuated by sobs. I went to her room and saw her lying with her face to the wall, sobbing. I was completely shaken. I didn't bargain for this. I watched her silently for a moment, and collected myself sufficiently to say: 'What is the use of crying, after committing a serious blunder?' Through her sobs, she sputtered: 'What do you care, what use is it or not. If I had known you cared more for a dilapidated clock.' She didn't finish her sentence, but broke down and wept bitterly. I was baffled. I was in an anguish myself. I wanted to take her in my arms and comfort her. But there was a most forbidding pride within me. I merely said: 'If you are going to talk and behave like a normal human being, I can talk to you. I can't stand all this nonsense.'

'You go away to your room. Why do you come and abuse me at midnight?' she said.

'Stop crying, otherwise people will think a couple of lunatics are living in this house ...'

I went back to my room – a very determined man. I lay on a mat, trying to sleep, and spent a miserable and sleepless night.

We treated each other like strangers for the next forty-eight hours – all aloof and bitter. The child looked on this with puzzlement, but made it up by attending to her toys and going to the old lady for company. It was becoming a torture. I could stand no more of it. I had hoped Susila would try to make it up, and that I could immediately accept it. But she confined herself to her room and minded her business with great concentration and never took notice of me. I caught a glimpse of her face occasionally and found that her eyes were swollen. I felt a great pity for her, when I saw her slender neck, as she was going away from the bathroom. I blamed myself for being such a savage. But I couldn't approach her. The child would not help us either; she was too absorbed in her own activities. It came to a point when I simply could not stand any more of it. So the moment I returned home from college next evening I said to her, going to her room:

'Let us go to a picture ...'

'What picture?' she asked.

'*Tarzan* – at Variety Hall. You will like it very much ...'

'Baby?'

'The old lady will look after her. We shall be back at nine. Dress up ...'

I was about to say 'Look sharp,' but I checked myself and said: 'There is a lot of time. You needn't hustle yourself.'

'No, I'll be ready in ten minutes...' she said rising.

By the time we were coming out of the Variety Hall that night we were in such agreement and showed such tender concern for each other's views and feelings that we both wondered how we could have treated each other so cruelly. 'I thought we might buy a new clock, that's why I gave away the old one,' she said.

'You did the best thing possible,' I said. 'Even in the hostel that wretched clock worried everyone near about. I am glad you have rid me of it.'

'They make such beautiful ones nowadays,' she said.

'Yes, yes, right. We will go out and buy one tomorrow evening,' I said. When we reached home we decided that we should avoid quarrelling with each other since, as she put it, 'They say such quarrels affect a child's health.'

Raja Rao (b. 1908)

Raja Rao published his first novel *Kanthapura* in 1939, about a remote South Indian village of the same name, penetrated and transformed by Gandhian politics in the days before Independence. It is narrated in the voice of an old and illiterate woman; thus, its diction – musical and unexpected, capable of making sudden transitions beween the contemporary and the atavistic, the local and the political at its best, ornate and deliberately mannered at other times – is said to owe something to the rhythms of the spoken Kannada vernacular. But Rao's invention of 'Indianness' has also always been partly a European project; and one might hear Hopkins's 'sprung rhythm' in the old woman's torrent of words. Rao waited more than twenty years before he published *The Serpent and the Rope* (1960), his second novel, from which an extract is included below. The narrator here is a cosmopolitan Hindu of South Indian ancestry, much like Rao himself. Indeed, this great novel takes as its subject-matter part of Rao's own life. It is about the gradual break-up of the marriage between an Indian and a Frenchwoman after the death of their son; it is situated, principally, in Benares, where, at the beginning of the story, the last rites of the protagonist's father is performed, and in a small town in France. Rao, or at least his protagonist in the novel, is not a Hindu mystic, as he has sometimes been made out to be, and contrary to what Rao has himself seemed to suggest in the past, in occasionally vatic pronouncements. At the very beginning of the novel, the narrator declares that 'I am a Brahmin', quotes from the Sanskrit, and then distances himself from the first half of the sentence with the colloquialism of 'and all that . . .' A sentence later, the abbreviation 'etc.' again ironizes and interrupts the ecstatic confession. Indeed, part of Rao's fascination with the high, Sanskritic culture of India comes to him from the Modernists and the European Orientalist scholars; and Europe itself, unusually for an Indian novel, is part of its theme and vision (rather than the colonial centre, England), as it might be in a Modernist text. *The Serpent and the Rope* is, in many ways, a Modernist text rewritten by a cosmopolitan Brahmin. It is, on the one hand, one of the first post-colonial fictions, about, like *The Mimic Men*, the transcultural marriage, exile, migration, and the relocation of identity (it was published seven years before Naipaul's novel); and this post-colonial exploration is inserted into, and qualifies, one of the last Modernist meditations on the limits of language and form, and on the disintegration, and the redemptive possibilities, of 'high' culture.

* * *

from *The Serpent and the Rope* (1960)

I was born a Brahmin – that is, devoted to Truth and all that.

'Brahmin is he who knows Brahman,' etc. etc. . . . But how many of my ancestors since the excellent Yagnyavalkya, my legendary and Upanishadic ancestor, have really known the Truth excepting the Sage Madhava, who founded an Empire or, rather, helped to build an Empire, and wrote some of the most profound of Vedantic texts since Sri Sankara? There were others, so I'm told, who left hearth and riverside fields, and wandered to mountains distant and hermitages 'to see God face to face'. And some of them did see God face to face and built temples. But when they died – for indeed they did 'die' – they too must have been burnt by tank or grove or meeting of two rivers, and they too must have known they did not die. I can feel them in me, and know they knew they did not die. Who is it that tells me that they did not die? Who but me.

So my ancestors went one by one and were burnt, and their ashes have gone down the rivers.

Whenever I stand in a river I remember how when young, on the day the monster ate the moon and the day fell into an eclipse, I used with *til* and *kusha* grass to offer the manes my filial devotion. For withal I was a good Brahmin. I even knew Grammar and the Brahma Sutras, read the Upanishads at the age of four, and was given the holy thread at seven – because my mother was dead and I had to perform her funeral ceremonies, year after year – my father having married again. So with wet cloth and an empty stomach, with devotion, and sandal paste on my forehead, I fell before the rice-balls of my mother and I sobbed. I was born an orphan, and have remained one. I have wandered the world and have sobbed in hotel rooms and in trains, have looked at the cold mountains and sobbed, for I had no mother. One day, and that was when I was twenty-two, I sat in an hotel – it was in the Pyrenees – and I sobbed, for I knew I would never see my mother again.

They say my mother was very beautiful and very holy. Grandfather Kittanna said, 'Her voice, son, was like a veena playing to itself, after evensong is over, when one has left the instrument beside a pillar in the temple. Her voice too was like those musical pillars at the Rameshwaram temple – it resonated from the depths, from some unknown space, and one felt God shone the brighter with this worship. She reminded me of Concubine Chandramma. She had the same voice. That was long before your time,' Grandfather concluded, 'it was in Mysore, and I have not been there these fifty years.'

Grandfather Kittanna was a noble type, a heroic figure among us. It must be from him I have this natural love of the impossible – I can think that a building may just decide to fly, or that Stalin may become a saint, or that all the Japanese have become Buddhist monks, or that Mahatma Gandhi is walking with us now. I sometimes feel I can make the railway line stand up, or the elephant bear its young one in twenty-four days; I can see an aeroplane float over a mountain and sit carefully on a peak, or I could go to Fathe-Pur-Sikri and speak to the Emperor Akbar. It would be difficult for me not to think, when I am in Versailles, that I hear the uncouth voice of Roi Soleil, or in Meaux that Bossuet rubs his snuff in the palm of his hand, as they still do in India, and offers a pinch to me. I can sneeze with it, and hear Bossuet make one more of his funeral orations. For Bossuet believed – and so did Roi Soleil – that he never would die. And if they've died, I ask you, where indeed did they go?

Grandfather Kittanna was heroic in another manner. He could manage a horse, the fiercest, with a simplicity that made it go where it did not wish to go. I was brought up with the story how Grandfather Kittanna actually pushed his horse into the Chandrapur forest one evening – the horse, Sundar, biting his lips off his face; the tiger that met him in the middle of the jungle; the leap Sundar gave, high above my Lord Sher, and the custard-apples that splashed on his back, so high he soared – and before my grandfather knew where he was, with sash and blue-Maratha saddle, there he stood, Sundar, in the middle of the courtyard. The lamps were being lit, and when stableman Chowdayya heard the neigh he came and led the steed to the tank for a swish of water. Grandfather went into the bathroom, had his evening bath – he loved it to be very hot, and Aunt Seethamma had always to serve him potful after potful – and he rubbed himself till his body shone as the young of a banana tree. He washed and sat in prayer. When Atchakka asked, 'Sundar is all full of scratches...?' then Grandfather spoke of the tiger, and the leap. For him, if the horse had soared into the sky and landed in holy Brindavan he would not have been much surprised. Grandfather Kittanna was like that. He rode Sundar for another three years, and then the horse died – of some form of dysentery, for, you know, horses die, too – and we buried him on the top of the Kittur Hill, with fife and filigree. We still make an annual pilgrimage to his tomb, and for Hyderabad reasons we cover it up with a rose-coloured muslin, like the Muslims do. Horses we think came from Arabia, and so they need a Muslim burial. Where is Sundar now? Where?

The impossible, for Grandfather, was always possible. He never – he, a Brahmin – never for once was afraid of gun or sword, and yet what depth he had in his prayers. When he came out, Aunt Seethamma used to say, 'He has the shine of a Dharma Raja.'

But I, I've the fright of gun and sword, and the smallest trick of violence can make me run a hundred leagues. But once having gone a hundred leagues I shall come back a thousand for I do not really have the fear of fear. I only have fear.

I love rivers and lakes, and make my home easily by any waterside hamlet. I love palaces for their echoes, their sense of never having seen anything but the gloomy. Palaces remind me of old and venerable women, who never die. They look after others so much – I mean, orphans of the family always have great-aunts, who go on changing from orphan to orphan – that they remain ever young. One such was Aunt Lakshamma. She was married to a minister once, and he died when she was seven or eight. And since then my uncles and their daughters, my mother's cousins and their grandchildren, have always had Lakshamma to look after them, for an orphan in a real household is never an orphan. She preserved, did Lakshamma, all the clothes of the young in her eighteenth-century steel and *sheesham* trunk, in the central hall, and except when there was a death in the house these clothes never saw the light of the sun. Some of them were fifty years old, they said. The other day – that is, some seven or eight years ago – when we were told that Aunt Lakshamma, elder to my grandfather by many years, had actually died, I did not believe it. I thought she would live three hundred years. She never would complain or sigh. She never wept. We never wept when she died. For I cannot understand what death means.

My father, of course, loved me. He never let me stray into the hands of Lakshamma. He said: 'Auntie smells bad, my son. I want you to be a hero and a prince.' Some time before my mother died, it seems she had a strange vision. She saw three of my past lives, and in each one of them I was a son, and of course I was always her eldest born, tall, slim, deep-voiced, deferential and beautiful. In one I was a prince. That is why I had always to be adorned with diamonds – diamonds on my forehead, chest and ears. She died, they say, having sent someone to the goldsmith, asking if my hair-flower were ready. When she died they covered her with white flowers – jasmines from Coimbatore and champacs from Chamundi – and with a lot of kumkum on her they took her away to the burning-ghat. They shaved me completely, and when they returned they gave me Bengal gram, and some sweets. I could not understand what had happened. Nor do I understand now. I know my mother, my Mother Gauri, is not dead, and yet I am an orphan. Am I always going to be an orphan?

That my father married for a third time – my stepmother having died leaving three children, Saroja, Sukumari, and the eldest, Kapila – is another story. My new stepmother loved me very dearly, and I could not think of a home without her bright smile and the song that shone like the copper vessels in the house. When she smiled her mouth touched her ears – and she gave me everything I wanted. I used to weep, though, thinking of my own mother. But then my father died. He died on the third of the second Moon-month when the small rains had just started. I have little to tell you of my father's death, except that I did not love him; but that after he died I knew him and loved him when his body was such pure and white spread ash. Even now I have dreams of him saying to me: 'Son, why did you not love me, you, my Eldest Son?' I cannot repent, as I do not know what repentance is. For I must first believe there is death. And that is the central fact – I do not believe that death is. So, for whom shall I repent?

Of course, I love my father now. Who could not love one that was protection and kindness itself, though he never understood that my mother wanted me to be a prince? And since I could not be a prince – I was born a Brahmin, and so how could I be king? – I wandered my life away, and became a holy vagabond. If Grandfather simply jumped over tigers in the jungles, how many tigers of the human jungles, how many accidents to plane and car have I passed by? And what misunderstandings and chasms of hatred have lain between me and those who first loved, and then hated, me? Left to myself, I became alone and full of love. When one is alone one always loves. In fact, it is because one loves, and one is alone, one does not die.

*

I went to Benares, once. It was in the month of March, and there was still a pinch of cold in the air. My father had just died and I took Vishalakshi, my second stepmother, and my young stepbrother Sridhara – he was only eleven months old – and I went to Benares. I was twenty-two then, and

I had been to Europe; I came back when Father became ill. Little Mother was very proud of me – she said: 'He's the bearing of a young pipal tree, tall and sacred, and the serpent-stones around it. We must go round him to become sacred.' But the sacred Brahmins of Benares would hear none of this. They knew my grandfather and his grandfather and his great-grandfather again, and thus for seven generations – Ramakrishnayya and Ranganna, Madhavaswamy and Somasundarayya, Manjappa and Gangad-harayya – and for each of them they knew the sons and grandsons – (the daughters, of course, they did not quite know) – and so, they stood on their rights. 'Your son,' they said to Little Mother, 'has been to Europe, and has wed a European and he has no sacred thread. Pray, Mother, how could the manes be pleased.' So Little Mother yielded and just fifty silver rupees made everything holy. Some carcass-bearing Brahmins – 'We're the men of the four shoulders,' they boast – named my young brother Son of Ceremony in their tempestuous high and low of hymns – the quicker the better, for in Benares there be many dead, and all the dead of all the ages, the successive generations of manes after manes, have accumulated in the sky. And you could almost see them layer on layer, on the night of a moon-eclipse, fair and pale and tall and decrepit, fathers, grandfathers, great-grandfathers, mothers, sisters, brothers, nephews; friends, kings, yog-ins, maternal uncles – all, all they accumulate in the Benares air and you can see them. They have a distanced, dull-eyed look – and they ask – they beg for this and that, and your round white rice-balls and sesame seed give the peace they ask for. The sacred Brahmin too is pleased. He has his fifty rupees. Only my young brother, eleven months old, does not understand. When his mother is weeping – for death takes a long time to be recognized – my brother pulls and pulls at the sari-fringe. I look at the plain, large river that is ever so young, so holy – like my Mother. The temple bells ring and the crows are all about the white rice-balls. 'The manes have come, look!' say the Brahmins. My brother crawls up to them saying 'Caw-Caw', and it's when he sees the monkeys that he jumps for Little Mother's lap. He's so tender and fine-limbed, is my brother. Little Mother takes him into her lap, opens her choli and gives him the breast.

The Brahmins are still muttering something. Two or three of them have already washed their feet in the river and are coming up, looking at their navels or their fine gold rings. They must be wondering what silver we would offer. We come from far – and from grandfather to grandfather, they knew what every one in the family had paid, in Moghul Gold or in Rupees of the East India Company, to the more recent times with the British Queen buxom and small-faced on the round, large silver. I would rather have thrown the rupees to the begging monkeys than to the Brah-mins. But Little Mother was there. I took my brother in my arms, and I gave the money, silver by silver, to him. And gravely, as though he knew what he was doing, he gave the rupees to the seated Brahmins. He now knew too that Father was dead. Then suddenly he gave such a shriek as though he saw Father near us – not as he was but as he had become, blue, transcorporeal. Little Mother always believes the young see the dead more clearly than we the corrupt do. And Little Mother must be right. Anyway, it stopped her tears, and now that the clouds had come, we went down the steps of the Harischchandra ghat, took a boat, and floated down the river.

I told Little Mother how Tulsidas had written the *Ramayana* just there, next to the Rewa Palace, and Kabir had been hit on the head by Saint Ramanand. The saint had stumbled on the head of the Muslim weaver and had cried Ram-Ram, so Kabir stood up and said, 'Now, My Lord, you be my Guru and I Thy disciple.' That is how the weaver became so great a devotee and poet. Farther down, the Buddha himself had walked and had washed his alms-bowl – he had gone up the steps and had set the wheel of Law a-turning. The aggregates, said the Buddha, make for desire and aversion, pleasure and ill, and one must seek that from which there is no returning. Little Mother listened to all this and seemed so convinced. She played with the petal-like fingers of my brother and when she saw a parrot in the sky, 'Look, look, little one,' she said, 'that is the Parrot of Rama.' And she began to sing:

> *O parrot, my parrot of Rama*

and my little brother went to profoundest sleep.

My father was really dead. But Little Mother smiled. In Benares one knows death is as illusory as the mist in the morning. The Ganges is always there – and when the sun shines, oh, how hot it can still be . . .

* * *

I wrote postcards to friends in Europe. I told them I had come to Benares because Father had died, and I said the sacred capital was really a surrealist city. You never know where reality starts and where illusion ends; whether the Brahmins of Benares are like the crows asking for funereal rice-balls, saying 'Caw-Caw'; or like the Saddhus, by their fires, lost in such beautiful magnanimity as though love was not something one gave to another, but one gave to oneself. His trident in front of him, his holy books open, some saffron cloth drying anywhere – on bare bush or on broken wall, sometimes with an umbrella stuck above, and a dull fire eyeing him, as though the fire in Benares looked after the saints, not the cruel people of the sacred city – each Saddhu sat, a Shiva. And yet when you looked up you saw the lovely smile of some concubine, just floating down her rounded bust and nimble limbs, for a prayer and a client. The concubines of Benares are the most beautiful of any in the world, they say; and some say, too, that they worship the wife of Shiva, Parvathi herself, that they may have the juice of youth in their limbs. That is why Damodhara Gupta so exaltedly started his book on bawds with Benares. 'O Holy Ganga, Mother Ganga, thou art purity itself, coming down from Shiva's hair.' When you see so many limbs go purring and bursting on the ghats by the Ganges, how can limbs have any meaning? Death makes passion beautiful. Death makes the concubine inevitable. I remembered again Grandfather saying, 'Your mother had such a beautiful voice. She had a voice like Concubine Chandramma. And that was in Mysore, and fifty years ago.'

I could not forget Madeleine – how could I? Madeleine was away and in Aix-en-Provence. Madeleine had never recovered – in fact she never did recover – from the death of Pierre. She had called him Krishna till he was seven months old. Then when he began to have those coughs Madeleine knew: mothers always know what is dangerous for their children. And on that Saturday morning, returning from her Collège Madeleine knew, she knew that in four weeks, in three and in two and in one, the dread disease would take him away. That was why from the moment he was born – we had him take birth in a little, lovely maternity home near Bandol – she spoke of all the hopes she had in him. He must be tall and twenty-three; he must go to an Engineering Institute and build bridges for India when he grew up. Like all melancholic people, Madeleine loved bridges. She felt Truth was always on the other side, and so sometimes I told her that next time she must be born on the Hudson. I bought her books on Provence or on Sardinia, which had such beautiful ivy-covered bridges built by the Romans. One day she said, 'Let's go and see this bridge at St-Jean-Pied-de-Port,' that she had found in a book on the Pays Basque. We drove through abrupt, arched Ardèche, and passing through Cahors I showed her the Pont de Valentré. She did not care for it. It was like Reinhardt's scenario at Salzburg, she said. When we went on to the Roman Bridge of St-Jean-Pied-de-Port she said, 'Rama, it makes me shiver.' She had been a young girl at the time of the Spanish Civil War, so we never could go over to Spain. Then it was we went up to some beautiful mountain town – perhaps it was Pau, for I can still see the huge chateau, the one built by Henry IV – and maybe it was on that night, in trying to comfort Madeleine, that

Krishna was conceived. She would love to have a child of mine, she said – and we had been married seven months.

At that time Madeleine was twenty-six, and I was twenty-one. We had first met at the University of Caen. Madeleine had an uncle – her parents had died leaving her an estate, so it was being looked after by Oncle Charles. He was from Normandy, and you know what that means.

Madeleine was so lovely, with golden hair – on her mother's side she came from Savoy – and her limbs had such pure unreality. Madeleine was altogether unreal. That is why, I think, she never married anyone – in fact she had never touched anyone. She said that during the Nazi occupation, towards the end of 1943, a German officer had tried to touch her hair; it looked so magical, and it looked the perfect Nordic hair. She said he had brought his hands near her face, and she had only to smile and he could not do anything. He bowed and went away.

It was the Brahmin in me, she said, the sense that touch and untouch are so important, which she sensed; and she would let me touch her. Her hair was gold, and her skin for an Indian was like the unearthed marble with which we built our winter palaces. Cool, with the lake about one, and the peacock strutting in the garden below. The seventh-hour of music would come, and all the palace would see itself lit. Seeing oneself is what we always seek; the world, as the great Sage Sankara said, is like a city seen in a mirror. Madeleine was like the Palace of Amber seen in moonlight. There is such a luminous mystery – the deeper you go, the more you know yourself. So Krishna was born.

The bridge was never crossed. Madeleine had a horror of crossing bridges. Born in India she would have known how in Malabar they send off gunfire to frighten the evil spirits, as you cross a bridge. Whether the gunfire went off or not, Krishna could never cross the bridge of life. That is why with some primitive superstition Madeleine changed his name and called him Pierre from the second day of his illness. '*Pierre tu es, et sur cette pierre ...*' she quoted. And she said – for she, a French woman, like an Indian woman was shy, and would not call me easily by my name – she had said, 'My love, the gods of India will be angry, that you a Brahmin married a non-Brahmin like me; why should they let me have a child called Krishna. So sacred is that name.' And the little fellow did not quite know what he was to do when he was called Pierre. I called him Pierre and respected her superstition. For all we do is really superstition. Was I really called Ramaswamy, or was Madeleine called Madeleine?

The illness continued. Good doctor Pierre Marmoson, a specialist in child medicine – especially trained in America – gave every care available.

But bronchopneumonia is bronchopneumonia, particularly after a severe attack of chickenpox. Madeleine, however, believed more in my powers of healing than in the doctors. So that when the child actually lay in my arms and steadied itself and kicked straight and lay quiet, Madeleine could not believe that Pierre was dead. The child had not even cried.

We were given special permission by the Préfet des Bouches-du-Rhône to cremate Pierre among the olive trees behind the Villa Ste-Anne. It was a large villa and one saw on a day of the mistral the beautiful Mont Ste-Victoire, as Cézanne must have seen it day after day, clear as though you could talk to it. The mistral blew and blew so vigorously: one could see one's body float away, like pantaloon, vest, and scarf, and one's soul sit and shine on the top of Mont Ste-Victoire. The dead, they say in Aix, live in the cathedral tower, the young and the virgins do – there is even a Provençal song about it – so Madeleine went to her early morning Mass and to vespers. She fasted on Friday, she a heathen, she began to light candles to the Virgin, and she just smothered me up in tenderness. She seemed so far that nearness was farther than any smell or touch. There was no bridge – all bridges now led to Spain.

So when my father had said he was very ill, and wished I could come, she said, 'Go, and don't you worry about anything. I will look after myself.' It seemed wiser for me to go. Madeleine would continue to teach and I would settle my affairs at home. Mother's property had been badly handled by the estate agent Sundarrayya, the rents not paid, the papers not in order: and I thought I would go and see the University authorities too, for a job was being kept vacant for me. The Government had so far been very kind – and my scholarship continued. Once my doctorate was over I would take Madeleine home, and she would settle with me – somehow I always thought of a house white, single-storeyed on a hill and by a lake – and I would go day after day to the University and preach to them the magnificence of European civilization. I had taken History, and my special subject was the Albigensian heresy. I was trying to link up the Bogomolites and the Druzes, and thus search back for the Indian background – Jain or maybe Buddhist – of the Cathars. The 'pure' were dear to me. Madeleine, too, got involved in them, but for a different reason. Touch, as I have said, was always distasteful to her, so she liked the untouching Cathars, she loved their celibacy. She implored me to practise the ascetic *brahmacharya* of my ancestors, and I was too proud a Brahmin to feel defeated. The bridge was anyhow there, and could not be crossed. I knew I would never go to Spain.

*

India was wonderful to me. It was like a juice that one is supposed to drink to conquer a kingdom or to reach the deathless – juice of rare jasmine or golden myrobalan, brought from the nether world by a hero or dark mermaid. It gave me sweetness and the *délire* of immortality. I could not die, I knew; and the world seemed so whole, even death when it was like my father's. So simple: when it came he said, 'I go,' and looked at us, with just one tear at the end of his left eye; then stretched himself out, and died.

The smell of India was sweet. But Madeleine was very far. Little Mother when she saw the photographs of Madeleine and the baby did not say anything, but went inside to the sanctuary to lay flowers on her *Ramayana*. She never spoke about it at all, but whenever she saw me sad she said, 'Birth and death are the illusions of the non-Self'. And as though before my own sorrow her unhappiness seemed petty and untrue, she seemed suddenly to grow happier and happier. She started singing the whole day; she even brought out her veena from the box where it had not been touched for three years, and started singing. My father who was still alive then said, 'Oh, I suppose you want to show off your great musical learning to the Eldest.' Even so he laid his book aside, a rare act for him to do, and started to listen to the music.

My grandfather said Father had such a wonderful voice when young – just like a woman's voice. 'Later, when that Mathematics got hold of him – for figures are like gnomes, they entice you and lead you away, with backward turned faces, to the world of the unknown–' he continued, 'your father never sang a single *kirtanam* again. Oh, you should have heard him sing *Purandaradasa*.' I never heard my father sing, but this I know, he had a grave and slow-moving voice such as musicians possess. His mathematics absorbed him so deeply that you saw him more with a pencil – his glasses stuck to the end of his nose (he had a well-shapen, but long and somewhat pointed nose) – than with a veena on his arm. Father was a mathematician, and when he was not able to solve a problem he would turn to Sanskrit Grammar. Panini was his hobby all his life, and later he included Bharthrihari among the great Grammarians. Father had no use for Philosophy at all – he called it the old hag's description of the menu in paradise. For him curry of cucumber or of pumpkin made no difference to your intestines. 'The important fact is that you eat – and you live.'

Father's greatest sorrow was that I did not take his mathematical studies a little further. He would say, 'The British will not go till we can shame them with our intelligence. And what is more intellectual than mathematics, son?' He worshipped Euler, and quoted with admiration his famous

saying on the algebraic proof of God. That Father's work on Roger Rama-
nujam's identities or on Waring's problem were accepted by the world
only made him feel happy that it made Indian Freedom so much the
nearer. He was happy though that I had taken the Albigensian heresy as a
subject for research, for he thought India should be made more real to the
European.

He had never been to Europe. First, Grandfather was against the eldest
son-in-law going across the seas. Then when Grandfather was reconciled
with the changing values of the world there were too many responsibilities
at home. And Father, in any case, did not care for travel. Like many persons
of his generation I think he could not forget his bath and the Brahmin
atmosphere of the house – the ablutions in the morning, with the women
singing hymns, the perfume of camphor, and the smell of garlic and
incense when the daughter came home for childbirth. He disliked my
marriage, I think chiefly because my wife could not sing at an Arathi; but
before the world he boasted of his intellectual daughter-in-law, and had a
picture of me and Madeleine on his table.

He never thought he would die, so he never thought of the funeral
ceremonies. Grandfather must have thought of it, for when I went to ask
his advice as to where and what should be done Grandfather had all the
answers ready: the ceremony had to be in Benares, and it had to be in my
brother's name. 'Not that I do not love you, Rama. How can I not love
my daughter's own eldest born? But that is what the elders have laid
down; and it has come from father to son, generation after generation.
Why change it today? Why give importance to unimportant things? God is
not hidden in a formula, nor is affection confined to funeral ceremonies.
Be what you are. I like the way you go about thinking on the more serious
things of Vedanta. Leave religion to smelly old fogeys like me,' he concluded, and I almost touched his feet. He was so noble and humble,
Grandfather was.

It was not the same thing with my uncles, but that is a different story.

*

Thus Benares was predestined, and as I went down the river with Little
Mother, Sridhara on her lap, I could so clearly picture Madeleine. She
would be seated at the left window of the Villa Saint-Anne, patching some
shirt of mine, and thinking that as the sun sets and the sun rises, she
would soon have the winter out. Then the house had to be got ready, and
before the house was ready I would be there, back in Aix. Not that it gave
her any happiness – but it had to be, so it would be. I was part of the

rotation of a system – just as July 14 would come, and she would spend the two weeks till the thirtieth getting the house in order before we went to the mountain for a month. After that we would go to see her uncle for three days on a family visit, take a week off in Paris, and then come down to Aix before the third week of September. On October 1 term begins and on waking up she would see my face.

Affection is just a spot in the geography of the mind.

For Madeleine geography was very real, almost solid. She smelt the things of the earth, as though sound, form, touch, taste, smell were such realities that you could not go beyond them – even if you tried. Her Savoyard ancestry must have mingled with a lot of Piedmontese, so that this girl from Charente still had the thyme and the lavender almost at the roots of her hair. She said that when she was young she loved to read of bullfights, and the first picture she had ever stuck against the wall of her room was of Don Castillero y Abavez, who had won at the young age of nineteen every distinction of a great *torrero*. She hated killing animals, however, and I did not have to persuade her much to become a vegetarian. But sometimes her warm Southern blood would boil as never my thin Brahmin blood could, and when she was indignant – and always for some just cause – whether about the injustice done to teachers at the Lycée de Moulin, or the pitiful intrigue in some provincial miners' union at Lens or St Étienne, she would first grow warm and then cold with anger, and burst into tears, and weep a whole hour. This also explains how during the occupation she was closer to the Communists than to the Catholics or Socialists, though she hated tyranny of all sorts. What I think Madeleine really cared for was a disinterested devotion to any cause, and she loved me partly because she felt India had been wronged by the British, and because she would, in marrying me, know and identify herself with a great people. She regretted whenever she read a Greek text not having been born at the time of the Athenian Republic; which also explained her great enthusiasm for Paul Valéry. I, on the other hand, had been brought up in the *gnya-gnyaneries* of Romain Rolland, and having read his books on Vivekananda and Ramakrishna, I almost called him a Rishi and a Saint. Valéry seemed to be too disdainful, too European. For me, the Albigensian humility seemed sweeter, and more naturally Indian.

Loving Valéry, Madeleine, who taught History at the Collège, loved more the whole of Ancient Greece. And when I introduced her to Indian History her joy was so great that she started researching on the idea of the Holy Grail. There is an old theory that the Holy Grail was a Buddhist conception – that the cup of Christ was a Buddhist relic which the Nestorians took over and brought to Persia; there the legend mingled with Manichaeism, and became towards the end of the Middle Ages the strange story of the Holy Grail. The Holy Grail also gave Madeleine's sense of geography a natural movement. She loved countries and epochs not our own.

Whereas I was born to India, where the past and the present are for ever knit into one whole experience – going down the Ganges who could not imagine the Compassionate One Himself coming down the foothpath, by the Saraju, to wash the mendicant-bowl? – and so for me time and space had very relative importance. I remember how in 1946, when I first came to Europe – I landed in Naples – Europe did not seem so far nor so alien. Nor when later I put my face into Madeleine's golden hair and smelt its rich acridity with the olfactory organs of a horse – for I am a Sagittarian by birth – did I feel it any the less familiar. I was too much of a Brahmin to be unfamiliar with anything, such is the pride of caste and race, and lying by Madeleine it was she who remarked, 'Look at this pale skin beside your golden one. Oh, to be born in a country where tradition is so alive,' she once said, 'that even the skin of her men is like some royal satin, softened and given a new shine through the rubbing of ages.' I, however, being so different, never really noted any difference. To me difference was inborn – like my being the eldest son of my father, or like my grandfather being the Eight-Pillared House Ramakrishnayya, and you had just to mention his name anywhere in Mysore State, even to the Maharaja, and you were offered a seat, a wash, and a meal, and a coconut-and-shawl adieu. To me difference was self-created, and so I accepted that Madeleine was different. That is why I loved her so. In fact, even Little Mother, who sat in front of me – how could I not love her, though she was so different from my own mother? In difference there is the acceptance of one's self as a reality – and the perspective gives the space for love.

*

In some ways – I thought that day, as the boat, now that evening was soon going to fall, was moving upstream, with a fine, clear wind sailing against us – in some ways how like Madeleine was Little Mother. They both had the same shy presence, both rather silent and remembering everything; they loved, too, more than is customary. Both knew by birth that life was no song but a brave suffering, and that at best there are moments of bridal joy with occasionally a drive over a bridge – and then the return to the earth and maybe to widowhood.

I remember very well that day, just three days before our marriage. We had been to Rouen, just because we had nothing better to do, and

Madeleine seemed so, so sad. She said, 'I have a fear, a deep fear somewhere here; I have a fear I will kill you, that something in me will kill you, and I shall be a widow. Oh, beloved,' she begged, 'do not marry me. Let us part. There is still time.' She was twenty-six then, and I twenty-one. I did not care for death and I said to her, as one does with deep certitude at such moments, 'I will never die till you give me permission, Madeleine.' She stopped and looked at me as though she were looking at a god, and turning laughed, for we were by the statue of Henriette de Bruges, who for the birth of her son Charles, later to become the Dark Hero of the Spanish Wars, had a statue erected to herself. The child Charles, with the crown of Burgundy already on his small plump head, was lying on her lap. The statue was stupid, but it seemed somehow an answer. And when we got back to Paris and were married at the Mairie of the VIIth Arrondissement – for I then lived in the rue St-Dominique – we bought ourselves a book on Bruges that is still with me. It is one of the few things I could save for myself when the catastrophe came.

Bruges must be beautiful though. I have never been to that city of canals and waterfronts, but the ugly, fat face of Henriette de Bruges will always remain a patron saint of some mysterious and unperformed marriage.

*

Little Mother, having recovered her peace, started reciting as at home Sankara's *Nirvana-Astakam*. I have loved it since the time Grandfather Kittanna returned from Benares and taught it to me. I would start on '*Mano-budhi Ahankara...*' with a deep and learned voice, for after all I had been to a Sanskrit school. Little Mother followed me, and verse after verse: '*Shivoham, Shivoham*, I am Shiva, I am Shiva,' she chanted with me. All the lights in Benares were by now lit, and even the funeral pyres on the ghats seemed like some natural illumination. The monkeys must have gone to the tree tops, and the Saddhus must be at their meals. Evening drums were beating from every temple, and one heard in the midst of it a train rumble over the Dalhousie Bridge. It was the long Calcutta Mail, going down to Moghul Sarai.

On the other side lay Ramnagarh – a real city for Rama. Every year people still came down to see the festival of Rama, and men and women and the Royal family with horses, fife and elephants enacted the story of Rama. Little Mother felt unhappy we were too late for it this year. I told her I would soon come back to India and take her on a long pilgrimage. I promised her Badrinath and even Kailas. I knew there would be no

Himalayas for me. Shridara woke and as Little Mother started suckling the
child again, I chanted to her the *Kāshikapurādinātha Kalābhairavam bhajé*:

> I worship Kalabhairava, Lord of the city of Kashi,
> Blazing like a million suns;
> Our great saviour in our voyage across the world,
> The blue-throated, the three-eyed grantor of all desires;
> The lotus-eyed who is the death of death,
> The imperishable one,
> Holding the rosary of the human bone and the trident
> *Kāshikapurādinātha Kalābhairavam bhajé*.

Benares is eternal. There the dead do not die nor the living live. The
dead come down to play on the banks of the Ganges, and the living who
move about, and even offer rice-balls to the manes, live in the illusion of a
vast night and a bright city. Once again at the request of Little Mother I
sang out a hymn of Sri Sankara's, and this time it was *Sri Dakshinamurti
Stotram*. Maybe it was the evening, or something deeper than me that in
me unawares was touched. I had a few tears rolling down my cheeks.
Holiness is happiness. Happiness is holiness. That is why a Brahmin should
be happy, I said to myself, and laughed. How different from Pascal's, '*Le
silence éternal des grands espaces infinis m'effraie*.'

The road to the infinite is luminous if you see it as a city lit in a mirror.
If you want to live in it you break the glass. The unreal is possible because
the real is. But if you want to go from the unreal to the real, it would be
like a man trying to walk into a road that he sees in a hall of mirrors.
Dushasana* is none other than the *homme moyen sensuel*.

For the bourgeois the world, and the bank, and the notary are real; and
the wedding ring as well. We spent, Madeleine and I, the last few thousand
francs we had, to buy ourselves two thin gold wedding rings the day
before our marriage. I still remember how they cost us 3,700 francs apiece,
and as we had a little over 9,000 francs we went up the Boulevard St-
Michel to eat at the Indo-Chinese Restaurant, rue Monsieur. We had rice
for dinner and Madeleine felt happy. It was her recognition of India.

The next day at eleven we went up to the Mairie with two witnesses.
One was Count R., an old and dear friend of Father's who had worked with
de Broglie; unable to go back to Hungary because of the Communist
revolution there, he had settled in Paris. The other, from Madeleine's side,
was her cousin Roland, who was an officer in the French Marine. Having

---

* A character in the *Mahabharata*, humiliated because he had walked into a mirror
thinking it was a path in the park.

seen a great deal of the world, an Indian was for him no stranger – he even knew Trichinopoly and Manamadurai – and he came to the marriage in his brilliant uniform.

Madeleine's uncle, of course, disapproved of all this outlandish matrimony. Oncle Charles was settled as a *notaire* at Rouen and he would not admit of any disturbance in his peaceful provincial existence. It was said of him that when he married his second wife – she was a divorcée – he married her without telling his old mother. It would have upset old Madame Roussellin too much – she lived in Arras. His second marriage was a most unhappy one, but he was proud of his brilliant wife; she made his position secure, and he loved her. Madeleine was her favourite, but lest the child should see too much of his married life the uncle very studiously avoided sending for her.

Madeleine was brought up by an unmarried aunt at Saintonge, in the Charente, but she saw her cousins from time to time, and they were gay with her. They teased her and said she would end up in a convent. Roland even discovered some mysterious tribe in the Australasian isles – they were called the Kuru-buri, I think – and said that on one of his expeditions he would land her on that blessed isle. 'Your virtue will be appreciated there, Mado,' he would say, 'and imagine adding twenty thousand more to Christendom, before some Gauguin goes discovering the beauty of their virgins and peoples the island with many blue-eyed children.' Such things were never said in front of me, but one day Madeleine, finding what a prude I was, told me the story with generous detail. 'Imagine me a Catholic Sister,' she said; 'I who love the Greeks. Tell me, Rama, am I not a pagan?'

I was the pagan, in fact, going down the Ganges, feeling such worship for this grave and knowing river. Flowers floated downstream, and now and again we hit against a fish or log of wood. Sometimes too a burnt piece of fuel from some funeral pyre would hit against the oars of the boat. People say there are crocodiles in the Ganges, and some add that bits of dead bodies, only half-burnt, are often washed down by the river. But I have never seen these myself. Night, a rare and immediate night, was covering the vast expanse of the Benares sky. Somewhere on these very banks the Upanishadic Sages, perhaps four, five, or six thousand years ago, had discussed the roots of human understanding. And Yagnyavalkya had said to Maiteryi, 'For whose sake, verily, does a husband love his wife? Not for the sake of his wife, but verily for the sake of the Self in her.' Did Little Mother love the Self in my father? Did I love the Self in Madeleine? I knew I did not. I knew I could not love: that I did not even love Pierre. I took a handful of Ganges water in my hand, and poured it back to the river. It was for Pierre.

Ruskin Bond (b. 1934)

Ruskin Bond was born in Kasauli, Himachal, in 1934, and grew up in Jamnagar, Dehradun, and Simla. He is an Anglo-Indian who has 'stayed on', though he does not write too often, or too explicitly, from the point of view of being an Anglo-Indian, but as one who has merged casually, almost calculatedly, with his surroundings, which have mainly been the hill-stations of North India, like the Mussoorie where he lives. His merging and self-effacement seemed to have been so complete that at one time it appeared he did not exist at all, despite having had an early and successful start: his first novel, *The Room on the Roof*, written when he was only seventeen, won the John Llewelyn Rhys Memorial Prize. After a long interim of depression and self-doubt in his middle years, he returned to his vocation first as a children's writer, a move that rejuvenated his creative powers. He is one of the few Indian writers who have proved, without the benefit of expensive publicity, that a local and healthy readership exists in India for Indian English writing; when, after a period of silence, he began to be published again by the relatively new Penguin India, his books found an immediate and receptive audience, which ensured that his fiction remained in print, and that new books appeared at regular intervals. He is an 'inner émigré', an outsider who has not moved far from where he began, either in terms of habitation or craft, and he has converted the habit of permanent residency, both in the hills of Uttar Pradesh, and in the genre of a certain kind of short story, into a virtue. The subtle tropes of dislocation in his writing have to do with, as in Larkin or Edward Thomas, the image of the train or the railway platform, where each unnamed stop on an Indian railway route has something of the unexpectedness of Thomas's Adlestrop. His intimacy with his locale has earned him comparisons with Wordsworth, but Bond is not an architect of overarching theoretical designs as Wordsworth was; a more apt analogy would be with John Clare, a kindred and similarly self-effacing 'spirit of place', whose seemingly naive vernacular had the ability to express the different, and tender, gradations of belonging.

* * *

'The Night Train at Deoli' (1988)

When I was at college I used to spend my summer vacations in Dehra, at my grandmother's place. I would leave the plains early in May and return late in July. Deoli was a small station about thirty miles from Dehra; it marked the beginning of the heavy jungles of the Indian Terai.

The train would reach Deoli at about five in the morning, when the station would be dimly lit with electric bulbs and oil lamps, and the jungle across the railway tracks would just be visible in the faint light of dawn. Deoli had only a lone platform, an office for the stationmaster and a waiting room. The platform boasted a tea stall, a fruit vendor, and a few stray dogs; not much else, because the train stopped there for only ten minutes before rushing on into the forests.

Why it stopped at Deoli, I don't know. Nothing ever happened there. Nobody got off the train and nobody got on. There were never any coolies on the platform. But the train would halt there a full ten minutes, and then a bell would sound, the guard would blow his whistle, and presently Deoli would be left behind and forgotten.

I used to wonder what happened in Deoli, behind the station walls. I always felt sorry for that lonely little platform, and for the place that nobody wanted to visit. I decided that one day I would get off the train at Deoli, and spend the day there, just to please the town.

I was eighteen, visiting my grandmother, and the night train stopped at Deoli. A girl came down the platform, selling baskets.

It was a cold morning and the girl had a shawl thrown across her shoulders. Her feet were bare and her clothes were old, but she was a young girl, walking gracefully and with dignity.

When she came to my window, she stopped. She saw that I was looking at her intently, but at first she pretended not to notice. She had a pale skin, set off by shiny black hair, and dark, troubled eyes. And then those eyes, searching and eloquent, met mine.

She stood by my window for some time and neither of us said anything. But when she moved on, I found myself leaving my seat and going to the carriage door, and stood waiting on the platform, looking the other way. I walked across to the tea stall. A kettle was boiling over on a small fire, but the owner of the stall was busy serving tea somewhere on the train. The girl followed me behind the stall.

'Do you want to buy a basket?' she asked. 'They are very strong, made of the finest cane . . .'

'No,' I said, 'I don't want a basket.'

We stood looking at each other for what seemed a very long time, and she said, 'Are you sure you don't want a basket?'

'All right, give me one,' I said, and I took the one on top and gave her a rupee, hardly daring to touch her fingers.

As she was about to speak, the guard blew his whistle; she said something, but it was lost in the clanging of the bell and the hissing of the engine. I had to run back to my compartment. The carriage shuddered and jolted forward.

I watched her as the platform slipped away. She was alone on the platform and she did not move, but she was looking at me and smiling. I watched her until the signal-box came in the way, and then the jungle hid the station, but I could still see her standing there alone . . .

I sat up awake for the rest of the journey. I could not rid my mind of the picture of the girl's face and her dark, smouldering eyes.

But when I reached Dehra the incident became blurred and distant, for there were other things to occupy my mind. It was only when I was making the return journey, two months later, that I remembered the girl.

I was looking out for her as the train drew into the station, and I felt an unexpected thrill when I saw her walking up the platform. I sprang off the footboard and waved to her.

When she saw me, she smiled. She was pleased that I remembered her. I was pleased that she remembered me. We were both pleased, and it was almost like a meeting of old friends.

She did not go down the length of the train selling baskets, but came straight to the tea stall; her dark eyes were suddenly filled with light. We said nothing for some time but we couldn't have been more eloquent.

I felt the impulse to put her on the train there and then, and take her away with me; I could not bear the thought of having to watch her recede into the distance of Deoli station. I took the baskets from her hand and put them down on the ground. She put out her hand for one of them, but I caught her hand and held it.

'I have to go to Delhi,' I said.

She nodded. 'I do not have to go anywhere.'

The guard blew his whistle for the train to leave and how I hated the guard for doing that.

'I will come again,' I said. 'Will you be here?'

She nodded again, and, as she nodded, the bell clanged and the train slid forward. I had to wrench my hand away from the girl and run for the moving train.

This time I did not forget her. She was with me for the remainder of the journey, and for long after. All that year she was a bright, living thing. And when the college term finished I packed in haste and left for Dehra earlier than usual. My grandmother would be pleased at my eagerness to see her.

I was nervous and anxious as the train drew into Deoli, because I was wondering what I should say to the girl and what I should do. I was determined that I wouldn't stand helplessly before her, hardly able to speak or do anything about my feelings.

The train came to Deoli, and I looked up and down the platform, but I could not see the girl anywhere.

I opened the door and stepped off the footboard. I was deeply disappointed, and overcome by a sense of foreboding. I felt I had to do something, and so I ran up to the stationmaster and said, 'Do you know the girl who used to sell baskets here?'

'No, I don't,' said the stationmaster. 'And you'd better get on the train if you don't want to be left behind.'

But I paced up and down the platform, and stared over the railings at the station yard; all I saw was a mango tree and a dusty road leading into the jungle. Where did the road go? The train was moving out of the station, and I had to run up the platform and jump for the door of my compartment. Then, as the train gathered speed and rushed through the forests, I sat brooding in front of the window.

What could I do about finding a girl I had seen only twice, who had hardly spoken to me, and about whom I knew nothing – absolutely nothing – but for whom I felt a tenderness and responsibility that I had never felt before?

My grandmother was not pleased with my visit after all, because I didn't stay at her place more than a couple of weeks. I felt restless and ill-at-ease. So I took the train back to the plains, meaning to ask further questions of the stationmaster at Deoli.

But at Deoli there was a new stationmaster. The previous man had been transferred to another post within the past week. The new man didn't know anything about the girl who sold baskets. I found the owner of the tea stall, a small, shrivelled-up man, wearing greasy clothes, and asked him if he knew anything about the girl with the baskets.

'Yes, there was such a girl here, I remember quite well,' he said. 'But she has stopped coming now.'

'Why?' I asked. 'What happened to her?'

'How should I know?' said the man. 'She was nothing to me.'

And once again I had to run for the train.

As Deoli platform receded, I decided that one day I would have to break journey there, spend a day in the town, make enquiries, and find the girl who had stolen my heart with nothing but a look from her dark, impatient eyes.

With this thought I consoled myself throughout my last term in college. I went to Dehra again in the summer and when, in the early hours of the morning, the night train drew into Deoli station, I looked up and down the platform for signs of the girl, knowing I wouldn't find her but hoping just the same.

Somehow, I couldn't bring myself to break journey at Deoli and spend a day there. (If it was all fiction or a film, I reflected, I would have got down and cleaned up the mystery and reached a suitable ending for the whole thing.) I think I was afraid to do this. I was afraid of discovering what really happened to the girl. Perhaps she was no longer in Deoli, perhaps she was married, perhaps she had fallen ill . . .

In the last few years I have passed through Deoli many times, and I always look out of the carriage window, half expecting to see the same unchanged face smiling up at me. I wonder what happens in Deoli, behind the station walls. But I will never break my journey there. It may spoil my game. I prefer to keep hoping and dreaming, and looking out of the window up and down that lonely platform, waiting for the girl with the baskets.

I never break my journey at Deoli, but I pass through as often as I can.

A. K. Ramanujan (1929–93)

The history of creative expression in Indian writing in English begins with poetry. The remarkable and precocious Anglo-Portuguese Henry Vivian Louis Derozio, who taught at the Hindu College in Calcutta in the early nineteenth century, saw himself as 'Indian', and was one of the first writers to address the 'idea of India' in his sonnets; he died at the age of twenty-three. The members of the Dutt family, again of Calcutta, wrote historical verse that arises directly out of the excitement at the time about the reconstruction of Indian history by Orientalist scholars. Much of this verse is accomplished, and, as a cultural phenomenon, an extremely significant but neglected part of our literary history; aesthetically, it remains as wooden and conventional as it was then. The break was made by Toru Dutt, a younger member of the family, who, in her tragically brief life, was educated in France and Cambridge, and returned to Bengal to write at least three great poems, 'Our Casuarina Tree', 'Baugmaree', and 'Sita'. These three works shift their gaze from the conventional subject-matter of Orientalist poetry to the realm of memory, language, exile, and the terrain we call 'home'. She had learnt something from the Symbolist poetry she'd read in France, some of which she'd translated. Although she died at the age of twenty-one, the kind of artist she represents – standing at the junction of European and Indian languages – points to the figure of A. K. Ramanujan. Ramanujan was born about eighty years after Toru Dutt, in Mysore in 1929; he taught for much of his adult life in Chicago, where he was William E. Colvin Professor; he was also a MacArthur Fellow. He died in 1993 at the age of sixty-four. In the seventies, he emerged, with two volumes of poetry, *The Striders* and *Relations*, as one of the most skilled practitioners of English verse in the latter half of the century, and was also part of a small but genuine efflorescence of Indian poetry in English that took place around the time. It became gradually clear that his bilingualism, or multilingualism, as a South Indian writing in English, was important not only to his work as a translator and cultural commentator, but to his creative practice as well; he saw modern Indian English poetry and contemporary reality in India not in terms of mimicry, or exile, but, most richly, as a continual act of translation, a negotiation between the brain's 'twin lobes' to which he composes a euphony in the essay below. In this, he appears to be the germination of the seed that was planted, all those years ago, at the beginnings of modern Indian poetry in English, with Toru Dutt; and, also, a paradigm for all the later Indian writers who wish to chart a course between the deprivations of exile on the one hand, and the equally alien, indefatigable sphere of postmodernist celebration on the other.

* * *

'Is There an Indian Way of Thinking?
An Informal Essay' (1989)

Walter Benjamin once dreamed of hiding behind a phalanx of quotations which, like highwaymen, would ambush the passing reader and rob him of his convictions.

I

Stanislavsky had an exercise for his actors. He would give them an everyday sentence like, 'Bring me a cup of tea', and ask them to say it forty different ways, using it to beg, question, mock, wheedle, be imperious, etc. My question, 'Is there an Indian way of thinking?', is a good one for such an exercise. Depending on where the stress is placed, it contains many questions – all of which are real questions – asked again and again when people talk about India. Here are a few possible versions:

Is there an Indian way of thinking?
Is there *an* Indian way of thinking?
Is there an *Indian* way of thinking?
Is there an Indian way of *thinking*?

The answers are just as various. Here are a few: There *was* an Indian way of thinking; there isn't any more. If you want to learn about the Indian way of thinking, do not ask your modern-day citified Indians, go to the pundits, the *vaidikas*, the old texts. On the contrary: India never changes; under the veneer of the modern, Indians still think like the Vedas.

The second question might elicit answers like these: There is no single

Indian way of thinking; there are Great and Little Traditions, ancient and modern, rural and urban, classical and folk. Each language, caste and region has its special world-view. So, under the apparent diversity, there is really a unity of viewpoint, a single supersystem. Vedists see a Vedic model in all Indian thought. Nehru made the phrase 'unity in diversity' an Indian slogan. The Sahitya Akademi's line has been, 'Indian literature is one, though written in many languages.'

The third question might be answered: What we see in India is nothing special to India; it is nothing but pre-industrial, pre-printing press, face-to-face, agricultural, feudal. Marxists, Freudians, McLuhanites, all have their labels for the stage India is in, according to their schemes of social evolution; India is only an example. Others, of course, would argue the uniqueness of the Indian Way and how it turns all things, especially rivals and enemies, into itself; look at what has happened to Indo-Europeans in India, they would say; their language gets shot with retroflexes, their syntax with nominal compounds, they lose their nerve – the British are only the most recent example (according to Nirad Chaudhuri). Look what happens to Buddhism, Islam, the Parsis. There is an *Indian* way, and it imprints and patterns all things that enter the subcontinent; it is inescapable, and it is Bigger Than All of Us.

The fourth question may question whether Indians think at all: It is the West that is materialistic, rational; Indians have no philosophy, only religion, no positive sciences, not even a psychology; in India, matter is subordinated to spirit, rational thought to feeling, intuition. And even when people agree that this is the case, we can have arguments for and against it. Some lament, others celebrate India's un-thinking ways. One can go on forever.

We – I, certainly – have stood in one or another of these stances at different times. We have not heard the end of these questions – or these answers.

II

The problem was posed for me personally at the age of twenty in the image of my father. I had never taken a good look at him till then. Didn't Mark Twain say, 'At seventeen, I thought my father was ignorant; at twenty, I wondered how he learned so much in three years'? Indeed, this essay was inspired by contemplation of him over the years, and is dedicated to him.

My father's clothes represented his inner life very well. He was a south Indian Brahman gentleman. He wore neat white turbans, a Sri Vaisnava caste mark (in his earlier pictures, a diamond earring), yet wore Tootal ties, Kromentz buttons and collar studs, and donned English serge jackets over his muslin dhotis which he wore draped in traditional Brahman style. He often wore tartan-patterned socks and silent well-polished leather shoes when he went to the university, but he carefully took them off before he entered the inner quarters of the house.

He was a mathematician, an astronomer. But he was also a Sanskrit scholar, an expert astrologer. He had two kinds of exotic visitors: American and English mathematicians who called on him when they were on a visit to India, and local astrologers, orthodox pundits who wore splendid gold-embroidered shawls dowered by the Maharaja. I had just been converted by Russell to the 'scientific attitude'. I (and my generation) was troubled by his holding together in one brain both astronomy and astrology; I looked for consistency in him, a consistency he didn't seem to care about, or even think about. When I asked him what the discovery of Pluto and Neptune did to his archaic nine-planet astrology, he said, 'You make the necessary corrections, that's all.' Or, in answer to how he could read the Gītā religiously having bathed and painted on his forehead the red and white feet of Vishnu, and later talk appreciatively about Bertrand Russell and even Ingersoll, he said, 'The Gītā is part of one's hygiene. Besides, don't you know, the brain has two lobes?'

The following poem says something about the way he and his friends appeared to me:

> Sky-man in a man-hole
> with astronomy for dream,
> astrology for nightmare:
>
> fat man full of proverbs,
> the language of lean years,
> living in square after
>
> almanac square
> prefiguring the day
> of windfall and landslide
>
> through a calculus
> of good hours,
> clutching at the tear

in his birthday shirt
as at a hole
in his mildewed horoscope,

squinting at the parallax
of black planets,
his Tiger, his Hare

moving in Sanskrit zodiacs,
forever troubled
by the fractions, the kidneys

in his Tamil flesh,
his body the Great Bear
dipping for the honey,

the woman-smell
in the small curly hair
down there.

(Ramanujan, 1986)

III

Both Englishmen and 'modern' Indians have been dismayed and angered by this kind of inconsistency. About twenty years ago, *The Illustrated Weekly of India* asked a number of modern Indian intellectuals to describe the Indian character – they did not seem to be daunted by the assignment and wrote terse, some quite sharp, columns. *They* all seemed to agree on one thing: the Indian trait of hypocrisy. Indians do not mean what they say, and say different things at different times. By 'Indians' they did not mean only servants. In Max Müller's lectures on India (1883), the second chapter was called 'Truthful character of the Hindus', in answer to many complaints.

Recently I attended a conference on *karma*, a notion that is almost synonymous in some circles with whatever is Indian or Hindu. Brahmanical texts had it, the Buddhists had it, the Jains had it. But when I looked at hundreds of Kannada tales, I couldn't find a single tale that used *karma* as a motif or motive. Yet when their children made a mess, their repertoire of abuse included, 'You are my *karma*!' When Harper (1959) and others after him reported that many Indian villagers didn't know much about reincarnation, such a discrepancy was attributed to caste, education, etc.

But the 2,000 Kannada tales, collected by me and others over the past twenty years, were told by Brahmans, Jains (both of whom use *karma* in their explanations elsewhere quite readily), and by other communities as well. What is worse, Sheryl Daniel (1983) independently found that her Tamil village alternately used *karma* and *talaividi* ('headwriting') as explanations for the events around them. The two notions are inconsistent with each other. *Karma* implies the self's past determining the present, an iron chain of cause and consequence, an ethic of responsibility. *Talaividi* is one's fate inscribed arbitrarily at one's birth on one's forehead; the inscription has no relation to one's prior actions; usually in such explanations (and folk tales about them) past lives are not even part of the scheme.

Another related characteristic seems to preoccupy observers. We have already said that 'inconsistency' (like my father's, or the Brahman/Jain use of *karma*) is not a matter of inadequate education or lack of logical rigour. They maybe using a different 'logic' altogether. Some thinkers believe that such logic is an earlier stage of 'cultural evolution' and that Indians have not developed a notion of 'data', of 'objective facts'. Edward Said's *Orientalism* cites many such Eurppean stereotypes about the 'Third World'. Here is Henry Kissinger's explanation:

> Cultures which escaped the early impact of Newtonian thinking have retained the essentially pre-Newtonian view that the world is almost completely *internal* to the observer ... [Consequently] empirical reality has a much different significance for many of the new [old] countries than for the West because in a certain sense they never went through the process of discovering it. (Said, 1978)

Such a view cannot be dismissed as peculiar to Kissinger's version of Newtonian optics. One meets with it again and again in travelogues, psychological writings, novels. Naipaul quotes Sudhir Kakar, a sophisticated psychoanalyst, deeply knowledgeable in matters Indian as well as Western, an insider/outsider:

> Generally among Indians there seems to be a different relationship to outside reality, compared to the one met with in the West. In India it is closer to a certain stage in childhood when outer objects did not have a separate, independent existence but were intimately related to the self and its affective states ... The Indian 'ego' is underdeveloped; 'the world of magic' and animistic thinking lie close to the surface; so the grasp of reality is 'relatively tenuous'. (Naipaul, 1977)

In a memorable and oft-quoted section of Foster's *A Passage to India*, Mrs Moore muses vividly on the relations between inside and outside in India; the confounding of the two is not special to humans in India:

> Going to hang up her cloak, she found the tip of the peg was occupied by a small wasp. She had known this wasp or his relatives by song; they were not as English wasps, but had long yellow legs which hung down behind when they flew. Perhaps he mistook the peg for a branch – no Indian animal has any sense of an interior. Bats, rats, birds, insects will as soon nest inside the house as out, it is to them a normal growth of the eternal jungle, which alternately produces houses, trees, houses, trees. There he clung, asleep, while jackals bayed their desires and mingled with the percussion of drums. (Foster, 1952)

And sympaticos, like Zimmer, praise Indians for not being hung up on an objectivity that distinguishes self from non-self, interior from exterior; what for Naipaul is a 'defect of vision', is for Zimmer vision itself:

> India thinks of time and herself ... in biological terms, terms of the species, not of the ephemeral ego ... We of the west regard world history as a biography of mankind, and in particular of Occidental Man ... Our will is not to culminate in our human institutions the universal play of nature, but to evaluate, to set ourselves against the play, with an ego-centric tenacity. (Zimmer, 1946)

A third trait should be added to 'inconsistency', and to the apparent inability to distinguish self and non-self. One has only to read Manu after a bit of Kant to be struck by the former's extraordinary lack of universality. He seems to have no clear notion of a universal *human* nature from which one can deduce ethical decrees like 'Man shall not kill', or 'Man shall not tell an untruth'. One is aware of no notion of a 'state', no unitary law of all men. Manu 8.267 has the following:

> A Kshatriya, having defamed a Brahmana, shall be fined one hundred (*panas*); a Vaisya one hundred and fifty or two hundred; a Sudra shall suffer corporal punishment. (Quoted in Müller, 1883)

Even truth-telling is not an unconditional imperative, as Müller's correspondents discovered.

> An untruth spoken by people under the influence of anger, excessive joy, fear, pain, or grief, by infants, by very old men, by persons labouring under a delusion, being under the influence of drink, or by mad men,

does not cause the speaker to fall, or as we should say, is a venial not a mortal sin. (Gautama, paraphrased in Müller, 1883)

Alexander Wilder adds, in a footnote, further extensions:

At the time of marriage, during dalliance, when life is in danger, when the loss of property is threatened, and for the sake of a Brahmana ... Manu declared ... whenever the death of a man of any of the four castes would be occasioned by true evidence, falsehood was even better than truth. (Müller, 1883)

Contrast this with Kant's well-known formulation of his imperative: 'Act as if the maxim of your action were to become through your will a Universal Law of Nature' (Copleston, 1946).

'Moral judgements are universalizable,' says Mackie (1977). Universalization means putting oneself in another's place – it is the golden rule of the New Testament, Hobbes' 'law of all men': do not do unto others what you do not want done unto you. The main tradition of Judeo-Christian ethics is based on such a premise of universalization – Manu would not understand such a premise. To be moral, for Manu, is to particularize – to ask who did what, to whom and when. Shaw's comment, 'Do not do unto others as you would have they should do unto you. Their tastes may not be the same' (Mackie, 1977) would be closer to Manu's view, except he would substitute 'natures or classes' for 'tastes'. Each class (*jāti*) of man has its own laws, its own proper ethic, not to be universalized. Hegel shrewdly noted this Indian slant: 'While we say, "Bravery is a virtue", the Hindoos say, on the contrary, "Bravery is a virtue of the Cshatriyas"' (Hegel *c.* 1827).

Is there any system to this particularism? Indian philosophers do not seem to make synoptic 'systems' like Hegel's or Kant's. Sheryl Daniel (1983) speaks of a 'tool-box' of ideas that Indians carry about, and from which they use one or another without much show of logic; anything goes into their 'bricolage' (Lévi-Strauss, 1962). Max Weber, in various writings, distinguished 'traditional' and 'rational' religions. Geertz summarizes the distinction better than other writers:

Traditional religions attack problems opportunistically as they arise in each particular instance ... employing one or another weapon chosen, on grounds of symbolic appropriateness, from their cluttered arsenal of myth and magic ... the approach ... is discrete and irregular ... Rationalized religions ... are more abstract, more logically coherent, and more generally phrased ... The question is no longer ... to use a classical example from Evans-Pritchard, 'Why has the granary fallen on my brother ...?' but rather, 'Why do the good die young and the evil flourish as the green bay tree?' (Geertz, 1973)

IV

It is time to step back and try a formulation. The grammarian sees grammar in all things; I shall be true to my bias and borrow a notion from linguistics and try it for size.

There are (or used to be) two kinds of grammatical rules: the context-free and the context-sensitive (Lyons, 1971). 'Sentences must have subjects and predicates in a certain relation' would be an example of the first kind of rule. 'Plurals in English are realized as -*s* after stops (e.g. dog-s, cat-s), -*es* before fricatives (e.g. latch-es), -*ren* after the word *child*, etc.' – would be a context-sensitive rule. Almost all language rules are of the latter kind.

I think cultures (may be said to) have overall tendencies (for whatever complex reasons) – tendencies to *idealize*, and think in terms of, either the context-free or the context-sensitive kind of rules. Actual behaviour may be more complex, though the rules they think with are a crucial factor in guiding the behaviour. In cultures like India's, the context-sensitive kind of rule is the preferred formulation. Manu (I have already quoted a law of his) explicitly says: '[A king] who knows the sacred law, must imagine into the laws of caste (*jāti*), of districts, of guilds, and of families, and [thus] settle the peculiar law of each' (Manu; see Doniger and Smith, 1991).

In an illuminating discussion of the context-sensitive nature of *dharma* in its detail, Baudhāyana enumerates aberrant practices peculiar to the Brahmans of the north and those of the south.

> There is difference between the South and the North on five points. We shall describe the practices of the South: to eat with a person not having received Brahmanical initiation: to eat with one's wife; to eat food prepared the previous day; to marry the daughter of the maternal uncle or paternal aunt. And for the North: to sell wool; to drink spirits; to traffic in animals with two rows of teeth; to take up the profession of arms; to make sea voyages.

After this admirable ethnographic description, he notes that all these practices are contrary to the precepts of *śruti* and *smrti*, but these *śistas* (learned men) know the traditions and cannot be blamed for following the customs of their district. In the north, the southern ways would be wrong and vice versa. (Lingat, 1973)

Add to this view of right and wrong behaviour, the ethical views of the *āsramadharma* (the conduct that is right for one's stage of life), *svadharma* (the conduct that is right for one's station, *jāti* or class, or *svabhāva* or given nature), and *āpaddharma* (conduct that is necesssary in times of distress or emergency, e.g. one may even eat the flesh of dogs to save oneself from death by starvation, as sage Viśvāmitra did). Each addition is really a subtraction from any universal law. There is not much left of an absolute or common (*sādhārana) dharma* which the texts speak of, if at all, as a last and not as a first resort. They seem to say, if you fit no contexts or conditions, which is unlikely, fall back on the universal.

I know of no Hindu discussion of values which reads like Plato on Beauty in his *Symposium* – which asks the initiate not to rest content with beauty in one embodiment but to be drawn onward from physical to moral beauty, to the beauty of laws and mores, and to all science and learning, and thus to escape 'the mean slavery of the particular case'. (I am reserving counter-instances for later.)

Or take Indian literary texts. No Indian text comes without a context, a frame, till the nineteenth century. Works are framed by *phalaśruti* verses – these verses tell the reader, reciter or listener all the good that will result from his act of reading, reciting or listening. They relate the text, of whatever antiquity, to the present reader – that is, they contextualize it. An extreme case is that of the Nāḍiśāstra, which offers you your personal history. A friend of mine consulted the Experts about himself and his past and future. After enough rupees had been exchanged, the Experts brought out an old palm leaf manuscript which, in archaic verses, mentioned his full name, age, birthplace, etc., and said suddenly, 'At this point, the listener is crossing his legs – he should uncross them.'

Texts may be historically dateless, anonymous: but their contexts, uses, efficacies, are explicit. The *Rāmāyana* and *Mahābhārata* open with episodes that tell you why and under what circumstances they were composed. Every such story is encased in a meta-story. And within the text, one tale is the context for another within it; not only does the outer frame-story motivate the inner sub-story; the inner story illuminates the outer as well. It often acts as a microcosmic replica for the whole text. In the forest when the Pāṇḍava brothers are in exile, the eldest, Yudhiṣṭhira, is in the very slough of despondency: he has gambled away a kingdom, and is in exile. In the depth of his despair, a sage visits him and tells him the story of Nala. As the story unfolds, we see Nala too gamble away a kingdom, lose his wife, wander in the forest, and finally, win his wager, defeat his brother, reunite with his wife and return to his kingdom. Yudhiṣṭhria, following the full curve of Nala's adventures, sees that he is only halfway through his own, and sees his present in perspective, himself as a story yet to be finished. Very often the Nala story is excerpted and read by itself, but its poignancy is partly in its frame, its meaning for the hearer within the fiction and for the listener of the whole epic. The tale within is context-sensitive – getting its meaning from the tale without, and giving it further meanings.

Scholars have often discussed Indian texts (like the *Mahābhārata*) as if they were loose-leaf files, rag-bag encyclopaedias. Taking the Indian word for text, *grantha* (derived from the knot that holds the palm leaves together), literally, scholars often posit only an accidental and physical unity. We need to attend to the context-sensitive designs that embed a seeming variety of models (tale, discourse, poem, etc.) and materials. This manner of constructing the text is in consonance with other designs in the culture. Not unity (in the Aristotelian sense) but coherence seems to be the end.

Tamil (and Sanskrit) lyrics are all dramatic monologues; they imply the whole 'communication diagram'; who said what to whom, when, why, and often with who else overhearing it. Here is an example:

WHAT HIS CONCUBINE SAID ABOUT HIM
(within earshot of the wife's friends, when she heard that the wife had said disparaging things about her)

> You know he comes from
> where the fresh-water sharks in the pools
> catch with their mouths
> the mangoes as they fall, ripe
> from the trees on the edge of the field.
>
> At our place
> he talked big.
>
> Now back in his own
> when others raise their hands
> and feet,
> he will raise his too:
>
> like a doll
> in a mirror
>
> he will shadow
> every last wish
> of his son's dear mother.

Kuṟuntokai, 8 (Ramanujan, 1967)

The colophons give us the following frames for this poem:

Genre: *Akam*, love poetry, the 'interior'.
Landscape: agricultural, with pool, fresh-water fish, mango trees.
Mood: infidelity, sullenness, lovers' quarrels.

The poetry of such a poem depends on a taxonomy of landscapes, flora and fauna, and of emotions – an ecosystem of which a man's activities and feelings are a part (see Ramanujan, 1967). To describe the exterior landscape is also to inscribe the interior landscape. What the man has, he is: the landscape which he owns, in which he lives (where sharks do not have to work for the mango, it falls into their open mouths) represents him: it is his *property*, in more senses than one. In Burke's (1946) terms, *scene* and *agent* are one; they are metonyms for one another.

The poem does not use a metaphor. The human agents are simply *placed* in the scene. Both parts of the comparison (the man and shark) are part of one scene, one syntagm; they exist separately, yet simulate each other. The Tamils call such a figure *ullurai* 'inward speaking'; it is an 'inset', an 'inscape'. In such a metonymic view of man in nature – man in context – he is continuous with the context he is in. In Peircean semiotic terms, these are not symbolic devices, but indexical signs – the signifier and the signified belong in the same context (Peirce, 1931–58).

One might say, from this point of view, that Hindu ritual (e.g. Vedic sacrifice, or a coronation; see Inden [1978]) converts *symbols*, arbitrary signs (e.g. sacrificial horse), into *icons* where the signifier (the horse) is *like* what it signifies (the universe), and finally into *indexes*, where the signifier is *part* of what it signifies: the horse is the universe is Prajāpati, so that in sacrificing and partaking of it one is sacrificing and partaking of the universe itself (see the passage on the horse in the *Bṛhadāraṇyaka Upaniṣad, adhyāya* 1, *brāhmana* 1; Hume, 1931).

Neither in the Tamil poem nor in the upaniṣadic passages (e.g. the horse), does the Lévi-Straussian opposition of nature–culture make sense; we see that the opposition itself is culture-bound. There is another alternative to a culture vs. nature view: in the Tamil poems, culture is enclosed in nature, nature is reworked in culture, so that we cannot tell the difference. We have a nature–culture continuum that cancels the terms, confuses them even if we begin with them.

Such container-contained relations are seen in many kinds of concepts and images: not only in culture–nature, but also god–world, king–kingdom, devotee–god, mother–child. Here is a *bhakti* poem which plays with many such concentric containments:

My dark one
    stands there as if nothing's changed,

after taking entire
into his maw
all three worlds
the gods
and the good kings
    who hold their lands
    as a mother would
    a child in her womb –

and I, by his leave,
have taken him entire

and I have him in my belly
for keeps.

                Nammāḻvār, 8.7.9 (Ramanujan, 1980)

Like the Nala story in the *Mahābhārata*, what is contained mirrors the container; the microcosm is both *within* and like the macrocosm, and paradoxically also contains it. Indian conceptions tend to be such concentric nests: the view of the 'sheaths' or *kośas*, the different 'bodies' or *kāyas* are examples (Egnor, 1975). Such impressions are so strong and even kinesthetic that analysts tend to think in similar terms: one example is Dumont's notions of hierarchic encompassment, where each higher category or *jāti* encompasses all the earlier ones: the *ksatriya* is distinct from but includes the *vaiśya*, as the Brahman encompasses the *ksatriya*. Many Indian lists, like *dharma-artha-kāma*, tend to be successive encompassments. (For the separation of *mokṣa*, see below).

Even space and time, the universal contexts, the Kantian imperatives, are in India not uniform and neutral, but have properties, varying specific densities, that affect those who dwell in them. The soil in a village, which produces crops for the people, affects their character (as liars, for instance, in E. V. Daniel's village [1984]); houses (containers par excellence) have mood and character, change the fortune and moods of the dwellers. Time too does not come in uniform units: certain hours of the day, certain days of the week, etc. are auspicious or inauspicious (*rāhukāla*); certain units of time (*yugas*) breed certain kinds of maladies, politics, religions (e.g. *kaliyuga*).* A story is told about two men coming

*   Editor's note: The last, 'dark' age in the Hindu time-cycle.

to Yudhiṣthira with a case. One had bought the other's land, and soon
after found a crock of gold in it. He wanted to return it to the original
owner of the land, who was arguing that it really belonged to the man
who had now bought it. They had come to Yudhiṣthira to settle their
virtuous dispute. Just then Yudhiṣthira was called away (to put it
politely) for a while. When he came back the two gentlemen were quarrelling furiously, but each was claiming the treasure for himself this
time! Yudhiṣthira realized at once that the age had changed, and *kaliyuga* had begun.

As hour, month, season, year, and aeon have their own properties as
contexts, the arts that depend on time have to obey time's changing
moods and properties. For instance, the *rāgas* of both north and south
Indian classical music have their prescribed appropriate times. Like the
Tamil poems, the genres and moods are associated with, placed in, hours
of the day and times of the season. Even musical instruments have their
caste properties; a *viṇā*, no less than the icon of a god, has to be made by
a particular caste, or family, after observing certain austerities (*vrata*), made
on an auspicious day; the gourd from which it is made has to be taken
from certain kinds of places. Their *guṇas* (qualities of substance) affect the
quality of the instrument, the music.

The same kind of contextual sensitiveness is shown in medical matters:
in preparing a herbal medicine, in diagnosis and in prescription. As Zim-
mermann's work (1980) is eloquent on the subject, I shall say little. The
notion of *ṛtusātmya* or appropriateness applies to poetry, music, sacrificial
ritual as well as medicine. As Renou points out, *ṛtu*, usually translated as
'season', means articulation of time; it is also the crucial moment in Vedic
sacrific. *Ṛta* ('order', the original notion behind *dharma*) is that which is
articulated. *Kratu*, sacrifice, is a convergence of events, acts, times and
spaces. The vocabulary of *ṛtusātmya*, 'appropriateness', *rasa*, 'essences,
flavours, tastes', *doṣa*, 'defects, deficiency', and of landscapes is common to
both medicine and poetry: the arts of man reading and re-forming himself
in his contexts.

Thus, all things, even so-called non-material ones like space and time
or caste, affect other things because all things are 'substantial' (*dhātu*). The
only difference is that some are subtle (*sūkṣma*), some gross (*sthūla*).
Contrary to the notion that Indians are 'spiritual', they are really 'material
minded'. They are materialists, believers in substance: there is a continuity,
a constant flow (the etymology of *samsāra*!) of substance from context to
object, from non-self to self (if you prefer) – in eating, breathing, sex,
sensation, perception, thought, art or religious experience (Marriott, 1976,

1980). This is the grain of truth glimpsed by many of the stereotypes cited in the earlier parts of this essay. Zimmerman (1979) points out that in Indian medical texts, the body is a meeting-place, a conjunction of elements, they have a physiology, but no anatomy.

Where Kissinger and others are wrong is in not seeing that this view has nothing to do with the Newtonian revolution, education or (in)capacity for abstract thought. Cognitive anthropologists like Richard Shweder (1972) have studied descriptive phrases used by highly intelligent Oriya and American adults and shown that they describe persons very differently: Americans characterized them with generic words like 'good', 'nice', Oriyas with concrete contextual descriptions like 'he brings sweets'. The psychoanalyst Alan Roland (1979) suggests that Indians carry their family-context wherever they go, feel continuous with their family. He posts a familial self, a 'self-we regard', sees no phase of separation, individuation from the parental family as in modern American; hence there seems to be no clear-cut adolescent phase through which one rebels, and thereby separates and individuates onself in opposition to one's family (the exceptions are in 'modern' urban-centred families). Roland remarks that Indians develop a 'radar' *conscience* that orients them to others, makes them say things that are appropriate to person and context. (No wonder Max Müller had to insist that Indians were truthful!) Roland also found that when directions to places are given, Indians always make reference to other places, landmarks.

Such a pervasive emphasis on context is, I think, related to the Hindu concern with *jāti* – the logic of classes, of genera and species, of which human *jātis* are only an instance. Various taxonomies of season, landscape, times, *guṇas* or qualities (and their material bases), tastes, characters, emotions, essences (*rasa*), etc., are basic to the thought-work of Hindu medicine and poetry, cooking and religion, erotics and magic. Each *jāti* or class defines a context, a structure of relevance, a rule of permissible combinations, a frame of reference, a meta-communication of what is and can be done.

It is not surprising that systems of Indian philosophy, Hindu, Buddhist, or Jain,

> confine themselves to the consideration of class-essences (*jāti*) called genera and species in Western philosophy. They never raise the question of whether there are universals of other types, namely identical qualities and relations. The assumption seems to be that qualities and relations are particulars, though they may be instances of universals. (Dravid, 1972)

The most important and accessible model of a context-sensitive system with intersecting taxonomies is, of course, the grammar of a language. And grammar is the central model for thinking in many Hindu texts. As Frits Staal has said, what Euclid is to European thought, the grammarian Pāṇini is to the India. Even the *Kāmasūtra* is literally a grammar of love – which declines and conjugates men and women as one would nouns and verbs in different genders, voices, moods and aspects. Genders are genres. Different body-types and character-types obey different rules, respond to differrent scents and beckonings.

In such a world, systems of meaning are elicited by contexts, by the nature (and substance) of the listener. In the *Bṛhadāraṇyaka Upaniṣad, adhyāya* 5, *brāhmana* 2, Lord Prajāpati speaks in thunder three times: 'DA DA DA'. When the gods, given to pleasure hear it, they hear it as the first syllable of *damayatā*, 'control'. The antigods, given as they are to cruelty, hear it as *dayādhavam*, 'be compassionate'. When the humans, given to greed, hear it they hear it as *dattā*, 'give to others' (Hume, 1931).

V

All societies have context-sensitive behaviour and rules – but the dominant ideal may not be the 'context-sensitive' but the 'context-free'. Egalitarian democratic ideals, Protestant Christianity, espouse both the universal and the unique, insist that any member is *equal* to and *like* any other in the group. Whatever his context – birth, class, gender, age, place, rank, etc. – a man is a man for all that. Technology with its modules and interchangeable parts, and the post-Renaissance sciences with their quest for universal laws (and 'facts') across contexts intensify the bias towards the context-free. Yet societies have underbellies. In predominantly 'context-free' societies, the counter-movements tend to be towards the context-sensitive: situation ethics, Wittgensteinian notions of meaning and colour (against class-logic), the various relativisms including our own search for 'native categories' in anthropology, holistic movements in medicine (naturopaths who prescribe individually tailored regimens) are good examples. In 'traditional' cultures like India, where context-sensitivity rules and binds, the dream is to be free of context. So *rasa* in aesthetics, *mokṣa* in the 'aims of life', *sannyāsa* in the life-stages, *sphoṭa* in semantics, and *bhakti* in religion define themselves against a background of inexorable contextuality.

Where *kāma, artha* and *dharma* are all relational in their values, tied to place, time, personal character and social role, *mokṣa* is the release from all relations. If *brahmacārya* (celibate studentship) is preparation for a fully relational life, *grahasthāśrama* (the householder stage) is a full realization of it. Manu prefers the latter over all other states. *Vānaprastha* (the retiring forest-dweller stage) loosens the bonds, and *sannyāsa* (renunciation) cremates all one's past and present relations. In the realm of feeling, *bhāvas* are private, contingent, context-roused sentiments, *vibhāvas* are determinant causes, *anubhāvas* the consequent expressions. But *rasa* is generalized, it is an essence. In the field of meaning, the temporal sequence of letters and phonemes, the syntactic chain of worlds, yields finally a *sphoṭa*, an explosion, a meaning which is beyond sequence and time. In each of these the pattern is the same: a necessary sequence in time with strict rules of phase and context ends in a free state.

The last of the great Hindu anti-contextual notions, *bhakti*,* is different from the above; it denies the very need for context. *Bhakti* defies all contextual structures: every pigeon hole of caste, ritual, gender, appropriate clothing and custom, stage of life, the whole system of *Homo hierarchicus* ('everything in its place') is the target of its irony.

> Did the breath of the mistress
> have breasts and long hair?
> Or did the master's breath
> wear sacred thread?
>
> Did the outcaste, last in line,
> hold with his outgoing breath
> the stick of his tribe?
>
> What do the fools of this world know
> of the snares you set,
> O Rāmanātha?

Dāsimayya, 96 (Ramanujan, 1973)

In European culture, one might mention Plato's rebellion against (even the limited) Athenian democracy. Or Blake in the technocratic democracy of the nineteenth century railing against egalitarianism, abstraction, and the dark Satanic mills, calling for 'minute particulars', declaring 'To generalize is to be an idiot' (generalizing thereby); and forming the slogan of all context-sensitive systems: 'one law for the lion and the ox is oppression'. I would include the rise of minute realism in the nineteenth-century novel

---

* Editor's note: Medieval devotional movement within Hinduism.

and various 'indexical' movements of modern art in this counter-thrust towards particularism in the West.

Neither the unique, nor the universal, the two, often contradictory concerns of Western philosophy, art and polity, are the central concern of the Indian arts and sciences – except in the counter-cultures and in modern attempts, which get enlisted and remoulded (witness the fate of *bhakti* movements) by the prevailing context-sensitive patterns.

VI

In conclusion, I would like to make a couple of observations about 'modernization'. One might see 'modernization' in India as a movement from the context-sensitive to the context-free in all realms: an erosion of contexts, at least in principle. Gandhi's watch (with its uniform autonomous time, governing his punctuality) replaced the almanac. Yet Gandhi quoted Emerson, that consistency was the hobgoblin of foolish minds. Print replaced palm-leaf manuscripts, making possible an open and egalitarian access to knowledge irrespective of caste. The Indian Constitution made the contexts of birth, region, sex and creed irrelevant, overthrowing Manu, though the battle is joined again and again. The new preferred names give no clue to birth-place, father's name, caste, sub-caste and sect, as all the traditional names did: I once found in a Kerala college roster, three 'Joseph Stalins' and one 'Karl Marx'. I have also heard of an Andhra named 'Bobbili Winston Churchill'.

In music, the *rāgas* can now be heard at all hours and seasons. Once the *Venkateśasuprebhātam*, the wake-up chant for the Lord of Tirupati, could be heard only in Tirupati at a certain hour in the morning. Since M. S. Subbulakshmi in her devotion cut a record of the chants, it wakes up not only the Lord, but anyone who tunes in to All India Radio in faraway places.

Cultural borrowings from India to the West, or vice versa, also show interesting accommodations in the prevailing system. The highly contextualized Hindu systems are generalized into 'a Hindu view of life' by apologues like Radhakrishnan for the benefit of both Western and modern Indian readers. The individual esoteric skills of meditation are freed from their contexts into a streamlined, widely accessible, technique. And when T. S. Eliot borrows the DA DA DA passage (quoted earlier) to end *The Waste Land* (1922), it becomes highly individual, introspective, as well as universal.

In reverse, Indian borrowings of Western cultural items have been converted and realigned to fit pre-existing context-sensitive needs. When English is borrowed into (or imposed on) Indian contexts, it fits into the Sanskrit slot; it acquires many of the characteristics of Sanskrit, the older native father tongue, its pan-Indian elite character – as a medium of laws, science and administration, and its formulaic patterns; it becomes part of Indian multiple diglossia (a characteristic of context-sensitive societies). When Indians learn, quite expertly, modern science, business, or technology, they 'compartmentalize' these interests (Singer, 1972); the new ways of thought and behaviour do not replace, but live along with older 'religious' ways. Computers and typewriters receive *ayudhapuja* ('worship of weapons') as weapons of war once did. The 'modern', the context-free, becomes one more context, though it is not easy to contain.

In modern thought, William James with his 'sub-universes', or Alfred Schutz with his 'finite provinces of reality' and 'relevance' as central concepts in any understanding, should be reread in the light of what I have said about context-sensitive and context-free modes. The most recent kinds of science can hold together inconsistent systems of explanation – like wave and particle theories of light. The counter-movements in the West toward Schumacher's 'small is beautiful', appropriate technologies, and the attention paid to ethnicity rather than to a melting pot, though not yet successful, are straws in the wind – like the ethnography of communication in linguistics.

My purpose here is not to evaluate but to grope toward a description of the two kinds of emphases. Yet in each of these kinds of cultures, despite all the complexity and oscillation, there is a definite bias. The Buddha (who said, 'When we see a man shot with a poisoned arrow, we cannot afford to ask what caste he or his enemy is') also told the following parable of the raft. Once a man was drowning in a sudden flood. Just as he was about to drown, he found a raft. He clung to it, and it carried him safely to dry land. And he was grateful to the raft that he carried it on his back for the rest of his life. Such was the Buddha's ironic comment on context-free systems.

Dom Moraes (b. 1938)

Dom Moraes, son of Frank Moraes, eminent journalist and one-time editor of the *Indian Express*, was born in Bombay in 1938. He read English at Jesus College, Oxford; Stephen Spender, reading the teenager's poems, was astonished by their accomplishment; Moraes astonished the literary world again by winning the Hawthornden Prize for his first book of poems, *A Beginning* (1957), published when he was only nineteen. Approval in the form of English literary prizes was unheard of at the time for Indian writers in English. He published two more volumes of poetry at fairly acceptable intervals; instead of tracing a meteoric or radical development, they returned to the subject proclaimed by the title of his first book: his beginnings. Arvind Krishna Mehrotra notes: 'Moraes's burden, especially in his early poetry, is dispossession: the loss, on growing up, of boyhood visions.' For seventeen years after his third volume of poems appeared, Moraes wrote little poetry, seeming to have dried up, wandering, instead, the wilderness of the modern world writing commissioned travelogues, studies, biographies, and journalism; and a classic memoir, *My Son's Father*. In 1982 he began to write poetry again; much of the journalism and prose he wrote before he made his second 'beginning' in verse is of the ephemeral kind, but it is surprising to rediscover the quality of some of the writing, lucid, measured, and lugubrious, and to be reminded that, in contrast to other parts of the world, some of the best prose in India has been written by poets. Those seventeen years in which the famous poet did nothing in terms of poetry gave Moraes a fund of metaphors, images, and figures – to do with wandering, travelling barren, unyielding landscapes, and discounted prophets – that he would use in his later poetry. The extract below from *Answered By Flutes*, a marvellous travelogue and study commissioned by the Madhya Pradesh Government that is now forgotten and out of print, should not be seen, thus, as an accurate or serious anthropological work, but as part of the endeavour of a poet constructing, in elegant and ironical sentences, a metaphor for his own failed creativity, his failed quests, someone who would return to that metaphor later in 'Prophet': 'I followed desert suns/ Alone, these thirty years,/ A goatskin knotted round my sex ...' The book, then, is a form of disguised autobiography. 'I have it in me so much nearer home,' Frost once said, 'to scare myself with my own desert places.' It also rehearses, dourly but effectively, in the guise of disinterestedly amassing facts, a theme to be found elsewhere in this volume: the sense of dislocation and paradoxical discovery the bourgeois sensibility experiences upon encountering the underdeveloped interstices of small-town India. We find here a very early, and striking, instance of the sort of detached, solitary journalism that is now a familiar element of diasporic Indian English writing, but which, at the time, had hardly come into existence.

* * *

from *Answered by Flutes* (1983)

THE PILGRIM DAYS

When I first flew into Bhopal in February, the last effects of winter were still apparent in the air. The nights demanded blankets, and green trees rustled pleasantly around the small, off-white houses and offices of the city. It was a scattered city, except where the comparatively recent housing colonies crouched together around their shopping centres. The impression of space was pervasive: two man-made lakes, one large and one small, lay quietly among the houses, bordered with trees from which, at dusk, black bats fluttered, squeaking like unpleasant children. Between the city and the low blue hills on the horizon, the plains spread away, badged with wheat-fields and water.

The Gothic menace conveyed by the twilight apparition of the bats was not unsuited to the lakes. There has been blithe conversation in the city as to how well adapted they are for the use of swimmers and yachtsmen. In actual fact they are so heavily polluted by sewage that one writer has remarked, 'even after chlorination and filtration the water cannot be guaranteed as safe for drinking'. He adds, 'The water of the upper lake lacks in calcium, as a result of which a large part of the population suffers from stomach trouble . . .' To dredge the lakes, an expert assured me, 'is not like emptying a bathtub. The cost would be inordinate, more than it would be to put up two dams to double the water storage.' But the lakes, blue under the sun and deceptively beautiful, add to the peaceful, indeed rather somnolent atmosphere of the place.

I was rather surprised, at first, when people who took me out to dinner left their front doors unlocked and open, and their houses empty behind them. Driving back after dinner, we would pass stray parties of strollers, or lovers with hands entwined, murmurous by the lakes. It was late and lonely, but they apparently welcomed the darkness which causes keys to be turned and bolts shot in most other cities. Nevertheless, the local English paper carried a daily police diary, and seemed to find no dearth of matter with which to fill it. According to the 1981 census estimate, the total population of the city is about 672,000. Most of the crimes committed are in the old town, poorer and more densely populated than the new one. The green new city still possesses horizons, and in its purlieux it is still possible to listen to silence.

But the low and decrepit houses of the old city seem to exude noise. The narrow roads are cluttered with people and domestic fauna. Beside the roads are uneven lines of small shops and wayside stalls: on grimy mats, fruit and vegetables are spread out for sale. Bargains are made by means of hoarse shrieks swapped between buyer and seller. Five times a day the wailed cadences of Muslim prayer rise towards Allah. Film music blares from radio sets in the tea shops. Through all this hubbub, however, the people drift slowly, as though drugged, the male population like whiteclad wraiths, the women often in black burkas, long dresses like Bedouin tents, with hoods and veils to cover heads and faces. The drift-wood of history has washed up in the quarter: doors studded with brass open upon squalid courtyards, massive plastered arches lead nowhere.

At the heart of all this chaos are two narrow main streets, exactly parallel, and connected to each other by nine alleys, even narrower, but also parallel to one another. This grid system endures, ancient and solid, amidst the formless sprawl around it: like the studded doors, like the arches. The bricks of forgotten forts prop up the skewed walls of the houses: chipped mosques and crumbled mansions, where noblemen once lived, unexpectedly seize the eye at the corners of the miserable lanes. The gateways that once provided entry into the city no longer exist and now it is open to the world beyond, and seems to resent it, for soon it may cease to exist in its present form, in an era where renovation is all the rage. From the viewpoint of aesthetics, health and improved facilities, the renovation of the old city is highly desirable: from the romantic viewpoint, not.

The Bhopal area has always been haunted by life. Plants, animals and people have inhabited it since prehistory, then, generation by generation, gone back into the black and fertile soil. Glaciers and wind once carved out the landscape: the glaciers melted and turned into rivers, the rivers dried up and left few relics. The effect of all these evanescences has been to populate the countryside around the city with a host of memories, memories of the Buddhist, Hindu, and Muslim dynasties, enshrined in myth and, sometimes, in stone. The memories travel back beyond the frontiers of known history, to when the Bhopal district was a place without a name.

From 1956 onward, a great deal of construction work was done in Bhopal. At several building sites, prehistoric tools and weapons were found in the upturned earth, and identified by archaeologists. When proper excavations started, many more such primitive artefacts were dug up. It seemed as though if the topsoil were to be lifted like a lid off the city, a museumful of paleolithic relics would be discovered underneath. Fragments of chalcolithic pottery, with black motifs on redware, reminiscent of Harappan work, have also been unearthed. Even more importantly, a considerable number of painted rock shelters have been found all over Bhopal district, some within the city limits.

For millions of years through prehistory, the weather ripped at the rocks, and hollows were formed in the hills. For thousand of years, down to the present day, these hollows were used as human inhabitations. The ceilings and walls of these shelters were painted by their inhabitants, and each group tended to paint over the work of previous artists. This has caused some confusion: the earliest paintings have been tentatively dated back to a time some 25,000 years back, but there are others which were obviously done much later, in a historical period. Indeed a certain number of scholars have said that none of the paintings are, in their opinion, prehistoric.

Be that as it may, they exist. Green and yellow, red and white, the colours were taken from mineral deposits in the raw earth and rock, and were mixed with water and a fixative, tree resin or animal tallow. The brushes used were probably made of treated palmetto twigs or, for delicate work, porcupine quills. Some critics say that the shelter people only painted when they had nothing better to do, but the paintings cannot be described as idle scribbles. The use of a fixative indicates a desire to preserve the work, and the preparation of the colours and the brushes would in itself involve a lot of time, energy, and trouble. After all this, it is difficult to believe that the artist would start to paint merely because he was bored.

The best work, when examined in detail, has an awed and mysterious quality about it. The eye of the painter seems newly dipped in air: freshly washed by the world, it seems to see everything for the first time, to commemorate and record all this newness and mystery. Since prehistoric man was much enmeshed in ritual, the earliest stick-like but identifiable animals depicted in the caves were probably deified. Then stick-like men appear, hunters, whose sex the artist defined with a penis, as he defined the sex of a woman by her breasts. Later the stick-like men and animals disappear, and clearly outlined shapes stand out on the sallow rock. The hunters are now also warriors.

Over thousands of years, the weapons of hunters and warriors developed. The very early hunters carried axes and spears, but there is a multiplicity of bowmen. A kind of *bolas*, a throwing weapon which consisted of two round stones, fastened to either end of a rope, also appears. Much later in time, men are seen mounted on horses or elephants, and now many are equipped with shields and swords, but in all the periods covered by the paintings, the bowmen are present. The armed figures in the paintings are shown killing all sorts of animals, and also other men. But in the very earliest work there seems to be no mystique about death: killing seems taken as a natural human activity.

Themes of a less sanguinary type recur: women with children, dancers and musicians, men roasting their kill above a fire: honeycombs, fish, and isolated animals, all sources of food. Of the animals shown, the wild boar and the gaur are often depicted on a very large scale, possibly to define their hugeness in the eyes of the hunter, possibly because they were tribal totems. The bowmen are everywhere: their weapons, which obviated the necessity to approach a potentially dangerous prey too closely, look small and frail as their wielders, but were clearly effective. They were probably without flights, but the bamboo shafts were tipped with delicate brutal stone heads that pecked and bit their prey.

Female archers are also portrayed, so that it is conceivable that the whole tribe would take part in a hunt. Women would appear to have been in relatively short supply. However: there are descriptions of group sex, two men to a woman, and of bestiality practised on what appears to be a bitch. These, like the portrayals of killing, possess a certain rather occluded innocence: they are not pornography, but statements of situations. There is no attempt anywhere in the rock paintings to portray an individual. This is perhaps not only due to a deficiency of technique, but because the earliest painters in the rock shelters did not clearly perceive people as individuals, whether they were to be copulated with or killed.

Who these early painters were is an issue that has been much disputed. However, before the Dravidian and Aryan cultures manifested themselves in India, a shy and primitive people must have haunted the landscape: in all probability they were the ancestors of the present tribals, who still form a quarter of the population of Madhya Pradesh. The rocky hills where the painters left their presences form a strip from east to west across the entire state, and the motifs and style of some contemporary tribal art are not unlike those found in the rock shelters. The shelter dwellers of Madhya Pradesh have turned in the minds of later races into the 'demons' of Indian legend, as the goblins and trolls of Europe probably derive from racial memories of an earlier people.

*

Goblins and trolls would not have been unhappy at Bhimbetka. Some thirty miles south-east of Bhopal city, on a hogback ridge that rises above a once densely forested plain, stand the astonishing rock formations where people lived (as a fossilized human skull found there proves) more than 25,000 years back. Seen from a distance, they look like deformed Gothic castles strung out on the ridge: closer to, they are even more extraordinary, ridged and serrated masses of yellow and reddish rock which appear to have been splintered into pieces at some period in the past: so that great slabs and boulders seem to balance upon one another as though ready at any moment to come down.

The plain below is tame now, and under cultivation, and when I first visited the place, seemed friendly under a mild sun. This was in February: we scrambled about on the scree around the hills: green trees stood around us, sibilant in themselves, each populated by a musical curia of birds. A pleasant spot for a picnic, and indeed it is used as such by weekend trippers from Bhopal: on the walls where *sambar* and blackbuck in red and white outlines were perpetually poised for flight, numerous people had written their names, driven perhaps by the same instinct towards posterity as the original painters. Arrowheads and beads lay amidst pebbles round the excavation sites.

I thought of the stone implements and weapons the curator in the museum had shown me. The very placing of such artefacts in a museum civilizes them in some sense: at least when in glass crypts, between concrete walls, under artificial illumination, they seem to belong to our day, or anyway to some period not too far removed. The arrowheads and beads I picked up and threw away on that first visit to Bhimbetka seemed to belong to another place and time, but they evoked no associations in me or not very many more than discarded ice cream cartons would in a public park. It was all that sunlight, perhaps, an anodyne to the senses: or the visible presence of people farming on the plain below.

At Lascaux and Altamira, I always experienced a sense of mystery and, in the early days, before the tourists became tidal, of slight fright. These labyrinthine caves were proper places for a mystery: animal sacrifices took place within the painted walls, and ritual torches flamed, the paintings were themselves the mystery, and nobody appears to have actually lived in their vicinity. They seem to have been visited at intervals and for a purpose. At Bhimbetka the caves had been inhabited, very possibly not only by man but by his immediate ancestors, for many thousands of years. Lying on the ridged, sloped floor of what is called the zoo cave, painted animals above and around me, it was possible to see why.

This was a fairly typical shelter, shaped like a V lying on its side. About it loomed a mass of rock yellowed with lichen. A sentinel on the summit could look down across the sandstone slopes to the plain, and across the plain to the hills beyond. Presences on the plain could thus be clearly seen by the shelter people as soon as they appeared: the presence of food in the shape of browsing herbivores, and of fear in the shape of advancing enemies. The caves were not difficult to defend, if the people were forewarned of attack, for the screes and the tangle of thorns below made approach difficult. A ragged river seems to have flown past the foot of the formations, providing a water supply and attracting animals.

The shelters cannot have been very comfortable to live in, but at least they kept off much of the rain, and, being slightly elevated and open at one end, afforded some relief from the summer heat. For many people, these caves had been a home: children had scrambled and played on the talus below, and the smudge fires, producing smoke by day and flame by night, were shekinahs to the hunters as they came home. As the centuries passed, however, warriors from higher cultures appeared on the plains, armed better than the hill dwellers, and armoured: mounted on elephants, inimical. The records in the rocks show conflicts between them and the scantily clad and poorly armed people of the shelters: skirmishes rather than battles.

My next visit to Bhimbetka was in June, shortly before the onset of the monsoon. As we drove across the plain, a sullen lid of cloud shut down on us. The whole landscape was shrouded in dust spiralled by the wind, and there were no cultivators in the fields. We neared Bhimbetka, and saw ahead of us, shrouded in low cloud and dust, the monolithic formations on the ridge: in that light, they seemed to have receded, both in space and time, back into their past. The birds, when we climbed to the caves, were silent, but the trees hissed like kettles in the wind, and their dry leaves brushed together with a sound like fire. While my companions went on ahead, I seated myself on a rock and looked over the plain.

All I could see was cloud overhead and dust below, through where there were occasional ghostly intimations of trees and fields. An eerie stillness held the air, like that within the eye of a cyclone, but unrelated sounds broke it now and then, the rustle of dead leaves in the wind, the snap of dry thorns, the distant cry of an animal. Deprived of daylight, Bhimbetka had become a place of fear. If it was so for me, a product of my century, it must have been unimaginably more so for the naked men who lived by instincts rather than ideas, who were aware of the forest around them and were apprehensive as to what might come out of it, who were full of a prescience of the unknown.

It was a day of discovery: I went after my friends, and we looked at the painted walls of the shelters. Even in the stygian atmosphere of that afternoon, the colours, dim as they were, seemed to leap off the walls, as much a source of comfort as food and a fire. In the lee of a huge rock we kindled cigarettes. Beyond it was a cave which contained the picture of a colossal bull in pursuit of a hunter whose two companions stood helplessly by. The snout of the bull, dwarfing the hunter, nearly touched him, and for him there was no escape: he was being driven towards a monstrous crab-like creature that rose from the shadowed wall in a posture of menace. Perhaps in the end the images of bull and crab, dreamlike lords of death, most fully expressed the ethos of Bhimbetka.

*

By the time India had moved into a period of ascertainable history, death by violence was a commonplace in the country. The *Mahabharata* and *Ramayana* had already recorded bloody battles that had been lost and won in prehistory. The sombre cavalry and infantry depicted in some of the rock paintings may have had brief clashes with the shelter dwellers, but must usually have been on their way to some more consequential conflict. Greed and lust have been the prerogatives of princes everywhere and always: by 600 BC northern India was a cockpit of warlords and princes in continual combat. The overspill of blood from the north found its way into the forests of what is now called Madhya Pradesh.

Some princes sickened on this bloody surfeit. Blades clashed and widows keened all over the country: this terrible harmony drove the Buddha from his paternal palace into the forest, in whose thorny arbours he separated truths and founded one of the seminal philosophies of the world. In the third century BC the Maurya prince Asoka, weary of warfare, accepted the Buddhist doctrines. He planted his empire with pillars, each inscribed with an edict that mainly pertained to the proper conduct of life.

His own life was somewhat bound up with the land which is now Madhya Pradesh, for while still crown prince he was made Viceroy of Malwa, the spacious plateau which today ocupies the centre of the state.

His duties took him around the territory. He visited a prosperous town called Vidisha, some thirty miles north of modern Bhopal. Vidisha was famous for its money lenders, one of whom had a daughter, Devi. Asoka married her, and she bore him three children. But when Asoka eventually departed for Patna (the ancient Indian kings tended, for political reasons, to have a wife in every fort) he left a disconsolate Devi behind in Vidisha. Since he took the children with him, she had little to do: she occupied herself in the establishment of a Buddhist retreat on a hillock not far from her home. The hillock was called Sanchi, and Asoka in turned crowned it with a Buddhist stupa and built a school there for monks.

Sanchi is one of the most famous Buddhist shrines in the world, but its provenance was not entirely to do with Asoka. After he died, and the Maurya dynasty was succeeded in 187 BC by the Sungas, more stupas were built. Another seven centuries were to pass before the last additions were made to Sanchi, for successive dynasties renovated it and built upon its slopes. During this lengthy period, Buddhist monks and scholars flocked to the hillock, pilgrims and students. They still do: when U Nu, the exiled Burmese Prime Minister, fled to India, where he spent ten years, he elected to live in Bhopal, so that he could be near Sanchi. The Dalai Lama did not take so extreme a step, but has been there.

It is a lonely place, though lonely in a different way from Bhimbetka. The gateways hewn from golden stone, glow gently around the dome of the main stupa. Whenever I visited it, I was effusively welcome by a pack of crossbred terriers who appeared to be resident: going up towards the stupa, I was ambushed by trees, in most seasons covered by flowers so intricately frail they seemed to have been painted on enamel. There was a tranquil incantatory murmur from indubitably Buddhist birds and the whole hillock was apparently drenched in sleep. Nothing in the entire place demanded anything much from the visitor: not amazement and not awe: only, as it were, a kind of participation in its peace.

The gateways, four of them, introduced rather than admitted me into the circular inner courtyard. Steps lead up from it to a parapet that circles the dome. I used to walk around it slowly, looking down beyond the gateways to the luminous trees and the smaller stupas cloaked in their benison of shadow. The Jatakas, episodes in the life of the Buddha, are shown in stone on the gateways, each winged with a scroll that uncurls on either side, an indication of how serenely and endlessly that life unfolded.

Some of the figures were mutilated, centuries back, by Muslim steel: but even these barbarously hacked statues, crouched on their plinths like victims of torture, seem to live beyond sadness and to accept.

Time had left milestones all round the Bhopal district. The Sunga kings who replaced the Mauryas, though themselves, Hindus, built new stupas at Sanchi. But they also put up temples: one, dedicated to Vishnu, was erected in 113 BC at Bhesnagar, now a suburb of the modern Vidisha. Its sculptured walls fell away with the years, like petals from the calyx of a stone tulip. An inscribed pillar, the solitary stamen, remained. It now stands in a dusty enclosure near Bhesnagar: the local cattle loaf about round it, somnolent with their cuds: it is fronted by a bemerded lane. The inscription on the pillar records the conversion to Hinduism, in particular to Vaishnavism, of Heliodorus, an ambassador sent by a Greek satrap to the Sunga court two centuries before Christ.

The dynasties rose and fell in northern India, too many to enumerate, some Hindu, some Buddhist. The power of each dynasty swelled and shrank, by processes too complex to explain. Each left its tidewrack in Malwa. Pillars with indecipherable inscriptions, copper and silver coins which are perforated and rusted, have been found and dusted and comfortably lodged in museums. They are cold to the touch, and convey no hint of any human dream, though they must have passed through many. The conniving courts, with their truculent or timorous kings, their sumptuous queens who smelt of musk and honey, led a sealed and hermetic life in their own day, and have carried their possibly unpleasant secrets, intact, down the centuries to ours.

We know their names, however, and their approximate dates. A Paramara ruler, Bhoj, held uncertain sway over Malwa for nearly half a century from AD 1010. He was singularly luckless in his battles, a pity, since he was embroiled in a considerable number. The Kalyani Chalukyas not only invaded his territory but plundered his capital, Dhar. Further defeats followed, administered by the Chandelas and the Kalachuris respectively. How he continued to keep his throne is a mystery, since he was no learner from experience. Towards the end of his life, he made a quixotic attempt to attack another branch of the Chalukyas. Predictably, he was defeated once more: inadvisedly preparing for further combat, he fell ill and died.

Apart from his remarkably poor martial record, there seems little reason to remember him. He dabbled in literature, which may explain his inability to master more physical skills, but none of his work has survived. However, he is said to have been responsible for the dam that created the twin lakes of Bhopal. The unfortunate monarch's primary claim to fame rises from these polluted waters. It has been authoritatively stated that from a corruption of the word Bhojpal, Bhoj's dam, comes the name of the capital of Madhya Pradesh. If that is so, the king has his memorial, and a legacy of water, however insanitary, is a more beneficial bequest than that of most kings, a legacy of blood.

If the lives of the shelter dwellers were commemorated in paints, the lives of the ancient and medieval Indian courts were commemorated in stone. Ever since the historical period commenced, the more powerful kings busily built temples. Not only were masons necessary, but sculptors: sculpture was essential to a temple, with friezes on the facade, and large statues for the inner courtyards and shrines. Since temples proliferated all over the country, thousands of highly talented sculptors must have existed all over the subcontinent for this plethora to be possible. This is remarkable in itself, especially since India has no subsequent history of noteworthy sculpture.

When the temples were first built they were brightly painted, to stand out at a distance. The coats of paint have been stripped from the statues by weather and years, so that we see them now devoid, as it were, of their outer habiliments. They were probably not meant to be seen like this, but it is equally probable that they look better now than they did when new. The conceptual passion and precision, the delicacy of delineation in the statues, especially when the number produced was so immense, is incredible. Sculpture in ancient India was by no means a mechanical art: the elaborate coiffures and rather scanty raiment are precisely portrayed, but the expression, not only in the faces but the flesh of the statues, reveal deep empathy between the perception of the sculptor and the properties of his material. If modern European sculptors tend to fight the nature of their medium, the ancient Indian sculptors seemed to become part of the nature of theirs. They answered the needs of the stone, and the difficult stone answered them.

The sculptors did not set out to depict the lives of the poor. There was as little room for the problems of the masses in the temple friezes as there was in the courts. The gods and heroes portrayed in the friezes had to look physically perfect: the diseased had no place among deities, nor the malnourished among monarchs. The sculptors conformed to the prevalent idea of physical beauty, that is to say the court ideal. It is difficult to believe that all the courtiers were as physically perfect as the statues, but the sculptors must have had models. Even today there are Indian women, though not men, who look like their counterparts in the temples. I personally do not find it difficult when I encounter such women, to transpose them mentally to a temple frieze: admittedly with no very devout intentions. I doubt if the intentions of the sculptors differed much from mine.

The sculptors ceased their activities abruptly when the Muslims, who disliked idols, conquered India. By the fourteenth century, Malwa was Muslim. The conquerors beheaded statues, Hindus, and one another for some years. The plateau was transformed, not for the first time, into a backdrop for battle. Fortifications were in fashion, and the hills were strewn with soldiers. Islamnagar, near modern Bhopal, became the capital. Its ruins, not unreasonably dilapidated, remain: unkempt tombs and desiccated fountains, shabby, silent palaces. By the nineteenth century Bhopal had supplanted it as the capital. Much of the old city already existed, lying by its lakes in the forest while its future approached it.

Such a multiplicity of statues existed in the temples and shrines of Bhopal district that it is not peculiar that many of them have turned up in the city itself, and some in unexpected locations. Two statues of Ganpati are preserved in a mosque. The compound of the police headquarters contains what are described as '41 images' fixed in its walls. These date back to the Paramara period, as do the Jain statues and pillars situated behind the office of a large bank. Whether the statues were found at these sites or brought there seems a little unclear. The present and past are rather confused in Bhopal: an archaeological map of the city marks, among other historic sites, the bus stand and the railway station.

The provenance of all the sculptures lying around Bhopal cannot be exactly ascertained, but Madhya Pradesh has become a state much visited by antique dealers. It abounds in ruined or deserted temples watched over only by stray dogs and trees, and some of these temples contain sculpture which, if broken off the wall by an expert, can be profitably disposed of in Delhi or Bombay. Moreover, cultivators sometimes find hacked heads or even small statues in their fields: terracotta pieces too: and the dealers are ready to buy them. Destitute priests in unattended temples can be bribed to turn a blind eye if statues are taken from the shrine: so can underpaid watchmen. An immense fortune has been smuggled out of the state in art treasures, one expert told me, and more than half the illegally acquired pieces of temple art in India come from Madhya Pradesh, taken away by thieves.

The difficulty about prevention of theft lies in the size of the state. Some shrines and temples have been declared national monuments, and are administered and watched over by officers from Delhi: others, protected monuments, are looked after by the state. But there are a number of sites which have not really been taken account of, remote and hard to protect which the agents of the dealers are fairly free to plunder. Village temples are impossible to preserve: the local people, when offered money, are perfectly willing to part with a few chipped pieces of stone. 'It's very systematic,' said one officer, 'and because the dealers have such a network, very difficult to keep under control.'

Apart from the thieves of the present, the museums of the world have, in the past, systematically depleted Madhya Pradesh of its antiquities. 'The British Museum and the Victoria and Albert in London,' an archaeologist remarked bitterly, 'have more pieces from central India than all the museums in Madhya Pradesh. Bharhut, which was a sort of sister to Sanchi, was destroyed by the French and the British: destroyed in the sense that the best pieces were taken away for exhibition in the West. Sanchi was protected by the fact that it stood on a hillock and was surrounded by thick forest. Even so, one of the Napoleons wanted to carry the northern gateway of Sanchi away to a Paris museum.

'The logistics were too difficult for him, luckily. But even Indian museums, all those more than sixty or seventy years old, have collaborated in destroying the archaeological sites in the state. The total number of ancient works of art taken out of Madhya Pradesh, not only by unlicensed thieves but by museums, comes to much more than the total number removed from the rest of India. Apart from all this, there's excavation. Mortimer Wheeler said, "archaeological excavation is only destruction". University students are carelessly issued with licences to excavate; and they cause irreparable harm. They aren't guided properly. For an important operation, you have to put a knowledgeable surgeon in charge. He'll do what's necessary with the least damage. In an archaeological excavation, much depends on the leader. We are very careful, now, about issuing any licences for excavation.'

My informant sank back in his office chair, tired after this tirade. A peon brought in a file, which he examined carefully. He initialled the pages, sent the peon and the file away, and resumed his discourse. 'Now,' he said, 'our main task is one of preservation. The rock shelters, for example. The paintings survived exposure to the weather, but now they are also exposed to the public, who can damage them more quickly and severely than natural processes could do. We cannot remove them from the shelters. All we can do is to maintain a photographic record, and find enough money in the budget to keep a proper watch over the shelters. It's exactly the same with the shrines and temples. They must be guarded against people as well as natural processes. Chemists have now been asked to cooperate in the preservation of ancient monuments and prevent more deterioration.'

Most Indian museums exhibit antiquities without details as to the nature of the site and the physical position of the objects when they were found, both of which are important to the researcher. So the archaeological department is trying to ensure that all sites in the state are completely documented before anything is removed from them. After this they want to start small museums in the Panchayat halls of villages, and to distribute popular literature and picture books on archaeological sites in Madhya Pradesh to primary schools. The idea is to educate people into a realization of the importance of old stones, 'though,' said the archaeologist frankly, 'we aren't sure whether this will work'. Full-scale replicas of certain temples have been built in the original materials, and are to be exhibited at the Gwalior museum. 'They will be painted: they'll look as they originally were.'

The Department of Culture in Madhya Pradesh, under which the archaeological department comes, has allotted it a budget of Rs. 57.5 lakhs for the 1980–2 period. This is part of what is called, in a rather Wellsian way, 'The Sixth Plan for Culture in Madhya Pradesh.' The other components of the Plan include various schemes for teaching and popularizing the arts, and, perhaps more practically, for providing opportunities and money to indigent artists. According to the blueprint, special efforts are to be made to preserve tribal and folk culture in an authentic manner. This may be more difficult to do in practice than it would seem to be while its existence is confined to paper, for the scheme has various aspects, and the doubtless multifarious files it will create will inundate several different departments and ministries. Everything in life is connected: so is everything in administration.

*

It is difficult for the administration to know how to deal with the tribals. 'It's said on the one hand that we must preserve their culture,' said a senior official of the tribal welfare department, 'and on the other that we must improve and modernize their lives. That means that we have to introduce them to a new culture. It is as certain as night follows day that this will destroy the old one.' The problem inherent in all development schemes in the state is that each involves a certain amount of destruction. A great deal of deforestation has taken place and has benefited irrigation and industry, but not tribal culture, for it is essentially a forest culture.

It is not only that a number of essential elements of tribal diet disappeared wherever the mixed forest was lopped down, but the fact that the thinking and behaviour of the tribals were created and shaped by the forest. The forest was a part of their lives, and offered education: effort and money went towards the establishment of schools and polytechnics in tribal areas. But teachers complained that tribal children, whose parents were illiterate, did not come from a background that encouraged the educative process: moreover, their thinking patterns were different from those of other children.

Tribal children, the educators in the field said, were very likely to drop out of the system, never to be scooped back into it: while they were in it, they impeded the advance of the other children. It was also true that those who endured the system to the end and acquired posts (often as teachers) thereafter, tended to seek employment in the towns, and to look down upon the tribal lives they had left. Equally, their people in the forest treated those who were educated and employed as outcasts. It would take a generation to remove all the barriers: meanwhile, there was the question of the preservation of tribal culture in, as the Plan stipulated, an authentic manner.

When I was told about all this in Bhopal, I had not yet been to the tribal areas. But I was impressed by the number of departments involved in the cultural issue: tribal welfare, forestry, and education, directly, and several others, like irrigation and industry, indirectly. The administrative system, however, is flexible, and absorbs both present and, anticipatorily, future shock. Its ability to bend is more noticeable than its capacity to break, a legacy from the British administrative system which is followed in Madhya Pradesh as in every other Indian state. The system banks on the adaptability and resourcefulness of the officers in the field, without which it could not survive.

When the state was founded, there was no proper Secretariat: now there is one, Vallabh Bhavan, half a dozen storeys in pink and white sandstone, inhabited by hundreds of ministers and officers and thousands of files. Herbivorous clerks ruminate at their heaped desks over *paan* and cups of tea, swap stories in the corridors, or disappear for hours on unspecified errands. Government service is secure: and in thirty years they will be able to peg their lives to a pension. Surveying them, it is difficult to see how anything is ever done, though the scene is no different from that in any other Government office in India. But things are done, and the teleprinters are busy all day.

This is largely because of the senior officers. I was amazed, in Bhopal, to see that many chose not to take holidays: 'in fact,' one said, 'I get more work than usual done on Sundays, because there's nobody around to disturb me.' This was in the late afternoon of a weekday, and the clerks had fixed expectant eyes on the clock. At five precisely, they all rose and left, chattering happily as they went. 'It's the only time in the day,' said my friend, 'when they are particular about punctuality.' He would himself remain in the office a couple of hours more, so that he could start the next day from a clear desk. His key personnel would stay with him, voluntarily. 'We have to get things done.'

*

The Vidhan Sabha, or Legislative Assembly, squats with a lowering look in the middle of the new city. It is not far from the lower lake, and next door to the Aquarium, in both of which places torpid fish, fortunately mute, also open and close their mouths all day. Madhya Pradesh is for some reason one of the major Indian states without an Upper House; but it does not seem to feel the loss much: indeed its tranquillity is, if anything, increased thereby. As the largest Indian state, it has a plentiful supply of MLAs: 320 in 1981. Some come from towns and cities, others are backwoods boys: it is only natural, therefore, that the standard of debate should be uneven.

Bhopal, in comparison to most other state capitals, is not a very political city. The interests of the people are confined to local issues, and indeed this is true of most parts of the state, where the political involvement is largely parochial. A geographer of repute explained this to me: 'Until recently,' she said, 'because of the difficulties of transport and terrain, the people in many parts of the state were isolated, not only physically but mentally. Anything that happened outside their own area didn't concern them. Even their social attitudes stayed fixed in the past: stagnant. They may have been curious about the outside world, but they were also completely insulated from it.'

Smiling from a sofa, a friend told me a story. 'In the 1980 elections,' he said, 'a lady politician badly wanted to spread her party message to the interior of her constituency. This was a remote area, with no roads, but she was rich. At great expense, she hired a helicopter. Then she sent a courier to the interior to inform the people of her arrival. She landed in a village and was delighted: there were hundreds of people there, not only from that village but from every village in the neighbourhood, all cheering and clapping.' I said, 'So it was a worthwhile expense.' My friend replied, 'No. They hadn't come to see the politician. They had come to see the helicopter.'

Geographical factors have played a very important part in the history of Madhya Pradesh. They have kept some parts of it isolated from others: also, for centuries, they kept large tracts of what now forms the state isolated from other parts of India. There were densely forested hills, thought to be the abode of demons, deep streams and rivers with no way across, no bridge, no ford. Central India, then, acted as a buffer zone, an unknowing keeper of the peace between north and south. It was very difficult for the fierce northern kings to invade the south, or for the ambitious southern kings to lead their armies north, over the bulwark of rivers, hills and forests in between.

In my first days in Bhopal, I was immersed in the past: like a medieval pilgrim in the capital of a new land, I browsed over the rock shelters, the monuments, and the libraries in and around the city. I talked to many people, and absorbed into myself the aura of huge lands beyond the horizon. A brobdingnagian burden of inaction waited to be shed from my shoulders: like the medieval pilgrim, I wanted to be on my way, though I did not expect anthropophagi or unicorns to cross my path. Steel mills and tribal polytechnics were more like it, but even these, at a distance, and still to be seen, acquired an aura of romance. I was ready for the road, and itched to be off.

My photographer and I were accompanied by a senior Government official, P. S. Dhagat. A gentle person, he often had a rather concerned look about him, understandable enough in anyone forced to accompany me on a long trip. However, he made some order out of my chaos, and shepherded me through the state with a continual murmured flow of information on every topic from agriculture to zoology. He had been a journalist and a labour leader, and a quarter of a century in Government service did not affect his socialism or prevent him for believing the best of everybody else, often to his undoing. Because he was so exceedingly unmilitary, I nicknamed him the General. Led by him, we departed into the distances.

Arvind Krishna Mehrotra (b. 1947)

Arvind Krishna Mehrotra was born in the year that the nation-state we presently call 'India' also came into being. According to some, it was a year of portents, of angels and monsters with peculiar gifts coming into the world. One wonders how Mehrotra fits in with that creation-myth, born as he was in Lahore, brought into India in the time of Partition in a train when he was a few months old, and growing up in Allahabad, a colonial centre of education and culture already in decline, the son of a dentist. His childhood, unlike Saleem Sinai's, was not immediately prophetic in any way, but was outwardly tranquil, inwardly agitated by the imagination, and in location surburban, as these lines from his poem 'Continuities' reveal:

> At seven-thirty we are sent home
> From the Cosmopolitan Club,
> My father says, 'No bid,'
> My mother forgets her hand
> In a deck of cards.
> I sit on the railing till midnight
> Above a worn sign
> That advertises a dentist.

As a young man, he discovered, with some friends, Corso, Ferlinghetti, Ginsberg, and the French Surrealists, and, negotiating these paradigms, made it his purpose, in his poetry, to renew and to impart a fresh, sometimes mysterious, sometimes threatening, gleam to the 'worn signs' of which a suburban existence in a declining colonial city is composed. His latest book of poems is the *The Transfiguring Places* (1998), and he has also produced an excellent anthology of Indian poetry in English. Neither angel nor monster, Mehrotra has emerged as a hyphenated mutation, the poet-critic, of exceptional quality, in a country among whose several unremarked calamities is the unhappy state of its criticism; in this, at least, he is a miracle. He teaches us, as in the essay below, which began as a riposte to a fellow-poet on the subject of A. K. Ramujan's poetry, and developed as a subtle exploration of the issues of bilingualism, translation, and 'Indianness' in contemporary Indian English poetry, that it is possible to write criticism of a high order about Indian writing in English without either entirely abandoning the world of 'English literature', or fully belonging to it, or without situating oneself exclusively in the politics of post-colonial theory. The piece reminds us, too, that it was really the poets, and very seldom the novelists, who were intent upon discussing, and theorizing, in the sixties, seventies, and early eighties, the psychological and technical complexities of what it means, as an Indian, to write in English; it is a discussion and debate which, for its quality and vigour, and the way in which it was initiated by and involved actual practitioners, has had no successor.

* * *

from *The Emperor Has No Clothes* (1982)

The letters of Indian writers in English may never be published, but in case they are they will open up several unmapped areas of the literary terrain. One of these was recently suggested by Adil Jussawalla. In 'Six Authors in Search of a Reader' he uses the letters he has received from friends to show what a generation of Indian writers did in the late 1960s when they were abandoned by Indian publishers and had to improvise ways of contacting their readers on their own. Sandipan Chattopadhyay's Minibooks, Vilas Sarang's stories in *Encounter* and *TriQuarterly*, the establishment of Clearing House and Newground were some of their strategies. The strategies worked and Chattopadhyay sold 1,000 copies of the first Minibook within a week; Sarang's stories will be brought out by New Directions;* Clearing House and Newground have so far published nine books of poems between them and more titles continue to be added.

Not every story resurrected from a writer's files is so absorbing. Should the executors of the literary estate of R. Parthasarathy allow the publication of his letters to Jayanta Mahapatra, the reader of the future will find that the terrain is different. On 4 August 1979 Mahapatra wrote me a letter. In it he quoted a paragraph from one of Parthasarathy's letters to him, and I reproduce it here since it refers to this essay:

---

* They were eventually brought out by Penguin India in 1990.

I have serious doubts if you ought to encourage dilettantish writing of the sort displayed by Rabi S. Mishra [see 'A. K. Ramanujan: A Point of View' in *Chandrabhāgā*, No. 1, Summer 1979]. It is easy to disclaim responsibility by saying 'Opinions expressed in *Chandrabhāgā* are not those of the editor but of individual contributors.' But, in fact, the editor *is* responsible as it is published only with his approval. I wonder if this is the first in a series of exercises at literary demolition. I wish you would stop it. I enclose a letter which I hope you would be gracious enough to publish in *Chandrabhāgā*, No. 2, Winter 1979. This kind of irresponsible writing must not go unanswered. I learn Arvind Krishna Mehrotra is sharpening his knife to cut *Rough Passage* to size. If this is true, I don't think I am going to be amused by it. If this is *Chandra-bhāgā*'s editorial stance, I am not sure you are serving any useful purpose, and whatever support you might expect, even that would soon be eroded.

Before I come to Parthasarathy's letter in *Chandrabhāgā* and his poem *Rough Passage*, I want to look at the ten sentences above. They illuminate a period of our history in a way nothing else does; they are also a network of roads which will lead the traveller to the heart of *Rough Passage*.

In his first avian move, Parthasarathy circles over Rabi Shankar Mishra and then rushes towards the irresponsible editor of *Chandrabhāgā* who encouraged the Sambalpur dilettante to fling mud at A. K. Ramanujan. While he leaves Mishra alone, he pecks at the editor. 'But, in fact, the editor *is*...' Pleased, he hops back two steps and waits. Is this really, he thinks to himself, the first in a series of 'literary demolitions' to be carried out by a suicide squad from Tinkonia Bagicha? Well, if it is there is little our bird can do about it and he may have already overreached himself. So what does he do? In one ear he hisses, 'I wish you would stop it.' And in the other hums, 'I enclose a letter which I hope you would be gracious...' By now half the neighbourhood's children have fallen in love with the bird, and the bird wonders if it has not gone too far in the other direction. He changes tack and begins to speak in the voice of the town's senior citizen, who spends his waking hours in writing letters to the editor, complaining about the poor street lighting arrangements. 'This kind of irresponsible writing must not go unanswered.' His duty done, the bird prepares to leave, but not before he has surprised everyone in the crowd by coming back instead. He is not any more the friendly uncle but a mixture of bawling child, school bully, and streetcorner hood: 'I learn Arvind Krishna Mehrotra is sharpening his knife ... I don't think I am going to be amused by it ... I am not sure you are serving any useful purpose, and whatever support you might expect, even that would soon be eroded.' In the end the hood crushes his cheroot and blows a smoke ring. While I, I suppose, put my knife to the grinder and watch the sparks fly.

*

> Mishra's is an irresponsible and unfortunate exercise in debunking a poet who is generally considered significant. In 1976 ... I had remarked: 'Ramanujan's repossession, through his poetry, of the past of his family and of his sense of himself as a distillation of that past is to me a signal achievement...' Unaware of this fundamental aspect of Ramanujan's contribution, Mishra, the English teacher, chastises him for not writing like Pope, Yeats, Eliot or Neruda. Irrelevant as this comparison is, Mishra's attitude is not: it is potentially dangerous ... Might I suggest that Mishra stay clear of the treacherous waters of Indian English literature when he is so patently unfamiliar with the topography?

So Parthasarathy in his letter to *Chandrabhāgā*, No. 2, Winter 1979. But what was that cataclysmic event which turned the azureous waters of Indian English literature into a treacherous swamp? Rabi S. Mishra begins 'A. K. Ramanujan: A Point of View' by saying,

> A study of A. K. Ramanujan's poetry leads one to the uncomfortable conclusion that he is incapable of broad patterns of experience ... He reflects an inherently narrow range, and with the intellectual thinness of his poems he cannot achieve the depth that should qualify him for a significant poet.

Mishra knows this to be a minority opinion and admits his discomfort at the outset. Though ten years ago, writing on Ramanujan in *Contemporary Indian Poetry in English*, S. Nagarajan made a similar observation: 'Almost all the poems in the new volume [*Relations*] suffer to some extent from ... intellectual thinness.' Parthasarathy fires a warning shot at the trawler when he says it is unfortunate that Mishra has debunked a poet who is 'generally considered significant.' In the language of the Opies the phrase would translate as follows:

> There was an old man,
> And he had a calf,
>   And that's half;
> He took him out of the stall,

> And put him on the wall,
> And that's all.

Having done this, Parthasarathy reminds Mishra that in 1976 he had decided, on everyone's behalf, the precise nature of Ramanujan's achievement and therefore the subject was closed. By way of advice he adds that English teachers should approach the calf without making irrelevant allusions to poets from Pope to Neruda; he feels that the attitude underlying it is 'potentially dangerous'. The argument is odd. If some comparisons are so meaningless and trivial, there should be nothing to fear in them. And even if we heed the warning, is it true that the shell will burst in our faces if we read a poem by Ramanujan alongside one by Yeats? Other questions put themselves: should readings take place in cork-lined rooms or where voices from outside can enter? Should we attempt to further isolate Indian English poetry or should we see if it can still find a place under the sun? Should we stifle criticism which seeks to express another point of view or should we watch it with interest? And should we terrorize the editor who publishes this criticism?

Now Parthasarathy is no fool; elsewhere in the same letter to *Chandra-bhāgā* he says that 'responsible criticism' is absent from the Indian English literary scene. 'What exists ... is invariably laudatory in tone or is intended to damn with faint praise ... There is no evidence in them of either scholarship or of the critical faculty at work.' (Though a sentence in his personal communication to Mahapatra shows how keen he is to hear criticism other than laudatory: 'I wish you would stop it.') He continues, 'Those who write are familiar with British or American literature; their terms of reference are usually borrowed from that literature. The exercise becomes, as a result, as in Mishra's case, inappropriate and futile.'

A lot hinges on how we take the ubiquitous phrase 'responsible criticism' or, for that matter, 'the critical faculty'. Through certain clues provided by Parthasarathy himself we know what he would like excluded from its scope: everything which runs counter to his opaque statements on the nature of poetry; selected acts of literary demolition; most references to British or American literature. I have a lot to say on Parthasarathy's opacities and will not go into them just now. So far as demolition is concerned one knows it to be an inseparable part of the literary process, and Parthasarathy, who has himself been a teacher, could not have so quickly lost the perspective which comes in the classroom to not see that if poets are struck down by one generation of readers they can always bounce back with the next; and on the critical necessity of placing a work both among its near (Tamil Brahmin, Poona Parsi, Goan Catholic) *and* distant (Jesuit, WASP, Mormon) relatives, there is Octavio Paz's essay 'On Criticism':

> ... the space created by critical action, the place where works meet and confront each other, is a no man's land in our countries. The mission of criticism is not to invent works but to establish relations between them ... In this sense, criticism has a creative function: it creates a literature (a perspective, an order) out of individual works. This is precisely what our criticism has failed to do. And that is why where is no Hispano-American literature, even though there exists a whole body of important works. (*Alternating Current*)

There are, Paz says, two complementary tasks before the critic: 'to show that Hispano-American works are a *single literature*, a field of antagonistic relations; and to describe the relationships of this literature to other literatures.'

Parthasarathy and I attach different charges to 'responsible criticism'. I would say that if criticism has the health of the literary community in mind its framework should not be coterminous with the country's political boundary. The superstitous manner in which Parthasarathy refers to 'British or American literature' and to critics who 'borrow' from them was analysed by Pound in a 1917 essay. He begins 'Provincialism the Enemy' by saying,

> PROVINCIALISM consists in:
> (a) An ignorance of the manners, customs and nature of people living outside one's own village, parish or nation.
> (b) A desire to coerce others into uniformity.
> Galdos, Turgenev, Flaubert, Henry James, the whole fight of modern enlightenment is against this. It is not of any one country. I name four great modern novelists because, perhaps, the best of their work has been an analysis, a diagnosis of this disease.
> Provincialism is more than an ignorance, it is ignorance plus a lust after uniformity. It is a latent malevolence, often an active malevolence. (*Selected Prose*)

The word 'Provincialism' brings into focus the drift of Parthasarathy's Hindu revivalist mind.

Indian English literature is in its pupal stage, which we can either preserve as a specimen or leave alone in the open to face the often mild but sometimes inclement weather.

*

The poems of A. K. Ramanujan are a case in point. How are they to be seen? Much as I enjoy them, are they going to be buried like a treasure and guarded by a hound; worshipped like a village deity; turned into a two-headed freak with a long tail (minus the tail, its two-headedness could be a way of looking at it, but that is not what I here mean)? Or are they going to be read and commented on, praised and condemned, as poems are?

These are some of the issues raised by Parthasarathy's *Chandrabhāgā* letter, but peripherally. In its main part he says

> ... that Ramanujan's work offers the first indisputable evidence of the *validity* of Indian English verse. Both *The Striders* (1966) and *Relations* (1971) are the heir of an anterior tradition, a tradition very much of this subcontinent, the deposits of which are in Kannada and Tamil, and which have been assimilated into English. Ramanujan's deepest roots are in the Tamil and Kannada past, and he has repossessed that past, in fact made it available, in the English language. I consider this a *significant* achievement ... Ramanujan has successfully conveyed in English what, at its subtlest and most incantational, is locked up in another linguistic tradition. He has ... indicated the direction Indian English verse is likely to take in the future. 'Prayers to Lord Murugan,' overlooked by Mishra, is ... embedded in, and arises from, a specific tradition. It is ... the first step towards establishing an indigenous tradition of Indian English verse.

Both here and in his 1976 essay on Ramanujan, 'How It Strikes a Contemporary', the 'responsible critic' will find much that is vacuous, tautological, and ipse dixitish.

The languages inherited by the multilingual Ramanujan may not conform to Parthasarathy's geological model. For the model to hold we first have to grant that Ramanujan arranges Tamil and Kannada in the lower stratas, English in the upper, and each time he writes he descends into Tamil/Kannada with a Davy lamp. Unless we know more about how languages are positioned in multilingual sensibilities – do they always keep this inflexible order? – and how writers relate to them, it is premature to dogmatize about the 'anterior tradition'.

The phrase presents other difficulties. Does it mean that the Tamil and Kannada traditions are anterior *per se*, and the poet with access to their 'deposits' has an edge over those who do not? This is like saying that A. K. Ramanujan's pre-eminence as a poet lies solely in his being Attipat Krishnaswami Ramanujan of Mysore. In its context the phrase can also mean that Ramanujan's 'roots' in the subcontinent go deep because he spoke a native language first and learnt English subsequently (as if he were given a choice). Barring a few, most Indian English writers acquire the language they write in and seldom lick it off their mothers' teats. Everyone equally inherits the tradition which is 'very much of this subcontinent', and everyone has access to its 'deposits' in the Indo-Aryan and Dravidian languages. If sometimes the poet skips the ritual of offering a prayer to Lord Murugan or his collaterals, it does not follow that he stands disinherited. This whole question of multilingualism should be looked at less jingoistically if it is to have any meaning, as I think it does.

We will remember that 'Prayers to Lord Murugan' is given as the example of a poem which transfers to English what is 'embedded in, and arises from, a specific tradition.' This is what translations try to do and Ramanujan, writing about his attempts in the Translator's Note to *Speaking of Siva*, says, 'I have tried to ... *map* the medieval Kannada onto the sound-look of modern English ... The few liberties I have taken are towards a close structural mimicry, a re-enactment in English, the transposition of a structure in one texture onto another.' I therefore find it a little strange that when Parthasarathy talks about Ramanujan successfully conveying 'in English what, at its subtlest and most incantational, is looked up in another linguistic tradition', he does not have *The Interior Landscape* and *Speaking of Siva* in mind but *The Striders* and *Relations*. Should we not say that since poems in English and translations from Dravidian languages, though done by the same person, are materially different, they ought to be read in different ways? Or did M. R. Satyanarayana's nonsensical statement that Kolatkar's *Jejuri* nowhere reads like a translation conceal an important truth? And has Parthasarathy not done the same thing by describing Ramanujan's achievement as a poet in terms which are similar to those which Ramanujan employs to write about his aims as a translator? These questions are too arcane to be answered with any definiteness at present. Indeed, the line which separates the Indian English poem as a weak act of cultural transmission, a much-maligned monster, from one which is a work of art in its own right, a 'meta-translation', has never been so missed.

Parthasarathy also refers to 'Prayers to Lord Murugan' in 'How It Strikes a Contemporary'. Taking his ideas from a headmaster's uplifting speech, he says that the poem 'examines a tradition gone to seed, and invokes its relevance to our own times.' He does not tell us anything about the tradition's functioning and how it went to seed, how the poem examines it, how the invocation takes place, and what its relevance 'to our own times' is. Instead, he doles out bits of information about Murugan's changing fortune: in the sixth century he is eclipsed by Vishnu and Siva; there is a revival of the cult a thousand years later. He approvingly quotes the poem's second section in which Murugan, in the tradition of Tamil heroic poetry, 'is vividly invoked'. He calls Ramanujan's tone 'bantering' and points out three paradoxes. He concludes his account of the poem 'overlooked by Mishra' with the following sentence: 'Paradox is a form of indirection, and indirection is a feature of poetic language.' (There are moments, and this is one of them, when Parthasarathy does not get even his platitudes right. Indirection is not a feature of 'poetic language'; it is a feature of language.)

We have before us all the evidence Parthasarathy brings to support his claim that Ramanujan is a significant poet. Since his method is fallacious – the thing to be examined (Ramanujan's 'roots' in Tamil and Kannada) is assumed in the premises (he is the heir of an 'anterior tradition') – we are still in the dark about Ramanujan's significance. Where should we look for it? What is 'anterior tradition'? Where are the 'deposits'? How are they penetrated? Where is that miraculous English poem conjoining these elements? These questions become more persistent once we accept Parthasarathy's geological model. His simple answer to them is 'Prayers to Lord Murugan'. Ask him how and he hands you his circular argument. Parthasarathy's treatment of the presence of Tamil and Kannada in Ramanujan is so inept that even the idea of interlingual contact is thrown into doubt. He believes these languages are crucial to the work; he handles them like appendages.

There are several reasons for this. The one role Murugan's parents did not train him for was to be a mould for Indian English poetry and so, given his physique, he wobbles away each time Parthasarathy tries to catch him. As I look at it, the poem is a risky example to choose to show how Ramanujan's work connects with his native idiom: a reader like Parthasarathy will not think twice about making the figure of the Dravidian god its symbol. When Parthasarathy says the poem is embedded in another tradition which Ramanujan makes available to us, he is already reducing languages which are tissued in the multilingual sensibility to pictural shreds, to the framed surfaces of oleographs. The other tradition does not enter Indian English literature in the guise of a god, a river, a place, a cow named Gopi, or a Tipu Sultan; nor as a poetic shell: a *rubai*, a *doha*, a *vacana*, or an *abhanga*. Their presence alone does not reflect the inlay of, for instance, Tamil and Kannada in Ramanujan, and their absence will not mean that no inlaying has taken place. Ramanujan writes in the manner of Tamil heroic poetry, Adrienne Rich writes seventeen poems based on the ghazal, and American poets in Cedar Rapids write haikus by the score. Have they not taken their forms from a common pool? Is there any difference in the way non-English traditions operate in Ramanujan and Rich? There is none if we restrict Tamil and Kannada to being suppliers of poetic forms and colourful gods. Ramanujan's multilingualism therefore is so inlaid in his work that in order to trace it we will have to look outside the obvious signs. Once this is accepted we can further say that if Ramanujan had written bucolics instead of *vacanas* and closed *Relations* with 'The Goatherd versus the Shepherd' instead of 'Prayers to Lord Murugan', his 'deepest roots' would not have ceased to participate in the writing, but certainly their mode of participation would be more difficult to plot.

A two-line note at the bottom of page 57 of *Relations* describes Murugan as the 'Ancient Dravidian god of fertility, joy, youth, beauty, war, and love. He is represented as a six-faced god with twelve hands.' Does one need to know more? Perhaps one does and a disinterested scholar could profitably study the origins of the 'cockfight and banner-/dance' and the 'painted grey/pottery' mentioned in the poem. It is, however, necessary to keep in mind that Kolatkar in *Jejuri* and Mahapatra in *A Rain of Rites* situate their work similarly in 'specific traditions', and I hope too much fuss is not made about this aspect of their work since specificity is almost the first exercise in the book. To a poem the location – whether cultural, historical, geographical, or fictive – is everything:

> At Rochecoart,
> Where the hills part
>   in three ways,
> And three valleys, full of winding roads,
> Fork out to south and north,
> There is a place of trees . . . grey with lichen.
> I have walked there
>   thinking of old days.
> At Chalais
>   is a pleached arbour;
> Old pensioners and old protected women
> Have a right there –
>   it is charity.

I have crept over old rafters,
                    peering down
Over the Dronne,
                    over a stream full of lilies.

                    . . .

I have gone in Riberac
                    and in Sarlat,
I have climbed rickety stairs, heard talk of Croy,
Walked over En Bertran's old layout,
Have soon Narbonne, and Cahors and Chalus,
Have seen Excideuil, carefully fashioned.

                    . . .

I have lain in Rocafixada,
                    level with sunset,
Have seen the copper come down
                    tingeing the mountains,
I have seen the fields, pale, clear as an emerald,
Sharp peaks, high spurs, distant castles.

                    . . .

That age is gone;
Pierre de Maensac is gone.
I have walked over these roads;
I have thought of them living.

                    (Ezra Pound, 'Provincia Deserta')

The atlas has these qualities: it reveals the forms of cities that do not yet have a form or a name. There is the city in the shape of Amsterdam, a semicircle facing north, with concentric canals – the princes', the emperors', the nobles'; there is the city in the shape of York, set among the high moors, walled, bristling with towers; there is the city in the shape of New Amsterdam known also as New York, crammed with towers of glass and steel on an oblong island between two rivers, with streets like deep canals, all of them straight, except Broadway.

                    (Italo Calvino, *Invisible Cities*)

By going to a library the reader can identify most references to myth and religion, folklore and history, in the poems of Ramanujan, Kolatkar, and Mahapatra. What the library cannot gloss is the prismatic interlingual space in each poet. This space Parthasarathy has filled with Murugan's torso. Multilingualism could well be the crux of Indian English poetry, but unless the perimeter around the space is cleared and we know more about the deployment of Tamil-Kannada, Marathi, Oriya, and Russian in the English work of Ramanujan, Kolatkar, Mahapatra, and Nabokov respectively, we need to tread like angels. All the plums in Ramanujan's basket are found growing in Tamil and Kannada orchards; all are but nodules lying at the bottom of the Palk Straits. Pluck, dredge, and make it 'available' in English: is that all to the manual?

I have attached Nabokov's name to the list because his position is analogous to ours and George Steiner, through his example, raises issues which are common to multilinguists:

> It would be by no means eccentric to read the major part of Nabokov's opus as a meditation – lyric, ironic, technical, parodistic – on the nature of human language, on the enigmatic coexistence of different, linguistically generated world visions and of a deep current underlying, and at moments obscurely conjoining, the multitude of diverse tongues. (*Extraterritorial*)

When Steiner moves away from subterraneity and looks specifically for the 'sources and fabric' of 'Nabokese' – the Anglo-American interlingua in which Nabokov wrote after his move to the United States in 1940 – he marks out an area and asks questions which we should be putting to Ramanujan, Kolatkar, and Mahapatra if we are to stay in the business as readers:

> We need really detailed study of the quality and degree of pressure which Russian puts on Nabokov's Anglo-American. How often are his English sentences 'meta-translations' of Russian? To what extent do Russian semantic associations initiate the images and contour of the English phrase? ... Is a good deal of Nabokov's English a piece of smuggling, an illicit conveyance across the frontier, of Russian verse now captive in a society he contemns?
>
> We also require careful analysis of the local and literary background of Nabokov's English ...
>
> All these would be preliminary lines of enquiry toward getting right the 'strangeness', the polysemic nature of Nabokov's use of language[s]. They would clarify not only his own prodigious talent, but such larger questions as the condition of multilingual imagining, of internalized translation, of the possible existence of a private mixed idiom 'beneath', 'coming before' the localization of different languages in the articulate brain.

Jorge Luis Borges and Samuel Beckett are the other 'new "esperantists"' in *Extraterritorial*. Though Borges writes only in Spanish,

> His intimacy with French, German, and, particularly, with English is profound. Very often an English text – Blake, Stevenson, Coleridge, De Quincey – underlies the Spanish statement. The other language 'shines through', giving to Borges' verse and to his *Fictions* a quality of lightness, of universality. He uses the vulgate and mythology of Argentina to ballast what might otherwise be almost too abstract, too peregrine an imagination.
>
> As it happens, these multilinguists (Ezra Pound has his place in this context) are among the foremost writers of the age. The equation of a single pivot of language, of native deep-rootedness, with poetic authority is again in doubt.

Steiner writes in *After Babel* that Borges moves among languages 'with a cat's sinewy confidence'. Though he has a keen sense of the irreducible quality of each particular tongue, 'his linguistic experience is essentially simultaneous and, to use a Coleridgean notion, reticulative. Half a dozen languages and literatures interweave. Borges uses citations and literary-historical references, often invented, to establish the key, the singular locale of his verses and fables.'

Read, for its Borgesian inventiveness, the following sentence from the Acknowledgements page in *Relations*: 'Among my conscious debts are a phrase from Vinda Karandikar (page 22), one from Pablo Neruda's prose (page 20), and an incident from a Kannada magazine story (page 51).'

The two examples of Nabokov and Borges are enough to show that the Indian English poem needs to be read in a radically different way: not as a delectable slice of reality which the critic – and sometimes Parthasarathy – applies to his nose, but as a place, a construct, housing two or more ways of seeing; four-eyed; Chang and Eng. Ramanujan emblematizes this in his recent work:

> Watch your step. Sight may strike you
> blind in unexpected places.
>
> The traffic light turns orange
> on 57th and Dorchester, and you stumble,
>
> you fall into a vision of forest fires,
> enter a frothing Himalayan river,
>
> rapid, silent.

On the 14th floor,
Lake Michigan crawls and crawls

in the window. Your thumbnail
cracks a lobster louse on the windowpane

from your daughter's hair

and you drown, eyes open,

towards the Indies, the antipodes.
And you, always so perfectly sane.

('Chicago Zen')

*

The questions which should be asked: what is a multilingual sensibility?
How do languages tenant it? How does this tenancy register on the poem?
Steiner is the only critic who tries to answer these questions, but even he
does not answer as much as ask in *After Babel*. The area is uncharted and
all findings are tentative. Perhaps they will always be so.

> When a natively multilingual person speaks, do the languages not in
> momentary employ press upon the body of speech which he is actually
> articulating? Is there a discernible, perhaps measurable sense in which
> the options I exercise when uttering words and sentences in English are
> both enlarged and complicated by the 'surrounding presence or pressure'
> of French and German? If it truly exists, such tangential action might
> subvert my uses of English, making them in some degree unsteady,
> provisional, off-centre. This possibility may underlie the pseudo-scientific
> rumour that multilingual individuals or children reared simultaneously
> in 'too many' languages (is there a critical number?) are prone to
> schizophrenia and disorders of personality. Or might such 'interference'
> from other languages on the contrary render my use of any one language
> richer, more conscious of specificity and resource? Because alternative
> means lie so very near at hand, the speech forms used may be more
> animate with will and deliberate focus. In short: does that 'intertraffique
> of the minde,' for which Samuel Daniel praised John Florio, the great
> translator, inhibit or augment the faculty of expressive utterance? That
> it must have marked influence is certain.
>
> (*After Babel*)

Parthasarathy has implied one way in which languages tenant a polyglot's mind: they are kept in layers and so the relationship between them

is that between source-language (Tamil-Kannada) and receptor-language (English). '"Layers" is,' says Steiner, 'of course, a crass piece of shorthand. It may mean nothing. The spatial organization, contiguities, insulations, synaptic branchings between, which account for the arrangement of different languages in the brain of the polyglot, and especially of the native bilingual, must be of an order of topological intricacy beyond any we can picture' (*After Babel*). There are several other ways in which languages can be arranged and each arrangement will affect the interlingual relationship. In other words, one could provide the field with new metaphors: languages as sources of light, attended by eclipses and penumbral zones; languages as lightning conductors, earthing each other's electric storms; languages as geological faults, sending mild tremors through each other; languages as conjugate mirrors. Since languages are motile, no single metaphor or cluster of metaphors is final.

> [N]o topologies of *n*-dimensional spaces, no mathematical theories of knots, rings, lattices, or closed or open curvatures, no algebra of matrices can until now authorize even the most preliminary model of the 'language-spaces' in the central nervous system ... The membranes of differentiation and of contact, the dynamics of interlingual osmosis, the contraints which preserve equilibrium between the blandness of mere lexical, public usage and the potentially chaotic prodigality of private invention and association, the speed and delicacy of retrieval and of discard involved in even the barest act of paraphrase or translation ... of [these] we can, at present, offer no adequate image let alone systematic analysis.
>
> (*After Babel*)

Following the anthropologists' division of establishment Hinduism into 'great' and 'little' traditions and Ramanujan's description of the terms in his Introduction to *Speaking of Siva*, we can devise a heuristic model to show the interplay of languages in the central nervous system. In Hinduism the 'great' tradition is Vedic, whereas the 'little' is woven from 'saints' legends, minor mythologies, systems of magic and superstition ... local animal sacrifices ... wakes, vigils, fairs ... worship of stone, trees, crossroads and rivers'. In the context of Indian English poetry, the 'great' tradition would be English and the 'little' revolve around the native idiom. Ramanujan has described how the two traditions coexist within the structure of Hinduism.

> ... traditions are not divided by impermeable membranes; they interflow into one another, responsive to differences of density as in an osmosis. It

is often difficult to isolate elements as belonging exclusively to the one or the other.

A Sanskrit epic like the *Mahabharata* contains in its encyclopedic range much folk material, like tales, beliefs, proverbs, picked obviously from folk sources, refurbished, Sanskritized, fixed forever in the Sanskritic artifice of eternity. But in a profoundly oral culture like the Indian, the Sanskrit *Mahabharata* itself gets returned to the oral folk-traditions, contributing the transformed materials back to the 'little' traditions to be further diffused and diffracted. It gets 'translated' from the Sanskrit into the regional languages; in the course of the 'translations', the regional poet infuses it with his rich local traditions ... Thus many cycles of give-and-take are set in motion.

Though Ramanujan and Steiner are discussing subjects as dissimilar as Hinduism and multilingual imagining, both use osmosis as a metaphor to describe their inner workings. If what Steiner says about the reticular nature of Nabokov's and Borges's linguistic experience is correct, then languages have porosity just as religious traditions do, the 'great' and the 'little' are 'not divided by impermeable membranes' in either. The native idiom (the 'little') has to seep through the English poem (the 'great'); how could it not? And if this is so, then each poet writes in an idiolect as distinctive as 'Nabokese': Ramanujan's consists of English-Kannada-Tamil, Kolatkar's of English-Marathi-Bombay Hindi, Mahapatra's of English-Oriya, and so on. Each poet belongs to a tribe of one or two, seldom more than of six or eight, and Indian English literature becomes a dream dreamt outside the several bodies of these phenomena. It is the dream of Gondwanaland.

The osmotic process of the multilingual common factor explain Indian English literature's mottled look and its incohesiveness: for this reason we can hardly speak of Indian English literature as we do of Bengali or French. What I call mottled look has a parallel in India's tribal art. The latter, according to Stella Kramrisch, lacks 'stylistic certitude', and her insight is based on the recognition of osmosis in Hinduism and its percolations into adjoining forms. Though there can be few outward resemblances between Hinduism and Indian English literature, there is at least one between Indian English literature and India's tribal art. The model I have proposed for the 'dynamics of interlingual osmosis' is supplemented by what she writes in *Unknown India*:

Tribal art throughout India for the last two thousand years at least must be assumed to have coexisted with traditions commanding greater means and more complex organization. The Buddhist stone railings of the Stupa of Bharut and the Stupa of the Saints, in Sanchi, both collective monuments of sculpture of the second to first century BC, show the work of many different hands. These stone railings with their carvings are each a symposium of styles, some of which bear affinity to tribal carvings such as those of the Gond who to this day live not far from the sites of these ancient monuments. Buddhism was open to members of any group. The sculptors, however, were not necessarily Buddhists, they were from the lower Hindu strata of ancient Indian or tribal stock. Progressing Hinduization, while dissolving much of the self-supporting and self-sufficient tribal communities, absorbed as much as it destroyed of tribal traditions while these tribes, where they survived as solid groups, assimilated much from their suppressors who were also their neighbours. But Hinduism from the start is an alloy of the Brahmanic tradition and the many other and older Indian traditions. Due to this long process of osmosis, tribal art in India, on the whole, lacks stylistic certitudes and perfectedness of the tribal art of Africa, Oceania, and of the American Indian.

Between Nabokov's English and Russian, between Borges's Spanish and English, between Ramanujan's English and Tamil-Kannada, between the pan-Indian Sanskritic tradition and folk material, and between the Bharut Stupa and Gond carvings 'many cycles of give-and-take are set in motion'. The Buddhist stone railings are imprinted with tribal motifs; the tribe, in its turn, assimilates the culture of its suppressor: it is the 'great' tradition getting 'translated' into the regional language. Nabokov's 'Russian version of *Alice in Wonderland* (Berlin, 1923),' writes Steiner, 'has long been recognized as one of the keys to the whole Nabokovian oeuvre' (*Extraterritorial*).

There is another aspect to the model. When Ramanujan says that traditions in Hinduism interflow into one another 'as in an osmosis', he is referring, obliquely, to an analogous structure: his poems. His statement quoted in *Ten Twentieth-Century Indian Poets* is explicit:

English and my disciplines (linguistics, anthropology) give me my 'outer' forms – linguistic, metrical, logical and other such ways of shaping experience; and my first thirty years in india, my frequent visits and fieldtrips, my personal and professional preoccupations with Kannada, Tamil, the classics and folklore give me my substance, my 'inner' forms, images and symbols. They are continuous with each other, and I no longer can tell what comes from where.

The semicolon in the first sentence is the osmotic membrane; the binaries of 'great'/'little' are substituted by 'outer'/'inner'; in Hinduism 'It is often difficult to isolate elements as belonging exclusively to the one or the other'; in his poems 'They are continuous with each other, and I no longer can tell what comes from where.'

Ramanujan is not without the necessary cunning.

The answer to the third question, how do the 'language-spaces' register on the poem? is dependent on how we answer the first two. If a multilingual sensibility is a bed where languages deposit their silt and the 'spaces' are stratified, they will register on the poem but marginally. On the other hand if we look on the sensibility as a crucible in which languages change their properties, the effect is molecular. To Nabokov's sentences they give an intricacy not elsewhere found in English prose; to Borges's what Alastair Reid calls 'a mysterious balance':

> At a time when the validity of literature is often in question, Borges reads and writes as one who has no doubt at all of the power of words to illumine and disquiet. I always think of him occupying that netherworld of the translator and the bilingual, backstage in the great silence behind language, taking his careful daily walk from the silence to the word, to the sentence, to the book, to the library, and back again. I think that what we are most grateful for in Borges's work is that from such disparate elements, such diverse reading, such multilingual experience, he has found a focal point, a mysterious balance, an equilibrium in a way that we, his readers, no longer thought possible in books. ('Borges as Reader')

In brief: for various phrenetical reasons – among them a suspicion that Ramanujan has been carried away by a pack of Oriya werewolves – Parthasarathy wrecks the axiom that links exist between Ramanujan's English poems and his native languages. Parthasarathy need not have repeated this four times in the same paragraph of his *Chandrabhāgā* letter. Moreover, the axiom, as he understands it, has nothing to do with Ramanujan's significance.

Most Indian English poets are bilingual and, though it is too early to say how or where, the other language is the torsional force in their work in the same way that Russian presses on 'Nabokese' and non-native French, German, and English glow beneath Borges's Spanish. Indian English literature belongs with the work of these 'new "esperantists"'.

*

... words and language are not wrappings in which things are packed for the commerce of those who write and speak. It is in words and language that things first come into being and are. For this reason the misuse of language ... destroys our authentic relation to things.

Martin Heidegger, *An Introduction to Metaphysics*

Words are not a medium in which to copy life. Their true work is to restore life itself to order.

I. A. Richards, *Philosophy of Rhetoric*

Parthasarathy stands the two epigraphs on their heads and says in his Introduction to *Ten Twentieth-Century Indian Poets* that there are two problems the Indian English writer must come to terms with:

The first is the quality of the experience he would like to express in English. The Indian who uses the English language feels, to some extent, alienated. His development as a poet is sporadic. And it is partly because of this that there is, today, no perspective at all in which to evaluate this phenomenon. The second is the quality of the idiom he uses. There has always been a time-lag between the living, creative idiom of English-speaking peoples and the English used in India. And this time-lag is not likely to diminish, although it has today considerably narrowed down.

It should be kept in mind that Parthasarathy is here not talking about the modernist crisis: the inward collapse of words, the fragments of speech, the crowded subway of language which everyone rides. 'The poet's language,' writes Valéry, 'constitutes ... *an effort by one man* to create an artificial and ideal order by means of a material of vulgar origin.' A haunting description of the crisis is Hugo von Hofmannsthal's *Lord Chandos' Letter* (1902):

For me everything disintegrated into parts, those parts again into parts; no longer would anything be let itself be encompassed by one idea. Single words floated round me; they congealed into eyes which stared at me and into which I was forced to stare back – whirlpools which gave me vertigo and, reeling incessantly, led into the void.

In Parthasarathy's account the Indian English writer, who seems to have fallen off the footboard of twentieth-century literature, faces a singular difficulty. The quality of his experience as an Indian – whatever that is – and the language in which he is fated to express himself do not fit. The problem – alienation – will presumably disappear if the poet removes English and wears his native idiom. Kolatkar, by this reasoning, is wasting his time fashioning Kolatkarese when he has the other cupboard stacked with Marathi readymades. Buridan's ass was 'given a choice to eat from two equal bales of hay situated at equal distances from him. But being unable to decide between the two equally balanced alternatives, he chose to starve himself to death.' Kolatkar and Ramanujan are better off. The bales of Marathi and Tamil are so much nearer than the straws of English. Why, then, are they giving up an uninterrupted poetic development for one which is 'sporadic'? And why should they occasionally choose to strut about in ill-shapen trousers when they can, instead, dress their experience in flowing robes? The problem of finding the right garments for the tailor's dummy of course does not exist. On the night of 18–19 February 1913 Kafka wrote to Felice Bauer:

> I am not of the opinion that one can ever lack the power to express perfectly what one wants to write or say. Observations on the weakness of language, and comparisons between the limitations of words and the infinity of feelings, are quite fallacious. The infinite feeling continues to be as infinite in words as it was in the heart. What is clear within is bound to become so in words as well. This is why one need never worry about language, but at sight of words may often worry about oneself. After all, who knows within himself how things really are with him? This tempestuous or floundering or morass-like inner self is what we really are, but by the secret process by which words are forced out of us, our self-knowledge is brought to light, and though it may still be veiled, yet it is there before us, wonderful or terrible to behold.

> (*Letters to Felice*)

Kafka's confidence in words was short-lived (who could have sustained it?) and, within a month, he was writing to the same correspondent:

> … hardly a word comes to me from the fundamental source, but is seized upon fortuitously and with great difficulty somewhere along the way. When I was in the swing of writing and living, I once wrote to you that no true feeling need search for corresponding words, but is confronted or even impelled by them. Perhaps this is not quite true, after all.

One has to bring Parthasarathy's problem alongside Kafka's crisis to see how puerile it is. There are some moments when the writer has all the garments for the dummy; there are others when he has none at all. Some mornings language – the bale of hay – is responsive to 'the swing of writing and living'; on others words have to be 'seized upon fortuitously' and the hay has disappeared. Kafka's father, incidentally, grew up a Czech, never quite mastering written German, and his son was aware that he too was a foreigner to the language. Three years before he died, in a letter to Max Brod, Kafka likened German to 'foreign capital' which had not been earned but 'boisterously or secretively or even masochistically' appropriated. 'This accounts,' Erich Heller says, 'at least partially for Kafka's unending scruples about publishing what he wrote. But sometimes he was confident that he had succeeded in hammering out that "most personal" German style that was truly alive.'

Hofmannsthal, Valéry, and Kafka – and indeed several others – realized that language, the sensitive plant, had withered. In extreme cases the writer, like Lord Chandos, felt that words had crumbled in his mouth 'like mouldy fungi'. The sensation that words sometimes fail to embody the quality – the 'what-ness' – of individual experience cuts across languages. 'There can,' writes Steiner,

> hardly be an awakened human being who has not, at some point, been exasperated by the 'publicity' of language, who has not experienced an almost bodily discomfort at the disparity between the uniqueness, the novelty of his own emotions and the worn coinage of words ... The secret jargon of the adolescent coterie, the conspirator's password, the nonsense-diction of lovers, teddybear talk are fitful short-lived ripostes to the binding commonness and sclerosis of speech.
>
> (*After Babel*)

To the list of short-lived ripostes, add Edward Lear's 'The Cummerbund'.

> She sate upon her Dobie,
>   To watch the Evening Star,
> And all the Punkahs as they passed
>   Cried, 'My! how fair you are!'
> Around her bower, with quivering leaves,
>   The tall Kamsamahs grew,
> And Kitmutgars in wild festoons
>   Hung down from Tchokis blue.

When the curtain lifts on the modern period we are witnessing the spectacle of this breach of contract between word and world. A little before Lord Chandos came on the scene, Rimbaud, looking under the disintegration, said,

> Old tricks of poetry played a large part in my alchemy of the word.
>   I became habituated to simple hallucination: I clearly saw a mosque in place of a gasworks, a school of drummers composed of angels, open

carriages on the roads of heaven, a drawing room at the bottom of a lake; monsters, mysteries; a title from light comedy would raise terrors before me.

(*A Season in Hell*)

(Remember that festooned waiters hung from blue police *chowkis* in Lear's 'Indian' poem.) Later, Louis Aragon will draw his inspiration from the same alchemical fount: 'Life is a language; writing is a completely different one'; and Eugene Jolas' *transition* will publish 'The Revolution of the Word': 'The writer expresses. He does not communicate. The plain reader be damned.' 'Hence the desire,' writes Renato Poggioli, 'to create new languages,'

attempts like that of young Stephan George or old James Joyce, or of the Russian poet Velimir Chlebnikov throughout his career. Each man constructed his own artificial and private idiom, conventional and arbitrary, based on onomatopoeic and etymological criteria, on the suggestiveness of ambiguity and equivocation ... Such a search for new languages ... is perhaps the most striking inheritance left to modern poetry by French symbolism and its numerous offshoots in Europe and America.

(*The Theory of the Avant-Garde*)

'The lacking word' and its aftermath is a rubric and Parthasarathy should have noticed it. The backstage chatter is loud enough to be heard:

The principal division in the history of Western literature occurs between the early 1870s and the turn of the century. It divides a literature essentially housed in language from one for which language has become a prison.

The poet no longer has or aspires to native tenure in the house of words. The languages waiting for him as an individual born into history, into society, into the expressive conventions of his particular culture and milieu, are no longer a natural skin. Established language is the enemy.

A modern poem is an active contemplation of the impossibilities or near impossibilities of adequate 'coming into being'. The poetry of modernism is a matter of structured debris: from it we are made to envision, to hear the poem that might have been, the poem that will be if, when, the word is made new.

(*After Babel*)

The rift is between language and experience rather than between a particular language and, in Parthasarathy's thoughtful phrase, 'everyday

Indian reality'. The rift, moreover, does not vary from place to place: wide here, narrow there. So let us not say that the development of the Indian English poet is 'sporadic' because he is down with a mild attack of alienation complicated by 'time-lag'. English is his 'foreign capital' and it is up to him to steal it and hammer out that 'most personal' style. In this he can either succeed or fail. Am I also to believe that if Parthasarathy and Shiv K. Kumar had written in Tamil and Punjabi respectively, their contributions to those literatures would have been any more remarkable?

Adil Jussawalla (b. 1940)

Adil Jussawalla was born in 1940 in Bombay. He was educated there, at the Cathedral and John Connon School, and later at University College, Oxford. He was in England for thirteen years, as a student and also as a schoolteacher; in 1970, he went back to Bombay. Those were the days when Indians spent a period of time abroad, and then returned to lead the life, as Jussawalla did, of partial exiles in the city of their birth, never entirely at one with the landscape, condemned to be singular, yet passionately concerned about not relinquishing their open-ended, slightly ambiguous status. The literature of the so-called diaspora is mainly to do with migration and memory; to this Jussawalla, in his two books of poems, *Land's End* and *Missing Person*, published in the sixties and seventies, adds a small but valuable chapter about the maladjustments and disappointments of return, implying that the return to the mythic 'homeland' is not, as Cesar Pavese showed in a perhaps more tender light, only a simple physical fact, but a long-drawn-out, stubborn, and estranging process, even an aesthetic. His fine poems can be astringent and theoretical; his essays (some of the best to have been written by an Indian) come, on the other hand, from some secret, erotic side of himself, and can arise, with an unexpected intimacy, from a buried family anecdote or a throwaway remark. They appear now and again in popular periodicals and Bombay newspapers; and they raise the interesting question of what their strategic self-revelations tell a harried and itinerant readership, in trains, buses, and drawing-rooms, about itself.

* * *

'Make Mine Movies' (1994)

I remember there was this blood-red sky and a whale singing in it. The whale was spotted. I know. We had drawing books of Minnie the Whale, the outlines to be filled in with paint. I remember the heron shedding a tear, one sole tear that hung from its eye till it distended, detached itself and splashed into the lake. The course of that tear changed the course of my life. Minnie was dead.

The whale that sang for bird, bee, flower and tree had been harpooned, I think, and the heron was in mourning. So were the lake, the forest and the sky. Are these memories false? No one's been able to tell me. No one seems to have seen or heard of the film I saw, an animation film called *Make Mine Music.*

I remember my mother and her elder sister Freny in whose flat we were staying at that time. I remember the humiliation of trying to keep out of their sight, moving from room to room in that flat on Altamount Road, so that they would not see that I was crying. Shoulders hunched, head lowered, I had *become* the heron, grieving for its dead friend. I don't think I've ever felt such pain in my chest before or since. My heart was broken. I remember the two formidable women confronting each other:

'Did you say something? Why is he crying?'

'*You* must have said something. Why else would he cry?'

Six-year-olds weren't supposed to cry, so the tears came slowly, squeezed out by a pressure of my chest which, after several bouts of pneumonia, was more like a tube than a chest. I couldn't bawl.

Exasperated at not being able to place the blame anywhere, neither on each other, nor the servants, nor the neighbours, they warily approached me one last time – children know when it's one last time; they *have* to say something, even if it meant bursting into uncontrollable sobs at that very moment; and I wasn't known to speak.

'*Chullee rurtu thun.*' The bird was crying, I said in reply to their question.

Now they were alarmed, questions about my sanity, I imagine, whirling through their heads.

'Bird? Bird? Which bird are you talking about?!'

'Film *nu.*'

*

Hundreds, perhaps thousands of films later, I wonder if it was that scene with the heron in *Make Mine Music* that set the pattern of my responses to every film I see. Minnie the Whale does sing again, from Heaven – that

---

* Editor's note: Jussawalla has since confirmed that the film does, indeed, exist. Not only does it exist, but it is singled out by the Bengali filmmaker Ritwik Ghatak as one of Disney's most experimental films.

was the whale in the sky at the end of the film – and all creation is happy but I wasn't. Perhaps the ending seemed false to me.

The moment of truth, for me, was in the heron's grief and in the suddenly shattering fact that loved and loving creatures do die, even in what we called cartoons then. I'd witnessed such deaths before. Bambi's mother dies but I barely remember the scene in the film. And nothing very bad happens in *Dumbo. The Wizard of Oz*, with its tin and lion men terrified me as did the forest fire in *The Jungle Book* (in colour). I still remember the fire, the whole screen a sheet of flame, but barely recall Mowgli. And Mowgli was Sabu, the very Sabu my parents were so proud of, the one Indian actor in Hollywood.

Such is the intensity of the moment of truth films provide that I try not to see them any more, at least not in public. When I do, I become a six-year-old again – tears, terror and all. That's not a nice thing to have happen to you when you're in your fifties, so I've decided to stop. Even recalling a film's moments of truth can be distressing. Films devour me as a sponge devours plankton. At the end of its meal, I'm spat out of cinema halls, drained, a wreck.

We had no 1.30 shows when I was a child but even to be excoriated at the end of the 3.30 show, the matinee, was to hit the pavements in the harsh light of day. The contrast between the wild prairies of the cinema hall and the streets of Bombay couldn't have been greater. It disoriented me, as it has done others, further.

It's not as though I didn't try to do something about it. I did. I decided to contain my experience of films, control it, as it were, by putting it down on paper. On the pages of a ruled exercise book I drew further rules, vertical, making a box of, I think, four columns: Film, Director, Music, Photography. After every film I saw, I put down the names of those that fell under the appropriate category and in a space under Remarks, wrote what I thought about the film I'd seen.

In the beginning, what I thought was mostly what *The Times of India* critic thought, there was no one else in 1951 but gradually I came to have views of my own. I think the process steadied me a little, helped distance myself from the sponge. Till the next time round.

*

We were a regular film-going family, in the sense that we saw films together about once a week, almost always on Sundays. After a generally silent drive to the cinema hall and the customary purchase of packets of wafers and chocolates there'd be a far-from-pregnant pause. Once the film got going my father would get involved in the action perhaps more than anyone else, punctuating the goings-on on screen with whoops and cries. Suddenly, on occasion, he would rise from his seat in an attempt to ward off a sword, descending, let's say, from Basil Rathbone's hand on Errol Flynn's neck.

Since my mother was the strong, silent kind and my brother and I the weak, silent kind – what relatives pityingly called 'the quiet type' – my father would take it upon himself to comment briefly on the film after the show.

'*Ghela ganda*.' Silly nonsense, he would say after a disappointing *Abbot And Costello* or an improbable action adventure. Or he'd say '*Soo* fine acting' (what fine acting) of a star whose performance impressed him. Sometimes his comments had a more sinister purpose. Stated casually, almost in the air, while opening the door of his car, say, to drive us back home from the cinema, the comment would be directed to one or other member of his family, with the intention of making him or her think. 'What? Can there only be unhappiness in an artist's life? No happiness at all?' he said after we saw *Lust For Life* at the Metro.

This was meant for me, the artist, whose glum and acned mien tried him greatly in those days. I was meant to respond. Needless to say, I didn't. After *Pather Panchali* at the Liberty, he said, 'You see what befell the family after she treated her mother-in-law that way?' This for my mother who he felt, quite wrongly, was mistreating his.

It was generally my father who decided on which Hindi films we should see. The films themselves would have been suggested to him by his patients, some of whom were film stars. In this way we saw, among others, *Barsaat, Baiju Bawra, Anarkali* and *Aan*. Meena Kumari had invited us to see her on the sets of *Anarkali* – a dungeon scene which we saw. But the Anarkali we went to see had been replaced by Bina Rai. My father couldn't believe his eyes. What had happened to one of his favourite patients? As for *Aan*, billed as India's first completely technicolour movie – it was a mish-mash. The colour held but nothing else did. A mixture of Cadillacs and swordfights, good acting and bad, confused us so much that I never wanted to see a Hindi movie again. And the beginnings had been so propitious.

In those years, in the forties, there used to be a tradition, now made irrelevant by video. At children's birthday parties, if the children were too many or too small, they wouldn't be taken to the cinema, the cinema would be taken to them. At one such party, or was it my *navjote*?, my father decided to show *Andaz*. The patients' waiting room, emptied of its sofas, became the darkened cinema hall and as the hired projector whirred and the hired screen came to life, hundreds of eyes, young and old, watched enthralled.

It was some years after my first 'moment of truth' in cinema but in *Andaz* too they came thick and fast. Two I remember most vividly are Nargis in a state of shock after her father's death, spilling a glass of milk; and the moment Raj Kapoor swats Dilip Kumar over the head with a tennis racket, sending him rolling down the stairs like a dazed fly. So that's how men fought over a beautiful woman. Great. I was growing up.

*

Did I spend my childhood only seeing sad films? No. But funny films had their problems too. If sad films led to uncontrollable tears, funny films led to uncontrollable piss – if I laughed too much I wet my pants. Several cinema seats in Bombay must have borne evidence of my affliction.

But the one I remember most clearly was borne not by a seat but a carpet. It belonged to my best friend's mother and, at the moment of urinary epiphany, held about twenty children watching 8mm cartoons. (It must have been a party.) The evidence, mercifully, was attributed to the pet Australian terrier Trixie, though, as I left the flat surreptitiously, I heard ominous cries and exclamations. The servants were insisting that Trixie had been tied up near the kitchen, a considerable distance away from the carpet, right through the show. The cries come from my best friend's mother and his aunts.

That was a narrow escape but at the Strand, watching Bob Hope in *Fancy Pants*, I peed quite openly. There was an incredibly funny dialogue which involved gold stones, gall stones and gold gall stones, so I just hitched up a side of my shorts and peed. I can still hear the hiss, amazed that an elder cousin sitting next to me didn't (or he pretended not to), the effusion gradually settling around the shoes of the man sitting in front of me. If he'd been wearing sandals I'd have been thrashed.

It wasn't only with family that we saw films. Sunday morning (10.30) shows could be seen with friends; so it was that my best friend, whose mother's carpet I'd wetted, and I went to several. Avid readers of comics (his father ran New Book Co. and had stacks of them), we saw the first (black-and-white) versions of *Superman, Batman, Captain Marvel* and *Flash Gordon*, and unanimously felt they were trash. Once, at a morning show, we crept into a cinema hall to see a film which wasn't meant for the eyes of persons under twelve. It was Jean Cocteau's *Beauty and the Beast.* It scared the shit out of us. So did the gentleman who, leaning over to us from the row behind, asked us how old we were. 'Twelve,' we said, quaking. 'You don't look twelve,' he said and chuckled, the chuckle rippling through the whole row behind. We watched the rest of the film not just terrorized but mortified.

We watched the comic hero films at the Capitol, *Beauty and the Beast* at the Empire and films I've forgotten at the Excelsior. These cinema halls are close to where I work now and together with the Metro, Eros and the Regal, formed an acre of my childhood. Three-D came and went with *Bwana Devil, House of Wax* and others. Cinemascope came and went with *The Robe, River of No Return* and others. The wide screen has come and will go. But the acre remains, only its magic's gone.

I don't want to go back to it, really go back to it, by having someone play the film backwards, let me be six again. Though I'd like to tell my father, as someone in *Finnegans Wake* does: 'Carry me along, taddy, as you done through the toy fair.' But he can't.

Once we were teenagers, we saw films on our own. *Rock Around The Clock* came to the Strand, the audience went wild, it was great, it danced in the aisles and seats were broken. It was the end of a chapter. But it was at the Excelsior where a bird broke my heart.

Salman Rushdie (b. 1947)

Salman Rushdie was born in Bombay in 1947. Like Jussawalla, he was a pupil at the Cathedral and John Connon School, before leaving for England when he was thirteen and a half. He was at Rugby, and later at Cambridge, where he read History. His first novel *Grimus* went unnoticed on publication; it was while reading Günter Grass's *The Tin Drum* that he felt the urge to write a novel, mixing desire, memory, autobiography, and national narrative, that might appropriate the discourse we call 'India', even while mocking its own ambition. *Midnight's Children*, published in 1981, also went unremarked when it first appeared; then, through the good offices of Malcolm Bradbury (who played an indirect part in shaping U. R. Anantha Murthy's first, remarkable novel), won the Booker Prize. Ever since then, the celebrations have been in progress, and modern Indian history has acquired the air of a fancy-dress party or the Mardi Gras, full of chatter, music, sex, tomfoolery, free drinks, and rock and roll, an occasion to which everyone is invited provided they can join in the fun. Another noteworthy metamorphosis has taken place after *Midnight's Children*: a whole generation of apparently normal people who also happen to be Indian have discovered that they were, all along, writers; they are a further effect, not to be discounted, of Rushdie's hallucinatory prose.

Midnight's Children is the story of Saleem Sinai, the narrator who, born at midnight on 15 August 1947 into an upper-middle-class Muslim family in Bombay, chooses to identify his own history with the history of his identical twin, the new nation-state born at exactly the same time. Rushdie's ability to relocate the spiritual world of visions and miracles in the world of popular culture and history was foreseen by Dalí, with his Christs on skyscraper-tall crosses and his Mae West sofas; and, indeed, the narrative tone, which veers, sentence to sentence, from the egotistical sublime to the ridiculously egotistical, might owe something to Dalí's *Diary of a Genius*. Sinai bears a close resemblance to another amiable egotist of literature, Walt Whitman, who, too, in his poetic autobiography, *Leaves of Grass*, claimed he was writing about every member of a new and great democracy in writing of himself: 'I am large, I contain multitudes...' Rushdie conflates Whitman's assertion in 'Song Of Myself' with Nabokov's observation that the novel is a democracy in which every character has his place in the sun; in *Midnight's Children*, India is that democracy, India that novel. The idea of democracy is, here, a crucial literary conceit, though it is one that calculatedly militates against the author's celebration of the singularity of the freakishly gifted Saleem Sinai. Rushdie employs and parodies the structures and rhetoric of religious myth, rejecting, at once, the systems of belief those myths belong to, in order to describe Saleem Sinai's extraordinary birth and life in a secular country; born, seemingly, of a virgin mother, attended to by magi like Prime Minister Nehru upon his birth. This habit of using religious mythology in order to create new meanings in secular fiction, or literature, began in India with Michael Madhusudan Dutt, when he wrote his epic poem in 1861; he, too, could reject belief while embracing mythology, and, basing his poem on the *Ramayana*, say, 'I hate Rama and all his rabble.' The thin line, wavering between art and heresy, which the secular Indian creative imagination, starting with Dutt, has repeatedly explored, would get Rushdie into all kinds of trouble with the publication of *The Satanic Verses*.

In one crucial regard, Rushdie is different from most of the other writers in this volume, especially from those who precede him. The narrative of modern Indian writing begins, with Dutt, with the twin processes of disowning and recovery; with disowning, or rejecting, the autochthonic, constituting world of the indigenous self as superstitious, constraining, and irrational, and then recovering, through the vantage-point of the colonial, modern self and through the secular act of creative expression, that very world of superstition, high tradition, language, and inherentness as one that creates meaning and identity. There has been, then, in the construction of 'Indianness', a profound and necessary impulse towards self-loathing, and then a profound impulse towards recognizing, and rehabilitating, the very thing one had rejected as being essential to one's creative centre. In Rushdie's fiction, however, one does not note the workings of these two related processes; there is, oddly, no impulse towards disowning; tearing the veil of that deep-rooted conflict, or tension, or ambivalence, his fiction, promiscuously, embraces everything. It is as if, to understand Rushdie's fiction properly, we must place it in a different psychological space from that which most other writers in this volume occupy; for him, there is no need to escape from the dark but mysterious womb to the bright, unfamiliar world outside, and then to make the journey wombward. However far Rushdie travels, whether towards history or some peculiar mutation of popular culture, he remains in a womb, which he calls the 'world', as vast as nature and as heterogeneous and artificial as discourse, where every stimulus is excitement, discovery, and nourishment.

* * *

from *Midnight's Children* (1981)

ACCIDENT IN A WASHING-CHEST

It has been two whole days since Padma stormed out of my life. For two days, her place at the vat of mango *kasaundy* has been taken by another woman – also thick of waist, also hairy of forearm; but, in my eyes, no replacement at all! – while my own dung-lotus has vanished into I don't know where. A balance has been upset; I feel cracks widening down the length of my body; because suddenly I am alone, without my necessary ear, and it isn't enough. I am seized by a sudden fist of anger: why should I be so unreasonably treated by my one disciple? Other men have recited stories before me; other men were not so impetuously abandoned. When Valmiki, the author of the *Ramayana*, dictated his masterpiece to elephant-headed Ganesh, did the god walk out on him halfway?* He certainly did not. (Not that, despite my Muslim background, I'm enough of a Bombayite to be well up in Hindu stories, and actually I'm very fond of the image of trunk-nosed, flap-eared Ganesh solemnly taking dictation!)

How to dispense with Padma? How give up her ignorance and superstition, necessary counterweights to my miracle-laden omniscience? How to do without her paradoxical earthiness of spirit, which keeps – kept? – my feet on the ground? I have become, it seems to me, the apex of an isosceles triangle, supported equally by twin deities, the wild god of memory and the lotus-goddess of the present ... but must I now become reconciled to the narrow one-dimensionality of a straight line?

I am, perhaps, hiding behind all these questions. Yes, perhaps that's right. I should speak plainly, without the cloak of a question-mark: our Padma has gone, and I miss her. Yes, that's it.

---

*   Editor's note: One of the many deliberate errors strewn through the novel. Actually, it
    was the *Mahabharata* that was dictated to Ganesh by Vyasa. On the one hand, these
    deliberate errors construct the archetypal postmodernist 'unreliable' narrator; on the
    other, they suggest a narrator who likes to be in control of everything, even his errors.

But there is still work to be done: for instance:

In the summer of 1956, when most things in the world were still larger than myself, my sister the Brass Monkey developed the curious habit of setting fire to shoes. While Nasser sank ships at Suez, thus slowing down the movements of the world by obliging it to travel around the Cape of Good Hope, my sister was also trying to impede our progress. Obliged to fight for attention, possessed by her need to place herself at the centre of events, even of unpleasant ones (she was my sister, after all; but no prime minister wrote letters to her, no sadhus watched her from their places under garden taps; unprophesied, unphotographed, her life was a struggle from the start), she carried her war into the world of footwear, hoping, perhaps, that by burning our shoes she would make us stand still long enough to notice that she was there ... she made no attempt at concealing her crimes. When my father entered his room to find a pair of black Oxfords on fire, the Brass Monkey was standing over them, match in hand. His nostrils were assailed by the unprecedented odour of ignited boot-leather, mingled with Cherry Blossom boot-polish and a little Three-In-One oil ... 'Look, Abba!' the Monkey said charmingly, 'Look how pretty – just the exact colour of hair!'

Despite all precautions, the merry red flowers of my sister's obsession blossomed all over the Estate that summer, blooming in the sandals of Nussie-the-duck and the film-magnate footwear of Homi Catrack; hair-coloured flames licked at Mr Dubash's down-at-heel suedes and at Lila Sabarmati's stiletto heels. Despite the concealment of matches and the vigilance of servants, the Brass Monkey found her ways, undeterred by punishment and threats. For one year, on and off, Methwold's Estate was assailed by the fumes of incendiarized shoes; until her hair darkened into anonymous brown, and she seemed to lose interest in matches.

Amina Sinai, abhorring the idea of beating her children, temperamentally incapable of raising her voice, came close to her wits' end; and the Monkey was sentenced, for day after day, to silence. This was my mother's chosen disciplinary method: unable to strike us, she ordered us to seal our lips. Some echo, no doubt, of the great silence with which her own mother had tormented Aadam Aziz in her ears – because silence, too, has an echo, hollower and longer-lasting than the reverberations of any sound – and with an emphatic '*Chup!*' she would place a finger across her lips and command our tongues to be still. It was a punishment which never failed to cow me into submission; the Brass Monkey, however, was made of less pliant stuff. Soundlessly, behind lips clamped tight as her grandmother's, she plotted the incineration of leather – just as once, long ago, another monkey in another city had performed the act which made inevitable the burning of a leathercloth godown...

She was as beautiful (if somewhat scrawny) as I was ugly; but she was from the first, mischievous as a whirlwind and noisy as a crowd. Count the windows and vases broken accidentally-on-purpose; number, if you can, the meals that somehow flew off her treacherous dinner-plates, to stain valuable Persian rugs! Silence was, indeed, the worst punishment she could have been given; but she bore it cheerfully, standing innocently amid the ruins of broken chairs and shattered ornaments.

Mary Pereira said, 'That one! That Monkey! Should have been born with four legs!' But Amina, in whose mind the memory of her narrow escape from giving birth to a two-headed son had obstinately refused to fade, cried, 'Mary! What are you saying? Don't even think such things!' ... Despite my mother's protestations, it was true that the Brass Monkey was as much animal as human, and, as all the servants and children on Methwold's Estate knew, she had the gift of talking to birds, and to cats. Dogs, too: but after she was bitten, at the age of six, by a supposedly rabid stray, and had to be dragged kicking and screaming to Breach Candy Hospital, every afternoon for three weeks, to be given an injection in the stomach, it seems she either forgot their language or else refused to have any further dealings with them. From birds she learned how to sing; from cats she learned a form of dangerous independence. The Brass Monkey was never so furious as when anyone spoke to her in words of love; desperate for affection, deprived of it by my overpowering shadow, she had a tendency to turn upon anyone who gave her what she wanted, as if she were defending herself against the possibility of being tricked.

... Such as the time when Sonny Ibrahim plucked up his courage to tell her, 'Hey, listen, Saleem's sister – you're a solid type. I'm, um, you know, damn keen on you ...' And at once she marched across to where his father and mother were sipping lassi in the gardens of Sans Souci to say, 'Nussie auntie, I don't know what your Sonny's been getting up to. Only just now I saw him and Cyrus behind a bush, doing such funny rubbing things with their soos-soos!' ...

The Brass Monkey had bad table manners; she trampled flowerbeds; she acquired the tag of problem-child; but she and I were close-as-close, in spite of framed letters from Delhi and sadhu-under-the-tap. From the beginning, I decided to treat her as an ally, not a competitor; and, as a result, she never once blamed me for my pre-eminence in our household, saying, 'What's to blame? Is it your fault if they think you're so great?' (But when, years later, I made the same mistake as Sonny, she treated me just the same.)

And it was Monkey who, by answering a certain wrong-number telephone call, began the process of events which led to my accident in a white washing-chest made of slatted wood.

*

Already, at the age of nearlynine, I knew this much: everybody was waiting for me. Midnight and baby-snaps, prophets and prime ministers had created around me a glowing and inescapable mist of expectancy ... in which my father pulled me into his squashy belly in the cool of the cocktail hour to say, 'Great things! My son: what is not in store for you? Great deeds, a great life!' While I, wriggling between jutting lip and big toe, wetting his shirt with my eternally leaking nose-goo, turned scarlet and squealed, 'Let me go, Abba! Everyone will *see*!' And he, embarrassing me beyond belief, bellowed, 'Let them look! Let the whole world see how I love my son!' ... and my grandmother, visiting us one winter, gave me advice, too: 'Just pull up your socks, whatsitsname, and you'll be better than anyone in the whole wide world!' ... Adrift in this haze of anticipation, I had already felt within myself the first movings of that shapeless animal which still, on these Padmaless nights, champs and scratches in my stomach: cursed by a multitude of hopes and nicknames (I had already acquired Sniffer and Snotnose), I became afraid that everyone was wrong – that my much-trumpeted existence might turn out to be utterly useless, void, and without the shred of a purpose. And it was to escape from this beast that I took to hiding myself, from an early age, in my mother's large white washing-chest; because although the creature was inside me, the comforting presence of enveloping soiled linen seemed to lull it into sleep.

Outside the washing-chest, surrounded by people who seemed to possess a devastatingly clear sense of purpose, I buried myself in fairy tales. Hatim Tai and Batman, Superman and Sinbad helped to get me through the nearlynine years. When I went shopping with Mary Pereira – overawed by her ability to tell a chicken's age by looking at its neck, by the sheer determination with which she stared dead pomfrets in the eyes – I became Aladdin, voyaging in a fabulous cave; watching servants dusting vases with a dedication as majestic as it was obscure, I imagined Ali Baba's forty thieves hiding in the dusted urns; in the garden, staring at Purushottam the sadhu being eroded by water, I turned into the genie of the lamp, and thus avoided, for the most part, the terrible notion that I, alone in the universe, had no idea what I should be, or how I should behave. Purpose: it crept up behind me when I stood staring down from my window at European girls cavorting in the map-shaped pool beside the sea. 'Where do you get it?' I yelped aloud; the Brass Monkey, who shared my sky-blue room, jumped half-way out of her skin. I was then nearlyeight; she was almostseven. It was a very early age at which to be perplexed by meaning.

But servants are excluded from washing-chests; school buses, too, are absent. In my nearlyninth year I had begun to attend the Cathedral and John Connon Boys' High School on Outram Road in the old Fort district; washed and brushed every morning, I stood at the foot of our two-storey hillock, white-shorted, wearing a blue-striped elastic belt with a snake-buckle, satchel over my shoulder, my mighty cucumber of a nose dripping as usual; Eyeslice and Hairoil, Sonny Ibrahim and precocious Cyrus-the-great waited too. And on the bus, amid rattling seats and the nostalgic cracks of the window-panes, what certainties! What nearlynine-year-old certitudes about the future! A boast from Sonny: 'I'm going to be a bullfighter; Spain! Chiquitas! Hey, toro, toro!' His satchel held before him like the muleta of Manolete, he enacted his future while the bus rattled around Kemp's Corner, past Thomas Kemp and Co. (Chemists), beneath the Air-India rajah's poster ('See you later, alligator! I'm off to London on Air-India!') and the other hoarding, on which, throughout my childhood, the Kolynos Kid, a gleamtoothed pixie in a green, elfin, chlorophyll hat proclaimed the virtues of Kolynos Toothpaste: 'Keep Teeth Kleen and Keep Teeth Brite! Keep Teeth Kolynos *Super* White!' The kid on his hoarding, the children in the bus: one-dimensional, flattened by certitude, they knew what they were for. Here is Glandy Keith Colaco, a thyroid balloon of a child with hair already sprouting tuftily on his lip: 'I'm going to run my father's cinemas; you bastards want to watch movies, you'll have to come an' beg me for seats!' ... And Fat Perce Fishwala, whose obesity is due to nothing but overeating, and who, along with Glandy Keith, occupies the privileged position of class bully: 'Bah! That's nothing! I'll have diamonds and emeralds and moonstones! Pearls as big as my balls!' Fat Perce's father runs the city's other jewellery business; his great enemy is the son of Mr Fatbhoy, who, being small and intellectual, comes off badly in the war of the pearl-testicled children ... And Eyeslice, announcing his future as a Test cricketer, with a fine disregard for his one empty socket; and Hairoil, who is as slicked-down and neat as his brother is curly-topped and dishevelled, says 'What selfish bums you are! I shall follow my father into the Navy; I shall defend my country!' Whereupon he is pelted with rulers, compasses, inky pellets ... in the school bus, as it clattered past Chowpatty Beach, as it turned left off Marine Drive beside the apartment of my favourite uncle Hanif and headed past Victoria Terminus towards Flora

Fountain, past Churchgate Station and Crawford Market, I held my peace; I was mild-mannered Clark Kent protecting my secret identity; but what on earth was that? 'Hey, Snotnose!' Glandy Keith yelled, 'Hey, whaddya suppose our Sniffer'll grow up to be?' And the answering yell from Fat Perce Fishwala, 'Pinocchio!' And the rest, joining in, sing a raucous chorus of 'There are no strings on me!' ... while Cyrus-the-great sits quiet as genius and plans the future of the nation's leading nuclear research establishment.

And, at home, there was the Brass Monkey with her shoe-burning; and my father, who had emerged from the depths of his collapse to fall, once more, into the folly of tetrapods ... 'Where do you find it?' I pleaded at my window; the fisherman's finger pointed, misleadingly, out to sea.

Banned from washing-chests: cries of 'Pinocchio! Cucumber-nose! Goo-face!' Concealed in my hiding-place, I was safe from the memory of Miss Kapadia, the teacher at Breach Candy Kindergarten, who had, on my first day at school, turned from her blackboard to greet me, seen my nose, and dropped her duster in alarm, smashing the nail on her big toe, in a screechy but minor echo of my father's famous mishap; buried amongst soiled hankies and crumpled pyjamas, I could forget, for a time, my ugliness.

Typhoid attacked me; krait-poison cured me; and my early, overheated growth-rate cooled off. By the time I was nearlynine, Sonny Ibrahim was an inch and a half taller than I. But one piece of Baby Saleem seemed immune to disease and extract-of-snakes. Between my eyes, it mush-roomed outwards and downwards, as if all my expansionist forces, driven out of the rest of my body, had decided to concentrate on this single incomparable thrust ... between my eyes and above my lips, my nose bloomed like a prize marrow. (But then, I was spared wisdom teeth; one should try to count one's blessings.)

What's in a nose? The usual answer: 'That's simple. A breathing appa-ratus; olfactory organs; hairs.' But in my case, the answer was simpler still, although, I'm bound to admit, somewhat repellent: what was in my nose was snot. With apologies, I must unfortunately insist on details: nasal congestion obliged me to breathe through my mouth, giving me the air of a gasping goldfish; perennial blockages doomed me to a childhood without perfumes, to days which ignored the odours of musk and chambeli and mango kasaundy and home-made ice cream: and dirty washing, too. A disability in the world outside washing-chests can be a positive advantage once you're in. But only for the duration of your stay.

Purpose-obsessed, I worried about my nose. Dressed in the bitter garments which arrived regularly from my headmistress aunt Alia, I went to school, played French cricket, fought, entered fairy tales ... and worried. (In those days, my aunt Alia had begun to send us an unending stream of children's clothes, into whose seams she had sewn her old maid's bile; the Brass Monkey and I were clothed in her gifts, wearing at first the baby-things of bitterness, then the rompers of resentment; I grew up in white shorts starched with the starch of jealousy, while the Monkey wore the pretty flowered frocks of Alia's undimmed envy ... unaware that our wardrobe was binding us in the webs of her revenge, we led our well-dressed lives.) My nose: elephantine as the trunk of Ganesh, it should, I thought, have been a superlative breather; a smeller without an answer, as we say; instead, it was permanently bunged-up, and as useless as a wooden sikh-kabab.

Enough. I sat in the washing-chest and forgot my nose; forgot about the climbing of Mount Everest in 1953 – when grubby Eyeslice giggled, 'Hey, men! You think that Tenzing could climb up Sniffer's face?' – and about the quarrels between my parents over my nose, for which Ahmed Sinai never tired of blaming Amina's father: 'Never before in my family has there been a nose like it! We have excellent noses; proud noses; royal noses, wife!' Ahmed Sinai had already begun, at that time, to believe in the fictional ancestry he had created for the benefit of William Methwold; djinn-sodden, he saw Mughal blood running in his veins ... Forgotten, too, the night when I was eight and a half, and my father, djinns on his breath, came into my bedroom to rip the sheets off me and demand: 'What are you up to? Pig! Pig from somewhere?' I looked sleepy; innocent, puzzled. He roared on. '*Chhi-chhi!* Filthy! God punishes boys who do that! Already he's made your nose as big as poplars. He'll stunt your growth; he'll make your soo-soo shrivel up!' And my mother, arriving nightdressed in the startled room, 'Janum, for pity's sake; the boy was only sleeping.' The djinn roared through my father's lips, possessing him completely: 'Look on his face! Whoever got a nose like that from sleeping?'

There are no mirrors in a washing-chest; rude jokes do not enter it, nor pointing fingers. The rage of fathers is muffled by used sheets and discarded brassières. A washing-chest is a hole in the world, a place which civilization has put outside itself, beyond the pale; this makes it the finest of hiding-places. In the washing-chest, I was like Nadir Khan in his underworld, safe from all pressures, concealed from the demands of parents and history ...

... My father, pulling me into his squashy belly, speaking in a voice choked with instant emotion: 'All right, all right, there, there, you're a good boy; you can be anything you want; you just have to want it enough! Sleep now . . .' And Mary Pereira, echoing him in her little rhyme: 'Anything you want to be, you can be; You can be just what-all you want!' It had already occurred to me that our family believed implicitly in good business principles; they expected a handsome return for their investment in me. Children get food shelter pocket-money longholidays and love, all of it apparently free gratis, and most of the little fools think it's a sort of compensation for having been born. 'There are no strings on me!' they sing; but I, Pinocchio, saw the strings. Parents are impelled by the profit motive – nothing more, nothing less. For their attentions, they expected, from me, the immense dividend of greatness. Don't misunderstand me. I didn't mind. I was, at that time, a dutiful child. I longed to give them what they wanted, what soothsayers and framed letters had promised them; I simply did not know how. Where did greatness come from? How did you get some? *When*? . . . When I was seven years old, Aadam Aziz and Reverend Mother came to visit us. On my seventh birthday, dutifully, I permitted myself to be dressed up like the boys in the fisherman picture; hot and constricted in the outlandish garb, I smiled and smiled. 'See, my little piece-of-the-moon!' Amina cried cutting a cake covered with candied farmyard animals, 'So *chweet*! Never takes out one tear!' Sandbagging down the floods of tears lurking just beneath my eyes, the tears of heat discomfort and the absence of One Yard Of Chocolates in my pile of presents, I took a slice of cake to Reverend Mother, who was ill in bed. I had been given a doctor's stethoscope; it was around my neck. She gave me permission to examine her; I prescribed more exercise. 'You must walk across the room, to the almirah and back, once a day. You may lean on me; I am the doctor.' Stethoscoped English milord guided witchmoled grandmother across the room; hobbling, creakingly, she obeyed. After three months of this treatment, she made a full recovery. The neighbours came to celebrate, bearing *rasgullas* and *gulab-jamans* and other sweets. Reverend Mother, seated regally on a takht in the living-room, announced: 'See my grandson? he cured me, whatsitsname. Genius! Genius, whatsitsname: it is a gift from God.' Was that it, then? Should I stopy worrying? Was genius something utterly unconnected with wanting, or learning how, or knowing about, or being able to? Something which at the appointed hour, would float down around my shoulders like an immaculate, delicately worked pashmina shawl? Greatness as a falling mantle; which never needed to be sent to the dhobi. One does not beat genius upon a stone . . . That one clue, my grandmother's one chance sentence, was my only hope; and, as it turned out, she wasn't very far wrong. (The accident is almost upon me; and the children of midnight are waiting.)

*

Years later, in Pakistan, on the very night when the roof was to fall in on her head and squash her flatter than a rice-pancake, Amina Sinai saw the old washing-chest in a vision. When it popped up inside her eyelids, she greeted it like a not-particularly-welcome cousin. 'So it's you again,' she told it. 'Well, why not? Things keep coming back to me these days. Seems you just can't leave anything behind.' She had grown prematurely old like all the women in our family; the chest reminded her of the year in which old age had first begun creeping up on her. The great heat of 1956 – which Mary Pereira told me was caused by little blazing invisible insects – buzzed in her ears once again. 'My corns began killing me then,' she said aloud, and the Civil Defence official who had called to enforce the blackout smiled sadly to himself and thought, Old people shroud themselves in the past during a war; that way they're ready to die whenever required. He crept away past the mountains of defective terry towels which filled most of the house, and left Amina to discuss her dirty laundry in private ... Nussie Ibrahim – Nussie-the-duck – used to admire Amina: 'Such *posture*, my dear, that you've got! Such *tone*! I swear it's a wonder to me: you glide about like you're on an invisible *trolley*!' But in the summer of the heat insects, my elegant mother finally lost her battle against verrucas, because the sadhu Purushottam suddenly lost his magic. Water had worn a bald patch in his hair; the steady dripping of the years had worn him down. Was he disillusioned with his blessed child, his Mubarak? Was it my fault that his mantras lost their power? With an air of great trouble, he told my mother, 'Never mind; wait only; I'll fix your feet for sure.' But Amina's corns grew worse; she went to doctors who froze them with carbon dioxide at absolute zero; but that only brought them back with redoubled vigour, so that she began to hobble, her gliding days done for ever; and she recognized the unmistakable greeting of old age. (Chock-full of fantasy, I transformed her into a silkie – 'Amma, maybe you're a mermaid really, taking human form for the love of a man – so every step is like walking on razor blades!' My mother smiled, but did not laugh.)

1956. Ahmed Sinai and Dr Narlikar played chess and argued – my father was a bitter opponent of Nasser, while Narlikar admired him openly. 'The man is bad for business,' Ahmed said; 'But he's got style,' Narlikar responded, glowing passionately. 'Nobody pushes him around.' At the same time, Jawaharlal Nehru was consulting astrologers about the country's Five Year Plan, in order to avoid another Karamstan; and while the world combined aggression and the occult, I lay concealed in a washing-chest which wasn't really big enough for comfort any more; and Amina Sinai became filled with guilt.

She was already trying to put out of her mind her adventure at the race-track; but the sense of sin which her mother's cooking had given her could not be escaped; so it was not difficult for her to think of the verrucas as a punishment . . . not only for the years-ago escapade at Mahalaxmi, but for failing to save her husband from the pink chitties of alcoholism; for the Brass Monkey's untamed, unfeminine ways; and for the size of her only son's nose. Looking back at her now, it seems to me that a fog of guilt had begun to form around her head – her black skin exuding black cloud which hung before her eyes. (Padma would believe it; Padma would know what I mean!) And as her guilt grew, the fog thickened – yes, why not? – there were days when you could hardly see her head above her neck! . . . Amina had become one of those rare people who take the burdens of the world upon their own backs; she began to exude the magnetism of the willingly guilty; and from then on everyone who came into contact with her felt the most powerful of urges to confess their own, private guilts. When they succumbed to my mother's powers, she would smile at them with a sweet sad foggy smile and they would go away, lightened, leaving their burdens on her shoulders; and the fog of guilt thickened. Amina heard about servants being beaten and officials being bribed; when my uncle Hanif and his wife the divine Pia came to call they related their quarrels in minute detail; Lila Sabarmati confided her infidelities to my mother's graceful, inclined, long-suffering ear; and Mary Pereira had to fight constantly against the most-irresistible temptation to confess her crime.

Faced with the guilts of the world, my mother smiled foggily and shut her eyes tight; and by the time the roof fell in on her head her eyesight was badly impaired, but she could still see the washing-chest.

What was really at the bottom of my mother's guilt? I mean really, beneath verrucas and djinns and confessions? It was an unspeakable malaise, an affliction which could not even be named, and which no longer confined itself to dreams of an underworld husband . . . my mother had fallen (as my father would soon fall) under the spell of the telephone.

*

In the afternoons of that summer, afternoons as hot as towels, the telephone would ring. When Ahmed Sinai was asleep in his room, with his keys under his pillow and umbilical cords in his almirah, telephonic shrilling penetrated the buzzing of the heat insects; and my mother, verruca-hobbled, came into the hall to answer. And now, what expression is this, staining her face the colour of drying blood? ... Not knowing that she's being observed, what fish-like flutterings of lips are these, what strangulated mouthings? ... And why, after listening for a full five minutes, does my mother say, in a voice like broken glass, 'Sorry: wrong number'? Why are diamonds glistening on her eyelids? ... The Brass Monkey whispered to me, 'Next time it rings, let's find out.'

Five days later. Once more it is afternoon; but today Amina is away, visiting Nussie-the-duck, when the telephone demands attention. 'Quick! Quick or it'll wake him!' The Monkey, agile as her name, picks up the receiver before Ahmed Sinai has even changed the pattern of his snoring ... 'Hullo? Yaas? This is seven zero five six one; hullo?' We listen, every nerve on edge; but for a moment there is nothing at all. Then, when we're about to give up, the voice comes. '... Oh ... yes ... hullo...' And the Monkey, shouting almost, 'Hullo? Who is it, please?' Silence again; the voice, which has not been able to prevent itself from speaking, considers its answer; and then, '... Hullo ... This is Shanti Prasad Truck hire Company, please?...' And the Monkey, quick as a flash: 'Yes, what d'you want?' Another pause; the voice, sounding embarrassed, apologetic almost, says, 'I want to rent a truck.'

O feeble excuse of telephonic voice! O transparent flummery of ghosts! The voice on the phone was no truck-renter's voice; it was soft, a little fleshy, the voice of a poet ... but after that, the telephone rang regularly; sometimes my mother answered it, listened in silence while her mouth made fish-motions, and finally, much too late, said, 'Sorry, wrong number'; at other times the Monkey and I clustered around it, two ears to earpiece, while the Monkey took orders for trucks. I wondered: 'Hey, Monkey, what d'you think? Doesn't the guy ever wonder why the trucks don't *arrive*?' And she, wide-eyed, flutter-voiced: 'Man, do you suppose ... maybe they *do*!'

But I couldn't see how; and a tiny seed of suspicion was planted in me, a tiny glimmering of a notion that our mother might have a secret – our Amma! Who always said, 'Keep secrets and they'll go bad inside you; don't tell things and they'll give you stomache-ache!' – a minute spark which my experience in the washing-chest could fan into a forest fire. (Because this time, you see, she gave me proof.)

And now, at last, it is time for dirty laundry. Mary Pereira was fond of telling me, 'If you want to be a big man, baba, you must be very clean. Change clothes,' she advised, 'take regular baths. Go, baba, or I'll send you to the washerman, and he'll wallop you on his stone.' She also threatened me with bugs: 'All right, stay filthy, you will be nobody's darling except the flies'. They will sit on you while you sleep; eggs they'll lay under your skin!' In part, my choice of hiding-place was an act of defiance. Braving dhobis and houseflies, I concealed myself in the unclean place; I drew strength and comfort from sheets and towels; my nose ran freely into the stone-doomed linens; and always, when I emerged into the world from my wooden whale, the sad mature wisdom of dirty washing lingered with me, teaching me its philosophy of coolness and dignity-despite-everything and the terrible inevitability of soap.

One afternoon in June, I tiptoed down the corridors of the sleeping house towards my chosen refuge; sneaked past my sleeping mother into the white-tiled silence of her bathroom; lifted the lid off my goal; and plunged into its soft continuum of (predominantly white) textiles, whose only memories were of my earlier visits. Sighing softly, I pulled down the lid, and allowed pants and vests to massage away the pains of being alive, purposeless and nearlynineyears old.

Electricity in the air. Heat, buzzing like bees. A mantle, hanging some-where in the sky, waiting to fall gently around my shoulders ... some-where, a finger reaches towards a dial; a dial whirrs around and around, electrical pulses dart along cable, seven, zero, five, six, one. The telephone rings. Muffled shrilling of a bell penetrates the washing-chest, in which a nearlynineyearold boy lies uncomfortably concealed ... I, Saleem, became stiff with the fear of discovery, because now more noises entered the chest: squeak of bedsprings; soft clatter of slippers along corridor; the telephone, silenced in mid-shrill; and – or is this imagination? Was her voice too soft to hear? – the words, spoken too late as usual: 'Sorry. Wrong number.'

And now, hobbling footsteps returning to the bedroom; and the worst fears of the hiding boy are fulfilled. Doorknobs, turning, scream warnings at him; razor-sharp steps cut him deeply as they move across cool white tiles. He stays frozen as ice, still as a stick; his nose drips silently into dirty clothes. A pyjama-cord – snake-like harbinger of doom! – inserts itself into his left nostril. To sniff would be to die: he refuses to think about it.

... Clamped tight in the grip of terror, he finds his eye looking through a chink in dirty washing ... and sees a woman crying in a bathroom. Rain dropping from a thick black cloud. And now more sound, more motion: his mother's voice has begun to speak, two syllables, over and over again;

and her hands have begun to move. Ears muffled by underwear strain to catch the sounds – that one: *dir? Bir? Dil?* – and the other: *Ha? Ra?* No – Na. Ha and Ra are banished; Dil and Bir vanish forever; and the boy hears, in his ears, a name which has not been spoken since Mumtaz Aziz became Amina Sinai: Nadir. Nadir. Na. Dir. Na.

And her hands are moving. Lost in their memory of other days, of what happened after games of hit-the-spittoon in an Agra cellar, they flutter gladly at her cheeks; they hold her bosom tighter than any bras-sières; and now they caress her bare midriff, they stray below decks … yes, this is what we used to do, my love, it was enough, enough for me, even though my father made us, and you ran, and now the telephone, Nadirnadirnadirnadirnadirnadir … hands which held telephone now hold flesh, while in another place what does another hand to? To what, after replacing receiver, is another hand getting up? … No matter; because here, in her spied-out privacy, Amina Sinai repeats an ancient name, again and again, until finally she bursts out with, 'Arré Nadir Khan, where have you come from now?'

Secrets. A man's name. Never-before-glimpsed motions of the hands. A boy's mind filled with thoughts which have no shape, tormented by ideas which refuse to settle into words; and in a left nostril, a pyjama-cord is snaking up up up, refusing to be ignored …

And now – O shameless mother! Revealer of duplicity, of emotions which have no place in family life; and more: O brazen unveiler of Black Mango! – Amina Sinai, drying her eyes, is summoned by a more trivial necessity; and as her son's right eye peers out through the wooden slats at the top of the washing-chest, my mother unwinds her sari! While I, silently in the washing-chest: 'Don't do it don't do it don't do!' … but I cannot close my eye. Unblinking pupil takes in upside-down image of sari falling to the floor, an image which is, as usual, inverted by the mind; through ice-blue eyes I see a slip follow the sari; and then – O horrible! – my mother, framed in laundry and slatted wood, bends over to pick up her clothes! And there it is, searing my retina – the vision of my mother's rump, black as night, rounded and curved, resembling nothing on earth so much as a gigantic, black Alfonso mango! In the washing-chest, unnerved by the vision, I wrestle with myself … self-control becomes simultaneously imperative and impossible … under the thunderclap influence of the Black Mango, my nerve cracks; pyjama-cord wins its victory; and while Amina Sinai seats herself on a commode, I … what? Not sneeze; it was less than a sneeze. Not a twitch, either; it was more than that. It's time to talk plainly: shattered by two-syllabic voice and fluttering hands, devastated by Black

Mango, the nose of Saleem Sinai, responding to the evidence of maternal duplicity, quivering at the presence of maternal rump, gave way to a pyjama-cord, and was possessed by a cataclysmic – a world-altering – an irreversible *sniff*. Pyjama-cord rises painfully half an inch further up the nostril. But other things are rising, too: hauled by that feverish inhalation, nasal liquids are being sucked relentlessly up up up, nose-goo flowing upwards, against gravity, against nature. Sinuses are subjected to unbearable pressure ... until, inside the nearlynineyearold head, something bursts. Snot rockets through a breached dam into dark new channels. Mucus, rising higher than mucus was ever intended to rise. Waste fluid, reaching as far, perhaps, as the frontiers of the brain ... there is a shock. Something electrical has been moistened.

Pain.

And then noise, deafening manytongued terrifying, *inside his head*! ... Inside a white wooden washing-chest, within the darkened auditorium of my skull, my nose began to sing.

But just now there isn't time to listen; because one voice is very close indeed. Amina Sinai has opened the lower door of the washing-chest; I am tumbling downdown with laundry wrapped around my head like a caul. Pyjama-cord jerks out of my nose; and now there is lightning flashing through the dark clouds around my mother – and a refuge has been lost for ever.

'I didn't look!' I squealed up through socks and sheets. 'I didn't see one thing, Ammi, I swear!'

And years later, in a cane chair among reject towels and a radio announcing exaggerated war victories, Amina would remember how with thumb and forefinger around the ear of her lying son she led him to Mary Pereira, who was sleeping as usual on a cane mat in a sky-blue room; how she said, 'This young donkey; this good-for-nothing from nowhere is not to speak for one whole day.' ... And, just before the roof fell in on her, she said aloud: 'It was my fault. I brought him up too badly.' As the explosion of the bomb ripped through the air, she added, mildly but firmly, addressing her last words on earth to the ghost of a washing-chest: 'Go away now, I've seen enough of you.'

*

On Mount Sinai, the prophet Musa or Moses heard disembodied commandments; on Mount Hira, the prophet Muhammad (also known as Mohammed, Mahomet, the Last-But-One, and Mahound) spoke to the Archangel. (Gabriel or Jibreel, as you please.) And on the stage of the

Cathedral and John Connon Boys' High School, run 'under the auspices' of
the Anglo-Scottish Education Society, my friend Cyrus-the-great, playing a
female part as usual, heard the voices of St Joan speaking the sentences of
Bernard Shaw. But Cyrus is the odd one out: unlike Joan, whose voices
were heard in a field, but like Musa or Moses, like Muhammad the
Penultimate, I heard voices on a hill.

Muhammad (on whose name be peace, let me add; I don't want to
offend anyone)* heard a voice saying, 'Recite!' and thought he was going
mad; I heard, at first, a headful of gabbling tongues, like an untuned radio;
and with lips sealed by maternal command, I was unable to ask for comfort.
Muhammad, at forty, sought and received reassurance from wife and
friends: 'Verily,' they told him, 'you are the Messenger of God'; I, suffering
my punishment at nearlynine, could neither seek Brass Monkey's assistance nor solicit softening words from Mary Pereira. Muted for an evening
and a night and a morning, I struggled, alone, to understand what had
happened to me; until at last I saw the shawl of genius fluttering down,
like an embroidered butterfly, the mantle of greatness settling upon my
shoulders.

In the heat of that silent night (I was silent; outside me, the sea rustled
like distant paper; crows squawked in the throes of their feathery night-
mares; the puttering noises of tardy taxi-cabs wafted up from Warden
Road; the Brass Monkey, before she fell asleep with her face frozen into a
mask of curiosity, begged, 'Come on, Saleem; nobody's listening; what did
you do? Tell tell tell!' ... while, inside me, the voices rebounded against
the walls of my skull) I was gripped by hot fingers of excitement – the
agitated insects of excitement danced in my stomach – because finally, in
some way I did not then fully understand, the door which Toxy Catrack
had once nudged in my head had been forced open; and through it I
could glimpse – shadowy still, undefined, enigmatic – my reason for
having been born.

Gabriel or Jibreel told Muhammad: 'Recite!' And then began The Recitation, known in Arabic as Al-Quran: 'Recite: In the Name of the Lord thy
Creator, who created Man from clots of blood ...' That was on Mount Hira

* Editor's note: It is impossible, alas, to read this parenthetical aside innocently anymore.
  Both this and the previous paragraph are full of references and images oddly prescient
  of *The Satanic Verses*. The section ends with a blasphemous confession by Saleem Sinai
  that meets with a reaction from his immediate family almost as violent as the real-life
  accusations that would come later. The novel, here, inadvertently, and comically, poses
  the question: to what extent can art subsume belief and justify irreverence, and the
  secular imagination compete with divine prophecy?

outside Mecca Sharif; on a two-storey hillock opposite Breach Candy Pools, voices also instructed me to recite: 'Tomorrow!' I thought excitedly. 'Tomorrow!'

By sunrise, I had discovered that the voices could be controlled – I was a radio receiver, and could turn the volume down or up; I could select individual voices; I could even, by an effort of will, switch off my newly-discovered inner ear. It was astonishing how soon fear left me; by morning, I was thinking, 'Man, this is better than All-India Radio, man; better than Radio Ceylon!'

To demonstrate the loyalty of sisters: when the twenty-four hours were up, on the dot, the Brass Monkey ran into my mother's bedroom. (It was, I think, a Sunday: no school. Or perhaps not – that was the summer of the language marches, and the schools were often shut, because of the danger of violence on the bus-routes.)

'The time's up!' she exclaimed, shaking my mother out of sleep. 'Amma, wake up: it's time, can he talk now?'

'All right,' my mother said, coming into a sky-blue room to embrace me, 'you're forgiven now. But never hide in there again . . .'

'Amma,' I said eagerly, 'my Ammi, please listen. I must tell you something. Something big. But please, please first of all, wake Abba.'

And after a period of 'What?' 'Why?' and 'Certainly not,' my mother saw something extraordinary sitting in my eyes and went to wake Ahmed Sinai anxiously, with 'Janum, please come. I don't know what's got into Saleem.'

Family and ayah assembled in the sitting-room. Amid cut-glass vases and plump cushions, standing on a Persian rug beneath the swirling shadows of ceiling-fans, I smiled into their anxious eyes and prepared my revelation. This was it; the beginning of the repayment of their investment; my first dividend – first, I was sure, of many . . . my black mother, lip-jutting father, Monkey of a sister and crime-concealing ayah waited in hot confusion.

Get it out. Straight, without frills. 'You should be the first to know,' I said, trying to give my speech the cadences of adulthood. And then I told them. 'I heard voices yesterday. Voices are speaking to me inside my head. I think – Ammi, Abboo, I really think – that Archangels have started to talk to me.'

There! I thought. There! It's said! Now there will be pats on the back, sweetmeats, public announcements, maybe more photographs; now their chests will puff up with pride. O blind innocence of childhood! For my honesty – for my open-hearted desperation to please – I was set upon from all sides. Even the Monkey: 'O *God* Saleem, all this *tamasha*, all this performance, for one of your stupid *cracks*?' And worse than the Monkey was Mary Pereira: 'Christ Jesus! Save us, Lord! Holy Father in Rome, such blasphemy I've heard today!' And worse than Mary Pereira was my mother Amina Sinai: Black Mango concealed now, her own unnameable names still warm upon her lips, she cried, 'Heaven forfend! The child will bring down the roof upon our heads!' (Was that my fault, too?) And Amina continued: 'You black man! Goonda! O Saleem, has your brain gone raw? What has happened to my darling baby boy – are you growing into a madman – a *torturer*!?' And worse than Amina's shrieking was my father's silence; worse than her fear was the wild anger sitting on his forehead; and worst of all was my father's hand, which stretched out suddenly, thick-fingered, heavy-jointed, strong-as-an-ox, to fetch me a mighty blow on the side of my head, so that I could never hear properly in my left ear after that day; so that I fell sideways across the startled room through the scandalized air and shattered a green tabletop of opaque glass; so that, having been certain of myself for the first time in my life, I was plunged into a green, glass-cloudy world filled with cutting edges, a world in which I could no longer tell the people who mattered most about the goings-on inside my head; green shards lacerated my hands as I entered that swirling universe in which I was doomed, until it was far too late, to be plagued by constant doubts about what I was *for*.

In a white-tiled bathroom beside a washing-chest, my mother daubed me with Mercurochrome; gauze veiled my cuts, while through the door my father's voice commanded, 'Wife, let nobody give him food today. You hear me? Let him enjoy his joke on an empty stomach!'

That night, Amina Sinai would dream of Ramram Seth, who was floating six inches above the ground, his eye-sockets filled with egg-whites, intoning: 'Washing will hide him ... voices will guide him' ... but when, after several days in which the dream sat upon her shoulders wherever she went, she plucked up the courage to ask her disgraced son a little more about his outrageous claim, he replied in a voice as restrained as the unwept tears of his childhood: 'It was just fooling, Amma. A stupid joke, like you said.'

She died, nine years later, without discovering the truth.

ALL-INDIA RADIO

Reality is a question of perspective; the further you get from the past, the more concrete and plausible it seems – but as you approach the present, it inevitably seems more and more incredible. Suppose yourself in a large cinema, sitting at first in the back row, and gradually moving up, row by row, until your nose is almost pressed against the screen. Gradually the stars' faces dissolve into dancing grain; tiny details assume grotesque proportions; the illusion dissolves – or rather, it becomes clear that the illusion itself *is* reality ... we have come from 1915 to 1956, so we're a good deal closer to the screen ... abandoning my metaphor, then, I reiterate, entirely without a sense of shame, my unbelievable claim: after a curious accident in a washing-chest, I became a sort of radio.

... But today, I feel confused. Padma has not returned – should I alert the police? Is she a Missing Person? – and in her absence, my certainties are falling apart. Even my nose has been playing tricks on me – by day, as I stroll between the pickle-vats tended by our army of strong, hairy-armed, formidably competent women, I have found myself failing to distinguish lemon-odours from lime. The workforce giggles behind its hands: the poor sahib has been crossed in – what? – surely not *love*? ... Padma, and the cracks spreading all over me, radiating like a spider's web from my navel; and the heat ... a little confusion is surely permissible in these circumstances. Rereading my work, I have discovered an error in chronology. The assassination of Mahatma Gandhi occurs, in these pages, on the wrong date. But I cannot say, now, what the actual sequence of events might have been; in my India, Gandhi will continue to die at the wrong time.

Does one error invalidate the entire fabric? Am I so far gone, in my desperate need for meaning, that I'm prepared to distort everything – to rewrite the whole history of my times purely in order to place myself in a central role? Today, in my confusion, I can't judge. I'll have to leave it to others. For me, there can be no going back; I must finish what I've started, even if, inevitably, what I finish turns out not to be what I began ...

Yé Akashvani hai. This is All-India Radio.

Having gone out into the boiling streets for a quick meal at a nearby Irani café, I have returned to sit in my nocturnal pool of Anglepoised light with only a cheap transistor for company. A hot night; bubbling air filled with the lingering scents of the silenced pickle-vats; voices in the dark. Pickle-fumes, heavily oppressive in the heat, stimulate the juices of

memory, accentuating similarities and differences between now and then
... it was hot then; it is (unseasonably) hot now. Then as now, someone
was awake in the dark, hearing disembodied tongues. Then as now, the
one deafened ear. And fear, thriving in the heat ... it was not the voices
(then or now) which were frightening. He, young-Saleem-then, was afraid
of an idea – the idea that his parents' outrage might lead to a withdrawal
of their love; that even if they began to believe him, they would see his
gift as a kind of shameful deformity ... while I, now, Padma-less, send
these words into the darkness and am afraid of being disbelieved. He
and I, I and he ... I no longer have his gift; he never had mine. There are
times when he seems a stranger, almost ... he had no cracks. No spiders'
webs spread through him in the heat.

Padma would believe me; but there is no Padma. Then as now, there is
hunger. But of a different kind: not, now, the then-hunger of being denied
my dinner, but that of having lost my cook.

And another, more obvious difference: then, the voice did not arrive
through the oscillating valves of a transistor (which will never cease, in
our part of the world, to symbolize impotence – ever since the notorious
free-transistor sterilization bribe, the squawking machine has represented
what men could do before scissors snipped and knots were tied) ... then,
the nearlynineyearold in his midnight bed had no need of machines.

Different and similar, we are joined by heat. A shimmering heat-haze,
then and now, blurs his then-time into mine ... my confusion, travelling
across the heat-waves, is also his.

What grows best in the heat: cane-sugar; the coconut palm; certain
millets such as *bajra, ragi* and *jowar*; linseed, and (given water) tea and rice.
Our hot land is also the world's second largest producer of cotton – at least,
it was when I learned geography under the mad eye of Mr Emil Zagallo, and
the steelier gaze of a framed Spanish conquistador. But the tropical summer
grows stranger fruit as well: the exotic flowers of the imagination blossom,
to fill the close perspiring nights with odours as heavy as musk, which give
men dark dreams of discontent ... then as now, unease was in the air.
Language marchers demanded the partition of the state of Bombay along
linguistic boundaries – the dream of Maharashtra was at the head of some
processions, the mirage of Gujarat led the others forward. Heat, gnawing at
the mind's divisions between fantasy and reality, made anything seem
possible; the half-waking chaos of afternoon siestas fogged men's brains,
and the air was filled with the stickiness of aroused desires.

What grows best in the heat: fantasy; unreason; lust.

In 1956, then, languages marched militantly through the daytime streets; by night, they rioted in my head. *We shall be watching your life with the closest attention; it will be, in a sense, the mirror of our own.*

It's time to talk about the voices

But if only our Padma were here ...

*

I was wrong about the Archangels, of course. My father's hand – walloping my ear in (conscious? unintentional?) imitation of another, bodiless hand, which once hit him full in the face – at least had one salutary effect: it obliged me to reconsider and finally to abandon my original, Prophet-apeing position. In bed that very night of my disgrace, I withdrew deep inside myself, despite the Brass Monkey, who filled our blue room with her pesterings: 'But what did you do it *for*, Saleem? You who're always too good and all?' ... until she fell into dissatisfied sleep with her mouth still working silently, and I was alone with the echoes of my father's violence, which buzzed in my left ear, which whispered, 'Neither Michael nor Anael; not Gabriel; forget Cassiel, Sachiel and Samael! Archangels no longer speak to mortals; the Recitation was completed in Arabia long ago; the last prophet will come only to announce the End.' That night, understanding that the voices in my head far outnumbered the ranks of the angels, I decided, not without relief, that I had not after all been chosen to preside over the end of the world. My voices, far from being sacred, turned out to be as profane, and as multitudinous, as dust.

Telepathy, then; the kind of thing you're always reading about in the sensational magazines. But I ask for patience – wait. Only wait. It was telepathy; but also more than telepathy. Don't write me off too easily.

Telepathy, then: the inner monologues of all the so-called teeming millions, of masses and classes alike, jostled for space within my head. In the beginning when I was content to be an audience – before I began to *act* – there was a language problem. The voices babbled in everything from Malayalam to Naga dialects, from the purity of Lucknow Urdu to the Southern slurrings of Tamil. I understood only a fraction of the things being said within the walls of my skull. Only later, when I began to probe, did I learn that below the surface transmissions – the front-of-mind stuff which is what I'd originally been picking up – language faded away, and was replaced by universally intelligible thought-forms which far tran-scended words ... but that was after I heard, beneath the polyglot frenzy in my head, those other precious signals, utterly different from everything else, most of them faint and distant, like far-off drums whose insistent pulsing eventually broke through the fish-market cacophony of my voices

... those secret, nocturnal calls, like calling out to like ... the unconscious beacons of the children of midnight, signalling nothing more than their existence, transmitting simply: 'I.' From far to the North, 'I.' And the South East West: 'I.' 'I.' 'And I.'

But I mustn't get ahead of myself. In the beginning, before I broke through to more-than-telepathy, I contented myself with listening; and soon I was able to 'tune' my inner ear to those voices which I could understand; nor was it long before I picked out, from the throng, the voice of my own family; and of Mary Pereira; and of friends, classmates, teachers. In the street, I learned how to identify the mind-stream of passing strangers – the laws of Doppler shift continued to operate in these paranormal realms, and the voices grew and diminished as the strangers passed.

All of which I somehow kept to myself. Reminded daily (by the buzzing in my left, or sinister, ear) of my father's wrath, and anxious to keep my right ear in good working order, I sealed my lips. For a nine-year-old boy, the difficulties of concealing knowledge are almost insurmountable; but fortunately, my nearest and dearest were as anxious to forget my outburst as I was to conceal the truth.

'O, you Saleem! Such things you talked yesterday! Shame on you, boy: you better go wash out your mouth with soap!' ... The morning after my disgrace, Mary Pereira, shaking with indignation like one of her jellies, suggested the perfect means of my rehabilitation. Bowing my head contritely, I went, without a word, into the bathroom, and there, beneath the amazed gaze of ayah and Monkey, scrubbed teeth tongue roofofmouth gums with a toothbrush covered in the sharp foul lather of Coal Tar Soap. The news of my dramatic atonement rushed rapidly around the house, borne by Mary and Monkey; and my mother embraced me. 'There, good boy; we'll say no more about it,' and Ahmed Sinai nodded gruffly at the breakfast table, 'At least the boy has the grace to admit when he's gone too far.'

As my glass-inflicted cuts faded, it was as though my announcement was also erased; and by the time of my ninth birthday, nobody besides myself remembered anything about the day when I had taken the name of Archangels in vain. The taste of detergent lingered on my tongue for many weeks, reminding me of the need for secrecy.

Even the Brass Monkey was satisfied by my show of contrition – in her eyes, I had returned to form, and was once more the goody-two-shoes of the family. To demonstrate her willingness to re-establish the old order, she set fire to my mother's favourite slippers, and regained her rightful place in the family doghouse. Amongst outsiders, what's more – displaying a conservatism you'd never have suspected in such a tomboy – she closed ranks with my parents, and kept my one aberration a secret from her friends and mine.

In a country where any physical or mental peculiarity in a child is a source of deep family shame, my parents, who had become accustomed to facial birthmarks, cucumber-nose and bandy legs, simply refused to see any more embarrassing things in me; for my part, I did not once mention the buzzings in my ear, the occasional ringing bells of deafness, the intermittent pain. I had learned that secrets were not always a bad thing.

Vikram Seth (b. 1952)

Vikram Seth was born in Calcutta in 1952, and was educated in Delhi and at the Doon School in Dehradun. He later read PPE at Oxford, before moving to the sunnier climes of Stanford in California to do a Ph.D. on the economic demography of China. He never completed the doctorate, but spent part of his life as a graduate student learning Chinese, and travelling to China, an experience from which came, later, his travel book, *From Heaven Lake*, and some of the excellent and underrated poems in *The Humble Administrator's Garden*. His career has been one of ceaseless reinvention; from economist to poet, to travel writer, to novelist-in-verse, to popular literary novelist, to librettist, to who knows what next. Skipping from genre to genre, it's as if he's not just a writer, but a microcosm of the cultural ethos – the ethos of the post-Independence, urban, English-speaking middle-class – to which he belongs, an ethos that too has felt the need indefatigably and restlessly to reinvent itself. Lacking a clearly defined tradition to fall back on, the Indian writer in English, working in isolation, has laid claim, like Borges's Argentinian writer, to all of Western and European tradition, besides his own, in a way that perhaps no European can; and so has Seth, taking whatever, and whenever, he chooses, whether it is Pushkin, or George Eliot, or the poetry of the Movement. For him, writing is partly a matter of creating genres, as if it's not enough to create an oeuvre, but a whole tradition in miniature, by which he, and his contemporaries, might be evaluated. Like Rushdie, and the eighteenth- and nineteenth-century novelists he loves, he has been flirting, although in an absolutely different way from either, with popular culture; this presumably led Dom Moraes to call *The Golden Gate* (from which an extract appears below) a 'Mills and Boon novel' when he first read it. Rereading it, one is reminded of Matthew Arnold's advice that writers should concentrate on great action and great characters, and struck by how thoroughly Seth, in his tribute to Mediterranean sunniness, to California, to human beings composed equally of maudlin emotion and a hunger for seriousness, has ignored this advice. As small and well-travelled as Puck, Seth, like Puck, has, in this novel, delighted in bringing together and separating his mortals, in fuelling their confusions and resolving them, and both chafing and transubstantiating them with his magic.

* * *

from *The Golden Gate* (1986)

2.1

That midnight, after strenuous drumming
And an hour's drive for Liquid Sheep,
After the catcalls of homecoming,
Janet's arm hurts. She cannot sleep.
For hours she stands and views Orion,
The Bear, the Dog, the Goat, the Lion,
The cats asleep now, slackly curled
Upon the surface of the World
Of Counterpane. Then, suddenly smiling,
A light within her almond eyes,
To her grandmother's desk she flies,
Seized by a notion so beguiling
That she must – must? – she thinks a bit –
She must act instantly on it.

2.2

The fitful pen moves on the paper,
It pauses to delete a phrase,
Doodles a face, attempts to caper
Across a dubious word, but stays
Poised in midair. 'If injudicious,
At least this won't be meretricious;
But individuality –
How do I strike that note? Let's see,
If I used ...' Outside, day is dawning.
Opus complete, and at the sill
She stands in thought. Eight. Nine. But still
The city sleeps. (Ah, Sunday morning,
Most blessèd of all times.) She sets
Her breakfast out, and feeds the pets.

2.3

Sated with requisite nutrition
They eye her milk and Weetabix
As she reads out her composition:
'*Young handsome yuppie, 26,*
Straight, forward, sociable, but lonely,
Cannot believe that he's the only
Well-rounded and well-meaning square
Lusting for love. If you, out there,
Are friendly, female, under 30,
Impulsive, fit, and fun, let's meet.
Be rash. Box — . Cuff, off that sheet!
It's just been typed, and now it's dirty.
I guess your paw prints ... (The cats purr.)
... Can serve in place of signature.'

2.4

Brown paper packets, marked discreetly,
From the *Bay Guardian* arrive
Each week: within lie, nested neatly,
A clutch of envelopes. When five
Such packets lie on Janet's table
(Thinner each week) and she is able
To sense a dwindling of the tranche
That seemed at first an avalanche,
She slits the packets to examine
The postmark on each envelope,
Thinking, 'I wonder if he'll cope
As sanguinely with glut as famine.'
She counts the letters – eighty-two –
And wonders, fiercely, what to do.

2.5

'So many! Jesus! Should I vet them,
Select a few and pass them on,
Or curb myself, abstain, and let them
Wing their uncensored way to John –
Expectant, uncurtailed, each letter
Pleading its own defense? It's better,
Surely, to yield to laissez-faire
And burden him with bulk than dare
Presume to cull his choice by proxy,
Picking my path through torrid lines,
Pert promises and suave designs
From dulcet Deborah to foxy
Farah – a world of tendered joys,
A passion play of pleas and ploys.'

2.6

Two mornings after Janet fires
Her postal charge, she's roused from sleep.
A chilled voice on the phone enquires:
'You sent it? Janet, you're a creep.
You didn't fool me for a minute –
But would you care to know what's in it?
It's wasted, I would say, on me –
My interest in pornography
Is somewhat jaded. Still, I'm curious:
Why did you choose to loose this host
Of bacchantes on me through the post?
Ought I to thank you?' 'You sound furious.'
'Your crazy ad – ' she hears him shout,
'Was garbage in and garbage out!'

2.7

'Come, John, where is your sense of humor?'
'It's dormant since last night.' 'But since
A good man wrote it, I'd assume a
Few pleasant women might evince
A favorable – who knows? – inviting
Response; I'd find it quite exciting.
How could they all be maenads mad
With morbid lust? Is it that bad?'
'Well, while we're on the subject, Janet,
Since you're charmed by your scheme, and I
Am a mere blameless passerby,
I think it's better if you ran it.
No doubt your modest maidens will
Quiver to your responsive quill.'

2.8

'John, don't get mad. Just think it over.'
'You're too much. Look, I'm late for work.
I've got to go.' 'O demon-lover,
Drive carefully.' 'I will, O jerk.'
But loosed upon the frenzied freeway,
He gives no quarter, grace, or leeway
To lesser cars within the law.
Tight-lipped, he hears the Peugeot roar
Past little Bugs and harmless Hondas
At 90 m.p.h., his mind
Pulsing with anger, while behind,
Unnoticed, the deft anacondas
Of the road-jungle glide in fast:
The cops catch up with him at last.

2.9

Lights flash. 'Oh God! This means a ticket.'
The siren wails. John brakes. 'Well, I'm
Just going to tell them they can stick it . . .'
A cop comes. 'License, please . . . This time
It's just a fine. The speed you're going
Is hazardous. How about slowing
Your pace a little, Mr Brown?'
John hears him with a restive frown,
With more impatience than repentance.
'Officer, work begins at eight.'
The cop says, 'Better late than "late,"'
Signing his ticket on that sentence.
'Have a good day, now!' But John, cross,
Can't work, and quarrels with his boss.

2.10

A fellow engineer's been fired.
John pleads his cause. ('What's done is done,'
His boss replies.) At evening, tired,
He drives back on Route 101.
Above the rush-hour droves, commuting
Bumper to bumper, horns are hooting.
Through the concussive gas fumes John
Sees *Goodnight, Lemmings!* scrawled upon
An overpass. A stern contralto
Bays Wagner out on 'Listener's Choice.'
An overripe announcer's voice
States, 'KDFC, Pah-lo Ahl-to.'
John turns his knob from rival bands
Till KOME's on his hands.

2.11

The freeway sweeps past humming pylons,
Past Canterbury Carpet Mart,
Warehouses, ads displaying nylons
On shapely legs that make John start.
A cigarette ad, sweet and suborning,
Subverts the Surgeon General's warning:
A craggy golfer, tanned, blue-eyed,
Insouciantly stands beside
A Porsche-caged blonde; coolly patrician,
He puffs a menthol-tipped King-size.
John tries to curb his vagrant eyes
And heed the poet's admonition:
'Beneath this slab John Brown is stowed.
He watched the ads and not the road.'

2.12

But in five minutes other features
Divert him: 'Honk for Jesus.' 'I
Swerve to run over little creatures.'
'The President is a lesbian spy.'
'Nuke the nukes,' 'Fan of David Bowie'
Or 'Here today – and gone to Maui,'
'I ♣ winos,' 'I ♥ L.A.'
Or 'Have you hugged your whale today?'
'Bartenders do it with more spirit.'
'Old beach boys do it with good vibes.'
John sighs, looks up. An ad describes
The Roach Motel's compelling merit:
'Roaches check in – but they don't check out!'
John thinks, 'That's what my life's about.'

2.13

Need John's life be so bug-infested?
He wasn't always so alone.
Entrepreneurial, double-breasted,
He's changed from what his friends have known.
Work, and the syndrome of possessions
Leave little time for life's digressions.
At college, walking down the hall,
You'd meet your friends. But now it's all
Too complicated ... Scattered, sifted,
From New York City to L.A.,
They write, 'We must meet up some day ...';
Yet even those who haven't drifted
– Like Phil, or Jan – too far from John,
He's chary to encroach upon.

2.14

His work's use does not disconcert him;
At least, not much. John feels that what
He chooses to ignore can't hurt him;
Some things are his concern, some not.
His politics have strongly, slowly,
Rigidified; nor does this wholly
Stem from his tenure in Defense.
It's a reflection, in a sense,
Of a rigidity deeper-seated.
A bit of an emotional waif
Since, a small boy, he used to chafe
Against the fate that he'd been meted,
The mother's love he'd never had,
He'd clung to 'standards,' good or bad.

2.15

Mumbling, as he turns off the freeway,
'Christ, what a day!' he drives his car
Beyond the Bay Bridge piers, the seaway,
The Ferry Building, to a bar,
In search of ... what? Oh, any dumb thing –
Love, company, oblivion – something
To breach this fearsome solitude.
Two bourbons down, in cheerier mood,
He thinks less of the ungiving fetters
Of his bleak life, the Universe,
And how things must get worse and worse,
Than of the intriguing cache of letters,
Almost untouched, back in his flat.
'I'll read a few. No harm in that!'

2.16

Back home, he spreads them in his study,
Boosts his intention with, 'Godspeed!
You've got to get your fingers muddy
When panning gold,' and starts to read.
The first one, waxing weird and wayward,
Comes from a doomed housewife in Hayward;
The next, from Kate in mad Marin,
Is redolent of Chanel and gin;
The third . . . but why describe the riot
Of paper, color, scent, device,
Construction, style? Let it suffice
That, dazed by this immoderate diet
('Too much confectionery, too rich'),
John can't remember which is which.

2.17

Yes, why describe the louche lubricious
Dreams of a Daly City Dame,
The half-enticing, subtly vicious
Burblings of Belle from Burlingame,
And then from Eve of San Francisco,
'Six novel ways of using Crisco,'
Or the Tigress of Tiburon
Who waits to pounce on hapless John.
Still, trapped in this traumatic traffic,
Silly and frilly, cool and hot,
John finds about a quarter not
Too evidently pornographic.
Of these he gingerly picks three.
'The others just aren't right for me.'

2.18

Selection made, John now dispatches
Three crisp and courtly notes, and waits
Unhurriedly. The act detaches
His heart from gloom, leaves to the Fates
What lies within their proper region.
To each of the residual legion
He sends in a plain envelope
The photocopied lines: *I hope*
You will excuse this xeroxed letter.
I do not think that you and I
Are matched, but thanks for your reply
To my ad, and I wish you better
Luck for the future. John. He signs,
But adds no surname to the lines.

2.19

In his notes, though, he begs the pleasure
On three successive Saturdays
(If they should chance to have the leisure)
Of the three women at three plays
Followed by dinner. Wasp Bluestocking
Accepts, and turns up with a shocking
Pink parasol. They see *Macbeth*,
Where John's bored to an inch of death
By her insistent exegesis:
Appearance and reality themes
And the significance of dreams
And darkness, and the singular thesis
That the Third Murderer is in fact
The central figure of each act.

2.20

Throughout the play she oozes jargon.
Throughout the meal she oozes French
Till John is numbed inert as argon.
He grows quite pale. 'Aroint thee, wench!'
He thinks, but keeps a fragile patter
Feebly afloat. 'Why, what's the matter?
You look as white as Banquo's ghost
Force-fed three slices of milk toast.'
She laughs genteelly at her sally.
'Just indigestion,' John replies.
When the time comes to leave, he sighs,
'Lately, my work in Silicon Valley
Leaves no time for *affaires de coeur,'*
And bids a glad adieu to her.

2.21

Belinda Beale's acceptance letter
Arrives (with photograph). John smiles.
'Surely Belinda will be better:
What eyes!' Unconscious of her wiles
John waits; exactly one week later
He goes with her to the theater
To see that interesting play
Cat on a Hot Tin Roof. Halfway
Through the third act, her dexterous digits,
With small attempt at camouflage,
Engage in passionate pétrissage*
Along his thigh. John squirms and fidgets.
He darts her a swift glance. She stops,
But not for long. The curtain drops.

* pétrissage: 'massage by longitudinal rubbing and lateral squeezing' (*Chambers Twentieth Century Dictionary*)

2.22

At dinner amorous Belinda
Stares deep, deep, with her peerless eyes
And tries to spark John's dampened tinder
With coos and flutings. 'Ah,' she sighs,
'You're such a fox!' John frowns and flushes.
Immune to his beleaguered blushes,
With 'Oh, your accent is so cute!'
She strikes her helpless victim mute,
While underneath the elegant table
Of coq au vin, to John's disgust,
Discomfiture, and rising lust,
She . . . John gets up, concocts a fable,
'Ten-thirty! – got to go – my wife – '
Leaves fifty bucks, and flees for life.

2.23

'Too bad,' he thinks, 'Well, third time lucky.'
He waits for A.T.F.'s response.
'I liked her letter; she sounds plucky
And amicable. For the nonce
I think that's what I need. Belinda
Would have combusted me to cinder
And Wasp stung me to learnéd death.'
Her letter comes. With indrawn breath
John reads the note, the friendly greeting,
The lines (as usual, typed). They say:
Since my job's taking me away
From San Francisco soon, our meeting
Would serve no aim. Forgive me, please;
I've just been told this. Anne T. Friese.

2.24

'The King's third daughter,' John thinks sadly.
'If this were just a fairy tale ...
Why am I taking this so badly?
She's just a name brought by the mail,
Gone with the wind.' To her box number
He writes: *Anne, I don't mean to lumber*
Once more into your consciousness,
But if you left me your address
We could maintain communication.
This is returned: *Box Number Changed.*
Thus Janet (alias Anne)'s arranged
Her creature's discontinuation.
She feels the note she wrote for fun
Would have been better unbegun.

2.25

At breakfast, sipping a Bacardi
And Coke, Jan meditates upon
Her guilt. She forwards seven tardy
Responses to the ad to John.
John reads these with faint aspiration.
Each seems a standard variation
On themes he's heard too loud and long.
'The Rhine maidens have sung their song;
This straggling coda is bathetic ...
(He reads the fifth one) ... It's a farce ...
(The sixth one) ... And it came to pass
That John stayed celibate and ascetic.
Good! Curtain down, and weak applause.'
The seventh letter gives him pause.

2.26

He reads it through twice, somewhat chary
Of yet one more time being had.
It goes: *Dear Yuppie, I am wary*
Of answering a personal ad.
This is the first time, I should mention,
That I have broken my convention
Of reticence. But, well, here goes:
I rather liked your literate prose.
As an attorney, the clear crafting
Of words (our stock-in-trade) excites
My admiration. Nothing blights
A document like sloppy drafting.
Your ad, if I may be allowed
To matronize you, does you proud.

2.27

I'm friendly, female 27,
Well-rounded too, and somewhat square.
I've not yet known romantic heaven,
But harbor hopes of getting there.
I'm fit – at least, I'm not convulsive;
And fun, I hope, though not impulsive.
To match the handsomeness you flaunt
(I do not mean this as a taunt;
I find immodesty disarming),
I have heard several people say
I am good-looking, in my way.
So if you'd like to meet, Prince Charming,
That shows discernment. If you flout
My charms, you are a tasteless lout.

2.28

With all good wishes. Yours sincerely,
Elisabeth Dorati (Liz).
John reads, but sees no image clearly.
At times it seems as if she is
Nervous and stern, at others hearty.
Who is Elisabeth Dorati:
A cool manipulating minx
Or a wise imperturbable sphinx?
The hand's italic, warm and vigorous,
Crossed out, at times, with a clean line.
The paper's cream, of plain design
(No scent or frill), the ink's a rigorous
Black, and the pen, though narrow-tipped,
Maintains the strength of the clear script.

2.29

How could John know that Liz Dorati
(Ex-Stanford Law School, last year's batch)
Is neither cool nor stern nor hearty,
And much sought after as a match
By more than one well-heeled attorney
At the staid law firm Cobb & Kearny?
Daily their sheepish, prurient eyes
Swerve from their statutes to her thighs.
Unmoved by this redundant bounty,
Liz spends her weekends at her folks':
A vineyard where she reads and soaks
The sunlight of Sonoma County,
Talks to her dad of must and vines,
Plays chess with him, and sips his wines.

2.30

Though Liz was brought up marinading
Near the jacuzzis of Marin,
She never reveled in parading
Her heart, her knowledge, or her skin.
She bloomed unhardened by her beauty,
Immune to 'Lizzie, you're a cutie!'
Though doting aunt and bleating beau
Reiterated it was so.
Her mother, anxious, loving, rigid,
Said, 'Liz, a pretty girl like you
Ought to be thinking of . . .' 'Et tu?'
Sighed Liz, 'Mom, do you think I'm frigid?
Just let me get my law degree
Out of the way – and then, I'll see.'

2.31

Though while at law school Liz had wandered
Into the odd affair or two,
So far at least she had not squandered
Her time or heart on someone who
Appeared a candidate for marriage.
Mrs Dorati might disparage
Her children (Liz and Ed and Sue)
For proving such a fruitless crew;
Yet all her gentle instigation
('When I was your age, Ed . . . don't frown . . .
You really ought to settle down . . .')
Had foundered in the generation
Of the desired posse of
Grandchildren she could spoil and love.

2.32

Liz seemed immersed in her career
(For which Miss Simms of fifth-grade math
Must bear the blame – who made Liz veer
Toward a more professional path
Than had been planned by Liz's mother).
Ed too had no 'significant other'
(Or none, at least, who could be seen).
And Sue in recent years had been
So captivated by the cello
That bows and rosin and Mozart,
Not beaus and roses, filled her heart.
Although life's autumn, sere and yellow,
Now pattered round their mother's days,
The kids preserved their childless ways.

2.33

Yet Liz, sweet Liz, a little lonely,
Sequestered in her city flat
(Unlike her student days), with only
The trusty Charlemagne, her cat,
A fearsome tabby, as companion –
Felt, as she swam the rapid canyon
Of her career, while crocodiles
Nibbled her toes with savory smiles,
That there must be some happy medium
Between a legal partner's life
And being a legal partner's wife.
O loneliness – or else, O tedium!
And so one day she hit upon
The personal ads and, through them, John.

2.34

In fact her letter cost Liz dearly.
Skimming the paper, flipping through
Its pungent *cris de coeur*, she nearly
Passed John's ad by. The word that drew
Her gaze was 'square.' She'd often pondered
Her own geometry, and wondered
About a possible congruence.
Could this be it? A second sense
Nudged second thoughts aside. Though cringing
At her unprecedented act,
With a brash pen and muzzled tact,
A quickening heartbeat and a singeing
Blush, she composed and swiftly wrote,
Signed, sealed, addressed, and sent her note.

2.35

On Sunday morning, groomed and waiting,
John sits in the Café Trieste.
A canny veteran of blind dating
(Twice bitten, once shy), it is best
To meet, he reckons, far from drama,
In daylight: less romantic, calmer,
And, if things should not turn out right,
Convenient for ready flight.
At noon, the meeting hour appointed,
A tall, fresh-faced blonde enters, sees
The suited John. 'Excuse me, please ...
(A little hesitant and disjointed)
... Would you be – John?' John smiles. 'Correct.
And you're Elisabeth, I suspect.'

2.36

'She's lovely,' John thinks, almost staring.
They shake hands. John's heart gives a lurch.
'Handsome, all right, and what he's wearing
Suggests he's just returned from church . . .
Sound, solid, practical, and active,'
Thinks Liz, 'I find him quite attractive.
Perhaps . . .' All this has been inferred
Before the first substantive word
Has passed between the two. John orders
A croissant and espresso; she
A sponge cake and a cup of tea.
They sit, but do not breach the borders
Of discourse till, at the same time,
They each break silence with, 'Well, I'm—'

2.37

Both stop, confused. Both start together:
'I'm sorry—' Each again stops dead.
They laugh. 'It hardly matters whether
You speak or I,' says John: 'I said,
Or meant to say – I'm glad we're meeting.'
Liz quietly smiles, without completing
What she began. 'Not fair,' says John.
'Come clean. What was it now? Come on:
One confidence deserves another.'
'No need,' says Liz. 'You've said what I
Would have admitted in reply.'
They look, half smiling, at each other,
Half puzzled too, as if to say,
'I don't know why I feel this way.'

2.38

Around them arias from Rossini
Resound from wall to wall. A bum
Unsoberly demands Puccini.
Cups clink. Aficionados hum
And sing along with Pavarotti,
Expatiate upon the knotty
Dilemmas of the world, peruse
The *Examiner* for sports or news
Or, best of all, the funny pages,
Where Garfield, that egregious cat,
Grows daily lazier and more fat,
And voluble polemic rages,
While praise by one and all's expressed
For the black brew of the Trieste.

2.39

The pair are now rapt in discussion.
Jan comes in, sees them, cannot hear
What they are saying – could be Russian
For all she knows; she does not steer
Too close, takes in the situation,
Sees John's face boyish with elation,
While Liz (Who's she?) with vibrant verve
In an exhilarating curve
Of explication or description
Looks radiant. Jan reflects, 'Somehow
I feel . . . Oh Christ! . . . I feel, right now,
I don't want coffee. My Egyptian
Deities wait at home for food.
I'll come back when I'm in the mood.'

2.40

Unnoticed, Janet leaves, abstracted
By her abortive coffee break.
Back in the café, Liz, attracted
By John's absorption, nibbles cake,
Sips tea, doffs her defensive armor
And, laughing, thinks, 'This man's a charmer.
I like him, and he likes me, though
I can't imagine why it's so.'
(O nightingales! O moon! O roses!)
In talk as heady as champagne
She mentions her cat, Charlemagne:
'A wondrous cat!' John laughs, proposes
A toast: 'The King and Queen of France
And England. Far may they advance.

2.41

Well may they reign. Long may they flourish.'
Happy (with just a dash of pain),
He drains his cup. 'But now to nourish
My hopes of meeting you again –
What do you say – next Thursday – seven –
For dinner at the Tree of Heaven –
Say that you'll come – it's in the Haight –
A movie afterwards at eight?'
Liz thinks, 'There's my gestalt group meeting.
I didn't go last week. I should
(The leader said) come if I could
This Thursday . . .' But the thought is fleeting.
She says, 'Thanks, John,' and the pair parts
By shaking hands (with shaking hearts).

2.42

The days pass in a picosecond –
The days pass slowly, each a year –
Depending on how time is reckoned.
Liz, floating in the stratosphere
Of daydreams, sees the hours go flying.
For John they linger, amplifying
The interval until they meet.
The sun seems almost to retreat.
At last it's Thursday. John, ecstatic,
Arrives first, stares at the decor
(Arboreal), then at the door . . .
And Liz's entrance is dramatic:
A deep blue dress to emphasize
The sapphire spirit of her eyes.

2.43

Her gold hair's fashioned, not severely,
Into a bun. From a gold chain
A single pearl, suspended clearly,
Allures his eye. John, once again,
Can't speak for wonder and confusion:
A woman, or divine illusion?
He overcomes his vertigo
And stands. He mutters, 'Liz, hello.
I hope . . . was it a hassle finding
This place?' His voice fails. He sits down.
Liz says, 'You're nervous, Mr Brown.
Don't worry; I too need reminding
That this is real.' In an unplanned
Gesture of warmth, she takes his hand.

2.44

John looks downwards, as if admonished,
Then slowly lifts his head, and sighs.
Half fearfully and half astonished
They look into each other's eyes.
The waiter, bearded, burly, macho,
Says, 'Madam, though it's cold, gazpacho
Is what I'd recommend. Noisettes
Of lamb, perhaps, or mignonettes
Of veal to follow . . .' Unavailing
Are his suggestions. Nothing sinks
Into their ears. 'Ah, well,' he thinks,
'They're moonstruck. It'll be plain sailing.
Lovers, despite delays and slips
And rotten service, leave large tips.'

2.45

Liz, floundering in a confusion
Of spirit, starts to speak: 'Today
We fought a case about collusion . . .'
John says, 'I don't know what to say.
Liz, since we met, I think I'm losing
My mind – O God, it's so confusing –
I thought it was a joke, but when
We met, I realized – and then
Today, once more – it seems I'm flailing
Around for something – and I feel
An ache too desperate for repeal
Or cure – as if my heart were failing.
I was transported Sunday. Then
You left; the pain began again.'

2.46

His voice is lowered, lost, appealing,
Rinsed of all wit, of all pretense.
Liz, helpless in a surge of feeling,
An undertow to common sense,
Finds that she has assumed the tender
Reincarnation of dream vendor.
Her eyes mist over with a glaze
Of sympathy. She gently says,
'Why do you find it so surprising
That you are happy? Are you sad
So often – tell me, John. I'm glad
That we've indulged in advertising,
But – having met you – it would seem
You feel all life's a shaky dream.'

2.47

As in an airless room a curtain
Parts to admit the evening breeze,
So John's exhausted and uncertain
Tension admits a transient ease,
And Liz's lenient mediation
Smooths out his doubt and hesitation.
She looks at him: 'Don't be afraid
I'll find what you say bland or staid.'
Relieved of the unspoken duty
Of cleverness and coolness now
John brings himself to speak, somehow,
Of truth, ambition, status, beauty,
The hopes (or dupes) for which we strive,
The ghosts that keep the world alive.

2.48

But talk turns, as the meal progresses,
To (heart-unsettling) movie stars,
The chef's (mouth-watering) successes,
The ills (mind-boggling) of their cars,
To cats, to microchips, flotation
Of corporate bonds, sunsets, inflation,
Their childhoods . . . while, along the way,
A bountiful, rich cabernet
Bestows its warm, full-bodied flavor
On everything they touch upon,
But most of all on Liz and John
Who, fluent as the draught they savor,
In phrase both fulsome and condign
Sing praise of California wine.

2.49

Cut to dessert. An apt potation
Of amaretto. They forgo
The cinema for conversation,
And hand in hand they stroll below
The fog-transfigured Sutro Tower,
A masted galleon at this hour,
Adjourn for ice cream, rich and whole,
At Tivoli's, near Carl and Cole;
Next for a drive – refreshing drama
Of changing streets and changeless bay
And, where the fog has cleared away,
The exquisite bright panorama
Of streetlights, sea-lights, starlight spread
Above, below, and overhead.

2.50

The night is cold. It's late November.
They stand close, shivering side by side,
Chilled by the ice cream, yet an ember,
A flare, ignited by the ride,
This staring at the lights together,
Defends them from inclement weather.
They stand, half shivering, half still,
Below the tower on Telegraph Hill,
Not speaking, with a finger tracing
The unseen lines from star to star.
Liz turns. They kiss. They kiss, they are
Caught in a panic of embracing.
They cannot hold each other tight
Enough against the chill of night.

2.51

Daybreak. John wakes to sunlight streaming
Across an unfamiliar bed.
'A cream duvet? I must be dreaming –
With the lilac hexagons – instead
Of my plain blanket – and the ceiling:
An open glass skylight revealing
Clear sky – and what's this on my feet?
A cat! My God! – ' With swift heartbeat
He starts as, through the door he's facing,
Liz enters with a coffee tray
In negligible negligee.
She pours two cups. Without embracing
They sit, their eyes infused with sleep
And love, and drink the potion deep.

2.52

It's Friday, though; the office beckons.
(No time for sleep or love, no time
To shave now.) John's boss frowns; he reckons
There's been a hitch: 'Oh, hi, John – I'm
A bit concerned about this bubble
Memory . . .' John strokes his stubble
And hums as beatifically
As a sun-sated bumblebee
Besotted by the soft vibration
Of his own pollen-dusted wings,
Oblivious to other things
Than his congenial meditation.
He says, 'What bubble memory?'
His boss gawks at him pityingly.

2.53

But Liz, with promptitude and pertness,
Displaying a resplendent smile,
A near-extravagant alertness,
And murmuring, 'When in doubt, file,'
Storms through (in spite of all distractions)
A block of six Secure Transactions
In record time. Her colleagues sigh:
'Poor Liz – I'm sure she must be high.'
(One mutters: 'Coke – she looks so hyper.'
Another: 'Acid can be rough.
I wonder where she gets the stuff.'
A third: 'Speed leads to speed.' With riper
Worldliness, her boss says: 'She's
Hooked on a stronger drug than these.')

2.54

John's watch beeps out the hour of seven.
Liz meets him, but this time outside
A theater near the Tree of Heaven
To see the movie they denied
Themselves last night. They choose to tender
Ill-judged obeisance to Fassbinder.
Ten minutes of *Veronika Voss*
And John says, 'Liz, I'm at a loss.
What's this about?' 'Beats me!' 'Your attic
Or my flat?' 'Either! Mine?' 'Let's go.'
Through the skylight the Pleiads glow
And soon, despite the operatic
Dissonances of Charlemagne,
The loving pair make love again.

2.55

The loving pair has bit the apple
Of mortal knowledge. As we see
The rosy half-light of love's chapel
Halo their ardent heads, should we
Hymn them in accents hushed and holy?
Forbear, O Gentle Reader. Slowly,
Ah, slowly, from their whim-swept height
Of rash delirium and delight
All sober inklings of perspective
Sink in the Wash of tenderness ...
Far better, since my life's a mess,
To spray the mooncalfs with invective.
Why do they look so pleased, when I
Am loverless, and pine, and sigh?

2.56

Who was it said, 'Love is the friction
Of two skins'? From 'Your place or mine?'
There follow weeks of sweet addiction
To insular if sparkling wine.
Liz, now addressed by John as 'honey,'
Responds to him with 'funny bunny.'
Their diction has, alas, become
Incomprehensible and numb.
Their brains appear to be dissolving
To sugary sludge as they caress.
In lieu of fire, force, finesse,
We have a ballet now involving
A pretty pas de deux instead,
With common Walkmans on their head.

2.57

Judged by these artless serfs of Cupid,
Love is not blind but, rather, dumb.
Their babblings daily grow more stupid.
I am embarrassed for them. Come,
Let's leave them here, the blesséd yuppies,
As happy as a pair of puppies,
Or doves, who with their croodlings might
Make even Cuff and Link seem bright.
Let's leave them to their fragile fictions –
Arcadia, Shangri-la, Cockaigne –
A land beyond the reach of pain –
Except for two slight contradictions,
To wit ... but what transpires next
Is furnished later in this text.

Amitav Ghosh (b. 1956)

Amitav Ghosh was educated at St Stephen's College, Delhi, and at Oxford, where he took a D. Phil. in Anthropology. His first novel, *The Circle of Reason* (1986) was clearly a response to his readings of Marquez and Rushdie; his second, *The Shadow Lines* (1988), still owed its tropes, which were to do with Partition and the national narrative, to Rushdie, but seemed to derive its lyricism and its belief in the power language has to convey reality from his cultural ancestry, the Bengal Renaissance. Ghosh stands, uneasily but intriguingly, at the confluence of two major cultural streams; that of postmodernism, which gives him his cerebral, self-conscious playfulness and his historicism, and that of the Bengal Renaissance, from which come his love for the inscape of words, his attendance to the mysteries of art and the world, and his troubled liberal conscience. He has had to negotiate these two, often antagonistic, value-systems in his work; it has been an occasionally difficult, but always gracefully executed, negotiation. Antithetical models and influences have enriched his exploration in more than one way; the possibility of writing about large themes and national narratives was opened up to him by Rushdie; from Naipaul he inherited the idea of travel through third-world landscapes and the solitary, introspective figure bearing witness, but with a compassion and tolerance, as the two pieces below show, that is neither really Rushdie's nor Naipaul's hallmark.

* * *

'Tibetan Dinner' (1988)

It was a while before the others at the table had finished pointing out the celebrities who had come to the restaurant for the gala benefit: the Broadway actresses, the Seventh Avenue designers, and the world's most famous rock star's most famous ex-wife, a woman to whom fame belonged like logic to a syllogism, axiomatically. Before the list was quite done, I caught a glimpse of something, a flash of saffron at the other end of the room, and I had to turn and look again.

Peering through a thicket of reed-necked women, I saw that I'd been right: yes, it was a monk in saffron robes, it really was a Buddhist monk – Tibetan, I was almost sure. He was sitting at the head of a table on the far side of the room, spectral in the flow of the restaurant's discreetly hidden lighting. But he was real. His robes were real robes; not drag, not a costume. He was in his early middle age, with clerically cropped hair and a pitted, wind-ravaged face. He happened to look up and happened to notice me staring at him. He looked surprised to see me: his chopsticks described a slow interrogative arc as they curled up to his mouth.

I was no less surprised to see him: he was probably a little less out of place among the dinner jackets and designer diamonds than I, in my desert boots and sweater, but only marginally so.

He glanced at me again, and I looked quickly down at my plate. On it sat three dumplings decorated with slivers of vegetables. The dumplings looked oddly familiar, but I couldn't quite place them.

'Who were you looking at?' said the friend who'd taken me there, an American writer and actress who had spent a long time in India and, in gratitude to the subcontinent, had undertaken to show me the sights of New York.

I gestured foolishly with a lacquered chopstick.

She laughed. 'Well, of course,' she said. 'It's his show; he probably organized the whole thing. Didn't you know?'

I didn't know. All I'd been told was that this was the event of the week in New York, very possibly even the month (it wasn't a busy month): a benefit dinner in the Indo-Chine, the in-est restaurant in Manhattan – one which had in fact defied every canon of in-ism by being in for almost a whole year, and which therefore had to be seen now if at all, before the tourists from Alabama got to it. My scepticism about the in-ness of the event had been dispelled by the tide of paparazzi we'd had to breast on our way in.

Laughing at my astonishment, she said, 'Didn't I tell you? It's a benefit for the Tibetan cause.'

More astonished still, I said, 'Which Tibetan cause?'

'The Tibetan cause,' someone said vaguely, picking at a curl of something indeterminately vegetable that had been carved into a flower shape.

It was explained to me then that the benefit was being hosted by a celebrated Hollywood star; a young actor who, having risen to fame through his portrayal of the initiation rites of an American officer, had afterwards converted to Tibetan Buddhism and found so much fulfilment in it he was reported to have sworn that he would put Tibet on the world map, make it a household word in the US, like Maalox or Lysol.

'The odd thing is,' said my friend, 'that he really is very sincere about this: he really isn't like those radical chic cynics of the sixties and seventies. He's not an intellectual, and he probably doesn't know much about Tibet, but he wants to do what little he can. They have to raise money for their schools and so on, and the truth is that no one in New York is going to reach into their pockets unless they can sit at dinner with rock stars' ex-wives. It's not his fault. He's probably doing what they want him to do.'

I looked at the Tibetan monk again. He was being talked to by an improbably distinguished man in a dinner jacket. He caught my eye, and nodded, smiling, as he bit into a dumpling.

Suddenly I remembered what the dumpling was. It was a Tibetan *mo-mo*, but stuffed with salmon and asparagus and suchlike instead of the usual bits of pork and fat. I sat back to marvel at the one dumpling left on my plate. It seemed a historic bit of food: one of the first genuine morsels of Tibetan *nouvelle cuisine*.

*

The last time I'd eaten a *mo-mo* was as an undergraduate, in Delhi.

A community of Tibetan refugees had built shacks along the Grand Trunk Road, not far from the university. The shacks were fragile but tenacious, built out of bits of wood, tin and corrugated iron. During the monsoons they would cover the roofs with sheets of tarpaulin and plastic, and weigh them down with bricks and stones. Often the bricks would be washed away and the sheets of plastic would be left flapping in the wind like gigantic prayer-flags. Some of the refugees served *mo-mos*, noodles and *chlang*, the milky Tibetan rice beer, on tables they had knocked together out of discarded crates. Their food was very popular among the drivers who frequented that part of the Grand Trunk Road.

In the university, it was something of a ritual to go to these shacks after an examination. We would drink huge quantities of *chlang* – it was very dilute, so you had to drink jugs of it – and eat noodle soup and *mo-mos*. The *mo-mos* were very simple there: bits of gristle and meat wrapped and boiled in thick skins of flour. They tasted of very little until you dipped them into the red sauce that came with them.

The food was cooked and served by elderly Tibetans; the young people were usually away, working. Communicating with them wasn't easy for the older people rarely knew any but the most functional Hindi.

As we drank our jugs of *chlang,* a fog of mystery would descend on the windy, lamp-lit interiors of the shacks. We would look at the ruddy, weathered faces of the women as they filled our jugs out of the rusty oil-drums in which they brewed the beer, and try to imagine the journey they had made: from their chilly, thin-aired plateau 15,000 feet above sea-level, across the passes of the high Himalayas, down into that steamy slum, floating on a bog of refuse and oil-slicks on the outskirts of Delhi.

Everyone who went there got drunk. You couldn't help doing so – it was hard to be in the presence of so terrible a displacement.

It was an unlikely place, but Tibetans seem to have a talent for surviving on unlikely terrain. Ever since the Chinese invasion of Tibet, dozens of colonies of Tibetan refugees have sprung up all over India. Many of them run thriving businesses in woollen goods, often in the most unexpected places. In Trivandrum, near the southernmost tip of India, where the temperature rarely drops below eighty degrees Fahrenheit and people either wear the thinnest of cottons or go bare-bodied, there are a number of Tibetan stalls in the market place, all piled high with woollen scarves and sweaters. They always seem to have more customers than they can handle.

Once, going past the Jama Masjid in Delhi in a bus on a scorching June day, I noticed a Tibetan stall tucked in between the sugar-cane juice vendors. Two middle-aged women dressed in heavy Tibetan *bakus* were sitting in it, knitting. The stall was stacked with the usual brightly coloured woollen goods. The women were smiling cheerfully as they bargained with their customers in sign language and broken Hindi. A small crowd had gathered around them, as though in tribute to their courage and resilience.

*

I found myself looking around the restaurant, involuntarily, for another Indian face, someone who had been properly invited, unlike me. I suppose I was looking for some acknowledgement, not of a debt, but of a shared history, a gesture towards the buyers of those hundreds of sweaters in Trivandrum. I couldn't see any. (Later someone said they'd seen a woman in a sari, but they couldn't be sure; it might have been a Somali robe – this was, after all, New York.)

When I next caught the monk's eye, his smile seemed a little guilty: the hospitality of a poor nation must have seemed dispensable compared to the charity of a rich one. Or perhaps he was merely bewildered. It cannot be easy to celebrate the commodification of one's own suffering.

But I couldn't help feeling that if the lama, like the actor, really wanted to make Tibet a household word in the western world, he wasn't setting about it the right way. He'd probably have done better if he'd turned it into an acronym, like TriBeCa or ComSubPac. And sold the rights to it to a line of detergents or even perhaps a breakfast cereal.

TiBet (where the Cause is): doesn't sound too bad, marketable even.

* * *

'Four Corners' (1989)

It becomes impossible to ignore the Four Corners once Route 160 enters Colorado's Montezuma County: chevroned signposts spring regularly out of the sand and scrub, urging you towards it. Even if you had never heard of it before, did not know that it is the only point in the USA where four states meet, you are soon curious: it begins to seem like a major station, a Golgotha or Gethsemane, on this well-worn tourist pilgrimage.

The size and sleekness of the trailers and travelling homes heading towards it are eloquent of its significance. These are not the trailers you have grown accustomed to seeing in small towns in the South and Midwest – those shiny aluminium goldfish bowls which sit parked in backyards until the ball game in the next town, when they get hitched on to pick-up trucks and towed out to the ball park to serve as adjuncts for tail-gate parties. Not these: these are no ordinary trailers, they are Recreational Vehicles (RVs) – if not quite palaces, then certainly midtown condos, on wheels.

You only get a real idea of how big they are when you try to pass one on a two-lane road in a Honda Civic which lost its fifth gear 8,000 miles ago. Before you are past the master bedroom, are barely abreast of the breakfast nook, that blind curve that seemed so far away when you decided to make a break for it is suddenly right upon you.

It teaches you respect.

Their owners' imagination are the only limits on the luxuries those RVs may be made to contain.

Once, on a desolate stretch of road in the deserts of western Utah, I watched an RV pull onto a sand-blown Rest Area, right beside my battered Honda Civic. It was almost as long as a supermarket truck and the air around it was sharp with the smell of its newness. A woman with white, curly hair stuck her head out of a window, tried the air, and said something cheerful to someone inside, over the hum of the air-conditioning. A moment later, the door opened, a flight of stairs clicked magically into place under it, and she stepped out, throwing a wave of a cheery 'How you doin'?' in my direction. She was carrying a couple of chairs and a rack of magazines. Her husband climbed out too, and in companionable silence they pulled an awning out of the side of the vehicle and unrolled a ten-foot length of artificial turf under it. She waved again, after the chair, the magazine rack, a pot of geraniums and a vase with an ikebana-ed orchid had been properly arranged on the patch of green. 'I call this my bower,' she said. 'Join us for cakes and coffee?'

Never had a wilderness seemed so utterly vanquished.

Often those RVs have striking names: Winnebago, Itasca ... The names of the dispossessed tribes of the Americas hold a peculiar allure for the marketing executives of automobile companies. Pontiac, Cherokee – so many tribes are commemorated in forms of transport. It is not a mere matter of fashion that so many of the cars that flash past on the highways carry those names, breathing them into the air like the inscriptions on prayer wheels. This tradition of naming has a long provenance: did not Kit Carson himself, the scourge of the Navajo, name his favourite horse Apache?

There are many of them on Route 160, those memorials to the first peoples of the Americas, bearing number-plates from places thousands of miles away – New York, Georgia, Alaska, Ontario. Having come this far, everybody wants to see the only point where four states meet.

*

There cannot be many places in the world quite as beautiful as the stretch of desert, mountain and canyon that sprawls over the borders of the four states of Colorado, Utah, New Mexico and Arizona. For the people who inhabited it at the time of the European conquest – the Diné, who came to be known as the Navajo – it was Diné Bikéyah, the country of the Diné, a land into which the First Beings climbed from the Underworlds through a female reed. To them it was the Fourth World, known as the Glittering.

Route 160 runs through some of the most spectacular parts of the Glittering World: around the caves and canyons of Mesa Verde, and through the spectacular mesas that border on Monument Valley. Curiously, its one dull stretch comes when it dips south of the little town of Cortez and heads towards the Four Corners monument. The landscape turns scraggy and undecided, not quite desert and not quite prairie, knotted with dull grey-green scrub, and scarred by a few shallow ravines and low cliffs.

That is why it is impossible to miss the Four Corners monument.

It springs up out of nowhere, perched atop nothing, framed by the only stretch of dull country in the region. There is nothing remotely picturesque about its surroundings – no buttes, no mesas, not even a salience of rock or an undulation in the plain. With the greatest effort of the imagination it would not be possible to persuade oneself that this may once have been, like so many places in the Glittering World, a haunt of the Spider Woman or the Talking God or the Hero Twins. Legends of that kind need visible metaphors – wind-scarred buttes or lava fields – to attach themselves to the landscape. For the Four Corners monument the landscape does not exist: it sits squatly on the scrub, like a thumbtack in a map, unbudging in its secular disenchantedness.

There is something majestic and yet uneasy about the absoluteness of its indifference to this landscape and its topography. It is simply a point where two notional straight lines intersect: a line of latitude, thirty-seven degrees North, and a line of longitude, 109 degrees and two minutes West, the thirty-second degree of longitude west of Washington. These two straight lines form the boundaries between the four states. These lines have nothing whatever to do with the Glittering World; their very straight-ness is testimony to a belief in the unpeopledness of this land – they slice through the tabula rasa of the New World leaving it crafted in their own image, enchanted with a new enchantment, the magic of Euclidean geometry.

*

The centre of the Glittering World was Diné Tah, which lay around Largo Canyon, about eight miles south-east of the Four Corners monument. To the Navajo it was the sacred heartland of their country. The first time they left it en masse was in the 1860s after Colonel Kit Carson and the US Army reduced them to starvation by scorching the earth of their Glittering World. Kit Carson felt no personal animosity towards the Navajo. He is said to have commented once: 'I've seen as much of 'em as any white man livin', and I can't help but pity 'em. They'll all soon be gone anyhow.' He was an unlettered man, given to expressing himself plainly. Unlike him, his commanding officer, General James H. Carleton, had had the benefits of an education. He was therefore able to phrase the matter more dispassionately, clothed in the mellow light of current trends in science and theology: 'In their appointed time He wills that one race of men – as in races of lower animals – shall disappear off the face of the earth and give place to another race ... The races of the Mammoths and Mastodons, and great Sloths, came and passed away: the Red Man of America is passing away.'

The Navajo were forced to march to an 'experimental' camp at the Bosque Redondo. It was soon clear, however, that the experiment was not going to work, and in 1868 a commission headed by General William T. Sherman was sent to New Mexico to decide what was to be done with the Navajo. Addressing the commission, the Navajo leader, Barboncito, said: 'When the Navajo were first created, four mountains and four rivers were pointed out to us, inside of which we should live, that was to be our country and was given to us by the first woman of the Navajo tribe.' Later, he said to the General: 'I am speaking to you now as if I was speaking to a spirit and I wish you to tell me when you are going to take us to our country.' They were permitted to return later the same year. On their return, Manuelito, the most renowned of the Navajo war chiefs, said afterwards: 'We felt like talking to the ground, we loved it so.' They were back in Diné Bikéyah, where every butte and mesa pointed to the sacred centre of Diné Tah.

The Four Corners monument evokes a centre too, in its own way. But that central point, the point from which its line of longitude takes its westerly orientation, that central zero degree from which its distance can be so exactly calculated, lies in another landscape, on another continent – far away in Greenwich, England. It is that distant place that the monument unwittingly celebrates.

*

The monument itself is modest by the standards of monuments in the United States. There is a wide, paved plaza, with plenty of parking space for cars and RVs. On the peripheries there are rows of stalls, manned by people from the neighbouring Ute and Navajo reservations.

In the centre of the plaza is a square cement platform, fenced off by aluminium railings. There is a state flag on each side of the square and towering above them a flag of the United States of America, on an eagle-topped mast. Two straight lines are etched into the cement; they intersect neatly at the centre of the platform. Somebody has thoughtfully provided a small observation post, at one end of the square. There would be little point, after all, in taking pictures of the Four Corners if you couldn't see the two lines intersect. And to get them properly into your frame you have to be above ground level.

You have to queue, both for your turn at the observation post and to get into the centre of the platform. If there are two of you, you have to queue twice at each end, unless you can get somebody to oblige you by taking your picture (and that is easy enough for there are no friendlier people in the world than American tourists). But queuing is no great trial anyway, even in the desert heat, for everyone is good-humoured and it is not long before you find yourself engaged in comparing notes on camp-grounds and motels with everyone around you.

There is good-natured spirit of competition among the people who walk into the centre of the cement platform: everyone tries to be just a little original when posing for their photographs. A young couple kiss, their lips above the centre and each of their feet in a different state. Another couple pose, more modestly, with one foot on each state and their arms around each others' shoulders. Six middle-aged women distribute themselves between the states, holding hands. An elderly gentleman in Bermuda shorts lets himself slowly down on to his hands and knees and poses with an extremity on each state and his belly-button at the centre. This sets something of a trend; a couple of middle-aged women follow suit. In the end a pretty, teenage girl carries the day by striking a balletic pose on one leg, her toes dead centre on the point where the lines intersect.

Men from the reservations lounge about in the shade of the stalls, around the edges of the plaza. Some rev their cars, huge, lumbering old Chevrolets and Buicks, startling the tourists. A boy, bored, drives into the scrub, sending whirlwinds of sand shooting into the sky. Others sit behind their stalls, selling 'Indian' jewellery and blankets and Navajo Fry Bread. When evening comes and the flow of tourists dwindles, they will pack the contents of their stalls into their cars and go home to their reservations. No one stays the night here; there is nothing to stay for – the attractions of the place are wholly unworldly.

They will be back early next morning: the cars and RVs start arriving soon after dawn, their occupants eager to absorb what they can of the magic of the spectacle of two straight lines intersecting.

Upamanyu Chatterjee (b. 1959)

Upamanyu Chatterjee, was educated at St Stephen's College, Delhi, where he read English. He later did what most conventional young men of ambition from New Delhi inexplicably do: he joined the Indian Administrative Services, the post-Independence incarnation of the Indian Civil Service. This is exactly what the studiedly unconventional young protagonist of Chatterjee's first novel, *English, August: An Indian Story* (1988), Agastya Sen ('the 'August' of the title is an Anglicized corruption of and nickname for Agastya) does; but finds that, instead of it leading to the expected accretion of privilege and status, or the powers due to an appointed member of the ruling cadre, his entry into the Administrative Service entails being banished to one of the innumerable small towns that dot the anonymous Indian veldts and outbacks that he would otherwise never have to come into contact with. The first casualty of exposure to the nothingness of small-town colonial, or post-colonial, life is normally bourgeois morality and ruling-class certainty; Kipling and Maugham enacted this in some of their stories, as did Forster in *A Passage to India*; Tagore's early story, 'The Postmaster', included in this volume, shifts the gaze to the duress that the self-definition of a minor member of the colonial, *bhadralok* Bengali community must come under when removed from an urban setting into the perpetual deferral of meaning and purpose that is small-town India. The question some of these, and other, writers seemed to have posed in such fictions in different ways is, 'Can the ruling class actually rule India?'; and the question is posed again, ironically, and comically, by Chatterjee in his first novel in relation to post-Independence India. The civil service left over by the departed English is itself transformed, by Chatterjee's satire, from the pivotal institution we imagine it to be to a purgatorial post-colonial or post-everything waiting room peopled by vague outlines in transit, their acts ranging from the oddly self-defeating to the self-abusive; he gives us a landscape in which noble gestures towards withdrawal, listening to rock music in solitude, and masturbation are seen to be at least as important as more direct forms of activism and social conscience in constituting our unnameable democratic life.

* * *

from *English, August: An Indian Story* (1988)

District administration in India is largely a British creation, like the railways and the English language, another complex and unwieldy bequest of the Raj. But Indianization (of a method of administration, or of a language) is integral to the Indian story. Before 1947 the Collector was almost inaccessible to the people; now he keeps open house, primarily because he does a different, more difficult job. He is as human and as fallible, but now others can tell him so, even though he still exhibits the old accoutrements (but now Indianized) of importance – the flashing orange light on the roof of the car, the passes for the first row at the sitar recital, which will not start until he arrives and for which he will not arrive until he has been ensured by telephone that everyone else who has been invited has arrived first. In Madna, as in all of India, one's importance as an official could be gauged by how long one could keep a concert (to which one was invited) waiting. The organizers never minded this of the officials they invited. Perhaps they expected it of them, which was sickening, or perhaps they were humouring them, which was somehow worse.

And administration is an intricate business, and a young officer who lacks initiative cannot really be trained in its artifices. There is very little that he can learn from watching someone else; Agastya learnt nothing. For a very short while he worried about his ignorance, and then decided to worry about it properly when others discovered it.

The Collectorate of Madna was one building among many in a vast field (which could not be called a compound, for it had no wall or gate) near the railway station. He had missed them all in the dark of the previous evening. The jeep inched its way through people and cattle onto an untarred metalled road. He saw a few flags against the hot clean sky. The national flag, he presumed, was over the Collectorate. 'What are the other buildings?'

'That's the office of the Superintendent of Police, sir,' said the naib tehsildar from behind, 'and over there are the Police Lines.' Whatever they are, thought Agastya. 'That's the District and Sessions Court, and behind, there, that big one, the District Council–'

'You mean, on which there's also the national flag?'

'Sir. And then that side, behind, the offices of the Sub-Divisional Officer, tehsildar, et cetera.' While the naib tehsildar was pointing out the buildings the driver nearly ran over a child defecating beside the road, and snarled at her in the vernacular.

On their left was some kind of pond, with thick green water and the heads of contented buffalo. Scores of people, sitting on their haunches, smoking, wandering, gazing at anything moving or at other people. Most were in white dhoti, kurta and Gandhi cap (or was it Nehru cap? wondered Agastya. No, Gandhi cap and Nehru jacket. Or Gandhi jacket and Nehru cap? And Patel vest? And Mountbatten lungi and Rajaji shawl and Tagore dhoti?), some had towels over their heads. The jeep chugged through them, honking petulantly. The people sitting on the road stood up and moved away at the last moment, reluctantly, some scowled. For them the road was the one stretch that the rains of Madna wouldn't immediately turn to mud; therefore it was a place of assemblage.

'They cover their heads because of the heat, no?'

'Yes, sir.'

It seemed wise, to bother not about appearance, but first about health. He tried his handkerchief over his head but it was too small. The naib tehsildar chuckled appreciatively. 'Too small, sir. Napkins easily available in the market, sir. If sir wants I'll get one.'

'Yes, thanks, please do that. How much will it cost?'

'Not to worry about price, sir.'

'Rubbish,' said Agastya, and offered him a twenty-rupee note.

The naib tehsildar raised his hands to ward off the horror. 'No, sir, not to bother, sir, hardly must, sir.' Agastya was momentarily distracted by the 'hardly must'. What could he mean? He reached over and, ignoring the naib tehsildar's giggles and soft shrieks, put the note in his shirt pocket, among the spectacle case, papers and pens.

In all those months he never got used to the crowds outside the offices.

'*All* these people have work here?'

'Yes, sir,' said the naib tehsildar, a little surprised, perhaps at the stupidity of the question. They all looked patient, as though waiting for entrance to the political rally of some awesome demagogue, Nehru perhaps, or one of his descendants. To him they also looked stoned. Their eyes were glazed, probably with waiting, and followed every movement around them without curiosity.

Just near the Collectorate he saw cannabis growing wild. That was nice and, he smiled, somehow symbolic. He would have to return alone one evening.

The Collectorate was a one-storey stone building. Its corridors had

benches and more people. The naib tehsildar led him to a biggish hall
full of mostly unoccupied desks, and through another door. A fat officious man said, 'Yes?' The naib tehsildar mumbled something and the
officious man immediately turned servile. 'Good morning, sir. Collector
sahib not yet come, sir. Myself Chidambaram, Reader to Collector. Kindly
accompany me to RDC's room sir.'

They moved through another door and down a central corridor, also
crowded with people, benches and water coolers. Another door, with 'C. K.
Joshi, RDC' above it. There were three men inside, Chidambaram mumbled
something. They all stood and shook hands, the two younger ones called
him sir. All introduced themselves, Agastya didn't catch a single name, and
didn't bother. Thank God for marijuana, he thought.

Formal pleasant conversation, someone brought in thick sweet tea,
which the others drank from their saucers. After some slow haphazard
guesswork he decided that the man on his right was Ahmed. Joshi was, or
should be, the old jovial man behind the desk. On his right was what had
sounded like Agarwal. Ahmed was immediately obnoxious, with blank
eyes and a false smile. He never listened when anyone else was speaking,
but always looked down at his thick forearms and flexed them. Both
Ahmed and Agarwal were 'Deputy Collectors (Direct Recruit), sir.' Whatever that was, thought Agastya, but nodded with what he hoped was
appropriate awe.

He eventually got to know, but by accident as it were, what a Deputy
Collector (Direct Recruit) was, and where a naib tehsildar stood in the
Revenue hierarchy. He himself made no effort to know his new world; as
it unfolded, it looked less interesting to him; and later, even to see how far
he could extend his ignorance became an obscure and perverse challenge.

Sitting with the three men, he was again assailed by a sense of the
unreal. I don't look like a bureaucrat, what am I doing here. I should have
been a photographer, or a maker of ad films, something like that, shallow
and urban.

'How old are you, sir?'

'Twenty-eight.' Agastya was twenty-four, but he was in a lying mood.
He also disliked their faces.

'Are you married, sir?' Again that demand that he classify himself.
Ahmed leaned forward for each question, neck tensed and head angled
with politeness.

'Yes.' He wondered for a second whether he should add 'twice'.

'And your Mrs, sir?' Agarwal's voice dropped at 'Mrs'; in all those
months all references to wives were in hushed, almost embarrassed, tones.

Agastya never knew why, perhaps because to have a wife meant that one was fucking, which was a dirty thing.

'She's in England. She's English, anyway, but she's gone there for a cancer operation. She has cancer of the breast.' He had an almost uncontrollable impulse to spread out his fingers to show the size of the tumour and then the size of the breast, but he decided to save that for later. Later in his training he told the District Inspector of Land Records that his wife was a Norwegian Muslim.

He went on like this, careless with details. His parents were in Antarctica, members of the first Indian expedition. Yes, even his mother, she had a Ph.D. in Oceanography from the Sorbonne. After a while the personal questions stopped. Later he felt guilty, but only for a very brief while.

Chidambaram poked his head in and said that the Collector had come. Joshi accompanied Agastya. Srivastav was short and fat and shouting at someone standing in front of him when they entered. He asked them to sit down and continued shouting. If you can tick off a subordinate in the language, thought Agastya, you're really fluent. On the far side of the desk stood a trembling black suppliant, weeping fresh tears, as though he had just been beaten. The other old man being shouted at turned out to be the District Supply Officer. Later Agastya would conclude that they all looked the same, the denizens of the Collectorate, ageing, with soft faces that hadn't seen much sunlight. They all wore pale shirts and loose pants. Their shirt pockets bulged outrageously with pens and spectacle cases. Most smelt nice, of some very Indian perfume, or scented hair-oil, or *paan.* They could withstand, like placid buffalo, anything that an industrious superior could shriek at them. The District Supply Officer's face shone gently in the volley from the Collector.

Lambent dullness, Agastya remembered abruptly, now where was that? Suddenly he was back in his college English class three years ago, with *Absalom and Achitophel* open in front of him, stoned and watching the new female teacher perform. Nervousness had made her aggressive. Narasimhan, beside him, also stoned, had asked her some stupid question. 'Your question doesn't make any sense,' she had said, arching her back. There had been giggles from the gigglers. Narasimhan had laboriously scrawled a long note on his Dryden and passed it to him. 'August, tell her, yes, my lovely bitch, when my hands are full with your flat buttocks, my mouth on either breast, I shall give you lust-gnaws between your absalom and achitophel.' His laugh had even woken up the back row. He had been sent out. The Supply Officer wiped his forehead with a many-coloured handkerchief. Yes, lambent dullness, definitely. That he could relate a phrase from an eighteenth-century English poet to this, a sweating Supply Officer in a Collector's office, in Madna, made him smile.

The Collector paused for breath, said, 'Hello, you've to get used to this. An administrator's job is not easy,' and returned to biting the Supply Officer's sweating head off. The shrieking stopped after a while and the Supply Officer left. At the door he again used his many-coloured handker-chief. The weeping man left too, after many namastes and two half-prostrations, forehead touching the Collector's desk.

Srivastav smiled at Agastya. His sideburns were like right-angled trian-gles, the hypotenuses of which looked like the shadows of his cheekbones. 'So? Agastya, what kind of name is Agastya, bhai?'

When you were in your mother's lap, you ignoramus, he said silently, drooling and piddling, didn't she make your head spin into sleep with the verses of some venerable Hindu epic? 'Agastya' is Sanskrit, he wanted to say, for one who shits only one turd every morning. But the Collector didn't really want any answer. Staccato conversation, while he rushed through his files. 'Someone was there to pick you up yesterday at the station?'

'Yes, sir.'

'How's the room at the Rest House?'

'Lots of mosquitoes, sir.'

The Collector threw every finished file on the ground. They landed, depending on their weight, with dull thumps or sharp claps. Thus he eroded the mountains on his desk, and the files lay like corpses in a battlefield, perhaps giving him the illusion that he was victorious.

'Oh, mosquitoes, yes, I can see that from your face.' A quick side-glance at him. 'I tell you, Madna must be one of the unhealthiest places in India. Hot, humid, disease, everything. Are you boiling your water? I told the naib tehsildar to tell you.'

'Thanks for that, sir. But I'm not quite sure whether the cook at the Rest House here understood yesterday what boiling means.'

'Yes, you'll face the problem of language in Madna. They can't even speak Hindi properly.' He rang the bell. 'Get some tea.' He suddenly leaned back and scowled. 'You see, in North India and Bengal and other places, everyone can follow Hindi.' Agastya was a little disconcerted by his Collector's scowls. Later he saw that that was his official face; at home, too, that face was occasionally donned, but only for office work, or when his wife or children behaved like his subordinates. 'And now everything from the State Government comes in the regional language. They think this'll increase administrative efficiency.' He wiped his face and forearms with a yellow hand-towel. 'Rubbish, these fellows.' he scowled at Joshi. 'Joshi sahib, arrange for some kind of a language tutor for Mr Sen. And later you must subscribe to a vernacular newspaper, that'll also help, but not the *Dainik*, that just publishes nonsense.' Joshi took notes, pen poised to record anything that the Collector might disgorge. Joshi's pad seemed to irritate Srivastav; it obliged him to emit noteworthy sentences. He rang the bell. 'Chidambaram, get Mr Sen the *District Gazetteer*.'

'Sir, may I have a look at the map?'

'Yes please, while I finish some of this.'

Agastya left his chair for the huge district map on the wall behind Srivastav. For the first few minutes nothing made sense. He finally located Madna town. God, the district was huge. The southern bits seemed heavily forested, that would be a good area to visit. Srivastav's voice penetrated intermittently. 'I want to suspend this Supply Officer bugger. That corrupt cement dealer in Pinchri taluka has again been passing off bloody sand as cement and this Supply Officer can't haul him up because he's getting his cut too . . .' Agastya contemplated the improbable, that soon, in a few months, he would be mouthing similar incomprehensibilities and acting appropriately. Chidambaram touched his elbow with a huge black book. He returned to his chair with the *Madna District Gazetteer*.

'Don't read that now, take it back with you. It's wonderful reading.'

Agastya opened it. 'It's ancient, sir. It hasn't been updated since 1935.'

Srivastav scowled. 'Who has the time? Either you work, or you write a history. Those fellows never worked.' He picked up his cup. 'You'll soon see how the people here drink tea. Always from the saucer, look.'

They watched a smiling Joshi pour his tea into his saucer. 'Tastes better this way,' Joshi said.

Srivastav, it seemed, had a lot to say to his protégé; he just didn't know where to begin, and bounded from one topic to another. 'You have a copy of your training programme. For the last two months you'll be Block Development Officer and before that you'll be attached to various district offices. The first three weeks is with the Collectorate. And this first week you sit with me and try to grasp the work of the Collector. After all, in a few months you'll be Assistant Collector, doing in a sub-division what I do at the district level.'

'Sir.'

'There's an Integration gathering at the Gandhi Hall at twelve-fifteen. We'll go for that.'

'Integration as in National Integration?'

'Yes, but here it's called something else, of course.' Srivastav rang the bell and said something to the peon. Joshi left. 'You just see how many people come to meet the Collector every day, like they'll meet you when you're Block Development Officer later,' scowled Srivastav at Agastya, and then at the villagers whom the peon had just ushered in.

Reverentially they unfolded and handed Srivastav a sheet of paper. Its black creases seemed to mark its tortuous journey, slipping off the hands of one unhelpful official into another's. A conversation ensued, Srivastav scowling less as he understood more, the voices of the villagers slowly gaining in confidence. Then while Srivastav scribbled the villagers waited, patient and passive, strong hands bent suppliantly. They had brought in a smell of sweat and the earth, but they weren't (thought Agastya irrelevantly, with a vacuous half-smile) remotely sexy, just sad, and then he felt vaguely guilty. Two of them looked at him now and again, he didn't fit into the Collectorate.

The visitors came all day. Agastya could eventually categorize them. Indeed, that was all he could do, since the conversations were beyond him. The petitioners always stood. Srivastav asked them to sit only if it seemed that they would take long; if they sat it was on the edge of the chair. The variety of complaints, from the little that Agastya grasped through instinct, gestures and the occasional tell-tale Hindi or English phrase, was bewildering, and the area of action spread over a district of 17,000 square kilometres (so the first paragraph of the *Gazetteer* had said). Someone had encroached on one petitioner's land, and the petitioner had received no help from the tehsildar. The police *patil* in a village had connived at a murder, and the entire police hierarchy seemed to be backing him up. Labourers on daily wages at some road site complained that the contractor paid them irregularly. A naib tehsildar somewhere seemed to be harassing a tribal's wife. A dealer in some village always adulterated his kerosene. Initially Agastya was impressed by the solidity and confidence in Srivastav's reactions; he seemed to know exactly what to do in each case. A few visitors after, he changed his view and thought, marvelling at the sideburns, that Srivastav *ought* to be confident because he had been dealing with such matters for years.

The petitioners partially explained the crowds outside the Collectorate. But there were others too, subordinate officers from various offices, who were summoned or came to report, and didn't sit until asked to. And then there were the gossips of the district, who were the most gluttonous about time, but whom Srivastav could not alienate, because they knew the pulse of Madna, and were also the politicians' groupies. Sycophants to the last, they wheedled like caricatures. Still others brought invitations, they would be honoured if the Collector and Mrs Collector (and later in the year some included Agastya, 'Sen sahib, IAS,' an afterthought in ink) graced with their presence the Sports Day of their school or the function to celebrate the eightieth birthday of some veteran freedom fighter of the district, who had perhaps had the overwhelming good fortune to have been jailed once with Gandhi.

Only a very few visitors breezed in before their names could precede them on slips of paper – the Member of Parliament from Madna, and two red-eyed Members of the Legislative Assembly. Agastya enjoyed his long speculative categorization, and placed at the apex the very select few for whom Srivastav moved forward in his chair to shake hands and to whom he offered tea – there were only two that day, the MP and the Managing Director of the paper mills somewhere in the district.

On the wall behind him hung a big teak board with the names of the District Magistrates of Madna since 1902. The earlier Collectors had been British, one Avery had been Collector for six years, 1917–23. He felt hungry and to dispel the pangs, thought of the horrors Vasant would feed him at lunch.

At twelve forty-five the Collector told the peon, 'I'll meet the others when I return. Get the driver.' Outside in the corridor the peons, the petitioners, the politicians' groupies and their groupies all stiffened and shut their babble when they saw Srivastav. They looked solemn and guilty, as though they'd been planning to strip him, thought Agastya.

The heat was terrible. The car began a slow furrow through the mass on the road. 'This car has an emergency siren apart from the light. I've always wanted to use both together just to get to my office.' They passed the wild cannabis and the pond. Children jumped from one buffalo to another. 'When it rains the cattle camp in the corridors of the Collectorate. The same thing used to happen in Azamganj, where I come from. Earlier I used to think that a Collectorate with cows and stray dogs in its corridors could only be found in Azamganj, now I think it's a common story.' A man poked his head in through the front window to gaze blankly at them. The driver snarled at him. 'You're from a city. This place will initially seem very different. Then you'll get used to it.' Someone thumped the back of the car in affection and boredom. Srivastav watched Agastya sweat. 'If you think it's hot you should be here in May. The old residents say that on some afternoons in May, even birds have dropped from the sky, dead.'

The car turned reckless as it left the field of offices. 'And this Integration meeting?'

'Oh, there was a big riot here a few months ago, Hindu–Muslim. It surprised everyone because Madna has never been communally sensitive. The last Collector, Antony, was transferred, I think, because of the riots. They said he'd bungled there, but more likely the politicians who were actually behind the riots just wanted a scapegoat. These politician bastards, you'll really know what they are like when you're Block Development Officer. So we formed an Integration Committee, it meets once a month. Both Hindu and Muslim goondas get together and eat and waste time. Have as little of the food as possible, it'll be poisonous.'

The brown curtains of the car couldn't keep out the town. Narrow streets and two-storeyed shacks, people and animals immune to the heat. Srivastav perhaps sensed Agastya's mood and said, 'The population of the town is only two lakhs. Sometimes I think the development of Madna must be a representative Indian story. Once it was just another district, very rich forests, and made to feel proud of its tribal traditions, which is another way of trying to make you forget your economic backwardness. Then they found coal here, mica, limestone, one of the country's richest industrial belts, now oil, too. Factories soon surrounded this town, new ones come up almost every day.' The car screeched its rage at a cyclist who cut across and darted down a side alley the width, or so it seemed, of a writing table. 'Development is a tricky business. There must be something wrong with development if it creates places like Madna. But priorities is the problem, how're we to spend our money, will it be on coal and oil, or town planning, or forests. And the pressure of time, there is never enough time. But you'll see another facet of development when you're BDO, the insane race to meet targets.' Srivastav talked on, with eyes half-closed, never looking at Agastya, as though he was speaking to a cassette recorder.

This bequeathing of wisdom was surprising, especially on first encounter; but the pattern was frequently repeated, with Srivastav and with the Superintendent of Police. Sharing the back seat of a car with a novice in administration, the senior officers always theorized, attempted to explain, to impress, to tutor, to justify.

The car was continually being trapped by cycles and rickshaws, which seemed to behave like out-riders who had suddenly decided to have some fun with the limousine. He saw snatches of other lives – veined hands on bicycle handlebars, and behind them a man emptying a bucket into a drain, the tensed calves of a rickshaw-wallah, sweat-wet shirts around a stall selling fruit juice. But in the months that followed he saw very little of the real Madna, the lives of its traders in wood and forest produce, the coal miners, the workers at the paper mills, the shopkeepers, the owners of cinema halls and restaurants. The district life that he lived and saw was the official life, common to all districts, deadly dull. This world comprised Collectors, District Development Officers, Superintendents of Police, and their legionary subordinates, many wielders of petty power, sulking or resigned if posted away from home, and buying furniture cheap and biding time till transferred to a congenial place.

Gandhi Hall stood beside the city police station, a three-storeyed building. For a moment he thought that it had been bombed, something out of a TV news clip on Beirut, broken window-panes, old walls, an uncertain air, a kind of wonder at not having collapsed yet. A red banner over the door, and outside, a statue of a short fat bespectacled man with a rod coming out of his arse. He asked in wonder, 'Is that a statue of Gandhi?'

Srivastav laughed shrilly. 'Yes. Who did you think?'

'Phew. What's the rod, sir?'

Srivastav laughed even more. 'That's to prop up the statue. It fell off a few weeks after it was installed. Madna will have many more surprises, Sen.' Then the goondas were upon them.

They enveloped Srivastav with effusion. A jumble of white *khadi* and red teeth, the scent of hair-oil distracting the nose from the stench of urine, a few black eyes glancing at Agastya oddly – he didn't fit. Srivastav introduced him to somebody, no one heard anything except 'IAS', then they began fawning on him, too.

Wide stairs, the walls splotched maroon with *paan* spittle, like the scene of some frenzied killings (and abruptly he remembered Prashant at school, when life had been simpler, pointing to horseshit on a hill road, 'English, I bet you can't lick that, I bet!' 'Oh I can easily do it, if you give me something good for it, like enough money every month for the rest of my life'), the press of people and an alien tongue. On the second floor a huge hall and another banner, and below it a fat complacent policeman. With spectacles, thought Agastya, he could've resembled that travesty outside, of the Mahatma in stone.

'Sen, meet Mr Kumar, the Superintendent of Police of Madna.'

They all moved in, Kumar asking Agastya questions to which he could not hear the answers. Coloured paper decorations, mattresses on the floor with white sheets and cushions, the fans somehow encouraging the humidity. When Kumar sat down his knees cracked sharply. A hooligan joined them and spoke Hindi, 'You are also IAS?'

'Yes. I'm here for training in district administration.'

More questions. His lies were restricted by the presence of Kumar, but he did slip in that he had climbed Everest last summer. The hooligan left to arrange for their eats. Kumar lolled on his bolster, and patting the outside of his (own) thigh, said, 'Hahn, Agastya, a very Bungaali name, yaar.'

'Yes, sir.'

'Bungaalis choose such difficult names for themselves, why, yaar?'

Agastya smiled. 'The Collector was saying that they hold these meetings every month, sir. But what happens here?'

Kumar frowned and looked around, to see what everyone else was doing and how many were looking at him. There was a biggish gang around the Collector. 'Nothing on the surface, we just eat some rubbish together, and nurse raw stomachs for a week. But it helps in many ways. We find out from them what's really happening in the district – gossip, the things that our police and Revenue officials won't tell us because they themselves might be involved.' His voice turned dictatorial. 'Effective administration really means meeting the people, and showing them that the Collector and the SP of a district are not uppity and high-handed, but like meeting them. This is India, bhai, an independent country, and not the Raj, we are servants of the people.' A hooligan offered Kumar a *paan* which he stuffed into his mouth. 'Hahn, you look the English type—'

'The English type?'

'Any Indian who speaks English more fluently than he speaks any Indian language I call the English type, good, no?'

'Yes, sir.'

'Hahn, so English type, do you want to watch English movies on video?'

'Yes, sir.'

'You come over then, any time. I got new films, *A Passage to India, Amadeus, The Jewel in the Crown*, lots of others, you come.' Kumar waved to someone across the hall, who salaamed him jovially. 'But tell me, why do these English movies about India all have rape? Black men raping white women? Sathe, have you met Sathe? the joker of Madna, he says to be raped by a black man was a white woman's fantasy.' Just then the one who had salaamed Kumar joined them and the two gossiped. A groupie provided Agastya with company.

'What do you use this hall for normally?'

The groupie looked puzzled by the question. 'Oh ... everything.' He shrugged. 'Family Planning vasectomy and tubectomy camps, school table-tennis championships, bridge tournaments, meetings of the Youth Club, marriage parties ... anything.' All at one time, I hope, thought Agastya.

'Who built that statue of Gandhi outside?'

'An Executive Engineer called Tamse. He was here some time ago, he's been posted in Madna two or three times.' The groupie's face creased with an unpleasant memory. 'He's very enthusiastic and untalented. He paints also, also very badly. I was here when they installed the statue. Everyone was very angry, but it was too late.'

An urchin handed Agastya a plate. On it were *laddus*, samosas and green chutney. He could almost hear the chutney say, 'Hi, my name is cholera, what's yours?'

'No, not for me.'

The urchin said, 'Hayn?'

Agastya turned to the hooligan beside him. 'I can't eat anything today. My mother died today.' The man looked puzzled again. 'I mean, this is the anniversary of my mother's death, and I fast.' For a moment he contemplated adding, 'In penance, because I killed her.'

The hooligan said slowly, face creased again, but this time with perplexity, 'But it's very tasty, try just a little.'

'OK,' agreed Agastya, and began eating rapidly. He was feeling very hungry, and even finished a second plate, all the while imagining the filth beneath the urchin's fingernails.

The conversation continued. Agastya ensured that the man's perplexity never really disappeared. Both the Collector and the SP were earnestly discussing matters. He was again besieged, as he had been that morning in Joshi's room, by the sense that he was living someone else's life. He looked at his watch. One forty-five. In his old life he would've been with his uncle at home, talking rubbish over brunch. He remembered Dr Upadhyay, his head of department, and his words at their last encounter. Dr Upadhyay was a small dissatisfied man. 'I'm happy for you Agastya, you're leaving for a more meaningful context. This place,' he'd waved his hands at the books around him, at the tutorials on his desk, 'is like a parody, a complete farce, they're trying to build another Cambridge here. At my old University I used to teach *Macbeth* to my MA English classes in Hindi. English in India is burlesque. But now you'll get out of here to somehow a more real situation. In my time I'd wanted to give this Civil Service exam too, I should have. Now I spend my time writing papers for obscure journals on L. H. Myers and Wyndham Lewis, and teaching Conrad to a bunch of halfwits.'

Anchorlessness – that was to be one of his chaotic concerns in that uncertain year; battling a sense of waste was to be another. Other fodder too, in the farrago of his mind, self-pity in an uncongenial clime, the incertitude of his reactions to Madna, his job, and his inability to relate to it – other abstractions too, his niche in the world, his future, the elusive mocking nature of happiness, the possibility of its attainment.

On the way back Srivastav asked, 'So, what did you think of our SP?' Agastya smiled stupidly. 'You must call on him formally at his office this week, also on the District Judge and the District Development Officer. No one else. Normally this meeting lasts much longer, some idiots make speeches, but I have a lot of work in office, so I cut it short. How many meals do you have a day?' Srivastav was again pogo-sticking topics.

Agastya wondered at the question. 'Three,' he said, thinking. Perhaps Srivastav knows people who have fifteen.

'When you start working you must reduce it to two, before and after office, that's my advice. Take my case. Office starts at ten-thirty, I reach at eleven sharp.' He made it sound like a virtue. 'But no going home for lunch. Now, our SP followed quite another pattern earlier, but I fixed that. He reached his office at ten-thirty but would go home for lunch at one and would sleep fill four! and then come back to office at five. I fixed that.' Srivastav smiled in memory of the triumph. 'For one whole week I telephoned him at office at about three for some work or the other. His office would say, he's at home. They couldn't lie, no, because Collector was asking, and say he'd gone out. So I used to ring him up at home. His constable couldn't say he was sleeping, not to the Collector, so he was woken up. And when he talked he couldn't pretend that he'd been sleeping. One week of this. You have to straighten out these people, who think they're being paid to sleep in the afternoons. Kumar is an interesting fellow. He talks real big, about serving the people, that you'll soon find out, but he's a hopeless policeman. Do you want to go back to the Rest House for lunch?'

'Uh ... yes, I think.' An unwise decision, because the Rest House room was much hotter than the Collector's office, but he wanted to get away from his Collector and his job, to his other life. His secret life that year was lived in his hot dark room in the Rest House, or in other hot dark rooms in other Rest Houses. His secret life became much more exciting and more actual than the world outside. In the afternoons the rooms were dark because the windows had to be closed against an incandescent world, and the window panes were painted an opaque pink ('Against the glare,' explained one Junior Engineer. 'For privacy,' said another). There would be marijuana and nakedness, and soft, hopelessly incongruous music (Tagore or Chopin), and the thoughts that ferment in isolation. There would even be something vaguely erotic about the heat, about watching his own sweat on his bare skin.

'OK, relax after lunch, no need to rush things. You'll take a few days to get used to the heat. But tomorrow you come home with me in the evening.'

At the Collectorate Agastya switched from the white Ambassador to the jeep. The naib tehsildar sweated and beamed at him. At the Rest House he said, 'I shall take your leave, sir.'

Agastya said, 'OK, thanks, come tomorrow.'

The naib tehsildar handed him a huge white napkin, with a blue border. 'This morning, sir.'

'Oh, of course.' He tried it on. The driver and the naib tehsildar chuckled appreciatively. He asked the driver to call Vasant. His room looked quite welcoming, with its high ceiling and Tamse's picture. He wasn't hungry but he wanted milk to delude himself that he was careful of his health. 'Vasant, is there some milk?'

'Milk?' asked Vasant, as though Agastya had just asked him for his wife's cunt. Vasant looked more insane with a green towel wrapped around his head, but he seemed in concert with Madna. Agastya asked for tea at five-thirty and sent him away. He had three hours to himself, and was looking forward to them. He closed the door and prepared a smoke, contemplating to which music he should change his clothes. He smoked very slowly, till time, and most other things, ceased to matter. In Madna funny things happened to time. Outside the room its passage was wearisome, but in his secret life Agastya was to savour the seconds. No action was automatic: changing clothes, even the brushing of teeth, they were to become sensuous acts. He decided on Keith Jarrett, a valedictory present from Dhrubo.

He went up to the mirror on the dressing table, bent forward till his nose pressed against the mirror and asked himself silently what was happening to him. Not even twenty-four hours over and he felt unhinged, without the compensations of insight or wisdom. He lay down and looked at the wooden ceiling. He could masturbate, but without enjoyment. What is it? He asked himself again. Is it because it is a new place? Yes. So do I miss the urban life? Yes. Is it because it is a new job? Yes. The job is both bewildering and boring. Give it time, not even twenty-four hours. He waited for the mosquitoes. The ventilator was open, the room filled with the stench of the excrement of others when the wind came his way. My own shit doesn't smell like that, he thought randomly. He absent-mindedly fondled his crotch and then whipped his hand away. No masturbation, he suddenly decided. He tried to think about this but sustained logical thought on one topic was difficult and unnecessary. No, I am not wasting any semen on Madna. It was an impulse, but he felt that he should record it. In the diary under that date he wrote, 'From today no masturbation. Test your will, you bastard.' Then he wondered at his bravado. No masturbation at all? That was impossible. But then the marijuana really hit him and even that ceased to matter. He lay down again.

Vikram Chandra (b. 1961)

Born in Delhi, Vikram Chandra was educated in Bombay, Ajmer, and later studied film in America; he now teaches creative writing in Washington DC. His first novel, *Red Earth and Pouring Rain*, was a considerable success; it is a postmodern extravaganza, populated by, among others, monkeys, actual figures from history, celebrated murderers, and American students; its landscape shifts strikingly from pre-colonial India to Victorian England to present-day America, in no particular order. In his next book, *Love and Longing in Bombay*, Chandra abandoned this panoply of event and colour for what is a difficult form, the long short story, and was transformed from being a very ambitious novelist into a very good writer indeed. Here, Chandra sets aside the burden and glamour of the post-colonial narrative in order to bring alive the physical presence of Bombay, a city where his family still lives, and where he himself spends part of the year; the stories (some of the best examples of Indian fiction in English), which open a window on to the city's underworld and also on to its real estate and its dazzling hierarchy of wealth, are littered with the corpses of criminals, dons, and, metaphorically, of upper-class society ladies who have been slain by irony and snobbery. Chandra belongs to a family of successful filmmakers in commercial 'Bollywood' cinema; perhaps inevitably, he has confessed, in his pronouncements, to an impatience with the pretensions of 'high' art, or with the artificial division separating it from 'popular' culture, although everything about his stories tells us that he is as careful with his sentences as any stylist. Yet his appropriation of the detective story is probably his means of charting a path between 'high' and popular culture, without colliding into either. The extract below is from a novel in progress; the well-mannered, single-minded Inspector Sartaj Singh has appeared before, in the story 'Kama'.

* * *

'Siege in Kailashpada' (1997)

from a novel in progress

'You're never going to get in here,' the voice of Gaitonde said over the speaker after they had been working on the door for three hours. They had tried a cold chisel on the lock first, but what had looked like brown wood from a few feet away was in fact some kind of painted metal, and although it turned white under the blade and rang like a sharp temple bell, the door didn't give. Then they had moved to the lintels with tools borrowed from a road crew; but even when the road men took over, wielding the sledgehammer with long, expert swings and huffing breaths, the concrete bounced their blows off blithely, and the Sony speaker next to the door laughed at them. 'You're behind the times,' Gaitonde crackled.

'If I'm not getting in, you're not getting out,' Sartaj said.

'What? I can't hear you.'

Sartaj stepped up to the door. The building was a precise cube, white with green windows, on a square plot of land in Kailashpada, which was on the still-developing northern edge of Zone 13. Here, among the heavy machinery groping at swamp, edging Bombay out farther and wider, Inspector Sartaj Singh had come to arrest the great Ganesh Gaitonde, gangster, don among dons, and wily and eternal survivor.

'How long are you going to stay in there, Gaitonde?' Sartaj said, craning his neck up. The deep, round video eye of the camera above the door swivelled from side to side and then settled on him.

'You're that *chodu* Sardar inspector,' Gaitonde said.

'That I am,' Sartaj said. There were two Sikh commissioners on the force, but he was the only Sikh inspector in the whole city, and so was used to being identified by his turban and beard. He was known also for the cut of his pants, which he had tailored at a very film-starry boutique in Bandra, and also for his profile, which had once been featured by *Modern Woman* magazine in 'The City's Best-Looking Bachelors'. His assistant, Katekar, on the other hand, had a large paunch that sat on top of his belt like a suitcase, and a perfectly square face and very thick hands. Katekar was a senior constable, and an old colleague, and now he came around the corner of the building and stood wide-legged, with his hands in his pockets. He shook his head.

'Where are you going, Sardarji?' Gaitonde said.

'Just some things I have to take care of,' Sartaj said. He and Katekar walked to the corner together, and now Sartaj could see the ladder they had going up to the ventilator.

'That's not a ventilator,' Katekar said. 'It only looks like one. There's just concrete behind it. What the hell is this place, sir?'

'I don't know,' Sartaj said. It was somehow deeply satisfying that even Katekar, Mumbai native and practitioner of a very superior Bhuleshwar-bred cynicism, was startled by an impregnable white cube suddenly grown in Kailashpada, with a black swivel-mounted Sony video camera above the door. 'I don't know. And he sounds very strange, you know. Isn't he supposed to be very polite?'

'Yes, like a congressman who wants a vote from you,' Katekar said. 'Polite like an oil massage, even with constables.'

'I've never met him. You?'

'No, but that's what everyone says. Never heard of him being rude to police.'

'Today he must not want anything,' Sartaj said.

'But what's he doing here, in Kailashpada of all places?'

Sartaj nodded. The Gaitonde they had read about in police reports and in the newspapers lolled in the stands during Sharjah cricket matches with bejewelled starlets, he bankrolled politicians and bought them and sold them, his daily skim from Bombay's various dark *dhandas* was said to be greater than annual corporate incomes, and his name was used to frighten the recalcitrant. Gaitonde bhai said so, you said, and the stubborn saw reason, and all roads were smoothed, and there was peace. But he had been on the run for many months, on the Indonesian coast in a yacht, it was rumoured, far but only a phone call away. Which meant that he might as well have been next door, or as it turned out, amazingly enough, in dusty Kailashpada. The tip-off had come from an anonymous male voice on Sartaj's direct line at the station, bringing them to Kailashpada in a hasty caravan bristling with rifles. 'I don't know,' Sartaj said. 'But now that he's here, he's ours.'

'He's a prize, yes, sir,' Katekar said. He had that densely snobbish look he always assumed when he thought Sartaj was being naive. 'But you're sure you want to make him yours?'

'He's already mine, only he doesn't know it,' Sartaj said, turning to walk back toward the door. 'All right. Cut off his power.'

'Hey, Sardarji,' Gaitonde boomed over the speaker. 'You were the one who *lurkaoed* Mahinder Mathu's wicket.' There was a strange rolling richness about his voice, even over the tinny speaker.

'I did,' Sartaj said. 'Friend of yours?'

'Not exactly,' Gaitonde said. 'But why the hell did you have to shoot him five times? In the face?'

'He was trying to bowl me out also, Gaitonde. And it was four times, and only twice in the head.'

'Mathu should have gotten you. But he thought too long,' Gaitonde said. 'Mahinder Mathu always—' And his voice stopped short, as if cut by a knife.

Sartaj turned from the door. Now it was a matter of waiting, and an hour or two under a hot June sun would turn the unventilated, unpowered building into a furnace that even Gaitonde, who was a graduate of Arthur Road Jail many times and many years over, would find as hard to bear as the corridors of Hell. And Gaitonde had been lately very successful and thus a little softened, so perhaps it would be closer to an hour. But Sartaj had taken only two steps when he felt a deep hum rising through his toes and into his knees, and Gaitonde was back.

'What, you thought it would be so easy?' Gaitonde said, chortling. 'Just a power cut? What, you think I'm a fool?'

So there was a generator somewhere in the cube. Gaitonde had been the first man in Arthur Road Jail, perhaps the first man in Bombay, to own a cellular phone. With it, safe in his cell, he had run drugs, *matka*, smuggling, and construction. 'No, I don't think you're a fool,' Sartaj said. 'This, this building is very impressive. Who designed it for you?'

'Never mind who designed it, Sardarji. The question is, how are you going to get in?'

'Why don't you just come out? It'll save us all a lot of time. It's really hot out here, and I'm getting a headache.'

There was a silence, filled with the murmuring of the spectators who were gathering at the end of the lane.

'I can't come out.'

'Why not?'

'I'm alone. I'm only me by myself.'

'I thought you had friends everywhere, Gaitonde. Everyone everywhere is a friend of Gaitonde bhai's, isn't it? In the government, in the press, even in the police force? How is it then that you are alone?'

'Do you know I get applications, Sardarji? I probably get more applications than you police fucks. Don't believe me? Here, I'll read you one. Hold on. Here's one. This one's from Wardha. Here it is.'

'Gaitonde!'

'"Respected Shri Gaitonde." Hear that, Sardarji?' "Respected." So then . . . "I am a twenty-two-year-old young man living in Wardha, Maharashtra. Currently I am doing my M.Com., having passed my B.Com. exam with seventy-one per cent marks. I am also known in my college as the best athlete, since I am captain of the cricket team." Then there's a lot of crap about how bold and strong he is, how everyone in town's scared of him. OK, then he goes on, "I am sure that I can be of use to you. I have for long followed your daring exploits in our newspapers, which print very often these stories of your great power and powerful politics, which make you the first man in Mumbai. Many times when my friends get together, we talk about your famous adventures. Like how you finished Dhanraj Kalia's game, in spite of his police guards. And of course I hope you are not offended if I mention your great love affair with our own Miss India, Miss Nandita Kumar. Please, Shri Gaitonde, I respectfully submit to you my vita, and some small clippings about me. I will do whatever work you ask. I am very poor, Shri Gaitonde. I fully believe that you will give me a chance to make a life. Yours faithfully, Amit Shivraj Patil."

'Hear that, Sardarji?' Gaitonde called out.

'Yes, Gaitonde,' Sartaj said. 'I do. He sounds like a fine recruit.'

'He sounds like a *lodu*, Sardarji,' Gaitonde said. 'I wouldn't hire him as a *bhangi* to clean my toilets. But he'd probably do well as a policeman.'

'I'm getting tired of this, Gaitonde.'

Gaitonde laughed. 'Are your feelings hurt, saab? Should I be more respectful? Should I tell you about the wonderful and astonishing feats of the police, our defenders who give their lives in service without a thought for their own profit?'

'Gaitonde?'

'What?'

'I'll be back. I need a cold drink.'

Gaitonde laughed long and very hard, and became avuncular, affectionate. 'Yes, yes, of course you do. Hot out there.'

'For you also? A Thums Up?'

'I've a fridge in here, *chikniya*. Just because you're so far and so hero-like good-looking doesn't mean you're extra smart. You get your drink.'

'I will. I'll be back.'

'What else would you do, Sardarji? Go, go.'

Sartaj walked down the street, and Katekar fell in beside him. The
cracked black tarmac seemed to swim and shimmer in the heat. The street
had emptied, the spectators bored by the lack of explosions and bullets
and hungry for lunch. Between Bhagwan Tailors and Trimurti Music, they
found the straightforwardly named Best Café, which had tables scattered
under a neem tree and rattling black floor fans. Sartaj pulled desperately
at a Coke, and Katekar sipped at fresh lime and soda, only slightly sweet.
He was trying to lose weight. From where they sat they could see Gaitonde's white bunker.

'Let's blow it up,' Katekar said.

'With what?' Sartaj said. 'And that'll kill him for sure.'

Katekar grinned. 'Yes, sir. So what, sir?'

'And what would the intelligence boys say?'

'Saab, excuse me, but the intelligence boys can suck my *lauda*. Why
didn't they know he was building this thing?'

'Now, that would have been very, very intelligent, wouldn't it?' Sartaj
said. He leaned back in his chair and stretched. 'You think we can find a
bulldozer?'

*

Sartaj had a metal chair brought to the front of the bunker, and he sat on
it patting his face with a cold, wet towel. He was sleepy. The video camera
was unmoving and silent.

'Ay, Gaitonde!' Sartaj said. 'You there?'

The camera made its very small buzzing machine noise, nosed about
blindly, and then found Sartaj. 'Yes, I'm here. I was searching this bastard
place. Sardarji, can you believe it? There's nothing to eat in here.'

'Nothing?'

'A brand-new two-lakh fridge big enough to walk into, and not a slice
of bread in it. I have idiots working for me.'

Sartaj thought suddenly that Gaitonde had learned that big voice from
the movies, from Prithviraj Kapoor in a smoking jacket complaining about
the servants. 'Can we send you something?' Sartaj said. 'Shrimp? Chicken?'

'No, you can't, and stop trying to be so *maderchod* smart.'

'You'll stay hungry?' Sartaj was trying to calculate the chances of
starving Gaitonde out. But he remembered that Gandhiji had lasted for
weeks on water and juice. The bulldozer would arrive in an hour – an
hour and a half, at most.

'I've been hungry before,' Gaitonde said. 'More hungry than you could
imagine.'

'Listen, it's too bloody hot out here,' Sartaj said. 'Come out and back at the station you can tell me all about how hungry you were.'

'I can't come out.'

'I'll take care of you, Gaitonde. There are all sorts of people trying to kill you, I know. But no danger, I promise. This is not going to turn into an encounter. You come out now and we'll be back at the station in six minutes. You'll be absolutely safe. From there you can call your friends. Safe, *ekdum* safe. You have my promise.'

But Gaitonde wasn't interested in promises. 'Back when I was a kid, I left the country for the first time. It was on a boat, you know. Those days that was the business: get on a boat, go to Dubai, go to Bahrain, come back with gold biscuits. I was excited, because I had never left the country before. Not even to Nepal, you understand. OK, Sardarji, establishing shot: there was the small boat, five of us on it, sea, sun, all that kind of crap. Salim kaka was the leader, a six-foot Pathan with a long beard, good man with a sword. Then there was Mathu, narrow and thin everywhere, always picking his nose, supposed to be a tough guy. Me, nineteen and didn't know a damn thing. And there was Gaston, the owner of the boat, and Pascal, his assistant, two small dark guys from somewhere in the South. It was Salim kaka's deal, his contacts there, and his money that hired the boat, and his experience, when to go out, when to come back, everything was his. Mathu and I were his boys, behind him all the time. Got it?'

Katekar rolled his eyes. Sartaj said, 'Yes, Salim kaka was the leader, you and Mathu the thin guy were the guns, and Gaston and Pascal sailed the boat. Got it.'

Katekar propped himself against the wall next to the door and spilled *paan* masala into his palm. The speaker gleamed a hard metallic silver. Sartaj shut his eyes.

Gaitonde went on. 'I had never seen such a huge sky before. Purple and gold and purple. Mathu was combing his hair again and again into a Dev Anand puff. Salim kaka sat on the deck with us. He had huge feet, square and blunt, each cracked like a piece of wood, and a beard that was smooth and red like a flame. That night he told us about his first job, robbing an *angadia* couriering cash to Bombay from Surat. They caught the *angadia* as he got off the bus, tossed him in the back of an Ambassador, and went roaring away to an empty chemical godown in the industrial estates at Vikhroli. In the godown they stripped him of his shirt, his *banian*, his pants, everything, and found sewn inside the pants, over the thighs, four lakhs in five-hundred-rupee notes. Also a money belt with sixteen thousand in it. He was standing there baby-naked, his big paunch shaking, holding his hands over his shrunken *lauda*, as they left. Clear?'

Sartaj opened his eyes. 'A courier, they got him, they made some money. So what?'

'So the story's not over yet, smart Sardarji. Salim kaka was closing the door, but then he turned around and came back. He caught the guy by the throat, lifted him up and around, and put a knee between his legs. "Come on, Salim Pathan," someone yelled to him, "this is no time to want to fuck a boy." And Salim kaka, who was groping the *angadia's* bum, said, "Sometimes if you squeeze a beautiful ass, as you would a peach, it reveals all the secrets of the world," and he held up a little brown silk packet, which the *angadia* had taped behind his balls. In it were a good gross of the highest-quality diamonds, agleam and aglitter, which they fenced the next week at fifty per cent, and Salim kaka's cut alone was one lakh, and this was in the days when a lakh meant something. "But," Salim kaka said, "the lakh was the least of it, money is only money." But after that he was known as a lustrous talent, a sharp lad. "I'll squeeze you like a peach," he'd say, cocking a craggy eyebrow, and the poor unfortunate at the receiving end would spill cash, cocaine, secrets, anything.

'"How did you know with the *angadia*, Salim kaka?" I asked, and Salim kaka said, "It is very simple. I looked at him from the door and he was still afraid. When I had my knife at his throat he had said to me in a child's little voice, "Please don't kill me, my *baap*." I hadn't killed him, he was still alive and holding his *lauda*, the money was gone, but it wasn't his, we were leaving, so why was he still afraid? A man who is afraid is a man who still has something to lose."'

'Very impressive,' Sartaj said. He shifted in his chair, and regretted it immediately as his shoulder blade found a curve of heated metal. He adjusted his turban and tried to breathe slowly, evenly. Katekar was fanning himself with a folded afternoon newspaper, his eyes abstracted and his forehead slack, while into the slow stirring of the air came Gaitonde's voice with its cool electronic hiss.

'I resolved to be sharply watchful for ever after, for I was ambitious. That night I laid my body down along the bow, as close as I could get to the onrushing water, and I dreamed. Did I tell you I was nineteen? I was nineten and I made myself stories about cars and a high house and myself entering a party and flashbulbs popping.

'Mathu came and sat beside me. He lit a cigarette for himself and gave me one. I drew hard on it like him. In the dark I could see the puff of his hair, his haggard shoulders, and I tried to remember his features, which were too bony to be anywhere close to Dev Anand's, but still every day he stroked talcum powder onto that pointy rat face and tried. I felt suddenly kindly toward him. "Isn't this beautiful?" I said. He laughed. "Beautiful? We could drown," he said, "and nobody would know what happened to us. We would disappear, *phat*, gone." His cigarette made spirals in the dark. "What do you mean?" I asked. "Oh, you pitiful *dehati* idiot!" he said. "Don't you know? Nobody knows we are out here." "But," I said, "Salim kaka's people know, his boss knows." I could feel him laughing at me, his knee jogging against my shoulder. "No they don't." He was leaning closer to me, whispering, and I could smell his *banian* and see the pale phosphorescence of his eyes. "Nobody knows, he didn't tell his boss. Don't you get it? This is his own deal. Why do you think we're on this little *khatara* of a boat, not a trawler? Why do you think we are with him, one *dehati* smelling of pig shit and farm dirt and a very, very junior member of the company? Eh? Why? This is Salim kaka's own little operation. He wants to go independent, and to go independent what do you need? Capital. That's what. That's why we're out here slopping away in this *chodu* wheezing tin trap, one pitch away from the big fishes. He thinks he's going to make enough to start himself all new and fresh and shiny. Capital, capital, you understand?"

'I sat up then. He put a hand on my shoulder and swung himself up. "*Beta*," he said, "if you want to live in the city you have to think ahead three turns, and look behind a lie to see the truth and then behind that truth to see the lie. And then, and then, if you want to live well, you need a bankroll. Think about it." Mathu patted my shoulder and drew back. I saw his face for a second in dim light as he lowered himself into the cabin. And I did think about it.'

Under the speaker Katekar turned his head, right and left, and Sartaj heard the small clicking noise of the bones in his neck. 'I remember this Salim kaka,' Katekar said softly. 'I remember seeing him in Dongri, walking around in a red lungi and a silk kurta. The kurtas were of different colours, but the lungi was always red. He worked with Haji Salman's gang, and he had a woman in Dongri, I remember hearing. Dongri was Bachchu Singh's area, but still Salim kaka came for the woman, in a red lungi and silk kurtas.'

Sartaj nodded. Katekar's face was puffy, as if he had just woken from sleep. 'Love?' Sartaj said.

Katekar grinned. 'Judging by the silk, it must have been,' he said. 'Or maybe it was just that she was seventeen and had an ass like a prancing deer's. She was an auto mechanic's daughter, I think.'

'Don't believe in love, Katekar?'

'*Saab*, I believe in silk, and in everything that is soft, and everything else that is hard, but ...'

Above their heads the speaker rumbled. 'What in God's name are you mumbling about, Sardarji?'

'Go on, go on,' Sartaj said. 'Just minor instructions.'

'Not giving up? Good, I like that. So listen. The next afternoon, we started to see tree branches in the water, pieces of old crates, bottles bobbing down and up, tyres, once the whole wooden roof of a house floating upside down. Gaston stayed on deck the whole time now, one arm around the mast, looking this way and that with binoculars, never stopping. I asked Mathu, "Are we close?" He shrugged. Salim kaka came up in a new kurta. He stood by the bow, looking to the north, and I saw his fingers dabbing at the silver medallion at his chest. I wanted to ask him where we were, but there was a narrow-eyed gravity on his face that kept me from speaking.'

Sartaj leaned forward toward Katekar. 'Do you think our friend Gaitonde really had an affair with Miss India?'

Katekar grinned. 'She was a very English-medium type, that one. But it's true, she stayed at his house in Hong Kong.'

'Maybe he learned English.'

'Maybe she liked his sweaters. He has a lot of sweaters.'

Sartaj remembered the pictures of Gaitonde, the medium-sized body and the medium face, neither ugly nor handsome, all of it instantly forgettable despite the bright-blue and red cashmere sweaters, everything quite commonplace. But now there was this voice, quiet and urgent, and Sartaj tipped his head toward the speaker.

'As night came, in the last failing light, there was a pinpoint of red winking steadily to the north. We dropped anchor, then headed toward it in a dinghy. Mathu rowed, and Salim kaka sat opposite, watching our beacon, and I between them. I was expecting a wall, like I had seen near the Gateway of India, but instead there were high rushes that towered above our heads. Salim kaka took a pole and pushed us through the feathered banks that creaked and whispered, and although I wasn't told to I had my pistol in my hand. Then the wood scraped under my feet, hard on ground. Flashlight in hand, Salim kaka led us up the island, that's what it was, a soft wet rising in the swamp. We walked for a long time, half an hour maybe, Salim kaka in front, under a rising moon. He had a brown canvas bag over his shoulder, big as a wheat sack. Then I saw the beacon again, over the top of the stalks. It was a torch tied to a pole. I could smell the tallow; the flames jumped two feet high. Under it there were three men. They were dressed like city people, and in the leaping light I could see their fair skin, their bushy black eyebrows, their big noses. Turks? Iranis? Arabs? I don't know still, but two of them had rifles, muzzles pointed just a little away from us. My trigger was cool and sweaty on my finger. I cramped and thought, You'll fire and finish us all. I took a breath, turned my wrist, feeling the butt against my thumb, and watched them. Salim kaka and one of them spoke, their heads close together. Now the bag was offered, and a suitcase in return. I saw a gleam of yellow, and heard the clicks of locks shutting. My arm ached.

'Salim kaka stepped backward, and we edged away from the foreigners. I felt the smooth wet rim of a stalk against my neck, and I couldn't find a way out, only the yielding pressure of vegetation, and panic. Then Salim kaka turned abruptly and slipped between the bushes, the faint beam of his flashlight marking his way, and then Mathu. I came last, sidewise, my pistol hand held low, my neck taut. I can still see them watching, the three men. I see the gleam of the metal bands around the rifle muzzles, and their shaded eyes. We were walking fast. I felt as if we were flying, and the tall grass that had pulled and clawed at me at first now brushed softly along my sides. Salim kaka turned his head, and I saw his frantic smile. We were happy, running.

'Salim kaka paused at the edge of a little stream where water had cut a drop of three feet, maybe four, and he reached down with his right foot and found a place for his heel. Mathu looked at me, his face cut into angles by the gaunt moonlight, and I looked at him. Before Salim kaka had completed his step, I knew where we were going. The report of the pistol bounced off the water into my belly. I knew the butt had bruised the base of my thumb. Only when the flare left my eyes could I see again, and my stomach was twisting and loosening and twisting, and at the bottom of the ditch Salim kaka's feet were treading steadily, as if he were still finding his way to the boat. The water thrashed and boiled. "Fire, Mathu," I said. "Fire, damn you." Those were the first words I had spoken since we'd come ashore. My voice was firm and strange, the sound of it alien. Mathu tilted his head and pointed his barrel. Again a flash brought the weeds out from the shadows, but still those feet clambered away, going steadily somewhere. I aimed my pistol into the round frothy turbulence, and at the first discharge all movement stopped, but I put another one in just to make sure. "Come on," I said, "let's go home." Mathu nodded, as if I were in charge, and he jumped into the ditch and scrabbled for the suitcase. The flashlight was glowing under the water, a luminous yellow bubble that embraced exactly half of Salim kaka's head and his green kurta collar. I snapped it up as I went through, though all the way back to the dinghy the fat moon was low overhead and lit us to safety.'

Sartaj and Katekar heard Gaitonde drink now. They heard, clearly, every long gulp and the glass emptying. 'Whisky?' Sartaj whispered. 'Beer?'

Katekar shook his head. 'No, he doesn't drink. Doesn't smoke either. Very health-conscious don he is. Exercises every day. Water he's drinking. Bisleri with a twist of lime in it.'

Gaitonde went on, hurrying now. 'When the sun came up on the boat the next day Mathu and I were still awake. We had spent the night sitting in the cabin, across from each other, with the suitcase tucked under Mathu's bunk but still visible. I had my pistol in my lap, and I could see Mathu's under his thigh. The roof above my head creaked out a stealthy step. We had told Gaston and Pascal that we had been ambushed by the police, the police of whatever country we had been in. Pascal had wept, and they were both moving very gently now, in respect for our mourning. Behind Mathu's head there was the dark brown of the wood, and the white of his *banian* floating and dipping with the swell of the waves. There was the hazy distance between us, and I knew what he was thinking. So I decided. I put my pistol on the pillow, put my feet up on the bunk. "I'm going to sleep," I said. "Wake me up in three hours and then you can rest." I turned to the wood, with my back toward Mathu, and shut my eyes. Very, very low down on my back there was a single circle on my skin which twitched and crawled. It expected a bullet. I could not calm it. But I kept my breathing steady, my knuckles against my lips. There are some things you can control.

'When I woke it was evening. There was a thick orange light pushing into the cabin from the hatch, colouring the wood like fire. My tongue filled my throat and mouth, and my hand when I tried to move it had become a loathsome bloated weight. I thought the bullet had found me, or I had found the bullet, but then I jerked once and my heart was thudding painfully and I sat up. My stomach was covered with sweat. Mathu was asleep, his face down on the pillow. I tucked my pistol into my waistband and went up. Pascal smiled at me out of his black little face. The clouds were piled above us, enormous and bulging, higher and higher into the red heaven. And this boat a twig on the water. My legs shook and I sat down and prayed. I said the Hanuman *chalisa*. I said it again and again. When it was dark, I asked Pascal for two sacks. He gave me two white sacks made of canvas, with drawstrings.

'"Wake up," I said to Mathu when I went downstairs, and kicked his bunk. He came awake groping for his pistol, which he couldn't find until I pointed to it, between the mattress and the wall. "Calm down, you jumpy *chut*. Just calm down. We have to share." He said, "Don't ever do that again." He was growling, stretching his shoulders up like a rooster heaving its feathers. I smiled at him. "Listen," I said, "you *bhenchod* sleepy son of *moderchod* Kumbhkaran, do you want your half or what?" He calculated for a moment, still all swollen and angry, but then he subsided with a laugh. "Yes, yes," he said. 'Half-half. Half-half.'

'Gold is good. It moves and slips on your fingers with a satisfying smoothness. When it is near to pure it has that healthy reddish glow that reminds you of apple cheeks. But that afternoon as we moved the bars from the suitcase into the sacks, one by one, one for one and then one for the other, what I liked best was the weight. The bars were small, a little longer than the breadth of my palm, much smaller than I had expected, but they felt so dense and plump I could hardly bear to put each in my sack. My face was warm and my heart congested and I knew I had done right. When we got to the last bar, which was mine, I put it in my left pants pocket, where I could feel it always, slapping against me. Then the pistol on the other side at the back of my waistband. Mathu nodded. "Almost home," he said. "How much do you think it's worth?" His smile was slow and faltering. I looked down at him and felt only contempt. I knew absolutely and for certain and in one instant that he would always be a *tapori*, nothing more, maybe even with ten or twelve people working for him, but always nothing more than a nerve-racked small-time local buffoon, jacked up into tottery brutishness with a gun and a chopper under his shirt, that's all. If you think in rupees you're a sweep-carrying *bhangi*, nothing more. Because lakhs are dirt, and crores are shit. I thought, What is golden is the future in your pocket, the endless possibility of it. So I shoved the sack under my bunk, nudging the last of it under with my foot as Mathu watched with wide eyes. I turned my back on him and climbed up to the deck laughing to myself. I was no longer afraid. I knew him now. That night I slept like a baby.'

Katekar snorted, and shook his head. 'And for years he slept a restful sleep every night, while the bodies fell right and left.' Sartaj held up a warning hand, and Katekar wiped the sweat from his face and muttered quietly, 'They're all of them the swinish same, *moderchod* greedy bastards. The trouble is when one gets killed, five come up to take his place.'

'Quiet,' Sartaj said. 'I want to hear this.'

The speaker growled again. 'The day after the next, I saw, over the water, a faraway hillock. "What is that?" I asked Gaston. "Home," he said.

From the bow Pascal called to another boat leaning out toward the horizon. "*Aaa-hoooooooo*," he called, and the long cry and its echoing reply wrapped about my shoulders. I was home.

'We helped to beach the boat, and then took leave of Pascal and Gaston. Mathu was whispering threats at them, but I shouldered him aside, not too gently, and said, "Listen, boys, keep this quiet, very quiet, and we'll do business again." I gave them a gold bar each – from my share – and shook hands with them, and they grinned and were my fellows for life. Mathu and I walked a little way down the road, to the bus stop, with our white sacks dragging over our shoulders. I waved down an auto rickshaw and nodded at Mathu. I left him standing there, buffeted by exhaust. I knew he wanted to come with me, but he thought more of himself than he was, and he would've forced me to kill him, sooner or later. I had no time for him. I was going to Bombay.'

*

The speaker was silent. Sartaj stood up, turned, and looked up and down the street. 'Eh, Gaitonde?' he said.

A moment passed, and then the answer came: 'Yes, Sartaj?'

'The bulldozer's here.'

Indeed it was there, a black leviathan that now appeared at the very end of the street, with its throaty clanking causing a crowd to appear instantly. The machine had a certain dignity, and the driver had a cap on his head, worn with the flair of a specialist.

'Get those people out of the road,' Sartaj said to Katekar. 'And that thing up here. Pointed this way.'

'I can hear it now,' Gaitonde said. The video lens moved in its housing restlessly.

'You'll see it soon,' Sartaj said. The policemen near the vans were checking their weapons. 'Listen, Gaitonde, this is all a farce that I don't like one bit. We've never met, but still we've spent the afternoon talking. Let's be gentlemen. There's no need for this. Just come out and we can go back to the station and we can get you something to eat. Shrimp.'

'Shrimp would be good,' Gaitonde said. 'But I can't do that.'

'Stop it,' Sartaj said. 'Stop acting the *fillum* villain, you're better than that. This isn't some bloody schoolboy game.'

'It never was, my friend,' Gaitonde said. 'It never was.'

Sartaj turned away from the door. He wanted, with an excruciating desire, a cup of tea. 'All right. What's your name?' he said to the driver of the bulldozer, who was leaning against a gargantuan track.

'Bashir Ali.'

'You know what to do?'

Bashir Ali twisted his blue cap in his hands.

'It's my responsibility, Bashir Ali. I'm giving you an order as a police inspector, so you don't have to worry about it. Let's get that door down.'

Bashir Ali cleared his throat. 'But that's Gaitonde in there, Inspector saab,' he said tentatively.

Sartaj took Bashir Ali by the elbow and walked him to the door.

'Gaitonde?'

'Yes, Sardarji?'

'This is Bashir Ali, the driver of the bulldozer. He's afraid of helping us. He's frightened of you.'

'Bashir Ali,' Gaitonde said. The voice was commanding, like an emperor's sure of its consonants and its generosity.

Bashir Ali was looking at the middle of the door. Sartaj pointed up at the video camera, and Ali blinked up at it. 'Yes, Gaitonde bhai?' he said.

'Don't worry. I won't forgive you' – Bashir Ali blanched – 'because there's nothing to forgive. We are both trapped, you on that side of the door and me on this. Do what they tell you to do, get it over with, and go home to your children. Nothing will happen to you. Not now and not later. I give you my word.' There was a pause. 'The word of Ganesh Gaitonde.'

By the time Bashir Ali had climbed up to his seat on top of the bulldozer he had understood, it seemed, his role in the situation. He put his cap on his head with a twirl and pointed it backward. The engine grunted and then settled into a steady roar. Sartaj leaned close to the speaker. The left side of his head, from the nape of the neck to the temples, was caught in a sweeping pulse of heat and pain.

'Gaitonde?'

'Speak, Sardarji, I'm listening.'

'Just open this damn door.'

'Oho, you want me to just open this door? I know, Sardarji, I know.'

'Know what?'

'I know what you want. You want me to just open this damn door. Then you want to arrest me and take me to the station. You want to be a hero in the newspapers. You want a promotion. Two promotions. Deep down you want even more. You want to be rich. You want to be an all-India hero. You want the President to give you a medal on Republic Day. You want the medal in full colour on television. You want to fuck film stars.'

'Gaitonde–'

'But you know I've had all that. And I'll beat you.'

'How? You have some of your boys in there with you?'

'No. Not one. I told you, I'm alone.'

'A tunnel? A helicopter hidden inside?'

Gaitonde laughed. 'No, no.'

'What then? You have a battery of Bofors guns?'

'Not even an AK-47. But I'll beat you.'

The bulldozer was shimmering on the black road, flanked by grim-eyed policemen. Their choices were narrowing rapidly, leading them inevitably to this metal door, and they were determined, and helpless, and afraid.

'Gaitonde,' Sartaj said, rubbing his eyes. 'Last chance. Come on, *yaar*. This is very, very stupid.'

'I can't do it. Sorry.'

'All right. Just stay back from the door when we come in. And for God's sake have your hands up.'

'Don't worry,' Gaitonde said. 'I will.'

Sartaj stood up straight, his back to the door, and checked his pistol. He rotated the cylinder, and the yellow cartridges sat fat and round in the metal. The heat came through the soles of his shoes, into his feet.

Suddenly the speaker came to life again against his shoulder blade. 'Sartaj, you called me *yaar*. So I'll tell you something. Build it big or small, there is no house that is safe. Love is an iron trap, and the game always wins.'

Sartaj could feel the tinny trembling in his chest from the speaker. The machine in front of him produced a blare that pressed him back against the door, and it was enough. He palmed the cylinder back into the pistol, and stepped off the porch. 'All right,' he shouted. 'Let's go, let's go, let's go.' He waved toward the door with the weapon. The speaker was buzzing again, but Sartaj wasn't listening. 'Come on, Bashir Ali, get that thing down.' Bashir Ali raised a hand, and Sartaj pointed a rigid finger at him. 'Get that thing moving.'

Bashir Ali crouched in his high seat, and the behemoth lurched forward, past Sartaj, and smashed against the building with a dull crunch, with a soaring cloud of plaster. But after a moment, when the bulldozer pulled back, the building still stood complete and sacrosanct, the door not even dented. Only the video camera had been injured: it lay next to the door, flattened neatly halfway along its length. A long jeer rose from the crowd down the street. It grew louder when Bashir Ali switched off his engine.

'What the hell was that?' Sartaj said when Bashir Ali stepped down on the shaded side of the bulldozer.

'What do you expect when you won't let me do it the way it should be done?'

They were both wiping plaster from their noses. On the sunlit side of the bulldozer the crowd was chanting '*Jai* Gaitonde.'

'Do you know the way to do it?'

Bashir Ali shrugged. 'I have an idea.'

'All right,' Sartaj said. 'Fine. Do it how you want.'

'Get out of my way then. And get your men back from the building.'

As Bashir Ali spun his steed on the gravel, Sartaj saw that he was an artist. He operated with flicks and thumps of his hands on the driving sticks, leaning into the direction of his turns, in sympathy with the groaning gears underneath. He raised and then lowered his blade, positioning it precisely, with its lower extended edge level with the door. He reversed ten feet, twenty, thirty, his arm jauntily on the back of his seat. He came at the building at a diagonal, and as he went past Sartaj he flashed a white grin. This time there was a scream of metal, and when the violet juddering of the bulldozer had ceased Sartaj saw that the door had been peeled back, inward. A crack ran three feet up into the masonry.

'Back!' Sartaj shouted. He was running forward, pistol held in front of him. 'Get back, get back.' Then Bashir Ali was gone, and Sartaj was leaning against one side of the doorway, and Katekar on the other. An icy wind came out and Sartaj felt it drying the sweat on his face and his forearms. Suddenly, for a moment, he envied Gaitonde all his air-conditioners, the frigid climate control won by his audacity. And for a moment, rising from somewhere deep in his hips, unbidden and nauseating, like a buoyant dribble of bile, was a tiny bubble of admiration. He took a deep breath. 'Do you think the building will hold?' he said.

Katekar nodded. He was looking in, through the door, and his face was dark with rage. Sartaj touched the tip of his tongue to his upper lip, felt the dryness, and then they went in. Sartaj went ahead, and at the first door inside Katekar went by him. Behind them followed the rustling of the others. Sartaj was trying to hear above the thunderous unclenching of his heart. He had done entries like this before, and it never got better. It was very cold inside the building, and the light was low and luxurious. There was carpet under their feet. There were four square rooms, all white, all empty. And at the exact centre of the building was a very steep, almost vertical, metal staircase. Sartaj nodded at Katekar, and then followed him down. The metal door at the bottom opened easily, but it was very heavy, and when Katekar finally had it back Sartaj saw that it was as thick as a hatch to a bank vault. Inside it was dark. Sartaj was shivering

uncontrollably. He moved past Katekar, and now he saw a bluish light on
the left. Katekar slid past his shoulders and went out wide, and then they
shuffled forward, weapons held rigidly before them. Another step and now
in the new angle Sartaj saw a figure, shoulders, in front of a bank of haze-
filled TV monitors, a brown hand near the controls on a black panel.

'Gaitonde!' Sartaj hadn't meant to shout – a gentle admonitory assertion
was the preferred tone – and now he squeezed his voice down. 'Gaitonde,
put your hands up very slowly.' There was no movement from the figure
in the darkness. Sartaj tightened his finger painfully on his trigger, and
fought the urge to fire, and fire again. 'Gaitonde, Gaitonde?'

From Sartaj's right, where Katekar was, came a very small click, and
even as Sartaj turned his head the room was flooded with white neon
radiance, generous and encompassing and clean. And in the universal
illumination Gaitonde sat, revealed, a black pistol in his left hand, and half
his head gone.

*

It was night when Sartaj came up the metal stairs. He left underneath him
the symmetrical rooms of the cube, which the two police commissioners
below were now calling a safe house. The three lab technicians were
dusting it, and Katekar was guarding it with a proprietor's fierce watchful-
ness. Sartaj stood shadowed in the lee of the metal door. There were
reporters waiting behind a row of police jeeps. He checked his collar, and
ran his hands along the sides of his turban, and stepped out. In the flare of
the flashbulbs, he found that he could not leave behind Gaitonde's stare.
Gaitonde had looked at him in the first sudden light; his right eye had
bulged with a manic intensity. Sartaj had seen the fragile tracery of pink
lines, the hard black of the pupil, the shining seep of fluid from the inside
corner, which despite himself he had thought of as a tear. But it was only
the body reacting to the gigantic blow that had exploded everything from
the chin up on the other side of his face, slicing from the left nostril into
the forehead.

'Enough,' Sartaj said, and shouldered his way through the photogra-
phers. Soon he was at the wheel of a Gypsy, winding through the heavy
traffic. He didn't know where he was going. He thought, It's finished,
Sardarji, finished. It's only work. Enough. But he could still see water
slapping against the rust-brown side of a boat, a cloud-laden sky, a figure
sitting in the bow looking toward the horizon.

Sartaj turned the jeep's wheel violently to the left and was now driving
along a familiar road, which led to the sloping beach at Kausa where he

used to go picnicking during college. The curving waterfront lined with tiny fishing villages had been a great secret then. Now there was a huge yellow hotel, built in an epic arc to match the bay. The hotel belonged to a family in the construction business, and the permission required to build in a protected area had come from a minister close to Gaitonde. There was nothing to be done about it now. The villagers' sons and daughters worked in it, as gardeners, waiters, and maids. The hotel was far ahead in the dark but Sartaj could see it clearly, like an enormous wall stretching from right to left. In its rooftop bar, Sartaj had once drunk a Scotch. He veered to the side of the road and stopped the Gypsy.

Sartaj sat for a long while. Then he moved the jeep in a slow half circle across the road, and went back to Kailashpada.

Sunetra Gupta (b. 1965)

Sunetra Gupta was born in Calcutta in 1965, and spent part of her child-hood in Africa. She studied at Princeton, and Imperial College, London; and is now a Reader in the Department of Zoology at Oxford. Her first novel, the Sahitya Akademi Award-winning *Memories of Rain*, was pub-lished in 1992; since then, three more novels have appeared, including the latest, *A Sin of Colour* (1999), which won the Southern Arts Literature Prize. She is one of the few genuinely talented writers to have emerged from that aggressively marketed group of practitioners called 'Indian writers in English'; and yet she seems to have missed out somewhat on the spotlight that has fallen on almost all those who, by luck or by merit, have found themselves to be part of the jamboree of Indian English writing. *Memories of Rain* (an extract from which appears below) is about a broken marriage, about belonging to two cultures, and owes its romanticism and poetry of exile to, via Tagore, Kalidasa's own tribute to the rains in *Meghdoot* (*The Cloud Messenger*). It was warmly received; but her subsequent work has been restricted to only a small circle of admirers. There may be any number of reasons for this, including the problematic, and increasingly complex, nature of Gupta's own writing, writing which divides her audi-ence into either admirers or detractors (sometimes even divides the admirer into surrendering wholeheartedly to certain sections of her work while being resistant to others). To engage with Gupta's writing, however, means that one has to be prepared to engage with the diffi-culties her writing presents, even challenges the reader with. She is a writer who seems to demand two distinct, seemingly irreconcilable, aesthetic responses; it is as if she inhabited two different cultural spaces, or spoke with two voices. On the one hand, she is capable of passages and images of marvellous exactitude and poetic suggestiveness, passages that link her not only to Modernism but to Bengali writers like Bibhuti Bhushan Baner-jee and Jibanananda Das. On the other hand, she can be seemingly fanciful, vague, abstract, melodramatic, tremulous – and these are the 'purple passages', the moments of overwriting, that have made some readers impatient with her work. Yet it is precisely in this dichotomy that the peculiar richness of Gupta's work lies. Gupta's world is a hybrid one; her writing is preternaturally sensitive to the trajectory of individual lives, of migrations across continents, of lower- and middle-class post-Partition Bengali culture; but it is also open to excess, to stereotypes and archetypes, to the vague, intense longings of the feminized, adolescent imagination. These psychological dichotomies mirror the two cultures – Bengali and English – that have shaped, vivified, and also fractured Gupta's sensibility, a sensibility, thus, in which nothing is ever finally resolved.

* * *

from *Memories of Rain* (1992)

She saw, that afternoon, on Oxford Street, a woman crushing ice cream cones with her heels to feed the pigeons. She saw her fish out from a polythene bag a plastic tub that she filled with water for the pigeons, water that they would not be able to drink, for pigeons, her grandmother had told her many years ago, can only quench their thirst by opening their beaks to drops of rain. And she remembered a baby starling that, in the exhilaration of her first English spring, she had reached to hold, her hands sheathed in yellow kitchen gloves, for within her, as her husband had once observed, compassion had always been mingled with disgust.

Even he, the first time she ever set eyes upon him, had disgusted and fascinated her, the dark hairs plastered to his chalk-white legs, for this was in the flood of '78, and he had just waded through knee-deep water, he and her brother, all the way from the Academy of Fine Arts to their house in Ballygunge. He had rolled up his jeans revealing his alabaster calves which dripped the sewage of Calcutta onto the floor of their veranda, and that was what caused her to tremble in excitement and loathing as she pushed aside the curtain with a tray of tea and toast, his large, corpse-white, muck-rinded toes pushed against the bamboo table, soiling the mats she had crocheted in school. She set down the tea, her brother did not bother to introduce her, but Anthony asked, is this your sister? And she had nodded vaguely and smiled, picked up the book that she had been reading all afternoon, there on the veranda, all afternoon, watching the rain. In her room, which she shared with her grandmother, the mouldy smell of a deep, long rain was settling in, compounded by the muddy strokes of the maid, who had picked this unlikely hour to wash the floors. She treaded gingerly across and flung open the shutters, letting in a spray of rain. Her grandmother, coming in with the sewing machine, pleaded with her to shut them, her old bones would freeze, she said, so she drew them in again and switched on the much-despised fluorescent light, and lay with her face towards the damp wall, lulled by the whirr of the sewing machine, and the ever loudening beat of the raindrops, until the lights went out, as they did every night, and every morning – the inevitable power rationing – and she was summoned to take out to her brother and his white friend a kerosene light. And so she appeared to him a second time, lantern-lit, in the damp darkness, a phantom of beauty, and his eyes roamed for a time after she had disappeared inside, the ghost of light that her presence had left, there beside him, in the rain-swollen dark. He saw her again at dinner, candlelit, their first dinner, and she sat well back in the darkness, so that he could only gaze upon the flames that danced upon her delicate fingers, the drapes of her sari that fell upon the formica tabletop, and as they were being served yogurt, the lights came on again, the house sprang into action, the fans whipped up the clammy cold air, the water pump revived, Beethoven resumed on the record player. I'd rather you didn't leave the player on during load shedding, said their father, their grandmother shivered, the rain will go on for a few days now, she said, I can feel it in my bones, those poor villagers.

She noticed he had changed into some clothes of her brother's, the long punjabi shirts that he wore over jeans or loose paijama pantaloons, which together with his thick beard (gnat-infested, I'm sure, she would tease him, a veritable ecosystem, their ornithologist uncle called it) set him apart as a man of letters, reaffirmed his association with an experimental theatre group. Last year her brother had visited her in London, he had been touring in Germany, and he had sat all day in his hideous check jacket which he always kept on, in front of the television, smelling of alcohol, Anthony had had no patience with him, they were glad when he left. And yet, the first evening that he was here, the two of them had sat and argued late into the night, and she had felt again the soggy wind of that first rain-filled evening upon her limbs, as she folded clothes in the laundry room, their voices drifting towards her, the quivering ring of heat around the edges of the iron. Later as she lay upstairs staring through the bedroom curtains at the haze of the streetlights, their voices rose in thin wisps to edge the darkness, as they had done that mouldy evening, when all of Calcutta was one large sea of mud and dung, and floating water-logged Ambassador cars, and children disappeared on their way home from school into open manholes, their covers wrenched off and sold long ago, to drown in the city's choked sewers, on a night like this, he had come to dinner, and been forced to stay, she had been ordered to spread clean sheets on her brother's bed in the living room, which during the day they called the divan, and make one up on the floor for her brother, and so she heard them talk, wide-eyed in the dark of her own bedroom, heard their laughter amid the gentle snores of her grandmother, the vacillating rain. She heard her brother's footsteps, the corridor light came on, she heard him rummaging at his desk, which lay in an alcove in the corridor where, as children, they had kept their toys, the little red tricycle that they rode together on the roof terrace, the silver-haired dolls her aunt sent from Canada. She emerged cautiously from her bedroom to meet his excited eyes.

'You're not asleep yet!' he exclaimed.

'You woke me up,' she retorted, but he brushed by her without a rejoinder, she struggled with the heavy latch on the bathroom door until it slid down suddenly, as it always did, and once within, she stood in the mossy darkness, and heard through the thin walls her brother translating to his English friend a play that he had just finished writing last week, his first (there, he had said to her, a week ago, after an afternoon of furious scribbling, what do you think, do you think your brother will make it as a playwright, tell me, Moni, if this isn't better than most of the crap that they call theatre, and she had put down her Agatha Christie novel to pick up with her calm fingers the foolscap booklet that he had flung on the bed, at her feet), the play was set in rural West Bengal, where, her brother had wanted to show, the peasantry were still as oppressed as they had been the past thousand years under feudalism, you must take me out there, she heard Anthony say, you must acquaint me with rural Bengal, that was what she had heard him say, her cheeks pressed against the damp bathroom walls, on a night of mad thunder and rains that swept away half the peasantry of their land, left them without the mud walls within which they had sheltered their grains, their diseased children, their voracious appetites, and their stubborn ignorance. For she had come to this island, this demi-paradise, from a bizarre and wonderful land, so Anthony's friends called it, was it true, they asked, that they still burn their wives, bury alive their female children? And she would nod numbly, although she had known only of those children that had escaped death, whether deliberate or from disease, those that had been sent out to serve tea in tall grimy glasses in roadside stalls, or to pluck the grey hairs of obese turmeric-stained metropolitan housewives, fill the gentleman's hookah, blow, blow until the green flame gushes, while the mother, helpless domestic, watches silently and trembles. And even these were often graven images, culled

from film and fiction. From such a land Anthony had rescued her, a land
where the rain poured from the skies not to purify the earth, but to spite
it, to churn the parched fields into festering wounds, rinse the choked city
sewers onto the streets, sprinkle the pillows with the nausea of mould, and
yet the poet had pleaded with the deep green shadows of the rain clouds
not to abandon him, the very same poet who wrote,

> You, who stand before my door in this darkness
> Who is it that you seek?
> It has been many years since that spring day, when there came a young
>   wanderer
> And immersed my parched soul in an endless sea of joy;
> Today, I sit in the rain-filled darkness, in my crumbling shack
> A wet wind snuffs my candle, I sit alone, awake;
> Oh, unknown visitor, your song fills me with sweet awe
> I feel I will follow you to the depths of uncharted dark.

But it was not this song, not yet, that ran through her rain-ravaged
mind as the grandfather clock in the living room struck two, interrupting
the awkward flow of her brother's translation, the grammatical mistakes
she shivered at, why was his English so terrible, and she stood in the
bathroom, splashed icy cold water out of the drum onto her feet, she
caught a ghost of herself in the cracked mirror, and a sudden embarrassment overcame her, she switched on the lights and took in the cracked
plaster, the dilapidated water closet, long since choked with lime, suspended over the Turkish toilet, the cracked mirror, the shelf cluttered with
bottles of coconut oil, toothpaste tubes, rusty razor blades, and she
compared it to the bathrooms at Amrita's, where she knew Anthony was
staying, marbled to the ceiling, with Western commodes and bathtubs, he
cannot be used to any of this, she thought, and now as she luxuriated in
the lavender-scented heat of her bath, she would wonder how she had
ever been used to it either. Yet, for many years, that bathroom had been
her only refuge, here she had soaped the corners of her growing body,
watched her breasts bud, shampooed the grime of the city out of her long
black hair, memorized poems with her face to the knife-edged drops of
water from the shower, and that night, before she drew back the latch and
stepped into the corridor, she whispered to herself from Keats's 'Ode on
Melancholy', which they had dissected that afternoon in her Special Paper
class, and saw in her mind's eye Anthony, crushing grapes with his
strenuous tongue against his palate fine: his soul shall taste the sadness of
her might, and be among her cloudy trophies hung.

She was jerked awake in the morning by her mother, it was still raining, the floodwater lapped at the outside walls, but somehow, even in all this, her father had managed to procure a whole chicken on his daily morning excursion to the market. On her way to the bathroom, she glimpsed the sleeping form of her brother, one dark arm grazing the floor, and for once, she shared the indignation of her uncles that it was still her father who went to the market every morning while he slept off his late nights, but let the boy sleep, their father would protest, I go for my morning walk anyway, it doesn't hurt me to stop by the bazaar, besides he is the artistic type, he does not comprehend life's practicalities. So who does the shopping now, who braves the early-morning sun to haggle over fish, fish smeared with goat blood to simulate freshness, you shake the flies from your face and palpate the aubergines, the king prawns are a hundred rupees a kilo today, but nothing is too good for my daughter's wedding, even if she is marrying an Englishman, they will still have it done the traditional way, that was all her father had asked of her. You alone are to blame for the ruin of your children, her uncles would tell him later, you indulged them, and now as you sit paralysed in your grandfather's rocking chair, your son lies sodden with drink at the Press Club and your daughter is lost to you, over the seas.

And yet that rain-laden morning, her mother had allowed her to wander through the living room in her nightdress, which she never would have tolerated if any other friend of her brother's had been asleep on the moist floor, but he, this white man, was too remote to be a threat, there was no need for modesty, and so she looked upon him, as he slept, the dark eyebrows, deep-set eyes, closed now, the sunburned chin, he did not look quite so European as those Germans that had been here last year, he could almost pass for a North Indian, but for that peculiar papery texture of his scorched skin. She brought in tea, and her brother sat up suddenly rubbing his eyes, but Anthony rolled over, turned his face to the wall, and continued to sleep the sleep of the dead, as he would later in the face of her despair, grey mornings through pale curtains, the finality of his striped pyjama back.

'So what should I do with his tea?' she asked her brother.

'Leave it, if he doesn't get up I'll drink it.'

The roar of thunder drowns the faint tinkle of rickshaw bells. Thick wet footsteps on the veranda, an umbrella shaken and opened out to dry, the smell of betel juice drifts through the damp air, her music tutor has arrived, on a morning like this, he picks his muddy way past the white man, glances at him with disgust, she leads him into the bedroom, pulls out the grass mat, all smells are magnified in this grand penetrating wetness. She drags out the harmonium from under the bed, the keys are moist with condensation, the notes slice through the damp air, her brother slams the bathroom door. She pulls out the heavy volume of Tagore songs, opens it to the right page, it is a song of rain that she has been learning these past few weeks, she has almost mastered it, but for a few delicate folds in the final phrases. Her tutor runs a gnarled finger across the lines, who but the poet could have captured the sorrow of the rain so well? he asks, as if she might have dared to suggest otherwise.

And so he woke, a strange chill in his limbs, to the sound of her windy voice, unfamiliar half-tones, words he would never understand,

> in the dense obsession of this deep dark rain
> you tread secret, silent, like the night, past all eyes.

Her voice rises, she is immersed in the words he cannot understand, although they come to him like the wet morning wind:

> the heavy eyelids of dawn are lowered to the futile wail of the winds
> clotted clouds shroud the impenitent sky
> birdless fields
> barred doors upon your desolate path.

He sits up, a weak cup of tea is pushed towards him, her voice rises again,

> oh beloved wanderer, I have flung open my doors to the storm
> do not pass me by like the shadow of a dream.

Many years later, huddled in a deserted tin mine on the Cornish coast, she translated the same song for him, staring into the sheets of rain that ran by like frozen phantoms across the crumbling entrance, and he sat back against the mouldy walls, paying only half heed to her eager, nervous translations, mesmerized instead by the duet of the storm and the sea, until, like the sudden spray, it hit her that he was not listening, he was not listening at all, but they had been rescued, then, by the sudden urge to see their child, the girl left behind at his mother's, was she staring glumly into the rain, her little elbows on the white sill, or was she wrapped up in her grandmother's lap, rocking back and forth to a story, her cold toes digging into the old woman's wrinkled palms. Wedged between two Swedish cars on the Cornish moorland motorway, she had watched the rhythm of her breath as it condensed on the car window, while he had mused of his afternoon with Anna, a curious half-smile flitting across his face from time to time, for he had long come to terms with his infidelity, he implored her silently, ever, to accept it, to reconcile the poetry of his passion for Anna with his deep affection for her and for her child, as he had done, after many evenings of gentle agony, desperately curling the child's hair in his agitated fingers, the unbearable stillness of a rare summer evening, her regular breathing, a child asleep on a summer evening, sun-warmed sheets billowing in the garden. The doorbell rings, she staggers in with the shopping, her face flushed, he holds her in his sad embrace, I will make dinner, you sit down and rest, and as they eat their scrambled eggs, he looks across at her in the dying light, that beloved darkness in the hollows of her eyes, perhaps she was what really held them together, Anna and himself, without her, there would be no substance to their relationship, he remembers a night, drenched with lavender, in the hills of Provence, where, among the olive groves, he had first kissed Anna's warm lips, he remembers his sad exhilaration grappling with an emotion long forgotten, an emotion that is there but in faint wisps, on the winding path back to the rented cottage he is divided between an excruciating guilt and an insane desire to preserve the passion that having climaxed in that one painful kiss seems now to be melting away. In the distance, he can hear Moni singing, she sits by the window, her song drifting towards them with the spiced winds, her foreign lament, was it sad, was it joyful, it was her song that had hypnotized them then, infused them with a gentle sustained lust, that was, perhaps, their doom,

> in this moonlit night, they have all gone wandering in the forest
> in this mad springtime wind, in this moonlit night

for the lush warmth of the South of France had taken her back to moonlit college picnics by broad tropical rivers, the spell of her song webbed across the wide fields

> I will not go into the inebriated spring winds
> I will sit alone, content, in this corner
> I will not go forth into the drunken winds

– the inscrutable elation of the poet, who shall not sip of the wild honey of spring, for he awaits a sterner intoxication, and he must remain watchful, lest those that wander in the forest should choke upon the spring breezes and the moonlight, the poet must remain awake,

> in this moonlit night, they have gone wandering in the forest
> drunk with the young wind of sprintime.

She turns around to face them, dense shadows in the doorway, a shadow shifts and sighs, Anna is beside her, the moonlight fringes her wet lashes, and Anthony moves quietly to her other side, they have surrounded her, for one perfect moment she is an integral part of their passion, they are circled by love. And it had become clear to her, as they picked their way through the gorges of the Ardèche, where the butterflies swirled like pieces of burnt paper, that this was no temporary lust, no flitting desire worked by the lavender breezes and the moonlight, no mild weekend enchantment that he would work off by listening to Mozart all day, these she had grown to tolerate, but here, among the charred butterflies, like a thin stream of blood in her mouth, came the first taste of her long tryst with fear. How would it happen, she wondered, would he seat her down gently, and explain, stroking with a kind hand, her long black hair, his other hand strumming on an airplane ticket, and how could she ever go home, home to the wild grief of her parents, the snickers of the neighbours, her brother's pity, his smugness – but no, how could he be smug, he who turned away his cloudy eyes at the airport, think of what you will miss, Moni, think of what you are giving up, how can you desert us like this, Moni? For he had been so terribly proud of her, her voice, her talents, his friends' roving eyes as she served them tea, her refinement, he had moulded her, told her what to read, how to appreciate it, taken her with him to plays and films, the right films, forbidden her to accompany her girlfriends to the trashy commercial films they all went giggling to see, not that he needed to, she and her group of close friends preferred English films anyway, he would drag her off to the film societies to see French and German films, Russian films, and now, she would surprise a group of Anthony's friends with a shy, yes, I have seen that, amid conversations where her only other contribution was her smile. A moment of silence, all eyes upon her, someone would ask kindly, how did you like it, trying to draw her into the conversation. Anthony would smile encouragingly, and she would voice some simple opinion and if they were in the mood they would try and tease some more out of her, but soon enough a rapid and incomprehensible debate would erupt, and she would get up to make the coffee. She did not mind it this way, indeed this was what she had been used to at home, among her brother's friends, opinionated, enthusiastic, they were terrifying, the stern, beautiful Amrita, the rotund Gayatri who always played the mother with her glorious, deep voice, the men, all in beards, blur in her mind now, she would sit among them, as she did here, now, among Anthony's friends, silent, smiling, absorbing their life, their determination, their warmth. Would she have become like them, like

Amrita, confident and eloquent, had she stayed there? Had she been
arrested in her development, remained the passive, attentive child, by
crossing the seas to an unfamiliar country, where, despite her half-finished
honours degree in English, she could not find the right words, the right
expressions, to voice her opinions, to participate but in the most banal of
conversations, or was she merely passive by nature, content to sit and
listen? Might she have burgeoned, shed the role of the adolescent sister,
nurtured by their admiration, their respect? In the summer months before
Anthony came to Calcutta, they had invited her to sing a few Tagore
songs, offstage, for one of their plays, it was her entrance to their world,
she loved the smoky school hall where they rehearsed in North Calcutta,
she would look out of the tall windows onto the narrow gutter-lined
streets where the little boys played cricket, square-cutting balls into the
gutter, to be fished out gingerly and washed under the burst hydrants, the
mossy courtyards where their mothers waited with glasses of milk that
they gulped and ran out again like a shot to join the game, and then some
gentle hand would fall upon her shoulder, could you sing '*Je ratey moir
duarguli*' for us now? Pull out the off-key harmonium, Ranjan fiddles with
the tabla, knocking about with a hammer, all right then, Polash has the
tape recorder ready, you may begin, Moni,

> On the night that my doors broke with the storm
> How was I to know that you would appear at my door?
> A blackness surrounded me, my light died
> I reached towards the sky, who knows why?

Her voice echoes through the old school hall, which creaks every morning
under hundreds of fidgety feet, identically shod, the sound of fluttering
hymn books, corners that have been creased a century ago by careless
sunburned fingers. Later, when they are all eating lunch, spicy meat in
earthenware containers, with paper-thin *rumali roti*, 'handkerchief bread',
she tries out the old piano, we should have used this rather than that
wretched harmonium, she remarks. Gayatri, swinging her legs from the
stage, asks her to eat something, but she shakes her head, she suspects
that the meat is beef, she knows that they all eat beef, and that the food
has been bought from the Muslim restaurant down the road. Her brother
teases her about her conservative Brahmanic habits, and embarrassed, she
retires to a corner of the vast hall, where behind heavy, dust-smothered
curtains there are worn gym horses, benches and bars, instruments of
torture in the hands of some terrifying gym mistress, her heart floods with
sympathy, and yet she feels detached, she is part of another world.

And now on Oxford Street watching a woman crush ice cream cones to feed the pigeons, she is seized by an overwhelming desire to return to that world, although she knows it is there for her no longer, that the experimental theatre group has long been dissolved, that her brother squanders his meagre journalist's income on alcohol, her mother arranges with her tired hands the disused limbs of her father over the divan in the living room, the divan which used to serve as her brother's bed, the same divan that had been offered to Anthony on that first night of incessant rain. But somehow he had ended up on the floor, perhaps the divan was not long enough to contain his vast frame, and that was where he had woken up to the rain-swollen syllables of her song, buried his face in the clammy pillow to drown his sudden burning desire to smell the rain vapour on her young skin, to run his hands through her moist cloud-black hair, there was a sound of wet feet on the floor beside him, he raised his face from the pillow to find her closing the front door, quietly, so as not to disturb him, and then to check that she had not woken him up, she turned, and so he looked upon her in the leaden morning light, tried to hide his naked desire with a smile, that she did not return, but ran past him, confused, and bumped into her brother, coming out of the bathroom.

'What's the hurry?' he asked her. 'I can't believe that bohonkus of a music teacher made it in this weather.'

'You had better telephone Amrita,' he told Anthony in English, towelling his hair as he came into the living-room. 'I don't think you can go back in this.'

And so he had stayed, shared their midday meal of chicken and rice after showering in death-cold water, and during the thunder-filled afternoon, they had played cards on the living-room floor, two young cousins had turned up, soaked to their waists, grinning proudly, they had walked all the way from Dhakuria, and they had produced from their sodden shoulder bags several packs of cards. They played rummy, until hypnotized by the rain, they drifted off, one by one, into a leaden monsoon slumber, only he and Moni were too conscious of each other to submit to the torpor of the ponderous rain. She brought pillows for them all, and for one painful moment, he was afraid she would leave, but she sat down to finish the game. For a while, a silence between them deepened with the slap of well-worn cards on the cold damp floor, the delicate snores of the two boys, the heavy wheeze of her brother whose oily hair grazed Anthony's toes. She was across from him, leaning against an armchair, her coal-black hair spread out over the chintz seat, lifted high on either arm, a valley of hair. She had wrapped her arms in her sari, faded print flowers pushed against her chin, and from there his eyes travelled up to her overflowing lips, her remarkable eyes under dark brows.

I heard you singing this morning, he said, you have a lovely voice.

He finds out from her that she is in her second year at college, he is strangely pleased that she is studying English, he leans back against the dank pillow and asks her what she likes to read.

Oh, everything, really – poetry, novels. She likes Thomas Hardy and Keats. They are reading Keats, now. 'Ode on Melancholy.'

Boldly, he begins to recite, No, no! go not to Lethe, neither twist wolf's bane, tight-rooted ... heavy words sink between them in the bloated afternoon. She listens with closed eyes, the rain ceases and the room is suddenly flooded with a lime-coloured syrupy light that deepens the shadow of her eyes. He cannot remember the rest of the poem, he asks her, could you translate to me the song you were singing this morning, it sounded so beautiful.

Oh no, she says, my English isn't good enough.

Your English is beautiful.

But she is too embarrassed. She will translate it for him, years later, in a mouldy tin mine on the Cornish coast, while he is lost in the thick swirl of lovemaking recollected, feeding deeply on the fresh memories of a recent afternoon of salt-encrusted passion. And the memories that her songs bring to him now are no longer laced with bitterness, not since he found that he could bring to their bed, in peace, the warmth of another woman. Yet, her silence becomes more and more inscrutable, there is dignity in her silence, in her excruciating grief of her untranslated songs, but does anger froth behind those long stretches of silence? He will hold her for hours in the morning, kiss her sleepless eyes, he wants to ask her if she would like to go home for a visit, her parents have not seen the child yet, but he cannot for fear she will think he is sending her away, she is like a small, soft bird in his arms, he does not dare to attempt to make love to her, he prays that through her songs she will come to appreciate the beauty of their situation, the only thing that can save them now, the intense beauty of their interwoven emotions, the poetry of the half triangle they form, he, Anna, and she, evenings that the three of them spend together, Anna dries while he washes up, and she dishes the remains of their quiet dinner into freezer containers, evenings she must spend alone while he and Anna make violent love in her studio flat, he envisages her sitting in the half-light of dusk, singing, or rocking the child to sleep, images of peace. She had been afraid once, he knew, afraid he would leave her, and he had been afraid too, that he would not be able to sustain his affection for her, but it had not happened, what had seemed inevitable in the valleys of the Ardèche, among the blackened butterflies, for him at least, it had not happened.

Aamer Hussein (b. 1955)

Aamer Hussein was born in Karachi in 1955, and grew up there, in Ooty, in Bombay and in Indore, among the vestiges of a landed Muslim aristocracy forced to redefine itself by history and Partition; it is a world that informs some of his stories, including the one below. He moved to London when he was 15, and has lived there ever since. Hussein studied Persian, Urdu and Indian history at the School of Oriental and African Studies, where he has also taught; for a while he was known more as a critic than as a short story writer, being, as he is, a regular contributor to the *Times Literary Supplement* and various national dailies in Britain. With the publication of two volumes of short stories, *Mirror to the Sun* and *This Other Salt* (published in India as *The Blue Direction*), albeit by small presses, there has been an increasing recognition of the fact that, scattered among the pieces in these books, are a handful of perfectly crafted stories that do honour to the language. Hussein has resisted turning to the novel, while far less gifted writers of fiction have leapt towards it, preferring to hone his skills in a form that is presently unfashionable to British publishers. Writing outside the penumbra of the spotlight, he is, thus, the kind of writer, rare these days, you chance upon and discover yourself; and if there is something these oblique, suggestive, and deceptively intimate fictions say to you directly, upon your having discovered them, it is: 'Yes, there are other things in subcontinental writing in English besides what you normally read'; this leads one to suspect that the reticence and obliqueness might be part of a literary programme more quietly aggressive than one might have believed at first. There is, about his fiction, an air of delicacy, and cosmopolitan finesse that is usually available less to Indian writers in English than to those who belong to the modern vernacular traditions, such as Bengali or Urdu, and to writers like Qurratulain Hyder. Yet in place of Hyder's little-girlish wisdom, we often find, in Hussein, the twilight emotions of our youthfulness; on the one hand, a tender credulity, and on, the other, the harrowings of our very first disillusionments.

* * *

'The Colour of a Loved Person's Eyes' (1990)

My father's laughing eyes changed colour like the leaves. A singer, a dreamer, a hunter, he rode like an arrow shot from the air. In my imagination he had the semblance of an eagle or a hawk; but whereas those predators went in search of food with cruel wing and beak and claw, my father went in search of stories and songs and visions. He enchanted me with anecdotes of his voyages to cities I had never seen, with stories of his hunting trips, with poems in Farsi and in Urdu: he knew every one of the one thousand and one Arabian Nights, every chronicle and lay of the ancient kings of Persia, every ballad by every bard. Often, in the midst of a recitation, he would pause like a thirsty bird in midflight swooping down to a pond, and abandon his account, to lose himself awhile in reverie; then, flight forsaken, he would fold his silken wings around himself leaving me in suspense until he returned to resume his tale, often from the start, and then take wing again.

His absences, though I grew accustomed to them, were for me a source of infinite grief. I rarely saw him, but when he appeared for brief periods, to rest between his trips to the great cities of India and his hunting expeditions, he was always amiable, more like an older brother than a father with his youthful appearance. I can hardly even claim I knew him; he died when he was barely forty and I only fourteen, but I loved him.

*

He had come as a young bridegroom to the mansion where my mother's family had lived for centuries: she was an only daughter, and my father, being the second son of an impoverished scion of the landed gentry, had consented to live in his father-in-law's household, playing the role of his son and heir until I, his third child and first son, was born. It was in his house that I lived until, in the manner of the time, I was sent away to school. It was a vast edifice, like a fortress or a walled city – indeed, it was surrounded by walls. But the many open courtyards and flights leading nowhere, the whitewashed walls and balustrades, the arabesques and tinted windows, all gave it an appearance of ease and light at variance with its vast proportions. I grew up here surrounded by a shifting population of women: my two sisters, somewhat older than I; aunts, cousins, maid-servants, seamstresses.

For playmates I had the children of the weavers and grooms and gardeners who entered the walls in search of employment and were usually not turned away or disappointed. For a few hours a day three tutors came to teach me, to be dismissed more or less as I chose to terminate a lesson.

Perhaps it was the somewhat sequestered nature of this life of mine that made my parents – or rather my mother, since it was she who made these decisions – decide to send me on to better things. This life, she said, was turning me into a useless person, a gentleman of leisure. In those days – it was 1934, and we were fast approaching the last decade of colonial rule – a growing man needed to learn the ways of the rulers of most of India and above all their language in order to deal with them on their own level. Somewhat lower than ours, my mother would have held: after all, we belonged to the India of the princes.

I cannot remember my father's reaction to this debate; if, indeed, he chose the boarding school in the hills above our town to which I would be sent. I think he would have been indifferent; to him, education was something to be acquired during the course of life; beautiful manners, graceful speech and a knowledge of the classics were a privilege of birth never questioned. But I – though I could read the Quran with some fluency – had only the rudiments of such an education. Provincial, as my father would have said, laughing, though he, like I, had a knowledge of English that was barely functional. Now, however, I was to replace the Arabic and Persian, the Urdu and Braj of my ancestors with the rude tongue of our usurpers. It was common practice in my generation for the children of the upper classes to be sent away to such schools at the age of seven or less to learn the foreigners' ways and language; bureaucratic employment as well as law were professions that even the higher echelons of society had come to accept under the influence of the British – though commerce, of course, was still frowned upon. Schools for the children of the rich were established all over India, especially in the hills of both North and South, and most families sent their children away to cold, distant places. But as I have said the school chosen for me was only a few miles above our town, a reputable establishment built within the walls of a fortress, with two precepts in mind: discreet colonization and the safeguarding of feudal dignity. It was not until I went to Aligarh that I was fired by the concepts that would guide me. The sojourn in the fortress-school was difficult; I was taunted for my lack of English, but I rapidly learnt the language in which I now write. The rules of the establishment were severe, almost militaristic; but I was a hardy child and survived, resilient as I was and used to solitude. I did not, however, form any close attachments, though one teacher took great care of my well-being.

During my holidays I found my father – when he was there – a better companion than ever; I was growing up, and was increasingly fond of sport. I could now accompany him on hunting and shooting trips; I could shoot almost as well as he, and he showed pride in my progress, though he took care to let me know, if I shot a stag, or a buzzard or a bear, that he, the superior marksman, had allowed me the opportunity; he would tell me how to improve my aim, demonstrate to me how he, the superior marksman, would have performed. Attributing my own frequent success to luck and an excess of youthful energy, I longed to be like him: elegant, controlled, even in the moment of the shooting and the kill, while I sweated and struggled.

But that fated summer – my fifteenth – my holidays were empty, and I bereft; there was a hole in my life like a fissure in a hunting tent through which the wind blew harsh around my head and the rain poured in. The walls hunted me with hollow echoes; my father's ringing voice was muted now, and his sarod lay in a corner, gathering dust. When my dreaming father died I was sent home for just three days to attend his funeral, to see his face one, final time. There was a hole in his temple: it seemed to me the passage into nightmare. They had neglected to tell me that while cleaning his gun he had shot himself in the head. They said it was an accident.

*

He had been wandering and when he came home from the hunt he found his wife had shut her door with the golden lion lock, shut her door and barred it, and he would never again lie in her bed. One morning at dawn his wife awakened to say her prayers and was performing her ablutions under the cold January sky when she heard an alarming explosion from his room below; she ran downstairs, her white garments in disarray, to find him dead with a hole in his temple and his massive shotgun in his right hand. Two soiled rags lay nearby and a smell of cleaning fluid filled the air. She stood there, silent, rooted to the stone floor like another stone; she did not cry, call out, or move. When she realized that her daughter, home for a while with her husband, was standing beside her, she said, he's dead, though the state of Jafar's face was enough to reveal the manner of his parting. An accident, she said, a mishap with his gun. Her daughter went towards her to embrace her, console her, but the woman like a phantom moved towards the whitewashed walls and broke her red and green bangles against the stone in grief's ritual gesture: God gives and he takes, she said, but she did not weep, did not even seem to feel, and her empty words echoed in the room like a crazed beggar's incantation.

This was the story of the death of Jafar Khan. His sombre widow Ismat Bano – so her oldest daughter told me – changed her bright silks for the white of mourning and issued instructions in a voice of preternatural calm, without once weeping. Her regal bearing became more rigid and her splendour faded; she seemed to grow in stature and in age. A thought, that had always lived within me like a silent enemy or a hidden disease, now attacked, a swift stab in my side: how could my dreaming father ever have loved this severe and hard-faced woman? Where did those poems come from, the lyrics and melodies arranged on his sarod and dedicated to her in the early days of their marriage, when he had taken her with him on his hunts and forays into the ravines? Why did he linger in the shadows, a petty appendage in this aristocratic establishment where his wife took over the reins of management, handling the affairs of her estates, dealing with overseers and debtors with her face unveiled in the manner of a modern city woman? Why did he escape to seek solace in petty infidelities with city trollops?

This woman had borne his children, and, once she had produced the requisite heir, and her father had died content, had been a wife to Jafar only in name. Had I ever seen him laughing with her, like my sisters laughed with their husbands? When had I ever seen him leave her room in the morning or ascend the open staircase to her in the evening to the summer terrace where she slept under the sky in the breeze heavy with jasmine and night-blossoms? Never. She had never been a companion to him. There must have been another love that inspired the longing poems he wrote. I could not share my sorrow or my mourning with my mother. Unable to turn to her, I turned away from her for ever. When I arrived from my school for my holidays, she would stiffly kiss me, and I stiffly accept her kiss. Is there anything you need? she would ask. No, thank you, I would respond, I have everything I need, and we would part: she to her various occupations, her duties and her charities, and I to my dreams, spending hours in the lower wing where my father had lived, looking through his books and his manuscripts and reconstructing from his beautiful calligraphy the life of his mind.

*

The princess is dressed in crimson, her hooded falcon on her wrist. She has reined in her white stallion to look at her companion, a beardless youth dressed in green. She is looking at him with a dry season's longing in her eyes. He is looking at the sky.

In the distance the blue of the sky melts into the clear waters of the Jamuna. In the lower left-hand corner the artist has inscribed in gold letters the following couplet:

> *and our living longings breathe*
> *and our dead longings cry*

Underneath the simple verse is the signature of the artist, who is the probable author of these words: Makhfi, The Hidden One.

The Hidden One was the pen-name of the princess Zebunnissa, Aurangzeb's incarcerated daughter and a gifted poet; but the couplet is not hers, and the miniature does not date from Mughal times. It is a modern pastiche, and Makhfi the style given to Ismat by Jafar in allusion to her epigrammatic talent which he once said outshone his.

I came across the signed miniature years later, marked with a handful of flowers, in an album of poems and pictures Ismat and my father had compiled. My mother had died some years ago, and I had left the old house to my sister and her family. I do not know what compelled me to dwell on this picture in particular; I knew my mother was an exquisite copyist, but there was something in this picture that far exceeded the skill of a mere imitation however proficient, some wild yearning concealed in the mannered strokes of the miniaturist's brush. The colours had, over the years, gained in intensity: the pellucid blue she had chosen was particularly striking. While painting the sky and the landscape and the distant sleeping river, she had engraved her vision in every stroke – this was our region, our province, our colours, the land she had known all her life and loved with the passion of her aristocratic ancestors and of the peasants who had often slept between their sheets. And the eyes of the nobleman in the picture were connected to the sky, to clear air and running water, by their cerulean colour and their gaze, just as the princess's eyes were connected to his face, and Ismat had bathed the scene in the colour of a loved person's eyes.

*

What was it, then, that drove these two apart: Jafar to his actresses and Ismat to the relentless categorization and cataloguing of her assets? Jafar, on his rare trips home, seemed to find solace only in his music, playing mournful ragas morning and evening on his *sarod* until that morning when he died as impetuously as he had lived.

And Ismat, enclosed within her walls, continued convoluted negotiations with her male staff, discarded her veil in her mid-thirties and shocked the town with her views on politics and progress, treating her husband as an outworn luxury tolerated for the sake of the past and because he was the father of her son. His death hardly seemed to affect her; he had become an absence in his lifetime, and his absence echoed the departure of the daughters, shy, laughing creatures with an overdrawn tendency to humility entirely contrary to their mother's fiery principles.

And I, the only son, who had absorbed instead of mother's milk – I had been fed at the breast of a peasant wet-nurse – the principles of the house of Ismat Bano, knew that I must make my mark on the real world of society and anti-colonial politics. As I did, only to leave behind me the haunted house of my ancestors, to find my life in Pakistan, wondering what my father would have made of his son's defection. Of my mother's reaction I can only say that she blessed me when I left with the conventional prayers of benediction, refusing to commit herself to approval or disapprobation; divided within herself, perhaps, as she looked across the border to the new nation promised by the political dreams of her Muslim brothers, and yet bound for ever to those acres of land in which her ancestors' blood mingled with the blood of their enemies, where their perspiration had nurtured the growth of the crops along with the sweat of the peasants they had exploited but also sworn to love. And I left that land where she now lies buried near her father and Jafar Khan.

What would she say now to her son, the fierce intransigent woman who died withholding the truth of her dead love even from the daughters she cherished? Could she explain to me the phantom of that dead love that roamed the corridors of the house in the years of my father's death? Would she approve of my successful career as a discreet diplomat, of the compromises I made to keep faith with my promise to a nation, of the slim volumes of verse I have irregularly produced, careful always to inscribe the mellow notes of universal humanism and eschew direct comment on the bitter crops yielded by our own beloved fields of Pakistan? I cannot say; I cannot even say that the woman I came to know through the few memories she left in the form of her scattered verses, her palimpsest miniatures, and the first women's educational establishment in our province founded by her and renamed in her honour after her death, I cannot say that this woman was a real reflection of the woman I had veiled in silence and blame. But I go ahead of my story. When I return to the past, to those years of silence and directionless recrimination, it is my dreaming father's voice I remember, echoing and ringing around me in the hollow walls, leading me to the choice I made to abandon my ancestral world of privilege and position, in some impotent attempt to vindicate the unlived life of Jafar Khan.

*

It was 1941, I think. I was seventeen. It was early summer and a heavy heat hung over our town, with portents of a dust storm and a longing for rain in the air. The weather was unbearable and our great white house was curtained with screens of perfumed straw to cool the oppressive interiors. We were faint with exhaustion from the heat; and I was restless, possessed by my father's restlessness, unable to be by myself or with his memory. I took his jeep and drove out slowly to the ravine where often we had hunted deer together. It was a wild place, on the edge of the jungle, bordered by a lake so close to the sky that in my childhood fancies it would summon up for me the sea that I had never seen. When the winds blew hard in the rainy months of Sawan and Bhadon, the water broke against the pebbles in white waves which I imagined played the sea's music. Deer came to this open, quiet place, to graze around the water; they were tame here, or nearly so. I would never kill a doe or a yearling; it seemed delinquent, and my father had reprimanded me for weeping once when he had shot a fawn. Often, by twilight, we heard peacocks loudly crying, and once or twice we saw one spread his fan and dance. My father would say that they danced when it was about to rain, and even though I had learned at school that the peacock's dance was a ritual of courtship to attract a mate, I did not contradict him – he was master here, and his word law. Once, as if to prove him right, there was a sudden storm and before we had the chance to draw the shelter over our heads, we saw a peacock fly through the air, alight on a grassy mound, and perform – for us, for the sky, for the approaching night. Perhaps he had not found shelter from the rain – but then again the birds had another accord entirely with the elements, lost to us mortal creatures who depended on roofs and fire, on wood and coal.

And then the sky fell: it began to rain as I parked the jeep by the shore of the lake, and the herons that had continued to paddle there beneath the first shower flew away when it turned into a torrent. I went out into the rain, washing away my grief, watching the colours of the water change: the sky's grey become nearly black, the leaf-green, so dark it seemed poisoned, battle with the gaudy flying colour of a parrot flock which took wing in unison, disturbed by my roaring engine. In the first moments of the storm the rain carried in it all the colours of herons and parrots and flamingos, the grey and green and black, the white and the offended pink. I wished my father were there to sail with me at random on a boat as we had often done, renting one for a rupee or two from a waterman. As the sky burst its tight skin I had to shelter in my jeep again: I sat there for what seemed an aeon, trying desperately to remember the verses of a poem he had written or loved. I had never acquired the art of reciting classical verse; even now, I shrink from reciting in public, and my laconic free verse and offhand declamatory manner is considered an affectation by my critics. Then the lines of an Urdu ghazal, by the master Mirza Ghalib, came to me:

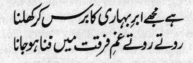

I repeated them to the rain, savouring the resonance of my clumsy recitation. I had never heard a grown man weeping, much less these dry, anguished sobs that seemed to come from elsewhere, tearing from my ribcage a sensation akin to retching. You have drunk his eyes, I called to the rain, and to the churning water, you are drunk on the colour of his eyes. Come back, Jafar, or I will never forgive you. Come back, said the lake, and the rain said, forgive you, forgive you.

How long I sat there I cannot say: the torrent abated and the air began to chill as it does in the wilderness even in the summer. Darkness began to fall upon me and upon the trees. I was not afraid to drive at night and even carried a gas lantern in the back of the jeep, but I was aware that the route home would take me through heavily wooded land, dangerous to traverse after a storm. There were no signposts and I might easily lose my way. Rumours of dacoits were as rife as dry grass and cows in our region. People said that my father had been friendly with the outlaws, and when he drove their way they would come out smiling and offer him a drink of their liquor, some sugar cane juice, curds, bread. I was afraid now; not of dacoits or of darkness or of rain, but of my own solitude. And yet, in grief, this was the only place to which I could lay claim, that laid claim to me.

I must have slept as I sat there in the darkness. And then some sound – a flying bird perhaps, or the harsh song of the cicadas – awakened me. As I opened my eyes, it seemed to me that the edges of the trees and the lake, and the sky, too, had caught fire; or that a gang of travelling outlaws was moving through the jungle with candles held aloft in the night. And then, as I turned down the shelter, feeling the dampness in the air, of dew now, not of rain, I was no longer afraid. One by one the lights moved towards me, around me, and I remembered how once I had fallen asleep against my father's shoulder and awoken, in this very place, to just such a sight: I had never seen fireflies before. On the way back to town he was telling me some tale when I asked him, Where do fireflies go in the morning, Father?

And he replied, Son, they only burn for a night.

*

The discovery of my mother's vision brought back to me the colours of a buried grief; I had long been locked in the traps of living, and interred all thoughts of my father's death and my mother's long silence. I had left the old country for the new and, in that first eventful decade, we were still optimistic; though we tried in every way to recreate the traditions of our forsaken homeland on the rougher terrain of the new country, we had made our choice – and land, privilege and heritage were only notions now, dull reflections of a reality for ever and wilfully abandoned.

Coming back to the place of my birth after so many years, I had tried to suppress my feelings of loss – only to be faced by the phantom of a mother I had never known. A dreamer, a poet, who had left behind this vision for an uncomprehending son, marked with a handful of dried flowers – *and our living longings breathe, and our dead longings cry*. She had lost three men – one to death, one to life, and me, her son, she had relinquished at birth, fulfilling a pattern etched by someone else, in some other time. I went through her writings, her journals, all exquisitely maintained in her graceful hand – but aside from these lines and the coded missive of her miniature, there was no other message.

And yet, what more could she have left? I saw her features superimposed on those of the princess; this is how she saw him, I thought, this is how she saw herself. Her love for my father, her grief at his defection, permeated the couplet. But another, more abiding link bound me to her over the years and the distances of two deaths; I saw, in the landscape she had painted, a vision not of the Jamuna, but of that lake where I had wept for my father. Perhaps the shadows of their love still played there, and had beckoned to me; I will never know.

Her gift to me, I thought, was greater than a secret revealed. For in the painted blue of the water and the sky, she had recaptured for me that moment when I had been bathed, on that rainy evening, in the lost colours of a dreamer's eyes, those laughing eyes that she had touched.

Ashok Banker (b. 1964)

Ashok Banker was born in Bombay, was educated there, and worked for a long time as a very successful copywriter before, presumably encouraged and impelled by the newly flourishing phenomenon of Indian writing in English, tried his hand at a genre that is still relatively uncommon in this body of writing, the detective novel. He produced three in quick succession, and then wrote a novel, *Vertigo*, which was something of a critical and certainly a commercial success; in spite of this, the book was allowed to go out of print, because Banker moved to a new publisher for his next novel. Banker is now a full-time writer, but has not really produced anything noteworthy since *Vertigo*; more novels have appeared, and he has been engaged in exhausting amounts of hack-writing for a number of newspapers and for the internet, and has been writing the script for the only English-language soap opera on Indian television. He is the only person in this volume who would not be recognised by his contemporaries as a serious "literary" writer. Yet *Vertigo*, from which an extract is included below, is a genuine addition to Indian English writing; it seems to be entirely forgotten for a number of reasons, among which the most important are probably that it is out of print, that it was never published in the West and therefore lacked its crucial approbation, and that Banker appears to lack proper literary and intellectual credentials. *Vertigo*, however, gives us a portrait of Bombay that has hardly, if ever, been written about. It is a Bombay in the first light of economic deregulation and liberalization; and it is about the 'great American dream', of the pursuit of happiness, material wealth, and capital, as it is dreamt in Bombay, and also the dark underside of that dream, dreamt as it is not only by the powerful, but by nobodies and minor players. The protagonist, Jay, is one such minor player; the novel is frankly autobiographical; it tells the story of a young copywriter, who comes from a dysfunctional family, his father a rich Gujarati businessman, his mother, abandoned by his father, and with whom Jay lives, an unforgettable character, a Goan Christian schizophrenic and alcoholic. Jay, too, is a repository of the huge material ambition and romantic desires this city nourishes, then kills; the buoyant scenes of office life have an ironical innocence. One thing that the novel clarifies powerfully is that the so-called 'English-speaking elite' in India is a mythic construct; that it is composed both of the powerful and the happy, and also of the thousands who catch their crowded local trains in the morning, listen to rock music, read novels, and struggle to stay in their jobs, those who have no backing or capital except the English language and the doubtful possibilities possessing it seems to offer.

* * *

from *Vertigo* (1993)

In the second half of 1984, as elections approach, two major changes take place in the country. One is the setting up of television transmission stations across the length and breadth of the subcontinent. Indira-bashers claim this is the iron woman's means of ensuring a massive self-publicity blitz since Doordarshan is more a Government spokesperson than a television network. Perhaps it is. But the fact is that by seeking her own aggrandizement through the nascent power of the boob tube, Mrs G also succeeds in spearheading the most incredible media expansion in the history of the world. Never before have so many LPGs, HPGs, et cetera sprung up at such a rapid rate anywhere on the planet. An observer looking down from a suitable vantage spot in orbit – from the ill-fated Skylab had it endured perhaps – would gawk at the proliferation of aluminium aerials across the rooftops of the subcontinent.

This immense propaganda juggernaut has already sprung into action by September '84. It opens up a world of opportunties – or so everybody thinks – for prospective film-wallahs and hopeful film strugglers everywhere. It will be some time before this dream is turned to cynical disgust by Doordarshan's bureaucratic inefficiency, pathetic programming and cantankerous corruption.

The second revolution that takes place is not in the homes of India, but on the roads. These potholed obstacle courses are honoured with the appearance of the country's first 'people's car'. Maruti is the dreamchild of Sanjay Gandhi, the late son of Mrs G, who had dreamed of producing a car which almost every middle-class Indian could afford. It's ironic that when the 'people's car' finally appears on the roads in '84, it costs more than the price of a modest flat in the far suburbs; or that there is a substantial premium charged by middlemen for early delivery. Despite this, the little

Suzuki-designed 8-cylinder *'khilona'** (as Ambassador owners call it deri-sively) is snapped up by the thousands, and soon, by the tens of thousands. The most remarkable thing that Maruti achieves is not the bringing of automobiles within everyone's reach – far from it – but the igniting of an explosive boom in the automobile industry and its allied industries. Before Maruti, the total annual production of all makes of cars in the country never exceeded a total figure of 50,000 cars. A year after Maruti's appear-ance, the industry's total production climbs to 75,000 cars annually. Three years after its inception, Maruti Udyog Ltd alone is rolling out 80,000 vehicles. Less than five years since that fateful launch, this one new company is producing twice as many cars as all the other manufacturers put together – against their total record of a combined 43 years in the business. A revolution on wheels has taken place.

Maruti's initial vehicles are manufactured under close supervision by Suzuki technicians. Suzuki's high standards of quality infect the whole industry. Peripheral manufacturers fight to acquire prestigious Maruti OEM status, or, at the very least, to offer Maruti-standard spares and peripherals. Several of these firms grow rich overnight. Along with them, their own suppliers also grow. Among the many suppliers to these OEMs are companies manufacturing metal dies and casts; forging companies.

The company that Conrad had chosen to invest Jay's money in was a forging company.

As the acceptance of Maruti's unqualified success spreads through the industry, futures of every company that produces any product that might someday find its way into a Maruti vehicle soar through the roof. Stock market investors run their stubby fingers down rows of names of listed companies, ticking off possible goldmines. Enforge Ltd is one of those which find a little tick beside its name.

In August '84, Enforge Ltd secures a Letter of Intent to supply several crores worth of vital dies and forgings to an important Maruti OEM.

Its share price, which has hovered between 17 and 21 over the last year or so since its equity issue, leaps to Rs 36 for a Rs 10 share by Indepen-dence Day, 15th August, 1984. By the 29th of the same month, Jay's mother's birthday, it has risen inexorably to Rs 50. And by September 30, it has touched the unbelievable figure of Rs 94. Then, for a week, it dips to Rs 67 and threatens to go lower, when rumours spread that Mrs G is contemplating declaring another Emergency on the eve of the elections. But when the rumour is discovered to be false and preparations for the

---

*   Editor's note: Hindu for 'toy'.

elections are seen to proceed beyond a point of no return, Enforge rises confidently again, cresting the magic peak of Rs 100, and finally pausing reluctantly at Rs 125 a share.

Jay has Rs 25,000 worth of Enforge shares, bought at the appetizingly low price of Rs 16 a share. This meant he had bought 1,562 shares. By October 18, these are worth 7.8 times the value Jay had bought them for; this translates into a total rupee value of Rs 1,95,250, or in words: Rupees One Lakh, Ninety-Five Thousand Two Hundred and Fifty Only. Jay's Rs 25,000 has grown to almost Rs 2 lakhs in less than six months. This apparent miracle is nothing more than the third revolution of the eighties that sweeps India by storm: The Stock Market Boom.

He sits down on the toilet seat of the Non-Management Gents Toilet in office and buries his face in his hands. He laughs a little, cries a little, does both at the same time, likes it, does it some more, and then stares at the white tiled floor for twenty minutes almost without blinking.

'Now what?' he asks Conrad. They are sitting in Conrad's cubicle, chairs drawn up close to the desk. Conrad jiggles his legs while thinking. Occasionally his left knee bumps Jay's right thigh.

Conrad spreads his hands. 'We celebrate.'

'I mean, about the shares. What do we do now?'

'What's to do? They're doing it all for us. We're rich, man!' Conrad tosses a 555 at Jay. Jay fumbles it and almost drops it, puts in his mouth and lets Conrad light it. He puffs nervously, unable to get satisfction from such a mild cigarette. 'No, I mean, shouldn't we sell? While it's up? Before it goes down, I mean? Shouldn't we? What do you think?'

'Are you nuts?'

'Why?'

'You don't fool with a thing like this. It's magic, pal. You don't fuck around with magic. Just let it happen and keep your hands ready.' Conrad makes a cupping motion with his palms, like a man waiting for manna to fall from the skies.

Jay thinks a bit. He's surprised to find that the 555 is finished. He presses the smouldering filter in the ashtray and takes another one. 'I don't know.'

'What? What do you want? You want to have your cake and eat it too?'

'Maybe—' Jay hesitates, afraid of Conrad's laugh. Conrad has a terrible laugh. Everybody turns and looks this way when Conrad laughs. Once a new Product Manager, Sreenivasan, came out of his cabin to find out who was dying: it was only Conrad laughing at one of his own jokes. 'Maybe we should sell them, cash in, you know, I mean,' voicing the thought that has been nagging him ever since the initial euphoria lessened enough to allow him to think, 'what good are they unless we sell them, right? I mean, what if they drop again? It'll all be down the drain, won't it?'

Conrad shakes his head sadly. 'Poor Jay-bird. Poor birdie. Scared, baby? Scared of your shares crashing?'

'Come on, Conrad. Think about it. Maybe we should sell now and get out while we're ahead. After all—'

'They'll cross Rs 200,' Conrad says. 'After the elections, when Mrs G comes back into power. Maybe even Rs 250. Bluechip in the making.' He crosses himself and knocks on the desk as he says this, lifting the little silver crucifix from around his neck and kissing it.

'But what if Mrs G doesn't come back? The Opposition may not support Maruti Udyog because they know it was her idea, her sentimental tribute to Sanjay's memory. What if—'

Conrad is grinning at him. 'Fuck off,' he says loudly, 'fuck off, pal.'

'Conrad, think about it.'

'Look, I'll tell you what I think. I think we should hold on to this paper' – he taps the share certificates in a plastic folder on his desk – 'until they touch Rs 200 at least. Then we can think about selling part of the portfolio – if, and only if – there's a better investment. That's what I think and that's what I'm going to do, OK? Now, you have the right to do what you please with your shares. You can take them into the loo and use them for toilet paper for all I care. That's your problem, buddy.'

Jay bites his lip. Conrad sweeps his shares into a drawer, slams the drawer shut and stands up. 'Coming for lunch? I'm going to have a few beers and celebrate.'

'Uh, I don't like to drink during the day. It gives me a headache.'

'Come on, man. Loosen your asshole. You just made an 800 per cent profit. Can you beat it? What are you crying for?' Conrad punches Jay playfully in the stomach.

'I don't know,' Jay says anxiously. 'What about tax?'

'Jay, that's wonderful. Are you serious? Wow!'

'Yes, yes, but what do you think, Tuli? I mean, don't you think it's risky keeping them any longer?'

'Oh, Jay. Now we can buy a flat of our own!'

'For two lakhs? Where?'

'At Bandra at least?'

'Are you joking? Do you know what the rate is at Bandra? Do you know what Mama's flat is worth?'

'Not a big flat. Maybe just a one bedroom hall.'

'Tuli, even a one bedroom hall will cost something like fifteen lakhs in a good area.'

'Really? I don't think so.'

'There's nothing to think. That's the going rate. Nothing less than Rs 2,500 a square foot, in a good area.'

'Anyway, there's no harm in looking, is there?'

'The second thing is, we don't have the money in hand, which is the point I've been trying to make but nobody seems to understand. The shares may be worth 2 lakhs, but we have to sell them to get the money.'

'What if we just look around a bit and if we find a place we like we can think of selling them off. Oh, Jay this is terrific. Let's celebrate!'

'But, Tuli, these damn shares may be worth nothing tomorrow for all we know. Besides, I don't have the money to celebrate with, you know. I'm still the same broke Jay Mehta, remember? All I have is some very expensive paper. Not money.'

'Jay, you're such a pessimist.'

'I'm practical. An idealist, yes, but a practical one. Say, that's nice. Practical idealist. That's me.'

'Anyway, is Saturday's lunch fixed?'

'With Araldite. Come over to office, we'll go to Purohit's together. Daddy and Dadiji will meet us there directly.'

'Jay, remember that bedroom set we saw in Benzer? The one with the mirror-work?'

'The one that costs fifty thousand bucks? Are you crazy?'

'Come on, we have the money.'

'I keep telling you. Doesn't anybody understand me? I don't have the money. All I have is fifteen hundred to manage till the end of the month, which is twenty-five days away.'

'Don't be mean.'

'I'm not – yeah? OK, tell him I'll be right there. Tuli, I have to go, Dave's calling us. See you Saturday, love. One sharp, OK?'

'The bedroom set, la-la-la-la!'

The next day, terrorists kill thirty-five people in Punjab, including three candidates for the forthcoming Lok Sabha elections. The stock market index slumps. Enforge's share price drops to Rs 117 by close of trading.

Conrad laughs away Jay's I-told-you look and repeats his confident assurance that the price will top Rs 200 by the elections.

But on Wednesday and Thursday, the price continues to plummet.

On Thursday evening, Jay panics and prevails on Conrad to call their broker and give him orders to sell. Conrad spends half an hour trying to persuade Jay, but he's adamant. Finally, Conrad picks up the phone in disgust and tells Chagganbhai to sell ten lots of Jay's Enforge shares at the current price of Rs 98 per share. Even the broker says its stupid to sell at this point. Jay prevails over all arguments. He can be stubborn when he's convinced what he's doing is right. He signs the required transfer forms and sends them to Chagganbhai the next morning. By that time, he is of a mind to sell the remaining 562 shares too but Tuli gets so upset when she hears of the sale that for her sake he relents and lets them stay. Conrad lets his investment – close to sixty thousand rupees initial capital in Enforge alone – stay. He passes biting comments on Jay's lack of 'balls' in the conference room while they are waiting for the ad agency to arrive with their storyboards for the launch commercial for Chamatkar. Jay has grown used to Conrad's witticisms. They bother him less and less as time goes by.

The day after Jay sells off the ten lots of Enforge shares, he and Tuli enter Purohit's Restaurant near Churchgate Station and find his father and grandmother sitting at a table, waiting. His grandmother's wizened round face cracks into a wide smile as she sees Tuli. She looks her up and down minutely, examining her clothes – a beige silk sari – and her looks. She evidently likes what she sees because she rises and lifts her hand in a gesture of blessing. Tuli, an orthodox Gujarati girl for all her convent education, bends unhesitatingly and touches first Jay's grandmother's feet and then his father's feet. Both pat her on the head and sit down again, exchanging an apparently expressionless glance which Jay knows to be more eloquent than Indira Gandhi's election speech.

They sit silently as the waiter lays down the inevitable steel thalis before each one. His grandmother mutters something to his father in Gujarati. Tuli shoots a sharp look at Jay, then lowers her eyes in keeping with her demure Gujarati bride-to-be image. Jay doesn't understand what was said but he can't help noticing that both his grandmother and father looked pointedly at Tuli's lower body for a moment. Only, he thinks they're looking at her sari, and he doesn't give it much attention. The waiter returns with his portable buffet and Jay's grandmother authoritatively supervises the feeding of her grandson and prospective daughter-in-law. Jay doesn't even bother to protest this time, but he promises himself that once they're married he will make sure that Tuli never cooks Gujarati food.

The lunch goes as well as can be expected. Tuli is a hit. Both his father and grandmother approve of her. Afterwards, he learns from Tuli that the muttered comment concerned the boyish slimness of her hips which was perceived as being not-ideal for childbearing.

Cows are treated better than women in India. And youth is regarded as an inferior state in a land where crabbed age and and silver locks are symbols of wisdom and authority. Jay tells himself he is lucky that he and Tuli happen to be of the same community and caste; their sub-castes and gotras don't match, but that ought to be possible to overlook after consideration of factors such as the parallel status of both families. He leaves Tuli to a cab and takes another cab back to office. Another painful inch of progress. Perhaps they will marry after all. He tries not to think of the all too likely possibility of Tuli's father summarily dismissing the proposal – especially in view of the fact that it is normally the girl's people who approach the boy's not vice versa as will happen in his case; this fact alone is bound to make the Jhaveris suspicious. If they suspect or learn that he and Tuli have actually been seeing each other for over four years, that itself could mark disaster. On the other hand, if they were to learn that she had already been 'polluted' by him, then it would surely guarantee a quick marriage; though not one that Tuli desires. 'Yes. Mr Jhaveri, I slept with your daughter,' he says softly to himself, looking out the window at the unseasonal October drizzle.

That day and the next he receives two surprises. One is seated on the couch in the reception when he returns from the Purohit lunch.

'Jay? Hi, man.'

Jay stops and stares at this apparition from the past. 'Mittal?'

They shake hands, grinning happily. Jay feels like he has aged five years in as many seconds. Just the sight of Mittal rolls back layer after layer of dusty memories. Can it be just one and a half years ago that he last met this man? Impossible!

'So what's happening? How's Chris?'

'Same, man. You know.'

'Is he still sowing his wild oats?' Jay glances at Suchitra as he says this, keeping his voice low but inflected with a touch of lightness. Mittal laughs: an abrupt coughing laugh.

'Same, man. Never change.'

'So what brings you here? Thinking of joining Synergetics?' As he says this, Jay is surprised to detect a hint of superior-than-thou in his own tone. Without knowing it, he has assimilated the puffed-up pride that infects this megahype multinational culture. It seems to him that his new soft-leather shoes look more sophisticated and elegant than Mittal's patent leather lace-ups. Then the shirts: he has on a Zodiac pinstriped formal while Mittal's is a tailor-stitched one with too-large too-dark *horizontal* stripes. Lastly, Jay's trousers are narrower and more elegantly fashionable than Mittals' wide-bottomed ones. Jay is glad he let Tuli talk him into spending Rs 780 of that money left over from the Rs 5,000 to buy this new set of clothes, and that he happens to be wearing it today. He is also sharply aware of all the hours of multinational brainwashing – the seminars and talks by visiting foreigners from the parent company, the exposure to international marketing and management information; systems, case histories, et al – and of how all this has created a gap between him and Mittal. All this passes through his mind as a series of emotional rather than logical impulses, little neuronic pulses of pleasurable realization, in the space of a few seconds. He does not understand it fully until several days later; but meeting Mittal makes him more aware of himself, of the new improved Jay, and of the direction in which he is now travelling.

'No, man. Where am I, where are you,' Mittal says in confirmation of his feelings of superiority. Mittal gestures around the reception lounge which Jay realizes – he's like a man with new eyes – is truly distinguished in contrast with DM's ostentatiously gauche decor: 'Big time, eh?'

Jay shrugs, grinning happily, letting the compliment settle comfortably on his shoulders. Dave and Sreenivasan stroll in, back from lunch. Dave is dressed in his usual suit with suspenders, missing only a hat to qualify him for Best Imitation Of A Western Manager; Sreenivasan sports a well-cut expensive suit over his gaunt but seasoned frame. Both look like portraits from a Business India feature. Both nod at Jay as they pass, casting a brief glance at his companion, and walk past. Dave pauses, turns and walks back to Jay: 'I say, Jayesh, about those storyboard changes. Did you brief the agency? They were waiting to start shooting the commercial tomorrow, you know. And we are spending eighty bloody lakhs on that accursed thing.'

'I did it first thing this morning, Dave. Arvind said he'd get back to us after the producer confirms whether he's shooting in Famous as planned or some other studio.'

Dave nods curtly and walks away without another word.

Jay turns back to Mittal, whose eyebrows are raised very slightly. 'Dave Rai. My superior.'

'MD?'

'No, no. Product Manager. But very senior. A martinet to work for. But brilliant marketing mind. One of the best.'

Mittal nods.

'So what brings you here, Mittal? Business or pleasure?'

Mittal looks down at his hands. 'Jay, I want a change.'

'You're leaving DM?'

'Want to.'

'Where are you going?'

'I don't know.' After a pause: 'Any vacancies?'

'What? Here? Oh ... well, I don't have any idea. This place is like a battleship. I don't think I've even met everybody here yet.' He laughs self-deprecatingly. Suchitra happens to be looking at him just then and she flashes one of her dazzling white smiles.

Mittal nods. Jay takes a pack of Benson & Hedges from his pocket and offers it to Mittal. He only bought three, but that was how many there were left in the 'loose' pack the *paan*-wallah had, so he got the handsome gold and white box too. What is it admen say about cigarettes? You can sell beedis for ten rupees a dozen if you put them in gold packs and create slick advertising to promote them? Mittal declines. 'Don't smoke.'

Jay lights the cigarette with the slim gold and black lighter he bought second-hand outside Andheri station a few days ago. He allows it to catch the light, clicks it shut and places it on the gold pack on the table, smoking the cigarette slowly and casually.

'How's your mother?'

The question shakes him.

Like a bolt of Rin lightning, it streaks across the dark blue surface of his gloating superiority and strikes right at the heart of his most vulnerable root. In the same flash it occurs to him that Mittal must have been present in office on the day his mother arrived drunk, semi-nude, and proceeded to create an absusive, violent, destructive spectacle which ended in her arrest and his getting sacked. He swallows. The cigarette loses its flavour, if it ever had any to begin with, and he stubs it out half-smoked, wasting 30 pice of B & H and not caring. 'Oh, fine, fine,' he says noncommittally. He remembers that he never did go to see her last Sunday as he'd intended to. A cold bead of sweat forms on his right temple: his palms and the soles of his feet grow damp.

Mittal nods. 'I was the one.'

'Uh?'

'That day?'

Jay knows which day he means but can't bring himself to admit it. 'When?'

'You know. The trouble.'

'Uh-uh.'

'I was the one who convinced Chris not to press charges against her. He wanted to file a criminal charge.'

Jay swallows again. His throat is very dry. The sweet-sour flavour of *shrikhand* lingers in his mouth. He looks at the clock on the wall behind Suchitra. 'I see.'

Mittal shrugs. Jay waits, but he doesn't say anything else. 'I see,' Jay repeats numbly. Then, several seconds too late: 'That was ... very nice of you. Uh ...' swallowing, 'thanks.'

Mittal waves away gratitude and compliments. He makes a show of looking at his watch. 'You must be having a lot of work.' He gets up, offering Jay his hand. Jay doesn't notice the hand; Mittal lowers the hand. Then Jay realizes he was just offered a handshake and puts out his hand, but by then Mittal has already started around the coffee table. 'So,' he says at the doorway, 'in case there's anything, any vacancy, let me know. I'll give you a call sometime?'

'Oh, sure. Sure.' Jay fumbles in the pocket of his Zodiac shirt and fishes out a visiting card. 'Anytime.'

Mittal puts the card in his pocket without looking at it. 'By the way, your old girlfriend is in town.'

Jay blinks several times. 'Yes, of course. I just had lunch with her.' He adds belatedly: 'You mean Tuli, don't you?'

Mittal grins wryly. 'Meera.'

'Oh. Oh.'

'She was asking about you. I said I was planning to drop and say hi to you one of these days. She said she might call you.' He makes a circle with his forefinger and thumb and gestures with it: 'Solid one, man.'

Jay smiles weakly. He doesn't know what to say. 'We had lunch together a couple of times,' he tries.

Mittal smiles inscrutably.

But when Jay comes into office the next day at 11.30 – after stopping en route at the ad agency – he finds enough good news waiting on his desk to wipe out all unpleasant and embarrassing old memories. This second surprise is a cheque for Rs 94,502 from Chagganbhai, the payment for the ten lots he asked him to sell the day before. Rupees Ninety-Four Thousand Five Hundred and Two Only, Payees Account only, Jayesh Mehta. Tolstoy,

Dostoevsky, Henry James, Conrad, Austen or George Eliot never wrote more exciting words. He sits down, his entire body numb with excitement, his eyes unable to focus clearly.

'Oh God oh God oh God oh God,' he whispers almost inaudibly, over and over again.

It takes him three misdialled numbers before he calms down enough to dial Tuli's number. The familiar voice of the servant calls out to Tuli as the phone is set down with a heavy wooden clunk. He taps his fingers rhythmically on the desktop. The tune of the Chamatkar jingle keeps playing in his head endlessly: La. La-la. La-la-la-la-la-la. Dum-dum-di-di. La-la.

'Tuli,' he says, when she comes on the line and says hello cautiously. 'Tuli, I'm rich. Can you believe it? I'm rich. Rich.'

Rohit Manchanda (b. 1963)

Rohit Manchanda was born in 1963; he grew up in Dhanbad, a major mining town in Bihar. Like Sunetra Gupta, he is a scientist, the latest in a line of scientists and doctors, beginning with Parashuram, to have enriched our literatures; he took a BA in Physiology from Oxford, and, later, a D.Phil. in Pharmacology from the same university; he is now Associate Professor at the Indian Institute of Technology, Bombay. Manchanda's under-publicized, episodic novel *In The Light Of The Black Sun*, appeared in 1996 from Penguin India; it won a Betty Trask Award. The novel, which is about an upper middle-class childhood in a mining town, far from an urban centre where such a childhood would naturally belong, is also about the comedy and wonder of the transformation of meaning such a mutation, or relocation, would involve. Others in this anthology have written about the desolation that is small-town India; Manchanda succeeds in transforming it, in certain episodes, into an unlikely, and talkative (for Manchanda is a master of dialogue) pastoral, where neither the unexpected nor the gleam of the seasons is too far away; at the same time, he tenderly mocks his pastoral, not by bringing to it the burden of fact, or social realism, but by inscribing into it, equally, comic books, coal-dust, and the minor perversities of the English language. Manchanda's great gift is his ability to convey joy even in the midst of the dubious benedictions of our middle-class life; he writes with a mock-gravity and a gracious lightness of touch that are rare among present-day Indian English novelists; but, if one listens to them, his sentences have a cadence that allow them to speak for themselves.

* * *

from *In the Light of the Black Sun* (1996)

SWAMIJI

Vipul had dreaded that after Veena masi's and Neha's departure from Khajoori, the month or so that remained of the summer vacation would prove difficult to pass, and that memories of their visit would make everything subsequently seem relatively barren. And for a few days after they left he did feel crushingly vacant and alone, most of all perhaps – he had to admit to himself – for lack of Neha's touch.

But a new preoccupation was very soon to commandeer most of Vipul's time and his thoughts, leaving him scarely any leisure to wax maudlin over this desideratum.

Vipul was getting on in years but was showing no signs of growing tall, and this was making both Vipul and his parents more than a little anxious.

The matter of the height of a child, or for that matter anybody's height at all, was of the greatest significance to the people of Jadugoda, as it was to the people of all of India's other towns and cities. Children and their parents, at all kinds of events and places – at parties, in school, or on social visits – were asked, 'So how tall have you grown?', or 'Has your son touched five yet?', as inevitably and as naturally as they might be asked their names. A good height mattered a great deal: tall people had personality: at five-six, you had begun to be noticed, a head of hair above the crowds; at five-nine you virtually towered above them; beyond six-zero – a dream – you rose like a monument. The inches mattered most of all for marriage. The parents of tall boys received proposals from the parents of the best-cultivated girls. Like the Alfonso mango, the gene for tallness was in demand as acute as it was in supply short.

And so all parents, including Vipul's, remained in perennial suspense about the state of elongation of their children, and particularly of boys. They measured their heights every few weeks, against walls, where little horizontal nicks marked the often painfully slow vertical progress of their bodies. The boys were administered growth-promoting tonics and fed vitamin-rich preserves. Parents whose children seemed never to emerge from the darkness of the Midgets' category in the school's annual sports day wore humiliated, cheated looks. They and their children prayed for sudden providential spurts of growth. In contrast parents whose children advanced unproblematically into the Seniors' looked becalmed, as though half the exhausting, lifelong task of decently settling their offspring had been automatically and effortlessly accomplished – which it was.

For Vipul there was further cause for dismay. The Bull, living up to his name, was growing prodigiously, and looked a likely six-footer; Koyala had recently enjoyed a providential spurt; and the Mosquito, though still only as high as Vipul, had taller parents, and therefore greater potential.

Vipul had tried many methods of accelerating his growth. He had suspended himself from the rusty rungs of the cast-iron stepladder that led to the roof till his arms felt hot and his muscles torn. He had given up carrom and table-tennis in favour of badminton and volleyball, which were supposed to stretch the body and provoke growth. He had jumped and jumped to try and touch with the tips of his fingers the leaves on increasingly higher branches of trees, hoping to recapitulate in this manner some of the evolutionary achievement of the giraffe. The springs in his legs grew commendably strong, but Vipul's spine remained inelastic.

There was a waking dream into which Vipul would often wilfully lead his mind. In it he would be stranded in a jungle, and hanging by his hands from a high branch of a tree. He would not have the strength to pull himself up, but only enough to keep hanging. He would not be able to let go and fall to the ground because on the ground, directly below him, there would be a cobra, fanning its hood and hissing. In this state Vipul would remain until rescued, which would perhaps be days later, and by this time he would have elongated by an extraordinary amount.

And finally there was the neck rack. Known as the 'Extender', this was a recently invented device, introduced by someone who had gauged cannily the magnitude of the anxiety of millions of height deficient Indians. He had collaborated with a Japanese firm to start its production in India. And he had grown very rich very suddenly. The advertisements for the neck rack said: 'First Time in India! Inches in Months, or Your Money Back! Your chance to Grow Tall the Same Way as Millions of Europeans and Americans.' The exact matter of how many inches in how many months, was left unaddressed. But the advertisements carried several persuasive 'Before and After' pictures of initially nondescript people blooming into svelte, lanky frames.

Tayaji, Vipul's father's elder brother, had gifted an Extender to Vipul through sympathetic concern: Tayaji's children, too were midgety. This how the Extender worked: the back of the head was placed in a fitting saddle; ropes that led from the saddle passed over high pulleys fixed to the wall; then the ropes hung down, ending in clasps. You now pulled the clasps downward – this hauled up the saddle, and along with it your head and neck, brought you to your toes, and stretched your spine; meaning thus to elongate it. Vipul did this exercise for hours every evening, feeling like a prisoner condemned to a rare routine of torture. It was an especially boring exercise: standing against the wall, staring at the blankness ahead, being stared back at by geckos with pensive cunning eyes, and simply pulling and stretching, no involvement of any skill whatsoever.

But even this drastic measure did not work. Vipul's spine was firm. The little horizontal nick on the wall stood callously still, an indifferent spectator of Vipul's worries. Something needed to be done urgently, but everybody had run out of ideas.

*

Then, in the summer, fresh hope arrived. A group of yogis set up camp in Khajoori. They came from Jadugoda, where they had a small headquarters. They came as evangelists, to instruct the people of Khajoori in the fundamentals and the benefits of yoga. In the early mornings, the air still crystalline and coal-dust free before the onslaught of the sun and industry began, the saffron-swathed yogis, sitting in the lotus position on the floor of the veranda of the Khajoori Guest House, told Khajoori's people how yogic exercises would tone their muscles, supple their limbs; or augment their powers of concentration and strength of will; or purge their viscera; or subjugate their bodies to their minds; or, most importantly for Vipul, impart chimeric physical virtues like height. And so it became imperative that Vipul should learn yoga.

The swamis at the camp had divided themselves into two groups. One, comprised of the elder swamis, took charge of Khajoori's adults. The other consisted of the younger Swami Suryaparmananda, in charge of the children. Vipul was glad of this arrangement. The elder swamis were intimidating. The most frightening thing about them was their preternatural serenity. It was almost deliberate; and it seemed to have been honed and perfected to an art. Theirs was the serenity that associates with abstinence and austerity. But it seemed to arise not from the abstinence itself, but from the sense of achievement of it, like the satisfaction that arises from doing a job well that may not really be worth doing. And the swamis wielded their serenity like an instrument, if not of castigation, then at least of reproof. People would wilt under the glare of their censorial serenity. Under its transmuting influence utilities seemed to turn into comforts, comforts into luxuries, and luxuries into sin. The elder swamis inspired strong feelings of guilt and self-indulgence: in tailored clothes, mattressed cots, good food, and the lack of will to renounce these pleasures. Their glances, as they swept about, seemed to reprimand the furniture, the hangings on the walls, the ornate lampshades and carpets, for simply being there. Often they came to Vipul's home for a meal, and every time, without uttering a word of recrimination, they succeeded, by the time they left, in leaving the family feeling inexplicably remorseful. And the collective remorse of Khajoori's families had the effect eventually of raising a handsome subscription for the camp.

Swami Suryaparmananda, in contrast to his elders, was milder. He was not more than a few years older than Vipul and his friends. His eyes spoke not of serenity but of a worldly restlessness which against his holy-looking shaven head and saffron robe made him appear an impostor, a fraud.

But he was most definitely a yogi, and he knew his yoga. Every morning, after he had instructed the children in the elementary *asanas*, he would stage demonstrations of the difficult ones. Then his body seemed to turn into rubber; it was as if his joints forgot that they existed, and his limbs turned into octopusine tentacles. His legs went over his head, and round his neck. His arms went under his legs and up his back. His back arched into a hairpin. His limbs were like infinitely adjustable flexible tubing: you could have knotted them. To some of his *asanas* he ascribed names which sounded as impossible as the postures themselves: *Poorna matsyendrasana, Parivritti janushirshasana*. Thus, at the end of each lesson, he showed off.

They called him Swamiji. He instructed them to bid him '*Hari Om Tatsat*' instead of '*Namaste*' in the mornings. He taught them a clip of the Gayatri mantra and made them chant it time after time, slowly, in one breath each time, until the mantra seemed to become a reflexive part of the very act of breathing, so that with each exhalation the incantation '*Om*' seemed to emanate naturally from the recesses of the lungs. And he taught them to sing:

> *Hari Om,*
> *Have no home,*
> *Food nor money nor wishes have I none,*
> *Still ... ll I will ... ll*
> *Be Aa ... aa ... anandam,*
> *Hari Om,*

over and over again. This they all chanted, the children who came from and returned to comfortable homes, who harboured a hundred ambitions

each, but who savoured, through the chant, a little of the arcane flavour
of the Swami's asceticism. It was somewhat like the Bible History lessons
Vipul had to take at school. They studied the parables of the Old and the
New Testament, they learned how to judge the allegorical significance of
the improbable events in the lives of the prophets; for forty minutes on
three days of every week they dived into all this, and for the remaining
nine thousand nine hundred and sixty minutes of the week quite forgot
about anything to do with the Bible, and turned heathen untutored minds
to marbles or ants or comics or Lord Krishna or Goddess Durga.

Swamiji taught them all the simple exercises, of strength, of endurance,
of agility, of meditation. He seemed at the time of the lessons to be much
older than they were, and much wiser. He knew mantras and shlokas,
could recite them offhand in Sanskrit, and casually said primal-sounding
things that seemed to make him an anachronism.

*

The days went by, many of the children, including Vipul, became plastic
and strong to varying degrees, but ... Vipul was not gaining any height.
Swamiji had not so far taught them any specific height-increasing *asanas*,
and Vipul was not bold enough to make the demand. His father or his
mother would ask after every lesson whether the necessary *asana* had
been taught or not. Then they would say, 'Probably there's a right time for
every *asana*; its time will also come.'

Eventually Vipul became impatient. After class one morning, and after
Swamiji had shown off some more of his contortionist tricks, he went up
to him and said, 'Swamiji, I want to learn a particular kind of *asana*.'

'What kind?' said Swamiji.

'One that can make me grow tall.'

Swamiji laughed. He said, 'I knew you would ask for this. Everyone asks
to be taught such *asanas*. I always teach these right at the end because
once they learn such *asanas* people forget about the others. All they want
is to grow tall, as high as date palms. How high do you want to grow?'

'As tall as Tarzan,' Vipul said.

'Tarzan! How tall is he?'

'Must be six-six at least, judging by the pictures. Or even as tall as Tony
Greig.'

'Which comic is that?'

'No, no. He's an English cricketer. Of South African-English mixture.
He's six-seven-and-a-half. He scored a century against Australia some days

ago and also took nine wickets in the match. A great all-rounder, and very good-looking,' Vipul said.

'Cricket I cannot understand. But listen. Do you have any Tarzan comics?'

'Tarzan comics? Of course. But why?'

'May I read them?'

'You?'

'I want to read them.'

'You must be reading only religious books, but.'

'Those I have to. But comics I like to.'

'Then you must read some of my comics.'

'Do you have any others? Richie Rich, Laurel and Hardy, the Phantom?'

'I have all these, and many others too. Swamiji you know a lot about comics.'

'When should I come to your home?'

Swamiji came the same evening. He looked around at the appointments in Vipul's home in a way that was quite different from the way the elder swamis looked. There was neither criticism in his eyes nor reprimand. He seemed fascinated by everything he saw.

Vipul showed him the collection of comics that he and Sameer had built up. Their father had sanctioned each of them the purchase of two foreign and two Indian comics every Saturday, when they went to the Jadugoda market. It was understood that this was their pocket money, in kind. Books were under a separate head, debited from their mother's account.

They bought comics sensibly. They collaborated with the Bull. They did not buy the comics he bought; and they exchanged comics with him. The Bull had different tastes. He preferred Superman and Wonder Woman and Flash Gordon and Zorro: Action Comics, he called them.

They cherished their comics. They handled them with a care that approximated reverence, turning their pages delicately as though they were archival material, sensitive to touch. They preserved them in neat stacks in cupboards, and had them bound into volumes of twenty-five each. Each volume, with its flower-papered hard cover, became a treasure box that would be periodically reopened and its contents re-examined with as much fresh enchantment as when they were first read.

They went through the comics studyingly. They looked long and deep into the clean simple luxurious world that they contained, illustrated in sunny colours, particularly in the American comics: just-right houses;

just-right lawns, skies, trees, avenues; everything pastel and easy on the eyes; placid dustless uncrowded manicured towns; and an all-pervading air of quaintness and of wealth. All so different from – so superior to – the coal-dust shrouded, glamourless, congested towns that Vipul knew. How spartan yet how voluptuous everything there seemed to be, and how lush yet how indigent everything here was.

Swamiji looked at the books greedily. He picked up all the loose comics one by one, and as he took up each one, said, 'Can I take this?'

Then he leafed through the bound volumes. Continually he made noises of recognition and of pleasure. He seemed to want to borrow them all. Eventually he picked two, Woody Woodpecker and Dennis the Menace.

Vipul's mother had prepared toasted curry-potato sandwiches and a sweet lime drink for the evening snack. Swamiji had his share with relish and at an astounding speed, and asked for more. He did not raise the issue of abnegation. As he ate he said to Vipul, 'You have a nice home,' 'Your mother is very nice,' 'Do you have snacks like this every day?' and 'What great comics! I shall really enjoy myself.'

Vipul asked Swamiji about life at the ashram. Swamiji said it was not easy. The swamis got up at three-thirty every morning. They said their prayers and freshened up by four. Then for two and a half hours without a break, they practised yoga exercises. After this they washed, bathed, put on fresh saffron cloths. Throughout the day there were several chores to do. Being the youngest and still an apprentice, he had to shoulder the largest fraction of the chores while the other swamis meditated, disputed, studied, and held court for visitors and sponsors. In the mornings he swept and swabbed the floors of the ashram, cleaned the toilets and bathrooms, prepared lunch. In the afternoons, after an hour's nap – that was granted – he swept the courtyard, tended to the ashram's vegetable garden, made tea. Then there was another hour of yoga, and another bath. Finally he helped prepare dinner. Dinner was at seven-thirty; by nine the ashram was asleep.

He said, 'Staying here at the camp is like a holiday. Everything is taken care of by the guest-house servants. I'll have plenty of time to read the comics.'

'But where will you read them?' Vipul said. 'Will the other swamis not object?'

'I have a padlocked trunk in which I keep a few things of my own. No one will see the comics. And sometimes I am on my own.'

As Swamiji was about to leave, Vipul said, remembering, 'Swamiji, those height-increasing exercises?'

'Of course, of course. In the next class I'll teach you one. Within weeks you will have learnt several of them. All the ones I know I'll teach you. You can be sure you'll grow tall. Yoga is like magic. *Hari Om Tatsat!*'

'*Hari Om Tatsat,*' Vipul said.

Swamiji turned to go, then turned around. 'In fact, we can have an arrangement,' he said. 'Among friends ... now we are friends.' He patted the bundle of comics that he was clutching under his armpit. 'You keep lending me comics, and I'll keep teaching you those *asanas.* Will that go?'

'It'll go fine,' Vipul said.

'*Hari Om Tatsat,*' Swamiji said, and walked away, and in the distance his vestment rippling about him was like an unquiet saffron vapour.

*

During the weeks that followed Swamiji taught Vipul a few height-increasing *asanas.* The most effective, he said, was the *Tadasana,* or the Heavenly Stretch Pose. For this Vipul had to stand on tiptoe, feet together; interlock his fingers, evert his palms; then raise his arms, stretch his neck and tilt his head so that he looked straight up.

To Vipul this felt suspiciously similar in both sensation and procedure to the neck-rack method of the Extender, and he voiced his misgivings.

But Swamiji said, 'That is artificial. This is natural, it is yoga. The natural way is the best way to gain height or to change the body's functioning in any way. In fact most probably the maker of the Extender got his idea from the *Tadasana* only. But remember, in yoga you must *meditate* on what you are doing. Bring your thoughts down to your backbone as you do the *Tadasana.* Try to feel each segment of it. And with the power of your mind, extend it, force it to stretch. You must feel yourself grow.'

Swamiji subsequently taught Vipul the *Chakrasana,* or the Wheel Pose, and the *Ushtrasana,* or the Camel Pose, which were also meant to have the same effect.

Vipul performed all these exercises with diligence. He did yoga for an hour every morning and for another hour every evening; of this he spent almost half the time on the *Tadasana.* Swamiji had also told him that the *Tadasana* could be performed informally – that is, by simply walking about in the prescribed posture, during the course of any normal activity. So Vipul started going about the house in this fashion, arms up, craning his neck, and trying at the same time to cast his eyes downwards to see the way.

While on tiptoe, Vipul projected his mind down onto his spine and dreamed of glorious imminent height. The nightmarish prospect of hanging from a high branch while a cobra fanned its hood below receded. Now, instead of stretching downward from above he would rise upward from below, with the help of the *Tadasana*.

Five ... six ... seven feet tall! Then he would show them all. He would show the Bull. Inch for inch, pound for pound, he was certain he was stronger than the Bull. But the Bull had so much more height and mass. Vipul determined first to grow tall, and then to put on weight. He would exercise profusely. Every day he would eat half a dozen fried eggs, and drink three big tumblers of milk. He was sure that if he had a spurt of growth he would immediately begin to relish milk and eggs: surely a taste for these was contingent upon proper growth, and not the other way around, as people in general, and in particular his mother, believed. He would insist on some non-vegetarian food every day. Up he would go, and beyond the Bull. He would thrash the Bull with ease, as he had done before the Bull discovered his self-respect. He would thrash many others, on the trivialmost counts. He would become a scourge. He would be particularly severe on Koyala.

'Good,' his mother said when she saw him going about in *Tadasana*. 'If you keep it up you'll soon cross five feet.'

Swamiji came twice again to Vipul's home and borrowed more bound volumes of the comics. He seemed as voracious and attentive a reader as Vipul and Sameer themselves. He had a precise memory of the frames of the illustrations; he could relate the stories in vivid detail, quoting accurately the bubbled dialogues.

He said that he enjoyed the Riche Rich comics especially.

'What a life it must be in America, no?' he said. 'Every second man is a millionaire.'

Vipul said, 'And even those who are not – even labourers – have cars and electric blankets and televisions.

'Labourers, even!'

'You don't see them in the comics. But I know. I once read an article about coal-miners in America. The pictures showed their cars, TVs and bungalows. And just look at Indian mineworkers.'

They reminded themselves briefly of Khajoori's mineworkers, housed in tight dark barracks, happy to afford a new bicycle or a medium-wave transistor radio or a shiny frilly nylon dress for a child once a year, around Diwali. Vipul felt ashamed.

Swamiji said, 'And how free children are with the elders. They call them by their names, Mr Wilson, Mrs Grundy, Mr this, Mrs that. None of this "auntie-uncle" business that goes on here.'

Vipul reflected upon the Bull calling his mother 'Mrs Uberoi' rather than 'Auntie', and felt almost enraged. However, he conceded that Swamiji had a point. He said, 'And children get pocket money, in dollars and cents. They can act like adults even when they are just our age.'

'Does your mother give you pocket money?' Swamiji asked.

'No, but she buys us books.'

'Not the same thing.'

'Not at all.'

'And boys and girls are able to meet each other freely there.'

'And how forward the girls are. They wear small clothes, they go here and there with boys unaccompanied by parents, imagine, for dinners and for picnics and for pictures.'

Swamiji said, 'But really, girls should be shy and should feel shame. Without shyness and shame what is a girl?'

'Yes, that's true,' Vipul said. In his heart he preferred shy girls to brash; Chetna, for instance, to Sushma didi; one could weave loftier romances around the former. But surely there could be a compromise – surely girls could shyly date?

'Still, it would be nice to be like Richie Rich.'

'That it would.'

*

The time came for the yoga camp to move on to Victoria Jubilee colliery, some distance away on the other side of Jadugoda. Swamiji came to Vipul's home to say goodbye.

He said, 'I'll be visiting Khajoori off and on, because I've made friends like you here. I'll return your comics by and by. At the moment I feel like rereading them. Now, since I won't be back for some time, can I take two more volumes?'

He took a volume of Classics Illustrated, saying that he would like to read *Moby-Dick* and *Kim* and *Tom Brown's Schooldays* because he had heard the names of these books, and a volume of Laurel and Hardy.

After the camp had departed, Vipul practised the entire set of *asanas* that Swamiji had taught him, every day for months. There was no appreciable result. The nick on the wall remained resolutely immovable.

Swamiji came to visit some six months later; the swamis were reviewing the results of their earlier efforts. Vipul was alone at home. Swamiji had not brought any of the comics back with him. He said, 'Vipul, I just forgot. But next time I'll return them all together. In any case, whenever you want them, you can come across to the ashram in Jadugoda and take them. But I can take just a couple of others?'

Vipul thought quickly and said, 'You'll have to ask Mummy.'

'But they are your comics, no?'

'I know. But Mummy has forbidden me to lend them to anyone without her permission. Even the Bull can't borrow them without Mummy's permission these days. Actually it's nothing to do with you, it's all that boy in my class...' here Vipul invented a name ... 'Dipen's fault. He started denying that he had borrowed them and even started stealing them.'

'I see...' said Swamiji.

'Swamiji, those *asanas* you taught me ...'

'Which?'

'Those ones for height.'

'Yes, yes, I remember.'

'Swamiji, there's no effect.'

'No effect?'

'My height – it's still the same.'

'Who says?'

'Papa measures it every month.'

'But Vipul you have grown, I'm sure. You *look* taller. I'm cent per cent sure. In fact the first thing I thought when I saw you today was, "Vah! Vipul has grown by inches!" But I wanted to say sorry first for the comics, so I didn't mention it.'

'But according to Sameer I haven't grown taller.'

'Where do you measure your height?'

Vipul led him to the spot and showed him the unmoving nick.

'Give me a book and a pencil,' Swamiji said. 'Now stand there. Straight. No, absolutely straight. Chest out. Head up. Neck straight. Up to your full height.'

Swamiji placed the book on Vipul's head and marked the wall. 'Of course you've grown! See? Look at this.'

Vipul came away from the wall. Swamiji's pencil mark was a clear inch above the familiar nick. 'I told you you had grown.'

'But, until a few days ago, there was nothing.'

'These things can happen suddenly. As a yogi I have seen incredible things happen. Do you know, we once had a swami in our ashram in Patna who came from Nepal and so he had very little chance of growing beyond five feet. One night he grew two and a half inches – overnight, while he slept! He woke up in the morning saying he was feeling thinner. We couldn't recognize him at first.'

'Could that have happened to me?'

'God can do anything. See this mark. You too must have had an overnight spurt. A couple more spurts like this one, and you'll soon be reaching where the Bull stands.'

Vipul felt warm and triumphant. He said, 'Swamiji, it's all due to your *asanas.*' He paused for a moment and said, 'Swamiji, I've thought of a way you can take the comics.'

'No, no, leave it if it's any trouble with your mummy.'

'No, listen. Mummy and Sameer are not here. You take them now. I'll explain to them later.'

That evening Vipul kept going to the wall and looking at the new mark. When Sameer came back, Vipul said to him, 'Do you know, I've grown taller.'

'Where?' Sameer said.

Vipul showed him the new mark.

'Stand there,' Sameer said. Vipul stood there and drew himself up to his maximum height.

'You're still at the old mark.'

'But this pencil mark?'

'Who made this?'

'Swamiji.'

'He was here?'

'He left a few minutes back.'

'Took more comics?'

Vipul was silent. Sameer slapped his head.

'Idiot!' Sameer said. 'Why did you let him?'

'He taught me those *asanas*. That's how I've grown.'

'But where have you grown!'

'Put a book on my head and see, properly.'

'Why put a book on your head, when I can see anyway.'

'I'm up to the new pencil mark.'

'Idiot.'

'Why do you keep calling me idiot?'

'Why not?'

'It's an abuse.'

'It isn't. Even if it is, you are an idiot, so you are.'

'You can't call me an idiot.'

'Who says? I'm calling you one now.'

They started grappling, and there was a fight; Vipul got beaten, and he cried.

*

It was some months before they could visit the ashram in Jadugoda. Vipul's parents thought that it was time they paid their respects once again to the swamis. They also needed to get professional advice on particular matters such as how to combat the stiffening of joints or the increasing rate of fall of hair.

They sat on a thin cotton sheet on the mud floor of a room that was bare but for a few framed pictures of gods and goddesses and of renowned swamis, and a squat earthen water-pitcher in a corner.

Vipul's parents told the swamis how beneficial yoga had turned out to be for them, how enlivening and how becalming, and invited the swamis to drop in at any time for a meal or even to stay. The swamis listened serenely – even the way they listened was reassuring, as though merely an audience with them would solve all problems. They then recommended specific *asanas* for each complaint that Vipul's parents had listed.

Vipul waited, keeping a discreet lookout for Swami Suryaparmananda, but he was nowhere to be seen. Vipul wondered how he might raise the question of the comics. He had assumed that he would find the Swami sweeping the courtyard or chopping vegetables, and had planned that he would act as though something or the other reminded him of something in the comics, and thus bring up the question. He was too scared of the elder swamis to ask them directly.

Then, as they were leaving, his mother said, 'But Swamiji, I don't see the younger Swami today? The one who was very popular with the children?'

Vipul said, quickly and audibly, 'Swami Suryaparmananda.'

'The little boy has a sharp memory,' the elder Swami said, considering Vipul beatifically. 'Our young Swami has left.'

'Why?' Vipul asked.

The elder Swami said to Vipul's parents, 'Everybody dreams and even thinks that he can live this life of hardship and penance, but in practice very few can.'

Vipul gathered courage. 'Swamiji,' he said, 'did Swamiji leave behind any comics for us?'

'Comics? My son, we devote ourselves to other kinds of studies,' the Swami said, through a laugh. 'We have given up comics along with a lot of other things.'

'No, Swamiji, not his own comics. They were ours. What had happened was...'

'Vipul, it doesn't matter, son,' his mother said. Her voice was coaxing but her eyes scolded him.

Vipul kept quiet.

Then his mother said, 'Swamiji, there was another small problem.'

'Speak, my daughter, speak,' the Swami said.

'You see how our Vipul is short for his age.'

'Is he? Which class are you in, son?' The Swami chucked him on his neck.

'Seventh,' Vipul said.

'Yes, a little short in that case,' the Swami said, sizing him with his eyes.

'Yes, just a little,' his mother said. 'But last summer the younger Swamiji had taught him some *asanas* for gaining height. But they don't seem to have had much effect.' Then she added, apologetically, 'Perhaps he is not doing the *asanas* properly?'

'Quite possible, quite possible,' Swamiji said. 'Just what I would have guessed. If instructions are not followed to the letter, yoga exercises cannot be expected to have their desired effect. Like mathematics. They may even harm. Are you following the instructions correctly, my son?'

'Just like Swamiji had taught me,' Vipul said. 'Exactly like that.'

Swamiji said, 'Good, very good. Then you're on the right track. There's no need to worry. Keep it up, continue with it, even increase the amount of exercise you do. You will certainly grow tall. One day you will find you have grown up overnight. *Hari Om Tatsat.*'

'*Hari Om Tatsat,*' they all said.

Notes on Translators

Elizabeth Bell is a writer, editor and translator of French and Spanish, based in San Francisco. Her translations from the Spanish have been widely published; and she received the Katha Award for Translation in 1997 for her translation of Naiyer Masud's 'Sheesha Ghat'.

Alok Bhalla received his PhD from Kent State University and teaches at CIEFL, Hyderabad. He has been an influential anthologist and editor, and his publications include *Writings From the Indian Subcontinent* (six volumes) and, with Peter Brooke, *Images of Rural India in the 20th Century*. He has translated, among others, the works of Nirmal Verma, Intizar Hussain and Manto.

Sukanta Chaudhuri was educated at Presidency College, Calcutta, and the University of Oxford. He is now Professor of English at Jadavpur University, Calcutta. His books include *Infirm Glory: Shakespeare and the Renaissance Image of Man, Translation and Understanding* and *The Select Nonsense of Sukumar Ray*.

Prodeepta Das was educated at Utkal and Essex universities. He is a London-based photographer.

Krishna Dutta, born and brought up in Calcutta, has lived and taught in London for many years, while frequently visiting Bengal. She holds degrees from Calcutta and London universities. She translated *Selected Short Stories* by Rabindranath Tagore, co-edited the anthology *Noon in Calcutta*, and wrote Tagore's biography *The Myriad-Minded Man*, all with Andrew Robinson. She has many other publications to her credit, and also writes in Bengali.

Lakshmi Holmstrom studied at Madras and Oxford. A freelance writer, critic and translator, she lives in England, and has published widely from India and from the UK. She is the author of *Indian Fiction in English: The Novels of R. K. Narayan*, and has edited *The Inner Courtyard: Short Stories by Indian Women*. Among her numerous translations from contemporary fiction are *A Purple Sea,* a collection of stories by Ambai, and Asokamitran's novel *Water.*

Ketaki Kushari Dyson was born in Calcutta in 1940 and studied English literature at Calcutta and Oxford, obtaining firsts from both universities. She also holds a doctorate from Oxford. Though she has lived in Britain for more than half her life, she belongs to that small minority of writers who write poetry in two languages; Bengali and English, in her case. Her latest book of poems is *Memories of Argentina and Other Poems.* She has received the Prafullakumar Sarkar Memorial Ananda Award and the Bhubanmohini Dasi Medal of the University of Calcutta for her contribution to contemporary Bengali letters. She is a distinguished translator and critical biographer of Tagore; among her publications in this regard are *I Won't Let You Go: Selected Poems by Rabindranath Tagore* and *In Your Blossoming Flower-Garden: Rabindranath Tagore and Victoria Ocampo.*

Nivedita Menon, the winner of Katha's A. K. Ramanujan Award for Translation in 1994, is a lecturer in Political Science at Lady Shri Ram College for Women, Delhi University. She is also currently Visiting Fellow at the Centre for the Study of Developing Societies, Delhi.

Tahira Naqvi was raised and educated in Lahore, Pakistan. Now settled in the US, she teaches English, has translated the works of Manto, Ismat Chughtai and, most recently, Khadija Mastur. She also writes fiction in English. Her first short story collection, titled *Attar of Roses and Other Stories of Pakistan,* was published in 1998; her second, *Dying in a Strange Country,* is expected to appear in the spring of 2001. She has just completed a translation of essays by Chughtai, the anthology titled *My Friend, My Enemy,* to be published by Kali for the Women's Press in the spring of 2001 as well. Currently Tahira is completing her first novel.

Mridula Nath Chakroborty took her M.Phil in English from Delhi University, and now teaches post-colonial literature at the University of Alberta, Canada.

Jatindra K. Nayak was educated at Ravenshaw College, Orissa and Merton College, Oxford. He teaches at the Post-Graduate Department of English, Utkal University.

William Radice was born in 1951 and went to Westminster School. After reading English at Oxford, where he won the Newdigate Prize for poetry, he gained high distinction in the Diploma in Bengali at the London School of Oriental and African Studies. He has published books of his own poetry, and also translated Tagore's poetry and stories for the Penguin Modern Classics series. He is now a Reader at the School of Oriental and African Studies.

A. K. Ramanujan – See headnote on Ramanujan in the 'English' section.

Andrew Robinson was born in Oxford. A King's Scholar of Eton College, he holds degrees from Oxford University and the School of Oriental and African Studies, London. He has written Satyajit Ray's biography *Satyajit Ray: The Inner Eye*, and collaborated on many projects with Krishna Dutta as biographer and translator, among which is the Tagore biography *Rabindranath Tagore: The Myriad-Minded Man.*

David Rubin was born in New England in the United States, and was educated at the University of Connecticut, Brown University and Columbia University, where he received his doctorate in English and Comparative Literature in 1954. He has taught English, American and Indian literature at Columbia, Sarah Lawrence College, Allahabad University and the University of Rajasthan at Jaipur. Since 1974, he has been Visiting Professor of Modern Indian Languages at Columbia. He has written novels, stories and a critical study, *After the Raj*; he is also one of Premchand's foremost translators.

Moazzam Sheikh was born in Lahore in 1962, and is now based in San Francisco. His stories have been published in the US and Canada. He received the Katha Award for Translation 1997 for 'Sheesha Ghat' by Naiyer Masud, and has recently finished a novel, *Sahab*.

Manu Shetty is on the faculty of the Department of Philosophy, University of Mysore. He has done his research with the Committee of Social Thought, the University of Chicago, on Tulu Oral narratives, and collaborated with A. K. Ramanujan on translating Kannada works into English.

Shivnath is a Dogri writer. He has written books on the history of Dogri literature, and has worked on the *Encyclopaedia of Indian Literature* and the *History of Literature* projects of the Sahitya Akademi. A retired civil servant, he now lives in Delhi.

Permissions Acknowledgements

The compiler and publishers wish to thank the following for permission to use copyright material:

Michael Madhusdan Dutt: from 'The Anglo-Saxon and the Hindu'(1854), Two Letters (1860).

Bankimchandra Chatterjee: 'A Popular Literature for Bengal' (1870), 'The Confession of a Young Bengal' (1872) extract from *Rajani* (1877) trans. from the Bengali by Nirad C. Chaudhuri.

Rabindranath Tagore: 'The Postmaster' (1891) trans. from the Bengali by Amit Chaudhuri (2001). Five Letters (1886–1895) trans. from the Bengali by Krishna Dutta and Andrew Robinson. Trans. reproduced by kind permission of Krishna Dutta and Andrew Robinson, taken from the Papermac edition 1991. 'An Essay on Nursery Rhymes' (1907) trans. from the Bengali by William Radice. From the introduction to *Thakurmar Jhuli* (1907) trans. from the Bengali by Amit Chaudhuri (2001). All work by Rabindranath Tagore reproduced by kind permission of Visva-Bharati, Calcutta.

Sukumar Ray: 'A Topsy-Turvy Tale' (1922) trans. from the Bengali by Sukanta Chaudhuri from *Select Nonsense of Sukumar Ray* edited and translated by Sukanta Chaudhuri © 1987 Oxford University Press India.

Bibhuti Bhushan Banerjee: from *Pather Panchali* (1920), trans. from the Bengali by Amit Chaudhuri. Original reproduced by kind permission of Taradas Banerjee. Trans. © 2001 Amit Chaudhuri.

Parashuram (Rajshekhar Basu): 'Blue Star' (1954) trans. from the Bengali by Ketaki Kushari Dyson. Trans. reproduced by kind permission of Samit Sarkar, M. C. Sarkar and Sons. 'The Jackal-Faced Tongs' (1955) translated from the Bengali by Ketaki Kushari Dyson. Trans. reproduced by kind permission of Samit Sarkar, M. C. Sarkar and Sons.

Buddhadev Bose: from *Tithidore* (1949) trans. © Dr Ketaki Kushari Dyson. From *An Acre of Green Grass: A Review of Modern Bengali Literature* (1948) from 'Pramatha Chaudhuri' – an essay. Reproduced by kind permission of

Papyrus, Calcutta. Both extracts reproduced by permission of the estate of Buddhadev Bose.

Mahashweta Devi: 'Arjun' (1984) trans. from the Bengali by Mridula Nath Chakraborty (from *The Wordsmiths*) © 1984 Katha. Reproduced by kind permission of the author.

Premchand (Dhanpat Rai): 'The Chess Players' (1924) trans. from the Hindi by David Rubin. First published as *The World of Premchand* © 1969 Penguin India. Copyright © 1969, 1988 The Sons of Premchand. Trans. © David Rubin 1969, 1988.

Nirmal Verma: 'Terminal' (1992) trans. from the Hindi by Alok Bhalla © 1992 Dangaroo Press Vol. XIX, No. 3 Anna Rutherford. Reproduced by kind permission of the author.

Krishna Sobti: from *Ai Ladki*! (1991) trans. from the Hindi by Shivnath, New Delhi. Trans. © 2001 Shivnath.

Sadat Hasan Manto: 'Peerun' (1950) trans. from the Urdu by Tahira Naqvi. Trans. © Tahira Naqvi. 'The Black Shalwar' (1942) trans. © Tahira Naqvi. First published in *The Life and Works of Saddat Hasan Manto: Another Lonely Voice*, published in 1985 by Vanguard Press, Pakistan.

Qurratulain Hyder: 'Memories of an Indian Childhood' (1965) trans. from the Urdu by the author © 1994 Sahitya Akademi and by kind permission of the author.

Naiyer Masud: 'Sheesha Ghat' (1996) trans. from the Urdu by Moazzam Sheikh and Elizabeth Bell © 1996 Naiyer Masud. Trans. appeared in *Katha Prize Stories*, Volume 7 © 1996 Katha.

U. R. Anantha Murthy: 'A Horse for the Sun' (1984) trans. from the Kannada by Manu Shetty and A. K. Ramanujan. Taken from *Indian International Centre Quarterly*, Vol. 19, No. 3, New Delhi.

Vaikom Muhammad Basheer: 'Walls' (1965) trans. from the Malayalam by Nivedita Menon © 1965 Vaikom Muhammad Basheer. Reproduced by kind permission of Smt Fatima Bi. Taken from *Katha Classic*. Trans. © Katha.

O. V. Vijayan: 'The Rocks' (1969) trans. from the Malayalam by the author © 1990 Penguin Books India.

Ambai (C. S. Lakshmi): 'Gifts' (1988) trans. from the Tamil by Lakshmi

Holmstrom © 1988 Ms. C. S. Lakshmi. Trans. © Lakshmi Holmstrom. Reproduced by kind permission of EastWest Books.

Fakir Mohan Senapati: from *Story of My Life* (1918, published 1927) trans. from the Oriya by Jatindra K. Nayak and Prodeepta Das.

Nirad C Chaudhuri: from *The Autobiography of an Unknown Indian* (1951). Reproduced by kind permission of Prithvi Narayan Chaudhuri. *The Autobiography of an Unknown Indian* was reissued in the UK & Commonwealth by Picador in 1999.

Aubrey Menen: from *Dead Man in the Silver Market* © 1954 Chatto & Windus.

Pankaj Mishra: 'Edmund Wilson in Benares' by Pankaj Mishra © 1998 Pankaj Mishra. Reproduced by kind permission of the *New York Review of Books* (April 9, 1998).

R. K. Narayan: from *The English Teacher* © 1945 R. K. Narayan. Reproduced by kind permission of the Wallace Literary Agency, Inc.

Raja Rao: from *The Serpent and the Rope* (1960).

Ruskin Bond: 'The Night Train at Deoli' (1988). From *The Night Train at Deoli and Other Stories* reproduced courtesy of Penguin Books India and the author © 1988 Penguin Books India.

A. K. Ramanujan: 'Is There an Indian Way of Thinking? An Informal Essay'. Taken from *The Collected Essays of A. K. Ramanujan* © 1989 OUP. Reproduced by kind permission of Oxford University Press India, and Mrs Molly A. Daniels-Ramanujan.

Dom Moraes: from *Answered by Flutes* (1983).Commissioned by the Madhya Pradesh Government. Reproduced by kind permission of the author.

Arvind Krishna Mehrotra: from 'The Emperor Has No Clothes' © 1982 Arvind Krishna Mehrotra, originally published in *Chandrabhaga* No. 7 (Summer 1982).

Adil Jussawalla: 'Make Mine Movies' © 1994 Adil Jussawalla. Reproduced by permission of *Filmfare*.

Salman Rushdie: from *Midnight's Children* © 1981 Salman Rushdie. Reproduced by kind permission of Vintage Books, The Random House Group Ltd.

Vikram Seth: from *The Golden Gate* © 1986 Vikram Seth. Reproduced by kind permission of Faber & Faber Ltd.

Amitav Ghosh: 'Tibetan Dinner', appeared in *Granta* 25, 'The Murderee', Autumn 1988. © 1988 Amitav Ghosh. 'Four Corners' appeared in *Granta* 26, 'Travel' Spring 1989. © 1989 Amitav Ghosh.

Upamanyu Chatterjee: from *English August: An Indian Story* © 1988 Upamanyu Chatterjee. Reproduced by kind permission of Faber & Faber Ltd.

Vikram Chandra: 'Siege in Kailashpada' from a novel in progress, *Siege in Kailashpada* © 1997 Vikram Chandra. Reproduced by kind permission of Janklow and Nesbit Associates. Originally published in *The New Yorker*.

Sunetra Gupta: from *Memories of Rain* © 1992 Phoenix House.

Aamer Hussein: 'The Colour of a Loved Person's Eyes' first appeared in *Critical Quarterly*, Winter 1990, and was included in the author's collection of stories *Mirror to the Sun* (Mantra 1993). Reproduced by permission of Mantra Publishing Ltd. Copyright © 1990 Aamer Hussein.

Ashok Banker: from *Vertigo* published by Rupa & Co. New Delhi © 1993 Ashok Banker. Reproduced by kind permission of the author.

Rohit Manchanda: from *In the Light of the Black Sun* © 1996 Penguin Books India. Reproduced by kind permission of the publisher and the author.